Lecture Notes in Computer Science 8500

Commenced Publication in 1973
Founding and Former Series Editors:
Gerhard Goos, Juris Hartmanis, and Jan van Leeuwen

Marian Bubak   Jacek Kitowski
Kazimierz Wiatr (Eds.)

eScience on Distributed Computing Infrastructure

Achievements of PLGrid Plus
Domain-Specific Services and Tools

Springer

Volume Editors

Marian Bubak
AGH University of Science and Technology
Department of Computer Science and ACC Cyfronet AGH
Kraków, Poland
E-mail: bubak@agh.edu.pl

Jacek Kitowski
AGH University of Science and Technology
Department of Computer Science and ACC Cyfronet AGH
Kraków, Poland
E-mail: kito@agh.edu.pl

Kazimierz Wiatr
AGH University of Science and Technology
ACC Cyfronet AGH and Department of Electronics
Kraków, Poland
E-mail: k.wiatr@cyfronet.pl

ISSN 0302-9743   e-ISSN 1611-3349
ISBN 978-3-319-10893-3   e-ISBN 978-3-319-10894-0
DOI 10.1007/978-3-319-10894-0
Springer Cham Heidelberg New York Dordrecht London

Library of Congress Control Number: 2014946919

LNCS Sublibrary: SL 3 – Information Systems and Application,
incl. Internet/Web and HCI

Typesetting: Camera-ready by author, data conversion by Scientific Publishing Services, Chennai, India

Printed on acid-free paper

Springer is part of Springer Science+Business Media (www.springer.com)

Preface

Nowadays, science requires powerful e-infrastructures: computing, data storage, visualization, and networking. One such e-infrastructure was built in Poland in the years 2009-2012, in the framework of the PLGrid project, whose main results were presented in the book: Marian Bubak, Tomasz Szepieniec, Kazimierz Wiatr (Eds.): Building a National Distributed e-Infrastructure – PLGrid, Scientific and Technical Achievements. Lecture Notes in Computer Science, vol. 7136. Springer 2012, ISBN 978-3-642-28266-9.

In spite of this progress, for many domain scientists direct, efficient, and transparent usage of such e-infrastructures often remains relatively difficult and time-consuming. Scientists frequently require assistance and close collaboration with service providers in order to access computational resources. Due to the diversity of scientists' requirements, a number of domain-specific computing environments have been developed. These include solutions, services, and extended infrastructures (including software) tailored to the needs of various groups of scientists. Such an effort has been undertaken in the framework of the PLGrid Plus project, the main results of which are presented in this book.

To help researchers from different areas of science understand and unlock the potential of the Polish Grid Infrastructure and to define their requirements and expectations, the following 13 pilot communities have been organized and involved in the PLGrid Plus project, helping refine and enhance the shared e-infrastructure: Acoustics, AstroGrid-PL, Bioinformatics, Ecology, Energy Sector, Health Sciences, HEPGrid, Life Science, Materials, Metallurgy, Nanotechnologies, Quantum Chemistry and Molecular Physics, and SynchroGrid.

Introduction of domain-oriented solutions for these communities enables various research groups of users to make further use of scientific data and computations. However, the scope is not limited to selected domains: indeed, by applying the generic infrastructure services more custom-tailored solutions, integration of new groups should proceed smoothly and at lower cost.

The book describes the experience and scientific results attained by project partners and the outcome of research and development activities carried out within the project. The book is split into three parts: the first (chapters 1 to 8) provides a general overview of research and development activities in the framework of the PLGrid Plus project with emphasis on services for different scientific areas and an update on the status of the PLGrid e-infrastructure, describing new developments in security and middleware. The second part (chapters 9 to 13) discusses new environments and services, which may be applied by all of the communities mentioned above. The third part (chapters 14 to 36) presents how the PLGrid Plus environments, tools and services are used by advanced domain-specific computer simulations performed by individual groups of researchers. These chapters present computational models, new algorithms, and ways, in which they are implemented with available tools and services. The book also provides a glossary of important terms and concepts.

We hope that this book, much like its predecessor mentioned at the beginning of this preface, will serve as an important intellectual resource for researchers, developers, and system administrators working on efficient exploitation of available e-infrastructures, promoting collaboration and exchange of ideas in the process of constructing a common European e-infrastructure.

We owe our thanks to all authors and reviewers for their diligent work in ensuring quality of this publication. We would like to express our sincere gratitude to Zofia Mosurska and Robert Pająk for their enthusiastic day-to-day management of the editorial process, for collecting new versions of papers and liaising with reviewers. We are also indebted to Bartosz Baliś, Włodzimierz Funika, Joanna Kocot, Piotr Nowakowski, and Milena Zając for their editorial contributions. Finally, we wish to thank Springer Verlag for very fruitful collaboration at all stages of the book's preparation.

We invite you to visit the PLGrid Plus web site (http://www.plgrid.pl/en), which carries up-to-date information regarding our e-infrastructure.

July 2014

Marian Bubak
Jacek Kitowski
Kazimierz Wiatr

Acknowledgments. This book, like all PLGrid Plus project activities, was co-funded by the European Regional Development Fund as part of the Innovative Economy Program.

Book Preparation

This book was prepared with the help of the members of the PLGrid Plus project.

Editors' Support Team

Help in editing the book: R. Pająk, M. Zając
English proofreading: B. Baliś, W. Funika, J. Kocot, P. Nowakowski

Reviewers

P. Bała
M. Baranowski
A. Belloum
K. Benedyczak
A. Bożek
I. Campos
R. Cushing
M. Czuchry
C. Engwer
N. Ferreira
M. Filocha
P. Flaszyński
W. Funika (2x)
P. Goryl
P. Grabowski
D. Groen
T. Gubała
M. Hanasz
I. Hidalgo-Gonzalez (2x)
S. Jezequel
M. Kasztelnik
M. Kęsek
J. Kocot
J. Komasa
J. Kozłowska
D. Kranzlmueller

V. Krzhizhanovskaya
M. Krzyżanowski
M. Kupczyk
J. Kusiak
W. Kuś
A. Kwiecień (2x)
Ł. Madej
G. Mazur
J. Meizner
N. Meyer
K. Michalek
Z. Mosurska
J. Mrozek
K. Muszka
K. Noga
A. Olszewski
P. Pałka
G. Papanikolaou
P. Petrov
M. Pietrzyk
T. Piontek
M. Płóciennik (2x)
P. Rafaj
Ł. Rauch (2x)
M. Romberg
R. Różańska

J. Rybicki (2x)
K. Rycerz (2x)
M. Schaap
B. Schuller
H. Siejkowski (2x)
G. Siemieniec-Oziębło
M. Sitko
P. Siudek
R. Słota
M. Stahl
M. Sterzel
M. Stolarek
C. Straube
W. Suwała
T. Szepieniec
R. Szwaba
T. Szymocha (2x)
J. Świrydczuk
M. Tomanek
I. Tsukrov
M. Uchroński
P. Wolniewicz (2x)
M. Zdybał
W. Ziajka

Table of Contents

Domain-Specific Services in Polish e-Infrastructure

Jacek Kitowski[1,2], Kazimierz Wiatr[1], Łukasz Dutka[1], Tomasz Szepieniec[1],
Mariusz Sterzel[1], and Robert Pająk[1]

[1] AGH University of Science and Technology, ACC Cyfronet AGH,
ul. Nawojki 11, 30-950 Kraków, Poland
[2] AGH University of Science and Technology, Faculty of Computer Science,
Electronics and Telecommunications, Department of Computer Science,
al. Mickiewicza 30, 30-059 Kraków, Poland

Abstract. Modern e-infrastructures provide huge computational power
and storage capacities to their users. While increasing capacity and
progressing with technological advancement is gradually ceasing to be
a problem, making these infrastructures easy-to-use for their users is
still a challenge. The barrier the users have to overcome to use an e-
infrastructure in their scientific experiments is still high – it is almost
impossible to do this without prior training on the infrastructure usage
and without knowledge of UNIX-like systems. At the same time, the
user is offered more and more easy to use tools in many other fields.
The increasing gap between the users' skills and competence required
to effectively use the e-infrastructure services needs to be bridged with
a new layer of services which are specific to a given domain of science and
more easy to use by researchers. The paper introduces the foundations
of the PL-Grid Infrastructure, the objectives of the PLGrid Plus project
and shortly describes several sample domain-specific services and tools,
developed and deployed in the Polish computational e-infrastructure to
overcome the aforementioned problems.

Keywords: domain-specific solutions, computing services, IT infrastructure.

1 Polish Grid Infrastructure

The Polish Grid Infrastructure [1] has been created within the PL-Grid project
(2009-2012) [2,3]. It was then that the basic infrastructure has been developed.
Soon, in March 2010, the PL-Grid Infrastructure turned out to be the first operational National Grid Initiative (NGI) in Europe. Since then, the users not only
have been able to conduct interdisciplinary research on a national scale, but also
have been given transparent access to international grid resources. Next, the
PLGrid Plus project (2011-2014) [4] was started, aiming at the infrastructure
extension with specific environments, solutions and services, developed according to the identified needs of different groups of scientists. Both projects were

M. Bubak et al. (Eds.): PLGrid Plus, LNCS 8500, pp. 1–15, 2014.

maintained by the Polish Grid Consortium [5] and co-funded by the European Regional Development Fund as a part of the Innovative Economy program.

This development was possible thanks to the experience the members of the Polish Grid Consortium had gained in previous years – by coordinating big infrastructure projects (e.g. [6]) or participating in their accomplishment [7], as well as in development of tools (e.g. [8]) or applications porting (e.g. [9]).

2   Domain-Specific Services – PLGrid Plus Solution

Contemporary science shows a great demand for networking, data storage, computing provided by e-infrastructures. However, from the point of view of a domain scientist, using the modern computing systems, services and tools of these infrastructures often becomes relatively difficult. Therefore, the scientists need assistance and close collaboration with service providers.

The main aim of the PLGrid Plus project [4] is to lower the barriers required for the researchers to use the infrastructure provided in PL-Grid, and, thus, attract new communities of the users, who need the computational power and large disk space of supercomputers but have no or little skills in using it. To achieve this, a number of domain-specific environments, i.e., solutions, services and extended infrastructure (including software) has been developed to serve researchers from specific domains of science. To enable and facilitate development of these domain-specific environments, the project relies on a broad cooperation with representatives of various disciplines (domain experts), often grouped in domain consortia. Direct cooperation with them, mostly through involvement in the project activities, ensures matching of computing, software, databases and storage services to the actual needs.

The domain-specific services are built on top of PL-Grid core services that are used to communicate with the computing and storage infrastructure (see Fig. 1). These core services include e.g. middleware – at present, PL-Grid Infrastructure users can choose from three major middleware suites to run their computations: gLite [10], UNICORE [11] and QosCosGrid [12].

The domain-specific services hide the complexity of the underlying infrastructure and, at the same time, expose the actual functions that are important to the researchers of the given domain (see Section 3). In this way, the users are provided with exactly the functionality they need. What is more, it is exposed to them in their domain-specific manner to achieve maximum intuitiveness and usefulness.

The activities realized in the PLGrid Plus project, aiming at the development of the domain-specific services, can be grouped into several categories:

- Integration Services: dedicated portals and environments, unification of distributed databases, virtual laboratories, remote visualization, service value (utility and warranty) facilities, SLA management – all at national and international levels,
- Computing-Intensive Solutions: specific computing environments, adoption of suitable algorithms and solutions, workflows, cloud computing, porting scientific packages,

- Data Intensive Computing: access to distributed scientific databases, homogeneous access to distributed data, Big Data (data discovery, processing, visualization, validation, etc.), 4th paradigm of scientific research (data intensive scientific discovery),
- Instruments in Grid: remote transparent access to instruments, sensor networks,
- Organizational: organizational backbone, professional support for specific disciplines and topics, rich international collaboration (EGI.eu [13], EGI-InSPIRE [14], EMI [15], PRACE [16], etc.).

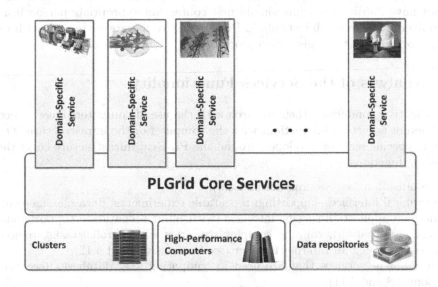

Fig. 1. Layered view of the PL-Grid Infrastructure

To provide support for building the domain-specific services, interdisciplinary teams have been established, gathering both e-infrastructure and domain experts. The teams work in short cycles providing the required functionality. The design of a particular service is based on the needs articulated by the researchers from a respective domain of science. Then, the service is developed in cooperation of computer scientists and domain experts, until it can be deployed and connected to the infrastructure. Finally, it is published and, after acceptance tests, made accessible to all the users who request it.

Currently, the PLGrid Plus project supports 13 different domains of science with their domain-specific services: Acoustics, AstroGrid-PL, Bioinformatics, Quantum Chemistry and Molecular Physics, Ecology, Energy Sector, Health Sciences, HEPGrid, Life Science, Materials, Metallurgy, Nanotechnologies, and SynchroGrid. Each of them requires different approach and different tools.

Introduction of domain-oriented solutions for these 13 communities [17,18] broadened the scope of use of the project's results to various research groups. Moreover, the experience in building domain services along with the existing offer of general services should make the integration of new groups smooth and much less expensive.

Access to the PL-Grid Infrastructure's computing resources is free to Polish researchers and everyone involved in scientific activities who is associated with a university or research institute in Poland. To obtain an account in the PL-Grid Infrastructure that enables access to its computing resources and domain-specific services, one needs to register using the PL-Grid portal [19]. Researchers who do not have Polish citizenship, should first contact an appropriate person from the university or research institute in Poland they cooperate with, and, with its help, proceed with the registration process.

3   Analysis of the Services Functionality

The scientists conducting their research with the use of computers have a need for different aspects of interactions with the computer or the infrastructure. The domain-specific services developed around the PL-Grid Infrastructure cover the following functions:

- visualization (see Sections 4.1 and 4.6),
- graphical interfaces supporting: repeatable experiments, data management, domain application-specific interface (with input preparation support, output visualization), running complex scenarios with parallel tasks, remote access through an Internet browser (see Sections 4.2 and 4.12),
- stand-alone services that are used in computing, e.g. databases (see Sections 4.8 and 4.11),
- efficient domain-specific data access, analysis and management (see Sections 4.3 and 4.7),
- deploying new, efficient algorithms solving domain-specific problems (see Sections 4.2 and 4.10),
- interfaces to complex physical instruments (see Sections 4.3 and 4.4),
- tools which enable management of computations from the users' personal devices, running both: Linux and MS Windows as well as mobile operating systems (see Sections 4.2, 4.11 and 4.12).

All the above-mentioned functions help to tailor the domain-specific services to the needs of different groups of scientists, thereby fitting the PL-Grid computational infrastructure to the topics of research.

4   Examples of Domain-Specific Solutions and Services Deployed in the PL-Grid Computational Infrastructure

It is not possible to provide in this paper a detailed view of all the domain-specific services including those already developed and deployed in the infrastructure, and the ones being planned for implementation. Therefore, only several sample services – already deployed or scheduled for deployment in the nearest future – representing all 13 scientific domains, have been chosen to be briefly presented within this section.

4.1 Acoustics

Hearing. The main part of the service is the Psychoacoustical Noise Dosimeter, which is based on utilizing the modified psychoacoustic model of hearing. The primary function of the Dosimeter is to estimate, in real time, auditory effects, which are caused by exposure to noise [20]. The user can define detailed conditions of exposure to noise such as: noise level, exposure time, and energy distribution in the frequency domain. The outcomes are presented in a form of cumulated noise dose and characteristic of temporary shift of the hearing threshold (see Fig. 2).

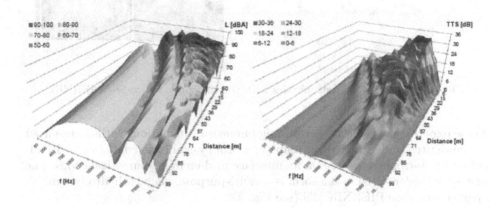

Fig. 2. Spectrum distribution of acoustic energy of noise source (left) and TTS (temporary threshold shift) effect evoked by the exposure to this noise expressed in critical bands as a function of distance from the noise source (right)

Noise Maps. The application generates noise maps in urban environments based on the data provided by the user. Integration of the software service with the network of distributed sensors allows for making automatic updates to noise maps for a specified time period. Operations are performed employing a dedicated noise prediction model, optimized for a computer cluster. In addition, predicted maps may be adjusted, using real noise level measurements [21,22].

4.2 AstroGrid-PL (Astrophysics)

InSilicoLab for Astrophysics. The service aims to support launching complex astrophysical computational experiments in the PL-Grid Infrastructure [23,24].

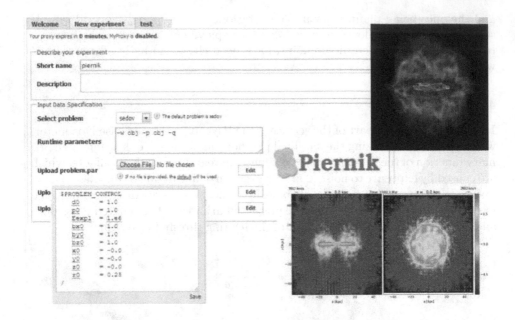

Fig. 3. InSilicoLab for Astrophysics with the first provided code – PIERNIK

These experiments facilitate performing numerical simulations without the need for unassisted and, often, very complex, astrophysical code compilation. InSilicoLab for Astrophysics serves as an interface grid-enabling numerical codes. The first code implemented in this form is a multi-purpose, magnetohydrodynamical, open-source code PIERNIK [25] (see Fig. 3).

4.3   Bioinformatics

Genetic Data Processing. The service allows to run a sequence of programs for analysis of bioinformatics data obtained from a genomic sequencer. Programs that can be activated in a cascade of data processing tasks, are: GS Run Processor, GS Reference Mapper, GS Reporter, GS Assembler and BLAST. Preparation of calculations is done in a graphical client of the UNICORE environment – UNICORE Rich Client [26,27].

Genetic Data Storage. The service implemented for all users who want to store – safely, in the long-term – large amounts of data on storage resources of the distributed computational infrastructure. The transmitted data is encrypted – ensuring confidentiality of the users data, and stored – providing an adequate level of security and access control [28].

4.4 Ecology

Automatic Phenology Observations Service (APheS). Gives an opportunity to observe the flora, together with important processes running in it [18]. The service is based on the KIWI Remote Instrumentation Platform – a framework for building remote instrumentation systems [29]. The platform provides a set of components to control and manage scientific equipment or sensors like cameras, weather, air pollution and water flow sensors, and others (see Fig. 4).

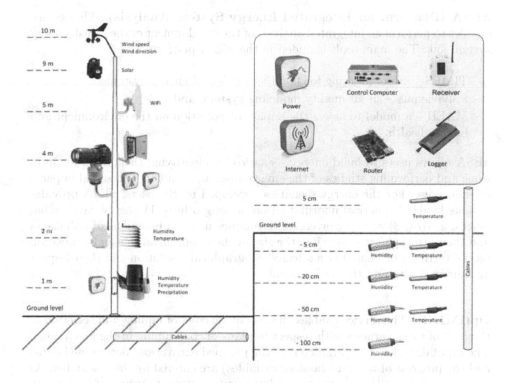

Fig. 4. Automatic phenology observations – infrastructure

Among several scenarios, designed to fully utilize the instrumentation system's potential and provide scientists with data, are:

- defining the phenological year seasons, climate local to the data-gathering site or phenophases for plants cultivated on the nearby arable area,
- examining the effects of cultivation conditions on the duration of vegetation,
- determining the relation between air humidity and wild plants growth.

For each scenario, in order to deliver results, analysis of raw and processed meteorological data and/or photos is performed. As a result of these studies, pictures accessible through the KIWI system may be tagged with information determined by the scientist.

The APheS service constitutes a unique and innovative tool that allows pheno-logical observations to become automated, remote measurements. This solution, developed and deployed within the PLGrid Plus project, is of great value, as it was developed in close collaboration with scientists from the natural sciences domain.

4.5 Energy Sector

πESA (Platform for Integrated Energy System Analysis). The service enables to perform an integrated analysis of the development of the Polish energy system [30]. The main tools included in the πESA platform are:

- TIMES – a tool allowing for building models of energy systems,
- Polyphemus – an air quality modeling system, and
- MAEH – a model to assess the impact of pollution on the environment and human health.

πESA allows users to build energy scenarios by identifying their main assumptions and performing studies of the environmental, economic and social impacts of energy use. For the energy scenarios developed by the users, πESA provides various kinds of practical information on, among others, 1) energy carriers balances, 2) cost, 3) energy conversion techniques used, 4) emissions of pollutants and their atmospheric dispersion, the size of their concentrations and deposition on the territory of Poland at a selected geographical resolution and their impact on human health and the environment.

OptiMINE. The service enables analysis of variants of mining and selection of the best of these variants with respect to plans of coal mining in the given mine. The input data, i.e.: the parameters of the planned excavation (determined data) and the progress of work (as random variables) are entered by the researcher. As a result of the application, the researcher receives adequate values of progress in the various workings and for a distribution of work over time which will ensure fulfillment of the planned extraction.

4.6 Health Sciences

Data Processing for Visualization. The service enables processing of medical data (segmentation, detection of distortion, comparison and search for relevant fragments) for advanced visualization, for scientific and diagnostic needs. Such an analysis is a key element to both research and medical diagnostics. This data processing requires high computing power, which is provided by the PL-Grid Infrastructure. Due to importance of the data, an adequate level of security and data access control is ensured.

4.7 HEPGrid (High Energy Physics)

CVMFS. The service provides catalogs of software and data needed to reconstruct and analyze data in HEP experiments (see Fig. 5). It operates on a dedicated server installation on a read-only virtual file system CERNVM-FS, installed by the FUSE module in the local user space. With this service, all the versions of the software and any modifications made to the central servers are immediately available ensuring reasonable usage of the local storage resources.

Fig. 5. Visualization of production and decay of the Higgs boson to two electrons and two positrons in the ATLAS detector (figure courtesy of CERN)

Proof on Demand (PoD). The service is designed to perform the final physical HEP analyses. It enables parallel data processing in the ROOT environment [31] using partitioning of input data and its processing by independent processes, and provides merging of the output results. In this way, the processing time of large quantities of data can be reduced by a factor of $1/n$ where n is the number of running PoD processes.

4.8 Life Science

Advanced Microarray Analysis Tool – Integromics. The service was developed for people conducting biological research using DNA microarrays, providing information on the level of gene expression in test samples [17]. Integromics is a tool that helps analyze this information and correlate expression levels with other clinical data on the studied organisms. The service is a unique web application, which supports a range of complex analyses, including, among others:

- quality control and normalization for the most popular microarray types (Affymetrix and Agilent), ensuring that differences in intensities are indeed

due to differential expression, and not merely printing, hybridization, or scanning artifacts,
- Artificial Neural Network (ANN) analysis, capable of creating and training a neural model (a perceptron), and subsequently using it to distinguish between healthy and abnormal tissue based on gene expression profile data (see Fig. 6),
- integromics analysis, which combines gene expression data with lipidomic or proteomic information in order to find interesting correlations, patterns and associations.

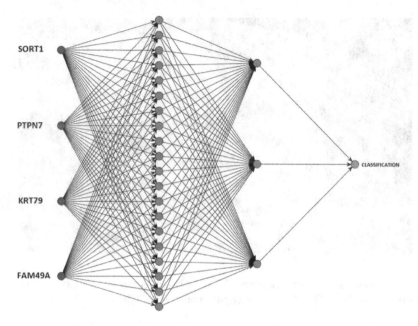

Fig. 6. Schematic representation of a sample artificial neural network, developed for classification based on gene expression profiles

4.9　Materials

Advanced Maintenance of the Material Modeling Software on the UNICORE Platform. The service provides grid access to some popular software packages used in the modeling of materials – VASP, Siesta, QE, Abinit and OpenMX through the UNICORE platform (middleware). It also provides support in executing typical task sequences.

Visualization of 3D Data in the VisNow Software Package. The results of programs such as VASP, Siesta, QE, Abinit, OpenMX are often large sets of data describing spatial distribution of a given quantity, e.g., electron density. Within the described service, a visualization software – VisNow – has been extended by a module enabling efficient preview of the aforementioned results, and, based on it, drawing required charts and maps.

4.10 Metallurgy

SSRVE. The service is used to generate a Statistically Representative Volume Element (called SSRVE) for microstructures of materials. The service is designed for people involved in large-scale modeling using a representation of microstructure of two-phase metallic materials [32] (see Fig. 7).

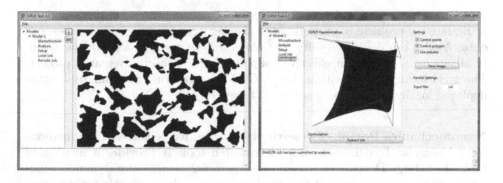

Fig. 7. Full representation of microstructure (left) and generated SSRVE (right)

Fig. 8. AuxEx service portals

Extrusion3d. The service relates to the modeling and optimization of extrusion profiles. It can assist a user in the process of designing tools and technologies. Owing to the implemented criterion of loss of cohesion, it also enables analyzing the extrusion process for cracks in the extruded material [33].

4.11   Nanotechnologies

AuxEx. The service is designed for teams of researchers, who, in their daily work, face the problem of managing and sharing large amounts of heterogeneous data. AuxEx is a dedicated software tailored to the needs of a particular team. It allows for a maximum effective cooperation in a specific research project. The service can be used within the PL-Grid Infrastructure or as an application deployed locally on the user's servers [34] (see Fig. 8).

Nanomechanics Portal. The service is designed for people who use methods from Molecular Dynamics as a basic research tool. It provides a number of tools, including: 1) tools to prepare and perform a molecular-dynamic simulation, 2) tools for analysis of the simulation results, in particular for structure characterization of materials simulated numerically.

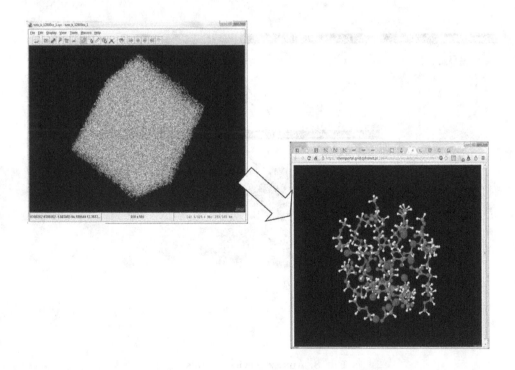

Fig. 9. An example of Trajectory Sculptor usage: an MD frame of 400 000 atoms reduced to a few selected molecules

4.12   Quantum Chemistry and Molecular Physics

InSilicoLab for Chemistry. The service supports launching of complex computational quantum chemistry experiments on the PL-Grid Infrastructure [23], [35,36]. These experiments facilitate planning of sequential computation schemes that require preparation of series of data files, based on a common schema. The first two experiments offered to the chemistry domain within InSilicoLab are: 1) general quantum-chemistry experiment and 2) Trajectory Sculptor [37]. The latter is a tool applicable to a wide range of systems, including binary or ternary solvent mixtures, electrolyte solutions or ionic liquids (see Fig. 9).

4.13   SynchroGrid

Elegant. The service developed for those involved in design and operation of a Synchrotron. The service consists in: 1) provisioning of the Elegant (ELEctron Generation ANd Tracking) application in parallel version on a cluster, 2) configuring the Matlab software to read output files produced by this application in Self-Describing Data Sets (SDDS) format and to generate the final results in form of drawings [38].

5   Conclusions and Future Work

The presented approach to construction of big e-infrastructures and opening their features to scientists, developed in the framework of the PL-Grid and PLGrid Plus projects, presents a way of providing advanced IT infrastructure to modern scientific research. The resulting solution provides Polish researchers with capability for collaboration with international research organizations.

The described approach also proves that the most important goal of the PLGrid Plus project – expansion of the existing computational infrastructure towards domain-specific solutions for research teams – allows for conducting more effective and valuable research. The results of most of these scientific computations can be applied in various branches of science and technology.

With the development of the domain-specific solutions, it became possible to reach beyond the traditional community of IT infrastructure users and create interdisciplinary teams, enabling them to achieve better scientific results, construct, implement and maintain domain services, as well as to introduce improvements to the functioning of the PL-Grid Infrastructure. Many of these users were directly involved in the PLGrid Plus project and supported its activities, thus, significantly contributing to the accomplishment of the final project's results.

In the future, we plan to focus on other domains of science and to offer a wider range of cloud and big data services. Modernization of software environments (i.e., toward EMI components) and hardware solutions (with more GPGPUs and Intel phi) are also foreseen.

References

1. The Polish Grid Infrastructure web site, http://www.plgrid.pl
2. The PL-Grid project web site, http://projekt.plgrid.pl
3. Bubak, M., Szepieniec, T., Wiatr, K. (eds.): PL-Grid 2011. LNCS, vol. 7136. Springer, Heidelberg (2012)
4. The PLGrid Plus project web site, http://www.plgrid.pl/plus
5. The Polish Grid (PL-Grid) Consortium web site, http://www.plgrid.pl/en/contacts
6. Bubak, M., Malawski, M., Zając, K.: Towards the CrossGrid architecture. In: Kranzlmüller, D., Kacsuk, P., Dongarra, J., Volkert, J. (eds.) PVM/MPI 2002. LNCS, vol. 2474, pp. 16–24. Springer, Heidelberg (2002)
7. Marco, J., Campos, I., Coterillo, I., et al.: The interactive European grid: Project objectives and achievements. Computing and Informatics 27(2), 161–171 (2008)
8. Dutka, Ł., Kitowski, J.: Application of component-expert technology for selection of data-handlers in CrossGrid. In: Kranzlmüller, D., Kacsuk, P., Dongarra, J., Volkert, J. (eds.) PVM/MPI 2002. LNCS, vol. 2474, pp. 25–32. Springer, Heidelberg (2002)
9. Funika, W., Korcyl, K., Pieczykolan, J.: Adapting a HEP application for running on the Grid. Computing and Informatics 28(3), 353–367 (2009)
10. gLite – Lightweight Middleware for Grid Computing, http://glite.cern.ch/
11. UNICORE – Uniform Interface to Computing Resources, http://www.unicore.eu
12. QosCosGrid Middleware, http://www.qoscosgrid.org/
13. EGI.eu web site, http://www.egi.eu/
14. EGI-InSPIRE project web site, http://www.egi.eu/about/egi-inspire/
15. EMI web site, http://www.eu-emi.eu/
16. PRACE web site, www.prace-ri.eu/
17. Kitowski, J., Dutka, Ł., Mosurska, Z., Pająk, R., Sterzel, M., Szepieniec, T.: Development of Polish Infrastructure for Advanced Scientific Research – Status and Current Achievements. In: Proceedings of 12th International Symposium on Parallel and Distributed Computing, ISPDC 2013, IEEE Conference (2013)
18. Kitowski, J., et al.: Development of Domain-Specific Solutions within the Polish Infrastructure for Advanced Scientific Research. In: Wyrzykowski, R., Dongarra, J., Karczewski, K., Waśniewski, J. (eds.) PPAM 2013, Part I. LNCS, pp. 237–250. Springer, Heidelberg (2014)
19. The PL-Grid portal web site, https://portal.plgrid.pl
20. Kostek, B., Kotus, J., Czyżewski, A.: Noise Monitoring System Employing Psychoacoustic Noise Dosimetry. In: Proceedings of the 47th AES Conference, Music Induced Hearing Disorders, New Technologies for Measurement and Prevention, Columbia College, Chicago, Illinois, USA, June 20-22 (2012)
21. Szczodrak, M., Kotus, J., Czyżewski, A., Kostek, B.: Application of Noise Mapping Tool Deployed in Grid Infrastructure for Creating Noise Maps of Urban Areas. The Computer Science Journal 14(2), 231–242 (2013)
22. Szczodrak, M., Kotus, J., Kostek, B., Czyżewski, A.: Creating Dynamic Maps of Noise Threat Using PL-Grid Infrastructure. Archives of Acoustics 38(2), 235–242 (2013)
23. Kocot, J., Szepieniec, T., Sterzel, M., Golik, M., Wojcik, P., Twarog, T., Grabarczyk, T.: A Framework for Domain-Specific Science Gateways. In: Bubak, M., Turała, M., Wiatr, K. (eds.) CGW 2013 Proceedings, pp. 93–94. ACK CYFRONET AGH, Kraków (2013)

24. The InSilicoLab for Astrophysics service web site, http://insilicolab.astro.plgrid.pl/
25. Ciecieląg, P., Hanasz, M., Kowalik, K., Kundera, T., Stachowski, G., Borkowski, J.: Grid-enabled platform for astronomers. In: Bubak, M., Turała, M., Wiatr, K. (eds.) CGW 2013 Proceedings, pp. 57–58. ACK CYFRONET AGH, Kraków (2013)
26. Borcz, M., Kluszczynski, R., Skonieczna, K., Grzybowski, T., Bala, P.: Using PL-Grid Infrastructure to Store and Process DNA Sequence Data from GS FLX Instrument. In: Bubak, M., Turała, M., Wiatr, K. (eds.) CGW 2012 Proceedings, pp. 67–68. ACK CYFRONET AGH, Kraków (2012)
27. Borcz, M., Kluszczyński, R., Skonieczna, K., Grzybowski, T., Bała, P.: Processing the biomedical data on the grid using the UNICORE workflow system. In: Caragiannis, I., Alexander, M., Badia, R.M., Cannataro, M., Costan, A., Danelutto, M., Desprez, F., Krammer, B., Sahuquillo, J., Scott, S.L., Weidendorfer, J. (eds.) Euro-Par Workshops 2012. LNCS, vol. 7640, pp. 263–272. Springer, Heidelberg (2013)
28. Borcz, M., Kluszczynski, R., Marczak, G., Chrupala, R., Benedyczak, K., Skonieczna, K., Grzybowski, T., Bala, P.: PL-Grid services for bioinformatics community. In: Bubak, M., Turała, M., Wiatr, K. (eds.) CGW 2013 Proceedings, pp. 67–68. ACK CYFRONET AGH, Kraków (2013)
29. KIWI Remote Instrumentation Platform web site, http://kiwi.psnc.pl/
30. Wyrwa, A., Pluta, M., Zysk, J., Skoneczny, S., Mirowski, T.: Modelling the mid-term development of the energy system with the use of technology explicit partial equilibrium model. In: Bubak, M., Turała, M., Wiatr, K. (eds.) CGW 2013 Proceedings, pp. 55–56. ACK CYFRONET AGH, Kraków (2013)
31. ROOT environment web site, http://root.cern.ch/drupal/
32. Rauch, L., Pernach, M., Bzowski, K., Pietrzyk, M.: On application of shape coefficients to creation of the statistically similar representative element of DP steels. Computer Methods in Materials Science 11(4), 531–541 (2011)
33. Milenin, A., Kustra, P.: Optimization of extrusion and wire drawing of magnesium alloys using the finite element method and distributed computing. In: Proceedings of the InterWire 2013 International Conference (2013) (in press)
34. Banach, G., Mikolajczyk, M.M., Uchronski, M., Tykierko, M.: Auxiliar Experimentorum – a different approach for creating and developing scientific applications. In: Bubak, M., Turała, M., Wiatr, K. (eds.) CGW 2013 Proceedings, pp. 65–66. ACK CYFRONET AGH, Kraków (2013)
35. Kocot, J., Szepieniec, T., Harężlak, D., Noga, K., Sterzel, M.: InSilicoLab – Managing Complexity of Chemistry Computations. In: Bubak, M., Szepieniec, T., Wiatr, K. (eds.) PL-Grid 2011. LNCS, vol. 7136, pp. 265–275. Springer, Heidelberg (2012)
36. Kocot, J., Eilmes, A., Szepieniec, T., Sterzel, M., Golik, M.: Molecular Modeling of Complex Systems with InSilicoLab. In: Wiatr, K., Kitowski, J., Bubak, M. (eds.) Proceedings of the Sixth ACC Cyfronet AGH Users Conference, pp. 45–46. ACC CYFRONET AGH, Kraków (2013)
37. Eilmes, A., Sterzel, M., Szepieniec, T., Kocot, J., Noga, K., Golik, M.: Comprehensive Support for Chemistry Computations in PL-Grid Infrastructure. In: Book of Abstracts of the Current Trends in Theoretical Chemistry VI Conference, pp. G9–G13. Jagiellonian University, Faculty of Chemistry, Kraków (2013)
38. Stankiewicz, M., Wawrzyniak, A., Goryl, P., Zajac, M., Nowak, M., Zytniak, L., Melka, F., Szymocha, T.: Services for Synchrotron deployment and operations. In: Bubak, M., Turała, M., Wiatr, K. (eds.) CGW 2013 Proceedings, pp. 63–64. ACK CYFRONET AGH, Kraków (2013)

National Distributed High Performance Computing Infrastructure for PL-Grid Users

Paweł Dziekoński[1], Franciszek Klajn[1], Łukasz Flis[2], Patryk Lasoń[2],
Marek Magryś[2], Andrzej Oziębło[2], Radosław Rowicki[3], Marcin Stolarek[3],
Dominik Bartkiewicz[3], Marek Zawadzki[4], Marcin Pospieszny[4],
Rafał Mikołajczak[4], Maciej Brzeźniak[4],
Norbert Meyer[4], and Marcin Samson[5]

[1] Wroclaw Centre for Networking and Supercomputing,
Wroclaw University of Technology, Wyb. Wyspiańskiego 27, 50-370 Wrocław, Poland
pawel.dziekonski@wcss.pl
http://www.wcss.pl
[2] AGH University of Science and Technology, ACC Cyfronet AGH,
ul. Nawojki 11, 30-950 Kraków, Poland
l.flis@cyfronet.pl
http://www.cyfronet.pl
[3] Interdisciplinary Centre for Mathematical and Computational Modelling,
University of Warsaw, ul. Pawińskiego 5a, 02-106 Warszawa, Poland
r.rowicki@icm.edu.pl
http://www.icm.edu.pl
[4] Poznan Supercomputing and Networking Center,
Institute of Bioorganic Chemistry of the Polish Academy of Sciences,
ul. Noskowskiego 10, 61-704 Poznań, Poland
mzawadzk@man.poznan.pl
http://www.psnc.pl
[5] Academic Computer Centre TASK, Gdansk University of Technology,
ul. G. Narutowicza 11/12, 80-233 Gdańsk, Poland
m.samson@task.gda.pl
http://www.task.gda.pl

Abstract. The article describes the PL-Grid computing infrastructure built as a result of the first PL-Grid-based project "Polish Infrastructure for Supporting Computational Science in the European Research Space", then enlarged, upgraded and improved during the PLGrid Plus project. Five Polish supercomputing sites joined forces to create a cross-country integrated computing service for our scientists. These sites were Cyfronet in Kraków, ICM in Warsaw, PSNC in Poznań, TASK in Gdańsk and WCSS in Wrocław. PL-Grid Infrastructure enables Polish scientists carrying out scientific research based on the simulations and large-scale calculations using the computing clusters as well as it provides convenient access to distributed computing resources.

Keywords: Grid, computing infrastructure, computing clusters.

M. Bubak et al. (Eds.): PLGrid Plus, LNCS 8500, pp. 16–33, 2014.

1   Preface

PL-Grid computing infrastructure started emerging in 2009 as a result of the first PL-Grid-based project – "Polish Infrastructure for Supporting Computational Science in the European Research Space" [1], when five Polish supercomputing sites joined forces to create a cross–country integrated computing service for our scientists. The sites were Cyfronet in Kraków [6], ICM in Warsaw [7], PSNC in Poznań [8], TASK in Gdańsk [9] and WCSS in Wrocław [10].

Our ultimate goal was, and still is, to provide as much as possible unified infrastructure. This is not an easy goal, because all centers are formally independent legal entities.

After 3 years of the first project, we delivered almost 260 TFLOPS[1] of theoretical peak performance of all HPC systems when only 215 TFLOPS was required as the project goal! We also delivered almost 3.7PB of all storage system whereas there was a demand for 2.5PB. The results of the first project were very successful.

In the second and current project – "Domain-oriented services and resources of Polish Infrastructure for Supporting Computational Science in the European Research Space – PLGrid Plus" [1] our goals are even higher. We want to provide additional 500 TFLOPS of computer power and additional 4.5PB (in addition to the previous values).

Besides deploying the computing and storage hardware, we continue to support other Work Packages of the project and – what is most important – our users.

One of the most interesting tasks is a detailed and unified accounting of the consumed computing time. This task is done in cooperation with Work Package 3. Fair accounting is a tough and sensitive subject. We need to be in control of how much computing time is utilized by our users, but we still want them to use our resources in an easy and friendly way. To help and ease the accounting, we developed a set of tools and enhancements:

- use of CPUSETS and CPUGROUPS,
- an interface for reservation system that works with all our batch systems and job schedulers – Moab[2], PBS PRo[3], TORQUE[4] and SLURM[5],
- integration of use of Modules in all supported grid middleware – gLite [11], QCG [12], UNICORE [13],
- unified labeling of all compute nodes in all sites,
- unified execution of most frequently used applications,
- monitoring of most frequently used applications,
- monitoring of cross-infrastructure license use – an approach for license provision between independent sites and using licenses as a resource,

---

[1] http://en.wikipedia.org/wiki/FLOPS
[2] http://en.wikipedia.org/wiki/Moab_Cluster_Suite
[3] http://en.wikipedia.org/wiki/Portable_Batch_System
[4] http://en.wikipedia.org/wiki/TORQUE_Resource_Manager
[5] http://en.wikipedia.org/wiki/
Simple_Linux_Utility_for_Resource_Management

– unified accounting of compute time across different compute nodes – every kind of compute nodes has been benchmarked and a formula has been developed to fairly account the compute time consumed in different sites and nodes,
– and other minor improvements.

The unification of computing resources also applies to the unification of User Interface (UI) machines – grid-enabled login/access nodes. We created a definition of standard or common configuration that the user can and should expect to be fulfilled by UI. This includes monitoring of all unified components to ensure a constant standard accordance. Five UI machines are deployed in five centers, but still they will be connected with 10Gbps Ethernet links using our Polish Optical Internet – PIONIER network [2]. At a later stage, there will be just two UI machines serving access to the Grid. They will be geographically separated – in Wrocław and Kraków – for high redundancy. Despite a long distance (300 km), there will be a shared storage system hosting user files.

There are also many smaller tasks, but equally important, like constant provision of different services like GridFTP[6], xrootd[7], DPM[8] (Disk Pool Manager), LDAP[9] and other, input for documentation – best practices for users, efficient use of computing and storage systems, general and basic user training for use of Linux, support for English-speaking, not only Polish users, and others.

PL-Grid Infrastructure is generally HPC-oriented and it is mostly beneficial to the users running heavy calculations in Linux environments.

To widen the offer, especially towards MS Windows users, PL-Grid Infrastructure was integrated by us with Platon U3 project [3], which provides an innovative, nationwide computing service by delivering applications on demand in a cloud-like style. Platon U3 is capable of providing a wide range of users from the scientific and research environments with an elastic and scalable access to specific applications, both in MS Windows and Linux systems. This takes also into consideration the needs of professional groups in these environments, including the implementation of an integrated system of services managing the grid resources.

By implementing a new web service and enhancing the Platon U3 middleware and the PL-Grid portal, it was possible to integrate both infrastructures in terms of the resource requesting mechanisms. Currently, virtual machines can be easily requested by PL-Grid users directly from the PL-Grid portal.

Another part of the Platon project is an archiving service – U4 [4]. PL-Grid users generate a lot of output data, which must be backed up and archived. To address these needs, we enhanced the PL-Grid portal to support automatic subscribing of our users to the Platon U4 service. Information exchange between PL-Grid and Platon U4 is instantly done by a set of LDAP servers. This allows transfer of users, groups and group membership, detection of addition of new

---

[6] http://en.wikipedia.org/wiki/GridFTP
[7] http://xrootd.org/
[8] http://en.wikipedia.org/wiki/GLite
[9] http://en.wikipedia.org/wiki/Lightweight_Directory_Access_Protocol

users and tracking their group membership, which may dynamically change over time.

Below, there are presented the detailed descriptions of all five sites' resources and infrastructures hardware and software layers. To simplify reading, they are roughly divided into common subjects: compute nodes, interconnect topology, local file systems and storage.

2   Academic Computer Centre Cyfronet AGH

2.1   Zeus – Compute Nodes

Cyfronet currently operates the largest Polish supercomputer named Zeus, providing more than 370 TFLOPS of theoretical performance, over 25000 x86 CPU cores, 200 GPGPUs[10] and about 60TB of RAM to PL-Grid scientific community.

As a heterogeneous computing cluster, it has been split to four basic classes of nodes (see Fig. 1):

- Classic CPU nodes with two Intel Xeon processors and about 2GB of memory per core,
- Fat CPU nodes with four AMD processors and 4GB of memory per core (256GB per node),
- GPU nodes with Intel Xeon CPUs and two Nvidia M2050 or eight Nvidia M2090 GPGPUs,
- Large vSMP nodes with Intel Xeon processors connected with a specialized virtual machine hypervisor, which allows for booting up the machines up to 768 cores and 6TB of memory.

Distinction of node types gives a possibility to fit applications to the hardware, which match at best its characteristics and special requirements. The CPU node group is dominated by serial and parallel (MPI) jobs, the second one is great for large memory jobs, the third allows some applications to benefit from GPGPU accelerators and the fourth one gives a possibility to run huge memory jobs or scale applications, which do not use any inter-node communication library, like MPI, for parallelism.

2.2   Queuing System

For users' convenience, all classes have been bound together and are accessible via the TORQUE queue system with Moab scheduler from a dedicated user interface machine, `zeus.cyfronet.pl`. Users may access the system through local queues with different computing time settings and also by the queues dedicated for the grid jobs. A big number of queues provides the PL-Grid users with a comfort of using the cluster and administrators can easier set up the limits for different types of resources.

---

[10] http://en.wikipedia.org/wiki/
General-purpose_computing_on_graphics_processing_units

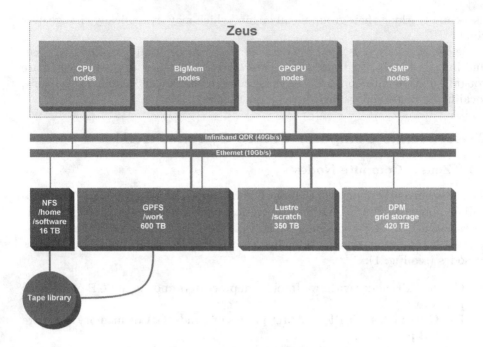

Fig. 1. Cluster Zeus in Cyfronet – logical layout

2.3 Interconnect Topology, Local File Systems

All cluster nodes are connected to an InfiniBand[11] QDR fabric in a fat-tree topology. There is also another 10Gbps network used to transfer remote data, stage in files from a local grid Storage Element, boot the nodes and for administrative communication. The cluster has a 10Gbps network uplink, which provides connectivity to the rest of Polish computer centers and a dedicated 10Gbps link for LHC[12] data transfers.

All nodes have direct access to shared file systems, and most of the nodes also contain a local hard drive, which might be used by, e.g., batch jobs that require low-latency file metadata operations. Currently, three shared network file systems technologies are used to provide disk resources for Zeus (see Fig. 1):

- NFS (/people and /software mount points), which is used for user home directories and software distribution among computing nodes,
- Lustre[13] (/scratch mount point), a parallel file system, which is used as scratch for temporary data storage during job lifetime,

---

[11] http://en.wikipedia.org/wiki/InfiniBand
[12] http://en.wikipedia.org/wiki/Large_Hadron_Collider
[13] http://en.wikipedia.org/wiki/Lustre_file_system

– GPFS[14] (/work mount point), a proprietary file system from IBM, which is used as a work space, for mid- and long-term storage of data, which are either job input or output files.

2.4 Storage

GPFS file system is also connected to a TSM system (IBM Tivoli Storage Manager), thanks to which Hierarchical Storage Management is being provided for the /work file system. This file system consists of three tiers: Tier-1 based on disk arrays with SAS drives (200TB), Tier-2 based on storage servers and nearline SAS drives (400TB) and Tier-3, which is based on LTO-5 tape drives and a few hundred tape slots in the library.

Beside the standard POSIX[15] file system storage, there is also an object storage service for grid users based on Disk Pool Manager technology. Currently, it provides 420TB of disk drives for PL-Grid and it is heavily used by High Energy Physics community focused on LHC analysis.

3 Interdisciplinary Centre for Mathematical and Computational Modelling – ICM

3.1 Hydra Cluster – Compute Nodes and Interconnect Topology

Compute nodes are booting using PXE (Preboot Execution Environment)[16]. Initrd with local modifications is a mounting root file system in read-only mode using NFS from NetApp 6080 NAS. We use neither unionfs nor other comprehensive solutions, instead all the needed logic is implemented in initrd and services init scripts. The directories, which need to work in read-write mode like: /var/lib or /tmp are mounted locally in /dev/ramX devices and synchronized with a frontend node state during the boot process. We apply special treatment for /etc where only some files (e.g. /etc/sysconfig/network) have to be different on all the nodes, these files are linked to /etc-local directory (similar to new Ubuntu systems).

Temporary directories for users are created in files on a Lustre file system at batch job startup and deleted directly after the job ends. This solution provides very fast metadata operations and higher throughput than local file systems. In such a configuration there is no need in local hard disks in compute nodes, which improves nodes reliability.

Interconnect topology is presented in Fig. 2. The main difficulty is the part of the nodes that does not have an InfiniBand connection. This part is mainly used for jobs with parallelism smaller than one node, hence there are 48 and 64 core nodes with AMD CPUs, this does not come as a real world limitation. However, one should remember that 10Gb for so large number of cores is a real performance

---

[14] http://en.wikipedia.org/wiki/IBM_General_Parallel_File_System
[15] http://en.wikipedia.org/wiki/POSIX
[16] http://en.wikipedia.org/wiki/Preboot_Execution_Environment

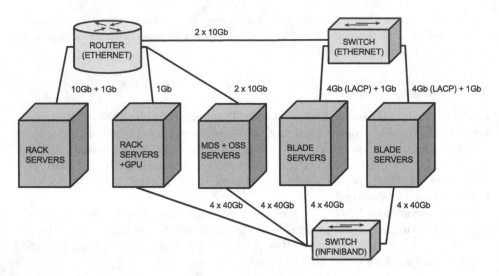

Fig. 2. Cluster Hydra in ICM – logical layout

bottleneck when high throughput to the Lustre file system is needed. A part of InfiniBand infrastructure in more detail is presented in Fig. 3.

3.2 Queuing System

ICM is using the SLURM batch system in version 2.6.1, with a variety of plugins, which are discussed below. One of the most important plugins is a topology/tree plugin, which allows us to fulfill the node scheduling policies based on a non-uniform interconnect topology presented in Fig. 2. The plugin is not only choosing nodes with the same interconnect (InfiniBand/Ethernet), but also prevents running jobs through a low bandwidth connection between InfiniBand islands.

The decision to use SLURM in PL-Grid and EGI e-infrastructures forced ICM team to implement some parts of federational requirements. These topics are covered in more detail in a separate paper [5]. An essential and important part of this work was implementation of PL-Grid accounting system into SLURM, which turned out to be a non-trivial task.

One of the new features introduced in the SLURM batch system is job profiling. Commonly available SLURM plugins are providing information about Lustre file system usage, electrical power consumption, InfiniBand links traffic and general information about RAM memory and CPU usage. Although job profiling sounds very promising and may play a great role in user education and resources monitoring, it is still suffering a lot of problems, especially in electrical power consumption, which is only available for the newest Intel CPUs.

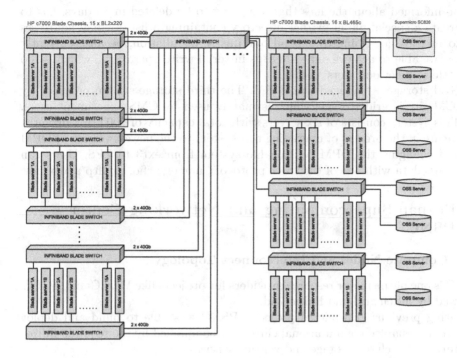

Fig. 3. Cluster Hydra in ICM – InfiniBand topology

3.3 Storage

In ICM we are supporting three types of storage: home directories, scratch directories and grid storage. We are briefly describing all these systems:

- Home directories – on the ICM cluster the users are divided into two groups. The first one are PL-Grid users, whose home directories are located on ZFS[17] shared over NFS from Solaris 10 server. ZFS configuration is using the caching of data on PCI-e SSD drive – Sun F20, and backend of 48 SATA disk. Maximal throughput efficiency from many clients is reaching 800MB/s The second group are local ICM users, their home directories are located on CNFS (cluster NFS distributed from four GPFS servers). This system supports the writing speed in one stream up to 1GBps.
- Scratch file systems – Hydra cluster provides a scratch file system on Lustre. Our Lustre installation consists of one metadata server (MDS) and eight object storage servers (OSS), each one with 10x 1TB drives in RAID 6[18] as object storage target (OST). The scratch does not provide any backup policy, quite the opposite we are realizing the policy of automatically removing files that have not been accessed for more than 60 days. Each user who wishes to

---

[17] http://en.wikipedia.org/wiki/ZFS
[18] http://en.wikipedia.org/wiki/RAID

be informed about the files that are going to be deleted in 10 days, has to create a special file in his/her directory containing a list of email addresses to use. We are going to expand our Lustre installation, because currently we are able to achieve only 3.5GBps in serial write operations, which is too little to meet our users' needs.

– Grid storage – managed with DPM. The third storage system provided by ICM site is grid storage, which is mainly used by CMS experiment users. This system consists of six servers with total capacity of 200TB. Currently, we are in the process of upgrading this system to the newest version of DPM and changing the DPM backing file system from ext3 to ZFS. Users can access data with one of the three protocols, namely: rfio, gridftp and xroot.

4   Poznan Supercomputing and Networking Center – PSNC

4.1   Compute Nodes and Interconnect Topology

PSNC is one of the major resource providers for projects like WLCG and EGEE, followed by int.eu.grid and BalticGrid.

During previous grid-related projects, PSNC was able to build and deploy several grid-enabled computational clusters accompanied by the required infrastructure that includes storage and various services.

For the PLGrid Plus project, PSNC delivers two grid-enabled computational clusters: a semi-homogeneous x86_64 Reef cluster and a hybrid Inula cluster.

The Reef cluster configuration consists of:

– 650+ Supermicro and HP BladeSystem nodes, each equipped with two x86_64 compatible processors (Intel Xeon 5160, Intel Xeon E5345, Intel Xeon 5410, Intel Xeon 5530, Intel Xeon 5520 or AMD Opteron 6164 HE),
– 10TB of RAM,
– subset of grid-services including:
  - user interfaces supporting multiple grid-middleware such as:
    * gLite/EMI,
    * QosCosGrid (QCG),
    * UNICORE,
  - storage services including:
    * DPM and Xrootd grid storages,
    * POSIX-compliant storage spaces,
    * Cloud-like storage,
  - grid-core services:
    * information and accounting services,
    * distributed directory information services.

The Inula cluster configuration consists of:

– 68 SGI/Rackable nodes with two 12-core processors (AMD Opteron 6234) and 1 or 2 NVidia Tesla M2050 GPGPU accelerator,

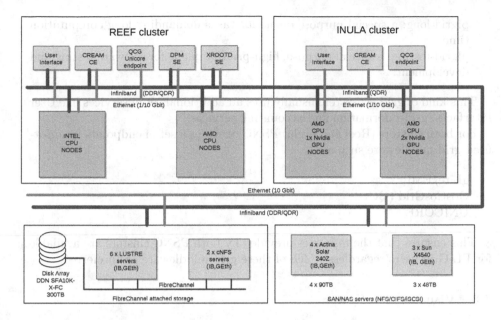

Fig. 4. Reef and Inula clusters in PSNC

- 48 or 64GB of RAM per node (1 or 2 GPGPU),
- The software stack consists of a subset of grid-services including user interfaces for gLite/EMI and QosCosGrid (QCG) grid middleware.

For both, the Reef and Inula clusters, we use two types of interconnects:

- 1Gb and 10Gb ethernet interconnect as a general purpose one. This network is used mainly for management, NFS file system and internet access medium.
- DDR/QDR (Reef) and pure QDR (Inula) InfiniBand interconnect as a dedicated network for data intensive tasks. The InfiniBand network is used for tasks, which require high throughput and low-latency data-intensive computations or high IOPS data access using the Lustre file system.

4.2   Queuing System

For both, the Reef and Inula clusters, PSNC deployed TORQUE Resource Management System, which, along with Maui scheduler[19], allows for flexible resource management.

A typical solution in this kind of environment is to use a subset of queues and resource partitions for tasks separation.

For PL-Grid users, both clusters, Reef and Inula, provide the following queues:

- plgrid: a general purpose queue for large quantity and scale jobs,

---

[19] http://en.wikipedia.org/wiki/Maui_Cluster_Scheduler

- plgrid-long: a special purpose queue for tasks demanding long computation times,
- plgrid-testing: a special purpose, high-priority queue for software testing and development.

This kind of grid-ecosystem usually uses an additional set of services like User Interfaces, grid-information and accounting services.

For both clusters (Reef and Inula) PSNC provides a set of endpoints for most-used grid middleware such as:

- gLite/EMI,
- QosCosGrid (QCG),
- UNICORE.

This ensures that the resources provided by both PSNC clusters are available for PL-Grid users regardless which of these grid middleware are preferred.

4.3   Visualization System

Along with the computational/HPC clusters, PSNC provides also visualisation services in form of a tightly-bonded visualisation cluster – Moss.

Moss is the visualization cluster operated by PSNC. It contains 7 fat compute nodes, 1 login node and 1 storage node. All its nodes are interconnected with a redundant 10Gb Ethernet. Users' home directories are located on a storage node, which consists of 14 SAS HDD – 4TB each. Home directories are shared among all Moss nodes via NFS. Moreover, compute nodes have its local fast scratch storage (2x 60GB SSD). All the nodes have also FC 8Gb HBAs to connect to an external backup storage and for future integration with a local disk array (12 fast 900GB SAS drives and 12 3TB SATA drives). Each compute node contains up to two accelerators. Accelerators installed on a single compute node are always of the same type, but Moss contains several different types of accelerators.

The detailed Moss configuration is as follows:

- Compute node 1-3: 2x Intel Xeon E5-2670, 512GB RAM, 2x SSD 64GB, 2x 10Gb Ethernet, 8Gb FibreChannel, 2x Nvidia Tesla K20,
- Compute node 4: 2x Intel Xeon E5-2670, 512GB RAM, 2x SSD 64GB, 2x 10Gb Ethernet, 8Gb FibreChannel, 2x Nvidia Tesla K10,
- Compute node 5: 2x Intel Xeon E5-2670, 512GB RAM, 2x SSD 64GB, 2x 10Gb Ethernet, 8Gb FibreChannel, 2x Intel Xeon Phi 5110P,
- Compute node 6: 2x Intel Xeon E5-2670, 128 RAM, 2x 10Gb Ethernet, 8Gb FibreChannel, 1x Nvidia Tesla M2090,
- Compute node 7: 2x Intel Xeon E5-2670, 256GB RAM, 2x 10Gb Ethernet, 8Gb FibreChannel, 2x Nvidia Tesla M2070Q,
- Storage node: 2x Intel Xeon E5-2670, 192GB RAM, 14x SAS HDD 4TB, 2x 10Gb Ethernet,

- Login node: 2x Intel Xeon E5-2450, 128GB RAM, 2x 10Gb Ethernet, 8Gb FibreChannel,
- Auxiliary equipment – 2x FC 8Gb Switch, 2x 10Gb Ethernet Switch, FC Disk Array (12x 900GB SAS, 12x 3TB SATA).

Moss is supposed to be used interactively by remote users. At the moment it is available via SSH (with X11Forwarding enabled). We plan also to enable remote users to access Moss via VNC in the nearest future. The following visualization application libraries are installed on Moss:

- vtk: a toolkit for scientific and information visualization,
- paraview: access to the Paraview visualization application,
- icarus, h5fddsm, hdf5-vfd, catalyst: paraview extensions to support visualization *in-situ*,
- vitrall: a distributed web based visualization system.

Other installed software:

- CUDA: software to develop programs for NVIDIA GPGPUs,
- OpenMPI: a Message Passing Interface open-source implementation,
- R: a freely available language and environment for statistical computing,
- Ansys: an advanced CFD simulator,
- Bowtie: an ultrafast, memory-efficient short read aligner,
- BWA: a tool to map low-divergent sequences against a large reference genome,
- Cufflinks: assembles transcripts, estimates their abundances, and tests for differential expression and regulation in RNA-Seq samples,
- FastQC: provides a simple way to do some quality control checks on raw sequence data coming from high throughput sequencing pipelines,
- RNA-SeQC: computes a series of quality control metrics for RNA-Seq data,
- RSEM: estimates gene and isoform expression levels from RNA-Seq data,
- TopHat: a fast splice junction mapper for RNA-Seq reads,
- atlas, mkl: linear algebra libraries,
- intel, gcc, python: programming languages,
- xkaapi: a library to facilitate development of parallel (multi-CPU/GPU) applications.

In the nearest future we plan to install also the following software packages:

- blender: an animation and video-stream editing application,
- ensight: access to CEI's Ensight visualization application,
- glew: a GL extension Wrangler library,
- idl: access to the IDL visualization application,
- mesa: access to a software implementation of OpenGL,
- sdl: a simple application development toolkit,
- silo: access to the Silo visualization application and associated tools and libraries,
- vapor: access to NCAR's Vapor visualization application,
- XSEDE: tools supporting XSEDE environment, including Globus.

4.4 Local File Systems

For end-user data, both clusters use NFS and Lustre partitions mounted across cluster nodes.

The storage on all clusters is divided into two classes: an NFS-based, home directory space that provides a shared workspace on all PSNC clusters and a Lustre-based, fast scratch storage space that is used by applications as a temporary workspace.

The data storage policy created over the duration of PL-Grid and PLGrid Plus projects allows users to store their data in several different locations.

For long-term storage, such as users' home directories and PL-Grid group storage, an NFS distributed file system is used.

For this purpose, we use a high throughput storage device (DDN disk array) exported using NFS distributed file system protocol. The back-end of the NFS storage is provided by a cluster of two GPFS-enabled NFS servers, working in ACTIVE-ACTIVE mode. The disk arrays work in protected RAID 5 or RAID 6 modes. The contents of the home directories is backed up on a tape storage using IBM TSM software.

For data protection we use both: RAID disk arrays and periodic data backup using tools like IBM TSM.

The Lustre file system consists of 10 server clusters and Infiniband as interconnect. Due to the storage policy that treats this space as a temporary scratch space, data on the Lustre file system is not protected by any means.

Unfortunately, this kind of storage (Lustre), due to usage pattern, is not really suitable for data protection. It is worth mentioning that no data loss was ever reported on PSNC's Lustre file system.

All these locally available storage spaces are POSIX-compliant.

The above mentioned storage device (DDN) provides storage space for both, NFS and Lustre file systems and ca. 12GBps aggregated throughput for PL-Grid users and 90.000 IOPS.

4.5 Storage Including Grid, Tapes and Hierarchical Storage Management (HSM)

For long-term large-scale data storage PSNC infrastructure contains a subset of grid-enabled storage elements like:

- DPM Storage Element, which provides:
  - 115TB of storage space distributed into 10 RAID 6 disk arrays,
  - standard grid access using the following protocols:
    * gridftp
    * SRMv2.2
    * xrootd
    * WebDav
- Xrootd Storage Element for dedicated for VO ALICE, which provides:
  - 187.3TB of storage space distributed into 20 RAID 6 disk arrays
  - xrootd protocol access.

DPM Storage Elements is available for PL-Grid users, Xrootd SE will be enabled "on demand".

The storage scheme and detailed description is available at [14].

Additionally, the following new storage systems have been recently purchased within the PL-Grid project:

- NetApp E5500 2x 360TB (disk array for home directory),
- NetApp EF540 SSD 9TB (ssd disk array for home dir. metadata),
- 6x IBM x3650 M4 FC/IB/10GE servers for GPFS.

5 Academic Computer Centre TASK

TASK provides access for PL-Grid users to HPC cluster Galera Plus. All batch queues are unified with other PL-Grid sites.

5.1 Compute Nodes and Interconnect Topology

There are currently two distinct flavors of compute node making up Galera Plus, with two different architectures.

- Regular cluster nodes – 2304 Intel Westmere cores are provided by 192 dual socket HP ProLiant BL2x 220c Generation 7 half-height blade servers. Each node consists of two 2.27 GHz six core processors, giving twelve cores in total, forming a single SMP unit with 16GB of RAM (1.3GB per core), 4GB of local flash storage and Mellanox ConnectX-2 VPI interconnect. Code run on these nodes should be optimized for CPUs supporting SSE4.2 instructions and using Intel MPI.
- vSMP nodes – 768 Intel Westmere cores are provided by 64 dual socket HP ProLiant BL490c Generation 6 half-height blade servers. Each node consists of two 2.93 GHz six core processors, giving twelve cores in total. These servers are aggregated to form InfiniBand connected virtual servers, seen as they would contain e.g. 192 cores and 1TB of RAM each.

The cluster is arranged into 10 blade chassis; 6 chassis hold up 32 individual nodes each (see Fig. 5). 4 chassis hold up 16 vSMP nodes. Between all nodes there is a QDR InfiniBand low latency network. In addition to the InfiniBand network, each compute node has a Gigabit Ethernet network for data access and administration.

5.2 Storage

The main storage consists of two shared volumes: the home volume (4TB) and scratch volume (8TB). These are all glusterfs file systems. In addition, there is grid storage (1TB) accessible from se.task.gda.pl server.

A new storage system is being developed with a capacity of 1.7PB. It will be based on the Lustre file system.

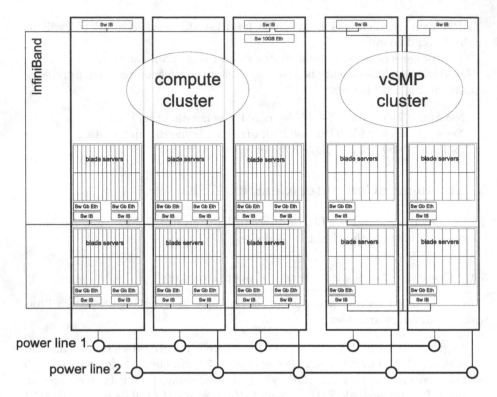

Fig. 5. Cluster Galera Plus in TASK

6   Wroclaw Centre for Networking and Supercomputing – WCSS

6.1   Supernova – Compute Nodes and Interconnect Topology

WCSS is currently operating HPC cluster Supernova. Cluster consists of various types of service and compute nodes:

- 152 Supermicro single-CPU 4-core Intel Xeon nodes,
- 176 Supermicro dual-CPU 4-core Intel Xeon nodes,
- 404 HP dual-CPU 6-core Intel Xeon nodes,
- 3 HP quad-CPU 16-core AMD Opteron nodes with 256GB of memory,
- numerous service nodes of different made and configurations.

Compute nodes are equipped with 2GB of memory per core, thus 8 to 24GB total per node, or 256GB total on fat nodes.

Nodes with 4 or 8 cores are connected to a local domain of InfiniBand DDR network based on Voltaire switches. This part of the network has a fat-tree topology.

12-core nodes are made in the blade technology and are connected to a local domain of InfiniBand QDR network based on Mellanox switches inside blade chassis and the core Intel/Qlogic QDR switch of modular design. Blade switches are connected with redundant links. This part of the network has a blocking factor 1:5, however, every connection provides 120Gbps of bandwidth, which is more than sufficient for users' needs.

Both DDR and QDR domains are connected together by Intel/Qlogic QDR switch. This switch also provides access to a Lustre file system.

Every compute node is connected to the Ethernet network with a single 1Gbps link using wire speed switches, which are then connected together using redundant 10Gbps links constituting an aggregation layer. The core network is based on 10Gbps switches working as one virtual chassis for the ease of management, scalability and redundancy. Core switches provide access to NAS and iSCSI servers and to an external network.

6.2 Local File Systems

All compute nodes are diskless and are being booted using PXE and a remotely mounted NFS root file system of custom design. There is no swap area on nodes. The root FS is served from high performance NAS heads of NetApp and Hitachi HNAS – 4 in total. Each node is booted from the same system image for the ease of management. One change made to the root image instantly propagates to all nodes. All the changes made locally on a node are saved only in a local ramdisk to guarantee the integrity of the image.

The access to home accounts, applications and all other utility volumes is done via NFS mounts from NAS heads. Total capacity of all head nodes is about 200TB. Total bandwidth provided by NAS heads is about 3GBps.

The scratch area is based on the Lustre file system, which consists of:

- three DDN S2A9900 disk arrays with InfiniBand DDR interfaces, total raw space about 30TB,
- one DDN SFA12K-40 disk array with InfiniBand FDR interfaces, total raw space about 420TB,
- two MDS nodes,
- 18 OSS servers.

Lustre provides an aggregated bandwidth of 35GBps – the fastest file system in Poland with a public access.

6.3 Storage

All users are able to archive their work in a backup-archive system based on IBM TSM. The primary archiving storage has a capacity of 20TB. The user data is automatically migrated in a transparent way using HSM mechanism to the LTO tape library with a capacity of about 3PB. The migration speed is estimated to about 2GBps using 16 LTO5 tape drives, thus the primary archiving file system can be emptied in just minutes when a migration threshold is triggered (see Fig. 6).

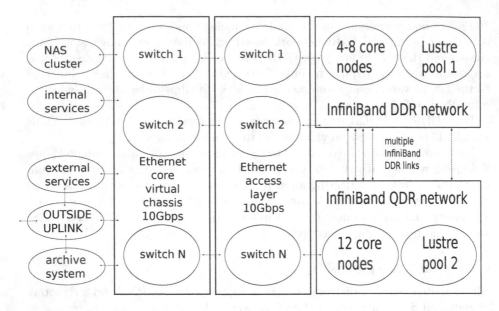

Fig. 6. Cluster Supernova in WCSS

7 Conclusions and Future Work

The actual computing infrastructure, described above site by site, is based on the PL-Grid Infrastructure built as a result of the first PL-Grid-based project. It was, and it is and will be, constantly enlarged, upgraded and improved during the PLGrid Plus project. The very important aim is to provide additional 500 TFLOPS of computer power (in addition to previous 260 TFLOPS) – not theoretical (Rpeak) but rather an effective one, with respect to the following formula:

$$effectiveTFLOPS = (80\% * CPU Rpeak) + (50\% * GPU Rpeak), \quad (1)$$

where two coefficients: 80% and 50% define approximately the realistic, usual computer performance with respect to the typical Linpack Benchmark.

We also want to provide additional 4.5PB (in addition to the previous 3.7PB) of available data storage. Both goals must be achieved by the end of December 2014.

Besides the enhancements and improvements of the computing and storage hardware and software, we will continue to support other Work Packages of the project and – of course – our users. All other important 'smaller' tasks, like constant provisioning of different services, input for documentation, efficient usage of computing and storage systems, user training and others, as well as integration with Platon U3 and U4 platforms and its users will be also continued and improved.

References

1. PL-Grid and PLGrid Plus projects web site, http://www.plgrid.pl/en
2. PIONIER, http://www.pionier.edu.pl
3. Platon U3, http://cloud.pionier.net.pl/index.pl
4. Platon U4, http://storage.pionier.net.pl/
5. Bartkiewicz, D., Benedyczak, K., Kluszczyński, R., Stolarek, M., Rękawek, T.: Integrating Slurm Batch System with European and Polish Grid Infrastructures. In: Bubak, M., Kitowski, J., Wiatr, K. (eds.) PLGrid Plus. LNCS, vol. 8500, pp. 106–117. Springer, Heidelberg (2014)
6. Academic Computer Centre Cyfronet AGH, http://www.cyfronet.krakow.pl/
7. Interdisciplinary Centre for Mathematical and Computational Modelling – ICM, http://www.icm.edu.pl/
8. Poznan Supercomputing and Networking Center – PSNC, http://www.man.poznan.pl/
9. Academic Computer Centre TASK, http://www.task.gda.pl/
10. Wroclaw Centre for Networking and Supercomputing – WCSS, http://www.wcss.wroc.pl/
11. gLite, DPM, http://en.wikipedia.org/wiki/GLite
12. QCG, http://www.qoscosgrid.org/
13. UNICORE, http://en.wikipedia.org/wiki/UNICORE
14. Storage at PSNC, https://hpc.man.poznan.pl/modules/resourcesection/category.php?categoryid=24
15. Binczewski, A., et al.: Polish Contribution to the Worldwide LHC Computing. In: Bubak, M., Szepieniec, T., Wiatr, K. (eds.) PL-Grid 2011. LNCS, vol. 7136, pp. 285–300. Springer, Heidelberg (2012)
16. Lasoń, P., et al.: Effective utilization of mixed computing resources on Zeus cluster. In: Bubak, M., Turała, M., Wiatr, K. (eds.) CGW 2012 Proceedings, pp. 105–106. ACK CYFRONET AGH, Kraków (2012)
17. Flis, Ł., Lasoń, P., Magryś, M.: Using Moab, Fairshares and TORQUE Filters to Guarantee Usage Agreements at Cyfronet. In: The MoabCon 2013, Utah, USA (2013)

New QosCosGrid Middleware Capabilities and Its Integration with European e-Infrastructure

Bartosz Bosak, Piotr Kopta, Krzysztof Kurowski,
Tomasz Piontek, and Mariusz Mamoński†

Poznan Supercomputing and Networking Center,
ul. Noskowskiego 10, 61-704 Poznań, Poland
{bbosak,pkopta,krzysztof.kurowski,piontek}@man.poznan.pl

Abstract. QosCosGrid (QCG) is an integrated system offering leading job and resource management capabilities in order to deliver
supercomputer-like performance and structure to end users. By combining many distributed computing resources together, QCG offers highly
efficient mapping, execution and monitoring capabilities for a variety
of applications, such as parameter sweep, workflows, multi-scale, MPI or
hybrid MPI-OpenMP. The QosCosGrid middleware also provides a set of
unique features, such as advance reservation, co-allocation of distributed
computing resources, support for interactive tasks and monitoring of
a progress of running applications. The middleware is offered to end
users by well-designed and easy-to-use client tools. At the time of writing, QosCosGrid is the most popular middleware within the PL-Grid
Infrastructure. After its successful adoption within the Polish research
communities, it has been integrated with the EGI infrastructure and
through a release in UMD and EGI-AppDB it is also available at European level. In this article, we focus on the extensions that were introduced to QosCosGrid during the period of the PL-Grid and PLGrid Plus
projects in order to support advanced user scenarios and to integrate the
stack with the Polish and European e-Infrastructures.

Keywords: grid computing, middleware, advance reservations,
co-allocation of resources, application monitoring, notifications.

1 Introduction

In the last years, there have been identified two distinctive groups of end users
interested in obtaining efficient access to computational resources belonging to
the national- or European-level e-Infrastructures such as PL-Grid and EGI. Both
groups of users differ primarily in their experience in running jobs on HPC
clusters and thus they expect different kinds of tools tailored to their needs,
habits and aforementioned levels of experience. The first group comprises the
researchers that usually have some computer science background and are familiar
with cluster solutions. They expect command-line tools similar to those known

M. Bubak et al. (Eds.): PLGrid Plus, LNCS 8500, pp. 34–53, 2014.

from queuing systems, but offering access to all resources of an e-Infrastructure. The second group consists of domain-oriented researchers, who have not used clusters yet, but who are willing to migrate from their desktop systems and to take full advantage of HPC computing. These users want to solve bigger instances of problems or to parallelize the execution of numerous application runs. They require intuitive tools resembling the tools they are accustomed to and breaking the technology barrier associated with the migration to the grid environment, in order to exploit them in their daily work.

To support the two groups of users, the QosCosGrid (QCG) middleware, developed in Poznan Supercomputing and Networking Center (PSNC), delivers an advanced multi-layered e-Infrastructure, which successfully integrates primary and brand-new services and tools capable of dealing with various kinds of computationally intensive simulations. Recently, all these services and tools were integrated with the European e-Infrastructure, and were made available through the EGI distribution channels, like Unified Middleware Distribution (UMD) [33] and EGI Applications Database (AppDB) [26] for the research communities outside PL-Grid.

Within this document, we present new capabilities of the QosCosGrid middleware developed in the time frame of the PLGrid Plus project that extend the core functionality described in [8]. The document focuses on the extensions provided to the basic QCG services and it describes several recently developed components that support new user scenarios and integrate QCG solutions with the Polish and European e-Infrastructures.

The remaining part of the article is organized as follows: Section 2, Related Work, provides a brief overview of existing grid middleware and available end user tools. The main objectives underlying the QosCosGrid middleware are presented in Section 3. Section 4 presents a high-level architecture of QosCosGrid along with a short description of its main components. In the next section we outline new features of the middleware, i.e. application scripts, improved brokering, advance reservation, co-allocation of resources and support for notifications. Section 6 describes the main QosCosGrid client tools, namely QCG-SimpleClient and QCG-Icon, and introduces the concepts of QCG-Data and QosCosGrid Science Gateway. The next section reports the status of the integration process of QosCosGrid middleware with the EGI infrastructure. Finally, a general discussion on the outcomes achieved so far and the plans for future development of the middleware are addressed in Section 8.

2   Related Work

The QosCosGrid is one of several advanced middleware distributions deployed on e-Infrastructures. Although each middleware provides an exhaustive set of functions required to efficiently run advanced simulations, the decision to select a particular system for grid calculation is complex as it usually entails the way how the scientific work will look like during a long period of time. Middleware differ in complexity, applied technologies, offered functions as well as in the features of end user tools. In some cases, small differences may cause serious problems or bring significant benefits in the future.

Undoubtedly, each of middleware has its loyal users, who historically or/and politically started to build their application scenarios based on specific environments and have no reason to change the selected system. A clear example may be the gLite framework massively exploited by the community associated with CERN LHC for their simulations [17]. Other groups of users, connected by specific projects, requirements or geographical location, decided upon different middleware technologies, e.g. UNICORE [4,5], ARC [16] or SAGA [32]. It is worth noting that the support for advance reservations and co-allocation of resources is not a common functionality and is available only in few middleware by adoption of specialized frameworks, such as HARC [18] or GridARS [22].

In turn, the number of various client programs that allow running the computations using one or many middleware systems is relatively large. Usually, a middleware introduces its own command-line tool(s), e.g. UNICORE provides UNICORE CommandLine Client [21], gLite provides its Command Line Interface [17], but often it also offers dedicated GUI applications, like UNICORE RichClient [10]. There are also advanced programs, capable of submitting jobs to many middleware, such as Migrating Desktop and gEclipse [19]. A different group of high-client tools includes web solutions, e.g. GridSpace2 [9] or science-gateways [11].

To help users select the optimal middleware, the work [8] provides a basic comparison of the QosCosGrid middleware with gLite and UNICORE.[1]

3   Goals of QosCosGrid

The QosCosGrid (QCG) middleware could be seen as a system that hides the complexity of many heterogeneous computing resources behind a single, intuitive and user-friendly interface. However, the functionalities offered by QosCosGrid are not simply limited to a direct mapping of particular functions available in queuing systems into the well-designed interface at a grid level. The aim was to design and implement a system driven by real requirements and expectations of researchers. Therefore, from the beginning, the development of QCG services and tools is carried out in a close collaboration with research groups representing various domains of science. This resulted in developing a system adjusted to specific needs and habits of scientific users, and provisioning functions often unavailable in queuing systems and other grid middleware. The list presented below outlines only some of them:

- "intelligent" brokering capabilities,
- support for advance reservations,
- co-allocation of heterogeneous computing resources,
- cross-cluster execution of jobs,
- support for multiscale computing,

---

[1] The comparison presents the state of year 2012.

- support for interactive tasks,
- flexible monitoring capabilities,
- intuitive command-line tools,
- user-friendly graphical interfaces.

The particular features of QosCosGrid are described in detail in the sections that follow.

4 High-Level QosCosGrid Architecture

Basically, the QosCosGrid middleware consists of two logical layers: grid and local one. Grid-level services control and supervise the whole process of execution of experiments, which are spread among independent administrative domains. One administrative domain represents a single resource provider (e.g. data center) participating in a certain grid environment by sharing its computational resources. The main component of a grid layer is the QCG-Broker metascheduling service whereas QCG-Computing services play the main role at a local level. We present the overall architecture of QosCosGrid system in Fig. 1.

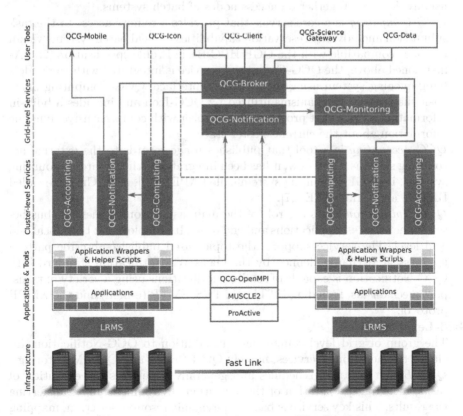

Fig. 1. The high-level architecture of QosCosGrid

QosCosGrid components, with respect to their function and placement in the architecture, may be divided into several groups marked on the left side of the diagram. On that basis, the description presented below aims to summarize the role of particular items building the whole QosCosGrid environment.

Infrastructure

QosCosGrid realizes an access to computing resources using LRMS/batch systems (e.g. Torque or SLURM). The integration between QCG services, i.e., QCG-Computing, and the underlying batch system is provided with the use of the DRMAA interface [23].

Applications and Tools

The QosCosGrid middleware is able to run practically every application installed on resources, including cross-cluster applications based on MUSCLE, MPI or ProActive libraries. In order to simplify the way of running popular applications, the middleware provides a number of scripts and tools that wrap certain commands.

Cluster-Level Services

At a cluster level, or more generally – local administrative level, QCG is represented by QCG-Computing, QCG-Accounting and QCG-Notification usually deployed together on access nodes of batch systems.

QCG-Computing is a core service that provides a remote access to the task submission and advance reservation capabilities of local batch systems via an interface compatible with the OGF HPC Basic Profile specification [28]. As mentioned above, the QCG-Computing service is integrated with the underlying queuing system using the DRMAA interface. QCG-Computing offers basic file transfer mechanisms utilized by QCG-Icon and includes a built-in information service that provides QCG-Broker with comprehensive dynamic information about the current cluster status.

QCG-Accounting is a tool that publishes usage records to the external accounting systems. Until now, it has been integrated with the three accounting systems, i.e, EGI accounting system called APEL [15], a PL-Grid one called BAT [8] and Grid-SAFE [27].

QCG-Notification plays the role of the main asynchronous message bus between the services, applications and end users. It is deployed at both local and grid level. The service supports the topic-based publish/subscribe pattern for message exchange defined by the Oasis WS-Notification standard [31]. QCG-Notification is capable of sending notifications using a variety of transport mechanisms, including HTTP/HTTPS, SMTP (e-mail) and the XMPP protocol.

Grid-Level Services

The group of grid level components, in addition to QCG-Notification, includes two additional services, namely QCG-Broker and QCG-Monitoring.

QCG-Broker controls, schedules and generally supervises the execution of tasks, including preparation of the execution environment and transferring the results. This key service is based on dynamic resource selection, mapping and advanced scheduling methodology, combined with the feedback control architecture. It operates within a dynamic grid environment and deals with resource management challenges, e.g. load-balancing among clusters, remote job control or file staging support.

QCG-Monitoring is a new grid-level service built on top of the QCG-Notification system. It offers end users a possibility of monitoring a progress of the application execution in a dedicated web portal. After processing, the application progress is displayed in a graphical way as a set of tables and charts in accordance with a selected predefined template.

User Tools

Capabilities of the QosCosGrid middleware are offered to end users by means of a number of client-tools, including command-line interface: QCG-SimpleClient, desktop GUI programs: QCG-Icon and QCG-Data, mobile application: QCG-Mobile, as well as high-level web-based solutions like GridSpace2 [6], [9] and QCG-ScienceGateway [11].

A detailed description of the core QosCosGrid services can be found in [8].

5   Primary QosCosGrid Functionalities

The objectives of the PL-Grid and PLGrid Plus projects have been defined in a way to significantly improve the collaboration between the QosCosGrid developers, end users and computing resource representatives. Owing to the given opportunities, it was feasible to organize frequent talks and discussions in order to improve the middleware, to prepare requested extensions and to implement better client tools. Within this section, we present several functionalities of QCG developed primarily under the umbrella of the PL-Grid/PLGrid Plus projects.

5.1   Application Scripts

Making application submission a transparent process and hiding its details from the user, regardless of where the application actually runs, was one of the foundations of grid computing. However, meeting this requirement implies operating within unavoidable heterogeneity of resources composing the grid system by the grid middleware. The same application can be installed in various locations on different systems. Moreover, the scratch file system locations can also differ among the systems and the way how the application is spawned may not be the same. Some of these problems can be solved with the help of Environment Modules [13], however, the module/environment variables' names may not be coherent among the sites. For this reason, QosCosGrid introduces an extra layer of computational resources with the abstract notion of an application. Within this approach, an application name (e.g. GROMACS) is mapped locally to the full path of an application's wrapper script. The wrapper script handles application execution, i.e., it loads a proper module, if needed, changes to scratch directory, spawns the application and removes temporary files after the application terminates. For some applications, like Gaussian, the input file is automatically preprocessed so that the number of application's threads and maximum available memory are set accordingly with the resources that were allocated to the job. What is worth mentioning, in QosCosGrid, we separate the script logic (which is global and updated periodically) from the script configuration (which is local).

5.2 Improved Brokering Capabilities

When submitting jobs to the grid environment, users expect that their applications will be started on a proper class of worker nodes and will provide results as quickly as possible. In the case of the QosCosGrid stack, the realization of this need is a part of a functionality of a specialized service called QCG-Broker. The service assigns jobs to clusters in a way that minimizes the time, in which jobs stay in queues waiting for resources. The decision to which cluster a job should be submitted is made based on a current status of the whole system returned by all currently active instances of QCG-Computing services. The brokering algorithm implemented in QCG-Broker includes two logical steps. In the first step, the clusters that do not meet user or system requirements are excluded from the list of potential sites. To be accepted, a cluster has to meet all verification criteria including, among others, the accessibility for a given user and grant, presence of a sufficient number of nodes of the requested characteristics, presence of the requested applications and software modules, or support for advance reservation. The clusters that passed the first step of the verification are graded. This evaluation is performed on the basis of the weighted sum of a set of metrics calculated for every cluster. An extensive list of plug-ins with configurable weights allows an infrastructure administrator to tailor the brokering policy to a specific system and to assign tasks to resources in the way that satisfies users (job owners) and meets their application requirements as well as takes into consideration the constraints and policies imposed by other stakeholders, i.e., resource owners and grid administrators.

Table 1 presents a subset of possible grading plug-ins with their defaults weights.

5.3 Advance Reservation and Co-allocation of Resources

The QCG middleware, to the best of our knowledge, as the first one, has offered advance reservation capabilities in a production environment. The advance reservation mechanism is exploited to provide end users with the following functionalities: reservation of resources to guarantee the requested quality of service and co-allocation of distributed heterogeneous resources to synchronize the execution of cross-cluster applications. QCG can automatically search, within a user-defined time window, for free resources for a requested period of time. Within QCG, it is possible either to reserve a given number of slots on any number of nodes or to request for a particular topology by specifying a number of nodes and slots per node. At present, the advance reservations can be created and managed using either command-line tools (the QCG-SimpleClient client) or

Table 1. QCG-Broker scheduler plugins

Plugin name	Default Weight	Description
RandomGrading	2	grades clusters in a random manner
SlotGrading	10	grades cluster based on free slots/total slots ratio
FreeNodeGrading	10	prefers clusters with more completely free nodes
NodesNumberGrading	1	prefers clusters with higher number of nodes
QueuesGrading	5	takes into consideration ratio between running and pending jobs
WaitingTimeGrading	5	grades cluster based on average waiting time of all already started jobs present in the system
LRUGrading	3	Last Recently Used – prevents submitting all jobs to a single cluster

a graphical, calendar like, web application (the reservation portal called QCG-QoS-Access) presented in Fig. 2. Currently, in QCG, advance reservations are created by calling the LRMS scheduler commands directly, while in the future a leverage of Advance Reservation API of Open Grid Forum DRMAA 2.0 specification [24] is planned. An extensive summary characterizing the concept of advance reservations can be found in [25].

The QosCosGrid's support for advance-reservation and co-allocation of various types of resources provides a good opportunity to create complex scenarios consisting of many demanding application modules. Within the MAPPER project [3], the QosCosGrid stack has been integrated with Multiscale Coupling Library and Environment (MUSCLE) [7], which enables cross-cluster execution of so-called multiscale applications. The common multiscale application consists of a number of single-scale modules that calculate some phenomena at different spatial or temporal scales and simultaneously exchange information one with another. Since the elementary modules can be written in different languages and have different resource requirements, the QosCosGrid ability to combine many clusters into the single virtual machine is crucial.

5.4 Application Status and Progress Notifications

The time needed to perform a simulation can differ in the cases of various input parameters and data, but even for the same ones, it can be unpredictable in complex and heterogeneous environments. Within the PL-Grid, for example, the waiting time needed to start a job can be dependent on the current load, while the execution time may be associated with the worker-node and processor type. This non-deterministic relation might be an obstacle for end users who often need to know in advance when they can expect results or what percent of the simulation has already been executed. Moreover, especially for long-running simulations,

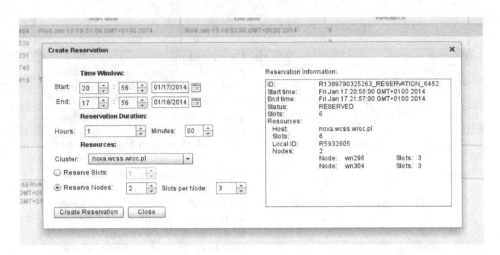

Fig. 2. The QCG-QoS-Access – Reservation Portal

it is important to know if the execution is performed properly and if produced partial results are correct in order to avoid aimless consumption of resources. Taking into account the above needs, the QosCosGrid middleware provides special notification capabilities. With the help of the QCG-Notification service and its support for e-mail and XMPP protocol, as well as QCG-Monitoring functionality, changes in the application execution may be immediately reported to the interested parties.

Users are provided with two basic types of notifications, respectively:

1. Notifications of a job status – users may register for obtaining e-mails or XMPP messages informing about a current status of their jobs (e.g. PENDING, RUNNING, FINISHED); whenever the job changes its state, the corresponding notification is generated and sent.
2. Notifications with an application's excerpt – users can also be provided with monitoring data consisting of a certain application's output, i.e., when a given phrase appears in an output file (e.g. "ENERGY=500") of the application, the system generates an appropriate notification. The application's excerpt notifications may be sent directly to users via e-mail or XMPP protocol, or alternatively, forwarded to the QCG-Monitoring service that is described later.

The procedure of the registration on notifications is simple and is performed with the use of the QCG command line client. The syntax of QCG-Simple provides several intuitive directives, which, if used, impose a flow of certain types of notifications to the specified recipient.

Dedicated Monitoring Solutions. To address specific needs of users, the QCG-Monitoring service was designed and deployed on top of the QCG notification system. The service offers end users a possibility of monitoring the

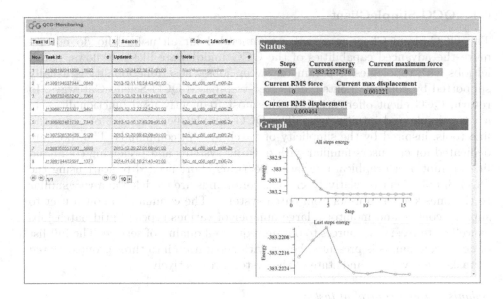

Fig. 3. QCG-Monitoring portal

progress of an application execution in a dedicated web portal. The application progress is displayed in a graphical way in a form of a set of tables and charts in accordance to predefined templates. Users can select from a set of general-purpose templates, they can also utilize templates for quantum chemistry and astrophysics applications that have been prepared in cooperation with domain-oriented researchers. Fig. 3 presents a visualization of energy changes in an example Gaussian simulation.

Mobile phone and tablet users may benefit from other QCG application called QCG-Mobile, which is available for the Android system. This application makes use of XMPP notifications and may be helpful in simple tracking jobs, especially when users do not have access to their PC's.

6   End User Access Tools

In this section we describe the most popular client programs used by QosCosGrid users within the PL-Grid Infrastructure, i.e., QCG-SimpleClient – a set of command-line tools, largely appreciated by the group of existing batch's systems' users, and QCG-Icon – a desktop GUI application suitable for users who have no particular knowledge about clusters or require a handy tool for accessing large computing resources. This section also presents our recent implementation, namely QCG-Data, as well as it shortly characterizes the concept of QCG-ScienceGateway.

6.1   QCG-SimpleClient

The QCG-SimpleClient is a tool recommended for all users who do not require the advanced capabilities of the QCG middleware like workflows, parallel jobs with topologies or parameter sweep jobs whose functionality is usually supported by domain-oriented, dedicated web-based QCG-ScienceGateways. In return, QCG client offers access to the most frequently used functionalities in a very simple and intuitive way. The QCG-SimpleClient is a set of command line tools, inspired by the simplicity of batch system commands. The tools are dedicated for end users familiar with queuing systems and preferring command line prompt over graphical interfaces. Learning effort needed to start using the QCG-SimpleClient is relatively small as commands are modeled in a way similar to the ones known to users from batch systems. The commands allow a user to submit, control and monitor a large number of various types of grid batch jobs as well as to reserve resources to obtain requested quality of service. The full list of qcg-* commands is presented below with separation into three groups related to tasks, reservations and state of the system, respectively.

Submission and control of tasks:

- qcg-cancel – cancel task(s),
- qcg-clean – clean the working directories of the given task(s),
- qcg-connect – connect with an interactive session to the task,
- qcg-info – display detailed information about the given task(s),
- qcg-list – list tasks in the system,
- qcg-peek – display ending of (stdout, stderr) streams,
- qcg-proxy – create a user proxy certificate,
- qcg-refetch – retry/repeat the transfer of output files/directories,
- qcg-refresh_proxy – refresh the user proxy certificate for the given tasks,
- qcg-resub – resubmit the task to be processed once again,
- qcg-sub – submit the task(s) to be processed by QCG services.

Resources reservation and control:

- qcg-rcancel – cancel reservation(s),
- qcg-reserve – reserve resources,
- qcg-rinfo – display information about the given reservation(s),
- qcg-rlist – list reservations in the system.

System information:

- qcg-offer – provide information about the current state of resources including their availability and supported applications.

Every task submitted to the system has to be described in a formal way. The default description format – QCG-Simple, is recommended and sufficient for majority of the tasks. The format does not yet allow users to describe more sophisticated scenarios like workflows, parameter sweep tasks, parallel tasks with topologies and these are supported by an XML-based format, called QCG-JobProfile. The QCG-Simple format description file is a plain BASH script annotated with #QCG directives, which is also a common approach for all nowadays queuing systems. The #QCG directives inform the system how to process a task (e.g. define resource requirements and input/output files for running an application). The main difference is that a user has to explicitly specify all files and directories that have to be staged in/out as there is no global shared file system for all sites. Fortunately, staging directives also accept short relative local paths beside the full URLs. Listing 1 presents an example of QCG-SimpleClient job description expressed in the QCG-Simple format. In this example, the NAMD application will be executed with the **apoa1/apoa1.namd** argument on the hydra cluster with the topology: 12 processes on a single node in the plgrid queue with the walltime limit set to 10 minutes. Prior to the execution, the apoa1.zip file will be staged in and unpacked. After the execution, the whole working directory of the task will be staged out to the results directory that will be created in the directory, from which the task was submitted. Moreover, standard output and error streams will be staged out to the apoa1.output and apoa1.error files, respectively. XMPP notifications concerning the status of the task will be sent to **tomasz.piontek@plgrid.pl** and additionally, every 20 seconds, the application output will be searched for a new line containing the ENERGY word, which, if present, is sent to the defined e-mail address.

```
#QCG note=NAMD apoa1
#QCG host=hydra.icm.edu.pl
#QCG walltime=PT10M
#QCG queue=plgrid
#QCG nodes=1:12:12
#QCG output=apoa1.output
#QCG error=apoa1.error
#QCG application=NAMD
#QCG argument=apoa1/apoa1.namd
#QCG stage-in-file=apoa1.zip
#QCG preprocess=unzip apoa1.zip
#QCG stage-out-dir=. -> results
#QCG notify=xmpp:tomasz.piontek@plgrid.pl
#QCG watch-output=mailto:tp@mail,20,ENERGY
```

Listing 1. An example QCG-SimpleClient submission script

One of the most frequently requested functionalities that have been recently added to the QCG-SimpleClient is the support for interactive tasks. Depending on particular needs, a user can get an interactive access to the cluster and either run his/her command line application in the interactive mode or compile their own code and process some test/debugging sessions. The support for this functionality is especially important in case of the systems that do not provide an interactive access at a queuing system level and offer entry only via middleware services.

In the last years we have learned how valuable it is for a user to obtain a detailed status of her/his simulations. Having access to the data produced only at the end of the job can be accepted in the cases of very short runs only. For this reason, QCG offers a possibility of viewing the output of any of its running jobs. Moreover, it is possible to establish an interactive session (using *qcg-connect* command) with an already started batch job. Once such an interactive session has been established, a user can inspect the task, for example: list the job directory, view any file or run *ps/top* commands to see if the program is not pending or swapping memory. Moreover, many of these erroneous situations can be detected by observing dynamic job metrics displayed in the QCG tools, namely *CPU efficiency* and *memory usage*. Another commonly asked question by end users is *"What time my job will start at?"*. The QosCosGrid services attempt to answer this question by extracting this information from the local scheduler. Although this is a best-effort metric, it provides a user with at least a rough estimation of the expected waiting time. Finally, what was mentioned in the previous section, QCG enables registering for notifications with application's output, i.e., whenever a given phrase appears in the output file, thus tracking the correctness of a simulation execution.

The QCG-Broker service provides brokering capabilities and, based on the information about a current state of the whole system, it can assign a task to the resource in a way that minimizes the waiting time in local queues. As an alternative, we provided users with the *qcg-offer* tool. It is a command-line tool that allows regular users to generate queries about free resources available in the Grid. The tool, at a QCG-Broker level, leverages the fine-grained information provided by the QCG-Computing services. It is possible to query a single site, to display a full or aggregated view of cluster nodes or to filter resources based on available memory, total/free number of cores, nodes attributes, etc. Listing 2 presents an example output of *qcg-offer*. Users can later utilize this information and their own experience to select a target resource adjusting job size and topology by changing the number of requested nodes and/or slots per node. Moreover, the *qcg-offer* tool is capable of searching for the applications and environment modules installed on all sites.

6.2   QCG-Icon

QCG-Icon is a desktop application written specifically for the Windows platform, but also available for Linux and Mac OSX distributions. It was designed to enable access to selected applications installed on the computing resources of the PL-Grid Infrastructure, and is made available through the QosCosGrid services. While developing QCG-Icon, the special emphasis was put on the following requirement: using an application installed in the grid environment should be as intuitive as using a locally installed application. At the moment, QCG-Icon supports a large portfolio of applications, including MATLAB, R, NAMD, Gaussian (also integrated with GaussView), GAMESS, Molpro, LAMMPS, Quantum

```
[plgpiontek@qcg ~]$ qcg-offer
HYDRA:
Summary:
      Metric Name          nodes/cores        share
      Total Resources:      279/5252     100%/100%
         Up Resources:      264/4968      94%/94%
       Used Resources:      141/2239      50%/42%
       Free Resources:       82/1432      29%/27% (FreeNodes=2x2,63x12,5x16,11x48,1x64)
    PartFree Resources:     117/2141      41%/40% (AvgFreeCoresPerNode=18)
    Reserved Resources:      34/408       12%/07% (Utilization=0%)

GALERA:
Summary:
      Metric Name          nodes/cores        share
      Total Resources:      194/2688     100%/100%
         Up Resources:      189/2628      97%/97%
       Used Resources:      113/1333      58%/49%
       Free Resources:        0/0          0%/00%
    PartFree Resources:       0/0          0%/00% (AvgFreeCoresPerNode=0)
    Reserved Resources:     151/2172      77%/80% (Utilization=61%)
```

Listing 2. An example of the *qcg-offer* output

ESPRESSO, Crystal09, NWChem, GROMACS and CPMD. Any other application can also be run as long as a proper BASH script is provided. Despite its simplicity, QCG-Icon delivers most of the functionalities offered by the QosCosGrid stack, including parallel jobs, live output monitoring and providing online statistics about the job resources usage. An overview of the QCG-Icon graphical user interface is shown in Fig. 4.

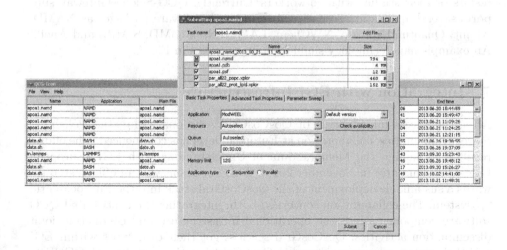

Fig. 4. The "Main" and "New Task" windows of QCG-Icon

6.3 QCG-Data

The purpose of QCG-Data is provisioning efficient and intuitive synchronization mechanisms for data exchange between a local user file system and the e-Infrastructure. At a low-level, QCG-Data utilizes the iRODS middleware [20] for data storage. The system is directly integrated with the QCG-Broker as well as with end user tools and it provides easy management of application input and output files in the QosCosGrid environment. It consists of two layers, which make use of iRODS: the server layer, which exposes links pointing to data chunks, and the client one, which creates and makes use of those links. The server part is built on top of the jargon library [30], whilst the desktop application that is integrated with a newest version of QCG-Icon, adapts and extends the iDrop code [29]. The integration carried out between QCG-Icon, QCG-Broker and QCG-Data allows users to process jobs, which require or produce large data sets.

6.4 QCG-ScienceGateway

The advanced graphic and multimedia-oriented web interfaces designed for scientists and engineers could change the way end users collaborate, deal with advanced simulations, share results and work together to solve challenging problems. With the use of the enhanced version of the Vine Toolkit portal [11,12], we created a platform called QCG-ScienceGateway. The Gateway consists of a general part displaying and monitoring computational resource characteristics as well as a set of domain-specific web applications developed for certain complex system use cases. Therefore, end users are able to use only web browsers to proceed with their complex simulations with the use of the Grid and to exchange the results of their studies with co-workers. Currently, QCG-ScienceGateway supports several application scenarios covering such software packages as NAMD, Abinit, QuantumEspresso, NWChem, LAMMPS, nanoMD, SIMPL and Anelli. An example nanotechnology simulation is presented in Fig. 5.

7 Integration with EGI Infrastructure

After the successful adoption of QosCosGrid solutions within the Polish research communities, collaboration at European level has commenced. The efforts resulted in signing the Memorandum of Understanding with EGI (European Grid Infrastructure) in November 2012[2]. This document was an official step towards a sustainable deployment of the QosCosGrid stack into the European grid ecosystem. The collaboration concerned both: integrating the contributed QCG software components into the operational infrastructure and conducting joint dissemination activities. QosCosGrid services got their own types within EGI and their instances were registered in Grid Configuration Database (GOCDB) – a registry containing general information about the sites and services participating in the production of the European e-Infrastructure. The QCG services were

---

[2] https://documents.egi.eu/secure/ShowDocument?docid=1350

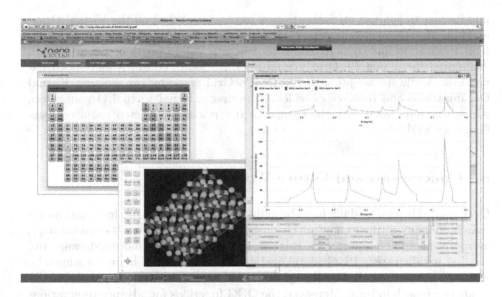

Fig. 5. The sample QCG-ScienceGateway application

also successfully integrated with the EGI Service Availability System (SAM) and APEL accounting system [15], where they continuously publish requested information. To support European research communities and end users, a dedicated QCG support unit was created in the structure of GGUS that is the EGI helpdesk. In September 2013, after meeting all mandatory requirements and a positive verification of all the core QosCosGrid components, the stack became a part of the Unified Middleware Distribution (UMD) [33]. Similarly, QCG end user tools became available in the EGI Applications Database (EGI-AppDB) [26], which is a repository of tools ready to use within the EGI infrastructure.

Moreover, on the basis of a collaboration between the MAPPER and PRACE projects, the QosCosGrid middleware has been initially validated and accepted for further installation on highly powerful supercomputers available in the PRACE infrastructure. Preliminary installations of basic QosCosGrid services were performed on SuperMUC, HECTOR and Huygens machines.

In August 2013, another Memorandum of Understanding was signed – between Poznan Supercomputing and Networking Center and BCC (Basic Coordination Centre) of Ukrainian National Grid[3]. One of the major objectives of this document is to *"provide robust, well-designed, user-centric services to scientific user"* based on the QosCosGrid services. This will be the first QosCosGrid deployment at such a scale outside Poland.

Quite recently, an LCAS/LCMAPS [2] based authorization plug-in has been developed for the QCG-Computing service. This work enabled the QosCosGrid

---

[3] http://infrastructure.kiev.ua/en/news/114/

middleware to support an authorization mechanism based on the Virtual Organization Management Support (VOMS) infrastructure [1]. Moreover, the QCG-Icon application had to be extended to generate VOMS proxy certificates when configured for a non PL-Grid virtual organization. The newly developed capabilities facilitate adoption of the QosCosGrid stack by the existing Virtual Organizations and resource providers. The first external Virtual Organization, which was integrated with the QosCosGrid services on selected resources, was Gaussian VO[4].

8   Conclusions and Future Work

QosCosGrid is used on daily basis by many researchers in Poland from various research domains, such as quantum chemistry [8], nanotechnology [11], metallurgy, astrophysics and bioinformatics. It is currently the most popular middleware and the first middleware in PL-Grid, taking into account the CPU hours consumed by its users. Tasks controlled by the QCG stack consume, in average, 2 million core-hours per month in total. Moreover, the QCG functions for advance reservations and co-allocation of resources proved to be of particular importance for several complex multi-scale applications developed within the MAPPER project [3], [14]. These successes would have not been possible without offering simple but powerful end user tools and comprehensive end user support.

What attracts users to the QCG solutions is the fact that the development of QCG tools and services is performed in a close collaboration with groups of domain researchers and is driven by their real needs. The fact that all the aforementioned QCG components are developed by a single group of programmers from Poznan Supercomputing and Networking Center in short development cycles causes that QCG can be adapted to specific requirements in a relatively short time. To the best of our knowledge, QCG currently provides the most efficient and powerful multi-user access to the job management and advance reservation features compared to other existing grid middleware services. QCG also offers unique functionalities and features, such as co-allocation of resources, cross-cluster execution of applications with heterogeneous resource requirements and communication topologies, interactive tasks, as well as asynchronous notifications and monitoring capabilities. In order to meet emerging end user requirements and sophisticated scenarios, QCG provides means, by which different e-Infrastructures like EGI, PRACE and EUDAT, as well as the GEANT one in the future, can be bridged.

The continous and sustainable development of QosCosGrid in order to provide a highest-quality product for existing and new users, remains a priority of Poznan Supercomputing and Networking Center. In the next few years, we plan to proceed with further deployments of QosCosGrid on Polish and European sites. We want to create extensions and improve the current functionalities of the middleware to support new and more demanding computing scenarios.

---

[4] https://voms.cyf-kr.edu.pl:8443/voms/gaussian

Finally, last but not least, we aim at rendering the use of e-Infrastructure as easy and user-friendly as possible.

References

1. Alfieri, R., Cecchini, R.L., Ciaschini, V., dell'Agnello, L., Frohner, A., Gianoli, A., Lőrentey, K., Spataro, F.: VOMS, an Authorization System for Virtual Organizations. In: Fernández Rivera, F., Bubak, M., Gómez Tato, A., Doallo, R. (eds.) Across Grids 2003. LNCS, vol. 2970, pp. 33–40. Springer, Heidelberg (2004)
2. Alfieri, R., Cecchini, R., Ciaschini, V., Gianoli, A., Spataro, F., Bonnassieux, F., Broadfoot, P., Lowe, G., Cornwall, L., Jensen, J., et al.: Managing dynamic user communities in a grid of autonomous resources. arXiv preprint cs/0306004 (2003)
3. Belgacem, M.B., Chopard, B., Borgdorff, J., Mamoński, M., Rycerz, K., Harężlak, D.: Distributed multiscale computations using the mapper framework. In: Alexandrov, V.N., Lees, M., Krzhizhanovskaya, V.V., Dongarra, J., Sloot, P.M.A. (eds.) ICCS. Procedia Computer Science, vol. 18, pp. 1106–1115. Elsevier (2013)
4. Benedyczak, K., Stolarek, M., Rowicki, R., Kluszczyński, R., Borcz, M., Marczak, G., Filocha, M., Bała, P.: Seamless Access to the PL-Grid e-Infrastructure Using UNICORE Middleware. In: Bubak, M., Szepieniec, T., Wiatr, K. (eds.) PL-Grid 2011. LNCS, vol. 7136, pp. 56–72. Springer, Heidelberg (2012)
5. Borcz, M., Kluszczyński, R., Skonieczna, K., Grzybowski, T., Bała, P.: Processing the biomedical data on the grid using the UNICORE workflow system. In: Caragiannis, I., et al. (eds.) Euro-Par Workshops 2012. LNCS, vol. 7640, pp. 263–272. Springer, Heidelberg (2013)
6. Borgdorff, J., Bona-Casas, C., Mamoński, M., Kurowski, K., Piontek, T., Bosak, B., Rycerz, K., Ciepiela, E., Gubała, T., Harężlak, D., Bubak, M., Lorenz, E., Hoekstra, A.G.: A distributed multiscale computation of a tightly coupled model using the multiscale modeling language. In: Ali, H.H., Shi, Y., Khazanchi, D., Lees, M., van Albada, G.D., Dongarra, J., Sloot, P.M.A. (eds.) ICCS. Procedia Computer Science, vol. 9, pp. 596–605. Elsevier (2012)
7. Borgdorff, J., Mamoński, M., Bosak, B., Kurowski, K., Belgacem, M.B., Chopard, B., Groen, D., Coveney, P.V., Hoekstra, A.G.: Distributed multiscale computing with muscle 2, the multiscale coupling library and environment. CoRR abs/1311.5740 (2013)
8. Bosak, B., Komasa, J., Kopta, P., Kurowski, K., Mamoński, M., Piontek, T.: New Capabilities in QosCosGrid Middleware for Advanced Job Management, Advance Reservation and Co-allocation of Computing Resources – Quantum Chemistry Application Use Case. In: Bubak, M., Szepieniec, T., Wiatr, K. (eds.) PL-Grid 2011. LNCS, vol. 7136, pp. 40–55. Springer, Heidelberg (2012)
9. Ciepiela, E., et al.: Managing Entire Lifecycles of e-Science Applications in the GridSpace2 Virtual Laboratory – From Motivation through Idea to Operable Web-Accessible Environment Built on Top of PL-Grid e-Infrastructure. In: Bubak, M., Szepieniec, T., Wiatr, K. (eds.) PL-Grid 2011. LNCS, vol. 7136, pp. 228–239. Springer, Heidelberg (2012)
10. Demuth, B., Schuller, B., Holl, S., Daivandy, J.M., Giesler, A., Huber, V., Sild, S.: The Unicore rich client: Facilitating the automated execution of scientific workflows. In: eScience, pp. 238–245. IEEE Computer Society (2010)

11. Dziubecki, P., Grabowski, P., Krysiński, M., Kuczyński, T., Kurowski, K., Piontek, T., Szejnfeld, D.: Online Web-Based Science Gateway for Nanotechnology Research. In: Bubak, M., Szepieniec, T., Wiatr, K. (eds.) PL-Grid 2011. LNCS, vol. 7136, pp. 205–216. Springer, Heidelberg (2012)
12. Kurowski, K., Dziubecki, P., Grabowski, P., Krysiński, M., Piontek, T., Szejnfeld, D.: Easy Development and Integration of Science Gateways with Vine Toolkit. In: Bubak, M., Kitowski, J., Wiatr, K. (eds.) PLGrid Plus. LNCS, vol. 8500, pp. 147–163. Springer, Heidelberg (2014)
13. Furlani, J.L.: Modules: Providing a flexible user environment. In: Proceedings of the Fifth Large Installation Systems Administration Conference (LISA V), pp. 141–152 (1991)
14. Groen, D., Borgdorff, J., Bona-Casas, C., Hetherington, J., Nash, R.W., Zasada, S.J., Saverchenko, I., Mamoński, M., Kurowski, K., Bernabeu, M.O., Hoekstra, A.G., Coveney, P.V.: Flexible composition and execution of high performance, high fidelity multiscale biomedical simulations. CoRR abs/1211.2963 (2012)
15. Jiang, M., Novales, C.D.C., Mathieu, G., Casson, J., Rogers, W., Gordon, J.: An apel tool based cpu usage accounting infrastructure for large scale computing grids. In: Data Driven e-Science, pp. 175–186. Springer (2011)
16. Krabbenhöft, H.N., Möller, S., Bayer, D.: Integrating ARC grid middleware with taverna workflows. Bioinformatics 24(9), 1221–1222 (2008)
17. Laure, E., Gr, C., Fisher, S., Frohner, A., Kunszt, P., Krenek, A., Mulmo, O., Pacini, F., Prelz, F., White, J., Barroso, M., Buncic, P., Byrom, R., Cornwall, L., Craig, M., Meglio, A.D., Djaoui, A., Giacomini, F., Hahkala, J., Hemmer, F., Hicks, S., Edlund, A., Maraschini, A., Middleton, R., Sgaravatto, M., Steenbakkers, M., Walk, J., Wilson, A.: Programming the Grid with gLite. In: Computational Methods in Science and Technology (2006)
18. MacLaren, J.: HARC: The highly-available resource co-allocator. In: Meersman, R., Tari, Z. (eds.) OTM 2007, Part II. LNCS, vol. 4804, pp. 1385–1402. Springer, Heidelberg (2007)
19. Palak, B., Wolniewicz, P., Płóciennik, M., Owsiak, M., Żok, T.: User-Friendly Frameworks for Accessing Computational Resources. In: Bubak, M., Szepieniec, T., Wiatr, K. (eds.) PL-Grid 2011. LNCS, vol. 7136, pp. 191–204. Springer, Heidelberg (2012)
20. Rajasekar, A., Moore, R., Hou, C.Y., Lee, C.A., Marciano, R., de Torcy, A., Wan, M., Schroeder, W., Chen, S.Y., Gilbert, L., Tooby, P., Zhu, B.: iRODS Primer: Integrated Rule-Oriented Data System. Synthesis Lectures on Information Concepts, Retrieval, and Services. Morgan & Claypool Publishers (2010)
21. Streit, A., Bala, P., Beck-Ratzka, A., Benedyczak, K., Bergmann, S., Breu, R., Daivandy, J.M., Demuth, B., Eifer, A., Giesler, A., Hagemeier, B., Holl, S., Huber, V., Lamla, N., Mallmann, D., Memon, A.S., Memon, M.S., Rambadt, M., Riedel, M., Romberg, M., Schuller, B., Schlauch, T., Schreiber, A., Soddemann, T., Ziegler, W.: Unicore 6 – recent and future advancements. Annales des Télécommunications 65(11-12), 757–762 (2010)
22. Takefusa, A., Nakada, H., Takano, R., Kudoh, T., Tanaka, Y.: Gridars: A grid advanced resource management system framework for intercloud. In: Lambrinoudakis, C., Rizomiliotis, P., Wlodarczyk, T.W. (eds.) CloudCom, pp. 705–710. IEEE (2011)
23. Troger, P., Rajic, H., Haas, A., Domagalski, P.: Standardization of an API for Distributed Resource Management Systems. In: Proceedings of the Seventh IEEE International Symposium on Cluster Computing and the Grid (CCGRID 2007), pp. 619–626. IEEE Computer Society, Washington, DC (2007), http://dx.doi.org/10.1109/CCGRID.2007.109

24. Distributed Resource Management Application API Version 2 (DRMAA), http://www.ogf.org/documents/GFD.194.pdf
25. Radecki, M., Szymocha, T., Piontek, T., Bosak, B., Mamoński, M., Wolniewicz, P., Benedyczak, K., Kluszczyński, R.: Reservations for Compute Resources in Federated e-Infrastructure. In: Bubak, M., Kitowski, J., Wiatr, K. (eds.) PLGrid Plus. LNCS, vol. 8500, pp. 80–93. Springer, Heidelberg (2014)
26. EGI Application Database (AppDB), http://appdb.egi.eu/
27. Grid-SAFE accounting framework, http://gridsafe.sourceforge.net
28. HPC Basic Profile Version 1.0, http://www.ogf.org/documents/GFD.114.pdf
29. iDrop – the client tool for iRODS,
    https://code.renci.org/gf/project/irodsidrop
30. Jargon library for iRODS, https://code.renci.org/gf/project/jargon
31. OASIS Web Services Notification,
    http://www.oasis-open.org/committees/tc_home.php?wg_abbrev=wsn
32. SAGA project, http://saga-project.org
33. Unified Middleware Distribution (UMD), http://repository.egi.eu/

Recent Advances of the Cloud Platform Delivered in the Infrastructure as a Service Model for the PL-Grid Scientific Communities

Jan Meizner, Maciej Nabożny, Marcin Radecki,
Tomasz Szepieniec, and Miłosz Zdybał

AGH University of Science and Technology, ACC Cyfronet AGH,
ul. Nawojki 11, 30-950 Kraków, Poland
j.meizner@cyfronet.pl, mn@mnabozny.pl, milosz.zdybal@ifj.edu.pl,
{m.radecki,t.szepieniec}@cyfronet.pl

Abstract. This paper describes the work done to provide production-grade Cloud system for the scientific communities of the PLGrid Plus project. Our goal was both to show generic architecture of the Open-Nebula-based platform as well as enhancements we had to provide in order to meet the needs of our users and the requirements of the platform. Numerous solutions have been developed and integrated such as the authentication and authorization mechanism working with the standard project accounts and based on X.509 proxy certificates, a group synchronization solution, flexible way to access cloud instances despite the need to conserve IPv4 resources either through Network Address Translation (NAT) mechanism or the Virtual Private Network (VPN). We also describe some security implications, which are crucial in the case of cloud systems.

Keywords: cloud, infrastructure, virtualization, KVM, Grid, X.509.

1 Introduction

Since some time the Cloud systems have become one of the most largely used e-infrastructures in both industrial and scientific communities. Their popularity is triggered by the specific needs of the modern eScience.

Nowadays, scientists require highly scalable and flexible solutions. Legacy cluster and grid systems, despite being well suited for a large number of scientists, are not always the best choice. Sometimes, it is necessary to deploy a highly customized, personalized middleware for a small group of researchers, not big enough to justify usage of all cluster resources. In such cases, it is very important to have the possibility to provide smaller, separated, virtualized environments, which could be dynamically adapted to the size required by the researchers.

Another good example involves researchers testing and developing software for different distributions or platforms. The cloud allows them to instantiate and recycle multiple different OS configurations for their tests in a safe environment.

M. Bubak et al. (Eds.): PLGrid Plus, LNCS 8500, pp. 54–60, 2014.

The goal of this paper is to present the Cloud infrastructure deployed in the scope of the PLGrid Plus project as part of the production PL-Grid Infrastructure [1]. The new cloud is located in th same server room as other PL-Grid services. Our goal is to overlay existing grid infrastructure with the cloud system up to a half of the Zeus supercomputer.

2 Description of the Problem Solution

2.1 General Overview

To fulfill the scientific needs of the use-cases described above, we have proposed and deployed the cloud platform as shown in Fig. 1.

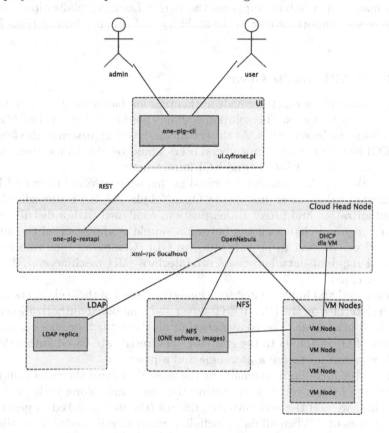

Fig. 1. Overall architecture of the PL-Grid cloud platform

As one can see, we have deployed a platform whose core is based on a well-known, open source solution OpenNebula [2]. However, in order to best suit the needs of the scientific community, we had to augment the platform. Our intention was to reach this goal by extending the solution with minimal need for integration into the core components of the OpenNebula. These extensions include creation of a REST API mechanism for easy and secure remote access to the Cloud API from the UI node, a mechanism allowing synchronization between users groups stored in LDAP and internal OpenNebula group representations, as well as network-related solutions for providing remote access to the instances itself based on NAT or VPN mechanisms. All these aspects are described in detail in the following sections.

2.2 OpenNebula Choice

OpenNebula was chosen due to its simplicity, scalability, and ease of extensibility of its API with new tools. Also, it already had most of the required features, so that only a few missing functionalities had to be implemented, as described below. Finally, OpenNebula supports the native Linux virtualization – KVM. This choice was important due to the stability and support from various Linux distributions.

2.3 REST API and Its Client

One of our main goals was to provide authentication based on the standard grid (X.509) proxy certificates. This solution is widely used in various grid middleware and is well-known by scientists. As the certificate-based approach is also featured by the EGI FedCloud task [3] members, users would be able to use their default certificate in both the PL-Grid and EGI infrastructures.

The solution for the platform described in this paper evolved from an LDAP-based authentication driver provided by OpenNebula. Adding features like LDAP based-authorization and proxy authentication, combined with a distributed architecture, required changes going beyond a simple modification of the authentication driver. We had to provide our own CLI (Command Line Interface) to transfer all required data between User Interface (UI) machine and the head node of the cloud.

The proposed and implemented solution is composed of three elements: a command-line interface on the UI, a REST server and a modified authorization driver on the cloud head node. The combination of all these parts provides a seamless experience of OpenNebula to the end user. The certificate-based authentication makes it unnecessary to use a username and a password.

The first step is calling a command by the user. We mirror the exact command-line interface of OpenNebula and capture the commands along with their arguments. Then, we add the user proxy certificate (the user is asked to generate it if it is not present). When all data, including input files if needed, are collected, the CLI makes a call to the REST server.

In the second step, the REST server prepares the OpenNebula command call and executes it.

In the last phase, OpenNebula attempts to authenticate and authorize user, using the modified driver. Instead of a simple user and password check, the user proxy certificate is verified. This process is made of multiple checks, where failing on any of them causes the rejection of the user call. First, we check if the user is allowed to use the Cloud infrastructure. Then, we verify that the provided proxy certificate is internally valid. Finally, signatures are checked: the proxy certificate must be signed with the user certificate registered in the PL-Grid LDAP database, and the user certificate must be signed by one of the trusted CAs (Certificate Authorities). When all these steps succeed, the result of the call is sent back to the user.

This approach simplifies requirements for the user who wants to use the cloud. A registered PL-Grid user needs to request access to the Cloud platform and generate (or register) a valid certificate. Both actions can be performed using the User Portal.

2.4   Group Synchronization

Despite the fact that the goal of scientific communities is usually to share results of their work through publications, even scientific service providers must ensure proper access control in multi-tenant systems such as Clouds, in order to safeguard early results from potentially malicious third parties.

The proper mechanism in OpenNebula is based on groups, which, in combination with ACLs, allows managing the access to resources such as OS images, templates, virtual networks, etc. To provide integrated access control based on the PL-Grid accounts, during development of the computing cloud platform, we had to provide a mechanism for LDAP and OpenNebula groups synchronization.

The goal described above could be reached by automatically executing every 6 hours a script responsible for group synchronization that performs necessary additions and deletions on the internal OpenNebula groups stored in its internal MySQL database on the basis of the entries in the LDAP catalog.

In addition to group synchronization, proper ACL entries are created to allow usage of these groups by authorized users. This ensures that the same information about groups is kept in the PL-Grid accounts system and in the cloud infrastructure.

2.5   Networking

The described platform allows users to access the cloud instances in numerous ways as shown in Fig. 2.

As the IPv4 address shortage is a well-known problem, we had to propose the solution that conserves these resources. Thus, cloud instances have private IP addresses and remote access to them is provided via one of the two solutions enabled in the PL-Grid Cloud.

Network Addresses and NAT. The first one is based on the NAT mechanism that could be controlled by the users to "redirect" the required TCP or UDP ports to the instance. In special cases, when port redirection is insufficient, it is possible to redirect the entire public IP (via a 1:1 static NAT mechanism). A good example of a use case requiring the entire IP address redirection

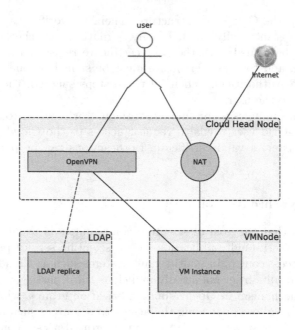

Fig. 2. Overview of the network solutions for the PL-Grid cloud platform

is SynchroGrid. Solutions used by this domain grid are based on legacy technologies whose complex communication patterns would not tolerate dynamic address/port translations. Another common protocol that needs special handling due to a typical communication patterns is FTP (and related ones, such as GridFTP). As users are frequently behind NATs and/or firewalls, FTP usually would require so-called passive mode, which opens multiple dynamic ports. As a result, in order to properly handle this protocol, it is needed to either redirect the full IP or a continuous range of ports in a static manner, which could be later added to server configurations.

As shown in Fig. 2, the HEAD node acts as a NATing router, which at the same time provides Internet access to the VM Instances through the SNAT mechanism as well as allow TCP/UDP ports or IP addresses redirection via the DNAT mechanism. From software point of view, the translation is handled by the netfilter mechanism being the part of Linux kernel controlled by the iptables tool.

Virtual Private Network. The second mechanism is based on OpenVPN [4] and allows establishing the (encrypted) tunnel to the platform from an arbitrary location and then direct access using the private IPs. The server is located on the Cloud HEAD node. The access is granted on the basis of the same X.509 certificate that is used by the Cloud API after verification that it corresponds with the user in LDAP having proper service activated. In this case, the VPN user gets, for the time of the connection, a dedicated private IP for the client machine. This type of a solution is perfectly suited for integration/configuration and testing phases when a single developer needs unrestricted access to the VM without the need to setup redirections for each port. Additionally, the VPN might be used if the service needs to be accessible just from a specific location(s) – e.g. a scientist's home institution. In this case, a so-called site-to-site VPN could be established in order to allow unrestricted access to the cloud.

Security Considerations. There are numerous security related issues related to the cloud, including those common to all or most IT systems, as well as specific to the cloud. The common ones include of course the need to provide secured communication between the user and the API as well as cloud instances. The secure communication between the user and the UI is ensured with the SSH protocol used to access the UI. Also, SSH is used to access and manage the cloud instances. The communication between the UI and the Cloud API features utilizes HTTPS [5], which is also encrypted using the TLS [6] protocol. Finally, if the user needs to access the cloud using a less secure protocol, the already mentioned encrypted VPN could be used.

Another more cloud-specific issue is related to the need to provide a mechanism for user authentication (including root) leaving out administration and OS configuration itself to the user, so in turn with minimum requirement for the software preinstalled on the machine. In the current platform we have achieved this goal through so-called contextualization. This mechanism requires just a few lines of code in the system initialization script, which injects the user-defined (via API) public key to the machine at the first boot-up and authorizes it as root. As a result, the user can use his/her private key to access the machine with administrators privileges.

Finally, we had to protect the machine from external attacks such as brute force attacks on SSH. Such types of attacks are nowadays very common and might be especially dangerous for cloud environments, in which users having full root access are acting as administrators, yet might not be so well versed in OS security-related aspects as full-time system engineers. As all communication goes through the firewall on a head node, by default all instances are protected from external attacks. When users are exposing some services on TCP/UDP ports or NAT 1:1 IP address, such services become vulnerable. However, in this case we can still discuss with the instance owner and provide a mitigation such as firewall rules on the cloud infrastructure side, limiting access to the services from trusted ranges, enable platform-wide IPS system, or at least instruct the users on how to use host based IPS (such as fail2ban) on their own machines.

3   Results

The described Cloud platform is currently deployed as a production service in the PL-Grid Infrastructure and available to scientists using the platform on the same rights as any other middleware. We are observing that scientists are very actively using the platform. At the time of writing this paper, our cloud is used by over 50 users, which are running over 100 VMs. In total, since production deployment, the cloud has been used to instantiate over 800 machines.

Specifically, the cloud is now actively used by the SynchroGrid [9] community and the group responsible for development of the VeilFS [7] system. Also some work has been done to Cloud-enable another PL-Grid service DataNet [8]. Additionally, members of the AstroGrid-PL [10] community are working on enabling their services on the cloud.

4   Conclusions and Future Work

In summary, the goal to fulfill scientific requirements to the cloud platform, described in the introductory section, have been reached. The functional Cloud platform has been deployed, integrated with the PL-Grid Infrastructure and provided to the users as a production service. The scale is of course still limited as the service is in its initial state, however, for the current stage of the project, we think that the number of users and provisioned resources is on a good level. Also, very promising is the fact that the interest in the services is constantly growing. Of course, the cloud needs to be constantly monitored and updated, which is our current and future task. We also plan to continue extending the platform, in order to respond to further scientific demands of the users. Additionally, we are looking for new solutions and middleware to further streamline users' access to the platform.

References

1. The PL-Grid Infrastructure (2013), http://www.plgrid.pl/en
2. OpenNebula Project (2013), http://opennebula.org/
3. EGI FedCloud (2013),
   https://wiki.egi.eu/wiki/Fedcloud-tf:FederatedCloudsTaskForce
4. Technologies, Inc., OpenVPN (2014), http://openvpn.net/
5. Rescorla, E.: HTTP Over TLS [RFC 2818]. The Internet Society (2000),
   http://tools.ietf.org/html/rfc2818
6. Dierks, T., Rescorla, E.: The Transport Layer Security (TLS) Protocol Version 1.2 [RFC 5246]. The IETF Trust (2008), http://tools.ietf.org/html/rfc5246
7. Słota, R., Dutka, Ł., Wrzeszcz, M., Kryza, B., Nikolow, D., Król, D., Kitowski, J.: Storage management systems for organizationally distributed environments PLGrid PLUS case study. In: Wyrzykowski, R., Dongarra, J., Karczewski, K., Wasńiewski, J. (eds.) PPAM 2013, Part I. LNCS, pp. 724–733. Springer, Heidelberg (2013)
8. Harężlak, D., Ciepiela, E., Kasztelnik, M., Wilk, B., Bubak, M.: DataNet – GridSpace Data Management Framework. In: Bubak, M., Turała, M., Wiatr, K. (eds.) CGW 2012 Proceedings, pp. 43–44. ACK CYFRONET AGH, Kraków (2012)
9. The SynchroGrid domain grid within the PLGrid Plus project (in Polish),
   http://www.plgrid.pl/projekty/plus/dziedziny_nauki/synchrogrid
10. The AstroGrid-PL domain grid within the PLGrid Plus project (in Polish),
   http://www.plgrid.pl/projekty/plus/dziedziny_nauki/astrogrid-pl

Multilayered IT Security Requirements and Measures for the Complex Protection of Polish Domain-Specific Grid Infrastructure

Bartłomiej Balcerek[1], Gerard Frankowski[2], Agnieszka Kwiecień[1],
Norbert Meyer[2], Michał Nowak[2], and Adam Smutnicki[1]

[1] Wroclaw Centre for Networking and Supercomputing,
Wybrzeże Wyspiańskiego 27, 50-370 Wrocław, Poland
http://www.wcss.pl
{bartlomiej.balcerek,agnieszka.kwiecien,adam.smutnicki}@pwr.wroc.pl
[2] Poznan Supercomputing and Networking Center,
ul. Noskowskiego 10, 61-704 Poznań, Poland
http://www.pcss.pl
{gerard.frankowski,meyer,michal.nowak}@man.poznan.pl

Abstract. The security of the Polish Domain-Specific Grid Infrastructure relies on applying appropriate security standards and practices by five Polish HPC centres participating in the PLGrid Plus project. We review both aspects of assuring in-depth security in the Polish Domain-Specific Grid Infrastructure: the conceptually lower level of underlying HPC centres and the topmost level of the project, comprising services and applications. We describe the security model in the PLGrid Plus project as a case-study in order to provide a best-practices example to be further developed, extended or adjusted in other Research and Development (R&D) projects, where resources available for ensuring security are visibly limited. We compare the available security measures and practices with those applied in other experienced grid and networking projects, both national (e.g. PL-Grid or National Data Storage 2) and European (e.g. EGI).

Keywords: IT security, HPC, Grid, security measures, NGI, NGI_PL.

1 Introduction

1.1 IT Security Landscape at a Glance

Although the relevance of security to information and communications technology (ICT) has not decreased over the past years, its shape has been altered by new attack techniques. Emerging threats include targeted attacks, such as large-scale Distributed Denial of Service (DDoS) and Advanced Persistent Threats (APT). According to the 2013 "Internet Security Threat Report, Volume 18" [25] there was a 42% increase in targeted attacks in 2012. As for APT, this is not a newly invented technique of attacking systems, but rather an advanced combination of different known attack types that results in obtaining a silent and

M. Bubak et al. (Eds.): PLGrid Plus, LNCS 8500, pp. 61–79, 2014.

secret backdoor to the attacked infrastructure, allowing the attacker to either control it or steal sensitive data (or both). APT attacks are usually long-term and, by definition, highly customised against the target.

The infrastructures of High Performance Computing (HPC) centres are attractive targets due to high bandwidth connections, extensive computational power and massive storage capacities [22]. Additionally, HPC centres may store valuable scientific data. According to [1], whilst the main targets of cybercriminals are web sites, e-commerce portals and payment processing infrastructures, HPC data centres and corporate infrastructures hold the 4th position (4% – not much, but HPC centres are not directly associated with financial assets). HPC systems are considered as a beachhead: once compromised, they may be utilised as a starting point for further attacks whilst remaining trusted by the attacked organisation.

Attacks are more sophisticated than ever, and keeping cybercriminals out requires a multi-faceted approach [1]. In order to combat sophisticated attacks, defence-in-depth strategies for specific information technology (IT) infrastructures should be designed. This type of strategy assumes that layered security mechanisms increase security of the system as a whole. If one security layer is breached in an attack, additional layers may stop the attacker (Open Web Application Security Project – OWASP [21]). Multilayered defence has a better chance of stopping a multilayered attack (like APT).

It is especially difficult to defend against APT attacks as they usually use social engineering and 0-day vulnerabilities (14 such vulnerabilities have been found in 2012 [25]). In the near future we cannot expect any single solution able to combat APT attacks – rather, we should try to combine the multilayered protection measures in order to decrease the probability of a successful attack.

1.2   Our Goal

Our goal is to review two aspects of assuring in-depth security in the Polish Domain-Specific Grid Infrastructure:

1. On the conceptually lower level consisting of five underlying HPC centres: Academic Computer Centre CYFRONET AGH (CYFRONET), Interdisciplinary Centre for Mathematical and Computational Modelling (ICM), Poznan Supercomputing and Networking Center (PSNC), Academic Computer Centre TASK (TASK), Wroclaw Centre for Networking and Supercomputing (WCSS).
2. On the conceptually higher level of the project, comprising services and applications.

Additionally, we would like to show how the situation changes over time. We have been able to observe the IT security landscape at Polish HPC centres in 2012, basing on research [14] performed in the Partnership for Advanced Computing in Europe (PRACE) project [6]. We have repeated the security assessment of the same centres in 2013 within the scope of the PLGrid Plus project. This

will allow us to assess the changing security level in the Polish HPC centres
themselves.

There is evolution on the project level as well. During the lifetime of the
project's predecessor, PL-Grid [23], certain activities were performed by its Security Center (Section 2). While in general these security actions were successful,
we found there was still room for improvement. An attempt was made to introduce such improvements in the new project.

The assessment of the evolution of security measures at Polish HPC centres
will be complemented with a description of technical and organisational solutions
designed and implemented in the PLGrid Plus project (including their evolution
since PL-Grid). We will try to determine whether there are still security gaps
at HPC centres and whether they are sufficiently remedied with security mechanisms built in PLGrid Plus.

1.3   PL-Grid Infrastructure Security

Only appropriate combination of security measures on the HPC level and the
project level may result in a secure project environment, even if the levels are
not quite dependent on each other – note that project teams may not have much
impact on HPC centre policies.

What Is the Security Level of HPC Centres? The security of the Polish
Domain-Specific Grid Infrastructure relies on appropriate security standards and
practices applied by five Polish HPC centres participating in the PLGrid Plus
project. All centres actively cooperate with their national and European partners, exchanging knowledge and experience, including information about the
most recent trends in IT attacks and suitable countermeasures. As a result, the
awareness of IT threats among security teams is sufficient. Good cooperation
practices on the project level have also been established, directly affecting the
security level of applications developed in the project, and facilitates appropriate
incident monitoring and response procedures. On the other hand, these are not
all layers where a security breach may occur. An attacker may find a vulnerability in the internal network of an HPC centre, or successfully prepare a social
attack. It is not an easy task to implement consistent security policies at different HPC centres as they operate in different environments and have different
security requirements, all of which bears influence on security measures.

What Is the Project's Security Level? The above-mentioned HPC centres
comprise the basis for assessment of security throughout the PL-Grid Infrastructure as they host the project services and data. This, however, is not enough.
A badly protected service may succumb to an attack using a port that is enabled on the HPC network firewall (otherwise the service would not be accessible
for legitimate users). Additionally, any grid-level or user-centric service may be
vulnerable to attacks, affecting security on different levels, e.g. Web OS code
execution compromises a machine (and usually upper layers as well) whilst SQL

injection affects the grid layer. Therefore, we need appropriate security measures on the level of the project itself. This creates another layer (which is technically composed of multiple sublayers). The PLGrid Plus project introduces new goals and aims to improve upon PL-Grid. As a consequence, the Security Center has to evolve as well. While these changes are difficult to measure, they define security evolution on the project level.

2   State of the Art

We will briefly describe how security issues are handled in selected Polish and European Union R&D projects. Even though security measures implemented in these projects have not been explicitly reviewed, or are unknown to authors, some of the applied security solutions were considered worthy of adoption in the PLGrid Plus project, and are analysed in this work.

2.1   PL-Grid

In [7], the authors described a way to maximise the level of protection of a heterogeneous grid environment. The PL-Grid Infrastructure is specifically referred to in [16]. In the PL-Grid project, a special task force, called the Security Center (SC), was established as an independent entity, with the National Grid Infrastructure (NGI) Security Officer as its head. The Security Center was engaged at every stage of development of the target infrastructure. The role of SC was both reactive – handling security incidents, and proactive – preventing security breach attempts. The latter work consisted primarily of preparing and applying security policies and procedures, developing a methodology for grid-oriented penetration tests [10] and performing security audits. Security monitoring was performed as well, using generic tools such as Pakiti [5] or more specific ones such as Acarm-ng [11] and SARA [15].

Appropriate procedures were created to ensure security on the HPC and other levels and to protect NGIs on the services level. As an example, "Security requirements for administrators" [8] applied to the lower level, whilst "Security requirements for programmers" pertained to the upper level of the software abstraction layer. The "Software deployment procedures" [12] document was an important example of the latter group. Among other issues, these procedures determined the role of the Security Center in the software deployment chain and stated an important rule, namely that SC must certify each software component developed within the project. Of note is also the "Simple CA user verification procedure" – part of [17], which allowed users to obtain certificates in a faster and more convenient manner, without significant detriment to the security of their software. During the project, penetration tests were conducted several times, in lockstep with changes in the infrastructure configuration. Two different approaches were applied: blackbox and whitebox. For the blackbox approach, a dedicated, custom methodology was used, whilst the whitebox part relied on a number of tools to automate the audit process. Owing to the higher degree of homogeneity on the OS level (compared to the application level), it was more feasible to apply automated tests in this layer. Thus, the whitebox toolkit helped secure the operating system level whilst heterogeneous services were thoroughly tested in a manual, blackbox-like manner.

A number of source code reviews were conducted within the lifetime of the project. The primary goal of the audits was to validate software created by various PL-Grid tasks. Audits of external, open- or closed-source grid software components considered critical to the NGI were performed. Since a decision has been made to manually review source code, and not simply use automatic code scanners, significant effort had to be invested in this task. As a result, a number of security bugs were found, affecting the European Grid Infrastructure as well.

As a result of the above described measures, the PL-Grid Infrastructure was only affected by a very limited number of known security attacks, all of which were detected early and successfully mitigated.

2.2 European Grid Infrastructure

The European Grid Infrastructure (EGI [3]) is a successor to the Enabling Grids for E-sciencE (EGEE) I/II/III projects. Its aim was to develop an integrated grid infrastructure among many National Grid Infrastructures (NGI) as well as many new grid-related services. One of those services was to create and maintain a dedicated operational IT security team, called the Computer Security Incident Response Team (EGI CSIRT [2]). The role of EGI CSIRT was mainly operational, providing several IT security services, including security incident response and management, computer forensics, vulnerability assessment and monitoring. Those services were performed on a global scale, for over 350 HPC sites located around the world.

The geographical scope and number of protected locations required a state-of-the-art approach, as security incidents can spread very quickly within a grid environment, due to shared credentials. In such a case, a single unpatched site poses a risk to all other sites, potentially leading to serious security incidents. To realise this task in an efficient way, a dedicated security monitoring system was developed as a precaution. The system checks for the presence of unpatched vulnerabilities at every HPC centre several times a day. Members of CSIRT constantly monitor public resources for new vulnerabilities. When these are identified, detailed advisories, mitigation instructions and patches are quickly distributed to all EGI member sites. EGI CSIRT advisories often spread beyond the EGI infrastructure, within the academic world, owing to their high quality. The rapid patching of all EGI sites was enabled by special policies, which required sites to either patch their systems or face suspension within 7 days.

To provide sufficient incident response quality, the position of a Security Officer on Duty was created: this person is responsible for quick reaction to all security issues within EGI. CSIRT members perform this role in shifts on a weekly basis. EGI CSIRT was successful in introducing a security incident information sharing model by introducing a policy, which requires sites to send detailed information about an incident to all sites within a given timeframe. This policy also requires sending head-ups to all sites as the investigation progresses. All security incidents within EGI are investigated thoroughly, providing very detailed reports, which sometimes take several weeks to prepare, but always point out the root cause of an incident. Many EGI sites were interested in receiving support from CSIRT forensics experts whilst running their own investigations. All of these measures combine to ensure a high level of service, which is very rarely seen in the commercial world and usually costs a lot. Additionally, CSIRT introduces a new service, which allows centralised user suspension. The aim of this service is to provide a quick way (under 1 hour) to block a given user's accounts on all sites should this account become compromised. This significantly limits the potential spread of security breaches to other EGI sites.

EGI CSIRT is involved in regular dissemination activities, improving overall security awareness among HPC users and administrators. It organises unique IT security training courses at HPC conferences and various CSIRT community meetings. CSIRT members are also responsible for performing risk assessment of the EGI infrastructure.

EGI CSIRT is a very unique team due to its structure – it is a virtual and distributed team, consisting of representatives of several NGIs. From among over 50 NGIs, slightly over 10 have nominated representatives, and the Polish NGI (NGI_PL) was among them, being represented by a member of the PL-Grid Security Center. EGI CSIRT is also a member of the TERENA Trusted Introducer TF-CSIRT workgroup with an accredited status, where many of worldwide CERT/CSIRT teams share their knowledge and experience.

2.3 National Data Storage 2

The purpose of the National Data Storage (NDS) project was to provide large secondary storage facilities for education and government in Poland [4]. National Data Storage 2 (NDS2) was a continuation and enhancement of NDS and was launched in May 2011. The project was addressed to deliver new features as well as enhanced security and performance stability to the basic NDS model [13]. The improvements were made on both technical and organisational levels. A Security Office has been appointed, consisting of security experts, with the project Security Officer and Security Office Coordinator as the managing body. Since the project team was relatively small (ca. 50 persons) and good cooperation between individual members had already been established, there were no requirements or serious demand to introduce security procedures concerning software validation. Nevertheless, the security team was free to cooperate with developers over the course of their work. As the number of software components was relatively small, it was not a difficult task for the Security Office to supervise all of them throughout their entire life cycle, including deployment. On the technical level, the Security Office operated in a similar fashion to its PL-Grid counterpart (the Security Center), with a similar approach to code audits and application penetration testing.

2.4 Partnership for Advanced Computing in Europe

The Partnership for Advanced Computing in Europe (PRACE) is an initiative started in 2008 with the first PRACE Preparatory Phase project, followed by Implementation Phase projects: PRACE-1IP, 2IP and 3IP [6]. During the course of these projects, the PRACE Research Infrastructure (PRACE-RI) was established as an international non-profit association, with 25 member countries, including Poland, represented by HPC centres. The goal of participating projects and the entire association is to create a pan-European supercomputing infrastructure, providing access to computing and data management resources and services for large-scale scientific and engineering applications. The PRACE Security Forum brings together representatives of each site contributing to the infrastructure. The goal of the forum is to discuss and formulate security policies and procedures on a project level. The forum closely collaborates with EGI CSIRT. Rapid communication channels for site security officers were instituted in order to spread information about emerging security issues. The state of security protection on PRACE sites was evaluated once, and the outcome was published as a set of general recommendations [14].

3 Layers and Measures of Security in a Grid

In this section we present the security measures that were used to perform an analysis of the security level of the PL-Grid Infrastructure (as described in the following sections). We will show that both previously presented abstraction layers of the grid infrastructure can be further divided into smaller components where specific security measures can be applied.

We will also divide the definition of grid security into two main areas: organisational and technical. Only an appropriate combination of these two areas may result in maintaining a sufficient level of security. A security policy, which does not translate into technical measures, is just a worthless piece of paper. Similarly, technical measures, which were not implemented in accordance with a common security policy, are usually applied in a chaotic way and often not according to best practices in the field. An additional problem emerges when technical staff members leave the organisation – their knowledge disappears with them, if undocumented.

Fig. 1 outlines both conceptual levels of the Grid: the project level and the HPC centre level, divided into sub-layers. Each layer can be assigned a security measure: either specific or shared by multiple layers. Each HPC-level component introduces distinct measures, e.g. a firewall, Network-based Intrusion Detection System (IDS) or anti-DDoS are reliable security metrics on the perimeter layer, whilst rootkit detector or Host-based IDS reflect security on the host layer. Security policies, Penetration tests and Security audits concern multiple layers.

3.1 Organisational Measures

Security cannot be approached in a consistent manner absent an organisational framework. Each organisation should employ a team of people tasked with

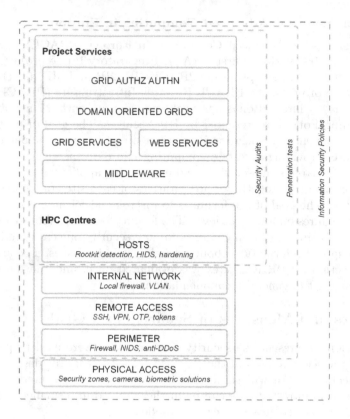

Fig. 1. Security levels and measures in a grid environment

taking care of security (a security team and/or internal audit department – the latter usually in larger organisations, especially big corporations). The existence of a separate security/auditing department or team is one of the best indicators of attitude towards security and of the degree of seriousness, with which this issue is treated within the organisation. The person whose daily duties include system or network administration should never be the one who audits those systems or infrastructures. They simply cannot do it well (i.e., in a completely unbiased and neutral way) even if they possess extensive knowledge about security. The situation resembles book editing – authors are generally not capable of consistently spotting and correcting their own mistakes.

Implementing state-of-the-art technical solutions and establishing a security team is still not enough: in the words of one of the greatest IT security gurus, Bruce Schneier: "security is a process, not a product" [24]. This is why level of security should be periodically evaluated and controlled. Periodical security audits should consist of various scenarios, such as configuration and source code reviews and penetration tests, both black-box and white-box, originating from the Internet and local networks. Naturally, security audits should be performed by people who are not directly involved in infrastructure maintenance. Besides audits performed by the security team, it is often prudent to periodically contract an external entity for a security test so as to obtain valuable third-party opinion, mitigating the risk of overlooking a crucial vulnerability. All of the above mentioned organisational means of maintaining a decent level of security have to be specified in the security policy. As well as being carefully prepared and thoroughly scrutinised, the organisational security policy should base on established norms and standards (such as ISO27001). The Information Security Policy should also settle some specific issues such as the terms of use or equivalent agreements for users to access the HPC centre, and the consequences of breaching these terms. The server room is a place with a significantly higher level of security. Therefore, not everyone is allowed to enter it.

3.2   Technical Measures

IT security cannot rely on security policies alone. Having an "it is forbidden" clause in a document will not convince an adversary to restrain themselves from performing attacks against the infrastructure. Some technical means have to be applied. A number of tools are available on the market; however, a perfect solution to security problems obviously does not, and will never exist. One should not rely on security provided by a single product. The key to establishing a decent level of security is defence-in-depth. While it does not guarantee absolute security, it nevertheless provides the means to make a successful attack so difficult as to become cost-ineffective for the attacker.

Firewalls. The main type of defence against threats coming both from the inside and outside of the HPC network is a firewall. In the easiest example it is a device installed on the network perimeter and examining all data sent between the internal and external networks. The key issue here is to examine the data as thoroughly and as deeply as possible. Application firewalls enable this by analysing all of the 7 ISO/OSI layers, including the topmost application level. It is also crucial to maintain high availability (HA) so as to secure the HPC infrastructure against the firewall's failure. According to the defence-in-depth principle, it is advisable to use not only network firewalls, but also local firewalls.

Antivirus Software. Another important type of local security system is antivirus software (AV). Unfortunately, whilst it should successfully detect known threats (based on the installed set of signatures), it may not be able to react to 0-day attacks or other unknown malware. In several categories of systems, not installing AV software may be justified (e.g. highly loaded HPC computational nodes that are protected on other layers, especially if these servers run an OS, which is not particularly susceptible to viruses or software vulnerabilities, e.g. Linux [1], [18]).

IDS Systems. Due to the fact that firewalls and antivirus systems are not sufficient to reliably secure organisations' IT infrastructure and prevent attackers from gaining unauthorised access to their internal networks, implementation of additional security measures is necessary. Systems able to monitor the processes and analyse network traffic are considered especially useful for HPC centres [22]. Solutions designed to help and support security administrators include Intrusion Detection Systems (IDS). An IDS monitors critical parts of the infrastructure in order to discover intrusions and intrusion attempts and immediately informs administrators about any irregularities. To reduce the likelihood and impact of a successful breach, it is crucial to minimise the window of opportunity for would-be attackers. Therefore, the aim of IDS is to discover and notify about attacks and intrusion attempts in (near-)real-time. Two main categories of IDS are:

- Host-based Intrusion Detection System (HIDS) – an application installed on a specified machine. Its main goal is to monitor certain operating system components as well as applications and network interfaces in order to discover suspicious activity that may be a sign of a break-in attempt.
- Network-based Intrusion Detection System (NIDS) – monitors network traffic and attempts to discover known attack patterns (signature-based approach) or unusual network activity (anomaly detection approach).

There are other IDS categories (for example Distributed Intrusion Detection System) and approaches to intrusion detection, but most of them are based on the two main categories presented above. Intrusion Detection Systems with active attack prevention mechanisms and features (blocking certain ports, resetting suspicious connections, etc.) are called Intrusion Prevention Systems (IPS), and may also be categorised as Host-based (HIPS) or Network-based (NIPS).

Authentication. Authentication basing on a username and a static password is, naturally, the most popular form of authenticating users. It is not, however, the most secure one (according to [1], 89% of networks contain a weak or blank system administrator password and 86% a database password of that sort). There are plenty of other, safer methods. The main idea of increasing authentication security is usually two-factor authentication. Under this approach, having a password, "something you know", is not enough for a user to authenticate. A second factor is required; typically a possession factor, i.e., "something you have". One of the relatively recent technologies currently gaining in popularity is the One-Time Password method (OTP). OTP is a password that is valid for only one login session, which helps avoid some of the shortcomings of static passwords such as vulnerability to replay attacks, i.e., even if the attacker obtains the password, it is not valid and cannot be used anymore. A special device is required to generate passwords, but the associated cost is not high. A better known technique is asymmetric cryptography. The user needs a public and a private key for successful authentication. The public key is placed on the server, which pre-authenticates the user. The user's identity is subsequently proven when a challenge encrypted with the public key is successfully deciphered. Possession of the private key and knowledge of the passphrase used for securing it is required at this step.

Remote Administration. Even the best authentication methods may prove ineffective and, as a consequence, insecure if other security practices are neglected. Remote access flaws were the most frequent cause of successful infiltration in 2012 (47% [1]). One should always bear in mind that remote administration does not come without a risk. It is crucial, whilst managing systems remotely, to use cryptographically secure protocols such as Secure Shell (SSH). Moreover, connections should be made to unprivileged accounts and administration privileges should be obtained locally, so as to add an additional layer of security.

Network Segmentation. Proper network segmentation must not be neglected. It is recommended to place public services in a separate network segment called the Demilitarised Zone (DMZ), with no access to the users' LAN. This can be achieved either by physical separation or by using VLANs (Virtual LANs), which enable the administrators to divide the physical network into logical subnetworks. In addition to easier network segmentation, VLANs help separate user traffic from administration traffic, which obviously increases the overall security level. In more complex environments, network segmentation can be further differentiated into several DMZs and several internal layers.

DDoS Attacks and Countermeasures. There is a specific group of network attacks that are of special interest to Security Administrators, as protecting against them is handled differently – the Denial of Service (DoS) attacks. Their concept bases on preventing legitimate users from accessing a certain service. A Distributed Denial of Service (DDoS) attack is a DoS attack that is additionally carried out from numerous locations. It introduces two main factors: the attack volume is much higher and it is much more difficult (or even impossible) to define the list of attacking source IP addresses. Combating DDoS attacks is a difficult task and a point of interest for security researchers. The most effective solution is geographical data distribution, aided by intelligent network filtering devices.

Advanced Security Solutions: Honeypots and DLP. More sophisticated technologies intended to further increase the security level are honeypots and DLP (Data Leak Prevention). Honeypots imitate badly secured systems in an attempt to attract real attackers who then spend time trying to compromise a throwaway system, whilst additionally revealing their methods of attack. DLP software tries to protect organisational data, but must be perfectly adjusted and configured for the protected infrastructure. As a result, neither solution is used extensively, which, in many cases is quite reasonable for an HPC centre. We have inquired about these measures to find out whether there is a trend to use some extra ("non-mandatory") protection techniques.

Physical Security. One should not underestimate the importance of physical security. Law #3 of Microsoft's 10 Immutable Laws of Security says: "If a bad guy has unrestricted physical access to your computer, it's not your computer anymore" [20] and is, as the name says, immutable, hence still valid. This is the reason for our focus on physical server room security. It is recommended to divide the server room into tiered security zones, besides keeping it under constant and uninterruptible surveillance and limiting access to authorised personnel. Several methods can be used to ensure staff authorisation – from conventional keys through electronic keys to biometric scanners.

4   Analysis and Evolution of Different Layers of Security

In this section we will try to review the security level of the PL-Grid Infrastructure. We will go beyond simple assessment of a particular point in time and instead attempt to show current infrastructure security facets and their dynamics. This is possible since we have performed two HPC security level measurements by requesting surveys from centre administrators. Although we treat HPC and project levels separately, it should be noted that they tend to affect each other (Section 5). Penetration tests are a good example as usually they are not bound to any particular layer and instead concern multiple layers, even if their results are only reported in HPC-level surveys.

Section 2 describes important aspects of PL-Grid security. The PL-Grid Infrastructure has evolved since then, as PLGrid Plus provided new goals and features, influencing security in a significant way. We are going to review these changes as well in order to provide a complete picture of the infrastructure-wide security evolution.

4.1   HPC Level

The Current State. As stated before, PLGrid Plus consists of two layers – the lower, hardware layer and the upper, application layer. Whereas the application layer has to be concise, the hardware layer may vary even within one HPC centre. Obviously, HPCs differ from each other and have different security requirements and different security policies. As a result, securing the PL-Grid Infrastructure does not have to account for the security of HPCs as a whole. Finally, the required set of mechanisms that should be used to secure an R&D project's infrastructure, depends on the project's nature, the sensitivity of processed data, etc. These factors may ultimately necessitate different approaches to IT security than those applied by HPCs.

Some security measures, however, are always present in an HPC infrastructure. Hence, core security tools, e.g. network and local firewalls, are immutably used at every HPC centre participating in the PLGrid Plus project. NIPS/NIDS systems are also widespread – 80% of HPCs have a network IDS/IPS solution deployed. HIPS and HIDS solutions are less common and have been implemented only at 40% of HPCs. One fifth (20%) of the surveyed centres use application firewalls and the same amount have antivirus software installed. However, 60% of the surveyed centres use rootkit detectors. More sophisticated security means, such as DLP, did not find any advocates among HPC administrators.

Physical security is approached very seriously at the surveyed centres – all HPC server rooms are under surveillance (Fig. 2) and every HPC centre has introduced an Acceptable Use Policy (AUP). Breaching the rules may lead to blocking the user's account, limiting privileges or suspending a grant. As mentioned in the previous section, the attitude towards security is reflected by the existence of a security team/department. Four fifths (80%) of the surveyed HPC centres either have a security team or employ people whose daily duties focus on security issues, but who do not belong to a separate organisational entity.

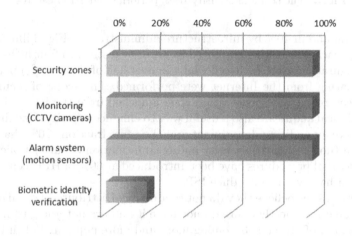

Fig. 2. Physical access control mechanisms used at HPC centres

The infrastructure at all HPC centres is properly separated using both VLAN segmentation and network filters, and all centres enforce secure communication channels to low-privileged accounts, requiring privileges to be upgraded locally, should the user need it. Moreover, 20% of HPCs provide a Virtual Private Network (VPN) service. Almost half (40%) have already introduced two-factor authentication in the form of security tokens.

The HPC infrastructure has to undergo regular security tests so as to maintain a proper level of security. Tests have been performed in all participating HPC infrastructures. The majority (60%) of the infrastructures go through periodical security tests, whilst the remaining ones (40%) have been tested at least once. In 60% of cases tests are performed by external entities, in 20% by dedicated

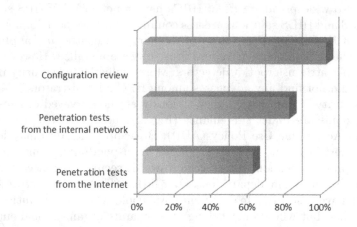

Configuration review

Penetration tests
from the internal network

Penetration tests
from the Internet

0%   20%   40%   60%   80%   100%

Fig. 3. The scope of security tests performed at HPC centres

security team and in 40% by infrastructure administrators. Fig. 3 illustrates the
various approaches to testing employed by security testers. In four fifths (80%) of
HPCs configurations were reviewed whilst in over half of them (60%) penetration
tests originating from the Internet were performed. The scope of security tests
in 40% of centres include penetration tests launched from the internal network.

Non-technical audits are also a useful way to enhance security. One fifth (20%)
of HPCs have an auditing department and the same fraction (20%) have under-
gone formal (non-technical) security audits. Information Security Policies (ISP)
based on internal procedures have been introduced at 60% of HPC centres whilst
40% of them have yet to introduce ISP.

Only 20% of sites believe they do not require any Distributed Denial of Service
(DDoS) protection and therefore do not have it and are not going to implement
it. Yet this kind of attack is becoming more and more popular. Polish High Performance Computing centres connected to the broadband National Research &
Education Network PIONIER are indubitably more resilient to DDoS attacks,
but definitely not immune. Therefore, 80% of the surveyed centres have introduced some countermeasures against this kind of attack. One fifth (20%) of sites
have procedures for combating DDoS attacks whilst 40% have implemented anti-
DDoS software or hardware solutions. One fifth (20%) of centres have plans to
introduce some countermeasures against DDoS attacks.

Progress Description. Besides assessing the current state, it is important to
analyse how the situation has changed since the survey conducted in [6] and the
one organised within the PLGrid Plus project (the approximate time elapsed
between both surveys is 12 months).

The most significant changes encountered through that period, are as follows:

- one (20%) HPC centre changed its organisational approach to IT security (a separate security team or department was created);
- one audit department was created and one HPC centre underwent a formal (non-technical) security audit;
- one HPC centre deployed a network IDS/IPS system (increase from 60% to 80%);
- as for local security systems, one HPC ceased to use local IDS/IPS; on the other hand 3 centres began using antirootkit tools;
- one centre ceased remote management of certain systems by direct remote login to privileged accounts (this was the only HPC centre, at which this practice had been used);
- one centre changed its policy stating that it did not require anti-DDoS techniques and began using technical (hardware) countermeasures;
- one centre (increase from 80% to 100%) implemented network segmentation in order to separate the HPC infrastructure from other systems, and deployed network filters;
- 2 centres (increase from 0% to 40%) began applying nonstandard authentication methods, more sophisticated than plain user-password pairs.

Whilst the scope of changes may seem low, twelve months is a relatively short time to handle the entire process of analysing, purchasing, deploying and configuring a new security system, especially in public research institutes, which have to conform to specific legal restrictions. In general, the direction of the encountered changes must be assessed positively.

4.2   Project Level

As already mentioned, PLGrid Plus can be regarded as a successor to PL-Grid. As such, PLGrid Plus builds on top of the PL-Grid Infrastructure, preserving the majority of its software services, as well as procedures and policies, including those related to security (e.g. validation procedures, penetration tests and audits, etc.) The new project also incorporates new significant features.

In general, the main enhancement relating to PL-Grid are the so-called domain grids – area-specific computing environments. 13 groups of scientists were invited to cooperate with infrastructure developers in order to address new computing challenges. From the security point of view, it is important to state that WWW services are the most frequently chosen interfaces enabling access to domain grids.

In the new project, development of the majority of existing project services was placed on hold, and developers instead started to issue patches and minor enhancements only. To fulfill grid user demands, a cloud infrastructure was also created, allowing users to access machines with administrator privileges. Unfortunately, whilst significant extensions have been made on the project level, the amount of resources dedicated to operational security was notably reduced. The Security Center now consists of representatives of only 2 project partners and operates at limited capacity. It can be clearly seen that in PLGrid Plus a number of new security challenges have arisen.

Software Validation Procedures. Since a feature freeze was instituted in production services (allowing only minor patches and enhancements to be accepted) corresponding procedural changes had to be introduced. For new releases, only binary packages are validated against security conditions, where the "rpmlint" tool is used as a validation base. Considering that the volume of such certification requests is high, the need for automation of the certification process has arisen. Each properly validated RPM package is digitally signed by the Security Center PGP key. A special service has been created in the infrastructure to accept upload of signed RPM packages. Once a package is uploaded to the infrastructure repository, it almost immediately appears in local package systems.

As for the new services, i.e., mostly domain grids, the verification procedure remains unchanged on the technical level, whilst a significant organisational change has been introduced in order to limit the usage of Security Center resources. Qualification factors now determine whether a given service will be thoroughly analysed by security experts. If the application's relevance to infrastructure security is below some defined level, only basic analysis is performed, or it will be skipped altogether. Usually, such applications include computational or user-side tools, without direct connections to the infrastructure. On the opposite end, components involved in user credentials processing or able to submit jobs are always scrutinised by the security team. A special variant of the verification procedure is used when a new version of an existing production service is submitted for auditing. If the release changelog lists modifications affecting authorisation or authentication mechanisms or the user input schema, an audit must be performed.

Cloud Infrastructure. The cloud is a novel and notable sub-environment introduced in PLGrid Plus [19]. As cloud computing is a young area of IT, there is still a lack of experience regarding it among IT specialists, even if they have good understanding of its concepts. This also affects computing security issues. The cloud brings new security factors and risks, including: immature technologies and applications, lack of staff experience, shared resources and environment (virtual machine hosts, network devices, storage, RAM, etc.) as well as changeability (hosts, possibly IPs and security domains). It becomes clear that special care have to be taken by the Security Center with regard to cloud resources.

In PLGrid Plus, an Infrastructure as a Service (IaaS) model was applied: the user is given a virtualised hardware layer where operating system images can be run. This model results in great convenience and flexibility of use: the user as now can have a dedicated machine in the Grid and directly install and manage software. On the other hand, new threats also emerge: the user is not expected to possess IT administrator knowledge and experience, in particular regarding protection of resources against unauthorised access and use. Compromising a virtual machine (VM) will not pose a problem to the user only, but also to the whole infrastructure, allowing attackers privileged access to other components of the environment (such as other VM network interfaces) whilst limiting the traceability of their activities. For the above reason, a detailed cloud infrastructure management and usage policy has been prepared [9]. The policy lists rules pertaining to both technical and organisational aspects. The technical issues addressed by the policy include: VLAN management, operating system image configuration (hardening), monitoring tools, which need to be installed, VM remote access methods, remote logging and monitoring configuration and active VM protection mechanisms (e.g. SSH scan protection).

The policy further covers organisational means to achieve cloud infrastructure security. The Virtual Machine repository is considered critical and, as such, has to be carefully protected. Thus, a number of duties have been defined concerning VM administrators as the repository itself. As for the VM images, they have to be periodically updated in order to secure them against known attacks. It is up to the administrator to do so, whilst the Security Center is responsible for periodically checking such a state. SC members not only monitor static images, but they are also allowed access to running VMs with administrator privileges in order to perform non-intrusive security tests of their own. The outcome of such tests may result in immediate suspension of a particular virtual machine.

Operations Management. A fundamental change in the management structure in PLGrid Plus has been made. The Security Center now operates as part of the Operations Center, instead of being a separate entity, subordinate to project technical director alone. In PLGrid Plus, each of the six work packages needs to perform periodic, formal actions concerning planning, reporting and communication. Since the Security Center was by far the smallest team among other main task teams, such activities consumed a notable amount of its time. In PLGrid Plus, these tasks are instead run on the Operations Center level, which enables the SC to spend more effort on content-related tasks. There are some potential drawbacks of such a transformation, as part of the SC autonomy was lost, but there is a way to overcome these issues with good cooperation and partnership skills.

5 Conclusions

Surveys have confirmed that different HPC centres use different security solutions (although the basic security mechanisms, especially on the network level, are applied rather consistently and without extensions). Additionally, positive progress may be identified – the centres gradually extend their security capabilities both on the technical and organisational level. However, the consistency of the protection layers instituted by the centres themselves is not sufficient to ensure acceptable protection level for specific services hosted in the HPC infrastructure within the confines of R&D projects – especially taking into account different security requirements on the project level, dependent upon the systems used and data processed.

Although some positive changes have been witnessed in HPC partners affiliated with PLGrid Plus (e.g. wider implementation of 2-factor authentication, proper network separation at all sites or improved DDoS awareness), there is still room for improvement, for example by implementing atypical security solutions. We would recommend creating opportunities for research on various types of security systems that could result in at least partial implementation by the participating centres. It must also be noted that several centres should complement the available technical security measures with formal or organisational support – there are (single) cases when particular centres do not have yet a dedicated security team or formal complex security policy.

Activities on the HPC and project layers may stimulate and support one another. Project-wide activities may contribute to the activities at each HPC partner. A real example may involve implementing recommendations from security audits of project services in everyday work of HPC administrators, or applying user agreements elaborated within the project to other projects pursued at HPC institutions.

To summarise, we believe that – both at Polish HPC centres and within the Polish Grid Infrastructure – there is a need to continue improving security activities both at the level of HPC operators and individual research projects. The centres should optimally apply all recognised security measures (including organisational ones). From the HPC-related R&D project perspective, this would decrease the amount of work required to secure project services against general infrastructure threats. On the other hand, the project security activities could then focus on customised security tests, covering mainly project-specific systems and services. Additionally, resources should be devoted to security-related research within the projects, addressing nonstandard and innovative solutions. Successful ideas could then be applied at all HPC centres, providing additional layers of protection, in compliance with the defence-in-depth principle. In a similar vein, transfer of security recommendations and best practices resulting from the project, should continue.

References

1. 2013 TrustWave Global Security Report,
   http://www2.trustwave.com/rs/trustwave/
   images/2013-Global-Security-Report.pdf
2. EGI Computer Security Incident Response Team,
   https://wiki.egi.eu/wiki/EGI_CSIRT:Main_Page
3. European Grid Infrastructure, http://www.egi.eu
4. National Data Storage Project, http://nds.psnc.pl
5. Pakiti: A Patching Status Monitoring Tool, http://pakiti.sourceforge.net/
6. Partnership for Advanced Computing in Europe, http://www.prace-ri.eu
7. Balcerek, B., Frankowski, G., Kwiecień, A., Smutnicki, A., Teodorczyk, M.: Security Best Practices: Applying Defense-in-Depth Strategy to Protect the NGI_PL. In: Bubak, M., Szepieniec, T., Wiatr, K. (eds.) PL-Grid 2011. LNCS, vol. 7136, pp. 128–141. Springer, Heidelberg (2012),
   http://dx.doi.org/10.1007/978-3-642-28267-6_10

8. Balcerek, B., Kosicki, G., Smutnicki, A., Teodorczyk, M.: Zalecenia bezpieczeństwa dotyczące instalacji klastrów lokalnych v0.95 (2010) (in Polish)
9. Balcerek, B., Smutnicki, A., Frankowski, G., Czarniecki, L.: Zalecenia bezpiecznej instalacji i użytkowania infrastruktury cloud (2013) (in Polish)
10. Balcerek, B., Smutnicki, A., Teodorczyk, M.: Testy penetracyjne infrastruktury PL-Grid (2011) (in Polish)
11. Balcerek, B., Szurgot, B., Uchroński, M., Waga, W.: ACARM-ng: Next Generation Correlation Framework. In: Bubak, M., Szepieniec, T., Wiatr, K. (eds.) PL-Grid 2011. LNCS, vol. 7136, pp. 114–127. Springer, Heidelberg (2012)
12. Baliś, B., Harężlak, D., Radecki, M.: Procedury wdrażania oprogramowania w infrastrukturze PL-Grid v1.2 (2010) (in Polish)
13. Brzeźniak, M., Jankowski, G., Meyer, N.: National Data Storage 2 – Secure sparing, publishing and exchanging data (2011),
    http://www.terena.org/activities/
    tf-storage/ws10/slides/20110204-nds2.pdf
14. Erdogan, O., Frankowski, G., Nowak, M., Meyer, N., Yilmaz, E.: Security in HPC Centres (2012), http://www.prace-ri.eu/IMG/pdf/wp79.pdf
15. Frankowski, G., Rzepka, M.: SARA – System for Inventory and Static Security Control in a Grid Infrastructure. In: Bubak, M., Szepieniec, T., Wiatr, K. (eds.) PL-Grid 2011. LNCS, vol. 7136, pp. 102–113. Springer, Heidelberg (2012)
16. Kitowski, J., et al.: Polish computational research space for international scientific collaborations. In: Wyrzykowski, R., Dongarra, J., Karczewski, K., Waśniewski, J. (eds.) PPAM 2011, Part I. LNCS, vol. 7203, pp. 317–326. Springer, Heidelberg (2012)
17. Krakowian, M.: Procedura rejestracji użytkowników v1.0.1 (2010) (in Polish)
18. Litton, J.: Why Linux Will Never Suffer From Viruses Like Windows (2012),
    http://hothardware.com/Reviews/
    Why-Linux-Will-Never-Suffer-From-Viruses-Like-Windows
19. Meizner, J., Radecki, M., Pawlik, M., Szepieniec, T.: Cloud services in PL-Grid and EGI infrastructures. In: Bubak, M., Turała, M., Wiatr, K. (eds.) CGW 2012 Proceedings, pp. 71–72. ACK CYFRONET AGH, Kraków (2012),
    http://dice.cyfronet.pl/publications/
    source/papers/023-B5-mp-c44-Szepieniec.pdf
20. Microsoft: 10 Immutable Laws of Security,
    http://technet.microsoft.com/library/cc722487.aspx#EIAA
21. OWASP: Defense in depth,
    https://www.owasp.org/index.php/Defense_in_depth
22. Patriot Technologies, Inc.: How to successfully secure a HPC system (2011),
    http://blog.patriot-tech.com/blog/bid/
    49004/How-to-successfully-secure-a-HPC-system
23. PL-Grid project web site, http://projekt.plgrid.pl/en
24. Schneier, B.: Crypto-Gram Newsletter (2000),
    https://www.schneier.com/crypto-gram-0005.html
25. Symantec: Internet Security Threat Report 2013 (2013),
    http://www.symantec.com/content/en/us/enterprise/
    other_resources/b-istr_main_report_v18_2012_21291018.en-us.pdf

Reservations for Compute Resources in Federated e-Infrastructure

Marcin Radecki[1], Tadeusz Szymocha[1], Tomasz Piontek[2], Bartosz Bosak[2],
Mariusz Mamoński†[2], Paweł Wolniewicz[2],
Krzysztof Benedyczak[3], and Rafał Kluszczyński[3]

[1] AGH University of Science and Technology, ACC Cyfronet AGH,
ul. Nawojki 11, 30-950 Kraków, Poland
`tadeusz.szymocha@cyfronet.pl`
[2] Poznan Supercomputing and Networking Center, Institute of Bioorganic Chemistry
of the Polish Academy of Sciences, ul. Noskowskiego 12/14, 61-704 Poznań, Poland
[3] University of Warsaw, Interdisciplinary Center for Mathematical and
Computational Modelling, ul. Pawińskiego 5a, 02-106 Warszawa, Poland

Abstract. This paper presents work done to prepare compute resource reservations in the PL-Grid Infrastructure. A compute resource reservation allows a user to allocate some fraction of resources for exclusive access, when reservation is prepared. That way the user is able to run his/her job without waiting for allocating resources in a batch system.

In the PL-Grid Infrastructure reservations can be allocated up to amount negotiated in a PL-Grid grant. One way of getting reservation is allocation by a resource administrator. Another way is to use predefined pool of resources accessible by various middleware. In both approaches once obtained, reservations identifiers can be used by middleware during job submissions. Enabling reservations requires changes in middleware. The modifications needed in each middleware will be described. The possible extension of existing reservation model in the PL-Grid Infrastructure can be envisaged: reservation usage normalization and reservation accounting.

The reservations are created and utilized in the user's context, so there must be a way to pass the reservation details from the user-level tools to a batch system. Each of PL-Grid supported middleware, namely gLite, UNICORE and QosCosGrid, required adaptations to implement this goal.

Keywords: QosCosGrid, UNICORE, gLite, advance reservations, co-allocation of resources.

1 Introduction

The scheduling of computing jobs at HPC clusters may be done in different ways according to the resource provider policy:

- *advance reservations*, when the user needs resources (limited to a single system, location) for a specific time span in future,

M. Bubak et al. (Eds.): PLGrid Plus, LNCS 8500, pp. 80–93, 2014.
© Springer International Publishing Switzerland 2014

- *co-scheduling*, when simultaneous access to resources that are part of different logical systems (or locations) is required,
- *on-demand scheduling*, when jobs for a time-crucial application should be
run as quickly as possible; the existing jobs are let to finish or running jobs
may be preempted to allow a new job to start,
- *workflows*, when jobs have dependencies between them and one job is waiting
for output of the other job (e.g. a visualisation job should start after core
computations have finished).

The scientists usually need computational resources to perform complex theoretical calculations. In most cases, typical submission of a job to the queuing
system is sufficient. The computations are done on shared resources at not exactly predictable time in future. But for some use cases it may be required to run
jobs without waiting in a batch system queue, at exclusive resource or/and at
specific time in future.

The PL-Grid Infrastructure is supporting *advance reservations, workflows* and
to a limited extent *co-scheduling*. The QCG middleware has pre-agreed pool of
reserved resources that provide the users with the global *co-scheduling* mechanism based on advance reservations at every PL-Grid Infrastructure computer
center.

The *advance reservations* are "expensive" meaning that a reserved resource
cannot be used by other users and if it is not occupied by jobs, it may be
considered as not optimally used. For this reason, the accounting of reservations
needs to be in place to efficiently manage a user's request. Thus, the *advance
reservations* are covered by the PL-Grid grant system. The user may apply for
a grant, in which he declares that the advance reservation will be needed and
specifies the general values for size, time-span and recurrence of the reservation.
Then, while the grant is active, the user can apply for setting the reservation
in advance, which is then manually set by a system administrator. The user is
informed about a reservation identifier and can specify it in his own scripts or
middleware tools. There is also some cost incurred by freeing resources needed
for the reservation. This is more substantial for large reservations and is similar
to freeing resources for executing a many-CPU job, however, in the PL-Grid
Infrastructure we decided to neglect this kind of cost.

2   Related Work

The advance reservation is of interest to users of different existing IT infrastructures. The need of advance reservation was tackled also by I. Foster et al. and
yielded in proposition of the Globus Architecture for Reservation and Allocation
(GARA) [1].

Parallel to the European infrastructure, the United States infrastructure was
developed within the TeraGrid and its continuator – the Extreme Science and
Engineering Digital Environment (XSEDE) [2] project. The metascheduling Requirements Analysis Team (RAT) recommended evaluation of tools facilitating

reservations management [3]. However, authors were not able to reach public documents describing technical implementation. The RAT indicated the Highly-Available Resource Co-allocator (HARC) [4] as recommended for further evaluation in the TeraGrid project. The goal of HARC is to provide co-allocation service for metacomputing and workflow applications, where diferent types of resources are reserved as they were a single, indivisible resource. So, the allocation process reminds database transaction.

An interesting approach of dealing with the issue of resource reservation at a middleware layer is use of a *pilot jobs* framework as presented in [5]. A pilot job occupies a resource and pulls down some other job to be executed at this resource. This way it is possible to avoid interaction with batch system mechanisms for resource reservation, which may be troublesome, having in mind a variety of batch systems in grid environment, but currently (2014) it is not used in the PL-Grid Infrastructure.

3   The Grid Resource Allocation and Agreement Protocol

The Grid Resource Allocation and Agreement Protocol working group (GRAAP-WG) [6] of the Global Grid Forum (GGF) defines methods and means to establish Service Level Agreements between different entities in a distributed environment. The advance reservation is one of the defined scenarios.

GRAAP-WG defines the advance reservations scenario as to perform a job submission within the context of an existing (or advance) reservation of capability or pre-established resource preferences. The difference from the simple job submission is that the user knows that he has an ongoing relationship with the job hosting service, and can expect his job offer(s) to be accepted as long as the requested parameters are kept within certain limits set by the relationship. For example, the reservation might guarantee availability of a certain kind of resource on a certain schedule, or with a particular cost model. Reservation is an abstraction for understanding this refined expectation about the handling of future jobs; whether the job hosting service uses preemption, predictive models, or the literal setting aside of resources is an implementation decision for the service. Another use of pre-established agreement is to specify resource preferences, e.g., choice of nodes with a certain amount of memory over others, via an agreement, that are to be used in all subsequent resource allocations to incoming jobs in the context of this agreement.

GRAAP-WG proposes an architecture comprising two main layers: the Agreement layer and the service provider layer. The Agreement layer implements the communication protocol used to exchange information about Service Level Agreements and defines its specification. The reservation and allocation request is issued by the agreement initiator. The Agreement layer is responsible for ensuring that the guarantees defined in the "contract" – the Agreement – are enforced by a suitable service provider. In addition, the Agreement layer defines the mechanisms:

- to expose information about types of a service and the related agreement offered (the Agreement templates),

– to handle the submission of service requests (the so-called agreement offers) and submit them to the Agreement layer; one offer needs to comply with at least one template exposed by the Agreement provider, to which it is dispatched, and it has to meet the agreement creation constraints specified in the corresponding Agreement template.

The Agreement layer relies on service providers. An Agreement is successfully created if one or more service providers are able to enforce the guarantees associated with it. The service provider is responsible for supervising the status of a pool of resources and enforcing the agreed guarantees associated with them. Each Agreement Factory can interact with one or more service providers. The actual enforcement mechanisms supported by a given service provider, depend on the type of technology the provider supports.

Generally speaking, not all the resource instances in one grid infrastructure need to support service providers for reservation and allocation. The possibility to do a reservation and an allocation depends on the type of technology the resource is based on.

4   Results

The reservations in the PL-Grid Infrastructure are delivered based on the following policy. In order to allocate a reservation on resources, the request for it should be registered in the PL-Grid grant system. Then, after the PL-Grid grant is active, a user can apply for preparation of reservation. The user specifies number of reserved slots and time of reservation (*Max. res. total walltime*). The agreed reservation allows the user to request the reservation up to the limits defined in the PL-Grid grant system, during application for the grant. There are restrictions in delivery of reservations due to the local resource provider policy: for example, minimum number of slots required, minimal walltime required or period of inactivity of the user. The reservation can be cancelled, but the user is charged for the time the reservation was active. The reservation time is accounted as if the resources were used for all the declared time by the user.

4.1   Reservations in gLite

Using LRMS and VOMS Based Reservations with gLite. The scheduling methods mentioned in Introduction form different requirements for service providers and resource managements systems.

Co-allocation is not supported in gLite, although there is a proposed extension to gLite architecture (see below).

Exclusive access to resources can be guaranteed by specifying in Job Description Language (JDL) job description file attribute *WholeNodes=yes*. The WholeNodes attribute indicates whether whole nodes should be used exclusively or not.

Most LRMS support advance reservation, but even if a user or a Virtual Organization (VO) manually agrees reservation with sites, it is impossible to request a specific reservation identifier (ID) in the JDL job description. JDL schema does not allow to specify additional parameters to be passed to LRMS. Another problem is that user accounts are assigned dynamically by LCMAPS, therefore there is no guarantee that the users can access reserved resources as they can be mapped to another account. Static mapping is possible, but not recommended. It is possible to create reservations for a Unix group, but then all users from the VO group mapped to these user accounts can access the reservation.

As gLite is strictly bound to Virtual Organisation concepts, it is recommended to use VO to manage users and their privileges with VOMS [7]. VOMS allows for elastic users management and users can have assigned specific roles, groups and attributes. This can be used to reserve some resources for some users by mapping different groups to different resources or can be used to specify a share in the resources by assigning different share and priority to groups. In site configuration, VOMS groups should be statically mapped to UNIX GIDs on CEs, LRMS shares are defined statically according to UNIX GIDs. This approach is simple, but static. It allows VO manager to dynamically assign individual users to different groups in VOMS, but changes in share assignment have to be arranged manually between VO manager(s) and sites. Dynamic share approach was implemented in GPBOX [8], which was a tool that provided the possibility to define, store and propagate fine-grained VO policies. It allowed to map users to service classes and to dynamically change the association between users and classes. Successors of GPBOX are AuthZ and Argus [9]. The working principle is simple. The Argus Authorization Service renders consistent authorization decisions basing on authorization policies defined in XACML. The Policy Administration Point (PAP) provides the tools to author authorization policies. The policies are then automatically propagated to the interested entities, where these are evaluated by a Policy Decision Point (PDP) and enforced by a Policy Enforcement Point (PEP). The VO managers define Group, Roles and capabilities within a VO. Then, they assign users to groups and grant them the possibility to ask for roles (e.g. /vo.plgrid.pl/normalpriority, /vo.plgrid.pl/highpriority). The site administrator on his side defines a set of policies, describing the mapping between service classes (e.g. low, medium, high), local unix groups and LRMS shares. The VO manager defines policy for describing mapping between groups/roles and predefined service classes and this policy can be changed dynamically. XACML semantics allows much more complex policies, not just related to fair share, e.g. for usage quota. By using VO groups, policies and additional VOMS attributes, it is possible to implement the PL-Grid grants concept in gLite.

gLite Implementation of Grid Resource Allocation and Agreement Protocol. The gLite Reservation and allocation architecture was proposed in [10], based on the agreement initiator, agreement service, agreement offer and service provider concepts defined by the Grid Resource Allocation and Agreement Protocol working group of the GGF. The agreement initiator uses the agreement service to obtain appropriate agreements with reservation and allocation service providers, which are typically co-located with physical or logical resources. In the gLite architecture, agreement initiators would include the workload management system (WMS), the data scheduler (DS), and the user, while reservation and allocation service providers would be associated with the logical representation of physical resources: the computing element (CE), the storage element (SE), and the network element (NE). Attributes defining reservation and co-allocation requests need to be specified in the agreement template/offer, which is initially expressed in JDL. Later on, during the translation to XML, attributes are placed in the Terms section of the agreement offer [WS-AG] and can belong to two alternative subsections depending on their nature: the Service Description Terms (SDTs) and Service Properties subsections. The Terms section provides a quantitative description of the service requested. Both SDTs and Service Properties need to be mapped to corresponding JDL attributes. The agreement template/offer expressed in JDL can specify general attributes: Type ("reservation", "allocation" or "coallocation"), ServiceCategory ("computeElement", "networkElement", "storageElement") and Functionality (e.g. "virtualLeasedLine", "spaceManagement", "bulkTransfer"). For each functionality, a set of specific attributes can be specified, e.g. "DurationTime", "SizeOfTotalSpaceDesiredInBytes", "Bandwidth", "FileTransferEndTime.

The proposed extension was not yet implemented in Workload Management System WMS [11] and computing elements like CREAM.

4.2   Advance Reservation and Co-allocation of Resources Capabilities in QosCosGrid Middleware

The QosCosGrid (QCG) middleware [12,13] is an integrated system, offering advanced job and resource management capabilities to deliver to end-users super-computer-like performance and structure. By connecting many distributed computing resources together, QCG offers highly efficient mapping, execution and monitoring capabilities for variety of applications, such as parameter sweep, workflows, multi-scale, MPI or hybrid MPI-OpenMP. However, for many application scenarios the typical best-effort model to access computational resources is not satisfactory, and they require more advanced one, guarantying the requested level of quality of service. Addressing such requirements, QCG, as a first grid middleware offering access to PL-Grid resources, has exposed advance reservation capabilities of the underlying Local Resources Management Systems to end-users.

Researchers can benefit from advance reservations offered by QCG in many ways. Firstly, the advance reservation can be directly used to book in advance resources for a specific period of time. The scenario corresponds to the situation, in which the scientist wants to perform series of experiments in known *a priori* time frame. The time is here usually determined by any event. For example, the access to resources must be synchronized with availability of some equipment, date of presentation or lecture. To the created in such a way reservation one can later submit many tasks to be started without typical delay caused by waiting in a queue.

While requesting for the reservation, a user can specify a list of potential resources (so called candidate hosts) as well as resource and time requirements. QCG can automatically search over all candidate hosts, within user-defined time window, for free resources and for the requested period of time. With QCG it is possible to reserve either a given number of slots located on arbitrary nodes or to request for particular topology by specifying number of nodes and slots per node.

At present, the advance reservations can be created and managed using command-line tools (the QCG-SimpleClient client) or graphical, calendar like, QCG-QoS-Access web application (the Reservation Portal) [14]. Both these tools are clients to the QCG-Broker service and can be used to create new reservations as well as to manage existing ones.

In the QCG-QoS-Access portal, the user can create a new reservation with the intuitive dialog, in which he can specify all requirements and preferences – see Fig. 1. The created reservations are displayed in the portal in a form of a list, where each position includes information about current status of reservation as well as provides a report about reserved resources. If the user wants to resign from the reservation, he can cancel it and release blocked resources.

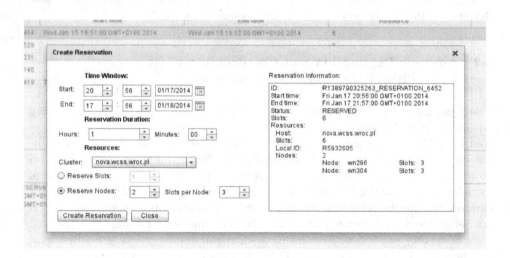

Fig. 1. The QosCosGrid reservation portlet

Creation and management of reservations can be also performed using QCG-SimpleClient. The QCG-SimpleClient is a set of command line tools, inspired by the simplicity of batch system commands. The tools are dedicated to end-users familiar with queuing systems and preferring the command line interface over graphical or web solutions. The learning effort needed to start using QCG-SimpleClient is relatively small as the commands are modeled after the ones known from batch systems. The qcg-* command-line tools allow a user to submit, control and monitor jobs as well as to create and manage reservations. The complete list of commands can be found in [12]. In the context of the advance reservation, the following tools are particularly important:

- qcg-reserve – creates the reservation and returns its identifier,
- qcg-rcancel – cancels the given reservation(s),
- qcg-rinfo – displays comprehensive information about the given reservation(s),
- qcg-rlist – lists reservation in the system meeting defined criteria.

Every reservation request has to be described in a formal way. The default description format supported by QCG-Client is QCG-Simple. The format does not allow yet to describe more sophisticated scenarios like co-allocation of resources (supported by the XML format called QCG-JobProfile), but is fully sufficient for most of typical cases. The QCG-Simple format description file is a plain BASH script annotated with #QCG directives, what is also a common approach for all modern queuing systems. The #QCG directives inform the system how to process the task and, in case of the reservation, about user's requirements and preferences. Listing 1 presents an example of a QCG-SimpleClient reservation request for 4 slots on *nova* cluster for one hour on 2014.01.25, between 8 am and 4 pm.

```
#QCG host=nova
#QCG walltime=PT1H
#QCG procs=4

#QCG not-before=2014.01.25 8:00
#QCG not-after=2014.01.25 16:00
```

Listing 1. An example of a QCG-Simple reservation description

Detailed information about the created reservation can be obtained with qcg-rinfo. The output of this command for our example reservation is presented in Listing 2.

In contrary to the scenario presented above, in which creation of a reservation and submission of jobs to it are separated steps, QCG also supports the scenario, where the reservation is created especially for a job as a part of submission process. This approach allows to provide the requested level of quality of service with granularity of a single task and to automate the process of managing resources. In such a case, the reservation directives extend directly the task description, while the created reservation is automatically canceled by the system at the end of task execution.

Except direct usage of the advance reservation by end-users, it can be also exploited internally by QCG services for more advanced scenarios like cross-cluster execution of parallel or multi-scale applications. For such applications, distribution across many resources may be required for two reasons. The first one is related to the heterogeneous resource requirements of processes constituting

```
qcg-rinfo R1389951946104__2181

UserDN: /C=PL/O=PL-Grid/O=Uzytkownik/O=PCSS/CN=Tomasz Piontek/CN=plgpiontek
SubmissionTime: Fri Jan 17 10:45:46 CET 2014
DescriptionType: QCG_SIMPLE
StartTime: Sat Jan 25 08:00:00 CET 2014
EndTime: Sat Jan 25 09:01:00 CET 2014
Status: RESERVED
TotalSlotsCount: 4
InUse: false


HostName: nova.wcss.wroc.pl
ProcessesGroupId: qcg
SlotsCount: 4
LocalReservationId: R5949627
Node: wn448 SlotsCount: 2
Node: wn452 SlotsCount: 2
```

Listing 2. An example output of qcg-rinfo command

an application, what is tightly connected with the QCG support for groups of processes and communication topologies. The second one addresses the problem of decomposition of a big task among many resources to enable more complex problem instances, decrease cluster "defragmentation" and to improve resource utilization on the whole system level.

The reservation mechanism is applied in the scheduling process to co-allocate resources and then to synchronize execution of application parts in a multi-cluster environment. QCG supports both the strict and best-effort approaches to resource reservation. In the former approach, resources are reserved only if user's requirements can be fully met (also known as the "all or nothing" approach), whereas in the latter case, the system reserves as much resources as possible, but gives no guarantee that all requested resources (cores) will be available. This feature allows to construct flexible algorithms of processes allocation, in which a whole group of processes can be assigned to a single node or even distributed across many clusters.

QosCosGrid successfully integrates various services and aforementioned tools to deliver to PL-Grid users an e-Infrastructure capable of dealing with various kinds of computationally intensive simulations, including ones that require the requested quality of services. The high-level architecture of the QCG middleware is shown in Fig. 2.

In general, the middleware consists of two logical layers: grid and local one. The basic advance reservation capabilities are offered by the local-level QCG-Computing service, usually deployed on access nodes of batch systems (like Torque or SLURM). The service provides remote access to capabilities of local batch systems. The job submission capabilities of QCG-Computing are exposed via an interface compatible with the OGF HPC Basic Profile [15] specification, while the integration with a queuing system is realized using DRMAA [16]. As

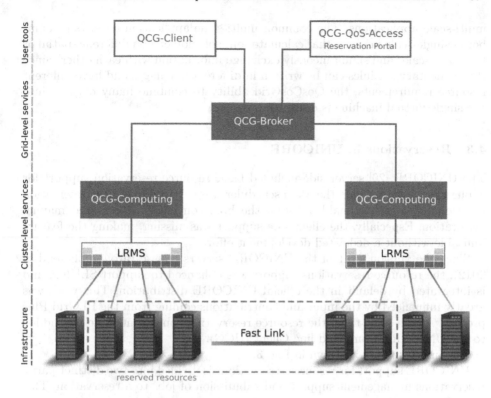

Fig. 2. The QosCosGrid middleware architecture

the first version of DRMAA specification does not address the advance reservation approach, the QCG-Computing specific interface (with a dedicated description language) was proposed to support this capability. Currently, in QCG, advance reservations are created by calling LRMS scheduler commands directly, while in the future leverage of Advance Reservation API of Open Grid Forum DRMAA 2.0 [17] specification is planned. What is important, flexible configuration allows the local system administrators to keep the full control over resources that can be reserved, limiting for example advance reservation capabilities only to a single system partition.

More advance scenarios, like reservations in multi-cluster environment and co-allocation of resources, are supported by the grid-level service, called QCG-Broker, which benefits from QCG-Computing capabilities for a single cluster. The QCG-Broker service, using the adaptive mechanism to determine a time window for a reservation, tries to allocate resources on machines meeting user's requirements. In order to gather the requested amount of resources, the procedure of selection is performed in a loop. If the amount of reserved resources is not satisfactory, the resources are released and the whole procedure is repeated for the next time window.

Within the MAPPER project [18], the QosCosGrid stack has been integrated with the MUSCLE library [19], enabling cross-cluster execution of so-called multi-scale applications. The common multi-scale application consists of number of single-scale modules that calculate some phenomena on different spatial or temporal scales and simultaneously exchange information with each other. Since the elementary modules can be written in different languages and have different resource requirements, the QosCosGrid ability to combine many clusters into the single virtual machine is crucial.

4.3   Reservations in UNICORE

The UNICORE [20] server side included basic resource reservation support for a long time, however only the Maui scheduler was supported and the reservation functionality was not enabled out of the box, conversely, it required manual integration. Especially, the client side support was missing, making the feature unusable without a dedicated development effort.

Since the version 6.5.1 of the UNICORE servers release (around the end of 2012), the resource reservations support was enhanced to support SLURM and is integrated by default in the official UNICORE distribution. This work was greatly influenced by the input and contributions coming from the PLGrid Plus project. At the same time, the resource reservation control interface was added to the UNICORE Command line Client (UCC).

The infrastructure is shown in Fig. 3.

UNICORE support for resource reservations is divided into two distinct parts: reservations management support and submission of jobs to a reservation. This

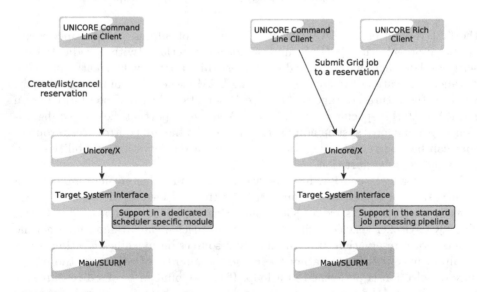

Fig. 3. UNICORE resource reservation processing: management (left side) and usage (right side)

approach covers a common situation where resource reservation functionality is not directly exposed to end-users and they can only submit jobs to reservations created by the site staff or external tools.

The UNICORE server side advertises for each grid site whether it supports reservations or not. For those sites supporting reservations, a user can create a reservation, list owned reservations and delete some of the previously created. It is worth to underline here that the complex reservation resources as CPUs, nodes or duration are all specified using the same syntax as the resource requirements for an ordinary UNICORE job. Therefore, the user is not faced with the differences between various schedulers.

Submitting a job to a reservation is a simple task: it is enough to set the reservation identifier in the job's resource requirements. While the reservations management support is only available in the UCC client, the submissions of jobs to reservations is available in both UCC and UNICORE Rich Client (URC).

Server side reservations handling is performed in a similar way to job processing: the Unicore/X Web Service component is the site's entry point talking to clients. It forwards the requests to the Target System Interface (TSI) server, which maps an abstract grid reservation related operation to something meaningful to the scheduler being used. It should be noted here that the reservation related operation, while similarly handled as a classic job, has its own (simplified) processing pipeline. This approach is probably correct, taking into account the fundamental lifecycle differences between a resource reservation and a grid job, however it also results in some limitations. Probably the most important one is that the functionality of the UNICORE incarnation tweaker[1] subsystem is not available for reservations.

The most significant contribution of the PLGrid Plus project to UNICORE resource reservations subsystem was a complete UNICORE TSI reservations management module for SLURM. What is more, the Maui module was updated and fixed in several places.

The most difficult parts of reservations handling in UNICORE are related to reservations accounting and authorization of reservation management. In the PL-Grid Infrastructure we have decided not to include any of those functions in the grid layer. This decision was dictated by the fact that direct access to computing sites is generally possible, so the accounting and authorization must be anyway solved on the lower, resource scheduler layer. Still, UNICORE provides some integration points with respect to those issues. It is possible to authorize reservation management operations on the Web Service level using the standard UNICORE authorization policy. The limitation of this approach is that the authorization is coarse grained: only the complete functionality access can be controlled, it is not possible to authorize basing on particular reservations or parameters (e.g. to ban reservations longer then a given value).

---

[1] Incarnation tweaker is a UNICORE server's feature allowing for nearly unlimited inspection and modification of the submitted job. It is used to fix common mistakes in a job description, add site specific settings, enforce required options and finally trigger additional actions for selected jobs.

The accounting of reservations in UNICORE is not supported. The only integration point is the TSI script, which can be modified to invoke accounting operations. However, besides the statistical knowledge about the amount of reservations made through UNICORE, the actual accounting of resource reservations should be made on the scheduler level to accommodate all reservation changes made externally to UNICORE.

We can conclude with the statement that our evaluation and deployment of UNICORE reservations was successful. All the basic features are currently enabled in the infrastructure and we support both Maui and SLURM schedulers, which are deployed in PL-Grid. The generally available SLURM support in UNICORE was contributed by the PLGrid Plus project. Beside those achievements, we can also point out limitations of the solution: PBS Pro is not supported while it is used by one of the PL-Grid Infrastructure sites. There is no support for higher, grid-level reservations. Functionality to broker reservations (i.e., to create them at any site fulfilling the given reservation resource requirements) is missing and could improve the user experience as well as the support for coordinated multi-site reservations. Nevertheless, we can underline that the above problems are rather minor, taking into account that not all sites in the infrastructure allow for the end user controlled resource reservation creation, due to well-known risks (related for instance to computational resource wasting).

5 Summary and Future Work

The functionality of the advance reservation is very comfortable for the user. However, it should be used in an efficient way in order not to waste resources at HPC clusters. Thus, usage of reserved resources is monitored and accounted. The user negotiates with a resource provider separately wall clock time to be spent on reserved resources and total time in the PL-Grid grant. The time spent in batch jobs is accounted based on PBS standard logs. The accounting of reservations requires additional logging. In Moab, they are triggered by pre-agreed actions, e.g. reservation ready, reservation removed. The next step would be integration of these two sources of information about reservations and jobs (PBS logs and reservation logs) to avoid double charging the user for jobs executed within reservation and to charge the user for unused reservations.

References

1. Foster, I., Kesselman, C., Lee, C., Lindell, B., Nahrstedt, K., Roy, A.: A Distributed Resource Management Architecture that Supports Advance Reservations and Co-allocation. In: Proceedings of the 7th International Workshop on Quality of Service, London, UK (1999)
2. XSEDE project web page, https://www.xsede.org/overview
3. Metascheduling Requirements Analysis Team report,
   http://www.teragridforum.org/
   mediawiki/images/b/b4/MetaschedRatReport.pdf

4. MacLaren, J.: HARC: The Highly-Available Resource Co-allocator. In: Meersman, R. (ed.) OTM 2007, Part II. LNCS, vol. 4804, pp. 1385–1402. Springer, Heidelberg (2007)

5. Casajus, A., Graciani, R., Paterson, S., Tsaregorodtsev, A.: DIRAC Pilot Framework and the DIRAC Workload Management System. Journal of Physics, Conference Series 219, 062049 (2010)

6. The Grid Resource Allocation and Agreement Protocol Working Group, Global Grid Forum, https://forge.gridforum.org/projects/graap-wg

7. VOMS home page, http://italiangrid.github.io/voms/

8. Guarise, A.: Policy management and fair share in gLite. In: HPDC 2006, Paris (2006)

9. Argus Authorization Service, https://twiki.cern.ch/twiki/bin/view/EGEE/AuthorizationFramework

10. Ferrari, T., Ronchieri, E.: gLite Allocation and Reservation Architecture. EGEE JRA1 technical report (2005), http://edms.cern.ch/document/508055

11. Job Description Language Atrribute Specification for the Workload Management System, https://edms.cern.ch/file/590869/1/WMS-JDL.pdf

12. Bosak, B., Kopta, P., Kurowski, K., Piontek, T., Mamoński, M.: New QosCosGrid Middleware Capabilities and Its Integration with European e-Infrastructure. In: Bubak, M., Kitowski, J., Wiatr, K. (eds.) PLGrid Plus. LNCS, vol. 8500, pp. 34–53. Springer, Heidelberg (2014)

13. Bosak, B., Komasa, J., Kopta, P., Kurowski, K., Mamoński, M., Piontek, T.: New Capabilities in QosCosGrid Middleware for Advanced Job Management, Advance Reservation and Co-allocation of Computing Resources – Quantum Chemistry Application Use Case. In: Bubak, M., Szepieniec, T., Wiatr, K. (eds.) PL-Grid 2011. LNCS, vol. 7136, pp. 40–55. Springer, Heidelberg (2012)

14. Kurowski, K., Dziubecki, P., Grabowski, P., Krysiński, M., Piontek, T., Szejnfeld, D.: Easy Development and Integration of Science Gateways with Vine Toolkit. In: Bubak, M., Kitowski, J., Wiatr, K. (eds.) PLGrid Plus. LNCS, vol. 8500, pp. 147–163. Springer, Heidelberg (2014)

15. HPC Basic Profile Version 1.0, http://www.ogf.org/documents/GFD.114.pdf

16. Troger, P., Rajic, H., Haas, A., Domagalski, P.: Standardization of an API for Distributed Resource Management Systems. In: Proceedings of the Seventh IEEE International Symposium on Cluster Computing and the Grid, CCGRID 2007, pp. 619–626. IEEE Computer Society, Washington, DC (2007)

17. Distributed Resource Management Application API Version 2 (DRMAA), http://www.ogf.org/documents/GFD.194.pdf

18. Ben Belgacem, M., Chopard, B., Borgdorff, J., Mamoński, M., Rycerz, K., Harężlak, D.: Distributed multiscale computations using the mapper framework. In: Alexandrov, V.N., Lees, M., Krzhizhanovskaya, V.V., Dongarra, J., Sloot, P.M.A. (eds.) ICCS. Procedia Computer Science, vol. 18, pp. 1106–1115. Elsevier (2013)

19. Borgdorff, J., Mamoński, M., Bosak, B., Kurowski, K., Ben Belgacem, M., Chopard, B., Groen, D., Coveney, P.V., Hoekstra, A.G.: Distributed multiscale computing with muscle 2, the multiscale coupling library and environment. CoRR, abs/1311.5740 (2013)

20. Streit, A., et al.: UNICORE 6 – Recent and Future Advancements. Annals of Telecommunications 65(11-12), 757–762 (2010)

Improving PL-Grid Operations Based on FitSM Standard

Marcin Radecki, Tadeusz Szymocha,
Tomasz Szepieniec, and Roksana Różańska

AGH University of Science and Technology, ACC Cyfronet AGH,
ul. Nawojki 11, 30-950 Kraków, Poland
tadeusz.szymocha@cyfronet.pl

Abstract. The goal of this paper is to present results of efforts to improve operations in the PL-Grid Infrastructure [1] based on applying a standard for lightweight IT Service Management – FitSM. There were a number of endeavors in PL-Grid community taken to streamline operations in past two years. All of them gave us valuable experience and better understanding of our specifics. Especially, the federated nature of the infrastructure appeared challenging.

From the organizational point of view, the PL-Grid Infrastructure consists of 5 largest Polish computing centres, which collaboratively provide resources to Polish researchers. On a technical level, this requires a number of processes running e.g. user registration, management of compute allocations (aka. computational grants), service availability monitoring, service reporting, incident handling, etc. Running these processes in a way spending minimum energy and reaching their goal to a maximum extent require good organization of activities. This is the task of PL-Grid operations.

Keywords: IT Service Management, operations, FitSM, ITIL, ISO20k.

1 Introduction

Large corporations and small business operate on a basis of processes. A car engine manufacturer or a photocopy point – they both perform some processes, either very complex like design of a fuel injection system or quite simple like making a copy of a document. They both have their clients, either simple like an anonymous person who just puts a pile of documents to be copied or more complex like a big company producing cars. There is a way to describe in a systematic manner structure and processes within an organisation and this is what a Service Management is about. For organisations supported by IT technology it is the IT-flavour of Service Management, in short ITSM.

PL-Grid is a name of consortium of 5 largest Polish academic computer centres. The consortium goal is to support Polish scientists by providing computing power and storage resources through the PL-Grid Infrastructure. Currently, the infrastructure provides access to more than 40 000 cores having power of

M. Bubak et al. (Eds.): PLGrid Plus, LNCS 8500, pp. 94–105, 2014.

588 TFlops and 5.6PB of storage space for more than 2000 scientists from Poland and their foreign collaborators. The consortium is led by ACC Cyfronet AGH, which is also a partner of FedSM EU project [2] aiming at improving IT Service Management practices in federated e-Infrastructures. The service to the users is offered by a single entity – namely PL-Grid – but resources are contributed collectively by the 5 computer centres. PL-Grid Operations Centre coordinates the daily operations and is responsible for the quality of the service to the users. This way, from the organisational point of view, the PL-Grid Infrastructure is a federation, rather than centrally managed entity.

The goal of introducing ITSM practices is to structure the processes that are taking place in an organization, in order to find a more efficient way of performing activities, have repeatable results each time the same process takes place. The focus does not necessarily is on some quality to be higher, but – what is true – it is hard to get better quality without any Service Management practices in place.

There is a number of standards that can back the works on introducing ITSM: ITIL, ISO-20k, COBIT, Microsoft Operations Framework – just to name perhaps the most important ones. But whichever will be adopted, it requires comparable steps: getting familiar with the framework concepts and terms, spreading the knowledge among staff and actual implementation of changes.

All frameworks, since they derive from and usually had been deployed in such environments, assume there is one central coordinating body with an authority to enforce implementing ITSM policy. Federated nature of the infrastructure influences the way how a service should be designed and how it is provided. In a federation, all members may contribute to a service delivery. Thus, designing a service, all federation members need to agree on the conditions and they must comply with their local policies. This causes management of federated IT infrastructure hard.

In order to introduce ITSM, an organisation needs to answer some questions, which allow to name things properly in context of ITSM terms and connect them together. Key questions are: who are the people providing a service and how are they structured? What is the service provided and to whom? What are the resources that the service is offered based on? As a result, a clear picture of an organisation can be made, where the customer, the provider, the service and resources are put together with right relationship and importance.

In this paper, we present the work on advancing PL-Grid Service Management System by introducing FitSM standard developed by FedSM project consortium. We describe briefly the FitSM, the approach proposed and the results that were obtained during the 1st year of implementing changes to PL-Grid operations.

1.1 Motivation for Implementing Service Management

Advances in long distance computer network links made possible large data transfers between geographically distant computer centres, making computations and, thus, research more mobile. They made possible building an IT infrastructure, which spans over different administrative domains. There was a number of projects building computational grids released in recent 10 years. In the beginning, these were research infrastructures where the level of quality of service was not as important as a prove of concept. With time, the concept proven true with the example of the European Grid Infrastructure, which is no longer perceived as a research infrastructure, but as a production environment where a certain level of service availability can be expected.

The same applies to the IT infrastructure for Polish Science – it is an environment for researchers' day-to-day work and even more – it allows to build-up their domain-specific services relying on PL-Grid basic services.

There is a number of requirements, which made necessary taking effort of adopting ITSM:

1. Defined, higher than best-effort level of quality. PL-Grid ITSM policy sets the focus on users' needs and makes them a driving force for the development.
2. Size and complexity. Large in size, complex in terms of software stack, geographically distributed and managed by different administrative domains IT infrastructure can hardly be managed without some ITSM practices in place.
3. Management in federation. The service is provided from one place (i.e. PL-Grid), but it is delivered by collective work of a number of computer centres. How to manage this environment? Who should be responsible for what? We had to define our approach to avoid confusion.

PL-Grid started its experience with ITSM at the end of 2011, after 2 years of developing basic infrastructure. Since 2012, the infrastructure has been fully supporting three middleware stacks: gLite, UNICORE [3] and QosCosGrid [4], each of them consists of a number of technical service instances. A number of 1000 users has been exceeded and the load on operations staff generated by them has grown significantly.

In order to provide a QoS, a service provider needs to learn how to build this relationship with a customer. This is what the ITSM is really focused on. Higher quality requires good preparation and efficiency. Some customers were raising their expectations over the "best effort" guarantees. Users coming with questions if they are able to finish computational part of their research at a given date were a new phenomenon for the computer centres serving academic community. It became clear that something must be done to streamline the operations and reach requested service quality levels.

1.2   Previous Experiences of Implementing ITSM in PL-Grid

It was identified that going beyond "best effort" level of support may only be done with adoption of some IT service management standards.

The first attempt was based solely on reading ITIL books, which seemed the most reputable source of ITSM knowledge. After a couple of months, a number of improvements to already existing processes was proposed and implemented [1]. This approach worked to some extent for making amendments to the processes that are existing, using the staff experience on them. But it was difficult to find a way to introduce organization-wide changes. There were ideas to produce completely new design from scratch, but they were abandoned as they seemed very complex and time consuming. We believe it would also prove impractical to carry out such big changes in an environment, which must work uninterrupted for users. It was also hard to understand how to map federation aspects onto ITIL processes.

While introducing ITSM practices, it is important to understand the overall level of maturity to identify the areas for improvements. The decision on what to improve should be preceded by an analysis of what is the most economically advantageous. So, the very bookish knowledge is not sufficient and this was hardly addressed by our first attempt.

2 FitSM Overview

Fortunately, ACC CYFRONET AGH, the coordinator of the PL-Grid Consortium, took part in the gSLM and FedSM EU projects [2], which had a positive influence of promoting IT Service Management in the PL-Grid Infrastructure.

In this article, we describe briefly the FitSM standard developed by the FedSM project consortium; what steps were performed in order to adapt FitSM in PL-Grid.

As indicated in Table 1, FitSM identifies 14 processes, which are vital for the operations of the federated e-Infrastructure.

Table 1. Operational processes proposed by the FitSM standard

Id.	Process acronym	Process name
1	SPM	Service Portfolio Management
2	SLM	Service Level Management
3	SR	Service Reporting
4	SCAM	Service Continuity and Availability Management
5	CapM	Capacity Management
6	ISM	Information Security Management
7	CRM	Customer Relationship Management
8	SRM	Supplier Relationship Management
9	ISRM	Incident and Service Request Management
10	PM	Problem Management
11	ConfM	Configuration Management
12	ChM	Change Management
13	RDM	Release and Deployment Management
14	CSI	Continual Service Improvement

The standard consists of 6 sections of average size of 15 pages as follows:

1. FitSM-0 – overview and vocabulary.
2. FitSM-1 – requirements for lightweight service management in federated IT infrastructures.

3. FitSM-2 – activities and objectives that are essential in implementing FitSM standard.
4. FitSM-3 – recommendation about the role model.
5. FitSM-4 – a guide on the application and implementation of ITSM.
6. FitSM-5 – contains samples and templates of recommended documents.

Requirements described in FitSM-1 are a base for maturity assessment.

2.1 ITSM Maturity Assessment Framework

Usually, it is not practical to start introducing ITSM with redesigning everything from scratch, especially in a working environment like the PL-Grid Infrastructure. It makes more sense to gradually improve processes and procedures. The key is to identify what should be improved first, how to proceed with changes to minimize service disruption and what dependencies should be kept in mind. An overall evaluation of the operations is useful to get a full picture of the area to be improved. The FedSM project helped with this task by providing an IT maturity evaluation framework, which evolved from the gSLM project [5].

The framework allows to evaluate an organisation's capability for each of 14 processes. A process capability describes how advanced the organisation is in operation of this process. There are 6 levels of process capability: *non-existent, ad-hoc, repeatable, defined, managed and measured,* and *efficient.* The overall organisation's maturity is derived based on process capabilities. There are 5 levels of overall maturity: *non-existent, aware, in-place, effective, advanced.* In order to achieve a certain maturity level, the processes' capabilities must be at a certain level, not necessarily all at the same, because usually more important processes are required to be at a higher level. This is the case for *in-place* maturity level where Service Portfolio Management should be at least at capability level *repeatable* while Service Level Management, which is more essential, should be at capability level *defined.* Fig. 1 presents the relation between process capability and overall ITSM maturity.

In order to obtain the organisations maturity, the organization must first answer to what extent it fulfills each of FitSM-1 requirements. The requirements are associated with each process and, as a result, a process capability is given. PL-Grid performed this assessment in 2013 and the results are presented in Fig. 2.

It was found there are 5 not met requirements for 7 processes selected for the assessment. They relate to Service Level Management, Service Reporting, Customer Relationship and Problem Management processes.

2.2 Goals for PL-Grid

ITSM overall maturity model of FitSM defines 5 levels of maturity, of which level 2 labeled: *in-place* is the goal proposed to PL-Grid to achieve. Taking this assumption and the result of the maturity assessment, we have to improve

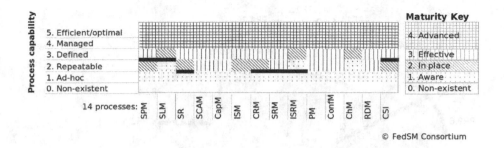

Fig. 1. FedSM assessment framework. Colours show relation between the processes capability and overall ITSM maturity, e.g. maturity *in-place* requires SLM process to be implemented at level *defined*. PL-Grid score in process capability is marked by black lines (e.g. SLM is at level 2 *repeatable*).

4 processes, namely: Customer Relationship Management, Service Reporting, Service Level Management and Problem Management.

Service Level Management (SLM) must be improved from level *repeatable* to level *defined*. By looking at our assessment we can easily find, which requirements are not met and should be improved in order to reach higher level. For SLM these are 2 requirements from FitSM-1: PR2.3 "Services and SLAs shall be reviewed at planned intervals" and PR2.4 "Service performance shall be monitored against service targets".

For each of requirements, an improvement plan needs to be created. For 2.4 example we first need to define a way of monitoring each service target that is possible in the PL-Grid SLA, then drive a development of our monitoring system to include these new metrics.

For PR2.3 the task is simpler as it only requires changes in the process that does not require development. It is sufficient to modify an SLA review procedure and a work instruction.

3   Results

This section presents the results of works aiming at improving ITSM in the PL-Grid Infrastructure. The advances can be observed in 4 areas: a) policy – where we define the overall direction and means for ITSM, b) documentation – which is essential for definition of Service Management System, c) processes – actual implementation of the system, d) tools – the supporting technology. We dedicated a subsection for each area mentioned above.

3.1   Defining ITSM Policy

Introducing ITSM requires changes across the whole organization. To be successful, this must be done with support from proper managerial bodies. In order

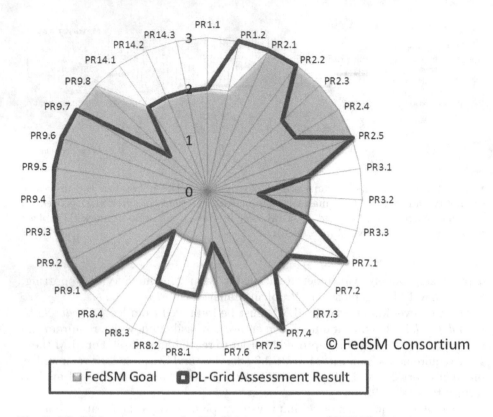

Fig. 2. PL-Grid score w.r.t each of FitSM-1 requirements (PRX.X). Requirement score is marked with the line, target is marked with the area. This area indicates requirements, which are not met by PL-Grid and thus need improvement. Correspondence between requirements and processes can be found in Fig. 1 where names of processes are given, e.g. PR1.X relates to Service Portfolio Management.

to ensure that works at PL-Grid are sufficiently supported, we created a policy, which key parts include:

1. Customer Alignment – the provision of IT services shall be aligned to customer needs.
2. Process Approach – to effectively manage all IT services and underlying components, a process-based approach to service management shall be adopted.
3. Continual Improvement – services and service management processes shall be continually improved.
4. Training and Awareness – through trainings and awareness measures, it shall be ensured that staff involved in service management activities can perform effectively according to their roles.
5. Leadership – senior management is committed to this policy and its implementation. It provides the resources required to implement and improve service management and enhance customer satisfaction with IT services.

The policy expresses also support for adopting ITSM from Infrastructure Development Board (pol. *Zespół Ewolucji Infrastruktury*) who approved the document.

3.2 Defining Documentation Approach

A Service Management System (SMS) must be defined in a set of documents. It is important to make sure the documentation is maintained in a consistent manner. In order to achieve that, a few steps have been made. First of them was to define documentation mechanism and document control mechanism. As a result, Documentation Management Policy was developed and approved. It covers the choice of the system used to document SMS, the structure of documentation, which documents are considered to be the ITSM documentation, how to introduce changes and verify documents. It also points out that all mentioned rules apply to documents created after the time of the introduction of Policy Document Management. Last but not least, it specifies the documentation control mechanism in the form of a table, in which each newly constructed or recently (after introducing the policy) changed document must be endorsed. Fig. 3 presents an example of a document control tag.

① Document info				
Status (szkic / gotowy do zatwierdzenia / zatwierdzony / zdezaktualizowany)		**Zatwierdzony (data/przez kogo)**	21.11.2012	Centrum Operacyjne + WP2
Wersja	major/minor /trailer	**Ostatnie zmiany wprowadzono (data/kto)**	20.11.2012	Roksana Różańska
Właściciel	Roksana Różańska			
Uprawnieni do wprowadzania zmian	Operator			
Data ostatniej weryfikacji	20.11.2013	**Wynik przeprowadzonej weryfikacji:**	do aktualizacji	
Data następnej weryfikacji	20.11.2014			

Fig. 3. Sample of a PL-Grid document control tag. Each PL-Grid operations document must contain it.

Next step is to categorize operations documents as: policies, specifications, procedures or work instructions by assigning them to the appropriate processes.

The essential documentation is the description of an operations process. Way of organizing this document is defined by a process documentation template, which defines the following subsections: Definition and objectives of the process, Process inputs, Process outputs, Process activities, Roles involved in the process, Key performance indicators (KPIs), Interfaces for other processes.

All documents involved in the process should be attributed to the process activities, in which they are involved. Preparing process documentation gives the opportunity to understand what should be done to fulfill process requirements as well as assess what is completed within the process with activities and functionalities already existing. So far, the documentation for SLM (Service Level Management) and ISRM (Incident and Service Request Management) has been completed. These are the two most important and most mature processes in PL-Grid.

3.3 Evolving the Processes

Adopting the FitSM standard assumes that operations processes will evolve towards more mature, stable and reliable form. In the first stage of evolving the processes, seven of them were taken into consideration. The selection of the processes was "chronological" in terms of steps that an organization must perform in terms of delivering a service to a customer. From this perspective, the first process is to identify what a service can they offer to a customer, which is performed in a frame of SPM. This must be followed by consideration of who is the customer and what agreements are going to take place. Another important process, which inevitably must be implemented at a relatively early stage, is ISRM, since the organization must be able to handle the issues related to disruption of their services. Processes included in the first stage are listed in Table 2. Remaining processes will be dealt in the second stage of improvements.

Table 2. Operational processes included in first phase of improvements

Id.	Process acronym	Process name
1	SPM	Service Portfolio Management
2	SLM	Service Level Management
3	SR	Service Reporting
7	CRM	Customer Relationship Management
8	SRM	Supplier Relationship Management
9	ISRM	Incident and Service Request Management
14	CSI	Continual Service Improvement

The SLM process will be shown as an example of how our work on improving it looked like. Our works started with preparing the process description according to a template and guidance from the FedSM project.

The FitSM standard defines requirements (PR X.X) for each of 14 processes. For SLM the following requirements are considered:

- services delivered to the customers and quality of such services should be agreed with them,
- the service catalogue must be maintained and updated when changed,
- delivered services and SLAs should be reviewed at regular intervals,
- the quality of service should be verified with respect to the standards set out in the SLA.

In PL-Grid most of them are realized by compute grants system, but at the same time not all aspects of these requirements are covered by features that already exist. So, along with identifying what we already have, comes realization what is still missing. The following activities were identified and documented: a) Applying for a compute grant, b) Review of the application, b) Negotiation, c) Exploitation of grants, d) Reporting grants, e) Accounting for grants, f) Renegotiation of grants.

The following activities were identified as missing: a) Changing the policies, b) Service Catalogue Management, c) Monitoring of compute grants.

After completing this assessment, a plan for development of each process was delivered. For SLM, the target level for the first process improvements phase is level 3 – *defined*. To achieve this goal, the capabilities addressed by the requirements PR2.3 and PR2.4 need to be raised from level 2 – *repeatable* to level 3 – *defined*. The PR2.3 reads: "Services and SLAs shall be reviewed at planned intervals. There is a defined and documented procedure for reviewing services and SLAs at planned intervals."

Within this activity, we already defined a procedure for reviewing services and SLAs at planned intervals and clarified how often and by whom reviews are carried out. What is still missing, is the template for recording the reviews and a place to store them. Simultaneously, we are improving tools used to process SLAs and services reviews.

The PR2.4 says "Service performance shall be monitored against service targets. There is a defined and documented procedure for service performance monitoring and reporting the results to relevant parties".

In order to achieve level *3 – defined* in this requirement, so far we identified ways of monitoring for each service target level and we are working on implementing a way to report the results of monitoring as well as working on solutions for highly performing monitoring. At the same time, a specialized tool is being developed to conduct activities connected with monitoring service performance.

A plan for process improvement delivered by FedSM contains requirements, target levels, tasks to be done, specifies documents that need to be produced and determines milestones, what allows to precisely plan steps needed to be taken in order to provide high quality IT services, which satisfy demands of Polish researchers.

3.4   Identifying Operations Tools Improvements

Effective management of ITSM processes should be supported with appropriate tools. Completing the first phase of the FedSM project required identifying improvements needed to be deployed in tools connected with processes, and planning them. Improvements might have been recognized in the areas of new tools to be introduced or existing tools to be changed, replaced, integrated or consolidated. Processes that had been taken into consideration were: SLM, CRM, ChM, ConfM and additionally General Requirements were given.

General requirements concerned the tools for storing and managing the ITSM related documentation. Exemplary identified missing functionalities within the PL-Grid Infrastructure are:

- a documentation structure where a Service Management Plan can be stored and accessed by PL-Grid staff,
- no possibility of linking SMP plans with tickets representing planned actions,
- a documentation structure where templates and documents for monitoring and reviewing SMS can be stored,
- ability to create and assign corrective actions related to SM nonconformities.

After recognizing the missing functionalities, we selected tools, which would implement them. The choice was to customize existing tools: JIRA and Confluence.

The same way was taken when considering specific processes. First, the missing functionalities in the process were identified, then the decision was made, which solution (new tool/changing existing tool, etc.) will be applied.

In conclusion, following tools (with relevant implementation or development) are considered to be needed within mentioned processes: Example of internal wiki (Confluence) improvements are listed in Table 3. Other tool improvements are planned for the project tracking tool (JIRA), Operations Portal, CMDB (Configuration Management Database) and Helpdesk Tool.

Table 3. Operations tools improvements intended for internal wiki (Confluence)

Related processes	Continual Service Improvement Management. Change Management.
Type of tool development	Existing tool customization.
Target functionality	A place where a Service Management Plan can be stored and accessed by PL-Grid staff. Ability to link SMP items with tickets representing concrete actions. Templates and documentation structure for monitoring and reviewing SMS. Ability to create and assign corrective actions related to SM nonconformities. Templates and structure for change planning.
Identification of needed actions	Create a structure where SMP and reviews and related templates can be stored. Create structure for Change Management documentation and templates.

4   Summary

With adopting FitSM standard, PL-Grid operations staff is able to tell where we are standing with regard to ITSM, what is more important and what less. Initially, it required a lot of consultancy and communication with FedSM project experts to understand ITSM concepts, but now we are able to describe our environment in ITSM terms.

A big asset of FitSM is the approach to introducing changes in Service Management System. It provides a guidance on what should be done and in what order. It is not sufficient to know where we are and where we want to be, but also how we want to get there.

During the lifetime of the FedSM project, the adoption of the FitSM standard was supported by free trainings, which are considered very fruitful to spread ITSM ideas among involved staff and facilitating understanding of key concepts. The training and direct contact with the experts was extremely helpful in terms of motivating people and convincing them to applying ITSM, especially for the federated environment.

5 Future Work

Ahead of PL-Grid there is a second stage improvement including remaining 7 processes. The challenge here is the parallel execution of tasks from phase one, together with assessment and execution of remaining 7 processes.

References

1. Radecki, M., Szepieniec, T., Szymocha, T., Szopa, M., Krakowian, M.: Towards Professional Service Operations in Grids. In: Bubak, M., Szepieniec, T., Wiatr, K. (eds.) PL-Grid 2011. LNCS, vol. 7136, pp. 27–39. Springer, Heidelberg (2012)
2. FedSM project web page (2013), http://fedsm.eu
3. Benedyczak, K., Stolarek, M., Rowicki, R., Kluszczyński, R., Borcz, M., Marczak, G., Filocha, M., Bała, P.: Seamless Access to the PL-Grid e-Infrastructure Using UNICORE Middleware. In: Bubak, M., Szepieniec, T., Wiatr, K. (eds.) PL-Grid 2011. LNCS, vol. 7136, pp. 56–72. Springer, Heidelberg (2012)
4. Bosak, B., Komasa, J., Kopta, P., Kurowski, K., Mamoński, M., Piontek, T.: New Capabilities in QosCosGrid Middleware for Advanced Job Management, Advance Reservation and Co-allocation of Computing Resources – Quantum Chemistry Application Use Case. In: Bubak, M., Szepieniec, T., Wiatr, K. (eds.) PL-Grid 2011. LNCS, vol. 7136, pp. 40–55. Springer, Heidelberg (2012)
5. Appleton, O., Radecki, M., Szepieniec, T.: Assessing Service Management maturity for the EGI/NGI ecosystem. In: Proceedings of EGI Community Forum 2012 / EMI Second Technical Conference, Munich, Germany, March 26-30. PoS(EGICF12-EMITC2)153 (2012)

Integrating Slurm Batch System with European and Polish Grid Infrastructures

Dominik Bartkiewicz, Krzysztof Benedyczak, Rafał Kluszczyński,
Marcin Stolarek, and Tomasz Rękawek

Interdisciplinary Centre for Mathematical and Computational Modelling,
University of Warsaw, ul. Pawińskiego 5a, 02-106 Warszawa, Poland
{bart,golbi,klusi,mstol}@icm.edu.pl,newton@mat.umk.pl
http://www.icm.edu.pl

Abstract. ICM, one of the major Polish HPC resource providers, migrated to the Slurm batch system as the first site in the PL-Grid and WLCG grid infrastructures. This article describes the Slurm integration issues and the solutions developed. The integration was focused on several areas where grid middleware interacts with the batch scheduling system, additionally taking into consideration the PL-Grid specifics. In particular, the resource usage accounting required a dedicated Slurm support and the scientific grants enforcement policy needed a new implementation. What is more, in this work we present the reasons of the Slurm adoption and other improvements that were necessary to handle the increasing load of the grid site.

Keywords: Slurm, accounting, gLite, UNICORE.

1 Introduction

The PL-Grid project [4], [8] was started in the year 2009 as a response to many requirements of Polish scientists for more user-friendly access to high-performance computing (HPC) resources. It consists of 5 main Polish supercomputing and networking centers, geographically distributed. The goals of the project were to build the Polish national grid infrastructure, provide users with computing and storage resources accessible in a uniform way. On top of this infrastructure, there are being prepared solutions and services for specific scientific environments, so called "domain grids" (addressed by the current PLGrid Plus project [7]). Unfortunately, distributed resources provisioned in PL-Grid are highly heterogeneous, what makes the integration sometimes not so easy as it was assumed at the beginning.

In the year 2012, ICM HPC system was migrated to the Slurm batch system [10], [14] as the first site in the PL-Grid and WLCG infrastructures. This change was dictated by the fact that Torque [13] became significantly inefficient under heavy load, what we describe in a next section.

The integration tasks included also the implementation of the PL-Grid scientific computational grants system, called POZO. POZO is an infrastructure wide

M. Bubak et al. (Eds.): PLGrid Plus, LNCS 8500, pp. 106–117, 2014.

resource access policy, which defines resource limits for scientists, granted by the infrastructure managers. The whole system is based on computing grants assigned to a user or scientific team. Every user has a small private grant issued every half a year to allow him/her to access the infrastructure for one thousand CPU hours. In case when the user needs much more time for simulations, he/she needs to create a scientific team and apply for a proper grant. For this purpose, the Bazaar [9], [12] system is used where HPC administrators negotiate with the user how many resources the user will need. After a successful agreement, no batch system used in PL-Grid should allow to access more resources than agreed.

POZO policy access describes how the system should behave when user resources are exhausted. All batch systems used in PL-Grid have to work according to the policy. In particular, Slurm used at ICM. The way of POZO implementation is described in the article.

The PL-Grid Infrastructure has complex requirements with regard to the accounting of the resource consumption by the grid jobs. It is required for billing both the individual users and also groups of users. Therefore, the accounting data needs to be collected and centrally stored for the internal management of the PL-Grid Infrastructure itself. This data must include records of both grid jobs (regardless of the middleware used) and jobs submitted locally, directly to the computing machines. The information about the middleware being used (if any) is also required for the purposes of internal reporting.

Besides the national accounting system, PL-Grid as a member of the European Grid Infrastructure (EGI) is additionally obligated to publish the accounting data to the European-wide database. The data exported to EGI typically should be pre-processed, to provide coarse-grained usage summaries only, and includes exclusively the grid job related records. Therefore, the accounting data required by EGI is different both in terms of the content, format and source jobs from the data being used in the National Grid Infrastructure (NGI).

As the vast majority of accounting data is collected from a resource management system, the newly introduced Slurm system needed to be integrated with the whole, complex accounting infrastructure. What is more, it turned out that the UNICORE accounting system [2] had, similarly as Torque, performance problems when tackling the constantly increasing stream of jobs. In this article we discuss the details of the observed problems and the developed solutions.

2   State of the Art

The Torque batch subsystem, used until recently at ICM, is properly supported by the grid infrastructure and the typical helper tools. This is true for the gLite job submission interface, the gLite APEL accounting system [5], UNICORE job submission and, eventually, Torque is properly supported by the UNICORE accounting system [2].

Unfortunately, in the recent years we observed that version 3.x of the Torque batch system (the latest one at that moment) was unstable under heavy load. It even came to solutions where a server daemon was checked if it responded and restarted in case if not. This was the reason why we have tested the Slurm batch system, which proved much more stable and efficient, especially with a load of thousands of jobs.

One of the grid systems supported by the PL-Grid Infrastructure is gLite with the Cream computing element (CE). CREAM accepts job submission requests described with Job Description Language (JDL) [6]. The CREAM support for the Torque batch system is well tested and works fine including the accounting subsystem. Unfortunately, JDL does not support any attribute, which can be used to express the PL-Grid grant. For authentication purposes, CREAM uses an LCAS/LCMAPS security stack. LCMAPS is a pluggable framework, implemented as a library that can be used by applications to map incoming grid identities to local POSIX identities, taking into account the local site policy. Therefore, LCMAPS plugin has been developed at ICM to allow efficient mapping grid-based users to their own POSIX LDAP accounts. Fig. 1 presents a decision rule used for the mapping.

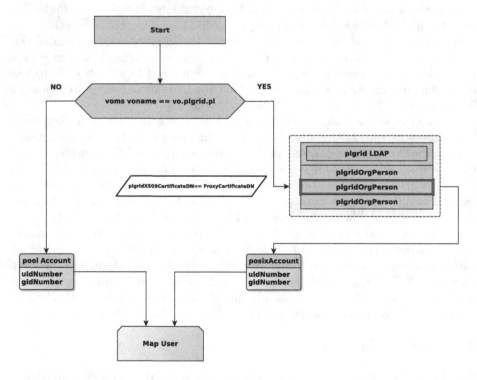

Fig. 1. The diagram of PL-Grid LCMAPS plugin. It shows decision rule based on the user's VO organization.

Such a method reacts in real time to changes in default grants or adding new users to the system. At the same time, it eliminates frequent generation of gridmapfile, which includes all users data. Support for Slurm in the gLite accounting system (called APEL) is officially available since its latest release, however it is immature and significantly buggy. Tests have shown that over 80% of job records were not handled correctly by the APEL Slurm module.

UNICORE, one of the three base grid solutions deployed in the PL-Grid Infrastructure [3], natively supports custom resource requirements. These requirements, among others, can be used to express the information about a requested PL-Grid grant in each UNICORE job. As all resource requirements are subject to brokering, a grant-aware site selection can be easily implemented in UNICORE. This, however, was not yet done as typically the grants are supported on all sites and in the rare cases when this is not true, the automatic job rescheduling solves the problem. Therefore, the integration with the PL-Grid POZO was not problematic from the UNICORE perspective.

UNICORE's accounting system developed at ICM was released back in 2010 and subsequently it has been deployed in the PL-Grid Infrastructure. Since this date, the system has processed several million of jobs using the Torque batch system, which was supported by the system since its beginning (next to Sun/Oracle Grid Engine). The situation with the UNICORE and Slurm was worse, as the Slurm batch system was not supported in the accounting system. To understand the required functionality, the details of the accounting deployment in PL-Grid need to be presented.

The PL-Grid Infrastructure features a complex accounting system or – more precisely – a set of cooperating accounting systems. The principal solution used for national and at the same time internal project accounting is called MWZ. Originally, MWZ was designed to collect accounting data from the gLite middleware. As PL-Grid exposes also QCG and UNICORE interfaces, their accounting solutions were deployed too, with additional plugins exporting the data to the central MWZ database. The export of accounting records to the EGI infrastructure should be done separately by each middleware installed. So far, it was only set up for the gLite system using its typical solution – APEL, the same software, which is used by EGI to receive and store the records in the central database.

The retrieval of the accounting data is as complicated as its distribution. The accounting data must be collected from two sources and then merged: from the resource management system (as Torque or PBS Pro) and from each middleware to enrich the low level data by grid related information.

To summarize this complex accounting landscape, the accounting deployment looks as follows from the ICM site perspective:

- APEL software is installed on the site and reports the accounting data of gLite jobs directly to the EGI central database.
- The UNICORE accounting system is installed and (independently of APEL) collects accounting data about all jobs submitted to the site from the batch subsystem (regardless of the middleware) and from the UNICORE middleware (in case of UNICORE jobs).
- Finally, the accounting data is exported to the central MWZ server and (what is planned) should be exported to the EGI central APEL service in case of UNICORE jobs.

In case of the remaining sites, typically the MWZ agent is installed to collect the data from the resource management system, and the UNICORE accounting module is responsible only for retrieving the grid part. The UNICORE grid part is sent first to the UNICORE accounting system at ICM and from that point it is forwarded (together with other records) to all configured consumers as MWZ or APEL. This scenario is presented in Fig. 2.

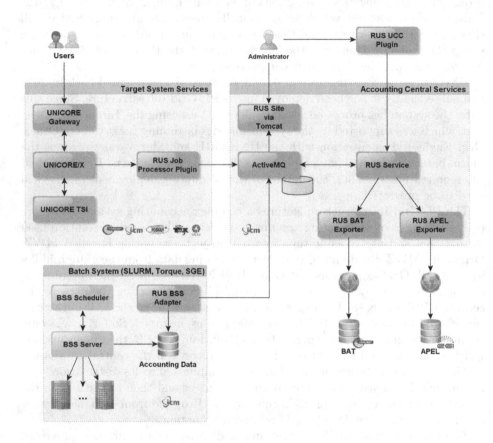

Fig. 2. UNICORE accounting deployment at the PL-Grid Infrastructure

The UNICORE accounting was tested with a typical HPC load and it handled thousands of jobs without any noticeable performance problems. However, as soon as a large amount of small high-throughput computing (HTC) jobs started to be processed, the database size reaches a much larger size. Around 1,000,000 records, the system started to consume large amount of CPU time during regular operation. It has become obvious that sooner or later the time needed to process a single job will be longer than an average delay between subsequent jobs collected by the system. Such a situation would nearly instantly lead to a crash of the whole system.

In the next section, a description of the Slurm integration module as well as the general performance and database model changes are presented.

3   Description of the Solution

The article describes the solutions for the Slurm integration with the gLite and UNICORE middleware as well as the implementation of the PL-Grid grants system in the gLite middleware.

The Slurm scripts from the gLite APEL were updated and the article discusses the issues and their solutions. What is more, the support for limiting the access to resources based on the PL-Grid grants specification (called POZO) with an ability to handle users' default grants has been implemented. The article describes the solution allowing for the enforcement of the PL-Grid POZO system with a new LCMAPS module. In this module, we use the data picked directly from the PL-Grid LDAP database, so the changes take place immediately, once the data is updated in the central PL-Grid database. However, it is important to emphasize that the main source of information about users' grants in POZO system is Bazaar [9], which provides data in XML format, available only for HPC administrators through a secure protocol. The Bazaar part of data contains more detailed information agreed between the site and the user, containing among others:

- maximal total walltime,
- maximal walltime for a single job,
- maximal parallelism of a single job,
- minimal memory value.

During the phase of implementation of POZO for the Slurm batch system three different solutions were tested, all of them having their advantages and disadvantages. All of them are using Slurm built-in associations. An association is a 4-tuple consisting of a cluster name, a bank account, a user and optionally a partition. If set correctly, only the users with valid associations will be enabled to run jobs. The bank account contains information about user's limits, which also are enforced during job execution. This is a convenient way to implement any computing policy, so we decided to use it during POZO implementation.

The first attempt was a simple script working periodically as a cron job. This solution was gathering data from PL-Grid LDAP and Bazaar and adding all users and account information into Slurm database using normal user space Slurm utilities. In this concept, all data was being processed by slurmdbd daemon. A schematic workload of this scenario is presented in Fig. 3.

Unfortunately, the PL-Grid Infrastructure supports more than seven hundreds users, all of them having their private grants. Running such a script in this situation was causing Slurm to be not responsive to any users' grant changes for more than two hours. Obviously, this cannot be accepted and another attempt to implement Slurm support was needed.

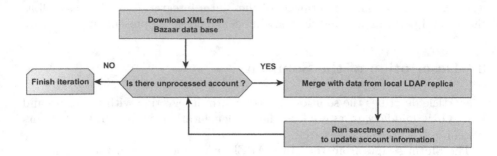

Fig. 3. The diagram of the first prototype of POZO implementation for Slurm

The first idea was to construct a buffer and run Slurm utilities only to update the users' grants data that have changed between a current and previous iteration. The implemented buffer database was almost a copy of Slurm accounting tables. This solution used SQLite [11], because its efficiency was not that important. Unluckily, another situation specific for the PL-Grid Infrastructure prevented this implementation from going into the production phase. The private grants, which are given by default to all PL-Grid users, are changing every half of year. This change is applied by the Bazaar system in several parts. Even though it still could cause efficiency problems every six months. This time it could cause Slurm to be immune to any grants changes for even three days. This again was not acceptable. A schematic design for this workflow is presented in Fig. 4.

While the previous implementations were tested, the Slurm version at ICM was upgraded from 2.4.3 to 2.6.1, allowing us to redesign the solution. The new version of Slurm supported reading the account information from backups with flushing the current state of the accounting database (in previous versions this operation was not able to delete users/accounts). In fact, this operation is not a simple flush. The dump file of the database is being compared with the current state of the database and, based on the results, a binary version of the new database state is prepared. Then, the whole new database is being imported through slurmdbd. This operation takes less than a minute, so with setting up proper timeouts it is possible to perform this action every day, which is a standard accepted by the PL-Grid Infrastructure (the existing solutions for Moab/Maui and PBS Pro work with the same interval constraint). A schematic workflow for this solution is presented in Fig. 5.

Batch system integration has also been done in the designated component of the UNICORE accounting, called BSS-Adapter. It orchestrates various batch system dependent modules, which have to implement a common internal SPI. The job records produced by a selected module are sent to the rest of the UNICORE accounting system using the ActiveMQ [1] message bus.

The Slurm support turned out to be the most difficult submodule of the BSS-Adapter. First of all, a difficult decision needed to be made on from what part

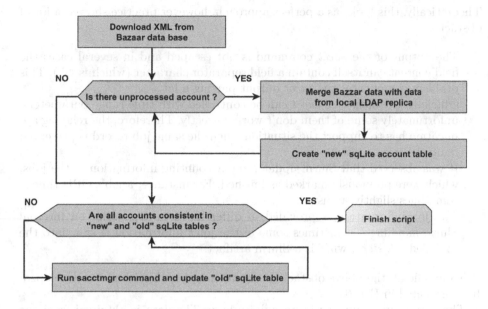

Fig. 4. The diagram of the second solution of integration of the POZO policy with the Slurm batch system

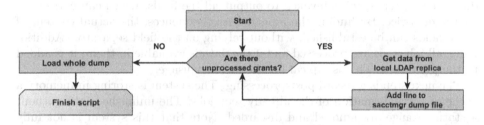

Fig. 5. The diagram of the final implementation of POZO used at the ICM. To be fully responsive, the solution needs at least 2.6.1 version of Slurm.

of Slurm the accounting data should be retrieved. As Slurm supports different storage backends for accounting data, it is possible to extract information directly from any of them (MySQL database and text files are the most common choices). Such an approach is easier from the development point of view, however in order to make the RUS BSS-Adapter independent from a SLURM backend, we developed a solution accessing the SLURM accounting data via its standard reporting *sacct* command.

The *sacct* command guarantees the same output format, regardless of the selected accounting storage backend. It also allows for changing its output format, with an ability to choose a format, which is suited to the machine processing.

Theoretically, this looks as a perfect approach, however practice showed a lot of obstacles:

- The output of the *sacct* command is not escaped and in several cases the field content can itself contain a field separator character (which is "|"). This problem complicates the *sacct* output parsing a lot.
- Officially, the output of *sacct* can be controlled with time range parameters, unfortunately some of them don't work correctly. Therefore, the relaying application has to support the situation when the same job record is presented multiple times.
- It was observed that Slurm updates the accounting information of the jobs, which were previously marked as finished. For instance, a job's CPU time is sometimes slightly adjusted.
- The job information is provided in different ways depending on internal Slurm handling – sometimes some of the job's information is split into the so called *job steps*, what is a Slurm artifact.

To handle all the above obstacles, a quite complex algorithm was developed. It is presented in Fig. 6.

The algorithm is invoked in an infinite loop. The data is obtained from the *sacct* command and the output is processed job by job. The parsing is using a special trick to detect inclusion of a field separator character used as an ordinary character: *sacct* is invoked to output all the fields, which can carry such characters twice. By finding the repeated text sequences, the actual content of those fields can be established, without relying on the field separator. Additionally, all job steps are processed and if the data is available in them, it is added to the job record. This is typical for the memory usage.

The next step is a record post-processing. The system is storing in memory a cache of key information of the already sent jobs. The unfinished jobs without a status change are ignored and discarded. Note that this system is not fully guaranteeing that a particular job record is absolutely never sent twice (for instance, this can happen if a BSS-Adapter is restarted and the sent records cache is cleared). However, this is not a problem for the accounting system as the central service ignores the unchanged job data. Therefore, this step is only reducing the network and processing load.

The second post-processing step is a workaround for the problem of Slurm changing the accounting information of a job, which is already in a terminal state and possibly could be already sent to the central accounting system. Therefore, the Slurm module ceases to send job records in a terminal state, which were finished only recently. The security time threshold is set to 2 minutes and tests confirm that after this time the job information becomes stable. Such jobs are going to be sent during the subsequent iteration of the Slurm module.

Besides the Slurm integration, the accounting system was redesigned to handle greater load and provide an unattended operation with a constantly growing

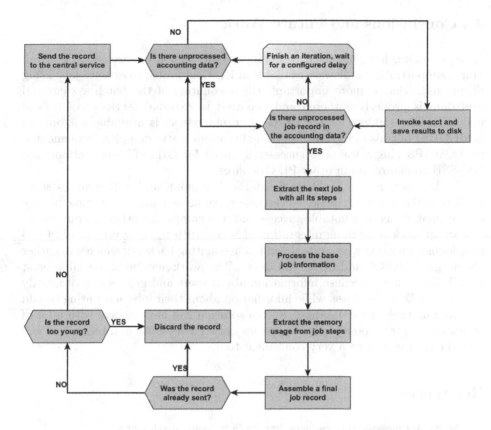

Fig. 6. Processing of the Slurm accounting data, using the *sacct* program as a source. The highlighted element is a good starting point to start following this infinite loop.

amount of processed records. The storage layer was redesigned and the new version is using a quite different persistence model. First of all, the daily usage summaries (kept for each user, site, queue and job status) become a fundamental element that is used for reporting and user-driven accounting data presentation. The measurements showed that such an approach provides a data amount reduction by approximately 20 times. The individual job records are still stored in the database, but only for a relatively short period of time (configurable, by default half a year) and after this period are automatically moved to a separate archive. This allows for keeping the advanced functionality of the system, which relies on the fine grained information stored in individual job records, yet keeping the amount of processed records at a reasonable level.

What is more, the same mechanism was implemented for the summary records, but with a much longer time period, after which the summaries are moved to an archive. Those two solutions together greatly improved the response time in case of accounting queries, reduced the everyday processing time and, finally, provide a promise that the system can work for many years to come.

4   Conclusions and Future Work

As a result, we have managed to deploy a new version of services with a full Slurm support. All middleware available in PL-Grid is able to execute jobs using Slurm and, what is more important, the accounting of the batch system and grid data is properly gathered and exported to external services in PL-Grid and EGI. The support for the PL-Grid grants system is available not only in UNICORE, but also in gLite. Additionally, users static mapping implemented by LCMAPS plugin was also successfully used for GridFTP connections and GSI-SSH configuration in other PL-Grid sites.

The integration was problematic at the beginning and still requires some work to make it more reliable. Nevertheless, we have managed to make it fully operational, which is a notable success and an example for others to pursue.

Further work concerning integration of Slurm with the new version of POZO may focus on writing a separate slurmdbd accounting backend, which will gather the usage of MySQL and LDAP databases. This work may be of special interest for all Slurm users, because information about users and groups is customarily kept in an LDAP database, while information about their jobs accounting should be saved in a relational database. Such a solution will have to deal with a lot of issues coming from possible incoherencies between separate databases, but will give the administrators a very convenient tool.

References

1. ActiveMQ message bus web site, http://activemq.apache.org
2. Bała, P., Benedyczak, K., Kluszczyński, R., Marczak, G.: Advancements in UNI-CORE Accounting. In: UNICORE Summit 2013 Proceedings, IAS Series 21, iii, Forschungszentrum Jülich GmbH Zentralbibliothek. Verlag Jülich (2013)
3. Benedyczak, K., Stolarek, M., Rowicki, R., Kluszczyński, R., Borcz, M., Marczak, G., Filocha, M., Bała, P.: Seamless Access to the PL-Grid e-Infrastructure Using UNICORE Middleware. In: Bubak, M., Szepieniec, T., Wiatr, K. (eds.) PL-Grid 2011. LNCS, vol. 7136, pp. 56–72. Springer, Heidelberg (2012)
4. Kitowski, J., Turała, M., Wiatr, K., Dutka, Ł.: PL-Grid: Foundations and Perspectives of National Computing Infrastructure. In: Bubak, M., Szepieniec, T., Wiatr, K. (eds.) PL-Grid 2011. LNCS, vol. 7136, pp. 1–14. Springer, Heidelberg (2012)
5. Byrom, R., Cordenonsi, R., Cornwall, L., Craig, M., Djaoui, A., Duncan, A., Fisher, S., Gordon, J., Hicks, S., Kant, D., Leake, J., Middleton, R., Thorpe, M., Walk, J., Wilson, A.: APEL: An implementation of Grid accounting using R-GMA. In: UK e-Science All Hands Conference (2005)
6. Pacini, F., Kunzt, P.: Job description language attributes specification. EGEE project (2006)
7. PLGrid Plus project web site, http://www.plgrid.pl/en/projects/plus
8. PL-Grid project web site, http://projekt.plgrid.pl/en
9. PL-Grid Resources Bazaar portal, https://bazaar.plgrid.pl
10. Slurm Workload Manager web site, http://slurm.schedmd.com
11. SQLite database web site, http://www.sqlite.org

12. Szepieniec, T., Tomanek, M., Radecki, M., Szopa, M., Bubak, M.: Implementation of Service Level Management in PL-Grid Infrastructure. In: Bubak, M., Szepieniec, T., Wiatr, K. (eds.) PL-Grid 2011. LNCS, vol. 7136, pp. 171–181. Springer, Heidelberg (2012)
13. Torque Resource Manager web site, http://www.adaptivecomputing.com/products/open-source/torque/
14. Yoo, A.B., Jette, M.A., Grondona, M.: SLURM: Simple Linux Utility for Resource Management. In: Feitelson, D.G., Rudolph, L., Schwiegelshohn, U. (eds.) JSSPP 2003. LNCS, vol. 2862, pp. 44–60. Springer, Heidelberg (2003)

Towards Provisioning of Reproducible, Reviewable and Reusable In-Silico Experiments with the GridSpace2 Platform

Eryk Ciepiela[1], Bartosz Wilk[1], Daniel Harężlak[1], Marek Kasztelnik[1], Maciej Pawlik[1], and Marian Bubak[1,2,3]

[1] AGH University of Science and Technology, ACC Cyfronet AGH,
ul. Nawojki 11, 30-950 Kraków, Poland
`eryk.ciepiela@cyfronet.pl`
[2] AGH University of Science and Technology, Faculty of Computer Science,
Electronics and Telecommunications, Department of Computer Science,
al. Mickiewicza 30, 30-059 Kraków, Poland
[3] University of Amsterdam, Institute for Informatics, Faculty of Science,
Amsterdam, The Netherlands

Abstract. The observed paradigm switch towards computational methods in research poses a serious challenge for e-infrastructure providers. Apart from delivering computing power, researchers are expected to create the foundation for complete and viable e-science environments. To address this demand, GridSpace2 was developed as a platform for provisioning reproducible, reviewable and reusable in-silico experiments. The resulting environment was applied in the scope of the PLGrid Plus project. In this work we analyze requirements, which should be met by in-silico experiments and describe how these requirements can be accommodated on the platform level, thus decreasing the costs of acquisition, preservation and curation of in-silico experiments. In order to evaluate our approach, we qualitatively assess how the features of GridSpace2 conform to these requirements and how the platform reduces the costs of provisioning in-silico experiments.

Keywords: e-science, in-silico experiments, reproducibility, problem solving environments, distributed computing.

1 In-Silico Experiments – e-Science Artifacts

Computational methods are becoming increasingly ubiquitous and often indispensable in scientific research in various domains. E-science can be treated either as a new standalone scientific paradigm or merely a specialization of the experimentation paradigm [1]. Correspondingly, data-driven and data-intensive research can be perceived either as "just another paradigm" or as the "original" paradigm [2]. Even though data-intensive and computational science paradigms are not necessarily new and disputes regarding their classification are still ongoing, what seems to be the most significant from the pragmatic standpoint is

M. Bubak et al. (Eds.): PLGrid Plus, LNCS 8500, pp. 118–129, 2014.

the difference between the established kinds of science and the so-called "new science", as well as the challenges brought about by these differences.

In particular, new means of conducting science should not result in shortcomings associated with methodological correctness and pragmatic usefulness. Scientific *artifacts*, by which we mean all kinds of apparatuses, tools and equipment used to obtain scientific findings, should always respect scientific method principles, supporting validation, verification and applicability within a reasonable timeframe and with modest effort. As computer science and information technologies have driven computational science, they should be harnessed to foster and aid the process of validation, verification and application of in-silico experiments. What is new and different here, are the definitions, dynamics and costs [3] related to new science artifacts, namely *in-silico experiments* characterized below.

The *initial cost* of **acquiring** in-silico experiments is relatively low compared to experimental science, but still significant when compared to theoretical models. The challenge is in streamlining – to a reasonable extent – the process of experiment development and distribution.

In-silico experiments are very different from both theoretical and experimental science. First, they are truly virtual, i.e., exist only as long as the computing hardware and software, which preserve them. Moreover, their growth in size and complexity is only restricted by the limitations of information technology. Therefore, the required ways of capturing, preserving and disseminating virtual experiments, are very different from methods used by traditional science. Finally, all virtual experiments incur *running costs* related to **preservation**.

In-silico experiments largely depend on technology (including hardware and software stacks), e-infrastructures and other experiments. Their dependencies continuously change, thus the experiments themselves are liable to change as well. This induces *recurring costs*, which are higher than for theoretical and experimental methods. Such costs comprise maintenance, i.e., refreshing, migrating, rebuilding, refactoring, etc. Resilience to such changes is important in terms of farsighted cost effectiveness when **sustaining** in-silico experiments.

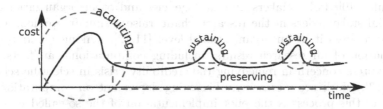

Fig. 1. Sample estimated cost of provisioning computational science artifacts over time as a combination of initial cost of acquisition, continuous cost of preservation and recurring cost of long-run sustainability. In farsighted cost analysis and optimization all these categories should be taken into account.

Bearing in mind the dynamic and complex cost structure of computational science artifacts, the meaning of provisioning becomes broader, covering not only acquisition, but also preservation and sustainability of experiments. Provisioning costs, as depicted in Fig. 1, are a combination of all these categories. A decrease of the costs in either category is desirable, however in practice we often need to resort to cost balancing. The more farsighted perspective we consider, the more crucial (in terms of overall cost) the trade-offs become.

In this regard, one of the goals of the PLGrid Plus project [4] was, given the e-infrastructure built in the scope of its predecessor, PL-Grid [5], to enhance the GridSpace2 platform [6,7] in order to enable provisioning of scientifically credible and pragmatically useful in-silico experiments in a cost-effective way by addressing key common aspects on the platform level. In the scope of this work we present and assess the approach adopted with GridSpace2.

2   Recognizing the Challenges of e-Science

The breadth and depth of the challenges that emerged with the advent of the e-science paradigm, induced various investigations that are related to this work and approach the problem from different angles.

The Royal Society, founded back in 1660 in order to advance the modern scientific method, is nowadays concerned with scientific conduct in the XXI century. Given all opportunities and challenges that emerge with the advent of e-science, it foresees e-science as an open enterprise [8] that would bring reproducibility back to scientific research of the future.

Reproducibility, being one of the main principles of the scientific method, has been recently discussed widely in the scientific community in the context of computational and data-intensive science. The problem of being unable to reproduce an entire experiment or study within a reasonable time and cost constraints, which is essential for credibility and reliability of scientific research, is raised more and more resonantly by various stakeholders. Such criticism is expressed by scientists themselves, who question the reproducibility of published findings. In extreme cases, this may result in retraction of papers [9]. Scientific programmers share the same concern when assessing the software engineering process, with tangled code and obscure ways, in which software arrives at scientific results [10]. Policymakers, funding agencies and other organizations, who are crucial stakeholders in the research chain, raise a similar problem and attempt to address it at an organizational level [11,12], making mandatory the dissemination of all research results, including computational artifacts. Publishers express concern in remedying the credibility crisis in scientific scholarly papers [13], which are increasingly becoming dependent on computations. An example of this process is the pilot implementation of the so-called *executable paper* concept [14,15]. Similarly, librarians are gradually switching to digital libraries where the notion of *enhanced publication* has emerged as a new means of disseminating research results [16] required by scientists and the general public. Last but not least, the problem becomes fully apparent for applicants of computational methods who, prior to implementing them in real-life cases, strive to reproduce or validate them. This applies especially to clinical research where the transparency, unambiguity and correctness of published computational methods are often questioned despite multilevel review policies [17].

This proves that while suitable e-infrastructure and software are needed, the entire e-science ecosystem built around should be enhanced with new means of recognizing and disseminating research results. New technologies are also expected to support and foster computational science by accommodating policies and strategies that policymakers, funding agencies and publishers impose in order to keep this ecosystem viable.

3   Towards Reproducible, Reviewable and Reusable In-Silico Experiments

To respond to this need, the GridSpace2 comes with its own approach that derives from the very fundamental definitions of *repeatability* and *reproducibility* as used in e.g. material engineering [18] and chemistry [19].

Repeatability is the ability of a method to obtain the same results (with some inaccuracy allowed) when applying it to the same case, under the same conditions: in the same laboratory, by the same operator, with the same apparatus, and in a short period of time; or close agreement between independent results obtained by applying such a method.

Reproducibility, in turn, is the ability of a method to obtain the same results (with some inaccuracy allowed) when applying it to the same case under different conditions: in a different laboratory, by a different operator, with a different apparatus, and/or at arbitrary time; or close agreement between independent results obtained by such reproduced methods. This concept logically extends repeatability, as shown in Fig. 2.

Reproducibility, in general, is indispensable in the process of *validation*, which determines whether a method "does the right thing". However, apart from "doing the right thing" in-silico experiments must "do it right" and this is what the *verification* process investigates. In this regard, another category of *reviewability* has to be introduced in order to embrace the capabilities of verifying in-silico experiments.

Reviewability is the quality or state of being reviewable, i.e., allowing for examination, verification, assessment, testing, scrutiny, etc. Reviewability can be considered as contrary to obscurity by accommodating concerns of structuring, transparency, traceability and expressiveness as depicted in Fig. 2.

Reproducibility and reviewability make experiments credible, although still not necessarily applicable to external real-life cases. Hence, another ability of *reusability* should be accommodated by in-silico experiments, which, in turn, can be borrowed from software engineering [21,22].

Reusability, in software engineering, is the ability to isolate, select, maintain and utilize existing software artifacts in the development of new systems. In the context of this work, new systems are understood as new experiments or different experiment cases. Therefore, we can define reusability as the ability to use an

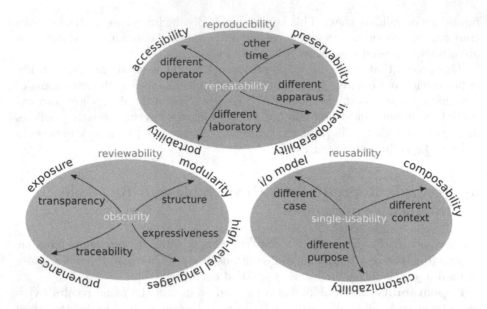

Fig. 2. Reproducibility (top) extending repeatability with the ability to apply the method at another time, by a different operator, in a different laboratory or with a different apparatus. An in-silico experimentation platform can support these features by properly addressing the aspects of preservation, accessibility, portability and interoperability respectively. Reviewability (left) carries the qualities of transparency, structure, expressiveness and provenance. These qualities can be built into an in-silico experimentation platform by properly addressing the aspects of exposure, modularity, high-level language support and traceability respectively. Reusability (right) enables the method to be applied to different cases, in a different context and/or for a different purpose. An in-silico experimentation platform can possess this ability by properly addressing the aspects of input/output models, composability and customizability respectively.

experiment again in a different case, for a different purpose and/or in a different context, as shown in Fig. 2, with slight or no modification. In effect, reusability expresses the measure of likelihood of such reuse.

The goal of GridSpace2 can be now more precisely defined as being to provide a software platform to support and foster reproducibility, reviewability and reusability of in-silico experiments, as opposed to mere repeatability, obscurity and single-usability. In order to enable the desired qualities that enhance in-silico experiments with reproducibility, reviewability and reusability, a number of aspects enumerated in Fig. 2 need to be properly addressed by the platform.

4   GridSpace2 Approach to In-Silico Experiments

In response to the above mentioned aspects we propose the GridSpace2 experiment meta-model as depicted in Fig. 3.

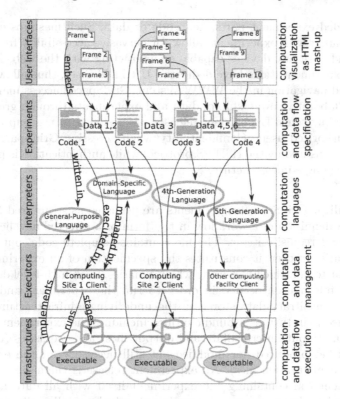

Fig. 3. GridSpace2 meta-model. Experiments are workflows composed of a number of interconnected *code* and *data items*. Code items are written in high-level programming languages and interpreted by *interpreters*, which are implemented as *executables* exccuted through *executors* on the underlying e-infrastructures. Executables run on e-infrastructures, carrying out computations. Executors manage and orchestrate computation flow, data staging and transfers. Data items are simply files that are read and written when executing code items. In the presentation layer code and data items are embeddable in HTML mashup pages.

Experiments are workflows composed of a number of interconnected *code* and *data items*. Code items are written in high-level programming languages that are interpreted by *interpreters*, which are implemented as *executables* executed through *executors* on the underlying e-infrastructures. Executables installed on the e-infrastructures carry out computations while executors manage and orchestrate computation flow and data transfers. Data items are simply files that are read and written when executing code items. In the presentation layer code and data items are embedded in HTML mashup pages. Referring to the requirements listed in the previous section we can now present how the GridSpace2 meta-model implements their respective aspects.

Accessibility. The GridSpace2 user interface is fully web-based. Users log in and interact with experiments using web pages, which are, however, enriched with embedded experiment parts, i.e., code or data. Such mashups combining web page content with experiments allow for pervasive accessibility from remote locations and with any devices capable of interacting with the web. Moreover, individual experiment items have dedicated URL addresses, thus allowing identification and navigation in the WWW system. GridSpace2 access management supports collaborative ownership of data and experiments through group-based access control systems. Experiment releases are assigned to a group that comprises all authorized users. Confidentiality when accessing GridSpace2 experiment items is ensured by the HTTPS protocol while authentication is performed by the underlying e-infrastructure.

Preservability. GridSpace2 experiments are persisted as structured XML files containing a definition of a workflow in the form of a directed acyclic graph of code, data and requisite items. The file contains complete code, but not data nor any binaries; rather, it constitutes the specification of an experiment plan, showing what to do, which files using which binaries. Such high-level description provides all information needed in order to run the experiment and is easily preservable in arbitrary data stores on the underlying e-infrastructure. An *experiment release*, in turn, is a bundle of files including the experiment plan and all data items (input, intermediate and output files) and requisites (other files that are neither produced nor modified yet still necessary for the experiment to run, e.g. configuration files). An experiment release is therefore a record of the experiment run containing the experiment itself with all data and requisite files involved in the course of experiment, which is still easily preservable as a bundle of files. Although the executables are not included but only mentioned in the experiment, they are uniquely identified as *interpreters* so that the system can lookup for any matching executables on underlying e-infrastructure and rerun the computations. For this purpose, GridSpace2 provides a registry of interpreters and matching executables installed on e-infrastructures.

Interoperability. GridSpace2 experiments support interoperability by relying on abstract entities of *interpreters* and *data formats*. An interpreter denotes any executable that is capable of interpreting a given language so that multiple alternative executables implementing the interpreter can be used to run an experiment code item. A data format is an abstract declaration of the syntax and semantics of a data file so that a number of alternative viewers and editors, commonly referred to as *openers*, supporting a given format can be used to edit or visualize an experiment data item. Experiments only indirectly depend on a particular executable or opener; instead, they depend on abstract interpreters and data formats. To enable matching between interpreters and executables as well as between data formats and openers, GridSpace2 provides a dedicated registry. GridSpace2 also allows for flexible configuration of openers and interpreters so that it can be adapted to existing or new e-infrastructures.

Portability. GridSpace2 introduces an abstraction layer over execution and data management capabilities of underlying e-infrastructures through the so-called *Executor API*. A number of e-infrastructure adapters implementing this API are already available and new ones can be developed and easily plugged into the system. GridSpace2 registry specifies what executor type to use to access a given e-infrastructure.

It is even possible to use multiple executors handled by the same or different executor type at the same time thus allowing for cross-infrastructure experiment runs.

Exposure. In GridSpace2 experiments code and data items are first-class citizens, fully exposed for viewing and editing in the user interface. Experiment items embedded in web pages are transparent and provide direct insight into the code and data files. Second-class citizens are interpreters whose code is not directly exposed. Nonetheless, interpreters' versions and distributions are explicitly specified in the experiment so that they can be investigated and analyzed independently. In the background, the "plumbing code" dealing with preparation, orchestration and monitoring of experiments, is moved out of the user's sight and hidden in the platform internals. Still, all relevant parameters are displayed to the users who can then study their impact on the experiment. With this selective exposure, GridSpace2 lets users focus on the business logic and rely on already-verified platform components. This approach to presenting experiments provides for a traditional, compact and uniform user experience with only code and data items arranged on the page.

Modularity. What makes even complex experiments manageable is their readable representation in the form of workflow, namely a directed acyclic graph comprising code and data items. Although not applicable to all classes of experiments, such representation accommodates a vast range of potential scenarios and naturally fits into the narrative of the scientific method. Modules like code, data and requisite items have explicit and well defined connections to one another, thus enabling scoped and isolated changes in individual items without impacting other modules. Moreover, workflow-based modularity facilitates clean and convenient rearrangement of workflow items.

High-Level Language Support. GridSpace2 enables execution of computations specified in an arbitrary programming language. Code items represent programs, algorithms, problem definitions or other specifications of computations and can be written in diverse general-purpose, domain-specific, 4th or 5th generation programming languages, which we refer to as interpreters. Interpreters, in turn, are implemented by executables, which ultimately evaluate code regardless of its nature. In this way, GridSpace2 fosters utilization of high-level languages making the experiment more expressive and easy to read and modify.

Provenance. As already mentioned, *experiment releases* bundle all code, data and requisite items involved in an individual experiment run. Since all experiment items are exposed to users, this allows for immediate introspection of primary data, intermediate results as well as final outputs. It is also easy to trace, which code was run against which data.

Input/Output Model. GridSpace2 adopts the file-based input/output model as the most straightforward, intuitive and popular approach to computing. Just like in the majority of operating systems, files can be organized in a directory tree and filename extension denotes their data types. Specific types can then be associated with compatible *openers*, which are tiny, dedicated web applications embedded in data item frames. Openers can either only visualize or allow for editing of data items.

Composability. In order to enable composition of complex experiments by reusing other experiments, the mechanism of *sub-experiments* was introduced in the GridSpace2 platform. The code items of the experiment can, at any moment of its execution, trigger an entire sub-experiment or just a single sub-item. The experiment passes input data items and receives output from the sub-experiment (or sub-code) according to the file mapping specified in the so-called *embedment* element. Behind the scenes, the executable evaluating the code item dispatches a REST request back to GridSpace2, which, in turn, executes the sub-experiment or sub-item and takes care of proper file staging.

Customizability. Taking advantage of the workflow meta-model wherein dependencies between code and data elements are explicitly defined, the user may decide, which parts of the workflow to detach, attach, replace or omit when repurposing the experiment. Similarly, changes to individual code and data items can be applied without affecting other parts of the workflow. In conjunction with the exposure of experiment items, any change that does not alter the workflow structure can be applied in situ and immediately executed.

5   Evaluation and Results

The GridSpace2 platform has been delivered as a platform-as-a-service hosted at the Academic Computer Center CYFRONET and available to registered PL-Grid users [23]. The platform is developed as an open-source project and is also available in the form of a binary distribution [24].

So far, the platform was successfully used in provisioning several in-silico experiments representing various domains both within the scope of PLGrid Plus and outside of it:

- analysis of hydrophobicity distribution in proteins [25],
- analysis of nanopore arrangement and structural features of anodic alumina layers [26],

- supporting the design process of mining operation in coal mines [27],
- simulation of nuclear fusion fenomena [28],
- simulation of in-stent restenosis in coronary arteries [29],
- simulation of irrigation canals in distributed high-performace computing infrastructures [30],
- imulation of clay-polymer nanocomposite materials [31].

It was also adopted as a technology empowering executable papers [15].

The usefulness of the solution can be evaluated against two criteria: (a) addressing the requirements of reproducibility, reviewability and reusability, and (b) the cost-effectiveness of provisioning in-silico experiments. Although the platform has already been used in numerous applications and evaluated in terms of general user experience, more in-depth evaluation and comparison with alternative approaches is still to be carried out.

6   Conclusions and Future Work

In this work we discussed the characteristics of in-silico experiments treated as artifacts of modern computational and data-intensive scientific research paradigms. We noticed that – apart from the benefits brought about by new technological capabilities – research, which relies on these methods, should remain reproducible in order to satisfy the basic principles of the scientific method. Hence, new policies for reviewing and disseminating models need to be urgently devised. Moreover, in-silico experiments – being first-class artifacts of e-science – should be provided in such a way as to enable reproducibility, reviewability and reusability. GridSpace2 is a software platform, which operates on top of e-infrastructures and addresses these requirements in a comprehensive fashion, thus lowering the cost of provisioning individual in-silico experiments, including the costs of experiment acquisition, preservation and sustainability.

In the future we would like to investigate whether the proposed meta-model and software platform can span multiple autonomous administrative domains and what business model would make this approach viable and adaptable to a wider ecosystem. We would also like to continue efforts towards making the GridSpace2-powered experiments embeddable in scientific publications through the Collage Authoring Environment [15]. Apart from that, we plan to incrementally improve the platform so that it supports more and more cost-effective provisioning of in-silico experiments.

References

1. Post, D.E., Votta, L.G.: Computational science demands a new paradigm. Physics Today 58(1), 35–41 (2005)
2. Bell, G., Hey, T., Szalay, A.: Beyond the data deluge. Science 323(5919), 1297–1298 (2009)
3. Nelson, M.L.: Data-Driven Science: A New Paradigm? EDUCAUSE Review 44(4), 6–7 (2009)

4. PLGrid Plus project web site, http://www.plgrid.pl/plus
5. Bubak, M., Szepieniec, T., Wiatr, K. (eds.): PL-Grid 2011. LNCS, vol. 7136. Springer, Heidelberg (2012)
6. Ciepiela, E., et al.: Managing Entire Lifecycles of e-Science Applications in the GridSpace2 Virtual Laboratory – From Motivation through Idea to Operable Web-Accessible Environment Built on Top of PL-Grid e-Infrastructure. In: Bubak, M., Szepieniec, T., Wiatr, K. (eds.) PL-Grid 2011. LNCS, vol. 7136, pp. 228–239. Springer, Heidelberg (2012)
7. Ciepiela, E., Harezlak, D., Kocot, J., Bartynski, T., Kasztelnik, M., Nowakowski, P., Bubak, M.: Exploratory programming in the virtual laboratory. In: Proceedings of the 2010 International Multiconference on Computer Science and Information Technology (IMCSIT), pp. 621–628. IEEE (2010)
8. Boulton, G., Campbell, P., Collins, B., Elias, P., Hall, W., Laurie, G., Walport, M.: Science as an open enterprise. The Royal Society (2012)
9. Retraction Watch, Archive for the "not reproducible" Category, http://retractionwatch.com/
10. Merali, Z.: Computational science: Error, why scientific programming does not compute. Nature 467(7317), 775–777 (2010)
11. Mervis, J.: NSF to ask every grant applicant for data management plan. ScienceInsider (2010), http://news.sciencemag.org/2010/05/
12. The Software Sustainability Institute, http://www.software.ac.uk/
13. Aalbersberg, I.J., Atzeni, S., Koers, H., Specker, B., Zudilova-Seinstra, E.: Bringing Digital Science Deep Inside the Scientific Article: the Elsevier Article of the Future Project. LIBER Quarterly 22 (2013)
14. Nowakowski, P., Ciepiela, E., Harezlak, D., Kocot, J., Kasztelnik, M., Bartynski, T., Meizner, J., Dyk, G., Malawski, M.: The Collage Authoring Environment. In: Proceedings of the International Conference on Computational Science, ICCS 2011. Procedia Computer Science, vol. 4, pp. 608–617 (2011), http://www.sciencedirect.com/science/article/pii/S1877050911001220
15. Ciepiela, E., Harezlak, D., Kasztelnik, M., Meizner, J., Dyk, G., Nowakowski, P., Bubak, M.: The Collage Authoring Environment: From Proof-of-Concept Prototype to Pilot Service. In: ICCS 2013. Procedia Computer Science, vol. 18, pp. 769–778 (2013), http://www.sciencedirect.com/science/article/pii/S1877050913003840
16. Bardi, A., Manghi, P.: A Rationale for Enhanced Publications. LIBER Quarterly 22 (2014), https://liber.library.uu.nl/index.php/lq/article/view/8445/9825
17. Baggerly, K.A., Coombes, K.R.: What Information Should Be Required to Support Clinical "Omics" Publications? Clinical Chemistry 57, 688–690 (2011)
18. ASTM Standard E177-13: Standard Practice for Use of the Terms Precision and Bias in ASTM Test Methods. ASTM International, West Conshohocken, PA (2003), http://www.astm.org, doi:10.1520/C0033-03E01
19. McNaught, A.D., Wilkinson, A.: IUPAC. Compendium of Chemical Terminology, 2nd edn. (the "Gold Book"). Blackwell Scientific Publications, Oxford (1997), XML on-line corrected version, http://goldbook.iupac.org, doi:10.1520/E0177-13, created by Nic, M., Jirat, J., Kosata, B.; updates compiled by Jenkins, A. (2006), doi:10.1520/E0177-13, ISBN 0-9678550-9-8
20. Department of Defense Documentation of Verification: Validation & Accreditation (VV&A) for Models and Simulations. Missile Defense Agency (2008)
21. Reese, R., Wyatt, D.L.: Software reuse and simulation. In: Proceedings of the 19th Conference on Winter Simulation, pp. 185–192. ACM (1987)

22. Robinson, S., Nance, R.E., Paul, R.J., Pidd, M., Taylor, S.J.: Simulation model reuse: definitions, benefits and obstacles. Simulation Modelling Practice and Theory 12(7), 479–494 (2004)
23. GridSpace2 platform installation in the PL-Grid Infrastructure, https://gs2.plgrid.pl
24. GridSpace2 project home page, https://dice.cyfronet.pl/gridspace
25. Ciepiela, E., Jadczyk, T., Harezlak, D., Kasztelnik, M., Nowakowski, P., Dyk, G., Bubak, M., Roterman, I.: Computations of protein hydrophobicity profile as virtual experiment in gridspace virtual laboratory. Bio-Algorithms and Medical-Systems 8(4), 361–372 (2011)
26. Zaraska, L., Stepniowski, W.J., Sulka, G.D., Ciepiela, E., Jaskula, M.: Analysis of nanopore arrangement and structural features of anodic alumina layers formed by two-step anodizing in oxalic acid using the dedicated executable software. Applied Physics A 114(2), 571–577 (2014)
27. Brzychczy, E.: A Modern Tool for Modelling and Optimisation of Production in Underground Coal Mine. In: Bubak, M., Kitowski, J., Wiatr, K. (eds.) PLGrid Plus. LNCS, vol. 8500, pp. 317–334. Springer, Heidelberg (2014)
28. Rycerz, K., Bubak, M., Ciepiela, E., Pawlik, M., Hoenen, O., Harężlak, D., Wilk, B., Gubała, T., Meizner, J., Coster, D.: Enabling Multiscale Fusion Simulations on Distributed Computing Resources. In: Bubak, M., Kitowski, J., Wiatr, K. (eds.) PLGrid Plus. LNCS, vol. 8500, pp. 195–210. Springer, Heidelberg (2014)
29. Borgdorff, J., Bona-Casas, C., Mamoński, M., Kurowski, K., Piontek, T., Bosak, B., Hoekstra, A.G.: A distributed multiscale computation of a tightly coupled model using the multiscale modeling language. Procedia Computer Science 9, 596–605 (2012)
30. Borgdorff, J., Mamoński, M., Bosak, B., Kurowski, K., Belgacem, M.B., Chopard, B., Hoekstra, A.G.: Distributed Multiscale Computing with MUSCLE 2, the Multiscale Coupling Library and Environment. arXiv preprint, arXiv:1311.5740 (2013)
31. Rycerz, K., Ciepiela, E., Dyk, G., Groen, D., Gubala, T., Harezlak, D., Bubak, M.: Support for Multiscale Simulations with Molecular Dynamics. Procedia Computer Science 18, 1116–1125 (2013)

A Framework for Domain-Specific Science Gateways

Joanna Kocot, Tomasz Szepieniec, Piotr Wójcik, Michał Trzeciak,
Maciej Golik, Tomasz Grabarczyk, Hubert Siejkowski, and Mariusz Sterzel

AGH University of Science and Technology, ACC Cyfronet AGH,
ul. Nawojki 11, 30-950 Kraków, Poland
{j.kocot,t.szepieniec,p.wojcik,m.trzeciak,m.golik,t.grabarczyk,
h.siejkowski,m.sterzel}@cyfronet.pl

Abstract. While modern Federated Computing Infrastructures – Grids, Clouds and other technologies – continuously increase their computing power, their use for research still stays lower than desired. The authors' diagnosis of this problem is a technology barrier hard to overcome to people who want to focus only on science. The federated infrastructures are difficult to use not only due to the physical distribution of the resources and, thus, need for remote access, but, mainly, due to the fact that everyday patterns of interaction with a computer cannot be directly used for these resources. The way of performing computing operations on them is different than the usual way the scientists do their research using laptops or personal computers.

The authors claim that the key to increase the use of modern federated infrastructures for science is making the processing on these infrastructures resemble using a personal computer. The paper collects requirements from different scientific use cases and, from these requirements, derives a processing model that could satisfy all of them, thus, allowing to build a system, in which computations on large infrastructures can be similar to everyday work. This model is implemented by a framework for creating Science Gateways – InSilicoLab.

Keywords: federated infrastructures, processing model, science gateway, framework, *in silico*.

1 Introduction

Modern Federated Computing Infrastructures offer almost endless computing power. The capacity provided by Grids, Clouds and other technologies is huge, however, the level of their use for research remains lower than desired. The reason for this might be that, for a researcher, moving from an everyday computation done on a personal computer to a large parallel machine is a very time-consuming process. It involves transferring data to and from a remote server, launching a computation – usually without any user interface other than command-line, managing the computation status, etc. Most of this is only a burden for a regular researcher, who usually possesses some kind of programmatic skills, but

M. Bubak et al. (Eds.): PLGrid Plus, LNCS 8500, pp. 130–146, 2014.

they are not the essence of his work. The amount of required purely technical operations might not be an obstacle for large communities, like LHC, who are able to invest in dedicated teams of computer scientists and programmers, but it almost eliminates smaller communities. For the latter, the inability to use the federated infrastructures might cause not only making slower progress – while running computations on a PC or laptop takes longer than on a parallel machine – but also prevent some of the research at all – as larger (usually more important) datasets could take years to be calculated on a standard computer. Apart from the difficulties related to technical specifics of the computations management, there are some objective obstacles that make using distributed computing infrastructures difficult, e.g.:

- overhead of running a computation – acceptable for very large ones, but too big for smaller tasks,
- problematic data transfer – e.g. for Grid: inefficient and difficult, for Clouds: expensive,
- inability to interact with a running computation.

The stakes are high, as often the research conducted in smaller or more dispersed communities is of great importance to humanity – take bioengineering or seismology as an example.

Fortunately, with successive identification of the aforementioned barriers, new tools have started to be created, leading also to evolution of Science Gateways – portals that aim at facilitating the operation on large computer infrastructures by providing interfaces adjusted to a given community, and offering many other tools that might be of use to researchers coming from these communities.

This paper presents a framework for creating Science Gateways – InSilico-Lab – that provides processing-related solutions tailored to specific domains of science. The gateways created with this framework, to facilitate the usage of the system, provide a user interface fully customized to a specific science domain, including the data types, possible operations and construction of the experimentation flow. On the other hand, they aim at reducing side effects of utilizing a computer infrastructure – not only the difficulties of performing operations on the infrastructure, but also indirect costs like time overheads and lack of interactivity (batch-style computations). The requirements for development of the gateway framework were based on several use cases concerning different domains of science or different areas of these domains.

The paper is constructed as follows: Section 2 gives an overview of computation use cases coming from different domains of science; summary of the requirements for a processing model identified on the base of these use cases is given in Section 3. Section 4 proposes an implementation of this model, while Section 5 specifies a framework for Science Gateways using it. The current status of work on the framework is summarized in Section 6. Section 7 gives an overview of the related work in the field of Science Gateways, and, in general, in computation models and tools for science. The article is summarized in Section 8.

2   Use Cases

This section presents several use cases from different domains of science or communities gathered around specific classes of problems within these domains.

2.1   Computational Chemistry

Computational chemistry is one of the domains that heavily utilize the resources of advanced computing infrastructures. Its computational methods are usually used to explain or predict empirical effects. Large computational power is necessary to improve accuracy of the simulation outcomes, extend the timescale of simulations or, sometimes, just to make modelling a large system possible. Computational cost of these methods can be the time needed to complete the calculations as well as large memory consumption and disk storage use.

Similar modelling is also used in other sciences, like nanotechnology or biological sciences. The significance of this work was recently confirmed by the Nobel Foundation who awarded the 2013 Nobel Prize in chemistry for "the development of multiscale models for complex chemical systems" [1,2].

A classic pattern for Quantum Chemistry computations is comparing similar systems (geometries), e.g. optimizing their energy or finding other properties. This requires preparing input data for different systems, launching computations for all of them and, then, repeatedly checking if the results are available. The results are text files containing the log of the whole computation process – sometimes including even the license and the 'message of the day'. Therefore, analyzing these files is difficult and tiresome, but often required, also while the computation is running – to control whether the processing is going to be convergent. If not, the process should be stopped and rerun with slightly different parameters. This is especially important in case of very time-consuming optimization procedures, that could otherwise run for days or weeks not giving eventually any correct results.

If the computations are launched on a distributed computing infrastructure, the user additionally has to transfer data to a suitable storage service, specify the computation description (usually, a file written in a description language specific to a given infrastructure), monitor the state of the jobs, and, afterwards, transfer the result data from a storage service to their computer. Even if it would further be used for next computations (which is a common scenario), the transfer to a local computer is required to analyze the contents of the file. What is more, in such case, watching the result (log) file during the computation is usually impossible or very difficult – and, in case of many parallel jobs – unmanageable [3].

Another scenario useful for the computational chemistry domain is an interactive "play" with a molecular system like Molecular Dynamics trajectory, where several parameters of the system reduction are chosen and tested on one of the trajectory frames. After the reduction is considered successful, the same operations can be applied to the whole trajectory or to a set of its chosen frames. In case of this scenario, implementing it using a traditional batch system would bring more inconvenience than benefits, as the operations required to run the program and transfer files take longer than the actual computation.

2.2   CTA

The Cherenkov Telescope Array (CTA) [4] is a large project from astrophysics domain that aims at building the next generation ground-based telescopes to observe very high energy gamma-rays. As the project is still in its preparatory phase, large simulations are needed to model the telescopes response with respect to different parameters – ranging from the telescopes size, placement and geographical location to the electronic trigger configuration. At this stage, heavy Monte Carlo (MC) computations are run to find the optimum values of these parameters, considering as well individual telescopes as the whole telescope array. The simulations often have a character of a parameter sweep – to thoroughly test the possible values of a range of parameters, usually also for different input files – which produces a very large number of parallel simulations. The simulations are based on data containing simulated atmospheric events, which tend to be very large (usually several GBs). Such large data cannot be stored on personal computers, and even their transfer from a dedicated storage takes considerable time. The duration of the computations themselves also depends on the data size as well as on the parameter values.

Within the next few years, CTA will enter its operational phase, when it will serve as an open observatory to a wide astrophysics community and will provide a deep insight into the non-thermal high-energy universe. The MC simulations will be needed in a limited number then, and the software will have to be targeted at analysis of the data produced by the telescopes. This has to be prepared earlier, to calibrate both the telescopes and the software parameters to provide reliable information to the astrophysics community. Such analysis requires multiple transformations of the telescope data to extract relevant information and to reconstruct the direction and the energy of the original atmospheric event, which are then compared against the simulated input values. This is done by several tools organized in a pipeline, for which some elements might be exchanged (e.g. for verification, some of the analyses have to be run twice, using different methods – only if they give similar outcomes, the resulting information can be considered valid).

Another important aspect of the telescope array operation will be consuming the data that come from the instrument. This will be streams of large data coming continuously – not being divided into individual files. To process data of such character, neither batch systems nor interactive applications are enough. Such data require completely different approach that would consider data not as files but as streams.

2.3   MHD Simulations in Astrophysics

Magnetohydrodynamic (MHD) simulations are an important way of modelling processes and studying their evolution in many astrophysical objects and environments. The codes used for this modelling have the highest requirements with respect to the computing infrastructure – e.g., one of the scientists performing these simulations every year reaches the first place in statistics of the resource consumption in the PL-Grid national grid infrastructure[1]. An important aspect of these simulations is monitoring the status of the physical system being modelled. Therefore, it is convenient to produce a significant amount of pictures delivered on the fly with their number and names not known prior to the calculations.

It is also useful to do a compilation test before the computation is submitted to the infrastructure. This allows the user to tune the compilation parameters and test whether they are valid and work with the application. This testing is of large significance, as the application could run for even as long as several months. A test compilation could be done several times until satisfactory configuration is reached, which requires that its results are returned almost instantly. Only the final, validated parameters are used for a real compilation in the infrastructure, which is done before the program starts.

2.4   Bioinformatics

The bioinformatics calculations are known for their complexity with respect to the number of different (often small) programs that have to be run in a specific order (see e.g. the Gromacs application [5]) – usually one taking output from the other as input. This order might be different for different classes of problems, therefore, different researchers have their own patterns of using these programs. A natural way of facilitating work with them would be connecting the individual programs in workflows or pipelines. However, automating that is very difficult due to the lack of formal semantic description. What is more, some of these programs cannot be run in batch mode, as they interactively ask the user for input. The interactivity is also often required on the level of constructing the workflow or pipeline – by dynamically choosing the subsequent processing steps. This is due to the fact that the decision on the next step of the experiment is often based on early obtained results of the previous step – e.g. the user observes a plot generated by one of the programs and decides whether to continue the experiment or recalculate the current step with different parameters.

The bioinformatics community has also created a well-developed set of protein databases (like Protein Data Bank [6]) or publication databases that publish a service API, which enables them to be used through service method calls (e.g. REST [7] operations).

3   Processing Model Based on Scientific Use Cases

The requirements gathered on the base of the presented use cases show that scientific computations not only need large computational resources, but also

---

[1]   According to the statistics presented on the forum of the PL-Grid Consortium.

immediate response and interactivity. Therefore, a comprehensive computing model targeted at research communities has to, on one hand, enable or facilitate access to large computer infrastructures, and, on the other, consider interactivity and responsiveness as key functionality.

We can summarize the requirements for such computing model by introducing the following three types of processing that have to be addressed:

- *Batch operations* – which usually take a significant amount of time to complete, therefore, their immediate result is not important. These operations often involve managing large datasets. There are also two features of such computations that are usually neglected by traditional computational systems:
  - Interaction with the application – the computational task run on an infrastructure might execute an application that, at some point, requires user input or simple decision.
  - Continuous preview of the application results – partial results should be available for preview during the computation (if the application produces such partial results before it completes).
- *Immediate operations* – requiring immediate response from the system. They would be usually used jointly with other types of processing – e.g. to test parameters for larger batch computation or to deploy a service.
- *On-demand deployment of services* – operations that deploy services to be later used by other components. The service endpoints will be distributed across the user infrastructure. The use of such services could enable processing data streams – which could not be handled by any other mechanism.

All of the above-listed types of processing require interactive mechanisms, where not only outputs are available immediately, but also processing units of all kinds can prompt for a user decision on a specific matter. This should be presented to the user in their interface or sent as a notification in case they are off-line.

Implementing this concept of performing computations brings us closer to the main aim a modern processing model for computing infrastructures should follow – i.e., preserving the same functionalities and usage patterns that the users have on their personal computers. Such model is already partially available through contemporary grid and cloud technologies (IaaS, PaaS), however, it is not yet accessible in a unified way. The authors believe that combining all these in a single system, which is a heart of a domain-specific portal solution, might be a vast change in the way of performing computing-aided research. A portal empowered with a system based on the presented processing model, on one hand, gives access to powerful processing mechanisms, and on the other, can offer a personalized user interface containing all necessary tools and applications required by a specific domain of science. We call it a Science Gateway.

4   Implementation of the Processing Model

To implement the computation model represented by the three classes described in Section 3, the following system architecture was designed.

The central component of the system (see Fig. 1) is a message broker (implemented as a message queue) that coordinates requests of the other actors: a requestor and a worker. The requestor is an entity (usually a portal interfacing the user) that defines the computation to be performed, whereas the worker is an actual program that performs the computation. Both the requestor and the worker can be deployed in multiple instances, either providing different functionality or duplicating an existing component – the latter providing means for load balancing. The message broker ensures a reliable asynchronous communication between all the actors. Fig. 1 shows this communication scheme.

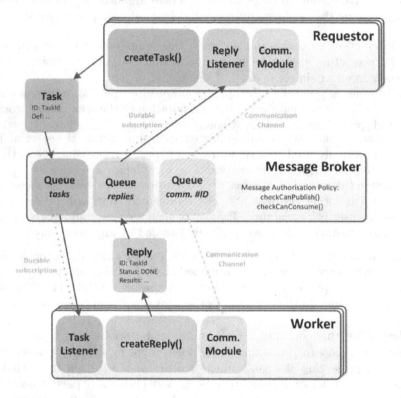

Fig. 1. Schema of the communication in the system: Requestor and Worker instances interacting through a Message Broker

Workers start their execution by subscribing to the queue and declaring what type of specific task they are able to process (e.g., a specific program, dynamically deployed visualization service, etc.). As the workers communicate with the rest of the system only via the message queue, they can be launched on any computer capable of running the specific task – regardless whether it is a node of an advanced distributed infrastructure or just a personal computer. Likewise, they can be implemented in any software technology or programming language. Workers of adequate type (able to process certain task type) can be spawned or terminated according to the system load.

The requestor is responsible for creating task definitions based on the user input, and submitting them to the message queue. The tasks are portions of work that have to be delegated from the requestor (e.g. portal) to workers. They are usually a specific set of parameters and/or input files for a concrete program run by the worker. When the requestor submits a task of a certain type to the queue, the message broker sends it to one of the workers, that are capable of processing it. The workers are usually built for a concrete application, and, therefore, need only a limited configuration and input files passed with the task description to start the computation. Such approach limits their use to only computations of a specified kind, however, the behavior of such workers is much more predictable and can be more easily handled and communicated to the user. Furthermore, implementing a general-purpose worker that would be able to execute an arbitrary script is also possible, to complement the system functionality.

At any time, the worker may send messages back to the requestor – also through the message queue. Such messages can include e.g. task results (also partial ones), execution status or error information. What is more, when receiving a task from the queue, the worker subscribes to a new, temporary queue, which serves as a channel for additional message exchange with the requestor (concerning only the given task). In this way, a two-way communication is possible, in which both sides may initiate the interaction and both sides await messages – e.g., the requestor can send additional data required by the task during its execution, or the worker may notify the requestor that it needs an input from the user. If a worker is deploying a service with an external interface, this communication channel will still be active, therefore, allowing the worker to communicate with the requestor in the usual manner (e.g. enabling the requestor to send a shutdown message), while external entities will be accessing it according to the service protocol and interface.

Relying on asynchronous message passing as the communication layer, adds an important quality to the system, namely, the persistence. Appropriate message broker policies ensure that task descriptions are not lost in case of worker failure or connection problems. Similarly, should the requestor side fail, all messages from the workers are persisted by the message broker and delivered as soon as the requestor restarts/reconnects. The message broker policies also ensure the integrity of the system – e.g., that one task request will not be consumed by many workers at a time.

The latency added by the communication through a queue is minimal, therefore, instant response of the system is assured assuming there is a free worker to perform the requested task, and that, in turn, may be managed by appropriate worker deployment and spawning policy.

The workers are owned by users who run them either manually – by executing them directly or starting through a dedicated interface – or automatically, by triggering a computation of a certain type. The owner can also set the worker policy to allow other users to utilize it. In this way, light, permanent workers can be deployed on dedicated resources to realize small computations and be available to all the users. Such workers can perform immediate operations, as they are constantly ready to receive and perform their tasks. Once they complete, the result is instantly put to the queue and dispatched to the requestor, which is waiting for it.

All workers are managed and monitored by a separate component – Worker Manager, which is aware how many workers, of what kind, and belonging to what users are alive, and what is their state (e.g. busy, waiting for reply, unoccupied). The manager would automatically adjust the pool of permanent workers to ensure the immediate operations are performed fast, and trigger notifications to the user whenever the user-managed pool of workers is overloaded.

5   Science Gateway Framework

To create a unique solution tailored to the needs of a specific research community, the generic computation model should be built into a larger framework that would specify how to create, on one side, the user interfaces, and, on the other, the connection to the underlying infrastructures.

5.1   Framework Architecture

The schema presented in Section 4 specifies the model of communication between the system components. This section specifies the architecture of a framework – InSilicoLab – that uses this communication model to build advanced Science Gateway solutions. It is composed of three layers:

- **Domain Layer** is the layer of contact with the user, providing specified tools for use in a concrete domain of science. These are usually exposed through a web portal to facilitate access from remote destinations. As responsible for the contact with the users, the Domain Layer has to assure maximum usefulness to them. Therefore, it operates only on actions and objects from the researchers domain or common to the research community – like Experiment, Analysis, Results, etc.
- **Mediation Layer** is responsible for performing the actions triggered in the user interfaces of the Domain Layer. The requests are handled with use of the InSilicoLab Core Services, that are able of interacting with the resources of the Resource Layer.
- **Resource Layer** is the layer of the computational and storage resources. The system interacts with these resources by calling resource-specific commands through the resource interfaces – e.g., submitting a computational job or saving entities to a database. The Workers (labelled with 'W' in the picture Fig. 2) reside on the members of this layer, serving as an additional interface for contact from the Core Services.

The user interaction with the system is realised through components of a Science Gateway (in the Domain Layer). It is responsible for taking the user input and sending it to the components of the Mediation Layer. They, in turn, translate

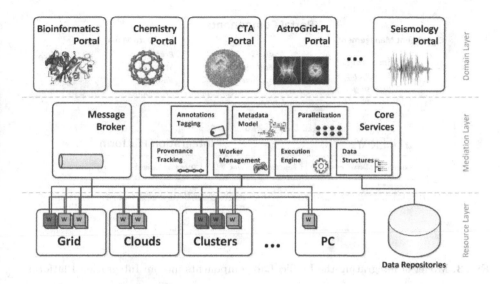

Fig. 2. Architecture of the InSilicoLab framework: Domain Layer, Mediation Layer with its Core Services, and Resource Layer. In the Resource Layer, Workers ('W') of different kinds (marked with different colors) are shown.

this request to task descriptions (in case of triggering a computation) or other messages (e.g. abort request message or response to an input request issued by a worker) and dispatch them to the appropriate queue. On the Resource Layer the workers process the messages compatible with their capabilities, and, whenever they need to communicate with the user or the system, they submit a message to another (or the same – depending on the communication purpose) queue. The Mediation Layer decides what should be further done with the message and, if needed, communicates it to the Domain Layer, which displays it correctly to the user.

The design of the framework makes it independent of the underlying infrastructure as customized workers may be deployed on any computing resources. This could prove useful also in situations where licensing issues prevent the researchers from running computations (with use of a proprietary software) on other computers than their own.

5.2   Integration Platform

The framework architecture enables creating Web components customized to the needs of a specific research domain. They are usually integrated in a standalone portal for the domain, however, they may also be composed into a larger integration platform – e.g., a Liferay portal [8]. In such case, apart from the usual In-SilicoLab components (e.g. Experiment Management, Result Management, Data Management), the community would be able to use additional functionality provided by the integration platform – like Wiki pages, blogs, social networking,

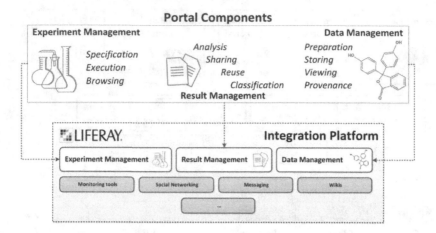

Fig. 3. Model of integrating the InSilicoLab components into an Integration Platform

etc. Furthermore, such platform as Liferay would also be capable of integrating more advanced services built for the research community – e.g. infrastructure monitoring service or other custom applications.

5.3   Science Gateway Instance Development Model

The most important aspect of developing a Science Gateway for a science community is understanding the way its researchers work. This is crucial to make the resulting solution useful and user-friendly. This cannot be done without analyzing the everyday work of a researcher, in order to extract common patterns, data flows and types, as well as tools they use. Having such knowledge, the work patterns can be recorded as science experiments understandable for a machine – algorithms. These algorithms become a base for the domain-related components required to create a new Science Gateway – i.e.: specialized workers, experiment logic (the algorithm of the experiment), and experiment-specific user interface.

The workers have a defined API and a set of utility methods they can use. Therefore, the development of a specialized worker requires only implementing several methods responsible for executing a domain application and transferring its results. The communication with the message queue, including serialization and deserialization of the messages, is implemented in the core classes each worker uses, therefore, it does not have to be separately handled by the worker developers. Likewise, communication with the Worker Manager, allowing for monitoring of the workers, is provided as a standard mechanism automatically included in each worker.

Experiment logic controls how the experiment is conducted – e.g., what operations are delegated to workers, what happens when a worker sends a reply or requests a user input. As in case of workers, this all can be implemented based on a common API and utility methods provided by Core Services of the Mediation Layer (see 5.1).

The last component of a new experiment in a Gateway is the user interface. It should provide forms for the experiment input, interaction with it, and the results display (e.g. tables, plots). Most of the user interface components – like input fields, upload forms, charts, etc. are provided with the InSilicoLab framework, therefore, for simpler experiments, the construction of the interface requires only to create a layout of a set of ready components.

To simplify the creation of a new Science Gateway, its developers are provided with a template project containing all the required components with empty methods to fill in with custom operations.

6   Current Status

This section provides information on the current status of the implementation of the framework itself as well as the status of development of gateways based on it.

6.1   Implementation Status

An implementation of the InSilicoLab framework architecture already resulted in several running gateway instances (see 6.2) – both exposed as standalone portals and as Liferay-integrated solutions. The implementation of the processing model was already tested for batch and immediate operations, with a proof-of-concept implementation of the mechanisms for interaction with the user.

The reference implementation uses Java-based workers, started manually and monitored through the message queue interface.

6.2   Running Instances

There are three production instances of gateways based on the InSilicoLab Science Gateway framework:

- CTA Science Gateway (http://cta-sg.grid.cyfronet.pl) – a portal for the Cherenkov Telescope Array community, integrated along with other CTA-specific services within Liferay. The gateway can be accessed by all CTA consortium members.
- InSilicoLab for Chemistry (http://insilicolab.grid.cyfronet.pl/) – a standalone portal for computational chemistry, featuring Quantum Chemistry experiments with the use of standard QC packages as well as a custom library for interactive management for Molecular Dynamics trajectories.
- InSilicoLab for Astrophysics (http://insilicolab.astro.plgrid.pl/) – a standalone portal for MHD simulations run by the community of astrophysicists in the PLGrid Plus project [9]. The portal was developed by one of the AstroGrid-PL scientists.

Three other Science Gateway instances are currently under development: a Thematic Node for Induced Seismicity for the EPOS project [10], and two portal instances for different communities in bioinformatics.

As the core components of the system are common to all gateway instances, the process of creating a new instance is simplified, and requires providing only domain-specific components (see also 5.3). Due to this fact, a new gateway instance can be created by domain experts, with only little help and guidance from the framework developers – which was already proved by InSilicoLab for Astrophysics and the Bioinformatics portals.

7   Related Work

This section describes other science gateway framework solutions (7.1) as well as works related to individual parts of the framework described in this paper.

7.1   Science Gateways and Science Gateway Frameworks

gUSE/WS-PGRADE and SCI-BUS. gUSE/WS-PGRADE (Grid And Cloud User Support Environment) is a science gateway framework developed by Laboratory of Parallel and Distributed Systems at MTA SZTAKI (http://www.lpds.sztaki.hu/) [11]. SCI-BUS (SCIentific gateway Based User Support) is a project aiming at providing a science gateway customization methodology based on gUSE/WS-PGRADE for different user communities and National Grid Infrastructures (NGIs) [12]. gUSE/WS-PGRADE provides a generic purpose, workflow-oriented graphical user interface to create and run workflows on various Distributed Computing Infrastructures (DCIs) including clusters, Grids, desktop Grids and Clouds. The technology is based on Liferay [8] and Liferay portlets, which enables it also to use the Liferay's community and social functionality.

The advantages of the system are undoubtedly large range of the supported DCIs and possibility to use and share common Liferay portlets. However, such tight integration with a portal technology might also be a disadvantage in the future. What is more, generality makes it relatively easy for a developer (a computer scientist) to create a new gateway in the gUSE/WS-PGRADE technology, however, still extremely difficult for a regular researcher (see e.g. [13]).

SCI-BUS offers also an extensive support for workflows, compatible with SHIWA [14], including interactive workflow nodes that enable users to have influence on the run of a workflow. Nevertheless, usually developing a priori workflows is not convenient for regular users – they would need help of workflow developers. What is more, interaction on the level of a workflow may not be enough, as the user would often like to interact with the computational job itself – thus, the requirement of interactivity is only partially met here and the framework allows only for broad range of batch operations.

Catania Science Gateway Framework. Catania Science Gateway Framework (CSGF) [15] is a tool for Science Gateway creation, developed by INFN, Division of Catania (Italy).

Like gUSE/WS-PGRADE, the Catania Science Gateway Framework is based on Liferay, however, the authors claim that the technology is compliant with JSR-168 [16] and JSR-268 [17] portlet standards – which could make the technology less Liferay (as specific solution) dependent. Nevertheless, as in case of gUSE/WS-PGRADE, CSGF's portal installation as well as portlet development is a process that only an application developer (not a researcher) can handle easily.

CSGF offers several authorization mechanisms, including SAML-compliant solutions as well as using one of the Social Networks account.

Unlike gUSE/WS-PGRADE, which use their custom layer – gUSE, the underlying technology of CSGF gateways for communication with DCIs is JSAGA [18], which makes the technology more standards-compliant.

The computing model of CSGF is very similar to the one of gUSE/WS-PGRADE, offering mainly batch processing with little interaction.

Apache Airavata. Apache Airavata is "a software framework for executing and managing computational jobs and workflows on distributed computing resources including local clusters, supercomputers, national Grids, academic and commercial Clouds" [19].

It provides a suite for building gateway solutions that are oriented mainly at workflow construction and execution. The framework is interoperable with many existing workflow standards. Nevertheless, as mentioned before, the mechanism of constructing workflows to run them later is difficult to realize by a regular scientist.

The architecture of the solution is based on Web Services communicating over SOAP protocol, what makes it a very flexible solution. However, in its current shape the framework is focused on heavy, large-scale applications, not implementing any support for lighter (instantaneous) operations, not mentioning any interactivity on the computation level.

7.2 Grid/Cloud Computing Frameworks

DIRAC. DIRAC (Distributed Infrastructure with Remote Agent Control) [20] is a software framework for distributed computing providing a level of abstraction above known middleware providing access to distributed resources – it is thus called Interware. DIRAC attempts to bridge some of the flaws of the existing middleware by providing a custom Workload Management System with Pilot Jobs, and therefore providing more reliability and efficiency of multi-job computations.

DIRAC provides also a custom file catalogue (DIRAC File Catalogue – DFC). The Catalogue proved to be more efficient [21] than the widely used LFC catalogue. DIRAC File Catalogue offers also metadata support, which largely improves its search capabilities and, as a consequence, its usability.

The DIRAC functionality is exposed through a command-line interface or through a web portal (http://dirac.ub.edu) as well as through a RESTful API. The portal provides functionality allowing for job and pilot control, file catalogue search, reporting, creating dashboards and many more. All DIRAC interfaces are job-oriented, which makes them difficult to use by a science community member with no knowledge about distributed computing. Creating job descriptions is largely facilitated in the DIRAC Web Portal, but, still, the users have to operate on scripts, files, servers, etc. instead of the concepts related to their research.

The range of the interfaces DIRAC provides, along with the advantages of the DFC catalogue and the system good reliability, makes it a good candidate to use as one of the means for running the workers of InSilicoLab, however, interaction of the computation with a user has to be provided by the InSilicoLab framework as DIRAC itself does not provide any support for such model of processing.

JSAGA. JSAGA [18] is an implementation of Simple API for Grid Applications (SAGA) [22], which is an attempt to provide a common interface for grid middleware. JSAGA can be used either as a command-line tool or as a library for a Java application. It offers a flexible mechanism of plugins (adaptors) that allows the users to include only the components that are required for a concrete application. The range of the available adaptors is large and still growing thanks to community support. It includes i.a. adaptors for different middleware like gLite, DIRAC and Unicore, as well as SSH and SFTP adapters.

JSAGA was already tested and used in InSilicoLab for access to the LFC catalogue and for submission of the workers. As DIRAC, it does not provide any means for interaction with a running job, but is a good candidate for submitting batch operations.

7.3 Specific GUIs

Another group of solutions related to the functionality that Science Gateways cover, are user interfaces provided only for a concrete science domain or even dedicated to a single application. They cannot be considered as broader frameworks, however, their interfaces can be used as a point of reference for the interfaces offered in gateways.

One of such solutions is WebMO [23] – a Web interface for computational chemistry packages – supporting several of them. It allows users to draw structures in a 3D java editor, run calculations, and view results from their web browser. Although the interface is very comprehensive as a tool for chemistry, it is not adjustable to other domains of science. Its more advanced features as well as the ability to compute larger systems are available only in commercial versions – WebMO Pro and Enterprise.

There are also many other Graphical User Interfaces supporting specific applications – like GaussView [24]. However, their use limits the user to only one application, not allowing to compare results or choose different computation method for the same input data.

8 Summary

Although the needs of different science communities are very different with respect to computing, they can be summarized by putting into several classes of processing patterns. To create a fully functional and intuitive to use processing model, all of these patterns have to be implemented. Without this, the resulting tools and frameworks for computing would serve only a limited set of research activities. InSilicoLab, on one hand, implements the processing model with consideration to all the aforementioned classes, and, on the other, provides a framework for creating domain- or community- specific gateways that enable the research communities to take advantage of this model with a specialized interface.

The framework was already used for development of several Science Gateways in different science domains.

References

1. The Nobel Prize in Chemistry (2013),
   http://www.nobelprize.org/nobel_prizes/chemistry/laureates/2013/
2. Eilmes, A., Sterzel, M., Szepieniec, T., Kocot, J., Noga, K., Golik, M.: Comprehensive Support for Chemistry Computations in PL-Grid Infrastructure. In: Bubak, M., Kitowski, J., Wiatr, K. (eds.) PLGrid Plus. LNCS, vol. 8500, pp. 250–262. Springer, Heidelberg (2014)
3. Kocot, J., Szepieniec, T., Harężlak, D., Noga, K., Sterzel, M.: InSilicoLab – Managing Complexity of Chemistry Computations. In: Bubak, M., Szepieniec, T., Wiatr, K. (eds.) PL-Grid 2011. LNCS, vol. 7136, pp. 265–275. Springer, Heidelberg (2012)
4. The Cherenkov Telescope Array project web site,
   http://www.cta-observatory.org/
5. Gromacs web site, http://www.gromacs.org/
6. Protein Data Bank, http://www.pdb.org/
7. Fielding, R.: Architectural Styles and the Design of Network-based Software Architectures, dissertation. Chapter 5 (2000)
8. Liferay portal web site, http://www.liferay.com/
9. PLGrid Plus project web site, http://www.plgrid.pl/projekty/plus
10. EPOS web site, http://www.epos-eu.org/
11. gUSE web site, http://guse.hu
12. SCI-BUS project web site, http://www.sci-bus.eu/
13. Gottdank, T.: Cookbook for Gateway Developers. Solutions and Examples for Advanced Usage and Development of gUSE Components and Related Programming Interfaces (2013)
14. SHIWA web site, http://www.shiwa-workflow.eu/
15. Catania Science Gateways web site, http://www.catania-science-gateways.it/
16. JSR 168: Portlet Specification, https://jcp.org/en/jsr/detail?id=168
17. JSR 286: Portlet Specification 2.0, https://jcp.org/en/jsr/detail?id=286
18. JSAGA web site, http://grid.in2p3.fr/jsaga/
19. Apache Airavata web site, http://airavata.apache.org/
20. DIRAC web site, http://diracgrid.org/

21. Tsaregorodtsev, A., Poss, S.: DIRAC File Replica and Metadata Catalog. In: International Conference on Computing in High Energy and Nuclear Physics 2012 (CHEP 2012). Journal of Physics: Conference Series 396, 032108. IOP Publishing (2012), doi:10.1088/1742-6596
22. Goodale, T., Jha, S., Kaiser, H., Kielmann, T., Kleijer, P., Merzky, A., Shalf, J., Smith, C.: A Simple API for Grid Applications, SAGA (2013),
http://www.ogf.org/documents/GFD.90.pdf
23. WebMO web site, http://www.webmo.net/index.html
24. GaussView web site, http://www.gaussian.com/g_prod/gv5.htm

Easy Development and Integration of Science Gateways with Vine Toolkit

Krzysztof Kurowski, Piotr Dziubecki, Piotr Grabowski, Michał Krysiński,
Tomasz Piontek, and Dawid Szejnfeld

Poznan Supercomputing and Networking Center, Poznań, Poland
{krzysztof.kurowski,deepres,piotrg,mich,piontek,dejw}@man.poznan.pl
http://www.man.poznan.pl

Abstract. Science Gateway is a set of tools for scientists to facilitate access to their computational resources in a comprehensive, efficient and easy manner. The most common instance of Science Gateway comes in the form of a web portal. It provides space for communities, collaboration, data sharing and visualization along with the possibility of defining, running and managing computational tasks. The main objective of such a portal is to allow users to access the computational resources, to process and analyze their data and to obtain results in a uniform and user friendly way. In this publication we briefly describe solutions for Nanomechanics, Quantum Chemistry and Molecular Physics fields with the use of Vine Toolkit and QosCosGrid tools and different domain-specific applications.

Keywords: Science Gateway, portal, Web2.0, Vine Toolkit, Lammps, NanoMD, SIMPL, Anelli, workflow, nanomechanics, advance reservations, QosCosGrid, monitoring.

1 Introduction

The advanced web-based graphic and multimedia oriented user interfaces designed for scientists and engineers can change the way users collaborate, share computing experiments and data, and work together to solve day-to-day problems. Moreover, future science and engineering gateways will influence the way users will not only access their data, but also control and monitor their demanding computing simulations. To allow users to interact remotely with supercomputers and large-scale computing environments in a more interactive and visual manner, we present a tool called Vine Toolkit that has been successfully used as a core web platform for various Science Gateways up to now [1,2,3,4]. Vine Toolkit is a modular, extensible and easy-to-use tool as well as high-level Application Programming Interface (API) for various applications, visualization components and building blocks to allow interoperability between many different HPC and grid technologies. Currently, the following modules, plugins and support for standards are available in Vine Toolkit:

- job submission and monitoring: QosCosGrid 3.0, Unicore 6, gLite3, GRIA 5.3, Globus Toolkit 4.0.x, 4.2.1 [5,6,7,8,9,10,11],

M. Bubak et al. (Eds.): PLGrid Plus, LNCS 8500, pp. 147–163, 2014.
© Springer International Publishing Switzerland 2014

- data access and management: iRODS, Storage Resource Broker, Storage Resource Manager, OGSA-DAI 2.2 [12,13,14],
- supported standards and services: BES, JSDL, RUS, Active Directory [15,16,17,18].

Moreover, it supports Adobe Flex and BlazeDS technologies in order to allow developers to create advanced and rich web applications similar to many stand-alone Graphical User Interfaces (GUIs). Additionally, Vine Toolkit has been integrated with well-known open source web frameworks such as Liferay and Gridsphere [19]. In the PL-Grid [20] and PLGrid Plus [21] projects, Vine Toolkit is tightly coupled with the QosCosGrid middleware. The QosCosGrid (QCG) middleware is an integrated system offering advanced job and resource management capabilities to deliver to end-users supercomputer-like performance and structure. By connecting many distributed computing resources together, QCG offers highly efficient mapping, execution and monitoring capabilities for a variety of applications, such as parameter sweep, workflows, MPI or hybrid MPI-OpenMP. Thanks to QosCosGrid, large-scale applications, multi-scale or complex computing models written in Fortran, C, C++ or Java can be automatically distributed over a network of computing resources with a guaranteed quality of service. The middleware provides also a set of unique features, such as advance reservation and co-allocation of distributed computing resources.

In this article, we briefly describe new technological solutions relevant to advanced scientific and engineering portals driven by various requirements defined by scientists, which we identified in the PL-Grid project. The rest of this article is organized as follows. In Section 2 there is presented related work in the area of Science Gateways and Science Gateway frameworks. In Section 3 we briefly describe our main motivations. Then, in Sections 4, 5 and 6 there are short descriptions of the used software, developed Scientific Applications and QCG Portal tools. Finally, in Section 7 there is a summary and information about future works.

2   Related Work

Currently, there are several approaches to the Science Gateway concept. There is a group of frameworks facilitating the design and creation of Science Gateways, there are also portals up and running ready to be used by the scientists. Among the tools available that help users to create advanced Science Gateways, P-GRADE is a good example of parallel application development system for the Grid and clusters [22]. It uses Globus, Condor-G, ARC, BOINC and MPICH-G2 as grid-aware middleware to conduct computations. The latest P-GRADE version, namely WS-PGRADE allows for cloud dispatching and similarly to Vine Toolkit offers Liferay portal container Graphical User Interface. EnginFrame is another good example of a web-based front-end for simple job submission, tracking and integrated data management for HPC applications and other services [23]. EnginFrame can be easily plugged on several different schedulers or grid middleware like: Platform LSF, Sun Grid Engine, PBS, or gLite middleware.

A slightly different approach to build an API providing the basic functionality required to build distributed applications is SAGA [24] – it focuses on delivering a set of programming interfaces covering the functionality of the HPC-aware application. Unfortunately, it does not provide a GUI support needed to create easy-to-use Science Gateways (see a comparison of Vine Toolkit and SAGA in Table 1).

Table 1. SAGA vs Vine Toolkit comparison

Middleware	Vine Toolkit	SAGA – Java adaptors
gLite 3 – Cream	Yes	Yes – JSAGA
gLite 3 – WMS	Yes	Yes – JSAGA
gLite 3 – JDL	Yes	under development – JSAGA
Globus Toolkit	Yes (4.0.x, 4.2.1)	Yes – JSAGA/JavaGAT
Globus Toolkit – MyProxy	Yes	Yes – JSAGA
Globus Toolkit – gsiftp	Yes	Yes – JSAGA
Globus Toolkit – WS-GRAM	Yes	Yes – JSAGA
BES	Yes	Yes – JSAGA
JSDL	Yes	Yes – JSAGA
GRIA	Yes (5.3)	No
Unicore 6	Yes	Yes – JSAGA
Active Directory	Yes	No
Java Keystore	Yes	Yes – JSAGA
X509 Certificates	Yes	Yes – JSAGA
Storage Resource Manager	Yes	Yes – JSAGA
Storage Resource Broker	Yes	Yes – JSAGA
(S)FTP, SSH, HTTP(S), ZIP	Partly (http, SSH applet)	Yes – JSAGA/JavaGAT
local data management	Yes	Yes – JSAGA
WebDav	Yes	No
VOMS	Yes	Yes – JSAGA
iRODS	Yes	Yes – JSAGA
NAREGI (Super Scheduler)	No	Yes – JSAGA
OGSA-DAI	Yes (2.2)	No
RUS	Yes	No
QosCosGrid 3.0	Yes	No
Nagios Monitoring Service	Yes	No

Fortunately, apart from the development environments, there are also several sites offering access to many specialist applications for the scientists directly. A good example of well-established Science Gateway is nanohub.org [25]. Its main purpose is to deliver tools, materials and helping with the education, research and collaboration in nanotechnology. According to the statistics provided by the nanohub.org site, there are over 10,000 simulation users and over 50,000 interactive users. That is the result of the wide range of nanotechnology applications and simulation/visualization available in the portal. Regarding the technical details, the web interface serves as a proxy between the remotely installed application and the end user. In order to achieve this, a Java applet with VNC plugin is used to connect the user to a remote GUI of the desired application. The next step in building Science Gateways in United States has been performed in the iPlant Foundation Agave API [26] and DNA Gateway agaveapi.co. Agave is a science-as-a-service platform for enabling the next generation of Science Gateways. Agave runs in the cloud as a hosted, multi-tenant service, so there is no need to install anything. It allows users to define their own compute and storage resources, so one can interact with the resources he/she has, as well as the ones Agave provides. Gateway DNA is a set of web-based components that run entirely within a web browser and provide access to all the core functionality of the Agave API. Another example is a collaborative environment where scientists can safely publish their workflows and experiment plans, share them with groups and find those of others, called myExperiment.org [27]. In this approach, workflows, other digital objects and bundles (called Packs) can now be swapped, sorted and searched like photos and videos on the Web. Unlike Facebook or MySpace, myExperiment fully understands the needs of the researcher and makes it really easy for the next generation of scientists to contribute to a pool of scientific methods, build communities and form relationships – reducing time-to experiment, sharing expertise and avoiding reinvention.

More comprehensive lists of available Science Gateways and Science Gateway frameworks can be found at EGI Applications Database [28] and XSEDE Science Gateways Listing [29].

3   Motivations

In this section, we briefly discuss our main achievements during the development and deployment phase of new Science Gateways. All achievements in the process of building Science Gateways are based on close collaboration with end-users conducting advanced Nanomechanics, Quantum Chemistry and Molecular Physics research in Poland. One of the main goals of the Science Gateway for nanomechanics was to integrate in one place all tools employed in the field of subtractive and erosion manufacturing with standard simulation tools used in nanotechnology and nanomechanics. To shorten the time needed for the development of a completely new portal, we use technologies and tools prepared within the scope of the PL-Grid project: the aforementioned Vine Toolkit and QosCosGrid middleware. The list of applications proposed by nanomechanics scientists from Gdansk University of Technology to be covered in the first release of the portal consists of the well-known LAMMPS Molecular Dynamics Simulator, NanoMD molecular dynamics code developed in Gdańsk, SIMPL and Anelli codes used to submit sophisticated nanomechanics workflows in Kepler system. There was a shortage of portal solutions for accessing QosCosGrid services for Advance Reservation, Monitoring and Data Management within Quantum Chemistry and Molecular Physics. Also in these cases Vine Toolkit was a technology of choice to quickly build services needed by users.

4 Software Used and PLGrid Plus Implementation

Starting from the top of the Vine Toolkit software stack (see Fig. 1), it provides an efficient and robust user interface framework based on the Adobe Flex and BlazeDs software.

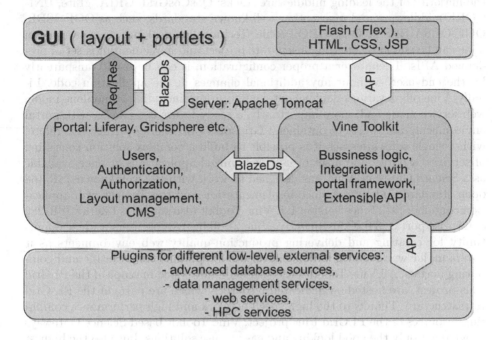

Fig. 1. Portal with Vine Toolkit generic schema

Vine allows for integration of the rich internet application standard directly to a browser and enables applications to act and look exactly as their stand-alone versions. Thus, it is possible to create advanced portal applications like Science Gateways where developers can create web-based versions of many legacy applications and their GUIs. One of the key new requirements for Vine Toolkit, regarding the integration with existing portal frameworks, was to enable web application developers to create rich and advanced user interfaces as quickly as possible. Initially, we tried to use JS/AJAX-based frameworks within Vine Toolkit. Various problems related to the software portability in different web browsers encouraged us to migrate to other frameworks for the development and deployment of cross-platform rich Internet applications. Eventually, Adobe Flex was chosen for developing rich and advanced user interfaces in Vine Toolkit. The main reason was the fact that at the time of the project's inception, Microsoft Silverlight was far behind Flex in terms of functionality [30]. Also, the licensing favored Flex, which is open source. On the other hand, the browser native solution HTML5, which still is far behind in terms of popularity and browser support, was not available those days. Obviously, the presentation layer is a front end to various components and services provided by Vine Toolkit, but it is getting more and more important once advanced web applications are available. Thanks to a pluggable Vine architecture it is possible to extend its base functionality in a uniform way. For instance, at the beginning Vine Toolkit offered only a support for the Globus Toolkit middleware. Currently, it is possible to use the majority of the leading middleware stacks: QosCosGrid, GRIA, gLite, UNI-CORE middleware and many other well-known standards, such as OGF JSDL, OGF OGSA-BES or OGF-HPC Profile. Technically speaking, a new service in Vine can be added by creating a separate project and implementing a set of pre-defined APIs. Then, after a proper configuration, it can be used transparently by the end user, without any additional changes in the application code. Finally, Vine offers various deployment configurations including standalone mode, web service mode and, more importantly, a ready to use integration with portal environments and portlet containers: Gridsphere or Liferay [31,32]. Therefore, with a single software stack it is possible to build a complex solution consisting of services, a portal and a set of user-customized applications at once available as a Science Gateway. Vine was designed to work with the well-known JSR-168 open standard and its reference implementation and the Tomcat web application container [33]. Since version 1.1, Vine Toolkit also supports Liferay JSR-286 enterprise portal [34]. Consequently, Vine Toolkit gives its users a great opportunity for creating and delivering production-quality web environments as it covers major web-based development aspects, especially for scientific and computing portals. All Vine Toolkit based services, developed in scope of the PLGrid Plus project, are hosted on dedicated resources, which are parts of the PL-Grid Infrastructure. Thanks to the high speed network and high performance computing resources of the PLGrid Plus project, Vine Toolkit based Science Gateways provide not only the good looking and easy to use solutions, but also the highest available in Poland speed of computations.

5   Scientific Applications

The most advanced part of our Science Gateway for nanomechanics research consists of four web-based interfaces for scientific applications: LAMMPS [35], NanoMD [36], SIMPL [37] and Anelli [38]. LAMMPS is a classical molecular dynamics code, and an acronym for Large-scale Atomic/Molecular Massively Parallel Simulator. LAMMPS has potentials for soft materials (biomolecules, polymers) and solid-state materials (metals, semiconductors) and coarse-grained or mesoscopic systems. It can be used to model atoms or, more generically, as a parallel particle simulator at the atomic, meso-, or continuum scale. NanoMD is a molecular dynamics code developed by PL-Grid scientists in Gdańsk. SIMPL and Anelli codes are used to submit sophisticated nanomechanics workflows in the Kepler system. Anelli is used in ring statistics of numerically simulated materials, it allows for characteristics of mid-range order. SIMPL allows for short-range order characteristics using Voronoi polyhedra analyses. LAMMPS, as a command-line tool, requires from the user not only domain-specific knowledge, but also experiences with LAMMPS in/out data structures. Moreover, in case of parallel or large scale deployment, the user has to be familiar with many complex IT and HPC technologies. In order to hide the complexity, we successfully developed a web-based collaborative access to LAMMPS, using Vine Toolkit and Adobe Flex [39]. Consequently, we are able to support the fully transparent web based access to parallel LAMMPS executions deployed on computing clusters in the PL-Grid Infrastructure. Instead of using SSH, file transfer protocols, or other tools, users can manage even complex simulation and data operations using web browsers. One should note that the inputs needed for LAMMPS job submission are coordinates files. Using another web-based tool, Vine Toolkit File Manager, users can easily access, copy and assign appropriate files that are stored on remote machines. What is even more important, the user is able to visualize data in the Science Gateway immediately after this simulation is completed. An example layout of the LAMMPS web application is presented in the Fig. 2. The example case consists of 4 parallel executions of LAMMPS using MPI processes on eight cores.

Another application, which was identified to be useful for nanomechanics, is NanoMD. NanoMD, like the aforementioned LAMMPS, is Molecular Dynamics code and similarly to LAMMPS is a command line application. Taking into consideration that both applications are used in the nearly same scope, we

Fig. 2. Web-based interface for LAMMPS simulation

decided to develop the NanoMD web application and LAMMPS web application as parts of larger entity, namely the Molecular Dynamics application. Graphical User Interface of the final solution is based on the work already done during the development of the ABINIT [40,41] simulator web application that was prepared in the scope of the PL-Grid project and described in [1]. In this approach, all user tasks are leafs of a four tier tree structure. The root of the tree is always the application itself (LAMMPS or NanoMD). The user can define cases – the tree branches. Each case, like a folder in filesystem, may contain many user computational jobs, each job is a group of computational tasks representing the parallel jobs submitted to the middleware. All information about the defined and executed task are stored in the portal database for further reuse. The same applies to the application results, however a larger content is stored only as a reference to files in the underlying Grid. In Fig. 3 there is presented the NanoMD and LAMMPS case manager window, from which the user may choose the stored jobs to be a base for the new submission.

Obviously, it is possible to create a new job from scratch, however, in most cases users have similar executions where only some parameters are changed, therefore the functionality of reusing the old job descriptions is highly desired by the user.

Fig. 3. NanoMD Case Manager layout

Once the user has defined his/her job with setting appropriate submission parameters for all tasks of the job, defined input files and set up domain specific attributes, he/she pushes the submit button. The simulation is submitted to the Grid through the QosCosGrid Broker, thus the user doesn't have to possess knowledge about the available resources. QosCosGrid broker checks all PL-Grid clusters for machine with the installed base application (NanoMD or LAMMPS packages) and chooses the least busy one. During the scheduling phase, the machines are also checked to meet the required resources amount. After the job is submitted, information about the execution in the form of a progress bar and text status is presented. Once the job is finished, the results section of the application is activated and the user can view or download the application results.

Anelli is another set of command line applications developed by nanomechanics from Gdansk University of Technology. In all the previous applications the workflow building mechanism provided by QosCosGrid Broker was sufficient. However, in the case of Anelli the workflow of applications being used is so complicated that the use of a dedicated workflow framework was feasible. The Kepler [42] framework has been chosen as the most sophisticated solution. As stated above, the Anelli web application like the Anelli package is used in the ring statistics of numerically simulated materials, it allows to build characteristics of mid-range order. The parameters of the whole workflow can be set in one simple form and similarly as in the previous cases the user does not have to contend with the grid related details and complexity of underlying services. In Fig. 4 there is presented the main form of the Anelli web application.

The last domain specific application being developed in the scope of the Nanomechanics Science Gateway is SIMPL. SIMPL allows for building short-range order characteristics using Voronoi polyhedra analyses. SIMPL requires from the scientists preparing complicated input files containing many execution param-

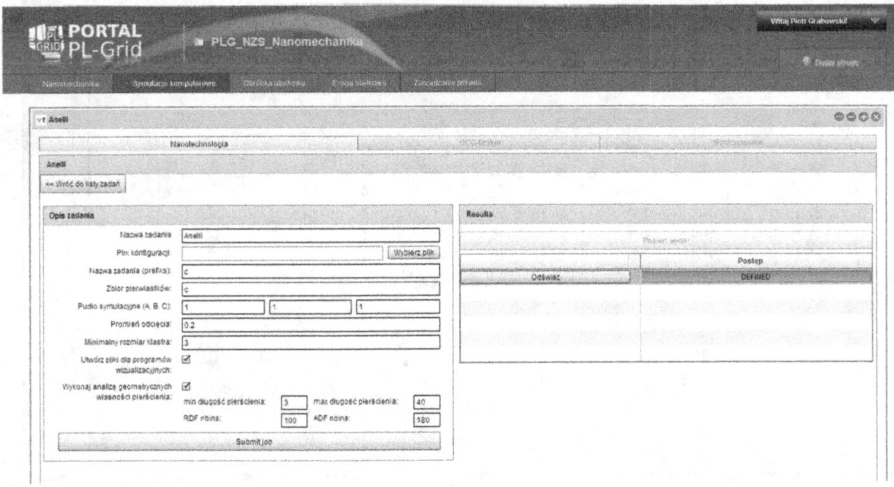

Fig. 4. Anelli web application main window layout

eters. The structure of the document is very strict and forces the user of the command line tool to remember which section, which order and which parameter fields should be used. Once again the portal tool is able to prepare such an input structure for the computational job after the user fills several tabs of data. For users who may be a little bit overwhelmed by the amount of the needed parameter fields to fill, there is prepared a helper application (prepareXYZ) that loads the coordinates file and saves the file needed by SIMPL. This conversion task is not submitted to the Grid – instead in Vine Toolkit we use a local submission mechanism, which launches prepareXYZ locally on the portal machine. The results are then used to initially fill the Analysis form fields. The filled-in Analysis tab of SIMPL is presented in Fig. 5.

Once the Analysis data is prepared, the user has to decide, which contraction method should be used. Additional possibilities available for the user before the job submission are requesting SIMPL diagrams, potentials files (PDB) and Common Neighbour Analysis (CNA) preparation. After the user submitted the SIMPL job to the Grid, he/she can watch the job status. From the user's perspective, everything up to this moment is done in the SIMPL web application. Once the job is finished, the user can download SIMPL output, together with requested diagrams, PDB and CNA files.

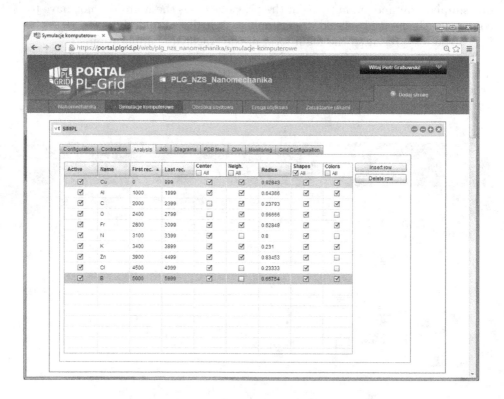

Fig. 5. SIMPL web application example tabs

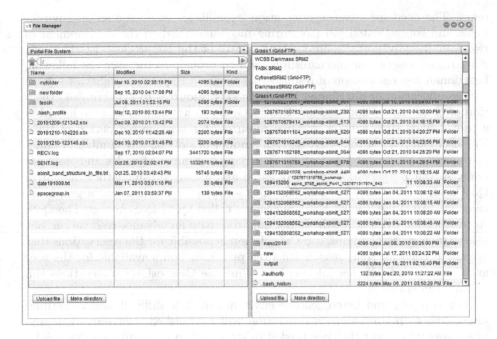

Fig. 6. Vine Toolkit File Manager using Single Sign-On

The Science Gateway for Nanomechanics consists of two kinds of components available to the logged-in user: standard Vine Toolkit components for user registration and login, file management and specialized components designed for Nanomechanics environments. Both component groups are designed according to the specific rules of grid portal design, based on the work in the BEinGrid project [45]. One of the most important portal design rule is incorporating Single Sign-On mechanism: it is fully supported in our Science Gateway based on Vine Toolkit – the user has to authenticate himself/herself only once, during the login procedure, then all credentials needed for accessing external services are used by the portal in the name of the user automatically. It means that even if the user needs to access files on remote hosts with the application input/output file manager, the process of authentication is performed entirely by the portal. The same applies to the Science Gateway File Manager application (see Fig. 6).

For the ease of use, it consists of two panels (each for one storage resource), the user can perform all the standard file operations (e.g. copy files with drag and drop between panels, delete, create folders, change names, download or upload files) without a need to authenticate himself/herself again – the only thing to do by the user is to choose an appropriate resource.

6   QosCosGrid Portal Tools

Another set of web applications was prepared in cooperation with scientists from Quantum Chemistry and Molecular Physics fields and core QosCosGrid

team. The need for advance reservation capabilities in a production environment and sophisticated job monitoring mechanism led to the development of
two user friendly portal solutions being parts of the larger QosCosGrid stack.
An advance reservation mechanism is used to provide to the user the following
functionalities: reservation of resources to ensure a requested quality of service
and co-allocation of distributed heterogeneous resources to synchronize execution of cross-cluster applications. QosCosGrid can automatically search, within
a user-defined time window, for free resources for a requested period of time.
The user can request to reserve a given number of slots on any number of nodes
or request a particular topology by specifying a number of nodes and slots per
node. Advance reservations can be created and managed using either the native
QosCosGrid command-line tool (the QCG-SimpleClient client) or a graphical,
calendar like, Vine Toolkit web application called QCG-QoS-Access. The QoS-
Access portlet (see Fig. 7) allows not only to create an advance reservation, but
also to manage reservations, e.g. Cancelation is possible for the reservations that
are not needed for some reason, thus the processor hours available for the user
grant are spared. Further information about the QosCosGrid reservations can
be found in [43].

In a complex and heterogeneous environment it is difficult and sometimes
impossible to predict when a simulation will be finished. Different loads and
processors type affect the time needed to start and run a simulation. Especially

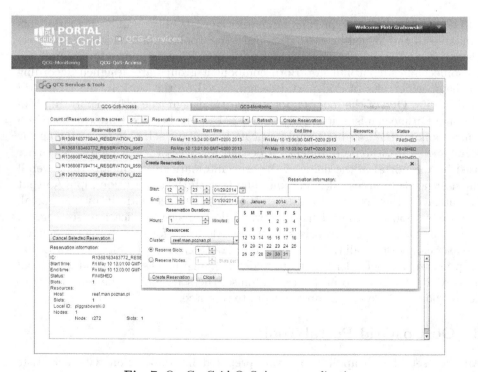

Fig. 7. QosCosGrid QoS-Access application

for long-running simulations, it is important to know if the execution is performed properly and if the produced partial results are correct to avoid aimless consumption of resources. For the user who needs to know when the simulation is finished or what percent of the task is done, QosCosGrid offers a Notification mechanism. There are two kinds of notifications: information about changes in a job status and notifications with an application result's excerpt. Job status information is presented in all Vine Toolkit based web applications for scientists. The application's excerpt notifications may be sent directly to users via e-mail or XMPP protocol, or alternatively, forwarded to the QCG-Monitoring service. The QCG-Monitoring web application being part of the QCG Tools and Services portal allows the user to view QCG-Monitoring service information. The application progress is displayed in a graphical way in form of a set of tables and charts in accordance to a predefined template. Users can select from a set of general-purpose templates, but also can utilize templates for quantum chemistry and astrophysics applications that has been prepared in cooperation with domain-oriented researchers. Fig. 8 presents an example content served for Gaussian application. Further information about the QosCosGrid notifications can be found in [44].

Following the user request for building easy to use mechanism for acquiring user grid credentials, the Credential Manager module existing in Vine Toolkit has been extended by PL-Grid KeyFS support. Instead of using Java-Webstart

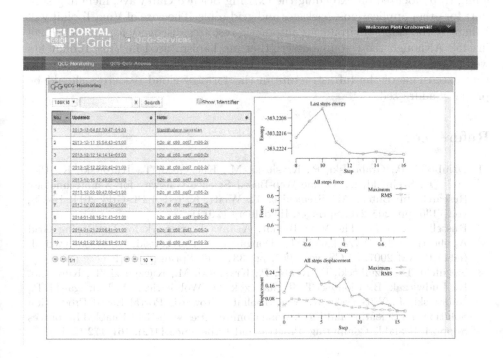

Fig. 8. QosCosGrid Monitoring application

Certificate Manager to upload a user proxy certificate to Vine Toolkit repository, the proxy certificate is produced in KeyFS enabled resource and copied over the secured channel to the portal repository. From the user's perspective, this process can be completely hidden – the credential is copied in the background at the login to the portal. The user only has to remember to export his/her certificate to KeyFS, which can be easily done from the main PL-Grid portal. This functionality has been initially introduced in QCG Tools and Services portal, however, other users of Vine Toolkit and users of Nanomechanics Gateway found it very convenient and the solution is working now for all Vine Toolkit based portals in PL-Grid.

7   Summary and Future Work

Science Gateways for Nanotechnology, Nanomechanics, Quantum Chemistry and Molecular Physics based on Vine Toolkit and QosCosGrid are available for PL-Grid users. In the scope of the Science Gateways, engineers and scientists can find domain specific applications together with visualization and middleware tools. The current list of applications consists of: ABINIT, Quantum Espresso, LAMMPS, NanoMD, SIMPL, Anneli, NAMD, NWChem, accompanied by specialized QosCosGrid services for Monitoring, Advance Reservation and Data Management. The future work on the Vine Toolkit-based Science Gateways is going to be focused on extending the existing Science Gateways, including support for other applications, packages and grid tools. The core of Vine Toolkit will benefit of the cloud environment automatic resource discovery feature described in [45]. Although the resource description mechanism used in Vine Toolkit fits well to the existing PL-Grid Infrastructure or small cloud environments, the future extensions of the Infrastructure in the form of cloud resources should be properly addressed.

References

1. Dziubecki, P., Grabowski, P., Krysiński, M., Kuczyński, T., Kurowski, K., Piontek, T., Szejnfeld, D.: Online Web-Based Science Gateway for Nanotechnology Research. In: Bubak, M., Szepieniec, T., Wiatr, K. (eds.) PL-Grid 2011. LNCS, vol. 7136, pp. 205–216. Springer, Heidelberg (2012)
2. Russell, M., et al.: The Vine Toolkit: A Java Framework for Developing Grid Applications. In: Wyrzykowski, R., Dongarra, J., Karczewski, K., Wasniewski, J. (eds.) PPAM 2007. LNCS, vol. 4967, pp. 331–340. Springer, Heidelberg (2008)
3. Szejnfeld, D., Dziubecki, P., Kopta, P., Krysinski, M., Kuczynski, T., Kurowski, K., Ludwiczak, B., Piontek, T., Tarnawczyk, D., Wolniewicz, M., Domagalski, P., Nabrzyski, J., Witkowski, K.: Vine Toolkit – Towards Portal Based Production Solutions for Scientific and Engineering Communities with Grid-Enabled Resources Support. Scalable Computing: Practice and Experience 11(2), 161–172 (2011)

4. Dziubecki, P., Grabowski, P., Krysinski, M., Kuczynski, T., Kurowski, K., Szejn-feld, D.: Nano-Science Gateway development with Vine Toolkit and Adobe Flex. In: Barbera, R., Andronico, G., La Rocca, G. (eds.) Proceedings of the International Worshop on Science Gateways (IWSG 2010). Consorzio COMETA, Catania (2010)

5. Agullo, E., Coti, C., Herault, T., Langou, J., Peyronnet, S., Rezmerita, A., Cappello, F., Dongarra, J.: QCG-OMPI: MPI applications on grids. Future Generation Computer Systems 27(4), 357–369 (2011), doi:10.1016/j.future.2010.11.015, ISSN 0167-739X

6. Kurowski, K., Piontek, T., Kopta, P., Mamoński, M., Bosak, B.: Parallel Large Scale Simulations in the PL-Grid Environment. Computational Methods in Science and Technology Special Issue, 47–56 (2010)

7. Kurowski, K., de Back, W., Dubitzky, W., Gulyás, L., Kampis, G., Mamonski, M., Szemes, G., Swain, M.: Complex System Simulations with QosCosGrid. In: Allen, G., Nabrzyski, J., Seidel, E., van Albada, G.D., Dongarra, J., Sloot, P.M.A. (eds.) ICCS 2009, Part I. LNCS, vol. 5544, pp. 387–396. Springer, Heidelberg (2009), doi:10.1007/978-3-642-01970-8_38

8. Streit, A., Bala, P., Beck-Ratzka, A., Benedyczak, K., Bergmann, S., Breu, R., Daivandy, J.M., Demuth, B., Eifer, A., Giesler, A., Hagemeier, B., Holl, S., Huber, V., Lamla, N., Mallmann, D., Memon, A.S., Memon, M.S., Rambadt, M., Riedel, M., Romberg, M., Schuller, B., Schlauch, T., Schreiber, A., Soddemann, T., Ziegler, W.: UNICORE 6 – Recent and Future Advancements. JUEL-4319 (2010) ISSN 0944-2952

9. gLite 3, http://glite.cern.ch/introduction (accessed April 10, 2014)

10. GRIA 5.3, http://www.gria.org/about-gria/overview (accessed April 10, 2014)

11. Foster, I.: Globus Toolkit Version 4: Software for Service-Oriented Systems. In: Jin, H., Reed, D., Jiang, W. (eds.) NPC 2005. LNCS, vol. 3779, pp. 2–13. Springer, Heidelberg (2005)

12. Moor, R.: Towards a Theory of Digital Preservation. The International Journal of Digital Curation 1(3) (2008)

13. Rajasekar, A., Wan, M., Moore, R., Schroeder, W., Kremenek, G., Jagatheesan, A., Cowart, C., Zhu, B., Chen, S., Olschanowsky, R.: Storage Resource Broker Managing Distributed Data in a Grid. Computer Society of India Journal, Special Issue on SAN 33(4), 42–54 (2003)

14. Antonioletti, M., Atkinson, M.P., Baxter, R., Borley, A., Chue Hong, N.P., Collins, B., Hardman, N., Hume, A., Knox, A., Jackson, M., Krause, A., Laws, S., Magowan, J., Paton, N.W., Pearson, D., Sugden, T., Watson, P., Westhead, M.: The Design and Implementation of Grid Database Services in OGSA-DAI. Concurrency and Computation: Practice and Experience 17(2-4), 357–376 (2005)

15. Foster, I., Grimshaw, A., Lane, P., Lee, W., Morgan, M., Newhouse, S., Pickles, S., Pulsipher, D., Smith, C., Theimer, M.: Open Grid Services Architecture Basic Execution Service, Version 1.0, GFD-R.108 (2008), http://www.ggf.org/documents/GFD.108.pdf

16. Anjomshoaa, A., Brisard, F., Drescher, M., Fellows, D., Ly, A., McGough, S., Pulsipher, D., Savva, A.: Job Submission Description Language (JSDL) Specification, Version 1.0, GFD-R.056 (2005), http://www.ggf.org/documents/GFD.56.pdf

17. OGSA Resource Usage Service, http://forge.ggf.org/sf/projects/rus-wg

18. Microsoft's Active Directory, http://www.microsoft.com/windowsserver2008/en/us/active-directory.aspx (accessed April 10, 2014)

19. Oleksiak, A., Tullo, A., Graham, P., Kuczynski, T., Nabrzyski, J., Szejnfeld, D., Sloan, T.: HPC-Europa single point of access as a framework for building science gateways: Research Articles. Concurrency and Computation: Practice & Experience 19(6), 851–866 (2007)
20. Bubak, M., Szepieniec, T., Wiatr, K. (eds.): PL-Grid 2011. LNCS, vol. 7136. Springer, Heidelberg (2012)
21. PLGrid Plus project web site, http://www.plgrid.pl/en/projects/plus (accessed April 10, 2014)
22. P-GRADE, http://www.p-grade.hu/ (accessed April 10, 2014)
23. EnginFrame, http://www.nice-software.com/web/nice/products/enginframe (accessed April 10, 2014)
24. Goodale, T., Jha, S., Kaiser, H., Kielmann, T., Kleijer, P., von Laszewski, G., Lee, C., Merzky, A., Rajic, H., Shalf, J.: SAGA: A Simple API for Grid applications, High-Level Application Programming on the Grid. Computational Methods in Science and Technology 12(1) (2006)
25. Klimeck, G., McLennan, M., Brophy, S.P., Adams III, G.B., Lundstrom, M.S.: nanoHUB.org: Advancing Education and Research in Nanotechnology. Computing in Science and Engineering 10(5), 17–23 (2008), doi:10.1109/MCSE.2008.120
26. Dooley, R., et al.: Software-as-a-Service: The iPlant Foundation API. In: 5th IEEE Workshop on Many-Task Computing on Grids and Supercomputers (MTAGS). IEEE (2012)
27. myExperiment, http://www.myexperiment.org/ (accessed April 10, 2014)
28. EGI Applications Database, https://appdb.egi.eu/store/software/ (accessed April 10, 2014)
29. XSEDE Science Gateways Listing, https://www.xsede.org/gateways-listing (accessed April 10, 2014)
30. Microsoft Silverlight, http://www.silverlight.net/ (accessed April 10, 2014)
31. Gridsphere, http://gridlab.org/Resources/Deliverables/B4.pdf (accessed April 10, 2014)
32. Liferay, http://www.liferay.com/ (accessed April 10, 2014)
33. JSR-168, http://jcp.org/en/jsr/detail?id=168 (accessed April 10, 2014)
34. JSR-286, http://jcp.org/en/jsr/detail?id=286 (accessed April 10, 2014)
35. LAMMPS Molecular Dynamics Simulator, http://lammps.sandia.gov/ (accessed April 10, 2014)
36. Bialoskorski, M., Rybicki, J.: Mechanical properties of the carbon nanotubes: simulation program and exemplary results. In: Proc. of the 8th Workshop of PTSK Gdańsk-Sobieszewo, p. 8 (2001)
37. Laskowski, R.: Pakiet SIMPL – metody geometrii stochastycznej w analizie strukturalnej. In: Sympozjum Symulacje MD w Polsce, Gdańsk (2000) (in Polish)
38. Bergmanski, G., Rybicki, J.: Pakiet ANELLI – analiza uporządkowania średniego zasięgu w strukturach symulowanych numerycznie. In: Sympozjum Symulacje MD w Polsce, Gdańsk (2000) (in Polish)
39. Adobe, Flex/BlazeDs, http://www.adobe.com/products/flex/ (accessed April 10, 2014)
40. Gonze, X., Amadon, B., Anglade, P.-M., Beuken, J.-M., Bottin, F., Boulanger, P., Bruneval, F., Caliste, D., Caracas, R., Cote, M., Deutsch, T., Genovese, L., Ghosez, P., Giantomassi, M., Goedecker, S., Hamann, D.R., Hermet, P., Jollet, F., Jomard, G., Leroux, S., Mancini, M., Mazevet, S., Oliveira, M.J.T., Onida, G., Pouillon, Y., Rangel, T., Rignanese, G.-M., Sangalli, D., Shaltaf, R., Torrent, M., Verstraete, M.J., Zerah, G., Zwanziger, J.W.: ABINIT: First-principles approach of materials and nanosystem properties. Computer Phys. Commun. 180, 2582–2615 (2009)

41. Gonze, X., Rignanese, G.-M., Verstraete, M., Beuken, J.-M., Pouillon, Y., Caracas, R., Jollet, F., Torrent, M., Zerah, G., Mikami, M., Ghosez, P., Veithen, M., Raty, J.-Y., Olevano, V., Bruneval, F., Reining, L., Godby, R., Onida, G., Hamann, D.R., Allan, D.C.: A brief introduction to the ABINIT software package. Zeit. Kristallogr. 220, 558–562 (2005)
42. Ludascher, B., Altintas, I., Berkley, C., Higgins, D., Jaeger-Frank, E., Jones, M., Lee, E., Tao, J., Zhao, Y.: Scientific Workflow Management and the Kepler System. Concurrency and Computation: Practice & Experience 18(10), 1039–1065 (2005)
43. Radecki, M., Szymocha, T., Piontek, T., Bosak, B., Mamoński, M., Wolniewicz, P., Benedyczak, K., Kluszczyński, R.: Reservations for Compute Resources in Federated e-Infrastructure. In: Bubak, M., Kitowski, J., Wiatr, K. (eds.) PLGrid Plus. LNCS, vol. 8500, pp. 80–93. Springer, Heidelberg (2014)
44. Bosak, B., Kopta, P., Kurowski, K., Piontek, T., Mamoński, M.: New QosCosGrid Middleware Capabilities and Its Integration with European e-Infrastructure. In: Bubak, M., Kitowski, J., Wiatr, K. (eds.) PLGrid Plus. LNCS, vol. 8500, pp. 34–53. Springer, Heidelberg (2014)
45. Karanastasis, E., Varvarigou, T., Grabowski, P.: Portals for Service Oriented Infrastructures. In: Dimitrakos, T., Martrat, J., Wesner, S. (eds.) Service Oriented Infrastructures and Cloud Service Platforms for the Enterprise, pp. 159–177. Springer, Heidelberg (2010) ISBN 978-3-642-04085-6

A Lightweight Method of Metadata and Data Management with DataNet

Daniel Harężlak[1], Marek Kasztelnik[1], Maciej Pawlik[1],
Bartosz Wilk[1], and Marian Bubak[1,2]

[1] AGH University of Science and Technology, ACC Cyfronet AGH,
ul. Nawojki 11, 30-950 Kraków, Poland
{d.harezlak,m.kasztelnik,m.pawlik,b.wilk}@cyfronet.pl
[2] AGH University of Science and Technology, Department of Computer Science,
al. Mickiewicza 30, 30-059 Kraków, Poland
bubak@agh.edu.pl

Abstract. Scientific computation is a source of many large data sets, which are often structured in a non-interoperable manner. Data and metadata are stored on computing infrastructures or local computers in databases or in files. The discoverability and verifiability of published results represented by such data are poorly established. It is also difficult to manage access to data by applying permission granting mechanisms in the available file systems or databases. Moreover, accessibility of data from external systems is limited by security restrictions imposed by storage facilities. In this paper we present a novel method for managing scientific data, addressing the aforementioned issues by providing a web-based data model management interface, which supports design of metadata structures and their relation to data stored in files, exposing REST-based repositories for data recording and providing easy access level configuration to limit data visibility during the publication process. The method implemented by DataNet tools exploits one of the available PaaS platforms. We present a typical use case scenario and provide an evaluation of DataNet deployment in the PL-Grid Infrastructure.

Keywords: data management, metadata recording, storage infrastructures, data sharing, discoverability, reproducibility.

1 Introduction

Modern large-scale computational resources generate a lot of scientific data. As stated in [29], the Large Synoptic Survey Telescope alone will produce around 20 TB of data per night. The idea is to store all data, because any dataset that is lost, might happen to be the relevant one. Even though the available storage infrastructures are able to cope with the amount of data which is produced, it is important to properly structure the data and annotate it in order to make future computing more efficient. Reproducibility of published results is a major challenge to be addressed. Besides the obvious requirement that results should be available for verification by third-party research groups, reproducibility is

M. Bubak et al. (Eds.): PLGrid Plus, LNCS 8500, pp. 164–177, 2014.

particularly important when trying to transfer the academic findings to the industry [19]. The main limitation in this regard is lack of access to published data as well as means to run the computation again and reproduce the results without contacting the authors. To tackle this problem, environments such as RunMy-Code [27] or GridSpace [3] support publication of code and processed data on dedicated resources through a web interface, to be retrieved by external users. The latter was integrated with the online publishing platform ScienceDirect [2], supporting result verification while viewing the article. Such systems greatly increase the manageability of reproducible scientific results, however with limited data management capacity, as only data stored in files can be used. Such limitations prevent the use of structured data stored in databases and also data comprising a mix of files and database records. It is also important to consider usage of different storage systems depending on the performance requirements of a given application. Scaling is an important aspect for large datasets during the data recording phase, when it is necessary to ensure that all data is saved for later analysis. The ability to share the collected data is essential in order to enable other researchers to verify the results and combine available datasets into new ones. Finally, enabling research teams to access data collections in a common and interoperable fashion completes the list of outstanding requirements.

The main objectives of this work are to investigate new methods for managing scientific data, ensuring better reproducibility of results, to design a scalable platform capable of processing large volumes of structured and file-based data, and to measure the performance of deployment in the PL-Grid Infrastructure. Beside the main goals, this work should provide a set of tools for building a DataNet service for data management within the PL-Grid Infrastructure and validate the proposed method on various use cases.

The paper is organized as follows: an overview of the available data publishing methods constitutes section 2 while requirements and architecture of the platform are presented in section 3. Each of the layers of the architecture is explained in sections 4, 6 and 7. Deployment in the PL-Grid Infrastructure and performance indicators are described in sections 8 and 9 respectively. The paper is concluded in section 10, which also points out future developments.

2 Overview of Scientific Data Publishing Methods

Preserving scientific experiment plans and the results of their execution is the focus of many teams. The workflow notation approach is adopted by Taverna [7], [18] and Kepler [17] while the scripting approach is used in GridSpace [3] to express computation plans. Each of these solutions applies a dedicated data representation mechanism. A more data-centric approach is taken by the wf4ever project [1], where different datasets related to a scientific workflow are collected and annotated within a so-called Research Object. This allows for storing information about the provenance of research results and improve their reusability and reproducibility. Another approach to data management is based on a semantic overlay pointing to different data resources represented by RDF links.

Ongoing development of these technologies and existing data repositories is described in [11]. It should be noted that using either of the aforementioned technologies imposes a specific data handling approach. Moreover, none of them offer a convenient way of querying the data and enabling support for different storage technologies.

Several available platforms can be used to publish scientific data. They allow users to assign a DOI identifier to a dataset and make it open for referencing. One such platform is Dataverse [5], which allows for advanced management of the research process with result versioning, citations and support for different file formats. Another such system is Dryad [13] based on DSpace [9] repository software and enabling journals to carry out a peer review of the published datasets. Figshare [10] can be used to manage and publish scientific results on cloud-based resources with advanced collaborative spaces. It provides access through a dedicated API allowing other applications to access its resources. For distributed file sharing on cloud resources the LOBCDER [16] service is available with the main benefit of easy integration with different systems using a WebDAV-based connector. A solution, which uses peer-to-peer processing of data represented as Nondeterministic Finite Automata [6], provides more insight into how scientific results are obtained.

All these platforms provide functional web-based user interfaces and make publication of scientific data easy and affordable by offering limited free space. The main drawback of these systems is the file format, which needs to be used – specifically, tabular data needs to be exported to files. Moreover, a dedicated infrastructure is required in each case, without the possibility to include resources on existing computational and storage sites. Another issue is the lack of computing power necessary to re-run the published experiments. To verify the published findings, the data has to be transferred back to a computing site and fed into the application. What is more, searching through exported tabular data is limited to a number of supported formats.

Regarding available PaaS platforms, the first requirement is to have the proposed solution available in a free and open-source version. DataNet is required to be free and operate at no extra cost to service providers. This requirement results in rejection of PaaS solutions available only commercially, for example Heroku [14].

Another requirement is enabling deployment of the solution to a variety of environments with particular focus on directly available machines and various Clouds with limited access rights. This is because the PL-Grid Infrastructure provides only a subset of cloud features, without administrative access; thus it is impossible to implement certain advanced configurations. Specific constraints include lack of public IPs, no network separation and lack of service reservation. This makes it impossible to use OpenShift [22] as it does not provide a router or gateway service, unlike CloudFoundry [23], which is able to operate on private Clouds with restricted access. Other available solutions, like Deis [8] and Cloudify [4] are not mature enough and their user base is small. This leaves CloudFoundry as the best solution for the DataNet PaaS platform.

The CloudFoundry project is supported by a large community, is available free of charge and is able to operate inside private Clouds by exposing relevant services to public networks. DataNet was extended with CloudFoundry deployment support and is able to manage deployed applications. Although the integration is tight, it is possible to adapt DataNet to work with other PaaS providers.

3   Requirements and DataNet Architecture

The shortcomings of the presented solutions in the area of data management and the lack of integration with the existing PL-Grid Infrastructure were the reasons behind development of a new method, as well as the design and implementation of a new system fulfilling the following set of requirements:

- creation of an abstract data model including file and structured data mixed together,
- versioning support for data models and the corresponding data repositories,
- managing access levels to repositories for third parties,
- programming language-independent access to deployed repositories,
- scalable infrastructure for handling a large number of repositories,
- integration with existing PL-Grid Infrastructure storage and security services.

The presented requirements were addressed by introducing the system architecture presented in Fig. 1. Three layers are used to decompose the functionality and make the solution modular. The topmost layer, built as a web interface, allows for managing abstract data models, versioning and deploying repositories, for which access restrictions can be set and the stored data can be viewed. The middle layer provides a scalable space for deploying data repositories. It is built on top of a PaaS platform, which ensures the means for using different storage engines for tabular data and can be easily expanded when the existing deployment capacity is exceeded. Each repository exposes a REST interface for data recording and retrieval. The bottom layer comprises the PL-Grid Infrastructure, where file data is stored through the GridFTP protocol.

4   Building Data Models

One of the views of the web interface allows users to build abstract data models. Building the model consists of creating a set of entities of simple data types and defining relations among them. Complex types such as arrays of simple types, relations and files can be modeled as well. The process is straightforward and allows users to express their data schema without knowing anything about complex data notations (e.g. RDF, XML or OWL often used in semantic modeling). When the model is ready, it can be saved as a version and deployed as a repository owned by a user or group of users. Following deployment, the repository exposes a REST endpoint, through which data management can be performed. Another view of the web interface allows accessing the API and presents the data

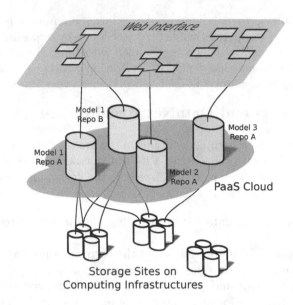

Fig. 1. DataNet architecture comprising three layers: the topmost layer (graphical user interfaces) allows for data model management and access to the data, the middle layer (data repositories) exposes REST interfaces for data management built on top of one of the available PaaS platforms, while the bottom layer (file storage) represents resources available on various computing infrastructures.

stored therein. The models stored in DataNet can be discovered by other users and, if the related data is publicly accessible, combined data sets (data coming from different repositories but belonging to the same model) can be acquired by a dedicated application. This constitutes a separate research area where data is no longer being produced but only queried to obtain valid scientific results. Queries are built by providing a set of search values in a URL pointing to a particular model entity. It is also possible to access repositories of different models and process the data within a single application.

Access to individual data repositories can be changed by their owners. Currently, public and private access options are available. In the private mode, a list of owners can be provided to limit access to a group of users. Public access exposes the data stored in a given repository to all users of the infrastructure.

The web interface integrates with the authentication mechanism offered by the PL-Grid Infrastructure, which is based on an OpenID [21] server. Users authenticating on the DataNet web page are redirected to the OpenID provider site where they input their credentials and, once successfully authenticated, are redirected back to the DataNet web page and switched to a secured area. During this process a valid user proxy certificate is generated and passed back to the DataNet web server. It is used to delegate user credentials to the repository (the REST API requires a valid user proxy certificate) and storage infrastructure (using the GridFTP protocol).

5   Provenance as a DataNet Generic Usage Scenario

The main advantage of DataNet is quick composition and deployment of data models. One common use case involving scientific data processing is recording of data provenance. The code of existing applications can be easily extended to record such a trace with the help of DataNet. Let us consider a generic case of results composed of one or more files, processed by one or more applications executing on computing nodes. Information about the results (including data), applications, computing nodes and users who ran the applications should be part of the provenance trace. The diagram presented in Fig. 2 shows how a DataNet model might look in the described scenario.

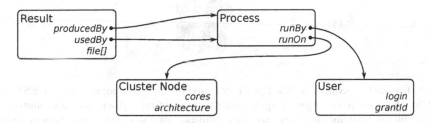

Fig. 2. Sample DataNet model representing provenance of results (consisting of one or more files) produced and used by processes executed on cluster nodes by users. Each of the entities may be extended with additional fields according to specific requirements of the application using the model.

Four entities are used to represent results, processes, cluster nodes and users respectively. In order to ensure proper associations between recorded entries, relations are modeled among them. In this way, each *Result* can be consumed or produced by a process (denoted by *usedBy* and *producedBy* relations respectively) and point to one or more files in the storage infrastructure. *Process* has relations to *Cluster Node* and *User* entities and can be associated with input and output results. Cluster node and user entities contain typical information that may be relevant when the provenance log is retrieved for inspection. Composition and deployment of the presented model is straightforward with the DataNet management interface. Another modification has to be applied in the application itself so that provenance metadata is recorded. This can be accomplished by modifying the enactment engine used to execute an application (e.g. through a Taverna plugin) or by modifying the application to contain proper REST requests.

6   Data Repository on PaaS Platform

Once the data model is created using the web interface described in the previous section, it is deployed into the CloudFoundry PaaS platform in the form of

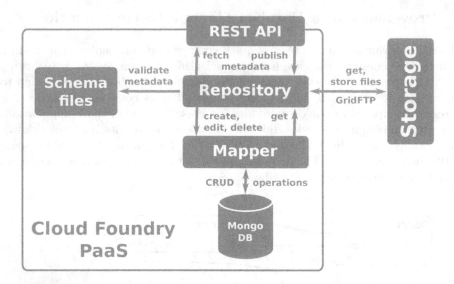

Fig. 3. Datanet repository architecture composed of the following elements: REST API used by the user or an external application to modify repository data and metadata, Schema files describing metadata structure, Mapper used to convert and store metadata in a document database and Storage used to archive annotated files

a Rack [24] application exposing the REST API and MongoDB [20] storage. Models – converted into JSON Schema files – are stored inside the application. They configure the application storage and REST API. Fig. 3 presents a detailed architecture of the repository.

The DataNet repository was conceived and designed in such a way as to allow integration with applications created in different programming languages. To simplify this process, a REST-based API was created. It provides a set of operations allowing users to create, edit, search and delete metadata according to a predefined schema (see Fig. 4 for details). It uses the Grape gem [12], which simplifies the creation of the REST interface thanks to a user-friendly DSL[1].

The DataNet repository API is versioned using the following rules: (1) existing API can be extended by introducing backward compatible changes, (2) all backward incompatible changes cause the API version to be incremented. The two most recent API versions are supported at any time. As a consequence, applications which use DataNet repositories will have enough time to upgrade their code when a new API version is released. All DataNet repository REST operations are secured using a *Grid Proxy*, which can be generated using PL-Grid Infrastructure tools. Owing to the delegation capability of the *Grid Proxy*, it can be used for authorization and authentication, as well as storage and retrieval of files from remote servers using the *GridFTP* protocol.

---

[1] Domain Specific Language

GET / List of all entity types defined in the repository
GET /{*entity_name*}.*schema* Entity type schema in JSON format
POST /{*entity_name*} Create new entity
GET /{*entity_name*} List all entities of a given type
GET /{*entity_name*}?*field_name=operator,value&*... Search for entities matching a given query
GET /{*entity_name*}/{*id*} Get entity identified by *id*
PUT /{*entity_name*}/{*id*} Update entity identified by *id*
DELETE /{*entity_name*}/{*id*} Delete entity identified by *id*

Fig. 4. Datanet repository REST API operations allow users and external applications to modify medatadata

Schema files are used to check if entities stored inside the repository are valid. Schema files allow users to define simple fields with specific datatypes (e.g. *experiment* entity has a *name* which is a *string*) and references to other entities (e.g. *experiment* has many *results*). All these constraints are modeled using the JSON Schema standard [15]. Storage is used to archive annotated files. In our deployment we rely on the Zeus computer cluster located at ACC Cyfronet AGH, however, other storage servers can be used as needed. The only requirement for a new server is to have the *GridFTP* library installed. Mapper is used to store metadata using the most appropriate storage technology. Currently, MongoDB is supported as the only storage backend. In the future we are planning to integrate other storage engines (e.g. relational databases or Hadoop solutions). The repository connects all elements presented above. It uses schema definitions to verify whether new metadata records are valid and converts queries defined in the REST interface into a form, which can be executed by the Mapper on a selected database engine. The *GridFTP* client is applied to store or retrieve annotated files from remote servers.

7 Integration with Storage Facilities

Integration with the PL-Grid Infrastructure was accomplished by implementing access to file resources with the GridFTP protocol. GridFTP, which is an established and well known protocol [28], was chosen due to its widespread use in the PL-Grid Infrastructure and support for credential delegation. Despite the adoption of GridFTP in scientific applications, only a handful of implementations of its client and server software exist. This may be due to the relatively complicated advanced features and lack of adoption in business communities, leaving implementation in the hands of several scientific teams.

The reference implementation of GridFTP software is available in the form of C and Java libraries. As the specific part of DataNet, which requires GridFTP support, was written in Ruby, the most optimal solution is to use the C library through the FFI (Foreign Function Interface) [25] Ruby extension. Extending

Ruby with C libraries is the most straightforward way to interface with external modules. The integration code was packaged as an external Ruby library *ruby-gridftp*, in order to simplify development, establish clear boundaries between GridFTP and repository code and allow for code reuse. The resulting library provides support for all GridFTP operations as well as most additional features and settings such as parallel transfers, relative and absolute paths, etc.

The main challenge in using the GridFTP C library is related to the asynchronous nature of operations. Executing every operation requires providing a callback and waiting for it to be called. This fact should be taken into consideration during development as operations do not have fixed time boundaries and may fail or return at any given moment. This needs to be handled and presented to the user accordingly, by implementing and forwarding the corresponding callbacks. On the other hand, the asynchronous mode is convenient for `put` and `get` operations, where it allows streaming data from and to the user without caching it all in one place. For the sake of convenience, a simple *Client* module was developed by wrapping most operations so that users can call them as plain blocking functions.

8   DataNet Deployment in the PL-Grid Infrastructure

DataNet is installed as a service in the PL-Grid Cloud infrastructure (see Fig. 5). The infrastructure provides IaaS-type services accessible to its users. The preferred way to manage cloud instances in the PL-Grid Cloud is through a CLI (Command Line Interface) client installed on the user-accessible *user interface node*. The standard operation of the PL-Grid Cloud assumes that virtual machines are given only local network connectivity with NAT (Network Address Translation) network setup providing Internet access. DataNet installation requires forwarding traffic addressed to the `datanet.plgrid.pl` domain to the main DataNet node.

The deployment and configuration of the service are performed by a service administrator and consist of installing DataNet web application and CloudFoundry. The administrator needs to establish a basic configuration where the main concerns are connectivity between the DataNet web application and the CloudFoundry installation, as well as storage provider details.

The most basic CloudFoundry deployment comprises a single virtual machine, which hosts all CloudFoundry services and runs user repositories. This setup is currently in operation and has proven sufficient to support operation by current PL-Grid users. Nonetheless, future usage scenarios might require distribution of user load to multiple nodes, which is enabled by CloudFoundry provisioning capabilities.

9   Assessment of DataNet Performance

Performance evaluation of DataNet repositories was performed using the CloudFoundry PaaS installation on PL-Grid Infrastructure resources. Each run was repeated 10 times and average values were calculated. We also measured

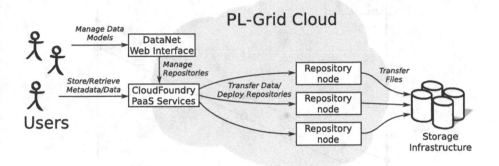

Fig. 5. Representation of a cloud-based DataNet installation. Each node located in the cloud represents a dedicated VM running DataNet components. DataNet Web Interface and CloudFoundry PaaS Service instances are exposed outside the cloud.

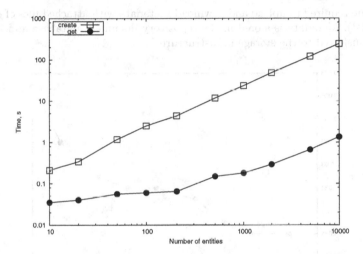

Fig. 6. Performance results presenting how DataNet repositories behave when large volumes of metadata need to be stored and retrieved

deviations of results, which proved relatively small and insignificant for result analysis – hence they are not presented in the figures.

At the beginning, we timed creation and retrieval of metadata. Results from this assessment can be found in Fig. 6. It shows how the repository handles creation and fetching of large volumes of metadata. There is a significant difference between the time needed to create and the time to fetch metadata entities. This is because the store operation checks data coherency (using a JSON validator [26]). This step is omitted when the entity is returned to the client. The DataNet repository also provides the possibility to store and fetch metadata together with files. Suitable performance evaluation was carried out to check how the repository behaves in such a situation (see Fig. 7 for details).

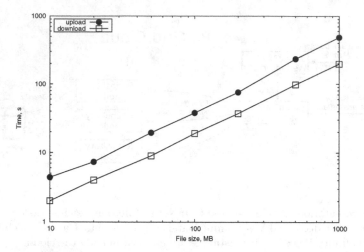

Fig. 7. Time required to upload and download metadata with attached files of different sizes (in MB). Metadata is stored in the repository document database and attached files are transferred to the storage infrastructure.

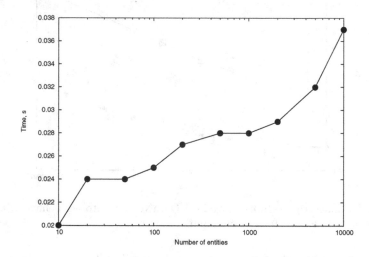

Fig. 8. Time needed to query the metadata repository as a function of the repository size. Only a document database is involved, with no interaction with the storage infrastructure.

We observe significant difference between the time needed to upload and download metadata with files. Two factors influence such behavior. The first is identical to the previous use case (i.e. involves entity validation). The second is connected with the CloudFoundry PaaS architecture, which uses *Nginx* as a load balancer for all deployed applications. *Nginx* supports data streaming while the file is being downloaded, but when uploading files, it stores the uploaded payload in a temporary file until the transfer is complete and only then passes it to the upstream application. A third assessment was executed to check for performance degradation while searching repositories of different sizes (but with the same search result size). Results of this evaluation are presented in Fig. 8. This shows that there are no significant differences between searching small (10 elements) and quite large (10,000 elements) repositories. This evaluation should be performed in the future for all storage technologies, which are to be integrated with DataNet repositories.

10   Conclusions and Future Work

In this paper a new method for managing structured and file data was presented. The method formalizes the process of managing data models and contents in a way, which ensures better reproducibility and accessibility of data once it has been published. The DataNet platform, which implements the method, is a convenient tool for managing scientific data, which can be shared and published for verification. Building abstract data models enables combining metadata and data into a single structure with many supported data types, including tabular data and files. A model can be deployed as a repository with a single user action, via a web interface, and then accessed from any application through a secured REST endpoint. The access model can be set to private or public, limiting data visibility accordingly. Extensions for different metadata storage technologies are feasible owing to the use of the CloudFoundry PaaS platform as the underlying service provisioning layer, which also ensures good scaling for an increasing number of repositories. DataNet integrates with the PL-Grid Infrastructure storage and security services, enabling users to easily adapt their code simply by delegating existing user credentials. Integration with the GridFTP library ensures effective file transfers to and from the storage infrastructure. As an approved PL-Grid service, DataNet is a reliable solution for data management in this infrastructure.

Future work will include integration with the group facility of the PL-Grid Infrastructure to support sharing repositories among user groups. Information about groups, to which a given user belongs, can be already retrieved as one of the attributes of the OpenID server. A detailed performance evaluation of file streaming is required to improve the upload characteristics for large files.

References

1. Belhajjame, K., Corcho, O., Garijo, D., Zhao, J., Missier, P., Newman, D., Palma, R., Bechhofer, S., García Cuesta, E., Gómez-Pérez, J.M., Soiland-Reyes, S., Verdes-Montenegro, L., De Roure, D., Goble, C.: Workflow-centric research objects: First class citizens in scholarly discourse. In: Proceedings of Workshop on the Semantic Publishing (2012),
https://www.escholar.manchester.ac.uk/api/
datastream?publicationPid=uk-ac-man-scw:192020&datastreamId=
POST-PEER-REVIEW-NON-PUBLISHERS.PDF

2. Ciepiela, E., Harężlak, D., Kasztelnik, M., Meizner, J., Dyk, G., Nowakowski, P., Bubak, M.: The collage authoring environment: From proof-of-concept prototype to pilot service. In: Proceedings of the International Conference on Computational Science. Procedia Computer Science, vol. 18, pp. 769–778 (2013), http://www.sciencedirect.com/science/article/pii/S1877050913003840

3. Ciepiela, E., et al.: Managing Entire Lifecycles of e-Science Applications in the GridSpace2 Virtual Laboratory – From Motivation through Idea to Operable Web-Accessible Environment Built on Top of PL-Grid e-Infrastructure. In: Bubak, M., Szepieniec, T., Wiatr, K. (eds.) PL-Grid 2011. LNCS, vol. 7136, pp. 228–239. Springer, Heidelberg (2012), http://dl.acm.org/citation.cfm?id=2184180.2184198

4. Cloudify – the open paas stack web page (January 2014), http://www.cloudifysource.org/

5. Crosas, M.: A data sharing story. Journal of eScience Librarianship 1, 173–179 (2013), http://escholarship.umassmed.edu/jeslib/vol1/iss3/7/

6. Cushing, R., Belloum, A., Bubak, M., Oprescu, A., de Laat, C.: Exploratory data processing using non-deterministic finite automata

7. De Roure, D., Belhajjame, K., Missier, P., Manuel, J., Palma, R., Ruiz, J.E., Hettne, K., Roos, M., Klyne, G., Goble, C.: Towards the preservation of scientific workflows. In: Procs. of the 8th International Conference on Preservation of Digital Objects (iPRES 2011). ACM (2011)

8. Deis web page (January 2014), http://deis.io/

9. Dspace web page (January 2014), http://www.dspace.org

10. Figshare repository web page (January 2014), http://figshare.com

11. Fundulaki, I., Auer, S.: Introduction to the special theme: Linked open data. ERCIM News 2014(96) (2014), http://ercim-news.ercim.eu/images/stories/EN96/EN96-web.pdf

12. Grape: an opinionated micro-framework for creating rest-like apis in ruby web page (January 2014), https://github.com/intridea/grape

13. Greenberg, J., White, H.C., Carrier, S., Scherle, R.: A metadata best practice for a scientific data repository. Journal of Library Metadata 9(3-4), 194–212 (2009), http://www.tandfonline.com/doi/abs/10.1080/19386380903405090

14. Heroku cloud application platform web page (January 2014), https://www.heroku.com/

15. Json schema web page (January 2014), http://json-schema.org

16. Koulouzis, S., Vasyunin, D., Cushing, R., Belloum, A., Bubak, M.: Cloud data federation for scientific applications. In: an Mey, D., et al. (eds.) Euro-Par 2013. LNCS, vol. 8374, pp. 13–22. Springer, Heidelberg (2014)

17. Ludäscher, B., Altintas, I., Berkley, C., Higgins, D., Jaeger, E., Jones, M., Lee, E.A., Tao, J., Zhao, Y.: Scientific workflow management and the kepler system: Research articles. Concurr. Comput.: Pract. Exper. 18(10), 1039–1065 (Aug 2006), http://dx.doi.org/10.1002/cpe.v18:10

18. Missier, P., Soiland-Reyes, S., Owen, S., Tan, W., Nenadic, A., Dunlop, I., Williams, A., Oinn, T., Goble, C.: Taverna, Reloaded. In: Gertz, M., Ludäscher, B. (eds.) SSDBM 2010. LNCS, vol. 6187, pp. 471–481. Springer, Heidelberg (2010), http://dx.doi.org/10.1007/978-3-642-13818-8_33

19. Mobley, A., Linder, S.K., Braeuer, R., Ellis, L.M., Zwelling, L.: A survey on data reproducibility in cancer research provides insights into our limited ability to translate findings from the laboratory to the clinic. PLoS ONE 8(5), e63221 (2013), http://dx.doi.org/10.1371%2Fjournal.pone.0063221

20. Mongodb web page (January 2014), http://www.mongodb.org
21. Openid foundation web site (January 2014), http://openid.net/
22. Openshift by red hat web page (January 2014), https://www.openshift.com/
23. Pivotal: Cloud foundry web site (January 2014), http://www.cloudfoundry.com
24. Rack – modular ruby webserver interface web site (January 2014),
    https://github.com/rack/rack
25. Ruby-ffi web page (January 2014), https://github.com/ffi/ffi/wiki
26. Ruby json schema validator web page (January 2014),
    https://github.com/hoxworth/json-schema
27. Stodden, V., Hurlin, C., Perignon, C.: Runmycode.org: A novel dissemination and
    collaboration platform for executing published computational results. In: 2012
    IEEE 8th International Conference on E-Science, pp. 1–8 (2012)
28. Toolkit, G.: Grid ftp web site (January 2014),
    http://toolkit.globus.org/toolkit/data/gridftp
29. Witt, S.D., Sinclair, R., Sansum, A., Wilson, M.: Managing large data volumes
    from scientific facilities. ERCIM News 2012(89) (2012),
    http://dblp.uni-trier.de/db/journals/ercim/ercim2012.html#WittSSW12

Uniform and Efficient Access to Data in Organizationally Distributed Environments

Łukasz Dutka[1], Renata Słota[2], Michał Wrzeszcz[1],
Dariusz Król[1,2], and Jacek Kitowski[1,2]

[1] AGH University of Science and Technology, ACC Cyfronet AGH,
ul. Nawojki 11, 30-950 Kraków, Poland
[2] AGH University of Science and Technology,
Faculty of Computer Science, Electronics and Telecommunications,
Department of Computer Science,
al. Mickiewicza 30, 30-059 Kraków, Poland
{dutka,rena,wrzeszcz,dkrol,kito}@agh.edu.pl

Abstract. In this article, the authors present a solution to the problem of accessing data in organizationally distributed environments, such as Grids and Clouds, in a uniform and efficient manner. An overview of existing storage solutions is described, in particular high-performance filesystems and data management systems, with regard to the provided functionality, scalability and configuration elasticity. Next, a novel solution, called VeilFS, is described in terms of objectives to attain, its architecture and current implementation status. In particular, the mechanisms used for achieving a desired level of performance and fault-tolerance are discussed and preliminary overhead tests are presented.

Keywords: storage system, data management system, virtual file system, distributed environment, Grid.

1 Introduction

We are observing a fast growth of the digital universe [7]. However, the increasing number of powerful computing environments is more challenging than the increase in the overall data volume. The data not only has to be stored, but it also has to be processed. This problem is often called the Big Data revolution [11] and addresses such issues as the variety of data and the processing speed required to unlock the potential of access to such an amount of information. The processing of large volumes of diverse data with a satisfactory performance requires use of appropriate storage systems. Moreover, different requirements of user groups make it necessary to install heterogeneous storage systems managed by advanced data management systems for efficient storage resources usage and provisioning.

We have investigated data access requirements of PL-Grid Infrastructure users [9]. Thirteen groups of users representing essential science disciplines are supported by the PLGrid Plus project, namely: AstroGrid-PL, HEPGrid, Nanotechnologies, Acoustics, Life Science, Quantum Chemistry and Molecular Physics,

M. Bubak et al. (Eds.): PLGrid Plus, LNCS 8500, pp. 178–194, 2014.

Ecology, SynchroGrid, Energy Sector, Bioinformatics, Health Sciences, Materials, and Metallurgy. As the PL-Grid Infrastructure spans across five biggest academic computer centers in Poland, most of these groups need to access their data located in different sites and storage systems. A common use case involves users who schedule computations to all available sites to generate data, e.g. as part of a data farming experiment [10], and then collecting the data in a single site to extract meaningful information.

The PL-Grid Infrastructure provides various storage systems fulfilling different requirements: "scratch" for intermediate job results, "storage" for final job results, and LFC/DPM for long-term data storage. "Scratch" and "storage" systems are file systems used locally within each site, while LFC/DPM is a global solution, accessible through a dedicated API, appropriate for data sharing between sites. Even within a single PL-Grid site, efficient data management is a challenging task, especially when involving the data access quality requirements, due to dealing with workload balancing between multiple storage resources abstracted by a single file system [14,15]. The users' quality requirements, defined using SLA, are an important aspect of resource management, as well as an important aspect of users' accounting [16].

The analysis of the PL-Grid Infrastructure users' requirements has shown that access to data is often too complicated [13]. The variety of possible storage solutions confuses users. Users expect that data access will be simple using one tool. The distribution of large scale computational environments should not create new barriers, but should provide new opportunities such as intra-community data sharing and collaboration.

The data access may be simplified by administrators of computing centers who can create special storage spaces for particular groups of users. However, it complicates the work of administrators and causes problems in the infrastructure maintenance when a lot of storage spaces is created and supported. Tools that will help the administrators with such management of various storage systems will be useful for them.

In this article, the authors introduce a system operating in the user space (i.e., FUSE), called VeilFS, which virtualizes organizationally distributed, heterogeneous storage systems to obtain uniform and efficient access to data. A single VeilFS instance works at a data center site level, but can also cooperate with instances from other sites to support geographically distributed organizations or separated organizations, which share resources on a federation level.

The rest of the article is organized as follows. Section 2 presents other possible solutions to the problem of accessing data in organizationally distributed environments and shows their shortcomings. The proposed VeilFS system architecture is widely described in Section 3. Section 4 shows the current state of VeilFS's implementation and preliminary tests results. Finally, Section 5 concludes the article.

2   State of the Art

In distributed environments, storage resources are provided to users through one
of two types of systems: (1) high-performance file systems and (2) data management systems. Solutions of the former type intend to provide access to storage
resources in an optimized for performance manner. They are built on top of
dedicated storage resources, e.g. RAIDs, and they expose a POSIX-compliant
interface. They can be used during computation to store results, which exceed the
capacity of a single hard drive. Examples of such solutions include GlusterFS [3],
CephFS [1], and Scality RING [5]. Despite providing similar functionality, these
systems differ in implementation, which influences their non-functional features.
For instance, to resolve the actual location of data, GlusterFS uses an elastic
hashing algorithm (each node is able to find the location of the data algorithmi-
cally, without use of a metadata server), CephFS uses a metadata server, while
Scality RING utilizes a routing-based algorithm within a P2P network. Most of
them are scalable, while strictly avoiding architectural bottlenecks. The choice
which one to use should depend on the actual requirements, e.g. low latency or
support for dynamic reconfiguration. However, they are not suitable for Grids
due to limited support for federalization, which is essential in organizationally
distributed environments such as Grids.

The second type of solutions for exposing the storage resources are data management systems. Such systems are oriented towards high-level data management,
e.g. to provide data accessibility between sites, rather than high-perfor-mance
data access. They aim at providing an abstraction layer on top of storage resources across multiple organizations, which exposes a single namespace for data
storage. In addition, many of such systems facilitate data management by enabling administrators to define data management rules, e.g. w.r.t. archiving the
unused data. Examples of such systems include Parrot [17], iRODS system [8],
[12], and DropBox [2]. The main goal of these systems is to enable data access
from anywhere in a uniform way, e.g. Parrot utilizes the *ptrace* debugging interface to trap the system calls of a program and replace them with remote I/O
operations. As a result, remote data can be accessed in the same way as local
files. Data integration in the iRODS system is based on a metadata catalog –
iCAT – which is involved in the processing of the majority of data access requests. The metadata catalog is implemented as a relational database, hence it
can be considered as a bottleneck of the whole system.

The analyzed systems were compared (see Table 1) according to the following
features:

- high-performance data access,
- data location transparency,
- support for data management rules,
- POSIX-compliant interface,
- decentralized management.

The first thing to notice is that there is no system, which would provide
all the mentioned features. High-performance file systems provide efficient data

Table 1. Comparison of storage exposing solutions

System	High-performance	Location transparency	Management rules	POSIX-compliancy	Decentralized management
GlusterFS	Yes	Yes	No	Yes	No
CephFS	Yes	Yes	No	Yes	No
Scality RING	Yes	Yes	Yes	Yes	No
Parrot	No	Yes	No	Yes	No
iRODS	No	No	Yes	Yes	Yes
DropBox	No	Yes	N/A	No	No

access, but they lack data management capabilities, while data management systems provide management-related capabilities, but they do not ensure high-performance. As a result, the users have to utilize high-performance systems during computations in one site, but a data management system has to be used during access to the generated data from other sites. Moreover, administrators have multiple storage solutions to manage, which can be error-prone and inefficient.

3   A Unified Data Access Solution for Organizationally Distributed Environments – VeilFS

Below we describe our solution to the problem of accessing data stored in organizationally distributed environments in an efficient and uniform way, named VeilFS, implemented as a virtual file system. We start with a summary of the functionality provided by our system. Next, we discuss its architecture and its internal components.

3.1   Functionality Overview

The VeilFS system provides a unified and efficient access to data stored in organizationally distributed environments, e.g. Grids and Clouds. From the user point of view, VeilFS:

– **Provides a Uniform and Coherent View on All Data Stored on the Storage Systems Distributed Across the Infrastructure.** The user of geographically distributed organization can perform many tasks simultaneously. The tasks may be executed in one or many locations. Using VeilFS, all user's processes see all data stored in all sites. If the needed data is not stored locally, it is migrated by the system. The user can also mount VeilFS on her/his PC and access the data as if it was stored on a local hard drive.
– **Supports Working in Groups by Creation of an Easy-to-Use Shared Workspace for Each Group.** Users are able to share data inside a group by simply moving the data to an appropriate directory.

- **Supports Data Sharing.** Users are able to publish a file obtaining a unique URL. Until canceled by the owner, anyone is able to download the file using the obtained URL. However, only the owner is able to modify the file.
- **Serves Data Efficiently.** The system is designed to minimize overheads and provide data from remote storages as fast as possible.

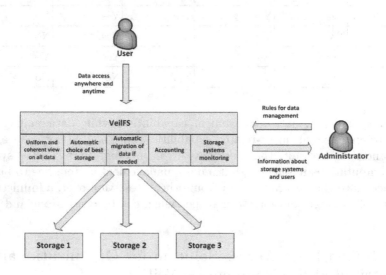

Fig. 1. Functionalities provided by VeilFS

However, simplification of the system for the users results in an increase in the number and difficulty of management tasks that have to be done by administrators or automaton. Hence, VeilFS provides functionalities that also facilitate administrators' work:

- Gathering and visualizing of the infrastructure state monitoring data – each storage system supervised by VeilFS is monitored to provide the administrators with an insight into storage utilization.
- Rule-based data management – automatic data management can be performed on the basis of rules specified by administrators, e.g. the rarely used data can be automatically migrated from fast to cost-effective storage. The optimization of use of storage resources is transparent to the users.
- Data protection from unauthorized access – the system is integrated with grid and Linux security systems to protect the data.

Both points of view are summarized in Fig. 1.

Such a wide set of functionalities implies that VeilFS can be perceived as a file system (it provides access to files), but on the other hand it can be treated as a data management system, because it manages the data on storage systems beneath it.

3.2   High-Level Architecture of VeilFS

An exemplary environment where VeilFS works is depicted in Fig. 2. This environment contains two sites. In each site an instance of VeilFS is installed. The most important element is Data Management Component, which coordinates the system's operation in the site and processes client requests. It consists of a set of cooperating modules, which may be deployed to a cluster to increase the throughput of the component. It is connected to a database (DB), which stores information about metadata, e.g. the mappings of logical filenames to the actual data location on a storage. Each site has its own Data Management Component with DB.

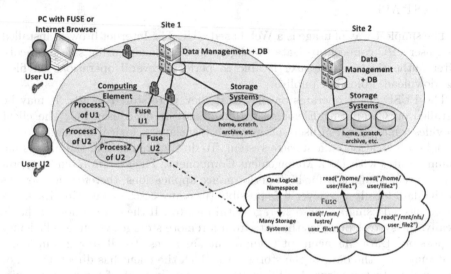

Fig. 2. Exemplary environment with VeilFS

The site usually contains many Computing Elements where users' processes are executed. Computing Elements are connected to Storage Systems where users' data is stored. Storage Systems in sites are usually organized as high performance systems with high capacity (e.g. Lustre) rather than simple hard disks. Not all Computing Elements must be connected to all Storage Systems, in contrary to the machines where Data Management Component is deployed.

There can be three levels of utilization of VeilFS:

- site level, i.e., a single data center being a part of a single organization,
- organization level (also geographically distributed organization), i.e., a single organization, which spans across one or more sites,
- federation level, i.e., separated organizations cooperating together to achieve a common goal, yet maintaining their autonomy.

There is no difference between the deployment of components when instances of VeilFS are cooperating within an organization or a federation. The difference is in the administration – VeilFS instances that belong to the same organization can cooperate more closely.

3.3 System Clients and Protocols

End users access the data stored within VeilFS through one of the provided user interfaces:

- FUSE client, which implements a file system in user space to cover the data location and exposes a standard POSIX file system interface,
- Web-based GUI, which allows data management via any Internet browser,
- REST API.

The simplest way of usage is a Web based GUI. The Internet browser installed on a user's PC connects to Data Management Component using safe protocols. After authentication, the user is able to perform several operations on files, e.g. download, upload or publish.

The FUSE client operates on files as if they were stored locally. It may be installed on Computing Elements within a site, or on a user PC. The client provides a file system in user space, which translates a logical file name to the actual data location on a storage system. To do the translation, the file system communicates with Data Management Component. The system intends to provide efficiency sufficient for high-performance applications, therefore it operates on the data locally whenever it is possible (in many cases Computing Elements are connected using a shared storage within a site). If the data is not reachable locally, the system provides the data from a remote storage system as efficiently as possible. Data Management Component has access to all storages in a site so it may copy the data to the storage, to which the client has direct access, or stream data to the client. VeilFS covers the management of temporary copies according to the rules specified previously by administrators, e.g. only the required blocks of a file can be copied in case of large datasets. If the client is located in a different site than the data, the instances of Data Management Component of both sites cooperate to increase the data transfer speed – the data is copied using an own protocol that allows for utilization of many hosts and many channels at the same time. The client from outside connects to the Data Management Component instance using DNS, where Data Management Component instances register information about users. When the data is not reachable locally, advanced buffering and prefetching algorithms are used.

VeilFS provides a REST programming interface to enable integration with other applications, which handle user data, e.g. domain-specific web portals. Another example is grid scheduling systems, which can decide to execute a grid job in a particular site, based on information about the required data location obtained through the REST API. Moreover, the scheduling system may request a transfer of the remaining data to the site where the job will run while this job is queued.

3.4   Data Management Component Architecture

Inside the Data Management Component we can distinguish between a few logical elements that perform specific tasks. We call them *modules*. The modules are listed below and shown in Fig. 3:

- *fslogic* – it is responsible for mapping the logical filenames to the real locations of data. It handles requests from FUSE clients.
- *dao* – this module performs operations in database.
- *rtransfer* and *gateway* – they are responsible for transfer of data between sites. One *rtransfer* can cooperate with many *gateways*. The *gateway* transfers parts of the data while the *rtransfer* coordinates requests (there may be many requests for transfer of the same data) and splits data between gateways to increase the transfer.
- *control_panel* – this module handles requests from web-based GUI.
- *remote_files_manager* – this module mediates between the FUSE client and storage during I/O operations when the FUSE client is not directly connected to the storage where data is located (e.g. it is installed at user's PC).
- *dns* – it provides answers to DNS queries. It is part of the load balancing system described later in this article.
- *cluster_rengine* – it handles the events used for monitoring and executes rules triggered by these events.
- *rule_manager* – this module allows for definition of management rules by administrators.
- *central_logger* – it gathers logs from all the nodes of the system in one place.

Analysis of exemplary use cases can help understand the functionality of each module. When a user writes some data using FUSE client on his/her PC, the client sends a DNS request to identify, to which machine it should connect to perform further operations. The answer is formulated by the *dns* module. Next, the client sends a request to *fslogic* to resolve the location of data. *fslogic* obtains this information from the database through *dao*. When the data should be written to a remote storage, the client writes this data sending it to *remote_files_manager*.

Afterwards, when the user wants to read other file, the client again uses *fslogic* to get location of the desired data. If the data is located in other site, it returns the information where the data will be copied and sends a request to *rtransfer* to download the needed data. *rtransfer* chooses instances of the *gateway* module that should perform the transfer and sends requests to them. The data may be split across many *gateways* when a large amount of data is requested (it is possible due to the use of the prefetching algorithms).

Administrators can define some rules, e.g. quota check every 10 000 writes performed by the user. It is done by defining a rule via the web-based GUI. GUI requests are handled by the *control_panel* module, which, in this case, sends a request of rule definition to *rule_manager*. *rule_manager* sends the definition of the rule to *cluster_rengine* and requests all connected clients to produce write events. The newly connected clients (e.g., recently installed on users' PCs) will download a list of events to be produced during the initialization. Then, when the

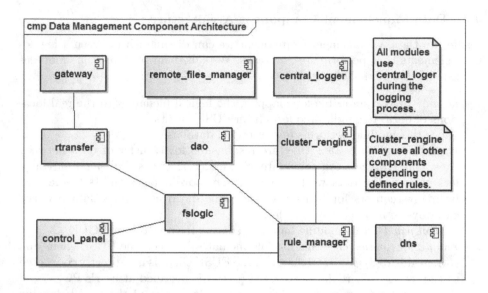

Fig. 3. Data Management Component modules

user performs a write operation, the write event is produced. If the administrator wishes to, the events are initially aggregated at the client-side, to reduce the load of network interfaces, and then sent to *cluster_rengine*, which counts events and performs the rule when at least 10 000 events have appeared.

3.5   Security

Data Management Component should be deployed on machines that are connected by internal network protected by a firewall. Only two ports should be opened: 53 for DNS and 443 for communication with clients, which is possible only using encrypted transmission (SSL).

The VeilFS authentication mechanisms are integrated with mechanisms already existing in PL-Grid so the user may use the PL-Grid certificate to mount the FUSE client or log-in to the web-based GUI. Additionally, proxy certificates generated with the PL-Grid certificates are also supported to enable the use of the FUSE client inside grid jobs. The web-based GUI cooperates with PL-Grid OpenID to automatically download additional information about users so the user is also able to log-in to GUI using the PL-Grid username and password.

The authorization mechanism is based on the fact that the sender of each request can be identified using data from his/her certificate or OpenID. Thus, the users' spaces in the database, that store information about data location, can be separated – the space connected with the request is automatically chosen. It is impossible to modify the data from other users' spaces.

The PL-Grid user accounts are automatically mapped to operating system accounts on all Computing Elements inside the sites. The data on the storage is created with adequate permissions so it is not possible to read the data that belongs to other user directly from the storage system.

FUSE clients installed outside all sites (on users' PCs) perform operations on the storage through Data Management Component that works with root permissions. Data Management Component verifies if the sender of a request has appropriate permissions to operate on a chosen data, because one might try to operate on other user's data by sending specially prepared requests of storage operations.

3.6   Deployment

Data Management Component has to manage thousands of clients working simultaneously. Furthermore, each client can generate several requests per second. Thus, one of the main non-functional requirements for Data Management Component is providing high-performance in terms of processed requests per second. For this reason, Data Management Component was written in Erlang, which provides very lightweight processes in comparison with standard operating system processes. To provide the implementation of basic language elements such as lightweight processes, Erlang has a dedicated Execution Environment – Erlang Virtual Machine. Erlang supports two types of applications – Erlang Application and Erlang Distributed Application. Erlang Application is executed inside a single Erlang Virtual Machine while Erlang Distributed Application links several Erlang Virtual Machines. At the start, Erlang Distributed Application is initialized on many Erlang Virtual Machines. However, all but one instances are paused immediately after the initialization. If the working instance fails, one of the paused instances is automatically resumed.

Data Management Component is deployed on a dedicated cluster of nodes using two types of applications that cooperate to provide the needed functionality:

- Erlang Worker Application (EWA), which hosts the modules (see subsection 3.4). It is a standard Erlang Application.
- Erlang Management Distributed Application (EMDA), which manages the cluster. It is an Erlang Distributed Application.

On each node, where Data Management Component is deployed, EWA is started. EMDA is started on chosen nodes. EWA and EMDA do not share Erlang Virtual Machine – if the node hosts them both, two instances of Erlang Virtual Machine are launched.

The nodes are physical or virtual machines. It is recommended to use physical machines to increase hardware fault tolerance (if a deployment is based on virtual machines, a hardware problem may cause a crash of many Virtual Machines – in the worst case it can be a crash of Virtual Machines that host all instances of EMDA). A deployment on a 5-node cluster is depicted in Fig. 4. Summarizing, the cluster nodes can be split into three groups:

- Management Master Node that hosts EWA and EMDA. On this node EMDA is working.

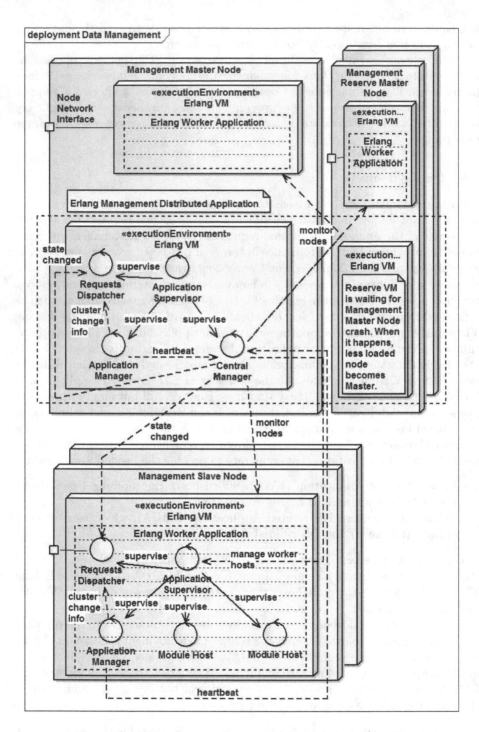

Fig. 4. Data Management Component exemplary deployment

- Management Reserve Master Nodes that host EWA and EMDA. Instances of EMDA are paused on these nodes.
- Management Slave Nodes that host only EWA.

When the Management Master Node fails, one of Management Reserve Master Nodes resumes EMDA and becomes the Management Master Node.

To provide the requested functionality and meet non-functional requirements, several application elements have been implemented using Erlang (see Fig. 4):

- Module Host – an element that executes the code of a chosen module (see 3.4).
- Central Manager – an element that coordinates all nodes, which are part of Data Management Component.
- Application Manager – an element that monitors the state of the node where the application is deployed and provides information about the node state to the Central Manager.
- Application Supervisor – an element that monitors the execution of application code and repairs the application after an error (Supervisor is an Erlang element that monitors Erlang processes and restarts them in case of failure).
- Requests Dispatcher – an element that is responsible for forwarding the requests to the appropriate Module Host.

EWA includes instances of Module Host, which provide modules' functionalities. Requests are processed by the modules concurrently – each request has its own Erlang process inside Module Host. The nodes and EWAs are independent. They cooperate due to the use of Central Manager, which coordinates their work. The Central Manager is the most important element of EMDA. It is not a single point of failure owing to the properties of Erlang Distributed Application described above. The set of nodes may change dynamically through the use of Application Managers. Application Manager periodically sends a heartbeat to Central Manager so Central Manager is able to discover new EWAs. Afterwards, Central Manager monitors Erlang Virtual Machine inside, which EWA works to notice when Erlang Virtual Machine is stopped, e.g. due to a failure. Application Manager also checks periodically if Requests Dispatcher (see subsection 3.7) has up-to-date information about the modules and triggers an update if needed.

Application Manager constantly monitors the load of a node. Module Host monitors the load of a module. Central Manager periodically gathers information about the load from all instances of Application Manager and Module Host. On the basis of this information, it dynamically starts/stops instances of Module Host working for chosen modules to provide load balancing and high availability of each module (for more details see subsection 3.7). Central Manager uses Application Supervisor available on each node to start/stop instances of Module Host. Application Supervisor is an element that monitors Erlang processes and restarts them in case of a failure so Central Manager is not involved in repairs.

Such a design of Data Management Component makes it scalable and resistant to failures. Central Manager is able to capture any changes and respond to them. Moreover, all nodes are able to work independently in case of a network failure, because they have own Supervisors. When the network is repaired, they connect once more and Central Manager is again able to reconfigure the node if needed.

3.7   Notifications and Requests

Clients send synchronous requests to Data Management Component to get/update metadata, e.g. get the mappings of logical filenames to the actual data locations on a storage or initiate metadata for the newly created files. Beside the standard requests connected with metadata, VeilFS heavily utilizes asynchronous notifications, which are processed by Data Management Component to exchange monitoring information across the system. Notifications provide useful information about the infrastructure state to administrators. The administrators use this information to create or parameterize data management rules, which are the basis of the effective data management subsystem, e.g. the rules that control data migration or system quotas. When the rules are defined, notifications are used as triggers of the rules (see exemplary use cases described in subsection 3.4). A typical rule concerns data management within a site. Data management that involves different sites is described in subsection 3.8. Notifications also enable detailed accounting. Beside the information about the amount of data stored in the system, other information such as the load of storage systems by read/write operations generated by user's processes can be controlled.

Types of requests/notifications may change with time. To meet this challenge, a scalable and elastic way of request handling has been designed. Central Manager controls DNS to inform clients, at which nodes a particular module works. However, Module instances may be started/stopped dynamically when types of incoming requests/notifications change. Therefore, a Module instances location may change before the mapping of modules to nodes provided by DNS is expired. Moreover, when many clients work simultaneously, a situation when no mapping is valid may never occur. For this reason, an instance of Requests Dispatcher works inside each application. It is used to route requests from a network interface to the nodes where a desired module is working. Having a Dispatcher instance, control over DNS is not required (requests are always redirected to an appropriate node), but is profitable, because an extensive use of DNS decreases the network traffic inside a cluster (requests usually go straight to the node, which hosts the required module). Additionally, Dispatcher provides a load balancing capability. The communication between instances of Module Host and Requests Dispatcher is not visualized in Fig. 4 – it would make the image too complicated. Instead, a request flow is depicted in Fig. 5.

3.8   Data Access in Organizationally Distributed Environments

The deployment of VeilFS is similar in the context of distributed organization and federation. The access to the data located in different sites was described in subsection 3.3. However, some requirements have to be fulfilled to provide a uniform and coherent view on data as well as an efficient access to data in the federation case. VeilFS supports rules, which operate between sites. Administrators of all organizations should agree on the management rules. Typically, the newly created data should be migrated to a site where the user has a granted storage when the data is no longer used by the process that has created it.

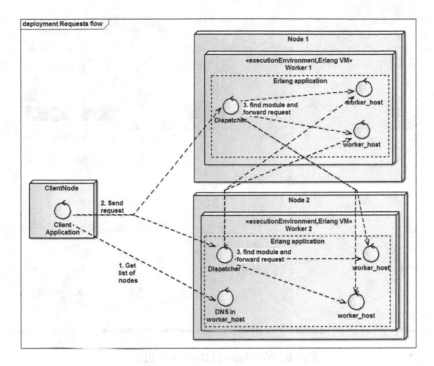

Fig. 5. Client request flow within VeilFS

However, when the user has an access granted to storage resources in multiple sites, different possibilities appear. For example, the data may be migrated to a site where it is used most frequently if all sites have activated rules that permit data send/receive in this case. It decreases the network traffic, because – once migrated – the data will be more frequently read locally than streamed.

4   Implementation Status

A prototype version of the presented system was implemented and evaluated. To provide high performance and scalability, Erlang, C programming languages and a NoSQL database were used. Erlang offers massive parallelism through its lightweight process mechanism, which is very important in the data management part, because Data Management Component cooperates with thousands of Computing Elements simultaneously. On the other hand, the C language enables efficient implementation of low level operations on the physical data. The information about metadata and the system state is stored in a fault-tolerant, high-performance, distributed NoSQL database to avoid performance bottlenecks and guarantee data security.

The implemented prototype version provides unification of namespace, support for group working and results publication. The FUSE client, web-based GUI

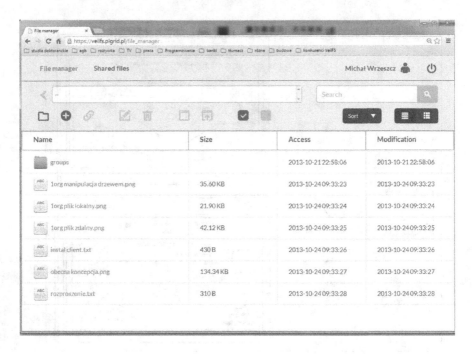

Fig. 6. Web-based GUI for VeilFS

Table 2. Preliminary overhead tests results

Number of threads used	1 thread			16 threads		
Test mode	RW	WR	RD	RW	WR	RD
Without VeilFS [Mb/s]	2,65	14,69	11,27	6,05	13,66	11,25
With VeilFS [Mb/s]	2,76	14,52	11,21	5,63	13,50	11,26
Difference [Mb/s]	0,10	-0,17	-0,06	-0,42	-0,15	0,01
Difference [%]	3,79	-1,12	-0,55	-6,99	-1,13	0,05

(see Fig. 6) and the REST API have been implemented using secure communication methods (SSL and GSI). The Data Management Component has been
equipped with mechanisms that provide load balancing and high availability.
Simple installators of client, Data Management Component and DB have also
been created.

The components implemented using different technologies are able to cooperate. In case of the FUSE client, the component implemented in the C language
communicates with modules on the server side implemented in Erlang. The requests are processed concurrently by light Erlang processes to minimize the
answer time on multi-core machines. Preliminary tests results have shown that
the overhead of VeilFS is low (see Table 2). The transfer rates measured by

SysBench [6] were similar when operations were performed directly using NFS [4] and when they were performed using VeilFS that exploited NFS to store data.

The current version of the system provides a complete set of functionalities for the end user – it provides a uniform and coherent view on all user's data, supports work in groups and data publication. Further work is going on to increase the functionality from the administrator point of view.

5 Conclusions and Future Work

A need for easy data access arises due to the continuously increasing diversity of storage systems. A users' requirements analysis has shown that access to files is often too complicated. Although there are a lot of tools that provide a single user interface for various storage management systems, they are too cumbersome to use in globally distributed environments.

The presented system addresses the issue of easy access to data along with administrators' requirements for effective managing federated, heterogeneous storage resources. The described solutions not only provide users with easy access to data anywhere and anytime, but also give administrators powerful tools for automated infrastructure monitoring and management. Moreover, the proposed architecture is able to process a large number of requests and notifications, which is needed to offer the described functionality. We believe that the system will be useful for all PL-Grid Infrastructure users and more users will be able to use all functionalities currently offered by the PL-Grid Infrastructure through the simplification of data management by VeilFS. We hope that the new functionalities offered by the system, e.g. a simple data sharing and publishing, will be appreciated by its users.

Future work will focus on further development of storage resources management, particularly in the areas of migration, caching and prefetching of data, as well as on creation the tools for administrators. Additionally, the authors are working to add a global level of VeilFS, which allows users data migration between different organizations that are not federated and globally unifies the access to data – the user will see all the data stored in all sites that belong to different federations regardless of the actual access point.

Acknowledgements. Thanks go to the rest of VeilFS team, especially to Rafał Słota, Łukasz Opioła, Darin Nikolow, Paweł Sałata, Beata Skiba and Bartosz Polnik for their support.

References

1. Ceph Filesystem web site, http://ceph.com/docs/next/cephfs/
2. Dropbox web site, https://www.dropbox.com/
3. GlusterFS community web site, http://www.gluster.org/about/
4. Nfs version 3 protocol specification, http://tools.ietf.org/html/rfc1813

5. Scality web site, http://www.scality.com/products/what-is-ring/
6. Sysbench: a system performance benchmark,
   http://sysbench.sourceforge.net/index.html
7. Gantz, J., Reinsel, D.: The Digital Universe in 2020: Big Data, Bigger Digital Shadows, and Biggest Growth in the Far East (2012),
   http://www.emc.com/leadership/digital-universe/index.htm
8. Hunich, D., Muller-Pfefferkorn, R.: Managing Large Datasets with iRODS: a Performance Analysis. In: Proceedings of the 2010 International Multiconference on Computer Science and Information Technology (IMCSIT), pp. 647–654 (2010)
9. Kitowski, J., Dutka, Ł., Mosurska, Z., Pająk, R., Sterzel, M., Szepieniec, T.: Development of Polish Infrastructure for Advanced Scientific Research – Status and Current Achievements. In: Proc. of IEEE Conf. 12th Inter. Symposium on Parallel and Distributed Computing (ISPDC 2013), Bucharest, Romania, pp. 34–41 (2013)
10. Kryza, B., Król, D., Wrzeszcz, M., Dutka, Ł., Kitowski, J.: Interactive cloud data farming environment for military mission planning support. Computer Science 13(3), 89–100 (2012),
    https://journals.agh.edu.pl/csci/article/view/19
11. Mills, S., Lucas, S., Irakliotis, L., Rappa, M., Carlson, T., Perlowitz, B.: DEMYSTIFYING BIG DATA: A Practical Guide to Transforming the Business of Government. Technical report (2012),
    http://www.ibm.com/software/data/demystifying-big-data/
12. Roblitz, T.: Towards Implementing Virtual Data Infrastructures – a Case Study with iRODS. Computer Science 13(4) (2012),
    http://journals.agh.edu.pl/csci/article/view/43
13. Słota, R., Dutka, Ł., Wrzeszcz, M., Kryza, B., Nikolow, D., Król, D., Kitowski, J.: Storage Systems for Organizationally Distributed Environments – PLGrid Plus Case Study. In: Wyrzykowski, R., Dongarra, J., Karczewski, K., Wasśniewski, J. (eds.) PPAM 2013, Part I. LNCS, pp. 724–733. Springer, Heidelberg (2013)
14. Słota, R., Król, D., Skałkowski, K., Kryza, B., Nikołow, D., Orzechowski, M., Kitowski, J.: A Toolkit for Storage QoS Provisioning for Data-Intensive Applications. In: Bubak, M., Szepieniec, T., Wiatr, K. (eds.) PL-Grid 2011. LNCS, vol. 7136, pp. 157–170. Springer, Heidelberg (2012)
15. Słota, R., Nikolow, D., Kitowski, J., Król, D., Kryza, B.: FiVO/QStorMan Semantic Toolkit for Supporting Data-Intensive Applications in Distributed Environments. Computing and Informatics 31(5), 1003–1024 (2012),
    http://dblp.uni-trier.de/db/journals/cai/cai31.html#SlotaNKOK12
16. Szepieniec, T., Tomanek, M., Radecki, M., Szopa, M., Bubak, M.: Implementation of Service Level Management in PL-Grid Infrastructure. In: Bubak, M., Szepieniec, T., Wiatr, K. (eds.) PL-Grid 2011. LNCS, vol. 7136, pp. 171–181. Springer, Heidelberg (2012)
17. Thain, D., Livny, M.: Parrot: an Application Environment for Data-Intensive Computing. Journal of Parallel and Distributed Computing Practices, 9–18 (2005)

Enabling Multiscale Fusion Simulations on Distributed Computing Resources

Katarzyna Rycerz[1,2], Marian Bubak[1,2], Eryk Ciepiela[2], Maciej Pawlik[2],
Olivier Hoenen[3], Daniel Harężlak[2], Bartosz Wilk[2], Tomasz Gubała[2],
Jan Meizner[2], and David Coster[3]

[1] AGH University of Science and Technology, Department of Computer Science,
al. Mickiewicza 30, 30-059 Kraków, Poland
{kzajac,bubak}@agh.edu.pl
[2] AGH University of Science and Technology, ACC Cyfronet AGH,
ul. Nawojki 11, 30-950 Kraków, Poland
{d.harezlak,b.wilk,e.ciepiela,t.gubala,m.pawlik}@cyfronet.krakow.pl
http://dice.cyfronet.pl
[3] Max-Planck-Institut fuer Plasmaphysik,
Boltzmannstr. 2, D-85748 Garching, Germany
{olivier.hoenen,david.coster}@ipp.mpg.de

Abstract. We describe a way to support the execution of multiphysics
simulations on PL-Grid resources. To achieve this, we extended the existing programming and execution framework for multiscale applications
to support execution of legacy, computationally intensive applications,
which apply various computational patterns. In particular, we focus on
a stability simulation involving the plasma edge in a Tokamak device.
We also show how to support the parameter sweep pattern of execution
used in that application.

We combine two approaches for building multiphysics applications:
visual composition enabled by the Multiscale Application Designer and
a script-based solution supported by the GridSpace platform. The usage
and benefits of the PL-Grid e-infrastructure for application execution are
outlined.

Keywords: distributed computing, multiphysics, multiscale, fusion,
workflow, e-Infrastructures, tools and environments.

1 Introduction

Multiphysics simulation is an important research field, which involves combining
models of multiple simultaneous physical phenomena [39]. Similarly, multiscale
simulations combine physical models acting at different scales [16], [23], [40].
In this paper we focus on simulations that are realized by complex applications
composed of independent software modules modelling physical phenomena. Such
modules often rely on advance scientific packages and require large-scale computational resources; therefore they might benefit from HPC (e.g. PRACE) or grid
(e.g. National Grid Initiative) projects such as PL-Grid [27]). In [34] we have

M. Bubak et al. (Eds.): PLGrid Plus, LNCS 8500, pp. 195–210, 2014.
© Springer International Publishing Switzerland 2014

proposed a method and framework for composing and running such applications. The way in which such modules are composed to form complex multiphysics or multiscale applications is dependent on various simulation patterns. We extend the presented solution to support parameter sweep applications, which can be found in most experimental science domains. Additionally, we also focus on mature legacy libraries for numerical simulations, such as fusion plasma physics applications used for magnetohydrodynamics (MHD) stability studies [4], [25], [38].

The objective of this work is to investigate methods of support for execution of legacy, mature and computationally intensive simulations. We facilitate creation of such applications in the form of "in-silico" experiments, enabling legacy modules to be flexibly combined, reflecting physical phenomena with new pre- or post- processing code, written using modern scripting languages without modification of legacy code. We focus on support for transparent control flow in interconnected modules, which form portable and reusable experiments. Last but not least, our goal is to show the benefits of using the PL-Grid Infrastructure for such a case study.

This paper is organized as follows: Section 2 overviews related work, Section 3 describes an example application simulating the fusion processes, Section 4 outlines the requirements of multiscale applications, Section 5 presents an environment, which supports the process of creating multiscale applications, Section 6 describes how the proposed environment is applied to the fusion application. Results are presented in Section 7, while the benefits of using the PL-Grid Infrastructure are discussed in Section 8. Section 9 concludes the paper.

2   Related Work

We based our approach to building and executing multiscale simulations on to-date experience with composing applications from existing software modules, including a system for building workflows with semantic and syntactic descriptions of the available services in the Grid [12]. In the Virolab[1] project [11], this approach was extended to support development of collaborative applications from elements available on distributed web and grid resources.

There are already many tools which support building and running scientific applications composed from independent modules (i.e., general workflows) [6], [32], [42]. For example, the Kepler workflow management system [3] offers various execution control features, implemented as directors: e.g. one director can be used to process one component at a time in a preordered sequence, while another may handle components running simultaneously [19]. There is also an approach based on scripts used as a coordination feature [2], [31]. Multiscale applications can, however, benefit from a more specific and problem-oriented approach. A good example of an environment which supports generic processing is the Astrophysical Multi-Scale Environment (AMUSE) [33], designed for astrophysical applications where different simulation models of star systems are incorporated into a coherent framework with a scripting approach, and can be

---

[1] http://www.virolab.org/

executed either sequentially or concurrently. Another example is MUSCLE [9], which supports cyclic multiscale simulations comprising modules executed concurrently and communicating directly in a distributed environment. The issue of using computational resources offered by grid or cloud e-infrastructures in multiscale applications has been addressed in projects such as QosCosGrid [10], Euforia [22], UrbanFlood [1], VPH-Share[2] or MAPPER[3], where applications are described using a dedicated Multiscale Modelling Language (MML) [15].

The approach presented in this paper extends the solutions mentioned above in a way, which is independent of the actual realization (i.e. implementation in a specific environment) of a multiscale application and supports combining modules from different environments. For example, it is possible to run MUSCLE-based applications [5] and join them with other non-MUSCLE modules. We also combine both approaches (i.e., script-based development and visual composition) in one solution, while most workflow management systems focus on one approach to the exclusion of all others. As a description language we have chosen MML, which, in contrast to general workflow languages such as MoML [30], is dedicated to multiscale applications [15]. We also support execution of scientific software components in various European e-Infrastructures by integrating different services [10], [41] with our solutions. In this paper we also focus on the usability and benefits of PL-Grid resources.

3   Characteristics of the Fusion Application

As a case study for our solution we have selected a computationally demanding application simulating fusion. This application consists of several legacy software components and follows the parameter sweep pattern. The chosen application simulates various phenomena involved in fusion reaction in magnetically confined plasma in a Tokamak experimental device. These phenomena exhibit different temporal and spatial scales whose modelling and simulation is a good match for multiscale approaches. In this work we concentrate on a use case which involves several physics models and requires a parameter scan: J-alpha stability analysis of the plasma edge.

This application is built upon two legacy components (for the sake of conciseness we disregard the initial equilibrium reconstruction from experimental data, a comprehensive description can be found in [28]): a high-resolution fixed-boundary equilibrium solver (HELENA) and an MHD stability component (ILSA). Both components are implemented in Fortran 77/90 and are mostly sequential (only a part of ILSA is parallelized with OpenMP). The interfaces of these components rely on a set of generic data structures [26] defined by the ITM-TF[4], providing a direct means of coupling different physics modules. Code-specific parameters (both physical and numerical) are passed in XML

---

[2] http://www.vph-share.eu
[3] http://www.mapper-project.eu
[4] http://portal.efda-itm.eu/itm/portal/

format through an additional input file. A simple *stability chain* consists of two following steps:

1. running HELENA to calculate a high-resolution equilibrium from a low-resolution version given by experimental data,
2. applying ILSA on this high-resolution equilibrium in order to determine the stability of the plasma in such a configuration.

Plasma stability is of high importance when trying to reach suitable conditions for a fusion reaction to occur. In order to find the best configuration, one can modify the pressure profile and the flux surface averaged current density. Such modification induces a slightly updated equilibrium, which might be proven more or less stable than the initial configuration. We use the parameter scan approach to simulate a range of different values for both pressure and current density. We thus obtain a J-alpha stability diagram which can be used to optimize an experiment. The application requires computational resources that can be provided by European e-infrastructures like PL-Grid.

4   Required Framework Capabilities

We use the aforementioned fusion application to illustrate the need for the following features:

- **Support for Mature, Legacy Computational Intensive Applications.** We aim to support a broad range of multiscale and multiphysics applications. Therefore, our solution is independent of actual software packages used in specific modules. In particular, we support mature legacy implementations of modules, which can be combined with new modules to form a full-fledged multiscale application.
- **Support for Parameter Sweep Applications.** Coupling between modules can follow many different patterns [8]. We aim to provide support for non-invasive execution control of different patterns. We consider the case of acyclic execution, where a designated module triggers many simulation instances with different sets of parameters.
- **Support for Building Different Multiscale Applications from the Same Modules.** We would like to give users the ability to experiment with different versions of modules provided they share the same interfaces (input and output description). This feature also enables validation of new module versions as well as benchmarking different implementations and numerics for a given physics module. Additionally, we would like to enable sharing the created modules (including the descriptions of their connections) and reusing them in different configurations.
- **Support for Accessing e-infrastructures.** Modules which belong to a multiscale application often have different computational requirements – some of them may be MPI parallel programs requiring a computational cluster, while others may perform best on GPU or SMP machines. Additionally, some models

may have different specialized proprietary software requirements. Therefore, there is often a need for running modules in distributed way to satisfy all their requirements. In this paper we focus on some details of providing access to the PL-Grid Infrastructure[5] for the multiphysics application developers.

5   Composition and Execution Control Framework

The environment presented in this paper allows for composition of multiphysics applications from submodels of single-scale phenomena. Following this step, the simulation is executed. We assume that the submodules are already created, deployed and properly described in MML by their developers. The development and deployment of particular submodules are out of scope of this paper.

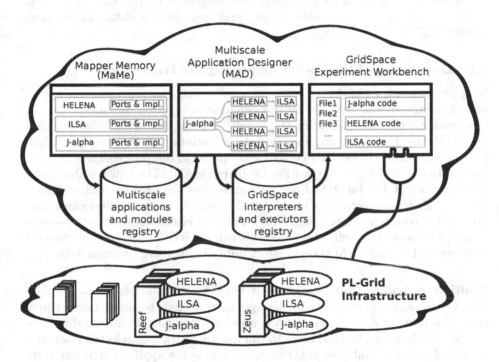

Fig. 1. Multiscale tools supporting modelling of fusion processes. Three modules needed to simulate MHD phenomena in Tokamak plasma are registered in the Mapper Memory (MaMe) registry: a high-resolution fixed-boundary plasma equilibrium module (HELENA), a linear magnetohydrodynamics stability module (ELSA), and a wrapper (J-alpha). An application is composed from these modules in the Multiscale Application Designer (MAD) and executed in the GridSpace Experiment Workbench.

The architecture of the framework of the presented tools is shown in Fig. 1. Mapper Memory (MaMe) is a registry for MML-based descriptions of

---

individual models used in the composition step supported by the Multiscale Application designer (MAD). In Fig. 1 three such modules, required to simulate MHD phenomena in Tokamak plasma, are depicted: a high-resolution fixed-boundary plasma equilibrium module (HELENA), a linear magnetohydrodynamics stability module (ILSA), and a wrapper (J-alpha), which embeds a small tool to modify plasma profiles (pressure and current density), along with equilibrium code (HELENA).

The Multiscale Application Designer supports application composition and transforms their high-level MML descriptions into an executable form of an "in-silico" experiment, which is then executed by the GridSpace Experiment Workbench. The user is able to select the appropriate resources and then start and monitor the execution from a single web-based entry point. Following the execution, the output data is fetched and presented to the user. The tools are web-based services available online[6] and described in detail in the next subsection.

5.1 Description of the Tools Comprising the Framework

Mapper Memory (MaMe). It is mainly responsible for providing a rich, persistent information store based on the semantic integration technology [20,21]. The semantic metadata model of MaMe relies on the Multiscale Modeling Language (MML) [15]. MaMe provides a web-based interface to record scripts, which the application developers have created and can use to compose complex applications with the Multiscale Application Designer (MAD). The registry also stores metadata about the input and output parameters required by such scripts – these are shown as ports to be connected. If a script simulates phenomena that possess the notion of scale, detailed information concerning this facet of operation can be stored as well. MaMe also provides a REST interface for external software tools – such as MAD – to store, publish and share common data.

Multiscale Application Designer. It fetches data from MaMe and enables visual composition of applications through a web page. The connection schema, generated from its visual view, is then translated into a portable executable experiment, which is used by GridSpace to run the application on selected resources. The application assembly in MAD supports saving the application at any state of composition, together with the parameters of individual models. The default values for these parameters are obtained from MaMe. It is also possible to share a precomposed application with other users through the application repository for collaborative work.

GridSpace Experiment Workbench. It executes the application in the form of "in-silico" experiments [13].

GridSpace was originally developed in the Virolab and PL-Grid projects [14] and was further extended to support multiscale applications. As can be seen

---

[6] https://gs2.mapper-project.eu

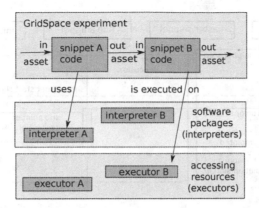

Fig. 2. Structure of a GridSpace experiment, which consists of a number of arbitrary executable code snippets and their input and output file artifacts (assets). Each snippet can be executed by a different interpreter, i.e., an arbitrary software package using a specific executor (i.e., infrastructure access service).

in Fig. 2, the experiments consist of a number of executable code snippets and their input and output file artifacts (assets). Each snippet can be executed by a different interpreter, i.e., an arbitrary software package. This can be a general-purpose scripting interpreter such as Python, Perl or Ruby, or any other software component used in scientific applications, e.g. MUSCLE supporting a cyclic multiscale connection schema [9], a JRuby script orchestrating HLA Components [35], [37], or a LAMMPS script executed as a parallel MPI application [18], [29], [36]. In this way, the GridSpace experiment concept matches the general multiscale description requirement.

GridSpace supports execution on a high level and interfaces with various services that access different e-infrastructures via so-called executors. Examples of such executors include the Application Hosting Environment (AHE) [41], which provides access to globus and UNICORE resources [7], and QCG-Broker [10], which provides co-allocation and an advanced reservation mechanism. The PL-Grid Infrastructure can be accessed directly by SSH on UI machines, by the QCG-Broker service and by the Elite middleware accessible with a dedicated GridSpace Grid executor.

5.2   Support for Complex Control Flow

In order to facilitate complex control flow in experiments, as required by certain fusion experiment scenarios, GridSpace was extended with a mechanism that enables reversed control of execution. It is possible to control the flow of the experiment from within the experiment itself. This is done by enabling a snippet to call for execution of other snippets, and oversee their execution. This mechanism is independent of other GridSpace features – in particular, it is possible to control execution of snippets distributed over different executors or infrastructures.

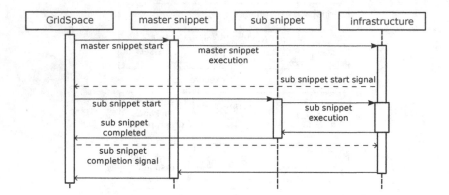

Fig. 3. Sequence diagram showing interactions between the GridSpace platform, the master snippet, a subsnippet and the underlying infrastructure. GridSpace controls execution of each snippet.

This permits transparent access to all the available infrastructures, regardless of compute site boundaries.

A simple scenario, which calls a snippet named *sub snippet* from inside of *master snippet*, is shown in Fig. 3. The four actors, depicted in this figure, can be treated as entities. They remain active during a given time period, are represented by blocks, and communicate with each other along arrows. The *GridSpace* actor is the presented platform, *snippets* contain code written by the user, while *infrastructure* is where the code actually runs.

GridSpace is an experiment execution management platform. As such, its main role is to start and keep track of snippet execution. This behavior is represented by outgoing and incoming arrows, which connect the GridSpace platform with the snippet entity. In turn, each snippet contains code that is executed on the designated infrastructure, represented by arrows pointing from the snippet entities to the *infrastructure* and back. The new functionality can be seen as calls represented by dashed arrows, occurring in the midst of snippet execution. Such calls communicate to GridSpace the need to start other snippets and signal their completion to the originator of the call.

The above mentioned functionality paves the way towards execution of nested snippets in loops and conditional statements which, in turn, facilitate experiments that follow popular application patterns such as parameter sweep studies.

6   Running the Fusion Application with GridSpace

To implement such an application within the framework presented in Section 5, we first need to register HELENA, J-alpha and ILSA through the MaMe tool, describing their properties in MML. In this description, HELENA and J-alpha have equilibrium data structures both as input and output, whereas ILSA has

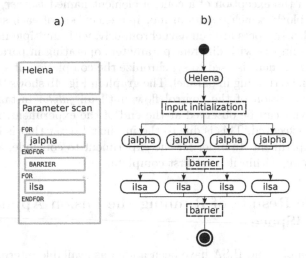

Fig. 4. Side by side comparison of (a) GridSpace UI experiment representation and (b) actual control flow scheme. The application consists of single *helena*, multiple *J-alpha* and multiple *ilsa* snippets. Multiple execution is controlled by the auxiliary *parameter scan* snippet.

equilibrium as input and an MHD data structure as output. Once this step is completed, the structure of the coupled application can be built graphically with the MAD tool, which connects components registered in MaMe. Once designed, each component of this coupled MAD application can be replaced by other implementations of the same component as long as they share the same interface (and thus the same data structure ontology defined by ITM-TF). Eventually, the coupled application is executed on the available computing resources through the GridSpace experiment workbench. In this specific application, HE-LENA and ILSA are treated as interpreters and their XML-specific parameters are considered code snippets. The subsnippet mechanism, newly added in GS and described below, enables execution of several instances of such a stability chain for different parameters, where J-alpha replaces the HELENA instance.

As shown in Fig. 4a, the GridSpace UI provides the ability to embed elements of the experiment (snippets and execution control elements) in other snippets.

The embedded snippets are treated as expressions with no return values; therefore their execution is governed by the control flow of the source code, from the containing snippet. As a result, *jalpha* and *ilsa* snippets can be invoked from within the *parameter scan* snippet.

An embedded snippet can be executed in two modes: *synchronously* and *asynchronously*. The first option means that control flow will be halted until the embedded snippet finishes executing, while the other mode means that control flow may advance. The example depicted in Fig. 4a shows that each of the embedded snippets, with the exception of a control element named *barrier*, is surrounded with a FOR block, which results in multiple execution of each snippet. In this case, embedded snippets are run asynchronously, with multiple instances of *jalpha* and *ilsa* snippets with different parameters operating in parallel.

The *barrier* element is used to synchronize the completion of a given group of snippet instances running in parallel. The graph in Fig. 4b shows that the *barrier* stops the progression of the control flow until all *jalpha* instances complete. Similar behavior can be observed at the end of the experiment, right after *ilsa* instances are executed. This is due to the implicit *barrier* that is inserted at the end of the experiment. In order for the experiment to conclude, all instances of snippets running within it must first complete.

7   Sample Results of Running the Fusion Applications in GridSpace

HELENA, J-alpha and ILSA have been added as available interpreters in Grid-Space. The J-alpha application snippet in GridSpace allows users to select the range of scaling parameters for modifying pressure and current density, given an initial high resolution equilibrium coming from HELENA. As a proof of concept, we have chosen to explore six different pressure and current density values (each additional value corresponds to the initial profiles being scaled by a given factor, i.e. from 0.6 to 1.1 with a 0.1 step).

- J-alpha requires between 1 and 30 minutes, depending on the selected resolution and other numerical parameters, which are fixed for a given simulation,
- ILSA requires between 1 and more than 24 hours, depending on the physics and profile scaling parameters, which are evaluated during the simulation.

Thus, this simulation consists of 36 different and independent equilibrium-stability chains, each of which is composed of three steps: creating the run directories with input files corresponding to the selected scaling parameter values, running J-alpha asynchronously to update the initial equilibrium to these parameters, and then running ILSA asynchronously on the updated equilibrium. J-alpha and ILSA runs are submitted to queues with respect to their expected wallclock time: The total time for such a parameter study simulation is 8.67 hours, from which each J-alpha job uses only 2 minutes, with all jobs started at the same time. Due to the heavy load, only 14 ILSA jobs are executed instantly after J-alpha jobs have produced an updated equilibrium. All jobs reach the execution state within 10 minutes, with ILSA running from 1.25 to 8.58 hours.

In addition to the experiment presented in Section 6, a post-processing tool based on Python and using Matplotlib [24] has been added as a new component to the framework, in order to visualize 1D and 2D data. Python is available as an interpreter in GridSpace and the code snippet corresponds to a Python script, which reads the data and builds a plot. Such a component is reusable for any ITM-TF data structure, and using it within the J-alpha coupled application allows preliminary results to be checked before the end of the simulation.

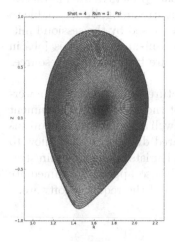

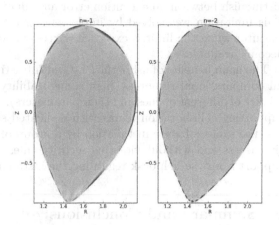

Fig. 5. High-resolution equilibrium mesh of a shaped plasma poloidal cross-section (ASDEX-Upgrade Tokamak), computed by HELENA using straight field-line coordinates

Fig. 6. Edge-localized mode structures of the plasma described by Fig. 5, for two different mode numbers computed by ILSA (in MISHKA mode). Blue and red colors represent the alternating phases of the mode.

Fig. 5 presents sample output from the Python script, which shows the structure of the high-resolution equilibrium mesh calculated by HELENA, given the experimental data from ASDEX Upgrade Tokamak. Subsequently, we performed a parameter study for each of the pressure and current density profiles, with a slightly different equilibrium mesh (sharing a common boundary). The results of edge structures for two sample parameter sets (modes) calculated by ILSA for such an equilibrium configuration are shown in Fig. 6. These results illustrate that the application was successfully run on the PL-Grid Infrastructure using the proposed framework. In the next section we will summarize our experience with the presented tools and the PL-Grid e-infrastructure itself.

8   Benefits and Limits of Using the PL-Grid Infrastructure

All the modules that constitute the fusion application (i.e., HELENA, J-alpha and ILSA) has been deployed on the PL-Grid Infrastructure (Zeus cluster at CYFRONET and Reef cluster at PSNC). We have used different configurations for each module of the application: J-alpha jobs are submitted to the *l_short* queue (3 hour wallclock time limit) and ILSA jobs are submitted to *plgrid* queue (72 hour wallclock time limit).

During our work we had to solve the problem of limits on interactive sessions. In the case of SSH access excessive interactive jobs are discarded, and an appropriate message is presented to the user. GridSpace prefers to use interactive job sessions, as they are required for real-time output streaming, but is unable to distinguish between an execution error and an error caused by the session limit. This limitation was solved by implementing a mechanism that queues jobs in executor when the limit is exceeded. Excessive jobs are held until the resources become available.

The main benefits of using the PL-Grid Infrastructure include access to powerful computational resources, high configurability of the execution environment (choice of different queues and their parameters), as well as extended mechanisms supporting collaboration teams with dedicated shared directories that allow to test the same software installation by a group of scientists without administrative access and without violating security rules. We also appreciate immediate support from the helpdesk regarding the installation of the required software.

9   Summary and Conclusions

In this paper we describe an extension to an environment for composing multiscale simulations from single-scale models [34], which are executed on various e-infrastructures. The proposed extension allows for advanced execution control of modules comprising multiphysics or multiscale applications that apply the parameter sweep pattern. We focus on a fusion simulation case study, which analyzes the stability of the plasma edge in a Tokamak device. We present how to build a fully functional application from mature, legacy components joined with additional modules written in a scripting language. Our application runs on resources provided by the PLGrid Plus project.

Compared to the usual homebrew scripting approach applied by physicists for similar parameters studies (which can sometimes involve advanced but non-portable capabilities), the usage of this framework offers a real advantage in terms of reusability and portability. It also supports heterogeneous computing resources, especially when dealing with coupled applications, where each sub-model might have different requirements. Quantifying the performance of the parameter study, we have conducted, is a difficult task as it depends heavily on the size of the system and on its load during the test. Nevertheless, the graphical user interface of the three main tools (MaMe, MAD, GridSpace) provides a very user-friendly experience, and conceals most of the technical complexity from the physicists who can thus focus their effort on the development of custom modules. Compared to other simulation platforms for running coupled applications, such as the one mentioned in [17], where all tools are available through a centralized Kepler installation, the web-based approach to design and execution of tools presented in this paper offers a more parameterizable experience.

Acknowledgements. The authors thank A.G. Hoekstra, J. Borgdorff, C. Bona Casas, E. Lorenz, M. Ben Belgacem, B. Chopard, A. Burckhart and W. Funika for helpful discussion and remarks.

References

1. Balis, B., Kasztelnik, M., Bubak, M., et al.: The UrbanFlood Common Information Space for Early Warning Systems. Procedia CS 4, 96–105 (2011)
2. Baranowski, M., Belloum, A., Bubak, M., Malawski, M.: Constructing workflows from script applications. Scientific Programming 20(4), 359–377 (2012)
3. Barseghian, D., Altintas, I., Jones, M.B., Crawl, D., Potter, N., Gallagher, J., Cornillon, P., Schildhauer, M., Borer, E.T., Seabloom, E.W., Hosseini, P.R.: Workflows and extensions to the Kepler scientific workflow system to support environmental sensor data access and analysis. Ecological Informatics 5, 42–50 (2010)
4. Batchelor, D.A., Beck, M., Becoulet, A., Budny, R.V., Chang, C.S., Diamond, P.H., Dong, J.Q., Fu, G.Y., Fukuyama, A., Hahm, T.S., Keyes, D.E., Kishimoto, Y., Klasky, S., Lao, L.L., Li, K., Lin, Z., Ludaescher, B., Manickam, J., Nakajima, N., Ozeki, T., Podhorszki, N., Tang, W.M., Vouk, M.A., Waltz, R.E., Wang, S.J., Wilson, H.R., Xu, X.Q., Yagi, M., Zonca, F.: Simulation of fusion plasmas: Current status and future direction. Plasma Science and Technology 9(3), 312 (2007)
5. Belgacem, M.B., Chopard, B., Borgdorff, J., Mamoński, M., Rycerz, K., Harężlak, D.: Distributed Multiscale Computations Using the MAPPER Framework. Procedia Computer Science 18, 1106–1115 (2013), http://www.sciencedirect.com/science/article/pii/S1877050913004195
6. Belloum, A., Inda, M.A., Vasunin, D., Korkhov, V., Zhao, Z., Rauwerda, H., Breit, T.M., Bubak, M., Hertzberger, L.O.: Collaborative e-Science Experiments and Scientific Workflows. IEEE Internet Computing 15(4), 39–47 (2011)
7. Benedyczak, K., Stolarek, M., Rowicki, R., Kluszczyński, R., Borcz, M., Marczak, G., Filocha, M., Bała, P.: Seamless Access to the PL-Grid e-Infrastructure Using UNICORE Middleware. In: Bubak, M., Szepieniec, T., Wiatr, K. (eds.) PL-Grid 2011. LNCS, vol. 7136, pp. 56–72. Springer, Heidelberg (2012), http://dx.doi.org/10.1007/978-3-642-28267-6_5
8. Borgdorff, J., Falcone, J.L., Lorenz, E., Bona-Casas, C., Chopard, B., Hoekstra, A.G.: Foundations of distributed multiscale computing: Formalization, specification, analysis and execution. Journal of Parallel and Distributed Computing 73, 465–483 (2013)
9. Borgdorff, J., Mamoński, M., Bosak, B., Groen, D., Belgacem, M.B., Kurowski, K., Hoekstra, A.G.: Multiscale Computing with the Multiscale Modeling Library and Runtime Environment. Procedia Computer Science 18, 1097–1105 (2013), http://www.sciencedirect.com/science/article/pii/S1877050913004183
10. Bosak, B., Komasa, J., Kopta, P., Kurowski, K., Mamoński, M., Piontek, T.: New Capabilities in QosCosGrid Middleware for Advanced Job Management, Advance Reservation and Co-allocation of Computing Resources – Quantum Chemistry Application Use Case. In: Bubak, M., Szepieniec, T., Wiatr, K. (eds.) PL-Grid 2011. LNCS, vol. 7136, pp. 40–55. Springer, Heidelberg (2012), http://dx.doi.org/10.1007/978-3-642-28267-6_4
11. Bubak, M., Gubala, T., Malawski, M., Balis, B., Funika, W., Bartynski, T., Ciepiela, E., Harezlak, D., Kasztelnik, M., Kocot, J., Krol, D., Nowakowski, P., Pelczar, M., Wach, J., Assel, M., Tirado-Ramos, A.: Virtual laboratory for development and execution of biomedical collaborative applications. In: Computer-Based Medical Systems (CBMS 2008), pp. 373–378 (2008)
12. Bubak, M., Gubala, T., Kapalka, M., Malawski, M., Rycerz, K.: Workflow composer and service registry for grid applications. Future Generation Comp. Syst. 21(1), 79–86 (2005)

13. Ciepiela, E., Harezlak, D., Kocot, J., Bartyński, T., Kasztelnik, M., Nowakowski, P., Gubała, T., Malawski, M., Bubak, M.: Exploratory programming in the virtual laboratory. In: Proceedings of IMCSIT 2010, Wisla, Poland (2010)

14. Ciepiela, E., et al.: Managing Entire Lifecycles of e-Science Applications in the GridSpace2 Virtual Laboratory – From Motivation through Idea to Operable Web-Accessible Environment Built on Top of PL-Grid e-Infrastructure. In: Bubak, M., Szepieniec, T., Wiatr, K. (eds.) PL-Grid 2011. LNCS, vol. 7136, pp. 228–239. Springer, Heidelberg (2012),
http://dx.doi.org/10.1007/978-3-642-28267-6_18

15. Falcone, J.L., Chopard, B., Hoekstra, A.: MML: towards a Multiscale Modeling Language. Procedia Computer Science 1(1), 819–826 (2010),
http://www.sciencedirect.com/science/article/pii/S1877050910000906

16. Fish, J.: Multiscale Methods: Bridging the Scales in Science and Engineering. Oxford University Press, Inc., New York (2009)

17. Frauel, Y., Coster, D., Guillerminet, B., Imbeaux, F., Jackson, A., Konz, C., Owsiak, M., Plociennik, M., Scott, B., Strand, P.: Easy use of high performance computers for fusion simulations. Fusion Engineering and Design 87(12), 2057–2062 (2012),
http://www.sciencedirect.com/science/article/pii/S0920379612002669

18. Gatsenko, O., Bekenev, L., Pavlov, E., Gordienko, Y.G.: From quantity to quality: Massive molecular dynamics simulation of nanostructures under plastic deformation in desktop and service grid distributed computing infrastructure. Computer Science 14(1) (2013), http://journals.agh.edu.pl/csci/article/view/106

19. Goderis, A., Brooks, C., Altintas, I., Lee, E.A., Goble, C.: Heterogeneous composition of models of computation. Future Generation Computer Systems 25(5), 552–560 (2009),
http://www.sciencedirect.com/science/article/pii/S0167739X08000915

20. Gubala, T., Bubak, M., Sloot, P.M.A.: Semantic integration of collaborative research environments. In: Cannataro, M. (ed.) Handbook of Research on Computational Grid Technologies for Life Sciences, Biomedicine and Healthcare, ch. XXVI, pp. 514–530. Information Science Reference IGI Global (2009)

21. Gubala, T., Prymula, K., Nowakowski, P., Bubak, M.: Semantic integration for model-based life science applications. In: Ören, T., Kacprzyk, J., Leifsson, L., Obaidat, M.S., Koziel, S. (eds.) SIMULTECH, pp. 74–81. SciTePress (2013),
http://dblp.uni-trier.de/db/conf/
simultech/simultech2013.html#GubalaPNB13

22. Guillerminet, B., Plasencia, I.C., Haefele, M., et al.: High Performance Computing tools for the Integrated Tokamak Modelling project. Fusion Engineering and Design 85(3-4), 388–393 (2010),
http://www.sciencedirect.com/science/article/pii/S0920379610000049

23. Hoekstra, A., Kroc, J., Sloot, P. (eds.): Simulating Complex Systems by Cellular Automata. Understanding Complex Systems. Springer (2010),
http://springer.com/978-3-642-12202-6

24. Hunter, J.D.: Matplotlib: A 2d graphics environment. Computing in Science & Engineering 9(3), 90–95 (2007)

25. Huysmans, G.T.A., Sharapov, S.E., Mikhailovskii, A.B., Kerner, W.: Modeling of diamagnetic stabilization of ideal magnetohydrodynamic instabilities associated with the transport barrier. Physics of Plasmas (1994-present) 8(10), 4292–4305 (2001)

26. Imbeaux, F., Lister, J.B., Huysmans, G.T.A., Zwingmann, W., Airaj, M., Appel, L., Basiuk, V., Coster, D., Eriksson, L.G., Guillerminet, B., Kalupin, D., Konz, C., Manduchi, G., Ottaviani, M., Pereverzev, G., Peysson, Y., Sauter, O., Signoret, J., Strand, P.: A generic data structure for integrated modelling of tokamak physics and subsystems. Computer Physics Communications 181(6), 987–998 (2010)

27. Kitowski, J., Turała, M., Wiatr, K., Dutka, L.: PL-Grid: Foundations and Perspectives of National Computing Infrastructure. In: Bubak, M., Szepieniec, T., Wiatr, K. (eds.) PL-Grid 2011. LNCS, vol. 7136, pp. 1–14. Springer, Heidelberg (2012), http://dx.doi.org/10.1007/978-3-642-28267-6_1

28. Konz, C., Zwingmann, W., Osmanlic, F., Guillerminet, B., Imbeaux, F., Huynh, P., Plociennik, M., Owsiak, M., Zok, T., Dunne, M.: First physics applications of the Integrated Tokamak Modelling (ITM-TF) tools to the MHD stability analysis of experimental data and ITER scenarios. In: EPS 2011. Europhysics Conference Abstracts, vol. 35G, p. O2.103 (2011), http://ocs.ciemat.es/EPS2011PAP/pdf/O2.103.pdf

29. LAMMPS: Large-scale atomic/molecular massively parallel simulator (2011), http://lammps.sandia.gov/

30. Lee, E.A., Neuendorffer, S.: MoML – a modeling markup language in XML Version 0.4. Technical Memorandum UCB/ERL M00/12, Electronics Research Lab, Department of Electrical Engineering and Computer Sciences, University of California, Berkeley, CA 94720 (March 2000)

31. Malawski, M., Gubala, T., Bubak, M.: Component-based approach for programming and running scientific applications on grids and clouds. IJHPCA 26(3), 275–295 (2012)

32. Montagnat, J., Taylor, I.: Guest editor's introduction: Special issue on workflow. Journal of Grid Computing 11(3), 337–339 (2013), http://dx.doi.org/10.1007/s10723-013-9270-7

33. Portegies Zwart, S., McMillan, S., Harfst, S., et al.: A Multiphysics and Multiscale Software Environment for Modeling Astrophysical Systems. New Astronomy 14(4), 369–378 (2009)

34. Rycerz, K., Bubak, M., Ciepiela, E., Harezlak, D., Gubala, T., Meizner, J., Pawlik, M.: Composing, Execution and Sharing of Multiscale Applications. Submitted to Future Generation Computer Systems, after 1st review (2013)

35. Rycerz, K., Bubak, M.: Building and Running Collaborative Distributed Multiscale Applications. In: Dubitzky, W., Kurowski, K., Schott, B. (eds.) Large-Scale Computing Techniques for Complex System Simulations. Wiley Series on Parallel and Distributed Computing, vol. 1, ch. 6, pp. 111–130. John Wiley & Sons (2011)

36. Rycerz, K., Ciepiela, E., Dyk, G., Groen, D., Gubala, T., Harezlak, D., Pawlik, M., Suter, J., Zasada, S., Coveney, P., Bubak, M.: Support for multiscale simulations with molecular dynamics. Procedia Computer Science 18, 1116–1125 (2013), http://www.sciencedirect.com/science/article/pii/S1877050913004201

37. Rycerz, K., Tirado-Ramos, A., Gualandris, A., Zwart, S.P., Bubak, M., Sloot, P.M.A.: Interactive N-Body Simulations on the Grid: HLA Versus MPI. IJHPCA 21(2), 210–221 (2007)

38. Strumberger, E., Günter, S., Merkel, P., Riondato, S., Schwarz, E., Tichmann, C., Zehrfeld, H.: Numerical mhd stability studies: toroidal rotation, viscosity, resistive walls and current holes. Nuclear Fusion 45(9), 1156 (2005)

39. Tong, M., Duggan, G., Liu, J., Xie, Y., Dodge, M., Aucott, L., Dong, H., David-chack, R., Dantzig, J., Barrera, O., Cocks, A., Kitaguchi, H., Lozano-Perez, S., Zhao, C., Richardson, I., Kidess, A., Kleijn, C., Wen, S., Barnett, R., Browne, D.: Multiscale, Multiphysics Numerical Modeling of Fusion Welding with Experimental Characterization and Validation. JOM 65(1), 99–106 (2013),
http://dx.doi.org/10.1007/s11837-012-0499-6
40. Weinan, E.: Principles of multiscale modeling, 1st edn. Cambridge University Press (2011),
http://www.amazon.com/exec/obidos/
redirect?tag=citeulike07-20&path=ASIN/1107096545
41. Zasada, S., Coveney, P.: Virtualizing access to scientific applications with the application hosting environment. Computer Physics Communications 180(12), 2513–2525 (2009),
http://www.sciencedirect.com/science/article/pii/S0010465509001830
42. Zhao, Z., Belloum, A., Bubak, M.: Special Section on Workflow Systems and Applications in e-Science. Future Generation Comp. Syst. 25(5), 525–527 (2009),
http://dblp.uni-trier.de/db/journals/fgcs/fgcs25.html#ZhaoBB09

Auxiliar Experimentorum – An Innovative Approach for Creating and Deploying Scientific Applications

Mikołaj M. Mikołajczyk[2], Mariusz Uchroński[1], Kamil Mowiński[1],
Marcin Lubimow[1], Sebastian Bijak[1], Marcin Teodorczyk[1],
Mariusz Hruszowiec[1], Sebastian Szkoda[1], Bartosz Majster[1],
Grzegorz Banach[1], and Mateusz Tykierko[3]

[1] Wroclaw Centre for Networking and Supercomputing,
Wroclaw University of Technology,
Wybrzeże Wyspiańskiego 27, 50-370 Wrocław, Poland
[2] Department of Physical Chemistry, Faculty of Pharmacy,
Wroclaw Medical University, ul. Borowska 211, 50-556 Wrocław, Poland
[3] Institute of Computer Engineering, Control and Robotics,
Wroclaw University of Technology,
Wybrzeże Wyspiańskiego 27, 50-370 Wrocław, Poland

Abstract. One of the primary assumption in the PLGrid Plus project proposal was expanding support for complex in-silico experiments. However, detailed analysis of scientific data workflows clearly shows that a data management solution for in-vivo or in-silico experiments may have major impact on the quality of research, laboratory administration and collaboration. The AuxEx (lat. *Auxiliar Experimentorum*) web application was developed in order to address experimentation requirements. It is a mixture of an electronic laboratory notebook, a knowledge base creator and a laboratory information management system, tailored for specific researchers. This article presents the authors' observations and experience gained during development of AuxEx for nanotechnology groups.

Keywords: ELN, LIMS, grid computation, cluster computation, in-vivo experiments, data processing, open data.

1 Introduction

The work of all scientists, whether theoretical or experimental, usually comprises gathering and analyzing large amounts of data. Unfortunately, the level of automation and computerization in many scientific societies is still disappointingly low. There are several reasons for this state of affairs. First of all, scientific groups are usually strongly attached to legacy data storage and analysis solutions.

Existing data storage systems typically depend on local hard drives and some external drives for backup. This makes data hard to access by fellow scientists as – in most cases – only archive owners know the structure of stored data and the backup methodology. There is no common mechanism for sharing or automatically publishing raw data. The metadata necessary for data analysis is

M. Bubak et al. (Eds.): PLGrid Plus, LNCS 8500, pp. 211–225, 2014.

usually restricted to filenames. This archiving method is quite common, but also very unreliable. Large archives are often difficult to browse due to their extensive content and human mistakes during file naming. It is also a common practice to store information about experiments in paper form.

The concept of paperless laboratories has been around for many years [1]. Unfortunately, the idea of paperless science is often understand as a laboratory without notebooks made of paper. The IT solutions, which make a laboratory paperless, usually propose data storage formats, which are specific to the scientific field, for which they were developed. This is a common problem related to experimental data management.

Experimentators often apply sophisticated software to very simple tasks. This sometimes results in poor readability and reproducibility of the results obtained through experimentation. Two members of a research group working on the same raw data may obtain different results due to nonstandard analysis procedures.

Our attempt to solve some of those problems has resulted in AuxEx – a mixture of an electronic laboratory notebook, a knowledge base creator and a laboratory information management system with features tailored for specific research groups. The following sections describe the current stare of computerization in laboratories, a case study, which applies our approach to application development, technological considerations and a summary.

2   Current Status of Computerization in Scientific Laboratories

It is hard to imagine a modern scientific laboratory without at least one computer. Even though many initiatives work to support the transition to computational science, the level of computerization of scientific experiments remains insufficient. The experimentator's work is usually related to producing and gathering large amounts of data. This includes standard data from standard experimental setups (for example microscope images or UV-Vis spectra) and nonstandard formats from experimental setups created by a particular scientific group (such as output from sensors representing internal air quality). Only the former pool is supported by commercial and open-source data management solutions. Measurement hardware suppliers typically provide solutions for data acquisition and analysis for specific experiments. However, large groups of researchers working on interdisciplinary projects often have greater needs. Handling data from a single experimental setup is not enough – instead, there is a need for a spectrum of tools specific to the experiments conducted in a given project. What is more, analysis of a single measurement or a single series of measurements may not provide the answer to a scientific problem. Advanced research leads to large and complex data repositories. Scientists often need to analyze data representing a long period of time, gathered from various experiments. Data from different experimental setups is often incompatible, which hampers further analysis. Finally, data analysis criteria may change over the course of a project. The available commercial solutions are suitable only for

standard measurements conducted in a standardized way. Usually it is difficult
to apply them to nonstandard experiments.

There are several ways, in which IT solutions can increase the efficiency and
quality of research work. To find these ways, we first need to study the main
reasons behind the observed inefficiencies. The following description focuses on
shortcomings related specifically to scientific information management.

2.1   The Problem of Unstructured Data

When dealing with measurements covering a long period of time, it is extremely
important to keep track of the entire experimental procedure. Measurement logs
can provide additional information useful in the analysis process, improving the
quality of results. This also helps establish repeatability and reproducibility of
results. The most common practice in creating experimental logs is still to write
down all information necessary to repeat an experiment. The idea of a paperless
laboratory is more than a decade old, but many stakeholders still interpret it
as a laboratory without notebooks made of paper. Scientist tend to use various
kinds of software to take notes in an electronic form. There is a large market for
electronic laboratory notebooks (ELN). Such software allows users to manage
metadata and notes produced during an experiment. Unfortunately, switching
from paper-based to electronic notebooks does not address problems related to
describing the experimental procedure itself. Records based on notes in some
kind of electronic diary can mitigate problems related to reading one's own (or
someone else's) bad handwriting. They can also be backed up automatically, preventing accidental loss of data. However, standardization of those notes remains
a problem as each experimentator takes notes in a different way. This manner
of computerization of scientific laboratories leads to completely unreadable and
unsearchable repositories. Without some consistent data structure and proper
ontology it is almost impossible to implement automatic data processing. When
dealing with unstructured data sets, even simple searches become very difficult.
Handling such data becomes a particularly pernicious problem when staff members leave a project. If a researcher responsible for a certain experiment leaves,
the organization incurs a loss of knowledge, even if a complete – but unstructured – data repository is left behind. While some advanced ELNs may improve
the searchability of data sets and even provide data sharing tools, the problems
associated with poor control over data structures persist.

Another solution may be to develop some sort of database for storing data
and metadata in a structured form. In fact, this solution is very often applied
in commercial software for laboratory management. There is a large spectrum
of laboratory information management systems (LIMS) [2], sometimes referred
to as laboratory information systems (LIS). Such software-based solutions keep
track of experimental procedures and data production and collection processes.
Unfortunately, they only work well for standardized experiments conducted in
a consistent manner. This is suitable for industry research labs, but usually
not for university research groups, where experimental setups are often modified

and the structure of gathered data and applied procedures changes. In such cases a more flexible solution for creating structured data repositories is needed.

2.2   Data Storage System

A particularly acute problem facing scientific information management is the lack of a central data storage system. It is quite common – especially in university research labs – for all data and metadata to be stored on researchers workstations. This scattering increases the risk of data loss. Data backups are typically stored on external drives, preventing loss in case of workstation disk failures, but exacerbating data security issues. With scattered data, the only form of data management is by periodic reports prepared for a scientific project manager. The existence of a central data storage system with access rights management would increase data security and allow project managers to track research progress in real time.

Another problem, which experimental scientists must face, is mistakes during data collection. Handling such errors is very important, especially when a large volume of experimental data is produced and when several scientists are involved in the data generation process. It is important to remember that errors not only in measurement files, but also in metadata describing those files, may bear great influence on the final result of the experiment. It is common practice to store some information about experimental files in the filenames. However, if more than one experimentator is responsible for data gathering, or if data acquisition is stretched in time, errors may creep into metadata stored in filenames. There is also a risk that changes in data naming conventions will make metadata unreadable. A centralized data storage system for experimental files and metadata with interfaces for data and metadata upload would solve this problem. However, it is still important to provide a high level of flexibility in the underlying database system. Lack of flexibility is the main issue facing commercially available LIMS software. Adapting this software for different metadata structures is usually nontrivial, reducing the usability of such tools.

2.3   Standardization of Data Formats and Data Processing

Another problem with making a laboratory paperless is the lack of a standard for storing experimental results. Quite often the suppliers of measurement devices equip their products with data analysis and tagging software. Saving full data with all available tags usually requires proprietary formats. This makes creating a universal format of scientific data storage even more difficult. It is important to change the way of thinking about experiment results and treat them as sets of information rather than files. It is also frequently necessary to connect data from different fields of science, especially in multidisciplinary and highly innovative projects. Proprietary file formats can present a serious obstacle on the way to achieving this task. One of the fields dominated by proprietary formats is optical microscopy. Microscope vendors often provide users with advanced image processing tools, which can read the closed format produced by the microscope. The user can export images, but only the microscope's native files include metadata, which describes the hardware setup applied when taking the picture. Without this information, image analysis becomes difficult or even impossible. In this way, users are forced to buy image analysis software from hardware vendors. Raw data, with all metadata stored in some propriety format, is often unreadable for external scientists, which is why only some partial information in the form of post-processed images can be shared.

Sometimes revealing hidden trends or correlations requires the researcher to analyze large volumes of data from a long period of time. In such cases it is extremely important to store data in some standard form. Data storage usually relies on XML standards. Good examples of such approaches include the AnIML project [3], which develops standards for data annotation in analytical chemistry or the PDB format [4] specifying how protein structural data should be stored. Unfortunately, well established standards only exist in a small minority of scientific disciplines.

2.4 Everyday Tools – Shooting Sparrows with Cannons

In everyday work scientists face the problem of analyzing and visualizing large sets of diverse data. In a large majority of cases, tools used for this purpose are either too sophisticated or too simple. Scientists tend to use very expensive and complicated software for simple tasks. The choice of software usually boils down to user habits. A good example of this problem is the Origin software [5]. It is an application for advanced data analysis and visualization, but it is usually used for drawing 2D charts. In fact, users often prefer purchasing costly software licenses to spending some time on learning new, arguably more suitable tools. Standard transformations of raw experimental data are often required before this data is shared with fellow scientists. Sometimes better understanding of data calls for visualization. Standard commercial tools usually cannot cope with those needs. The researcher needs to use more than one tool and switch between different interfaces. This makes data analysis very uncomfortable and increases the likelihood of errors during data transfer, due to incompatible input formats or different representations of numbers. Additionally, information regarding the parameters used for data analysis (for example curve fitting parameters) might be lost or become difficult to obtain/share automatically. Unification of interfaces for visualization and data analysis can definitely improve the efficiency and reliability of scientific work.

2.5 Lack of Collaboration Tools

Another problem with scientists' everyday work involves data sharing. In some cases, one person is involved in some experimental work while another person may require the results of this work for further experiments or data analysis. In some research groups, different people might be responsible for measurements and data analysis. In such a case it is crucial to have some data sharing solution enabling all stakeholders to access data and metadata. The most popular solution of this problem is to use FTP servers, email, http or some free cloud software such as Dropbox. Those solutions usually do not have proper access rights management, however. This can cause a lot of problems when some data needs to remain classified, for example due to IPR. The large diversity of experimental data structures makes almost all commercially available solutions difficult to use. In the course of our collaboration with different groups of scientist we observed that lack of information sharing inside a group often leads to measurements being repeated by different researchers. Poor access to information means it may be easier and faster to repeat a given experiment than to find out whether someone may already have performed it.

3 Features of Proposed Approach

3.1 Different Philosophy of Data Management

The philosophy of our solution is to develop a data management system dedicated for a specific scientific group, which would be able to share the data with other scientists representing a different field of science. This platform should be a bazaar of knowledge, where scientists from different fields can obtain information interesting from their point of view.

The available commercial software is usually dedicated for specific tasks and cannot be applied in different fields of science. Sometimes the application is a generic data management tool that causes problems related to configuration and adaptation for specific needs of a specific group. In our approach the application is dedicated to a particular scientific group and consists of modules managing experiments, laboratory, bibliography and collaboration. Such modules usually need to be personalized, which increases development costs. However, the proposed approach minimizes the most important cost factors – i.e. those related to changes in scientists' working habits and the overall learning curve. Application users obtain a clear and user-friendly interface, which minimizes the likelihood of human error when performing data annotation and standard preprocessing.

For a long time, data processing in client-server systems was restricted to high-tech, expensive and complex applications/solutions applied in large-scale IT projects. Overcoming barriers in development requires a new look at the basic aspects of resulting solutions:

1. Creating the right model of interactions between creators and consumers of an IT solution.
2. Applying modular architecture to the IT solution in all possible aspects, allowing the inclusion of all fields of scientific work and reliance on open standards.

In the traditional model of creating and implementing IT solutions, one may use many ways to structure the various stages of solution development – from design, through specialized programming and business analysis to implementation.

Adhering to strict rules of creating IT solutions produces solutions, which are expensive and reliant on complex business models. The maintenance and management of such solutions is expensive and requires advanced knowledge. Above all, it requires users to adapt their methods to the needs of the application. An alternative to this approach is a model based on close cooperation among all interested groups: users, developers (auditors), programmers and external experts. Due to the wide scope of cooperation, the management system must be highly flexible. This management model is usually referred to as "agile" [6,7,8] (see Fig. 1).

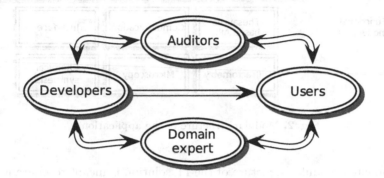

Fig. 1. Information flow during application creation process

Auditors and analysts continually translate users' expectations into application tools, which are then implemented by the development team. Complex issues going beyond the knowledge of those three groups are solved by domain experts. This model focuses on the realization of one task – an implementation, which is typical for the "agile" approach. Focusing only on the aspect of software development draws attention primarily to the effectiveness of small, "agile" IT projects, indicating that the construction of large-scale solutions requires the more structured waterfall (cascade) approach [9]. Such an approach ignores two important facts: the existence of a whole range of ready-to-use solutions (frameworks) created in recent years to streamline application development and involvement of the final recipient as an active participant and co-author of the resulting product.

The simplicity and effectiveness of the described cooperation model utilizes the modular architecture of the IT solution, as shown in Fig. 2.

General issues related to creating IT solutions can be divided into three main areas: hardware and software architecture, management and functionality. In the scope of the first area, the hardware virtualization module contains the definitions of all technical solutions, which support the project's or the end user's resources. This area also involves a licensing module, which defines the licensing policy of our solution and any other solutions in use, as well as their interactions. In particular, it contains legal scenarios for data storage and processing. The third module contains a coding platform for the applied programming languages, frameworks, documentation systems, communication and error tracking tools.

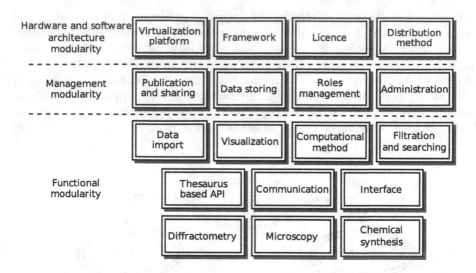

Fig. 2. Modular structure of the application

The adopted modular structure of the IT solution is meant to guarantee the ability to modify any aspect of the entire project in the scope of requirements of a given implementation while maintaining the integrity of the resulting solution/resources. The following management modules are distinguished: data storage, data publication/disclosure level and administration. Emphasizing the restrictions on role management and confidentiality of data leads to a typical Laboratory Information Management System [10,11,12] (LIMS) application, while more lenient role management and focus on data storage and the level of sharing leads to a typical Electronic Laboratory Notebook [13,14] (ELN) solution.

The final richest/most populous area of modularity involves the following components: data import, data presentation, search, dedicated computational methods, API dictionary and thesaurus, methods of communication, interface and domain modules already created on the basis of predefined modules such as microscopy, diffraction, etc. Any implemented solution in effect becomes a standalone module and can be further exploited.

Over the recent years a number of projects based on open licenses have been carried out, producing a number of advanced tools for easy selection of multiple alternatives for each of the above mentioned types of modules. Basing on such a structured repository, the PLGrid Plus project has produced a service, which enables IT support for research teams working in the field of nanotechnology, and ultimately, in the future, in any field of science. Currently existing modules allow users to build applications of any kind, ranging from restrictive LIMS modeled on ISO standards (e.g. ISO 17025), through arbitrarily complex ELN systems to KB knowledge gathering systems (*knowledge base*). These basic types of solutions are schematically depicted in Fig. 3. A KB-type system was created by using the existing implementations of data organization methods developed in the framework of the dictionary-thesaurus API module, which acts as an interface for querying available resources (through the publishing and sharing module) for each of the deployed applications. This is a completely new approach to managing scientific data in the process of conducting scientific research.

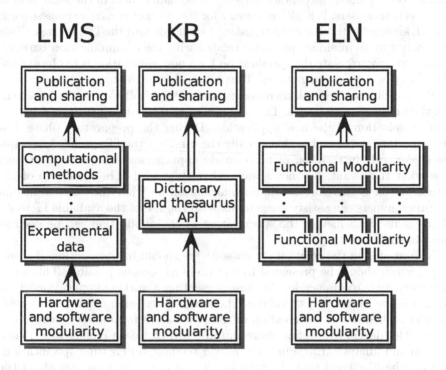

Fig. 3. Different module usage scenarios in the development of common solutions: LIMS, ELN and KB

3.2 Tailor-Made Software

In order to deliver personalized applications, it is very important to work out some mechanism of working with future application users. This is usually a non-trivial task. The most natural way to obtain the specification of a new feature or new application from the end user is via some kind of questionnaire. Unfortunately, creating a complete set of questions describing all aspects of a new feature is very difficult and even when done correctly, the answers to those questions are usually partial and paint a false picture of the end solution. Moreover, end users usually have a negative attitude towards any kind of questionnaires. Asking the user to fill in some kind of a form at the beginning of a collaboration is risky. The user can very easily lose interest and will not spend time on creating a proper specification. There are many other methods, which can be used to obtain a better description of user needs, but direct contact with future users is always required. It is also worth mentioning that meetings between end users and application programmers yield poor results. The first problem, which they need to face during such meetings is finding a common language. Usually this barrier is difficult to overcome. For this task a contact person is needed. The best situation occurs when the contact person is a domain expert in the same field of science as future users. It is also necessary for the contact person to possess some basic IT knowledge to be able to translate user needs into the IT language. This is the only way to minimize problems related with the communication barrier.

The best way to create the specification for a new application is to observe the natural way of work of future users. That allows developers to prepare very user-friendly workflows. Users will then understand the new software as it is consistent with their natural work habits. This will minimize the learning curve and permit faster exploitation of the new application. During the preparatory phase it is very important to remember that usually the user, not the IT specialist, is right. The golden rule in creation of tailor-made applications should be that users know what they want, but not always what they need. The main aim of the contact person is therefore to obtain information on what the users want and how programmers can satisfy these needs with the use of the available IT tools. If both goals are achieved, the specification of the application can be deemed complete and correct.

The next step in the creation of new software should be preparation of a prototype, which should be presented to end users as soon as possible. This haste in prototyping is recommended, because presenting a working application to the end user is the easiest way to validate the initial description of the new system. The user is involved in the creation of the application from a very early stage. This enables developers to find more suitable ways for data management, visualization and analysis. Engaging the user in testing and creating specifications increases the likelihood that the final result will meet the requirements of the user and will actually be used. Introducing corrections in the prototype and adding new features is an iterative process, related to information flow between programmers and users and brokered by the contact person. This is also the best way to develop new versions of the application after release.

Our solution is already used by several groups of scientists. In the course of our work with them, we have gathered significant experience mostly due to the diverse character of user groups. One of these groups is the NewLoks project research team [15]. In creating an application for this group, a very important consideration involved confidentiality as some of produced data might be patented. This group of users is geographically distributed. It was therefore important to implement safe and reliable data exchange and communications mechanisms. That was achieved by means of an elastic access rights system based on roles and integrated teleconferencing software. Another case where we needed to face different requirements, was our work with the OMinNANO group [16]. The main experiment conducted by this group helped determine photon absorption by novel photonic materials. As numerous students were involved in performing measurements, it was crucial to introduce some automated data analysis modules for standard processing of experimental data. Another requirement involved integrated bibliographic record management software. Our software was also used to manage the document flow in the HLA Proficiency Testing Program. The aim of this program is certification of laboratories from Central Europe conducting research in the field of immunogenetics. Altogether, 39 laboratories participated in this year's program. We are currently developing a module supporting chemical synthesis, electron microscopy and roentgenography experiments.

3.3   Module Development Case Study

What follows is a short case study describing the development of the most crucial module for managing data from the Z-scan experiment [17] conducted by the OMinNANO group. It can help understand how our solution was applied in the context of a specific research project.

The first step in the development of a new application module was to carry out interviews with users and observe their data management process. The main goal at this stage was to determine what the dataflow looks like and what tools users apply during data collection and analysis. Results of these observations are depicted in Fig. 4.

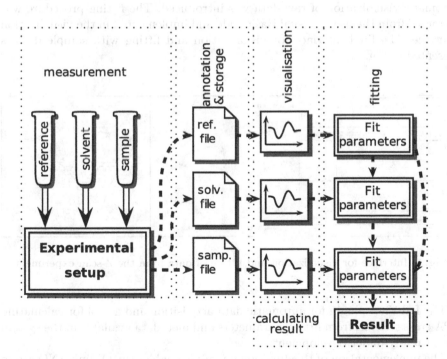

Fig. 4. Data flow for the Z-scan measurement and data analysis in the OMinNANO research group

The goal of the Z-scan experiment was to obtain a two-photon absorption (TPA) cross section, which implies carrying out three measurements: reference, solvent and target substance (sample). For each measurement an ASCII file with 4 columns of data was generated. Researchers then used paper notebooks to store some information about the samples and experimental conditions. Some of this information, for example laser wavelengths, was also stored in the names of raw datafiles. For each file some simple arithmetical operations were conducted, resulting in 2D plots. The Origin software was typically used for visualization purposes. At the next step of data analysis, experimental data needed to be fitted with theoretical curves. This part of data processing relied on Visual Basic based software written by one of the users. The fitting procedure is quite complex. Knowing all fitting parameters for the reference, solvent and sample enables users to calculate a TPA cross-section – this was typically carried out in MS Excel. It is worth mentioning that during standard data analysis users needed to change software interfaces several times and that each time they had to manually prepare input for a different software package. Knowledge of different software interfaces was also required. The basic idea for a functional module adapted to Z-scan data management was to implement tools supporting the entire workflow – from Fig. 4 data acquisition to results – in a single, unified interface.

In order to begin work on such a module, we prepared a relational database for raw data and all metadata required in the data analysis process. A tool for automatic visualization of raw data was introduced. The fitting procedure was extracted from the users' Visual Basic code and implemented in the visualization interface. The final interface for visualization and fitting with sample data is presented in Fig. 5.

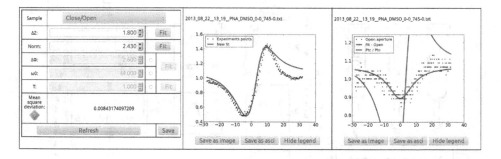

Fig. 5. Interface for visualization and fitting of data from the Z-scan experiment

The LabView plugin for automatic data acquisition and a tool for calculating TPA cross sections from fitting parameters and metadata available in the system are currently under development.

The implementation of this functional module enables the OMinNANO group to conduct all required data processing in a single interface. This not only improves efficiency, but also increases reliability and reproducibility of results.

At the current stage, basic features of the module are already in place and being used by researchers conducting Z-scan experiments. However, we are still working with users on further refinements. In addition to developing new features, which improve work efficiency and comfort, we continue to enhance existing solutions. As such, the introduction of a new application module is only the beginning of an iterative development process.

3.4 Technology

In order to create ready-to-use and platform-independent software, the web technology was chosen. This technology minimizes software requirements on the user side: the user only requires an Internet connection and a web browser to start using the electronic laboratory notebook developed by our group. The presented solution was built with the Django [18] framework. Django is a high-level Python [19] framework, which supports rapid development of elegant and efficient web applications. The availability of numerous extensions and plugins for Django eases the development process, for example by automating object permission management (django-guardian). Some core or common features can be moved to external modules and used in other instances of the system, for example a bibliography management module. An instance of the electronic laboratory notebook is running on a virtual machine at WCSS [20]. This approach facilitates resource adjustments (CPU cores, RAM, disk space) and enables the archive to be saved and redeployed as needed. Virtual machines are managed with Xen Server Cluster. For every instance of AuxEx two virtual machines are provided. The first is called the development machine and is used for functionality testing. The second, production machine handles real experiment data storage and management. Using a high-level web framework such as Django automatically protects the system from a host of common security vulnerabilities. Django provides the following security features: cross-site scripting (XSS) protection, cross-site request forgery (CSRF) protection, SQL injection protection, clickjacking protection, etc. Additionally, the system can start up in a production environment provided that an external security audit is performed. These features enable us to achieve a reasonable level of security. What is more, security policies are provided at the infrastructure level [21]. User data security is ensured via nightly backups with TSM (*IBM Tivoli Storage Manager*) software. Data is backed up on tapes and replicated at two geographical locations. Security policies concerning the stored user data protect the system against unauthorized access and data loss. In order to provide stable software, continuous integration has been applied. For this purpose, a Jenkins [22] open-source continuous integration server was used. On a lower level (Python language) unit tests have been provided. Functionality testing has been automated with the Selenium [23] portable software testing framework for web applications.

4   Summary and Future Work

There are still several obstacles on the way to paperless laboratories. Unfortunately, the main source of problems is quite often the human factor. The scientific society seems to appreciate the need for scientific data management solutions, however introducing such solutions is often very difficult when it requires changes in the researchers' work habits. We hope that the proposed approach will bring productive data management a little closer to becoming reality.

To develop fully searchable data repositories prepared for automated processing, a conceptual change is needed. Scientific data is no longer adequately represented by files produced by experimental devices and observation notes written by experimentators. It is necessary to begin thinking of data as a set of information elements associated with a specific experiment. Our next goal is to devise cross-repository data exchange mechanisms. This task will require developing suitable semantics and thesauri capable of translating metadata from one field of science to another.

References

1. Giles, J.: Nature 481, 430–431 (2012)
2. Gibbon, G.A.: A brief history of lims. Laboratory Automation & Information Management 32(1), 1–5 (1996)
3. AnIML...the markup language for analytical data,
   http://animl.sourceforge.net
4. PDB File Format,
   http://www.rcsb.org/pdb/static.do?p=file_formats/pdb/index.html
5. Origin, http://www.originlab.com/
6. Beck, K., et al.: Manifesto for Agile Software Development (2001)
7. Larman, C.: Agile and iterative development: A manager's guide, p. 27 (2004)
8. Ambler, S.: Agile modeling: Effective practices for extreme programming and the unified process, p. 12 (2002)
9. Bell, T.E., Thayer, T.A.: Software requirements: Are they really a problem? In: Proceedings of the 2nd International Conference on Software Engineering. IEEE Computer Society Press (1976)
10. McLelland, A.: What is a lims – a laboratory toy, or a critical it component?, p. 1 (1998)
11. Skobelev, D.O., Zaytseva, T.M., Kozlov, A.D., Perepelitsa, V.L., Makarova, A.S.: Laboratory information management systems in the work of the analytic laboratory. Measurement Techniques 53, 1182–1189 (2011)
12. Vaughan, A.: Lims: The laboratory ERP (2006), http://LIMSfinder.com
13. Myers, J.: Collaborative electronic notebooks as electronic records: design issues for the secure electronic laboratory notebook (eln). In: Proceedings of the 2003 International Symposium on Collaborative Technologies and Systems (2003)
14. Perkel, J.M.: Coding your way out of a problem. Nature Methods 8(7), 541–543 (2011)
15. Newloks, http://newloks.int.pan.wroc.pl
16. Ominnano, http://www.organometallics.pwr.wroc.pl/

17. Sheik-Bahae, M., Said, A.A., Wei, T.H., Hagan, D.J., Van Stryland, E.W.: Sensitive measurement of optical nonlinearities using a single beam. IEEE Journal Quantum Electronics 26(4), 760–769 (1990)
18. Django, https://www.djangoproject.com
19. Python, http://www.python.org
20. Wroclaw Centre for Networking and Supercomputing, http://www.wcss.pl
21. Balcerek, B., Frankowski, G., Kwiecień, A., Smutnicki, A., Teodorczyk, M.: Security Best Practices: Applying Defense-in-Depth Strategy to Protect the NGI_PL. In: Bubak, M., Szepieniec, T., Wiatr, K. (eds.) PL-Grid 2011. LNCS, vol. 7136, pp. 128–141. Springer, Heidelberg (2012)
22. Jenkins, http://jenkins-ci.org/
23. Selenium, http://docs.seleniumhq.org/

Domain-Oriented Services for High Energy Physics in Polish Computing Centers

Krzysztof Nawrocki[1,3], Andrzej Olszewski[2,4], Adam Padée[1,3], Anna Padée[1,3],
Mariusz Witek[2,4], Piotr Wójcik[2], and Miłosz Zdybał[2,4]

[1] Interdisciplinary Centre for Mathematical and Computational Modelling,
Warszawa, Poland
[2] AGH University of Science and Technology, ACC Cyfronet AGH,
ul. Nawojki 11, 30-950 Kraków, Poland
[3] National Centre for Nuclear Research, Swierk Computing Centre,
Otwock-Świerk, Poland
[4] Institute of Nuclear Physics PAN, Kraków, Poland

Abstract. The large amounts of data collected by the High Energy
Physics (HEP) experiments require intensive data processing on a large
scale in order to extract their final physics results. In an extreme case
– the experiments performed on the Large Hadron Collider at CERN –
even a dedicated computational grid, Worldwide LHC Computing Grid
(WLCG), had to be developed for the purpose of processing their data.
The central processing tasks, such as event reconstruction and selection,
are included in the computing models and managed by the central teams.
However, there is no uniform framework dedicated to final data analyses
carried out by research groups at the level of individual institutes. One
of the goals of the PLGrid Plus project was to provide such an analysis
framework for Polish scientific groups involved in HEP experiments. The
framework is based on a set of services dedicated to data analysis, data
access and software distribution constituting an efficient environment
built on top of distributed resources of the Polish computing centers.

Keywords: High Energy Physics, computational grid, WLCG, Proof
on Demand, CVMFS, XRootD.

1 Introduction

Polish High Energy Physics community is involved in many projects related to
experiments located all over the world and covering a wide range of research topics. The Large Hadron Collider (LHC) [1,2] in CERN is currently considered the
biggest scientific instrument on earth. The detectors built around LHC produce
a data stream of approximately 300 GB/s. This data is reduced by several stages
of hardware and software filters to a rate of about 25 PB per year. However, in
the following years, this amount will be significantly increased due to a higher
rate of collisions reached after the planned upgrade of the accelerator, as well as
due to higher processing capacities of the online computing farms. The challenging requirements of LHC are one of the main driving forces of the computing

M. Bubak et al. (Eds.): PLGrid Plus, LNCS 8500, pp. 226–237, 2014.
© Springer International Publishing Switzerland 2014

grid development. To accommodate and analyze the LHC data, a dedicated distributed computing infrastructure, the Worldwide LHC Computing Grid [3], has been built. Thanks to fast data processing in the WLCG grid, it was recently possible to announce the discovery of the Higgs particle only a few weeks after the end of the data taking period. Currently, WLCG consists of about 1 million computing cores and 500 PB of storage space in more than 150 computing centers from 40 countries all over the world. Polish contribution to WLCG is provided in the form of a large Tier-2 site [4], distributed among 3 computing centers: Academic Computer Centre CYFRONET AGH, Kraków (ACC CYFRONET AGH) (173k HS06, 900 TB disk), Interdisciplinary Centre for Mathematical and Computational Modelling, Warszawa (ICM) (89k HS06, 250 TB disk) and Poznan Supercomputing and Networking Center, Poznań (PSNC) (56k HS06, 110 TB disk). The computing sites are connected by multi 10 Gbps links of the PIONIER national broadband optical network.

The base part of the WLCG software stack is built upon components developed by the Globus Alliance [5] and the EMI collaboration [6]. They are usually integrated with more general tools prepared for managing the computing operations of the experiments that require large computing resources. Other experiments that do not need to use the grid infrastructure for data processing, adopt only selected elements of this environment – most often, the data management tools, which allow the members of the collaboration, who are often dispersed geographically, to share access to the data samples easily. The tools developed for the experiments provide advanced capabilities for central computing tasks, such as large scale data reconstruction and data pre-selection. The final data analyses, however, are carried out by physicists outside of the dedicated grid infrastructure – usually on clusters in local institutes or even on individual desktop computers. One of the aims of the PLGrid Plus project was to fill this gap by providing a convenient analysis environment deployed on dedicated computing resources for Polish research groups. Although the HEP experiments have developed different computing models and make use of various computational tools, some common elements can be identified between them. Most of their analyses are carried out using a popular package called ROOT [7]. Therefore, the tools based on ROOT were considered essential for efficient scientific research. One of the components developed with ROOT, XRootD [8], provides universal access to the distributed data across the Polish computing centers. The CERNVM project [9] is another example of a utility helping to provide easy access to the experiment analysis environment. CERNVM has been initially developed as a virtual desktop providing CERN with the computing environment for LHC experiments. Recently, its component, the CVMFS [10] file system, has turned out to be a convenient way for software distribution.

Within the PLGrid Plus project, common tools to facilitate end users' physics analysis are identified and provided in form of services. A schematic view of the topology of Polish distributed Tier-2 is shown in Fig. 1. The internal structure of a single Tier-2 center is shown only for ACC CYFRONET AGH, however, a similar structure is present also at ICM and PSNC centres. It includes the components of a typical WLCG site, such as Storage and Computing Elements. There are also additional elements indicated: Proof on Demand, which employs direct access to the batch system, and XRootD providing data access as a plugin to DPM [11] grid storage service. The CVMFS backend and XRootD redirector ensure the connection to central software repositories and access to remote data samples, respectively. A detailed description of the individual services is presented in the next sections.

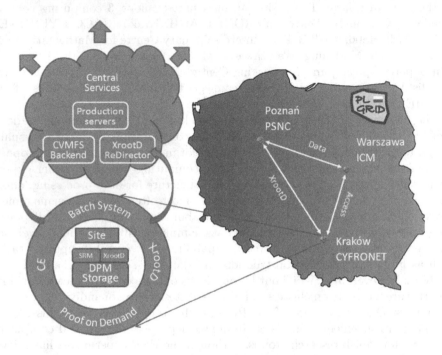

Fig. 1. Overview of HEPGrid services in the PL-Grid Infrastructure in Poland

2 HEP Experiments

The computing requirements for HEP experiments have increased rapidly since the introduction of large electronic detectors with digital readout about 50 years ago. The electronic detectors have replaced photographic experimental techniques, which used to be very successful (bubble chambers), but already have reached their limits. The main advantage of the digital readout is the possibility to increase the collision rates and to collect large samples of events. This makes it possible to run experiments such as those at the LHC accelerator (20 MHz collision rate), which aim at studying extremely rare processes on top of large background of ordinary and well-known interactions. The experiments require to store large amounts of data during the active run periods of the accelerator in order to analyze them later. A good example of such a pattern is the recent discovery of the Higgs boson, which is produced at rates of one per 10^9 proton-proton collisions at LHC. Massive volumes of data streaming from the experiment detector had to be first reduced online by sophisticated trigger systems (typically reducing the amount of data by a factor 50,000) due to the limited offline storage capacity. Although this online reduction is very efficient, the total size of the data to store and analyze is still huge – much too high to be handled by a single computing center. This is why the Worldwide LHC Computing Grid (WLCG) was invented.

The most important challenge for contemporary HEP experiments is to search for phenomena, which go beyond the Standard Model (SM) and form the so-called New Physics. Although SM is one of the most important theories of modern physics, it is not considered to be a final theory. In particular, SM does not quantitatively explain the dominance of matter over antimatter in the Universe and the composition of dark matter and dark energy representing 95% of the density of the Universe. Therefore, SM is widely regarded only as an effective approximation of a more fundamental theory, being able to describe well the interactions of elementary particles up to a certain energy scale. There are two main approaches to discovering New Physics – direct search and indirect search. The direct search relies on increasing the energy of colliders and on direct observation of new particles with high invariant masses. The second approach is based on indirect search for any deviation from SM predictions caused by virtual effects of new particles. Both of them are being used by the LHC experiments. There are also other projects exploring physics beyond SM, such as the neutrino experiments, the cosmic ray observations or search for dark matter particles. The Polish groups are involved in a variety of experiments carried out in most of the large HEP laboratories:

- direct searches at LHC: ATLAS, ALICE, CMS,
- indirect searches and flavor physics: B factories on e+e- colliders: Belle, Belle II, LHCb experiment at LHC,
- neutrino experiments: T2K, ICARUS, LArIAT,
- cosmic rays: Pierre Auger Observatory,
- dark matter: experiment WArP.

One may notice the diversity of both research goals and experimental techniques. The size of the experiments spans from the huge ones, which are run by collaborations of several thousands of people, to small projects with a few dozens of researchers working together. The experiments are in various stages of development. Some of them are in the R&D phase, while others are fully operational and already collect large amounts of data. What is more, most of the experimental collaborations are spread all over the world. The combination of all these factors make each of the experiments unique, and, as a consequence, causes that the central experimental software is developed individually. The same applies to the computing environments and models. Despite all these differences, one can distinguish some common elements in all HEP experiments or at least in the majority of them. With regard to distributed computing, the experiments may be classified into three categories, according to the level of integration with the grid tools:

- experiments fully employing the computational grid (mainly WLCG),
- experiments using selected elements of the grid middleware,
- experiments not using the Grid at all.

The first category comprises large projects supported by large number of people that have developed their own applications to interact with the grid middleware tools. The second type includes experiments of a medium size, which are already running or are in their preparation phase. The last type are experiments relatively small in size, which do not produce large data samples.

The aspects of final physics analysis will be described in the context of the LHC experiments, which make intensive use of the WLCG computing grid. The computing models are based on the hierarchic structure of WLCG, which is composed of three layers – Tier-0, Tier-1 and Tier-2. The resources are provided by computing centers, which all, down to Tier-2, have a well-defined role in the structure. The main Tier-0 center is located close to the LHC collider and the experiments at CERN. Its role is to store a copy of RAW data and participate in the data processing. The next layer is composed of a number of large Tier-1 centers located in different countries that participate in the WLCG project. They receive a second copy of data files, which are used later for reprocessing with improved calibration of the detector. In the third layer, there is a number of Tier-2 centers associated with a regional Tier-1 center. These centers share data analysis and production of the simulated data. The total capacity of resources at each layer (Tier-0, the sum of resources provided by Tier-1 centers and the sum of resources provided by Tier-2 centers) is comparable. The lowest level of WLCG, called Tier-3, is reserved for final analyses performed by scientific groups or individual users. However, the role of the Tier-3 centers is not defined precisely within the WLCG structure. The Tier-3 resources include small computing clusters or individual workstations and there are no general tools adapting the central production framework to the needs of users at Tier-3. Before their analysis can start, the whole data collected by the experiments has to be processed and pre-selected. This is performed using dedicated grid-aware applications. A large number of jobs has to be submitted to WLCG sites to select interesting events and to represent them in a reduced format. Only then the reduced data is passed to the Tier-3 resources and analyzed by the research groups.

The PLGrid Plus project aims at filling the gap between Tier-2 and Tier-3. Its domain-oriented services are focused on three aspects: efficient analysis of the data, software distribution and installation, and the data access and management. The computing tools used in HEP have evolved since the beginning of the PLGrid Plus project, therefore, the initial concepts of the tools supporting Polish HEP users were appropriately adjusted. The new general tools were implemented in Polish Tier-2 and Tier-3 centers to facilitate data access and data analysis.

Apart from LHC, there are also other experiments supported by PLGrid Plus. The ongoing experiments have relatively small requirements and use the Grid to a limited extent. Most of them use grid storage for sharing data sets among institutes spread around the world. Grid computing power is employed only for central Monte Carlo productions or for data processing, which are made available to all members of the collaboration. The end user's analysis is restricted to local clusters in individual institutes. In future experiments, such as Belle II or the experiment planned at the International Linear Collider (ILC), the requirements are comparable as in the LHC experiments and, thus, these experiments would need a distributed computing model. This model does not have to be the same as the one used in LHC, therefore, it is designed taking into account recent trends in computing. These trends, including one of the most influencing technologies – the Cloud Computing, will be shortly discussed in Section 5.

3   Domain-Oriented Services for HEP

Although each experiment is unique and uses specific software developed for its data processing and final physics analysis, one can distinguish a set of common elements in the activities at the Tier-3 level. Many of them are built around one of the main tools of the physics analysis – ROOT, a package widely used in particle physics for many years. ROOT was designed to create a universal environment for HEP experiments. In full form it is used by the ALICE experiment, other experiments use many of its features. The aim of the authors of this package was to create an object-oriented environment containing a set of generic tools for data analysis, data acquisition, event reconstruction, detector simulation and event generation. One of the most commonly used of its functions is storing data in form of C++ objects as compressed binaries. The data can be made available directly or via remote protocols, which are useful in a distributed system. The strength of the ROOT package are modules containing wide range of mathematical and statistical methods that enable advanced analysis of the data without the need to engage any external packages. Using the provided libraries, the user can create their own C++ applications. ROOT is also equipped with a set of graphical interfaces used for interactive data analysis and 3D graphics (visualization of the reconstructed events on top of the detector).

3.1   Data Analysis

The idea of Proof [12], which is built on top of ROOT, was to exploit simple parallel processing based on the segmentation of input data. The data from HEP experiments come in portions called events. The information stored in a single event corresponds to a collision of beam particles. Such collision produces a number of secondary particles observed in a detector and written to permanent storage. After the final selection, the events are stored in a binary compact format of ROOT, the so-called trees or ntuples. By dividing the input data for parallel processing, one can reduce the total processing time by a factor of $1/n$, where

n indicates the number of simultaneous processes. In ROOT, the Proof system can be used for this purpose. Originally, Proof was designed to be configured on a static cluster. The usual disadvantages of such a static structure that lead to underemployed computing resources, were overcome by a more dynamic solution, Proof on Demand (PoD) [13]. Its idea was to create a number of worker processes on demand, using existing resources, such as various batch systems and the grid resources. PoD enables the users to quickly create their own Proof cluster and to release the resources when the calculations are completed. First, the PoD server has to be launched on a master node. Then, a number of worker processes in form of batch jobs can be started. The worker processes register to the server as soon as they are ready. The ROOT script that is used to analyze the data has to be provided by the user. The script needs to be executed on the PoD server, which distributes the work among the available worker processes.

PoD was prepared as a service for the HEP domain within the PLGrid Plus project. The installation of PoD was performed on Scientific Linux operating systems, first on SL5 and later on SL6. For production, the SL6 version was selected. PoD requires ROOT with the XRootD plugin installed first. The ROOT installation requires appropriate compilation switches to be activated, for example, the one for the XRootD plugin. The PoD worker process can be started on various sorts of batch systems as well as on the Grid via the gLite middleware. The plugin for SLURM (Simple Linux Utility for Resource Management) [14] has been recently added to the set of PoD plugins[1]. The PoD service in PL-Grid is equipped with a simple activation procedure. The user applies for the service using the PL-Grid portal. A prerequisite of the activation of this service is access to related services enabling interactive work in the PL-Grid Infrastructure. From the interactive session, a simple configuration of the ROOT and PoD environment can be executed by means of a single command. After configuration, the PoD server can be launched. Then, a number of worker processes can be submitted to a batch system. It has to be noted that data processing can be started without waiting for all worker processes to report readiness. This feature is useful for both the batch system and gLite plugins. The processed data files can be accessed via the ROOT protocols. To avoid the bottleneck of concurrent access to the data, high performance storage should be used. In case of remote access, a fast network connection to worker nodes is also required. For example, in a small analysis that runs processing of 500 GB of data within 1 hour of time, a total data access rate of 140 MB/s is required and can be achieved by using 20 worker nodes in parallel.

3.2 Distribution of Software and Condition Databases

The CVMFS file system, used to distribute the experiments' software, was developed within the CERNVM project. The initial purpose of the project was

---

[1] The SLURM plugin was implemented by the PoD developers in collaboration with the authors of this report. The plugin was necessary as the SLURM system is used in one of the PL-Grid centers.

to provide the computing environment for the LHC experiments in the form of a virtual machine image containing Scientific Linux system with additional elements. The use of virtualization results independently from the underlying hardware and the native operating system. CERNVM can be run on any desktop or laptop equipped with one of the popular VM supervisors. One of the key elements is a dedicated file system – CVMFS. Its principal role is to provide the experiment's software for virtual machines without the need for manual installation each time a new version of the software appears. A similar mechanism is employed for the distribution of files with dump from condition databases, which are needed for data processing. CVMFS uses the standard HTTP caching mechanism for on-demand access to the catalogs placed on the remote server. The copy operation is performed from the remote repository to the local cache only when the file is requested to be opened locally. Due to its advantages, CVMFS has been chosen as the standard way to distribute software to the LHC experiments in WLCG sites, replacing the manual way of software installation initiated by the Grid managers.

The CVMFS service was implemented at all centers of Polish distributed Tier-2 as well as at several Tier-3 clusters used in Polish institutes involved in the LHC experiments. Although it is possible to install CVMFS on each working node, we use a cluster-wide implementation. A schematic view of the CVMFS implementation in PL-Grid centers is shown in Fig. 2.

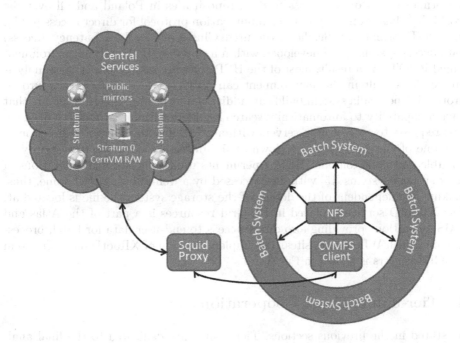

Fig. 2. A schematic view of the CVMFS implementation in a PL-Grid center

It relies on a server, which exports the CVMFS directory trees to worker nodes via NFS. The site server duplicates the structure of the directories and their file content, which is prepared by experiments on a Stratum-0 master server and the replica Stratum-1 servers all located at CERN. Operating in read-only mode and caching via standard http tools (squid cache) ensure good scalability and resilience. CVMFS is an attractive solution for non-LHC experiments as well.

3.3 Data Access

The experience of the first years of running analyses in the grid environment, on data collected by HEP experiments on the LHC accelerator, proved that quick and easy access to data is a key to the success. The original way of access by random distribution of data and sending computing jobs to sites where the data was placed was acceptable for central planned processing, but proved inconvenient for end-user analyses. It still required moving or replicating portions of data between the sites and then copying data from grid data servers to local disks. It required that physicists doing analyses to search for pieces of data they need download them to local computing systems or submit jobs to queues and wait, sometimes a long time, before they could see any results. If a site where the jobs were running went into a downtime or was broken, an even longer delay would occur. A solution for this weakness is XRootD. This service provides high performance and direct access to data repositories in Poland and all over the world. It is based on the xrootd communication protocol for direct access to files in ROOT format and Scalla (Structured Clustering for Low Latency Access) data access system, both developed within a popular HEP analysis environment called ROOT. As a result, most of the HEP software and, in particular, analysis applications built in this environment can natively access data via the xrootd protocol. The Scalla system builds an additional layer of redirection servers that have a capability to automatically search for file location and redirect data access requests to correct data servers with a possibility to repeat a redirection in case one of the data servers is down. This makes the data access system very scalable and fault tolerant. HEP experiments use Scalla to build federations of their storage systems [15] with files accessed by a well-known global name, thus, making it independent of the details of the storage system the file is located at. The XRootD service deployed in PL-Grid resources is a part of the Atlas and CMS federations providing also direct access to end-user data for batch processing on Polish WLCG grid sites. The implementation of XRootD data service in PL-Grid centers is shown in Fig. 3.

4   Tier-3 and Tier-2 Cooperation

As stated in the previous sections, Tier-3 sites are dedicated to the final analyses performed by scientific groups or individual users. Most frequently, the input

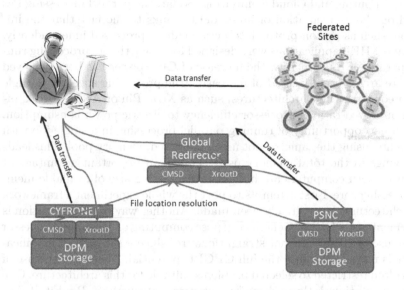

Fig. 3. Implementation of XRootD data service in PL-Grid centers

data for these analyses comes from reduction and pre-analysis of real or simulated data sets provided by central services of physics experiments (e.g. ATLAS, CMS, LHCb) and stored at Tier-2 sites. Such a reduction and pre-analysis typically require quite substantial computational resources. Therefore, it is very convenient to have a Tier-3 site very close to a Tier-2 site. In such case, the input data for analysis at Tier-3 can be easily accessed at Tier-2. This data is prepared in advance at Tier-2 and contain subsets of original data sets required by a given analysis. Then, the data can be interactively analyzed at Tier-3. Generally, there are two Tier-3 implementation models: in the first, Tier-3 is a site separated from a Tier-2 site; while in the second, Tier-3 is not completely isolated from Tier-2 infrastructure, but it becomes a dedicated partition of the resources supplemented by specific Tier-3 services. This model has been implemented at ICM. In this case, Tier-3 resources (e.g. queuing system, storage) are shared with the Tier-2 resources. This setup enables efficient use of resources, as the data sets can be shared between Tier-2 and Tier-3 parts of the cluster. Also, the assignment of the computing cores to different parts can be done dynamically within one queuing system, according to the current needs. Another important component, CVMFS described in the previous sections, gives unified access to experiment software repositories at Tier-2 and Tier-3.

5   Outlook

The new trends in computer technology are reflected in the evolution of computing models of HEP experiments. The two main aspects of these trends are parallel computing and Cloud Computing. So far, the parallel processing has been based on the segmentation of input data thanks to the fact that the initial collision, such as proton-proton interaction can be processed independently. Therefore, most HEP applications were designed for single thread processing running on separate CPUs. Recently, the increase of CPU power has been achieved by many-core architecture instead of increasing the processing speed of a single thread. Moreover, the new architectures, such as Xeon Phi or ARM-Cortex, offer a much improved ratio of processor efficiency to electric power consumption. This offers a new opportunity of running parallel processing in a single job with multiple events, using the same, or not much increased, memory pool. This leads to great savings in the total memory used. This is an important advantage at times when modern computers are built with decreasing size of available memory per processing core. First attempts to port the whole experiment's framework to these architectures have already been made. Another way of parallelization is the employment of GPGPUs (General-Purpose computing on Graphics Processor Units). The use of GPGPU is not straightforward, since a substantial modification of code is needed to utilize the full GPGPU potential. Therefore, the use of GPGPU is often restricted to selected problems suitable for this architecture. One of such implementations is the package for statistical data analysis, RooFit. Its implementation on GPGPU, called GooFit, is able to increase the speed of complex analyses by large factors, typically between 10 and 1000. The scope of potential applications of GPGPU is being studied within the PLGrid Plus project.

The Cloud Computing technology is of interest to new HEP experiments as well as to experiments that will be continued for the next decades. Cloud Computing is regarded as a complementary resource to WLCG and, in some cases, the computing models are entirely based on this technology. The integration of cloud-based centers with distributed computing models is explored by a subtask of the PLGrid Plus project.

6 Summary

The domain-oriented services for Polish High Energy Physics groups have been developed within the PLGrid Plus project. Their aim is to create an environment for efficient physics analyses for Polish research groups involved in HEP experiments. The general purpose tools have been implemented in Polish Tier-2 and Tier-3 centers. They include tools for automated access to the software repositories – CVMFS, tools for parallel analysis of large data samples in reduced formats, Proof on Demand, and the tools for universal access to the distributed data – XRootD. It has to be mentioned, that, despite the fact that the implementation of these tools in the PLGrid Plus project is closely connected to the formal WLCG tiered structure, they are also useful to other HEP collaborations. One example of such a successful use of HEP services in PL-Grid Infrastructure by a non-LHC experiment can be the preliminary data classification using MLP neural network prepared for the COMPASS (COmmon Muon Proton Apparatus for Structure and Spectroscopy) experiment [16] on the Tier-3 resources at Warsaw.

References

1. Myers, S., Bruning, O., Collier, P., Lebrun, P., Ostojic, R., Poole, J., Proudlock, P. (eds.): LHC Design Report. CERN-2004-003 (2004)
2. Myers, S.: The Large Hadron Collider. International Journal of Modern Physics A 28(25), 1330035 (2013), doi:10.1142/S0217751X13300354
3. Computing Grid, L.H.C.: Technical Design Report, LCG-TDR-001. CERN-LHCC-2005-024 (2005) ISBN 92-9083-253-3
4. Binczewski, A., et al.: Polish Contribution to the Worldwide LHC Computing. In: Bubak, M., Szepieniec, T., Wiatr, K. (eds.) PL-Grid 2011. LNCS, vol. 7136, pp. 285–300. Springer, Heidelberg (2012)
5. Globus Alliance, http://toolkit.globus.org/alliance
6. EMI Collaboration, http://www.eu-emi.eu/
7. Antcheva, I., et al.: ROOT – a C++ framework for petabyte data storage, statistical analysis and visualization. Computer Physics Communications 180(12), 2499–2512 (2009)
8. XrootD project, http://xrootd.slac.stanford.edu/
9. CERNVM Virtual Software Appliance, http://cernvm.cern.ch/portal/
10. Blomer, J., Aguado-Sanchez, C., Buncic, P., Harutyunyan, A.: Distributing LHC application software and conditions databases using the CernVM file system. Journal of Physics: Conference Series 331, 042003 (2011), doi:10.1088/1742-6596
11. DPM Storage Service, https://svnweb.cern.ch/trac/lcgdm/wiki/Dpm/
12. Parallel ROOT Facility, http://root.cern.ch/drupal/content/proof
13. Malzacher, P., Manafov, A.: PROOF on Demand. Journal of Physics: Conference Series 219, 072009 (2010), doi:10.1088/1742-6596
14. SLURM project, https://computing.llnl.gov/linux/slurm/
15. Bauerdick, L., et al.: Using Xrootd to Federate Regional Storage. Journal of Physics, Conference Series 396, 042009 (2012)
16. Abbon, P., et al.: The Compass Experiment at CERN. Nuclear Instruments and Methods A 577, 455–518 (2007)

Services for Synchrotron Deployment and Operation

Tadeusz Szymocha[1], Marek Stankiewicz[2], Adriana Wawrzyniak[2], Piotr Goryl[2],
Marcin Zając[2], Marcin Nowak[2], Łukasz Żytniak[2], and Fryderyk Melka[2]

[1] AGH University of Science and Technology, ACC Cyfronet AGH,
ul. Nawojki 11, 30-950 Kraków, Poland
tadeusz.szymocha@cyfronet.pl
[2] National Synchrotron Radiation Center Solaris,
ul. Gronostajowa 7, P. 1-6, Kraków, Poland

Abstract. The construction of the first synchrotron in Poland as well as its future operation have to be supported by adequate IT services. As there was no similar instrument in Poland before, new services have to be built especially for it. The intended target user groups of these services are: engineers and scientists preparing the synchrotron deployment and operation, its operators, accelerator physicists and beam scientists overseeing the synchrotron operation and delivery of light to the end-users' experimental stations, and, finally, end-users of the synchrotron who need to store and archive the data obtained during the experiment. This article describes the IT services supporting the Polish synchrotron built within the PLGrid Plus project.

Keywords: Synchrotron, Solaris, Synchrogrid, Elegant Service, Virtual Accelerator Service, Tracy Service.

1 Introduction

The Polish National Synchrotron Radiation Center, *Solaris* [1], is engaged in the process of constructing and building a synchrotron. A synchrotron is an instrument in which electrons, after initial acceleration in the linear accelerator, circle in the storage ring for a few hours. The circulating electrons are producing electromagnetic radiation, so-called synchrotron radiation, of a broad spectrum (from which the user can select a wavelength required for his experiment) and high intensity (allowing to shorten the time needed to obtain scientific results). The synchrotron radiation can be used in fundamental research in many scientific areas like physics, chemistry, material science and others.

The sychrotron constructed by *Solaris* is a replica of the MAX LAB [2] MAX IV synchrotron, adapted to local environment. The adaptations and construction of parts that will be unique to the Polish synchrotron, require significant computing power, and so will, later, the operation of the synchrotron. However, the latter will also require large volumes of data storage. This computing power and data storage are obtained from the PL-Grid Infrastructure. Based on this

M. Bubak et al. (Eds.): PLGrid Plus, LNCS 8500, pp. 238–249, 2014.

infrastructure, within the PLGrid Plus project, new services aimed at applications and software specific to the synchrotron domain have been developed. We present them in this article along with an outlook on the future work.

2 Related Work

The synchrotron radiation centers around the world (for more information about them and their research program see [3]) are using various data formats and protocols for device communication. Although there were attempts to standardize them, there are still too many standards in use. In the European synchrotron radiation centers, the control system is usually based on Tango [4]. It was chosen also for the Polish Synchrotron, as it is constructed and built with cooperation with MAX LAB, which uses the system as well.

The idea of using grid resources to support the synchrotron operation was already investigated within the DORII (Deployment of Remote Instrumentation Infrastructure) [5] project. However, this approach (remote instrumented infrastructure [6]) was not found appropriate for the *Solaris* control system built on an existing and well-tested Tango. What is more, many Tango modules were already prepared. However, the most important reason for not reusing the DORII software was the requirement to have the same interface both to the model and to the machine that will be built, and this DORII could not fulfill. The current implementation uses the same control room software regardless of whether it is run for the virtual accelerator or for the real machine; this is not the case for DORII. DORII itself provides an alternative communication layer that will need to be encapsulated in Tango anyway. Therefore, using it as a separate system would mean repeating the work required to provide this additional layer to the communication stack. An additional requirement for the *Solaris* control system was a virtual machine delivered as a cloud service for operation of the virtual accelerator service. The cloud services started to be available in the PL-Grid Infrastructure recently and could be used for this purpose.

3 Architecture

As a result of the development activities of the PLGrid Plus project [7], new services were built for the Polish synchrotron. They are aimed at facilitating everyday operation of staff as well as at providing data storage for the end-users studying the synchrotron radiation. For the daily operation, testing the synchrotron control software with the computing model of virtual accelerator is of great importance. On the other hand, for the end users, data management services are the most essential. Data management is also of great interest for other scientific domains, therefore, the PLGrid Plus project developed new generic services dedicated to this field, which can be used also by the Synchrogrid users. These data management services, along with the specific services developed especially for Synchrogrid (Elegant, Virtual Accelerator and Tracy) are presented in the next subsections.

General relations between the Synchrogrid services and the PL-Grid Infrastructure are shown in Fig. 1. The colors surrounding the name of the service correspond to the colors of arrows representing to which PL-Grid Infrastructure services the Synchrogrid services are linking. There are three basic services within the PL-Grid Infrastructure: Computing, Storage and Cloud. Elegant and Tracy are computing-oriented services that perform scientific calculations and store their results in the Storage service. Data services are helping the users to manage their files. The Virtual Accelerator service is run on a machine of the Cloud service, delegating some part of calculations to Computing service and, currently, saving results on the same Cloud machine in a local MySQL database. In the future, this service could be adjusted to use the generic Storage service as well.

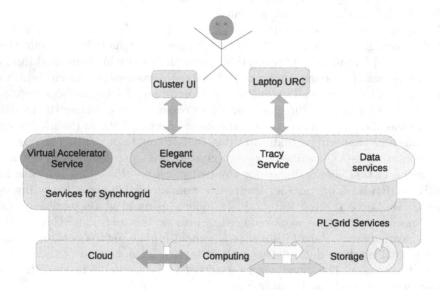

Fig. 1. General relations between Synchrogrid services and the PL-Grid Infrastructure services

There are two methods to access the Synchrogrid services. One of them is using the generic PL-Grid Infrastructure User Interface (depicted as the Cluster UI), which offers predefined modules available to the users. The second method is installation of a free, graphical UNICORE Reach Client on the user's personal computer (depicted as Laptop URC). Following the user documentation [8] allows the user to configure and access the PL-Grid Infrastructure Synchrogrid services with both methods. The URC Laptop is used as an access machine on the user side. It contains a directory with all the user job identifiers, allowing the user to download or store results locally or within the PL-Grid Infrastructure.

The Synchrotron users will be using the infrastructure in many ways. Firstly, the users can submit batch jobs to perform computations with their own code or with pre-installed generic software. Such computations are allocated to the resources on best effort basis. Secondly, it will be possible to make a reservation for resources (for example, correlated with beam time on the synchrotron). For Synchrotron operators, a "cloud" machine is foreseen to be delivered. The accelerator mock control system will be installed there to reflect the planned machine control system interface. In conjunction with models running on the computing clusters, it will provide a test suite for the software steering the accelerator. It could be also used to compare the behavior of the real and the simulated accelerator.

The developed services could also be of interest for scientists from abroad. In case of scientific collaboration between a Polish and a foreign scientist, the foreign user can register in the PL-Grid portal and request access to Synchrogrid services. It is also necessary (also for the Polish scientists) to request a PL-Grid grant (allocation) for resources and deliver reports (possibly, with scientific publications) of the grant usage.

The availability of Synchrogrid services is monitored by the PL-Grid Infrastructure monitoring system. In case of failures, alarms are raised and incidents are recorded in the ticketing Helpdesk system. There is also a support unit that handles incidents and answers the users requests.

3.1 Elegant Service

In order to properly design the synchrotron, and, consequently, ensure its best performance, it is necessary to perform a series of numerical calculations of the dynamics of the beam. Such calculations are aimed at optimizing the main parameters of the electron beam, such as emittance, beam size, life, dynamic aperture, tuning, etc. In order to do this, one needs a sophisticated optimization of both linear and nonlinear beam dynamics. Due to the complexity of the problem, dedicated programs, such as *Elegant* and *Tracy*, are used for this kind of calculation. They allow to choose from matrix, traditional or canonical integration methods. The advantage of these applications is the possibility to adapt the simulation to the user's needs. However, the calculations are time-consuming, since they require iterations between computation and optimization of other parameters.

To handle this issue and allow the users to perform computations and obtain results in satisfactory time (a few days), a parallel version of the dedicated software "ELEctron Generation ANd Tracking" (*pelegant*) [9] was compiled on the *Zeus* cluster computing nodes. Additional scripts and configuration files facilitating the use of the infrastructure were also developed and delivered to the service users. The users are now able to choose whether they want to submit the computing jobs locally (using just the cluster batch system) or to the Grid (using grid middleware), which adds the possibility to submit jobs to other computing centers supporting the Synchrogrid services.

One of the middleware deployed for the PL-Grid Infrastructure and facilitating the usage of the sites' resources is UNICORE [10]. We use the UNICORE Rich Client (URC), which is a graphical user interface for grid job management.

Owing to the prepared incarnation database (IDB) entries for the Elegant service (and supporting Matlab extension), the sites providing the Elegant service can be browsed in URC. When a user selects the Elegant service in a specific version, only sites supporting the given version of Elegant are presented (selectable). Another helpful functionality of the URC are workflows. The UNICORE workflow prepared for running the Elegant software as standalone application is presented on the right of Fig. 2. The workflow consists of two jobs: the first executes an MPI job on the cluster running *pelegant* software and passes its output to the second job. The second job executes several Matlab scripts in parallel to obtain visualization of the *pelegant* output. On the left of Fig. 2, panels helping to manage jobs already sent to the infrastructure and browsing their outputs are shown. A convenient feature is also the job description window, in which the user can input job parameters: numbers of slots, input, output files as well as the identifier of the reservation. One exemplary workflow was defined already, however, the URC facilitates creation of new workflows and saving them for later use. If saved in a common group area (shared between all the PL-Grid grant users) on the cluster UI, the workflow may be reused by other group members who load it to their own URC and configure it – setting paths, file names, etc.

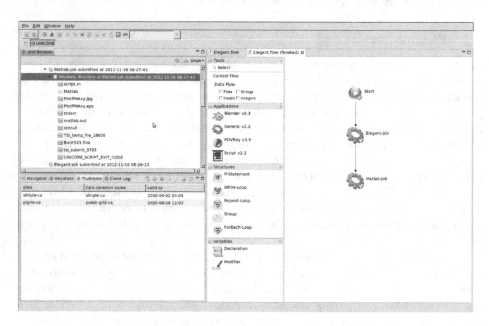

Fig. 2. The graphical user interface for defining workflows and allowing the job submission

Submitting a single job that is then split into large number of processes (tested up to 96 cores) leads to linear acceleration in obtaining the results (around 1h on 96 cores) with use of *mpirun*. The physics results are usually the parameters of beam line (see Fig. 3) which can be analyzed by end-users. If the results are unsatisfactory, the user may prepare a new set of parameters and submit a new job, quickly obtaining the results.

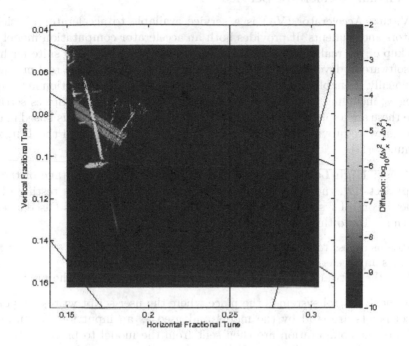

Fig. 3. Visualization of the Elegant service output

3.2 Tracy Service

The purpose of the Tracy service is similar as of Elegant. It is a tool used by accelerator physicist for various computations related to the accelerator design, simulation, tests and operation. Tracy is a set of C language libraries developed by the accelerator physicists community. It provides various algorithms, routines and data structures related to accelerator physics, mostly, to circular accelerators. The end-user utilizes these libraries to develop programs for their own computations.

Deployment of the service is similar to the deployment of Elegant – Tracy is provided as a module available to the service users. There is also a UNICORE workflow that defines all the required steps – similarly as in case of the Elegant service.

However, there is a slight difference in these two use cases. Usage of Tracy involves compilation of the code provided by the user against the Tracy library and its dependencies. It allows the user to link only the routines required by their actual task. Although that reduces the time needed for the computation itself, it adds the time needed for the compilation. The UNICORE workflow for

Tracy includes the compilation step, but it requires a makefile attached to users code.

3.3   Virtual Accelerator Service

The Virtual Accelerator (VA) is a service available to accelerator physicists, operators and students. It provides both an accelerator computation model and a mockup of the real machine control system. This creates a test suite for high-level software in development, similar to the environment on the real machines. Additionally, it enables examination of different accelerator operation modes and strategies, including electron beam filling patterns and magnet optics settings, before these are applied to the machine in operation. The service is based mainly on the software provided by Solaris, the MAX-IV laboratory and the Tango CS community [11].

Use Case: High-Level Software Testing. At the current stage of the Solaris project [12], the most important use case of the service is testing of the high-level control system software scripts that implement physics-based steering algorithms. To do this, the user:

1. Obtains access to the VA service.
2. Starts an accelerator model on the PL-Grid Infrastructure.
3. Runs the software to test on his/her local machine against the model.

The mock control system is the place where the user script writes set-points. The set-points are read by the model and used as an input for computation. Results of the computation are then sent from the model to proper attributes in the control system. The user has access to the results through the mock control system. There are, however, some prerequisites to this scenario. These are the computational model of the accelerator and the mockup of the control system interface. Both have to be delivered according to the user's request. Their implementation is done with tight collaboration between the service provider (the PL-Grid Infrastructure) and the user. The goal is to provide the user with an impression of working with a real machine. An important factor is also reducing the time needed for the computations – this is the area where the PL-Grid Infrastructure is of great utility.

Tango CS. The mock control system is based on the Tango CS [4] as in case of the Solaris machine [13]. Tango CS is an object-oriented distributed control system used to integrate accelerator devices. It provides SCADA (Supervisory Control And Data Acquisition) functionality successfully implemented in several accelerator facilities in Europe. It is based on CORBA and *zeromq* protocols hidden behind the Tango API. The devices, like magnets, power supplies, beam position monitors, are handled in Tango by so-called Device Servers. A device server translates the protocol used to communicate with a particular device into the common Tango protocol. Every physical device is represented in the system as an object with certain attributes, commands (methods) and properties [14] that reflect its characteristics (class).

Safety Issues and Consideration. The Tango CS uses CORBA protocol wrapped into Tango API to hide its implementation details. Although there is a Tango Access control device server, all authorization is handled on the client side and it is left to the client applications to use it or not. Each of the controlled devices is integrated into the system through so-called device servers. Each device server is listening for CORBA connections through an open TCP port. Through this port it accepts requests from client applications or from other device servers.

The Virtual Accelerator usage scenario involves accessing the mock Tango from different locations and in a multi-user environment – such as the PL-Grid Infrastructure. Moreover, a ModelServer device server enables the users to run an accelerator model on computation clusters by invoking a Tango command. To safeguard this, special precautions have been taken. One of them is the obligatory usage of a VPN to access the service. Another is a proper firewall configuration on the edge of the cloud network. This is later presented in the deployment description. Another precaution is also the procedure of stopping the model server when the user is not working with the service. This procedure is supplemented by a Nagios monitoring, that notifies the virtual accelerator service administrator.

Implementation. There are several software components that integrate the model and the control system interface. These are: device server providing ModelServer device, *tango2elegant* python tool and the *simple-tango* library. The ModelServer device provides functionality to configure and send a computation model to a queuing system through UNICORE. It allows a user to start an accelerator model using the Tango interface. *Tango2elegant* interfaces the Tango control system with the Elegant tool – a standard program to simulate accelerators and compute various beam parameters.

Simple-tango is a library that provides simplified tango interface for C/C++ programs. It is a tool focused on the Tracy users. It provides functions to read and write Tango attributes without any pre-initialization of the Tango client layer. The tools are described in [11].

Deployment. The static part of the deployment is showed in Fig. 4. There are two storage nodes. One of them provides a library of modules available to every user of the PL-Grid Infrastructure – these are, among others, tools provided by the accelerator community and dedicated to the modeling of the machine. The other storage node is a virtual accelerator users group directory that provides tools directly related to the virtual accelerator. Although these tools are still in development, in more mature stage, they will be converted to modules.

Fig. 5 shows the service in a dynamic state when there is a user working with it and a model is running on a cluster. It portrays the deployment of components and important relations between them, as well as relations between nodes.

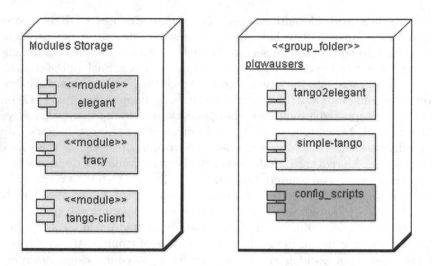

Fig. 4. The static (tools library) part of the virtual accelerator deployment

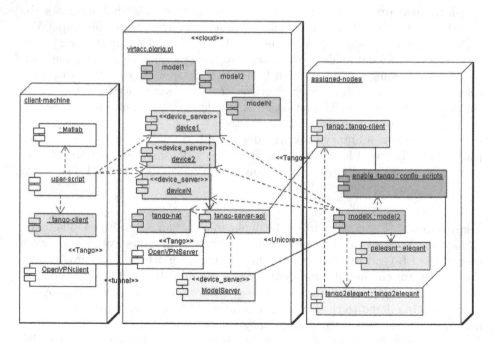

Fig. 5. The virtual accelerator deployment in dynamic state

The client machine is the user's local computer, containing a control room-like environment. It is an area where the user runs and tests his/her scripts (the user-scripts). The virtacc.plgrid.pl node is a machine in the cloud service of PL-Grid Infrastructure playing the role of a so-called service access machine.

It is the machine running the mock control system, as well as the place where the library of accelerator models is located. The user can, through the ModelServer, select one of the models and start it.

The model can be executed locally or on a remote site. However, in the latter case, it requires the Elegant service and Tango tools installed. Sites supporting the VA can be found by UNICORE on the basis of user job description.

The Tango layer is exposed through a local interface via one-to-one NAT to a public interface. To make the Tango work with NAT, a tool, called *tango-nat*, provides proper ORB endpoint information for the device servers. A firewall configured on the NAT public interface (not showed in the figure) allows access to Tango services only from the PL-Grid cluster nodes. This is a required safeguard. The user has to configure a VPN tunnel to obtain access to the service from their location.

3.4 Data Management Services

During the project realization, it appeared that many scientific domains require tools or services for data management. Some general-purpose services for data storage and management developed during the PLGrid Plus project were offered to the Synchrotron users to facilitate management of their files.

The end-stations collect data that the user needs to store. Usually, they have been stored using removable disks or pendrives. However, it was discovered that the users, after a long time, would like to come back to their historical data, thus, permanent storage is of great interest to them. As a similar need was identified also in other domain-specific grids, we are investigating the possibility to adopt some of the existing data management solutions – specifically: DataNet [15] and VeilFS [16]. For a long-term storage, including archiving large data sets, *Genetic Data Storage* was developed on top of the Platon U4 [17] service by the *Bioinformatics* domain grid. This storage offers geographic distribution and built-in encoding for increased data security.

The exact data storage workflows differ within the synchrotron users community, depending on experimental techniques or user groups. Due to this fact, specific tools shall be provided based on the requirements of the actual users. Currently, the synchrotron facility has defined two beamlines, and the potential users of one of them (the photoemission electron microscopy – PEEM – beamline) have already provided their requirements.

According to the requirements for the PEEM beamline, a service based on VeilFS with standard group access policies defined by the users will be sufficient for exporting, storage, management and sharing of the beamline experimental data. It is also worth to mention that the synchrotron community is now adopting the Nexus standard. It is a data format that combines metadata with experiment results [18], making the data files self-described.

The MySQL service provided within the PL-Grid Infrastructure is considered as a solution for backup and/or direct storage of the archive of machine operational data – so-called Historical Database (HDB). However, as the service is based on 24h, 7 days per week data injection into the database, it will require special solutions, like direct connection between Solaris and one of the PL-Grid data centers.

4 Outlook and Future Work

The PL-Grid Infrastructure is very well-suited for Synchrotron deployment and operation. During the deployment phase, it will be used for modeling of the elements required for the Synchrotron construction. After that, in the operation phase, the infrastructure will be used to test and validate the control system scripts. It will also enable storing of the data produced by the machine (operation parameters, data gathered by all users). For users requiring large computing power, data stored in the PL-Grid computing centers will be available for further processing. The time-scale and size of the data kept in the PL-Grid Infrastructure will be defined in service level agreements between the PL-Grid Infrastructure and the user, called PL-Grid grants. In case when the operations of the Synchrotron will have to be adjusted during its normal operation, the computations done by the virtual accelerator service will require short response times. For this purpose, advance reservations of the computing resources (supported by PL-Grid grants and the UNICORE middleware) are planned to be used.

One very important aspect for the Synchrotron users is the possibility of working collaboratively, with help of a collaborative environment with communication and message logging capabilities. During the Synchrotron construction and deployment phase, these aspects are not handled. Nevertheless, the requirements from the end-users will be collected after the initial start-up phase. Appropriate solutions will be offered to them then. Some of the functionality will be provided by the existing PLGrid Plus social services (Confluence, JIRA, etc.) available to the users of a given PL-Grid grant.

References

1. Solaris web site, http://www.synchrotron.uj.edu.pl/
2. MaxLab web site, https://www.maxlab.lu.se/maxlab
3. Ligth sources web site, http://www.lightsources.org/cms/
4. Tango control system web site, http://www.tango-controls.org/
5. DORII project web site, http://www.dorii.eu
6. Pugliese, R., Prica, M., Kourousias, G., Del Linz, A., Curri, A.: Integrating Instruments in the Grid for on-line and off-line processing in a synchrotron radiation facility. Computational Methods in Science and Technology 15(1), 21–30 (2009)
7. PL-Grid Infrastructure web site, http://www.plgrid.pl/
8. Synchrogrid services user manuals web page,
   https://docs.cyfronet.pl/display/PLGDoc/Synchrogrid
9. Pelegant Manual Version 24.0.1,
   http://www.aps.anl.gov/Accelerator_Systems_Division/
   Accelerator_OperationsPhysics/publish/Pelegant_manual/Pelegant.pdf

10. Benedyczak, K., Stolarek, M., Rowicki, R., Kluszczyński, R., Borcz, M., Marczak, G., Filocha, M., Bała, P.: Seamless Access to the PL-Grid e-Infrastructure Using UNICORE Middleware. In: Bubak, M., Szepieniec, T., Wiatr, K. (eds.) PL-Grid 2011. LNCS, vol. 7136, pp. 56–72. Springer, Heidelberg (2012)

11. Goryl, P., et al.: An implementation of the virtual accelerator in the Tango control system. MOSB3. In: Proceedings of the ICAP 2012, Rostock-Warnemünde, Germany (2012)

12. Wawrzyniak, A.I., et al.: Overview of the Solaris Facility. In: Proceedings of 3rd International Conference on Particle Accelerator (IPAC 2012), New Orleans, USA (2012)

13. Zytniak, L., et al.: GeoSynoptic Panel, TUPPC112. In: Proceedings of the ICALEPCS 2013, USA (2013)

14. The TANGO team: The TANGO Control System Manual Version 8.1 (2013), http://ftp.esrf.fr/pub/cs/tango/tango_81.pdf

15. Harężlak, D., Kasztelnik, M., Pawlik, M., Wilk, B., Bubak, M.: A Lightweight Method of Metadata and Data Management with DataNet. In: Bubak, M., Kitowski, J., Wiatr, K. (eds.) PLGrid Plus. LNCS, vol. 8500, pp. 164–177. Springer, Heidelberg (2014)

16. Dutka, L., Słota, R., Wrzeszcz, M., Król, D., Kitowski, J.: Uniform and Efficient Access to Data in Organizationally Distributed Environments. In: Bubak, M., Kitowski, J., Wiatr, K. (eds.) PLGrid Plus. LNCS, vol. 8500, pp. 178–194. Springer, Heidelberg (2014)

17. Platon storage service web site, http://www.storage.pionier.net.pl/

18. NEXUS, a common data format for neutron, x-ray and muon science, http://www.nexusformat.org/

Comprehensive Support for Chemistry Computations in PL-Grid Infrastructure

Andrzej Eilmes[1], Mariusz Sterzel[2], Tomasz Szepieniec[2], Joanna Kocot[2], Klemens Noga[2], and Maciej Golik[2]

[1] Jagiellonian University, Faculty of Chemistry, Kraków, Poland
eilmes@chemia.uj.edu.pl
[2] AGH University of Science and Technology, ACC Cyfronet AGH,
ul. Nawojki 11, 30-950 Kraków, Poland
{m.sterzel,t.szepieniec,ymkocot,klemens.noga,m.golik}@cyfronet.pl

Abstract. InSilicoLab for Chemistry with its experiments and QC Advisor are the tools assisting PL-Grid users in chemistry computations on grid infrastructure. The tools are designed to help the user at all stages of calculations – from the software choice and input data preparation, through job submission and monitoring to the retrieval of output files and analysis of results. General Quantum Chemistry experiment helps in launching QC computations on PL-Grid. A specialized tool – Trajectory Sculptor – is designed for manipulations with Molecular Dynamics trajectories and large sets of molecular structures in sequential computational experiments. QC Advisor collects information about availability of different computational methods in quantum-chemical programs and supports preparation of input files for the most popular software. The main idea behind the tools described in the paper is to reduce the effort needed to set-up the calculations, allowing users to focus on scientific content of their work.

Keywords: computational chemistry, experiments in silico, e-science, sequential modeling.

1 Description of the Problem

Computational methods of quantum chemistry and in silico experiments are valuable tools in materials science, biochemistry and related research areas allowing one to study properties of matter by performing calculations in order to explain (or even better – to predict) experimental results. Importance of such methodology has been recently recognized by the Nobel Foundation awarding the 2013 Nobel Prize in chemistry for "the development of multiscale models for complex chemical systems" [1]. Modern modeling and applications of advanced methods of computational chemistry require still increasing resources. Computational power is necessary to improve the accuracy of results and/or is needed to make larger systems tractable or to extend the timescale of simulations. The latter factors are of particular importance for current challenges of nanotechnology or biological sciences where systems consisting of thousands of atoms need

M. Bubak et al. (Eds.): PLGrid Plus, LNCS 8500, pp. 250–263, 2014.

to be modeled. Fortunately, constant progress in computer technology meets this demand from scientific community. However, successive application of modeling is not just a matter of available computational resources. Equally important is the proper choice of software and efficient management of huge amount of data used in often complicated workflows.

Quantum-chemistry (QC) uses a wide range of methods: from low-cost semi-empirical calculations, through Density Functional Theory methodology or ab initio Hartree-Fock calculations to accurate, but usually very demanding, post-Hartree-Fock methods. Computational cost of the method may be just related to the time needed to complete the calculations, but some methods have also large requirements for RAM memory and/or intensively use huge scratch files. Several packages using standard QC methods are available to the scientist. Some of them feature specific implementations which increase the efficiency of calculations (e.g. speed-up the calculations or reduce usage of scratch space), providing additional functionality or introducing the most up-to-date versions of certain QC methods.

A broad choice of available QC software is beneficial to scientists, in principle allowing them to find a program best suited to the needs of the researcher. However, quite often it may confuse less-experienced users who are trying to decide on which software to use. On the other hand, even experienced researchers usually tend to use one favorite package which they already know well. This behavior is caused by the time needed to learn how to prepare input files. A well-defined scientific problem (type of QC calculation and parameters of the method such as the basis set) may not be easy to express within the syntax of input files for a particular program. Even the most important keywords describing the problem may not be obvious; moreover, usually it is necessary to specify some additional parameters controlling the technical details of actual calculations. Strategies of specifying the input data and the syntax of input files differ completely between programs, therefore the learning curve is likely to prevent users from choosing another computational package; instead they try to master one program (usually the one they had used first).

Further complications are related to parallel computing. With quantum-chemical calculations that take long time (up to weeks or months) to complete, parallelization appears as a natural choice of increasing the speed of computations on modern computer architectures. For some quantum-chemical methods it may be easier, for other very difficult, therefore one may find a broad range of parallel implementations of QC methods: from purely serial to massively parallel. Even for one specific method its efficiency may drastically differ between programs. Regardless of the program, proper setup of parallel QC calculations usually requires additional knowledge that beginners or less experienced users simply do not possess. They usually are also unaware of technical details and lack necessary skills to be able to make use of the benefits parallelization brings.

All these factors lead to a rather undesirable scenario, in which many users choose not very well performing software, leading to inefficient use of available resources and overall performance degradation.

Another difficulty with input data faced by researchers is related to the number of necessary data files. Quantum-chemical modeling quite often requires preparation of numerous input files (based on molecular geometries, which sometimes need to be appropriately selected from larger systems), launching multiple jobs and monitoring their progress, extracting relevant information from output files and storing large amount of data for further use. Modeling of complex systems or use of more sophisticated methodologies make the data workflows even more complicated. Very often the whole process needs to be repeated, either with other data or for the same molecular data, but for a different computational method or its parameters. Data preparation and job execution may therefore consume a considerable amount of researcher's time and effort (and quite often it may require a knowledge of scripting languages). Maintaining the data integrity in such a process is an even more demanding issue, when grid resources are used and computational jobs and data files are distributed over multiple locations.

2   Related Work

There are several sources gathering information about the existing software for quantum-chemical calculations, e.g. Computational Chemistry List web site [2]. Such sites may be quite useful, but do not provide details about availability and efficiency of particular QC methods implemented in packages. They are rather starting points for the user who can follow links to the software sites and study the manuals of individual programs to learn about the capabilities of software. Of course, a single manual describes only the features of one particular program and to make a comparison between different programs, many sources of data have to be found and studied. This is a time consuming task and not many grid users want to pursue this route. Therefore, there is a need for a more friendly solution, which not only provides necessary information, but preferably should also encourage users to explore the variety of available software by assistance in job preparation and execution.

Most QC software suites have additional applications designed for data manipulation, usually Graphical User Interfaces. These tools are helpful in preparation of input files, some of them also support the job submission in simple computing environments and can analyze and visualize the results of calculations from outputs. Nevertheless, they are intended to operate with data files for a single chemical system, therefore do not allow for automated creation of sets of multiple jobs, neither support execution on grid-distributed resources nor are able to handle complicated workflows in sequential or multiscale modeling. Another disadvantage of QC GUIs is that some of them are non-free applications, thus incurring extra costs for the users. Necessity to install and configure (in some cases of free applications even to compile from sources) additional software (which often requires a specific version of the operating system) is another drawback of such a solution. There are also some tools available for parsing QC output files and extracting results, such as cclib [3] – a Python-based open source library.

Being a library, cclib is, however, not a ready-to-use application; instead it requires some programming knowledge from the user in order to successfully apply it to the problem.

Within the PL-Grid project there have also been developed services to support job management on the grid computing infrastructure – e.g. QosCosGrid [4] or Unicore [5] middleware. While they are helpful in job submission and execution, still do not solve the problem of automated preparation of input files. This stage of QC computing requires therefore some specialized tools to be developed and made available to researchers. The desired solution should be ready to use and do not depend on the operating system of the user machine – i.e. preferably a web-based one. An example of web portal of this kind may be the science gateway for nanotechnology [6].

3 Solution to the Problem

The PLGrid Plus project is aimed to provide Polish researchers with powerful computational infrastructure tailored to the needs of specific community, but also to address the problem of efficient use of resources by creating domain-specific computing environments for different fields of science, in order to make the scientists' computational work easier and more productive. In particular, domain services provide access to specialized software and support for performing common computational scenarios and multi-step experiments. Solutions and services for the community of quantum chemists are organized within the Quantum Chemistry and Molecular Physics domain.

Two kinds of services for computational chemistry are currently under development within the Quantum Chemistry domain: InSilicoLab for Chemistry and QC Advisor. They address the issues described in Sec. 1 – the question of choosing the software and the related problem of input file preparation as well as the issue of performing complicated experiments.

4 Results

4.1 InSilicoLab for Chemistry

InSilicoLab [7,8] is a platform that facilitates computations on distributed infrastructures as well as management of data involved in these computations. The idea of InSilicoLab is to provide a comprehensive workspace that would support the user in performing in silico experiments – that is: preparing application input data, executing the actual computation, storing, categorizing and searching relevant input and output data. Such experiments are repeatable and connected to the data they produce – allowing to easily monitor the process which led to a specific result.

InSilicoLab is organized as a framework of application portals and can be accessed using standard web browser with Java enabled (the latter is necessary, e.g., to view chemical structures in 3D). Therefore, there is no need for the user to install any additional software and the user may work in the portal from any machine, regardless of the operating system. No knowledge of how to use grid resources is necessary, unlike the case of manual job submission through a queuing system.

InSilicoLab in principle is designed to support different research areas. Currently, it offers two experiments for the chemistry domain: a general quantum-chemistry experiment and Trajectory Sculptor. Solutions for computational chemistry are organized as InSilicoLab for Chemistry.

General Quantum-Chemistry Experiment. This tool facilitates preparation of input files for typical quantum-chemical calculations, submission and monitoring of jobs on the PL-Grid Infrastructure and retrieval of output files with basic post-processing of results.

Setting-up the QC experiment requires a geometry specification of the molecular system. This can be done either by supplying a molecular structure in one of common formats (e.g. as XYZ file) or the geometry may be passed from a previous InSilicoLab experiment (including Trajectory Sculptor – see the next subsection). For verification purposes the structure can be easily viewed on-screen in 3D using Jmol [9] Java applets, allowing for rotation of the molecule and different rendering styles.

Next, the specification of a chosen quantum-chemical method with related parameters such as charge and spin multiplicity of the system or basis set are entered. The user can provide also some technical details of calculations (number of processor cores) or choose to save some intermediate files (e.g. Gaussian checkpoint files). Currently, three QC programs may be used in the experiment: Gaussian, Gamess and Turbomole. In the case of Gaussian it is possible to request a cube-file of specific type to be generated; these files are useful for visualization and analysis of molecular properties such as molecular orbitals, electron density or electrostatic potential.

The tool encapsulates the jobs into job description files, transfers them to the experiment directory on the grid storage system, submits the jobs to the infrastructure and controls their execution. Statistics about current status (submitted, running, finished) of jobs are presented to the user as well as information where the job is actually being executed. It is possible to download partial results from the running jobs for inspection.

Output files of successfully completed jobs are automatically retrieved and basic information about the calculated system parameters (like SCF energies, orbital energies, optical transitions, etc.) are extracted using cclib library parser [3] and written in XML format. Statistics for selected parameters (SCF energy) from multiple jobs can be summarized and displayed – an example is presented in Fig. 1. The user can also download the job files individually. Parameters of the experiment and associated job files can be stored on the storage system for future retrieval, reuse in another experiment or repeating the calculations.

Trajectory Sculptor. Molecular modeling of complex systems (e.g. solutions) quite often requires a two-stage approach. First, Molecular Dynamics (MD)

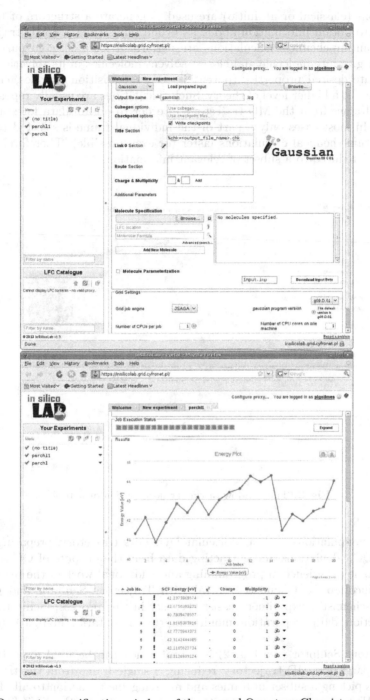

Fig. 1. Parameter specification window of the general Quantum Chemistry experiment (top) and an example of the summary of energy values computed from multiple jobs (bottom)

simulations (classical or ab initio) are used to generate a structure of the system and to obtain information about its evolution in time – a MD trajectory. Next, quantum-chemical calculations are performed for a selected part of the system (e.g. solute molecule and closest solvent molecules in its solvation shell) to calculate desired properties (potential energy, transition energies, chemical shifts, etc.) at a higher level of theory. Such calculations are usually repeated for series of frames from the MD trajectory in order to obtain data for statistical analysis. In most cases only a part of the individual frame is selected to make the quantum-chemical calculations faster (or even possible). Therefore, frames have to be reduced to a subset of relevant information.

Fig. 2. The window of the Trajectory Sculptor tool

Such manipulations with a Molecular Dynamics trajectory, preparing input files for QC calculations and extracting data from the outputs of QC software require some experience in programming and additional work of the researcher. The InSilicoLab for Chemistry portal with Trajectory Sculptor and general quantum-chemistry experiment assist the user in this process, facilitating system selection, data preparation, monitoring the computation and gathering the results.

Trajectory Sculptor (see Fig. 2) is a tool which can be used for extracting relevant parts of a MD trajectory, reducing a single frame from the trajectory as well as picking a subset of frames and applying the reduction to all of them.

The MD trajectory can be submitted in several formats, the XYZ file is preferred; other formats are automatically converted to XYZ using the OpenBabel software [10].

The trajectory reduction is performed in three stages:

- system definition – the user specifies the composition of the system and defines solute and solvent(s)
- distance definition – a metric of measuring the distance between each solute-solvent pair is supplied and the distance threshold to select solvent molecules is specified
- choice of frames – the relevant subset of frames is defined.

At each phase of system specification or reduction the user can preview the results. Reduced frames can be downloaded or used directly as inputs for InSilicoLab Quantum Chemistry experiment to launch QC computations. An example of frame reduction for a large simulation box is presented in Fig. 3.

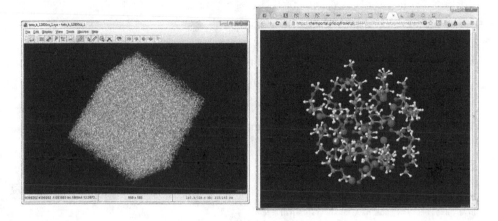

Fig. 3. An example of Trajectory Sculptor usage: Molecular Dynamics trajectory frame of more than 400000 atoms (left) reduced to a few selected molecules (right)

Support for different data formats (automated conversion of the trajectory file to XYZ format) and for periodic or open boundary conditions allows one to use trajectories generated by many popular Molecular Dynamics programs. A variety of available distance metrics and possibility to select either specified number of solvent molecules or to use a selection based on the distance thresholds makes the construction of the solvation shell very flexible. The Trajectory Sculptor tool is applicable to a wide range of systems including binary or ternary solvent mixtures, electrolyte solutions or ionic liquids.

InSilicoLab and its experiments for chemistry can be accessed at
http://insilicolab.chemia.plgrid.pl/.

4.2   QC Advisor

QC Advisor is intended to provide researchers with information about the implementation of different QC methods, especially in the software already available

PLGrid Dokumentacja / ... / Chemia

Chemia: Quantum Chemistry Advisor

Quantum Chemistry packages comparison

Software packages availability

Information about the newest quantum chemistry software versions available on PL-Grid clusters. See also PL-Grid In

HPC Centre	Gaussian	Turbomole	GAMESS	NWChem	ORCA	Terachem	ADF
ACK CYFRONET AGH	09.D1	6.5	2012.R2	6.3		1.5	2013.01
ICM UW	09.D1		2012.R2	?			
PSNC	09.D1		2009.R3	6.0			
CI TASK	09.D1		2012.R2	6.1.1			
WCSS	09.D1	6.5	2013.R1	6.3	3.0.1?		2013.01

Software packages capabilities

Legend

In all tables below symbols have meaning shown in legend:

Symbol	Meaning
energy	electronic energy calculations only
grad	analytic algorithm of computing gradients
num grad	numerical differentiation for computing gradients
freq	analytic algorithm of computing vibrational frequencies
num freq	numerical differentiation for computing vibrational frequencies
RI	Resolution of Identity/Density Fitting algorithm available
CD	Choleski Decomposition algorithm available

Fig. 4. A part of the QC Advisor knowledge base – support for quantum-chemical methods in different software

in the PL-Grid Infrastructure, to help them in finding alternative programs. At the first stage of development a knowledge base summarizing the capabilities of quantum-chemistry software covering common methods (but also some specific implementations reducing computational effort) was gathered and made available to PL-Grid users. A sample table is shown in Fig. 4.

The entries of the table describe what kind of calculation is possible in the chosen program using the requested QC method: energy, its gradient (analytic or numerical) or harmonic frequencies (requiring second derivatives of the energy).

At the second stage, QC Advisor will assist users in preparation of input files and job submission. This goal will be achieved through combining the Advisor with the general Quantum Chemistry experiment of InSilicoLab, allowing automated input preparation based on the user-provided geometry specification, chosen QC method and additional parameters (e.g. basis set) – see Fig. 5.

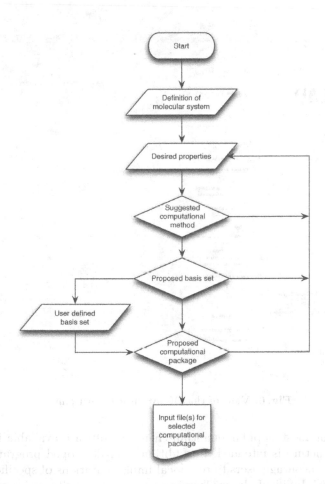

Fig. 5. Workflow diagram of data in the QC Advisor wizard

The idea of the tool is that the user supplies the molecular structure and selects from the context-sensitive menu the type of requested calculation and its parameters. In addition to the typical kinds of calculations (single point energies, geometry optimizations or frequency calculations for ground or excited states) it is possible to request some properties which will lead to launching multiple jobs (e.g. with different charges to obtain ionization potentials).

QC Advisor wizard guides the user through this process, so that only the options relevant to the chosen method are accessible (see Fig. 6). When the specification of the QC method and parameters is completed, the user can select a QC program from the suggestions offered by the wizard (only the software capable of performing the required computations will be suggested). Next, the input file is created, based on the stored syntax rules for the selected program. The user can download the input file or pass it to the general quantum-chemical experiment of InSilicoLab for instantaneous job submission.

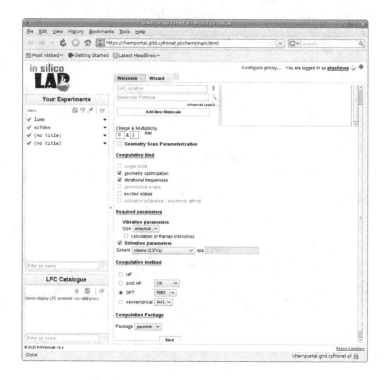

Fig. 6. View of the QC Advisor wizard panel

Support for most popular quantum-chemical software available in the PL-Grid Infrastructure is intended. In addition, user-developed programs may be supported to encourage users to test local implementations of specific methods. Integrated with InSilicoLab for Chemistry, this service will provide an easy way to set-up and launch QC calculations for an unexperienced user.

4.3   Use of the PL-Grid Infrastructure

The access to both services can be granted from the PL-Grid portal by activating the respective service. The authentication is performed using the PL-Grid OpenID which ensures Single Sign-On for all PL-Grid services. Additionally, for authentication to the InSilicoLab portal, grid certificates issued by either PL-Grid SimpleCA (and obtained from the PL-Grid portal) or PL-Grid CA [11] can be used.

The services for the chemistry domain exploit a dedicated PL-Grid machine for preparation of input files and analysis of the MD trajectory. Most of the computations triggered from the InSilicoLab portal is performed on the PL-Grid computing infrastructure, with use of quantum-chemical applications (Gaussian, Gamess, Turbomole) available for the PL-Grid community in virtual organization `vo.plgrid.pl`. The computational tasks are submitted to the infrastructure with use of the gLite [12] middleware.

5   Conclusions and Future Work

Efficient use of grid infrastructure requires supporting users in choosing software, job control or data management. Modern computational environment should provide sufficient assistance to allow users to focus on the scientific issues of the project, leaving technical details to specialized tools. Examples of such solutions are the services for computational chemistry in the PL-Grid Infrastructure.

InSilicoLab for Chemistry and its experiments for computational chemists are already implemented in PL-Grid Infrastructure and are ready for users. By the end of 2013 more than 40 users have registered for the service. A group of prospective users – PhD students at the Faculty of Chemistry of Jagiellonian University attended a tutorial introducing them to the use of InSilicoLab for Chemistry. The InSilicoLab for Chemistry web portal has been used for the computations of organic and metal-organic reactions important in electro-catalysis [13]. The development version of Trajectory Sculptor has been already applied in the production computations of real problems – sequential MD/QC modeling of an organic molecule in explicit water [14]. As of January 2014, the knowledge base of the QC Advisor is at the prototype stage and the wizard is currently under development.

Both tools will be further modified to support more software packages or to add new features and extensions that further facilitate input preparation according to the needs of PL-Grid Infrastructure users. This includes support for a QC program, `niedoida` [15,16], developed at the Faculty of Chemistry of Jagiellonian University in collaboration with Academic Computer Center CYFRONET AGH, featuring an implementation of dressed Time Dependent Density Functional Theory [17]. This promotes contributions from local groups for the benefit of the whole PL-Grid community.

References

1. The 2013 Nobel Prize in Chemistry – Laureates (2013),
   http://www.nobelprize.org/nobel_prizes/chemistry/laureates/2013/
2. Computational Chemistry List, http://www.ccl.net/
3. cclib, http://cclib.sourceforge.net/
4. Bosak, B., Komasa, J., Kopta, P., Kurowski, K., Mamoński, M., Piontek, T.: New Capabilities in QosCosGrid Middleware for Advanced Job Management, Advance Reservation and Co-allocation of Computing Resources – Quantum Chemistry Application Use Case. In: Bubak, M., Szepieniec, T., Wiatr, K. (eds.) PL-Grid 2011. LNCS, vol. 7136, pp. 40–55. Springer, Heidelberg (2012)
5. Benedyczak, K., Stolarek, M., Rowicki, R., Kluszczyński, R., Borcz, M., Marczak, G., Filocha, M., Bała, P.: Seamless Access to the PL-Grid e-Infrastructure Using UNICORE Middleware, ibid, pp. 56–72
6. Dziubecki, P., Grabowski, P., Krysiński, M., Kuczyński, T., Kurowski, K., Piontek, T., Szejnfeld, D.: Online Web-Based Science Gateway for Nanotechnology Research, ibid, pp. 205–216
7. Kocot, J., Szepieniec, T., Harężlak, D., Noga, K., Sterzel, M.: InSilicoLab – Managing Complexity of Chemistry Computations, ibid, pp. 265–275
8. InSilicoLab – an application portal supporting in silico experiments on e-Infrastructures, http://insilicolab.cyfronet.pl/
9. Jmol: an open-source Java viewer for chemical structures in 3D,
   http://www.jmol.org/
10. Open Babel: the Open Source Chemistry Toolbox, http://openbabel.org
11. Polish GRID Certification Authority, http://plgrid-ca.pl
12. gLite: Middleware for Grid Computing, http://glite.web.cern.ch/glite/
13. Romańczyk, P.P., Noga, K., Radoń, M., Rotko, G., Kurek, S.S.: On the role of noncovalent interactions in electrocatalysis. Two cases of mediated reductive dehalogenation, Electrochim. Acta 110, 619–627 (2013)
14. Eilmes, A.: Spiropyran to Merocyanine Conversion: Explicit versus Implicit Solvent Modeling. J. Phys. Chem. A 117, 2629–2635 (2013)
15. Niedoida: general purpose computational chemistry package,
    http://www.chemia.uj.edu.pl/~niedoida/
16. Mazur, G., Makowski, M.: Development and Optimization of Computational Chemistry Algorithms. Computing and Informatics 28, 115–125 (2009)
17. Mazur, G., Włodarczyk, R.: Application of the Dressed Time-Dependent Density Functional Theory for the Excited States of Linear Polyenes. J. Comp. Chem. 30, 811–817 (2009)

Supercomputing Grid-Based Services for Hearing Protection and Acoustical Urban Planning, Research and Education

Maciej Szczodrak[1,3], Andrzej Czyżewski[1],
Józef Kotus[1,3], and Bożena Kostek[2,3]

[1] Multimedia Systems Department, Faculty of Electronics,
Telecommunications and Informatics, Gdansk University of Technology,
ul. Narutowicza 11/12, 80-233 Gdańsk, Poland
[2] Audio Acoustics Laboratory, Faculty of Electronics,
Telecommunications and Informatics, Gdansk University of Technology,
ul. Narutowicza 11/12, 80-233 Gdańsk, Poland
[3] Academic Computer Center, Gdansk University of Technology,
ul. Narutowicza 11/12, 80-233 Gdańsk, Poland
{szczodry,andcz,joseph,bozenka}@sound.eti.pg.gda.pl

Abstract. Specific computational environments, so-called domain grids, are developed within the PLGrid Plus project in order to prepare specialized IT solutions, i.e., dedicated software implementations and hardware (infrastructure adaptation), suited for particular research group demands. One of the PLGrid Plus domain grids, presented in this paper, is Acoustics. The article describes in detail two kinds of the acoustic domain services. The first can be used to calculate noise maps of large city areas, and is called "Noise Map". The second, called the "Hearing" service, enables simulations of noise impact on the human hearing system. Several kinds of usage scenarios of the developed services are also presented and illustrated by exemplary results. The infrastructure and the software developed can be utilized mainly for research and education purposes. The engineered software is intended for creating maps of noise threat for roads, railways and industrial sources. Integration of the software services with a distributed sensor network enables to automatically update the noise maps for a specific time period. A unique feature of the developed software is the possibility to estimate the auditory effects, which are caused by the exposure to noise. This estimation is based on the calculated noise levels and on a given exposure period. The outcomes of this research study are presented in form of a cumulative noise dose and characteristics of the temporary threshold shift.

Keywords: noise, road noise, noise threat, supercomputer grid, noise dosimetry.

1 Introduction

Noise, the most ubiquitous pollutant found in an urban environment, may, imperceptibly, cause harmful effects to the human health. The problem is significant,

M. Bubak et al. (Eds.): PLGrid Plus, LNCS 8500, pp. 263–277, 2014.

particularly in heavily urbanized areas. Noise has an influence not only on the life quality in cities, but also on general health in the society. Therefore, an action aimed to assess the threat has been commenced by the European Parliament and Council, which has issued the European Directive 2002/49/EC. According to this legislation, the authorities of cities are obliged to prepare noise maps illustrating the sound level distribution in the city areas. To accomplish this task, dedicated software, which calculates the noise produced by sources such as road or railway traffic, is used. Computation of a noise map for large city areas would result in high computation time. Therefore, to solve this problem, software for calculating road and railway noise on a supercomputer platform was proposed and developed by the authors. A common problem related to hearing impairments is the exposition to an excessive sound level. The effect of high noise levels evokes serious consequences for the hearing system, like irreparable destruction of sensitive structures in the inner ear [9], [13]. Other issues related to the occupational threats of noise are extensively discussed in contemporary literature [3], [36]. It is also necessary to notice, that common access to audio equipment (such as portable MP3 players) and various types of entertainment could create a hidden health hazard for their users [12], [20]. The exposure to excessive sound level, both in form of urban noise and loud music, results in a temporary shift of the auditory threshold. The software for estimation of auditory effects, which are caused by the exposure to excessive noise, proposed and developed within the acoustic domain grid of the PLGrid Plus project, is described in the following sections.

2   State of the Art

The services described in this paper concern two different issues. First is the noise mapping, while the second concerns assessment of the noise dose and its influence on the human hearing system. The calculation of noise maps can be realized by means of one of the commercially available software packages [1,2], [4,5]. Most of them run on the Microsoft Windows operating system; only one can be used in a Unix-like environment [4]. They are also designed mainly as desktop applications. Optimization of the calculation engines includes multithread support when using multi-core computers with the PCSP (Program Controlled Segmented Processing) technique for distributed calculation. PCSP can also use multiple computers distributed in a network. To handle such a calculation task with PCSP, the entire project has to be first divided into rectangular sub-regions that match each other and, then, saved to a specific folder. The program loads independently a part of the project limited by a sub-region and an additional borderline. After completion of the calculation, the result for each sub-region is saved and the next portion is processed. The approach taken by the authors is different from the aforementioned. First of all, the solution proposed by the authors was designed to be used either on Windows or Unix-like platforms and uses a different method for parallelization of the calculations. Moreover, thanks to the availability of specific services in the PL-Grid platform, the users have flexible access to many calculation methods and to computational resources of the PL-Grid Infrastructure. A similar work, concerning noise mapping with use of a computational grid, has been accomplished in the GDI-Grid project [23]. However, the project's method was based on dividing the calculation area on smaller tiles and processing them in parallel.

The contemporary methods of hearing impairment risk evaluation are mostly based on the equal energies hypothesis [3], [36]. Such an approach focuses mainly on the assessment of the amount of energy that has direct impact on the human hearing system. Time characteristics of signals are ignored, while the main emphasis is put on the equivalent noise level. In many cases, such an approach turns to be insufficient. According to many literature sources on the subject of exposure to different noise types [7], [9], [21], both time characteristics and the spectrum significantly contribute to hearing loss [18], [33]. Having this in mind, the authors designed, implemented and evaluated a new method of hearing impairment risk estimation [6]. The method is based on modeling the consequences of a particular type of noise impact on hearing. The method and its effectiveness assessment are presented in the following papers: [16], [24,25,26,27], [28,29].

3 Description of the Solution

The authors developed tools for assessment of the noise threat, which consist of the noise map calculation and services for estimation of the noise influence on hearing. The software for calculation of the noise maps is based on open source programming libraries. Two kinds of services were prepared. The first can be used to calculate a noise map of large city areas, and is called the "Noise Map". The second, called the "Hearing" service, enables simulations of the noise impact on the human hearing system. The software was deployed on the supercomputers running within the PL-Grid Infrastructure. To fully exploit the computer cluster capabilities, a master-slave parallel programming paradigm was applied in connection with the MPI (Message Passing Interface) programming standard. The access to the services is realized by either QosCosGrid (QCG) or Unicore client software [8], [10]. The "Noise Map" service is intended for creating maps of noise threats for roads, railways and industrial sources. Integration of the software service with a distributed sensors network brings a possibility of making automatic updates to the noise maps for a specified time period. Two scenarios of use of the "Noise Map" can be distinguished. In the first scenario, the user has to provide input data by uploading it into the storage space available within the infrastructure. Therefore, it is possible to investigate various configurations of urban infrastructure and city acoustic climate. In the second scenario, a dynamic noise map and an estimate of influence of noise on hearing are produced periodically. A unique feature of the "Hearing" service is an evaluation of the auditory effects caused by exposure to an excessive noise. The main part of the "Hearing" service is the Psychoacoustical Noise Dosimeter, which is based on utilizing a modified psychoacoustic model of hearing. The primary function of the dosimeter is to estimate, in quasi-real time, the auditory effects which are caused by exposure to the noise. Owing to that, it is possible to recognize the character of the auditory threshold shift for a given type of noise. The user can define detailed conditions of exposure to noise such as noise level, exposure time and energy distribution in the frequency domain. The outcomes are presented in form of a cumulative noise dose and characteristics of temporary threshold shift (TTS) of hearing.

3.1 Noise Source and Propagation Model

The "Noise Map" service is devoted to calculating noise maps of an urban area. The method of creating a noise map is based on mathematical models of noise source and propagation. In case of a road noise, the source model consists of vehicle and traffic models. The sound power of a single vehicle is calculated on the basis of velocity as one of the input parameters. The traffic model is utilized to combine noise emission of numerous single vehicles according to traffic statistics. The output of the source model is the sound power per one meter of the linear source [32]. The resultant sound level is calculated in a defined grid of receiver points using the propagation model. The concept of sound propagation paths describing schematic lines of acoustic wave traverse paths from single point source to receiver is utilized in the model. The sound propagation paths are obtained by employing the acoustic ray tracing method [30,31].

The propagation method describes the attenuation between each pair of point source and the receiver [17], [31]. Point sources are introduced by segmentation of the linear source, which is done by ray tracing. A number of factors that affect the sound propagation in the real atmosphere has to be considered in the calculation process. The latter includes absorption of sound in the air, non-uniformity of the propagation medium due to meteorological conditions and interaction with an absorbing ground and solid obstacles [19]. Total sound level in each receiver is obtained by aggregation of the influence of sources found by ray tracing with respect to calculated sound attenuations on the propagation paths.

The main engine of the "Noise Map" service is the software implementation of noise source and propagation model. The developed software is highly parallel due to the applied method of noise level calculation and utilization of a master-slave parallel programming paradigm in connection with the MPI programming standard [14,15], [34].

The software was deployed on all supercomputers of the PL-Grid Infrastructure [35]. The integration with PL-Grid was made through usage of the QosCos-Grid and Unicore middleware [8], [10,11]. This integration gives users the ability to perform complex computational tasks in a convenient way, adapted to their experience and preferences.

The algorithm for noise mapping (NM) has a modular design, therefore, it is used in various configurations, depending on the use case. Typically, the calculation of sound level distribution over a specified urban area is performed using the algorithm shown in Fig. 1. In this configuration, the input data is uploaded into the PL-Grid Infrastructure and the result is provided in form of noise level values in the specified area.

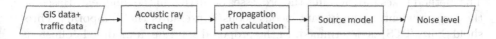

Fig. 1. NM algorithm for calculation of the noise map

A block diagram of another configuration is presented in Fig. 2. The intermediate results of the calculations are stored separately. They contain the attenuations obtained for each pair of source and receiver found by the acoustic ray tracing method. Since the computational cost of the latter is high, intermediate data can be utilized in further calculations of the noise map when the source parameters change. The diagram showing the algorithm, which uses the intermediate results, is presented in Fig. 3. Pre-calculated propagation path attenuations can be immediately combined with source emission level obtained by the source model.

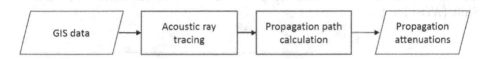

Fig. 2. NM algorithm for dynamic noise mapping: calculation of propagation path attenuations

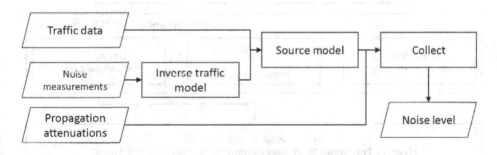

Fig. 3. Updating the dynamic noise map

3.2   Psychoacoustical Noise Dosimeter

Currently, a noise dose, to which a person is exposed, is determined based on the aggregated acoustic energy that he/she experiences in a certain acoustic environment. The proposed method uses a very different approach. It concentrates on a prediction of the threat incurred to a person due to a specific noise.

The method takes into account the processes occurring in the inner ear. Based on the measurement of the instantaneous acoustic pressure, the Temporary Threshold Shift (TTS) is determined. In the proposed solution, a modified Johnstons psychoacoustic model is used [22]. It enables to determine the global/maximal basilar membrane motion. Fig. 4 depicts a general block diagram of the psychoacoustic model of a noise dosimeter. Its performance is based on the analysis of the basilar membrane response to the noise in the critical bands of hearing. In the first step, the spectrum of the signal power is determined using the Fast Fourier Transform (FFT) (block 2). Then (in block 3), the spectrum is corrected by the outer to inner ear transfer function. In step 3, spectral factors are grouped into critical bands using the Bark scale. Next, signal levels in different bands are determined, and the result reflects the excitation of the basilar membrane. Its response is calculated through multiplexing levels of instantaneous excitation by the characteristics of the auditory filters relevant to particular critical bands. The obtained value of the basilar membrane deflection is then exponentially averaged. Such operation reflects the inertia of the processes occurring in the inner ear. The averaged values are used to resolve the Asymptotic Threshold Shift (ATS) level.

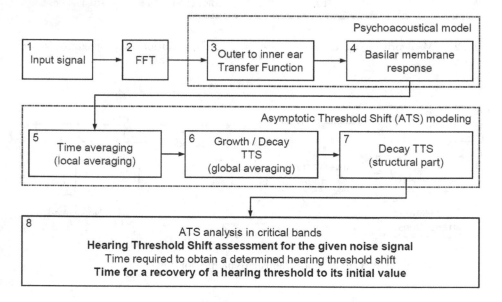

Fig. 4. Block diagram of the psychophysiological noise dosimeter

The ATS modeling block consists of three parts (blocks 5, 6, 7). In the subsequent step, the instantaneous ATS values are fed to block 5, which simulates the acoustic reflex mechanism. The algorithm used in this block averages the ATS level locally, operating accordingly to the time of the acoustic reflex duration. In practice, this enables to temporarily maintain the ATS level (local averaging), especially when the ATS level changes are abrupt. Such situations happen when a sudden change of a signal level occurs in a sound. This way, the processed ATS values are eventually exponentially averaged (block 6), which reflects the process of Temporary Threshold Shift of hearing (global averaging) during the noise exposure. Block 7 is activated right after the exposure is finished, when the level of noise does not cause the TTS effect any more. The blocks task is to reflect the changes in the process of TTS fading in response to mechanic strain put to delicate cochlea structures. The block is activated by the level of TTS existing in the moment the exposure is stopped. Block 8 produces final results, ready to be presented and stored in a file. Thus, the model enables to determine TTS values in critical bands, the time elapsing till the specified hearing threshold occurs, and the time necessary to restore the initial value of the hearing threshold. The proposed dosimeter has also an important feature, which is its ability to specify the shift of the hearing threshold at the time of exposure to a specified type of noise.

3.3   The Noise Harmfulness Indicators

The new concept of noise dosimetry uses a simple psychoacoustic model to determine the effects of exposure to excessive levels of noise. Such result-based approach to dosimetry leads to the assumption that the occurrence of the TTS effect is an inexpedient reaction. This assumption was the basis for the definition of two new indicators of noise-induced damages. The first links the values of the hearing threshold shift with the length of the noise exposure. The second relates to the time necessary for the TTS effect to fade. As already mentioned, the TTS effect is determined independently in different critical bands. Thus, during the exposure to noise, the characteristic of hearing threshold becomes variously deflected for different frequencies. The indicator is expressed by formula 1

$$L_{JK} = \frac{1}{N} \sum_{t=0}^{T+T_R} \sum_{i=0}^{N} \left(10^{\frac{L_{TTS}(i,t)}{10}} - 1 \right), \tag{1}$$

where: N – the number of analysed critical bands (24 critical bands), T – exposure time (expressed in minutes), T_R – resting time (time required for hearing recovery), $L_{TTS}(i,t)$ – instantaneous value of the TTS level for i-th critical band and for time t.

When using indicator L_{JK}, it is possible to determine the absolute aggregate value of the hearing threshold shift caused by a defined exposure to noise. It is done in conjunction with the time of the shift duration. The absolute value does not provide any direct information about the harmfulness of the particular exposure, neither does it show the degree of exceeding the limit of the noise dose. For the clarity of interpretation, a new parameter was introduced to reflect the amount of the hearing threshold shift. It is expressed by formula 2. The parameter directly links the value of L_{JK} for a considered exposure with the reference value. The D_{JK} parameter indicates the amount of hearing threshold shift caused by the exposure:

$$D_{JK} = \frac{L_{JKExp}}{L_{JK100}} \cdot 100, \tag{2}$$

where: L_{JKExp} – absolute value of the L_{JK} indicator for a given noise exposure, L_{JK100} – value of the L_{JK} indicator for the reference exposure.

The presented methodology was applied to the second type of the "Hearing" services. A unique feature of the developed service is the evaluation of the auditory effects caused by the exposure to excessive noise. The main part of the "Hearing" service is presented above the Psychoacoustical Noise Dosimeter, which is based on utilizing the modified psychoacoustic model of hearing. The primary function of this dosimeter is to estimate, in real-time, the auditory effects caused by the exposure to noise. Owing to that, it is possible to recognize the character of the auditory threshold shift for a given type of noise. The user can define detailed conditions of the exposure to noise, such as noise level, exposure time and energy distribution in the frequency domain. The calculation by means of real sound data are also possible. The outcomes are presented in form of a cumulative noise dose and characteristics of the temporary shift of the hearing threshold.

4   Results

Several use case scenarios of the developed grid-based services are presented in the paper. The "Noise Map" service use cases are twofold. The first scenario concerns simulation of the acoustic climate in an urban area. The user provides the input GIS data related to the considered area. The data contain both geometrical description of the infrastructure and source parameters, i.e., traffic volume and vehicle speed for road sources. The diagram of this use case is presented in Fig. 5.

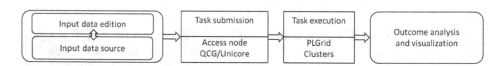

Fig. 5. Usage scenario of the "Noise Map" service in case of calculation of acoustic climate

Another illustration of the application of the "Noise Map" service is urban area noise monitoring. The map can be updated completely over a relatively short period of time, employing the PL-Grid Infrastructure.

Fig. 6 presents the discussed scenario. The result achieved by the use of the introduced setup is a dynamic noise map calculated with a 1-hour interval. The creation of dynamic maps, which show the disturbances evoked, for example, by variable road traffic, is one of the service use cases [35]. The data for modeling sound propagation can be provided by a system of municipal traffic sensors localized on the main transportation network. In addition, predicted maps may be adjusted using real noise level measurements, through means commonly referred as reverse engineering [35].

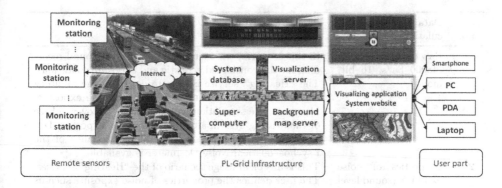

Fig. 6. "Noise Map" service architecture in case of creating dynamic maps

The "Hearing" service can be used in several different ways. The possible applications with a short explanation were listed in Table 1. The typical usage scenario of the service is presented in Fig. 7.

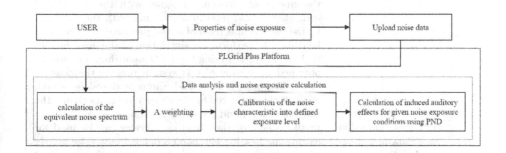

Fig. 7. Usage scenario of the "Hearing" service

Typical results obtained by means of the "Hearing" service for scenario 1 are shown in Fig. 8.

Another use case is related to the "Hearing" service with connection to the "Noise Map" service. In this scenario, a noise-induced temporary threshold shift during an outdoor concert at the city square was simulated. The considered auditory area, limited by the surrounding buildings, was about 100 × 130 meters, whereas the calculation area was 230 × 242 meters. The stage width was 10 m. Loudspeakers were modeled as two point sources located at both sides of the stage. We assumed that no other noise sources apart from the loudspeakers existed.

Table 1. Possible applications of the "Hearing" service on PL-Grid platform

Sc. no.	Data needed for calculation	Short explanation
1	Raw data of the noise (48000 Sa/s, 16 bit, mono)	In this scenario, the user should deliver the sound recording for the considered acoustic and exposure conditions. The "Hearing" service is able to calculate the auditory effects induced in hearing system during the exposure. Moreover, the simulation will include the recovery phase of the hearing system after the end of the exposure. During this kind of analysis, the full functionality of the Psychoacoustical Noise Dosimeter is available.
2	Properties of noise exposure (sound level defined in dB(A), time of exposure, sample of noise in the same format as in scenario 1)	This is a typical usage scenario of the "Hearing" services. The user defines the properties of noise exposure such us sound level (in dB(A)) and time (in minutes) of the exposure for the previously uploaded sample of noise data. At the beginning of the calculation, the service prepares an averaged spectrum (the FFT algorithm with 4096 point resolution was used for this purpose) of the noise. Subsequently, based on the average spectrum, the A-weighted equivalent sound pressure level is computed. Afterwards, a special coefficient rate is computed, which represents the chance of obtaining a signal with the A-weighted equivalent sound level in accordance with the value set by the user. A spectrum of sound prepared in such a way is utilized to perform the simulation of the noise impact on hearing system using the PND algorithm. The results obtained by means of this system present the changes of the Temporary Threshold Shifts produced by sound, which is characterized by the given average spectrum, the equivalent level end the exposure time.
3	Matrix of immission noise data in 1/3 octave bands	In this scenario, the "Hearing" service can be used for calculating hearing effects on a defined area. The matrix of immission noise data in 1/3 octave bands is required for this purpose. The user can obtain two kinds of results: the maximum TTS that will be evoked by the noise exposure for given immission point; the second kind of data, currently under development, is the full TTS characteristics for given calculation points.
4	Data needed for noise map	In this scenario, the "Hearing" service can be used together with the "Noise Map" service. During calculation of the noise immission levels, the maximum TTS values for every point are calculated.

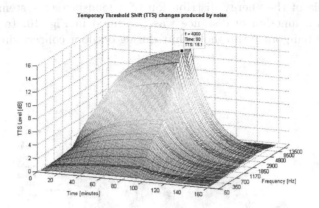

Fig. 8. Results obtained by means of the "Hearing" service for scenario 1. Real sound samples of the noise give the possibility to calculate detailed changes of the TTS in one minute time resolution.

The assumed duration of the concert was 3 hours. The spectrum distribution of the acoustic energy and the TTS effect evoked by the exposure to music were expressed in critical bands of hearing as a function of the distance from the stage. The observed temporary threshold shift exceeding 20 dB extends in radius of about 25 meters from the center of the stage. Fig. 9 presents the calculated maximum TTS values. The hearing recovery time required for the people who were present in this area was calculated at approx. 450 minutes.

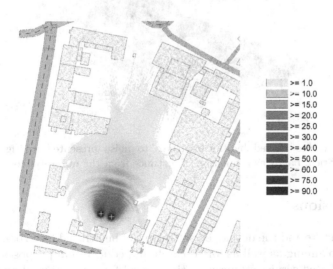

Fig. 9. The map of the maximum TTS values that could be evoked in the considered acoustic conditions

An example of the energy distribution of a loudspeaker system in 1/3 octave band as a function of distance was presented in Fig. 10. In Fig. 11 the noise-induced temporary threshold shift during outdoor concert simulation was presented.

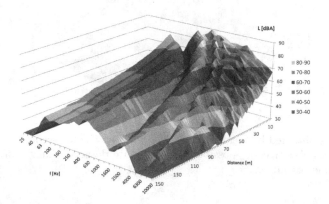

Fig. 10. Spectrum distribution of the acoustic energy of a noise source

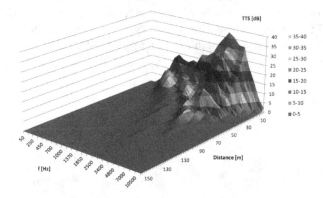

Fig. 11. TTS values evoked by the exposure to noise presented in Fig. 10; data expressed in critical bands as a function of distance from the noise source

5   Conclusions

The infrastructure and the developed software can be utilized for urban or sound enforcement planning as well as for research and educational purposes. The developed grid-based services, especially those used for estimation of auditory effects, which are caused by exposure to an excessive sound level, are dedicated to illustrate the harmfulness of noise. This method can be functionally integrated with the noise map service, what was illustrated in the text. It allows for presenting the environmental noise threat not only in a classical way (as an immission noise map), but also as the noise-induced hearing impairment risk. The presented software can be applied to conduct complex calculations on a selected number of cores. Such a flexible method of parallelization allows for achieving a proper computing cost balance. This methodology can also be integrated with both environmental noise monitoring system and road traffic flow sensors. The availability of the PL-Grid Infrastructure for education and research institutions allows for disseminating the knowledge about noise and its effect on health.

References

1. CadnaA, http://www.datakustik.com/en/products/cadnaa
2. IMMI – The Noise Mapping Software,
   http://www.woelfel.de/en/products/
   prediction-of-noise-and-air-pollution/immi-noise-mapping.html
3. Occupational exposure to noise: evaluation, prevention and control,
   http://www.who.int/occupational_health/
   publications/occupnoise/en/index.html
4. Predictor-LimA Software Suite Type 7810,
   http://www.bksv.com/Products/EnvironmentManagementSolutions/Noise
5. SoundPLAN Acoustics, http://www.soundplan.eu/english
6. Telewelfare, http://www.telezdrowie.pl/indexen2.html
7. Ahroon, W.A., Hamernik, R.P., Davis, R.I.: Complex noise exposures: An energy analysis. The Journal of the Acoustical Society of America 93(2), 997–1006 (1993)
8. Benedyczak, K., Stolarek, M., Rowicki, R., Kluszczyński, R., Borcz, M., Marczak, G., Filocha, M., Bała, P.: Seamless Access to the PL-Grid e-Infrastructure Using UNICORE Middleware. In: Bubak, M., Szepieniec, T., Wiatr, K. (eds.) PL-Grid 2011. LNCS, vol. 7136, pp. 56–72. Springer, Heidelberg (2012)
9. Borg, E., Engström, B.: Noise level, inner hair cell damage, audiometric features, and equal-energy hypothesis. The Journal of the Acoustical Society of America 86(5), 1776–1782 (1989)
10. Bosak, B., Komasa, J., Kopta, P., Kurowski, K., Mamoński, M., Piontek, T.: New Capabilities in QosCosGrid Middleware for Advanced Job Management, Advance Reservation and Co-allocation of Computing Resources – Quantum Chemistry Application Use Case. In: Bubak, M., Szepieniec, T., Wiatr, K. (eds.) PL-Grid 2011. LNCS, vol. 7136, pp. 40–55. Springer, Heidelberg (2012)
11. Bosak, B., Konczak, J., Kurowski, K., Mamoński, M., Piontek, T.: Highly Integrated Environment for Parallel Application Development Using QosCosGrid Middleware. In: Bubak, M., Szepieniec, T., Wiatr, K. (eds.) PL-Grid 2011. LNCS, vol. 7136, pp. 182–190. Springer, Heidelberg (2012)
12. Bray, A., Szymanski, M., Mills, R.: Noise induced hearing loss in dance music disc jockeys and an examination of sound levels in nightclubs. The Journal of Laryngology & Otology 118(02), 123–128 (2004)
13. Clark, W.W.: Recent studies of temporary threshold shift (TTS) and permanent threshold shift (PTS) in animals. The Journal of the Acoustical Society of America 90(1), 155–163 (1991)
14. Czyzewski, A., Kotus, J., Szczodrak, M.: Online urban acoustic noise monitoring system. Noise Control Eng. J. 60(1), 69–84 (2012)

15. Czyzewski, A., Szczodrak, M., Kotus, J.: Creating acoustic maps employing super-computing cluster. Archives of Acoustics 36(2), 1–24 (2011)

16. Czyzewski, A., Kostek, B., Kotus, J.: Multimedia services applied to noise and hearing monitoring and measuring. In: Tsihrintzis, G., Jain, L. (eds.) Multimedia Services in Intelligent Environments. SCI, vol. 120, pp. 275–295. Springer, Heidelberg (2008)

17. Embleton, T.F.W.: Tutorial on sound propagation outdoors. The Journal of the Acoustical Society of America 100(1), 31–48 (1996)

18. Emmerich, E., Richter, F., Linss, V., Linss, W.: Frequency-specific cochlear damage in guinea pig after exposure to different types of realistic industrial noise. Hearing Research 201(1-2), 90–98 (2005)

19. Engel, Z.: Environmental protection against vibrations and noise. PWN, Warsaw (2001) (in Polish)

20. Fligor, B.J., Cox, L.C.: Output levels of commercially available portable compact disc players and the potential risk to hearing. Ear and Hearing 25(6), 513–527 (2004)

21. Irle, H., Hesse, J.M., Strasser, H.: Physiological cost of energy-equivalent noise exposures with a rating level of 85 dB(A): Hearing threshold shifts associated with energetically negligible continuous and impulse noise. International Journal of Industrial Ergonomics 21(6), 451–463 (1998)

22. Johnston, J.: Transform coding of audio signals using perceptual noise criteria. IEEE Journal on Selected Areas in Communications 6(2), 314–323 (1988)

23. Kiehle, C., Mayer, C., Padberg, A., Stapelfeld, H.: Modelling noise propagation using Grid Resources. Progress within GDI-Grid. EGU General Assembly Conference Abstracts 12, 15285 (2010)

24. Kostek, B., Kotus, J., Czyzewski, A.: Noise monitoring system employing psychoacoustic noise dosimetry. In: Audio Engineering Society Conference: 47th International Conference: Music Induced Hearing Disorders (June 2012)

25. Kotus, J., Szczodrak, M., Czyzewski, A., Kostek, B.: Distributed system for noise threat evaluation based on psychoacoustic measurements. Metrology and Measurement Systems XIX(2), 219–230 (2012)

26. Kotus, J.: Nowa metoda oceny szkodliwości hałasu, uwzględniająca psychoakustyczne właściwości słuchu (in Polish). In: Krajowa Konferencja Radiokomunikacji, Radiofonii i Telewizji KKRRiT, Warszawa, Przegląd Telekomunikacyjny. Wiadomości Telekomunikacyjne, Wydawnictwo SIGMA NOT, June 17-19 (2009)

27. Kotus, J., Czyzewski, A., Kostek, B.: Evaluation of excessive noise effects on hearing employing psychoacoustic dosimetry. Noise Control Engineering Journal 56(6), 497–510 (2008)

28. Kotus, J., Kostek, B., Czyzewski, A.: A new methodological approach to the noise threat evaluation based on the selected physiological properties of the human hearing system. In: Audio Engineering Society Convention, vol. 126 (May 2009)

29. Kotus, J., Kozielecki, P., Kostek, B.: An Internet-based system for evaluation of the noise impact on hearing. In: NOVEM 2009, Noise and Vibration: Emerging Methods, Oxford, UK, April 5-8 (2009)

30. Kulowski, A.: A modification of ray-tracing acoustics modeling method in rooms. Scientific Books of Gdansk University of Technology 464, 1–117 (1991) (in Polish)

31. Li, K.M., Taherzadeh, S., Attenborough, K.: An improved ray-tracing algorithm for predicting sound propagation outdoors. The Journal of the Acoustical Society of America 104(4), 2077–2083 (1998)

32. Van Maercke, D., Defrance, J.: Development of an Analytical Model for Outdoor Sound Propagation Within the Harmonoise Project. Acta Acustica United with Acustica 93(2), 201–212 (2007)
33. Strasser, H., Chiu, M.C., Irle, H., Grünig, T.: Threshold Shifts and Restitution of the Hearing After Energy-Equivalent Narrow-Band and Wide-Band Noise Exposures. In: Proceedings-CD of the 37th International Congress and Exhibition on Noise Control Engineering, Internoise 2007, Istanbul, Turkey, vol. 12 (2010)
34. Szczodrak, M., Czyzewski, A.: Software for calculation of noise maps implemented on the supercomputer. Task Quarterly 13(4), 363–377 (2009)
35. Szczodrak, M., Kotus, J., Kostek, B., Czyzewski, A.: Creating Dynamic Maps of Noise Threat Using PL-Grid Infrastructure. Archives of Acoustics 38(2), 235–242 (2013)
36. US Department of Health and Human Services: Criteria for a recommended standard: occupational noise exposure. Revised criteria 1998. Centers for Disease Control and Prevention, National Institute for Occupational Safety and Health Pub. No. 98–126 (1998)

Kepler-Based Workflow Environment for Astronomy

Paweł Ciecieląg[1], Marcin Płóciennik[2], Piotr Spyra[2], Michał Urbaniak[2]
Tomasz Żok[2], Wojciech Pych[1], and Arkadiusz Hypki[1]

[1] N. Copernicus Astronomical Center,
ul. Bartycka 18, 00-716 Warszawa, Poland
[2] Poznan Supercomputing and Networking Center,
ul. Noskowskiego 10, 61-704 Poznań, Poland
pci@camk.edu.pl, {marcinp,pspyra,michalu,tzok}@man.poznan.pl,
{pych,ahypki}@camk.edu.pl

Abstract. With the recent advent of new-generation observational instruments, astronomy enters the 'data flood' era. The growing scale and complication of astronomical activities forces scientists to look for new technologies and tools. A workflow environment seems to be a good solution for many new requirements, but before scientists can use it commonly, it has to be suitably adapted and simplified. We have created a universal environment based on the Kepler workflow system that empowers scientists with such capabilities. It offers three access levels depending on the needs and skills of the user: 1) Kepler desktop application extended by our library of domain specific modules and workflows, 2) web application used to share workflows, 3) cloud service with on-demand Virtual Research Environment consisting of a set of tools and applications useful for astronomers. Our environment includes also interoperability mechanisms with the Virtual Observatory and other domain-specific tools and services.

Keywords: workflow, astronomy, data analysis, Grid, Cloud.

1 Introduction

Astronomy is a science relying greatly on observations and on numerical modeling; direct experimentation is extremely limited. Historically, both fields have their challenging aspects, which have been pushing the development of new computer technologies. On the observational side these are data archiving and cataloging (since even old data are valuable). On the numerical side it is the availability of computing power for more and more complex models. Nowadays, in both fields there is an increasing demand for automation of certain activities.

In observational astronomy, data reduction pipelines are a natural approach, and growing data streams from modern instruments have forced their wide adoption. Currently, astronomy enters the era of 'big data flood' – the upcoming sky surveys are designed to generate tens of TB per night (e.g. LSST project [4]).

M. Bubak et al. (Eds.): PLGrid Plus, LNCS 8500, pp. 278–292, 2014.

For such amounts of data, majority of steps between the observation and scientific result have to be automated. Since some observed phenomena are transient and can be observed only passively, it is crucial to analyze the data as fast as possible – if a phenomenon is detected early enough, the observational schedule on other available instruments can be adjusted in order to follow it. Obviously, such an *early warning system* has to be automated even for small data streams. For large streams it becomes a challenging task. The next step is usually an automatic dissemination of data to the remote data centers. A more detailed analysis of large data, sometimes from multiple instruments, is carried out there. It also involves automated or semi-automated tools. Finally, the data can be published in the world-wide, astronomical data grid: the Virtual Observatory [6] (hereafter VObs[1], see Section 4). Thanks to strict standardization of data formats and communication protocols, VObs provides services for automatic data search and retrieval, which enable large-scale analyses of vast amounts of observational data.

In the field of numerical modeling, astronomy was always one of the biggest consumers of computational resources. Magnetohydrodynamical simulations of interstellar medium or N-body simulations of the large-scale structure of the Universe are always needed to include additional physical processes or use higher resolutions. The growth of supercomputer power in the last decade has enabled scientists to carry out parameter studies even with large simulations. In addition, physical models get more complicated and require complex simulations involving more than one code. Scenarios of this type are perfect candidates for automation. Furthermore, bigger simulations often mean bigger data sets, so the same problems with storage and analysis arise as for observational data. Finally, the models are compared with the observational data. In some cases, this is implemented as the last step of complex, modeling workflows.

We have shown an increasing demand for automated services in astronomy. In practice, the whole scientific workflow displayed above is accomplished only in rare cases, mostly in large, international collaborations. For small groups or individual astronomers, the setup of a workflow environment is prohibitively difficult. While there are various environments for scientific workflows, they are not so easy to use and, what is even more important, they have to be integrated with available resources like clusters, Grids, storage systems and observational instruments. The latter task requires close cooperation between scientists and administrators of resources. The PLGrid Plus project has created a perfect opportunity for such activities by establishing an astronomical domain grid – AstroGrid-PL. In this article we present a universal environment built around the Kepler workflow system [1], which facilitates integration of different technologies, in particular two other AstroGrid-PL services: Astro-data and Polish Virtual Observatory Data Center. The Astro-data service is a domain data grid solution based on iRODS [5], while the Polish Virtual Observatory Data Center implements international VObs standards for sharing of astronomical data

---

[1] A commonly used acronym for Virtual Observatory is 'VO', but in the context of this book we prefer to use 'VObs' in order to avoid confusion with Virtual Organization.

and utilities. Both services are described in another article within this book. Together with the Astro-pipelines, they form a quite comprehensive ecosystem for astronomical research in the Grid.

2   General Requirements

During the planning of our environment, the main objective was simplicity. On the other hand, we wanted to create a universal service deployed in the PL-Grid Infrastructure, which would be beneficial for the whole astronomical community in Poland. In general, it is hard to reconcile both requirements, because simple interfaces usually are possible only for well-defined problems. Since we did not want to limit usability of the service, we finally opted for a three-component solution with the assumption that most users will use only one of them, so they should be independent.

As stated above, our target user group was the whole astronomical community in Poland (which anyway is relatively small). To start with, two broad classes of activities were identified as those benefitting most from using the workflow services: analysis of observational data and large, parameter-study kind of simulations.

Taking the above into account, we defined the following, more specific requirements for the service:

Interoperability with Other AstroGrid-PL Services. In a broader perspective, AstroGrid-PL was designed as a platform of generic services, which can cooperate to satisfy a user's needs. In particular, the workflow environment should be able to access storage provided by the Astro-data service.

Interoperability with Domain Software. Whenever it is possible, the users should be able to exploit existing domain-specific software, instead of learning new applications. Of course, the supported software has to be selected beforehand, which is an occasion to promote better, modern applications over old, but still popular ones.

Support for the VObs Standards. This was actually one of the most important objectives for the AstroGrid-PL grid. The VObs is gaining momentum world-wide and needs an extensive promotion in Poland. Standardization includes data formats and data exchange protocols – both are crucial for re-usable workflows. Of particular importance should be support for Simple Application Messaging Protocol (SAMP) [7], a protocol, which allows to exchange information between the existing VObs-enabled applications. Access to the vast archives of the VObs grid is also desirable for certain automated data analyses.

Support for Collaborative Work. The service should support sharing of workflows within working groups. Sharing should cover also auxiliary files needed for experiment as well as any editable workflow parameters.

Scalability from Workstation to the Grid Infrastructure. Here we mean the scalability of service and not that of workflows. It corresponds to the three access levels mentioned above. Users should be able to develop work-flows or adjust parameters on their workstations while later work can be carried out in the Grid with little changes to the workflow.

3   The Astro-pipelines Environment

3.1   Core Features

We have chosen to base our environment on the Kepler workflow system. Al-though the defined requirements could be fulfilled in various workflow systems, we have found Kepler favourable for a few reasons:

- strong orientation for data flow,
- ease of integration with other languages popular among astronomers: Python, C and Java (Kepler is written in Java),
- built-in support for grid technologies: iRODS, gLite, UNICORE and Vine Toolkit,
- existing presence and support in the PL-Grid Infrastructure,
- good documentation.

In the Kepler terminology, the basic building blocks of a workflow are called *actors* while *directors* define the order of their execution. The ability to mix dif-ferent execution models (directors) in a single workflow is another, quite unique feature of Kepler, making it very flexible.

Scientific workflow environments are particularly well suited to integration of different technologies although they are quite complicated to use. The main tech-nical goal of our environment is to simplify the usage of Kepler by astronomers. Thus, we have designed a flexible solution, which has powerful features, yet the user gets simple interfaces to start with.

Our environment extends Kepler with:

- a library of domain specific actors (plus a general tool to convert C codes into actors),
- dedicated actors for interaction with the user and with astronomical appli-cations,
- ready-to-use workflows for typical scenarios; they can access grid resources thanks to the Serpens suite distributed with the Kepler.

The environment is accessible in three ways depending on needs and advance-ment of the user. They are summarized in the sections that follow.

3.2   Desktop Application

In comparison to other methods, it allows use of a desktop computer, which is useful for running short workflows or prototyping; beginners do not have to deal with the sophisticated Kepler interface thanks to the simplified UI built in pre-defined workflows. There are ready-to-use sets of the packages to be installed on the local user workstations that include the Kepler workflow software itself, the workflow packages, all the necessary workflows (that are described in Section 5), the Serpens suite package that enables the submission to the Grid, and a set of suggested astronomical packages. Since each user has a different environment, there is also provided a general tool to convert C codes into Kepler actors.

3.3   Web Interface

A dedicated portal integrating the AstroGrid-PL services has been deployed using the Liferay content management system. One of its elements is a pipeline sharing portlet. The key feature of this application is to give users the ability to collaborate on Kepler scientific workflows, to speed up the process of solving common problems. The user can upload the workflows and then, through the web interface, modify the workflow's global parameters, save changes and download a modified workflow. The user is also able to share the workflows with another user or group of users. The group administrator can modify members' permissions, for example to restrict the rights to read-only for some group of users. There is also the possibility of describing every workflow, adding metadata tags to facilitate searching process, and also adding some extra files, like screenshots, etc. Fig. 1 shows the two main features of the web portlet for managing Kepler workflows: workflow manager and groups manager. The first one is used to upload/download workflows in two formats supported by Kepler: XML and kar. After uploading, the workflow parameters are detected and can be changed from the portlet. The user can also share the workflow and metadata within working groups. The groups can be created and managed via the groups manager.

3.4   Virtual Research Environment

The development and deployment of advanced middleware tools over e-infrastructures allows for creation of tailored work environments. These are so called Virtual Research Environments (VRE) systems helping researchers to collaborate. VRE plays an important role being exposed directly to users, frequently one of the preconditions of proper usage and uptake of the underlying technologies. Current networks provide new opportunities for the researchers in terms of remote access to the resources. Such software as e.g. VNC (Virtual Network Computing), works smoothly exporting remote desktops.

One of the common features of VRE is the use of virtualization and cloud technologies. The basic concept is to use a remotely predefined set of the ready to use environment on demand, without a need of local installation of software. This is very useful when there is a demand for sharing a desktop with running applications with other scientists, and for running longer workflows (also with usage of external grid resources), since it is not prone to local network or workstation problems. It is also convenient for users to make use of the whole predefined environment on demand.

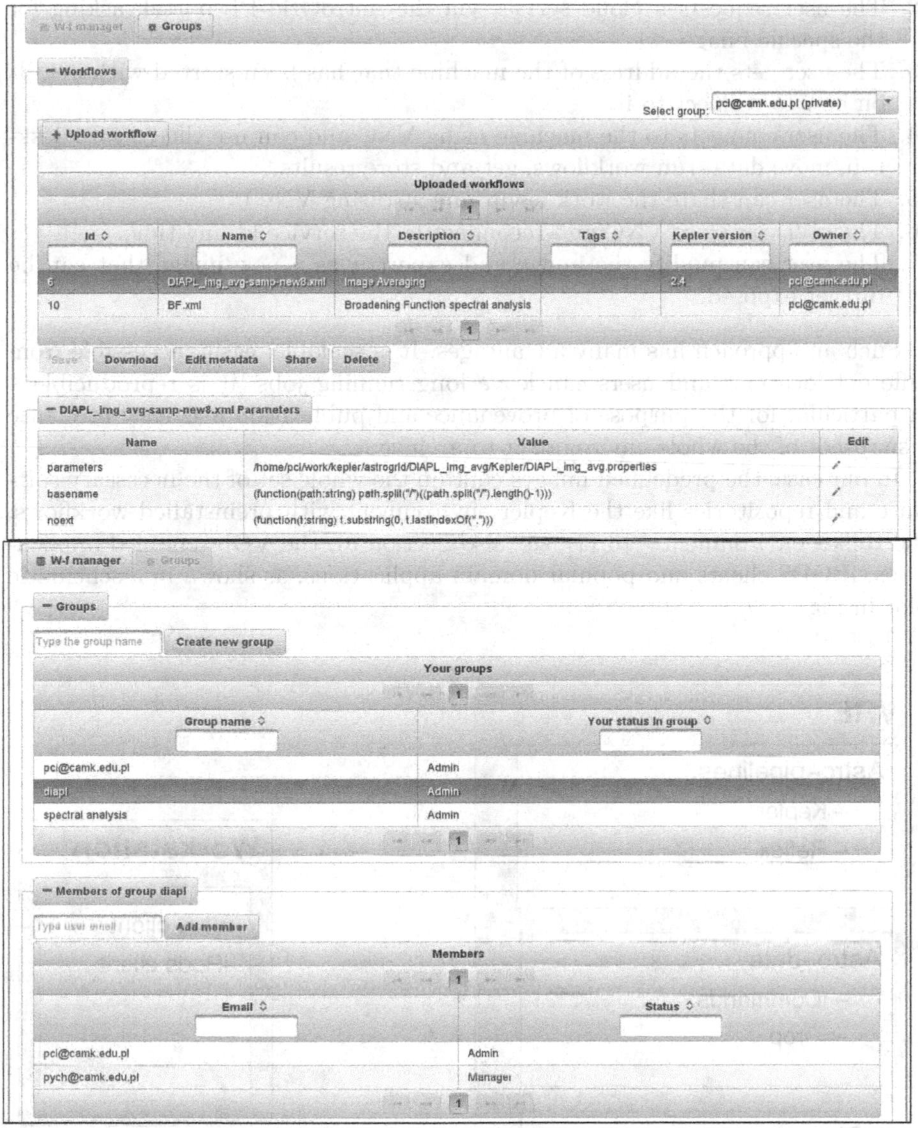

Fig. 1. Web applet for managing Kepler workflows. Upper panel: workflow manager allows editing of workflow parameters and to share workflows. Lower panel: group manager allows for definition of working groups, which share workflows.

A typical usage scenario consists of the following steps:

1. The administrator prepares an image with the whole demanding environment required by the scientist, including the libraries, software (e.g. scientific workflow engine like Kepler), common data sets and data, a graphical environment and a VNC server.

2. The user requests a cloud service via the AstroGrid-PL portal, asking for the specific image.
3. The user gets the address of the machine that has been started with details on how to connect to it.
4. The user connects to the machine using VNC and can use the remote desktop, move data, run workflows, get and store results.
5. The user can share the work environment (using VNC).
6. The user can close VNC and reconnect to the service at any time.
7. The user can modify the image and export it as a new image that can be further exposed.

Such an approach has many advantages. It is scalable, easily accessible from different locations and users can leave long running jobs. It is reproducible – in particular for the purpose of provenance and publication it is easy to create a snapshot of the whole environment to archive it.

In our case, the predefined images contain the whole set of the necessary software and repositories like the Kepler environment with preinstalled workflows, the Reflex environment ([16,17], see also Section 6), the VObs-enabled applications, iRODS clients and popular domain applications, as shown in a schematic plot in Fig. 2.

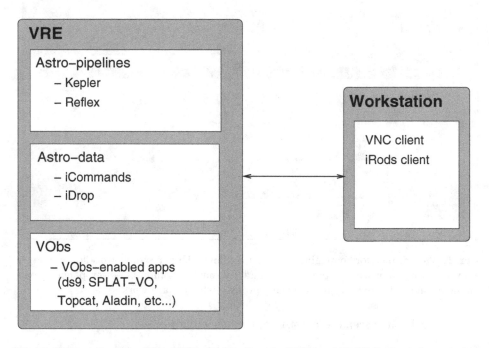

Fig. 2. Schematic plot of the VRE. To use it, only VNC and iRODS clients have to be installed on the user workstation.

4 Interoperability

An important aspect of our environment is its interoperability with other technologies. Scientific work is nearly always a complex process involving many tools. While we can help to automate certain parts of work, it is usually impossible to cover the whole process. Instead, we strive to provide means to integrate the workflow environment with other tools, and especially with other PLGrid Plus services.

Obviously, the most important for the user is ability to access the data from various storage systems or data sources. Kepler provides native support for a wide range of services: a local filesystem, a remote filesystem (ftp), databases, grid storage (GridFTP), web services (REST, SOAP). Of particular importance for our environment is native support for the iRODS data grid [5], since it is the core of other service, Astro-data. Astro-data is designed as a primary storage system for the whole astronomical domain grid. It integrates storage resources from astronomical institutions and supercomputing centers in Poland, thus making it easy to move data where they are used. Users operate it with a simple desktop or web application. For basic functionality, it can also be mounted as a fuse filesystem, what is implemented in our Virtual Research Environment.

An example of very successful solution for data sharing, driven by astronomical community, is the Virtual Observatory [6] – the world-wide standard for sharing data and related tools. The importance of using VObs standards has been already stressed before. There are multiple points where we apply this rule. Within the PLGrid Plus project, Polish Virtual Observatory Data Center has been set up. VObs specifies its own abstraction layer to access storage resources: VOSpace. In our VObs data center, iRODS is one of the backends to the VOSpace, so the data can be accessed in both ways. Since the current VOSpace standard defines RESTful bindings, it was easy to implement it in Kepler by wrapping native actors for web services. Another important VObs standard is SAMP (Simple Application Messaging Protocol), which allows to exchange data between applications. In fact, SAMP enables creation of simple workflows among the applications supporting it. We have implemented SAMP message sender as a Kepler actor. It is supplemented by another actor, which implements the execution of selected VObs-enabled applications [8]. The supported applications include a message router required in the SAMP infrastructure, but also standard data-analysis tools. Among them, an astronomical image analysis tool, ds9, is particularly well integrated, since it implements full asynchronous control via SAMP – it means that every operation can be done with the mouse or via sending SAMP messages.

Interoperability in the context of a grid project also means the ability to execute tasks in the Grid using different middleware solutions. This is fortunately assured by the official Kepler suite – Serpens [2]. It provides support for typical actions like job submission, monitoring and data handling in gLite and UNICORE stacks as well as for Vine Toolkit.

5   Usage Scenarios and Applications

Below we present specific details of several scenarios and applications developed within the AstroGrid-PL. From the users point of view, there are common preconditions and steps that allow them to use these services, which result from the PL-Grid Infrastructure characteristics. As a first step, users have to register in the PL-Grid portal and obtain their own certificate. Then, inside the portal, they have to activate Astro-pipelines service, which automatically implies activation of other services: cloud, Astro-data and VObs. All these common steps are described in the user guide book. PL-Grid provides also helpdesk services for any questions and problems users might have using any of the services.

5.1   DIAPL Workflows

DIAPL [9] is an astronomical package dedicated to photometry using the difference image analysis method. It consists of a number of command line programs in C language, which are typically invoked from a shell script. The package programs can be used in various configurations depending on the problem, so we have implemented them as Kepler actors and prepared ready-to-use workflows for typical applications.

Below we present the most basic workflow, which is typically the first step in analyses with DIAPL. The workflow takes a series of images of roughly the same sky region, re-grids them to common coordinates and averages. The purpose of this procedure is to increase the signal to noise ratio with respect to a single frame and to remove bad pixels from the image. The main steps are as follow:

1. Read in config files.
2. Start VObs-enabled applications: SAMP hub and ds9 (image viewer).
3. Display the reference image and camera bad pixels mask (in ds9). The user has an option to interactively modify the mask, before proceeding to the next step.
4. For each input image calculate basic statistics (min, max, sky level, full-width half maximum of star profiles).
5. Refining of the input selection of images. The user is assisted by a check box list of image names and calculated statistics; any change in the list loads the corresponding image into ds9 for inspection.
6. Calculate transformation between each image and the reference one. This is an automatic step done with a sophisticated algorithm provided by the DIAPL package.
7. Re-grid images to common coordinates and create an averaged template image. This is actually the most complicated step where a couple of DIAPL programs use data from previous steps (e.g. masks, statistics, transformations) to create the best image from the scientific point of view. An additional profit is an option to remove traces of cosmic rays from the input images.
8. Display both the reference and template images for comparison.

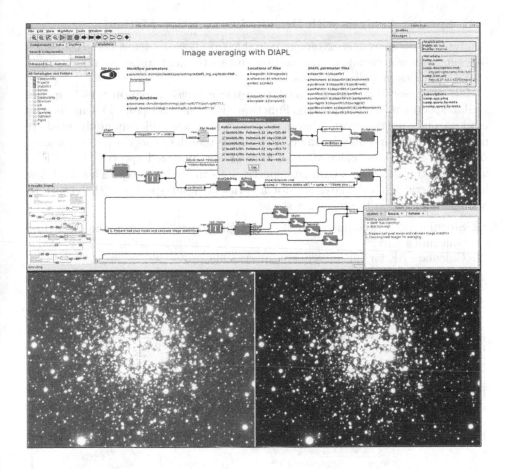

Fig. 3. Workflow for the averaging of a series of images. Upper panel: Kepler with central dialog widget corresponding to step 5, at the left edge parts of SAMP hub, image viewer ds9 and the workflow status window. Lower panel: reference image (left) vs. averaged template (right)

Fig. 3 shows an example screenshot made at step 5. The workflow is a good example of how we can assist the user in interactive tasks and how to exploit VObs standards. The interactivity is important, because the whole workflow may need to be repeated several times in order to find out best combination of input parameters. The use of VObs standards and applications enables the user to weave this workflow into other activities done outside of our environment.

The above workflow is the first step in other applications like: photometry of variable stars and deep photometry of dense stellar fields.

5.2   Spectra Analysis with Broadening Function Method

Analysis of star spectra is extremely valuable – it allows to determine parameters like temperature, chemical composition, magnetic field, rotation velocity and radial velocities in stellar systems.

The next workflow was designed to retrieve physical parameters from the stellar spectra using Broadening Function (BF) method [10]. The method is modern and superior over other methods, which are still commonly used. It consists of singular value decomposition of the template spectra (of well-known single star) and then calculation of the BF for analyzed spectra. The BF is a function transforming a template spectra into an analyzed one. This workflow is also generic – it calculates BF for a series of input spectra with respect to a single template in the following steps:

1. Singular value decomposition of the template spectra. This is the most time consuming part.
2. Calculate BF for the subsequent spectra file.
3. Smooth BF by convolution with the Gauss function.
4. Determine physical parameters of the object by fitting the model to the BF.
5. Go to step 2.

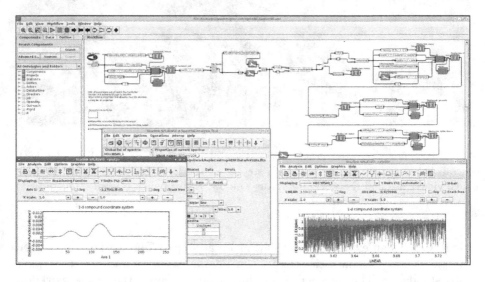

Fig. 4. Spectra analysis using the Broadening Function method. Kepler workflow is in the background. The three other windows show its results being analyzed in the SPLAT-VO application.

Fig. 4 shows the above workflow in a real application. The main benefit to the user is the ability to run the analysis multiple times in order to adjust the input parameters. As the results arrive, they can be displayed in another VObs-enabled application SPLAT-VO [11]. Moreover, this application can be also used to find the best template spectra for a given case from the vast VObs data.

5.3 Monte Carlo Simulations of Stellar Systems Dynamics

The MOCCA code [12] (MOnte Carlo Cluster simulAtor) is one of the most advanced codes able to simulate real size star clusters with tracking of the full dynamical history of all stars in the system. It follows the star cluster evolution closely to N-body codes, but is much faster [13]. Additionally, the MOCCA code is able to follow with great details the evolution of exotic objects like blue stragglers stars, black holes.

Results of one MOCCA simulation occupy on the average several gigabytes of disk space. Usually, the code needs to be run many times, which induces problems with shared storage space on the clusters. The use of a grid storage can help to overcome the problems, but the transfers have to be somehow managed at the runtime of the whole set of simulations. In general, handling of large-scale simulations is complex, non-trivial task and we employ Kepler to that end. In short, Kepler controls preparation of initial data, job execution, errors handling, and data transfers.

In the first step, Kepler generates the whole mesh of initial conditions using user supplied file with such a simple structure:

```
[StarCluster]
n = list 100000 500000 1000000
w0 = list 6.0 3.0
rbar = list 30.0 60.0 120.0
```

Each parameter from the file is combined with all other parameters and the result is merged with the template of a MOCCA initial conditions file. The whole problem is validated and divided into n jobs and corresponding input files that contain the parameters specific for each job are being generated. In the next step of the workflow, jobs are distributed in several packages of so called parametric jobs over the PL-Grid Infrastructure. This is implemented using a gLite middleware interface of the Serpens suite for Kepler [2]. The workflow is handling all kinds of possible problems, trying different strategies to redo failed actions. In general, the checkpoint-restart, retry and alternate resource failure mechanisms are combined and used to ensure the successful run, and collecting all the corresponding results. The whole procedure of failure handling in Serpens is described in [3]. Handling of external, job execution problems is a typical task for massive simulations. However, in the case of such a sophisticated code as MOCCA, we should also handle *internal* problems in the code. This is possible only by frequent monitoring of output files for unscientific results. Such jobs are also specially flagged in order to be re-run later, after the code is corrected.

In the last steps, the data generated by each job are initially preprocessed, optionally compressed and transferred to an iRODS resource in a given institute for further, interactive analysis. Careful handling of data transfers is important to avoid violation of local quota limits. Optionally, the results of MOCCA simulations can be registered in the VObs for use in a dedicated web service, which allows to compare the results of different codes.

Overall, the automation of MOCCA simulations minimizes their run time and greatly reduces handling costs.

6 Related Work

One of the 'astronomical' contributions to scientific workflows was the Triana system [14], initially designed for analysis of data from gravitational wave detectors. Over time Triana evolved into a general system with grid computing oriented or web services oriented components.

Reflex [16,17] is an environment that enables automated reduction of science data coming from the European Southern Observatory (ESO) [15] instruments of VLT/VLTI facility. It is built on top of the Kepler environment, which was extended with a dedicated installer, library of actors and ready-to-use scientific pipelines. The pipelines are very user friendly and provide advanced mechanisms of automatic data discovery and organization. The ESO instruments are very powerful and can be also used by Polish astronomers. Since the installation and usage of the environment requires some time and experience, we offer it preinstalled in our Virtual Research Platform. Because the environment uses Kepler, we are able to provide basic technical support for Polish users.

The great potential of VObs ecosystem for automation of work in astronomy has been recognized soon after its start. The AstroGrid project was the first VObs node in the world and it remains one of its driving forces. They have developed a specific workflow engine and a batch execution system for it [18]. AstroGrid developed also a plugin to Taverna workflow system [19], which implemented selected VObs standards. This work was further extended within wf4ever project [21] as AstroTaverna [20]. French VObs node and CDS (Strasbourg Astronomical Data Center) initiated a workflow working group [22] as early as in 2005. They have developed Astronomical Image processing Distribution Architecture (AIDA). AIDA consists of a server, execution part and a graphical composition part being GUI. HELIO-VO project [23] is a domain-specific VObs branch for solar physics and workflows are within its scope. Specifically, they have enabled Taverna workbench to run on the Grid or the Cloud. The whole HELIO infrastructure is built on the basis of service-oriented architecture and Taverna provides means to integrate various web services.

The future of astronomical workflows is researched within CyberSKA project [24]. In general view, it explores and implements cyber-infrastructure that will be required to address the evolving science needs of future radio telescopes such as Square Kilometre Array (SKA). This instrument will generate data streams order of magnitude higher than the whole current internet traffic and is planned to start operation in ten years. They are developing a web based workflow builder for image reduction and analysis. The system makes use of web services and is able to automatically determine optimal paths of operation.

7 Summary and Future Work

We have designed a universal solution based on the Kepler workflow environment that empowers scientists with new capabilities. The whole environment can be set up locally, or a cloud can be used to get on-demand Virtual Research

Environment that consists of the whole set of tools and applications useful for scientists in everyday work. Further work is foreseen mainly in deploying new applications into the environment, and development of additional tools for improving the interactive aspects of running workflows.

It should be stressed that presented work gained a lot from being part of the PLGrid Plus project. It gave us a unique opportunity to integrate with other domain services developed in parallel and to exploit general grid services like the cloud infrastructure. The integration of the environment into National Grid Infrastructure greatly enhances the available resources additionally simplifying the access to them. Furthermore, it ensures a long term availability of the service and technical support.

References

1. Altintas, I., Berkley, C., Jaeger, E., Jones, M., Ludascher, B., Mock, S.: Kepler: an extensible system for design and execution of scientific workflows. In: Proceedings of 16th International Conference on Scientific and Statistical Database Management, pp. 423–424 (2004)
2. Plociennik, M., Zok, T., Altintas, I., Wang, J., Crawl, D., Abramson, D., Imbeaux, F., Guillerminet, B., Lopez-Caniego, M., Campos Plasencia, I., Pych, W., Ciecieląg, P., Palak, B., Owsiak, M., Frauel, Y.: Approaches to Distributed Execution of Scientific Workflows in Kepler. Annales Societatis Mathematicae Polonae, Series 4: Fundamenta Informaticae 128, 281–302 (2013)
3. Plociennik, M., Owsiak, M., Zok, T., Palak, B., Gomez-Iglesias, A., Castejon, F., Lopez-Caniego, M., Campos Plasencia, I., Costantini, A., Yadykin, D., Strand, P.: Application Scenarios Using Serpens Suite for Kepler Scientific Workflow System. Procedia Computer Science 9, 1604–1613 (2012)
4. Large Synoptic Survey Telescope, http://www.lsst.org/lsst
5. iRODS – The Integrated Rule-Oriented Data System, https://www.irods.org
6. International Virtual Observatory Alliance, http://www.ivoa.net
7. International Virtual Observatory Alliance, SAMP protocol, http://www.ivoa.net/Documents/SAMP
8. VObs software, http://www.euro-vo.org/fc/software.html
9. Pych, W.: DIAPL, http://users.camk.edu.pl/pych/DIAPL
10. Pych, W.: BF, http://users.camk.edu.pl/pych/BF
11. Starlink SPLAT-VO, http://star-www.dur.ac.uk/~pdraper/splat/splat-vo
12. MOCCA code for star cluster simulations, http://www.moccacode.net
13. Giersz, M., Heggie, D.C., Hurley, J.R., Hypki, A.: MOCCA code for star cluster simulations – II. Comparison with N-body simulations. Monthly Notices of the Royal Astronomical Society 431, 2184–2199 (2013)
14. Triana workflow envirenment, http://trianacode.org
15. ESO, the European Southern Observatory, http://www.eso.org
16. Reflex, http://www.eso.org/sci/software/reflex
17. Freudling, W., Romaniello, M., Bramich, D.M., Ballester, P., Forchi, V., Garcia-Dablo, C.E., Moehler, S., Neeser, M.J.: Automated data reduction workflows for astronomy. The ESO Reflex environment. Astronomy & Astrophysics 559, id. A96 (2013)

18. Walton, N.A., Witherwick, D.K., Oinn, T., Benson, K.M.: Taverna and Workflows in the Virtual Observatory. In: Argyle, R.W., Bunclark, P.S., Lewis, J.R. (eds.) Astronomical Data Analysis Software and Systems XVII. Astronomical Society of the Pacific Conference Series, vol. 394, p. 309 (2008)
19. Wolstencroft, K., Haines, R., Fellows, D., Williams, A., Withers, D., Owen, S., Soiland-Reyes, S., Dunlop, I., Nenadic, A., Fisher, P., Bhagat, J., Belhajjame, K., Bacall, F., Hardisty, A., Nieva de la Hidalga, A., Balcazar Vargas, M., Sufi, S., Goble, C.: The Taverna workflow suite: designing and executing workflows of Web Services on the desktop, web or in the cloud. Nucleic Acids Research 41(W1), W557–W561 (2013)
20. AstroTaverna plugin to Taverna, http://wf4ever.github.io/astrotaverna
21. Belhajjame, K., Corcho, O., Garijo, D., Zhao, J., Missier, P., Newman, D.R., Palma, R., Bechhofer, S., Garcia-Cuesta, E., Gómez-Pérez, J.M., Klyne, G., Page, K., Roos, M., Ruiz, J.E., Soiland-Reyes, S., Verdes-Montenegro, L., De Roure, D., Goble, C.A.: Workflow-Centric Research Objects: A First Class Citizen in the Scholarly Discourse. In: Proceedings of the ESWC 2012 Workshop on the Future of Scholarly Communication in the Semantic Web (SePublica 2012), Heraklion, Greece (2012)
22. France VObs workflow working group, http://www.france-ov.org/twiki/bin/view/GROUPEStravail/Workflow
23. HELIO-VO project, http://www.helio-vo.eu
24. CyberSKA project, http://www.cyberska.org

High Performance Astrophysical Fluid Simulations Using InSilicoLab Framework

Michał Hanasz[1], Kacper Kowalik[1], Artur Gawryszczak[2],
and Dominik Wóltański[1]

[1] Centre for Astronomy, Faculty of Physics, Astronomy and Informatics,
ul. Grudziądzka 5, 87-100 Toruń, Poland
[2] CAMK, ul. Bartycka 18, Warszawa, Poland

Abstract. With the advent of the PL-Grid Infrastructure, Polish scientists have been equipped with substantial computational resources forming favorable conditions for the development of all research areas relying on numerical simulation techniques. To reduce the barriers inhibiting the start of the newcomers to the field of computational astrophysics, we have implemented a web-based workspace for astrophysical simulation codes based on InSilicoLab framework [19]. InSilicoLab for Astrophysics is a solution dedicated to astrophysicists intending to conduct a numerical experiment using the PL-Grid Infrastructure. It serves as an interface for the multi-purpose, magnetohydrodynamical, open-source software PIERNIK. InSilicoLab for Astrophysics vastly softens the learning curve of advanced astrophysical simulations, bringing new possibilities for scientists and students.

Keywords: in silico, experiment, computational astrophysics, astrophysical, magnetohydrodynamical simulations, numerical methods, grid codes.

1 Introduction

Fast progress in technical advancement of computational infrastructure together with increasing the availability of professional open-source astrophysical simulation codes create new opportunities for scientists and students to conduct leading-edge astrophysical numerical experiments. Successful utilisation of complex astrophysical simulation codes depends, however, on availability of proper configuration of software environment. Practically all modern hydrodynamical simulation codes require particular compilers, numerical libraries and specialised post-processing software for analysis of simulation results. Installation and configuration of the software environment require very specific technical knowledge that is, however, hard to gain in the community of researchers and students of astronomy. To reduce the barriers inhibiting the start of newcomers in the field of computational astrophysics, we implemented a web-based workspace based on the InSilicoLab environment for astrophysical simulation codes.

InSilicoLab [14], [19] is a framework that enables integrating simulation codes and running them in distributed infrastructures such as PL-Grid. The codes can

M. Bubak et al. (Eds.): PLGrid Plus, LNCS 8500, pp. 293–304, 2014.
© Springer International Publishing Switzerland 2014

be then compiled and executed from a web browser. The already accessible implementations offer GAUSSIAN, GAMESS and TURBOMOLE packages within the framework of InSilicolab for Chemistry [19], simulations of particle cascades in the Earth atmosphere for Cherenkov Telescope Array (CTA) [1]. A similar utility is needed to access easily the astrophysical fluid simulations on clusters of the PL-Grid Infrastructure. In this paper we describe the integration, within the InSilicoLab framework, of an open-source, multipurpose magnetohydrodynamical (MHD) code PIERNIK while using the up-to-date standard development tools (GIT, Jenkins [27]).

PIERNIK enables multifluid simulations of various astrophysical environments. An example of astrophysical environment that has to be investigated as a multi fluid system is the interstellar medium of galaxies. The interstellar medium is a composition of many interacting components: atomic and molecular gases, dust, magnetic fields, cosmic rays and electromagnetic radiation. The interstellar gas is a building material of forming stars and planets. The capability of the code to model the complexity of physical processes occurring in the interstellar medium is crucial for studying the cosmological evolution of the Universe. PIERNIK is equipped with a reach set of various physical modules to simulate multiple fluids interacting with magnetic and gravitational fields. The code is being enhanced with new modules, such as N-body module to simulate astrophysical system containing both particles and fluids. Examples of other codes developed for astrophysical fluid simulations including gas, magnetic field and a system of self gravitating particles are GADGET-2, RAMSES, FLASH, ENZO, ATHENA and many others.

The new solution is expected to ease the overall sequence of actions starting from preparation of necessary input data for the supported codes, submission of jobs to the queue, job execution and preliminary analysis of simulation results. The solution aims at popularisation of modern astrophysical fluid-dynamics and N-body simulation techniques among astrophysicists who exploit the PL-Grid Infrastructure.

The plan of our paper is as follows: in Section 2 we describe the functionality, scalability and exemplary applications of PIERNIK code, in Section 3 we present our prototype integration of PIERNIK into the InSilicoLab framework, hereafter named InSilicoLab for Astrophysics, in Section 4 we conclude our results.

2   MHD Code

PIERNIK is a grid-based MHD code using a simple, conservative numerical scheme, which is known as Relaxing TVD scheme (RTVD) [17]. The code relies on a dimensionally split, second order algorithm in space and time [23], [28]. The Relaxing TVD scheme is easily extensible to account for additional fluid components [4,5,6,7]: multiple fluids, dust, cosmic rays, and additional physical processes, such as fluid interactions, Ohmic resistivity effects and self-gravity. The simplicity and a small number of floating point operations of the basic algorithm is reflected in a high serial performance. A unique feature of PIERNIK code relies on our original implementation of anisotropic transport of cosmic-ray component in fluid approximation [8]. The basic explicit CR diffusion scheme has been recently supplemented with a multigrid-diffusion scheme.

2.1   Algorithms and Scaling

PIERNIK is equipped with advanced algorithms enabling multi-scale numerical experiments: Adaptive Mesh Refinement (AMR) and a Multigrid (MG) solver. The AMR algorithm allows to reach much bigger effective resolutions than it was possible with uniform grid. It dynamically adds regions of improved resolution (fine grids) where it is required by the refinement criteria. It can also delete grids, which are no longer needed to maintain high-quality solution. The MG, on the other hand, is one of the fastest known methods to solve parabolic and elliptic differential equations, which in our case are used to describe self-gravity of the fluid and diffusion of the cosmic rays, respectively. In addition, the isolated external boundaries for self-gravity use a multipole expansion of the potential to determine proper boundary values in a fast and efficient manner. Combination of AMR and multigrid algorithms make PIERNIK an ideal tool for simulations of multiphysics phenomena in gaseous disks of galaxies, active galactic nuclei, and planet-forming, circumstellar disks.

There are two main grid decomposition approaches in the PIERNIK code: the uniform grid (UG) and recently developed Adaptive Mesh Refinement (AMR). The UG algorithm divides the grid into smaller pieces, not necessarily of the same size, and assigns one piece to each process. Decomposition is performed in a way that minimizes the total size of internal boundaries between the pieces. Communication between all pieces is done via non-blocking MPI communication. The current implementation of AMR algorithm uses Hybrid-Block AMR approach, which means that at each level of refinement the grid is decomposed into relatively small pieces of the same size and shape (typically 16^3 cells) and each grid piece can be covered by some grid pieces at a finer level of refinement. The finer grid pieces do not cover more than one coarse grid piece and the coverage does not need to be complete (in contrast to standard Block AMR approaches) in order to save computational resources. The resolution difference between consecutive refinement levels is equal to 2. Typically there are many grid pieces that are associated with a given process. They are kept evenly distributed along a Morton or Hilbert fractal curves to decrease intracommunication and improve load balance.

The gravitational potential for the gas components is obtained by solving the Poisson equation inside the computational domain with an iterative, multi-grid solver [13]. The multigrid algorithm is based on a quick and simple V-cycle with some passes of a Red-Black Gauss-Seidel relaxation (smoothing) as an approximate solver. To minimize the effect of boundaries on the gravitational potential, a multipole expansion up to $l = 16$ moments is used to calculate the potential on the external boundaries [16]. The multigrid module creates a stack of coarse grids, each being coarsened by a factor of 2 (i.e., compatible with the AMR assumptions) to accelerate approximate solutions of elliptic equations by relaxation. An extension of the multigrid solver is the recently implemented parallel Multigrid-Preconditioned Conjugate Gradient Solver.

PIERNIK code is equipped with the cylindrical coordinate system implemented with the angular momentum-conserving form of the momentum equation [22], which with respect to Cartesian geometry introduces only one additional source term, minimizing possible nonphysical evolution of a system. Additionally, a new algorithm for a fast Eulerian transport [21] has been implemented for simulations of astrophysical disks to reduce the number of computational steps or to increase the resolution in the azimuthal direction.

The results of scalability tests are shown in Fig. 1. The scalability of PIERNIK code is predominantly dependent on the number of grid cells attributed to every MPI process. For big meshes of the overall size 1024^3, the code scales very well with respect to the ideal scaling curve up to 4096 CPU cores and shows further speed-up by 50% at 8192 cores (marked with squares in Fig. 1). For smaller meshes of the size 512^3, good scaling properties are apparent up to 2048 CPU cores.

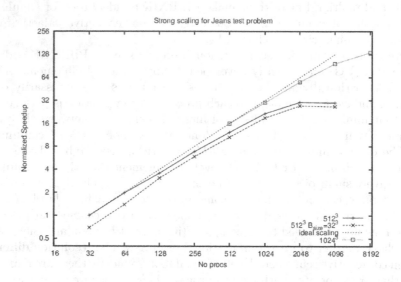

Fig. 1. Strong scaling of PIERNIK for the Jeans problem

Data I/O of PIERNIK code relies on HDF5 [12] library used in parallel mode. Current implementations allow for 2 scenarios of I/O: 1) one process collects data via MPI and writes to a single hdf5 file, 2) all processes write to (or read from) a single file using parallel HDF5 library routines. The checkpointing facility allows PIERNIK to split long computation time into small chunks and does not require the number of CPUs to be constant, making it very portable and flexible in utilizing available resources. The output produced by PIERNIK complies to Grid Data Format [34], which allows to utilize the yt package [29] for analysis and visualization purposes. The standard visualization is performed automatically, within the InsilicoLab workflow, by means of a high-level visualization routine 'yt plot' to produce color maps showing 2D-slices through the 3D simulation domain. As a result, the scientific results obtained using PIERNIK can be directly compared to the simulation output from other popular astrophysical codes such as FLASH, ENZO, ATHENA, GADGET, RAMSES and many others.

2.2 Application Examples

Below we present two examples of complex multi-fluid simulations of astrophysical disks: protoplanetary disks and galactic disks, resulting from PIERNIK simulations conducted in the PL-Grid Infrastructure. The main focus of astrophysics of those objects is their evolution. The relevant questions to address with the technique of astrophysical fluid simulations are: how planets form in disks consisting of dust and gas, how stars form from interstellar gas and what are the consequences of stellar explosions on the dynamics of interstellar medium, what is the origin of galactic magnetic fields and what is their impact on star formation.

Protoplanetary Disks. The basic concern of planet formation theory is how to grow dust from 1 m particles to km sized rocks and planetesimals that are basic building blocks for planets. There is a general agreement that dust particles can grow up to 1 m in radius due to collisions and interparticle interactions. However both theoretical models [3] and physical experiments [2] show that coagulation via collisional sticking is completely ineffective for large dust grains $(0.1 \div 1\,\mathrm{m})$. Moreover, particles of sizes $10\,\mathrm{cm} \div 1\,\mathrm{m}$ start to drift very rapidly towards the center of the disks, what results in a complete depletion of dust grains within timescales of hundreds of years [30]. A combination of these two processes is known as "meter barrier".

Despite these circumstances that are unfavourable for planet formation, there is a process that commences to dominate dust evolution when the local ratio of dust to gas density approaches unity. This mechanism was first presented in [33] and named the streaming instability. It appears that a combination of dust trapping in gas pressure maxima and aerodynamic coupling of gas and dust, enhancing the maxima even further, results in a significant dust pile-up [15]. Even without the presence of self-gravity, dust concentration may be risen up to the three orders of magnitude, which could possibly lead to gravitationally bound objects [18].

In our recent paper [20] we investigated for the first time the streaming instability in quasi-global protoplanetary disks (see Fig. 2). We have found that nonlinear evolution of the streaming instability leads to suitable conditions for the formation of gravitationally bound dust blobs. Our model extends the previous work of other authors [18] by taking into account the full dynamics of protoplanetary disk, e.g. radial migration that leads to significant variations in physical quantities, such as gas pressure gradient, and were previously treated as constant. This is an important step towards understanding the mechanism

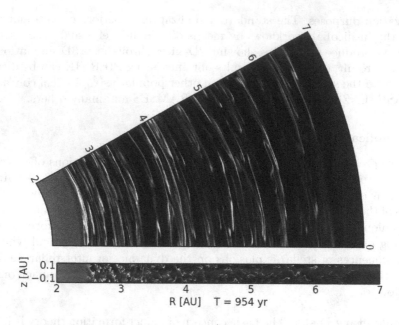

Fig. 2. Two-fluid hydrodynamical simulation of early stages of planet formation as a result of combined action of streaming and gravitational instabilities in protoplanetary disks. The picture shows dust condensations that emerged due to the action of streaming instability from an initially smooth dust distribution. The dust condensations are plausible progenitors of planetesimals, intermediate objects on evolutionary tracks towards rocky planets. The 3D simulation in the highest resolution ($2560 \times 480 \times 160$ consumed 1M CPUh in the PL-Grid Infrastructure).

responsible for planetary formation. In the currently ongoing project we incorporate self gravity, aiming to verify the hypothesis that planets can form due to combined action of streaming and gravitational instabilities.

Galactic Disks. PIERNIK has been successfully used in computationally demanding simulations of cosmic ray driven galactic dynamo [10,11]. We focus on the case of galactic disks, which involve many physical ingredients and processes, such as magnetic field generation, cosmic-ray transport and gravitational instability induced star formation. In such cases we need to resolve multiscale environment ranging from parsec scale, gravitationally bound star forming regions, up to tens of kiloparsec long cosmic-ray-driven outflows.

We have shown that the contribution of cosmic rays to the dynamics of the ISM on a global galactic scale leads to a very efficient magnetic field amplification on the timescale of galactic rotation. The model reveals a large scale regular magnetic field with an apparent spiral structure in the face-on view and an X-shaped structure in the edge-on view. In the presence of spiral arms in the

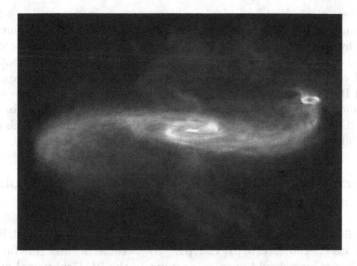

Fig. 3. Magnetohydrodynamical simulation of magnetic field generation in a spiral galaxy interacting with a companion dwarf galaxy [32]. The system resembles the famous M51 (Whirlpool) galaxy and its companion NGC5195. This is an example of hybrid simulation that includes N-body simulation of stars and dark matter component, performed with the VINE code [31], and MHD simulation including cosmic ray dynamics performed with the PIERNIK code.

distribution of stars, the magnetic field reveals a well pronounced spiral component closely corresponding to the material arms. Dynamical magnetic field structures with opposite polarities develop within the disk and are present even at the saturation phase of the dynamo. Moreover, during the coalescence phase of the two galaxies shown in Fig. 3 the magnetic field structure becomes irregular as observed in M51. An important part of the CR-driven dynamo is the galactic wind, which reaches velocities of a few hundred km/s at galactic altitudes of a few kpc.

Recently, we performed high-resolution simulations of the magnetized interstellar medium (ISM) in gas-rich star forming disk galaxies at high-redshift [9]. In our models, type II Supernovae locally deposit cosmic rays into the ISM. Our initial work indicates that cosmic rays produced in supernova remnants contribute essentially to the transportation of a significant fraction of gas in a wind perpendicular to the disk plane. The wind speeds can exceed the escape velocity of the galaxies and the global mass loading factor, i.e., the ratio of the gas mass leaving the galactic disk in a wind to the star formation rate, is approximately 10. These values are very similar to values observed for high redshift ($z = 2 \div 3$) star forming galaxies. Therefore, cosmic ray driven galactic winds provide a natural and efficient mechanism to explain the low efficiency for the conversion of gas into stars in galaxies as well as the early enrichment of the intergalactic medium with metals. This mechanism can be at least equally important as the usually considered momentum feedback from massive stars and thermal feedback from supernovae.

The aforementioned astrophysical problems pose a serious challenge from the computational point of view, as we deal with several nonlinear and mutually interacting physical processes that happen on various time and length scales. This implies that the undertaken numerical experiments require great spatial resolution and could not be tackled without significant amount of computational power. PIERNIK simulations, such as those presented above, require a specific configuration of software environment that may be hard to obtain for unexperienced HPC users. Such difficulties encountered by newcomers in the field can be successfully alleviated with tools like InSilicoLab for Astrophysics.

3   Description of the Solution and Results: Insilicolab for Astrophysics

The InSilicoLab for Astrophysics service is available at http://insilicolab.astro.plgrid.pl. To become a user of InSilicoLab for Astrophysics, one should open an account in the PL-Grid portal and apply for activation of the InSilicoLab for Astrophysics service. Activation of *Global gLite access* in the *Global services* section is also necessary. User manuals (only in Polish) are available at the web page [25].

Access to the service is possible with the aid of a certificate, which has to be registered in a web-browser, or via the OpenId system of the PL-Grid Infrastructure. Furthermore, configuration of a *proxy* certificate will be required for running simulations in the PL-Grid Infrastructure and for getting access to the data stored in the PL-Grid filesystems. After having configured the *proxy* certificate, one can start a user's experiment.

To start a new simulation, one should select **PIERNIK** from the menu. An empty card of a new experiment, shown in Fig. 4, opens and the user is promoted to fill in text fields to specify a problem name and problem description. One of the predefined experiments can be selected from the list including the following test problems:

1. **sedov** – the Sedov explosion experiment demonstrating spherical shock wave propagating after explosion of supernova in a uniform interstellar medium,
2. **otvortex** – evolution of sinusoidal perturbation of gas velocity and magnetic field, named Orszag-Tang vortex, leading to strong shock waves in a magnetised medium,
3. **tearing** – experiment demonstrating magnetic reconnection and formation of magnetic islands in plasma.

Sedov explosion test is perhaps the most common test of astrophysics fluid simulation codes, because its results can be confronted with a corresponding analytical solution. To explore one of the options in more detail, we select **sedov** from the list of test problems. Our choice implies that three problem-specific files, available for optional modifications, will be checked out from the repository:

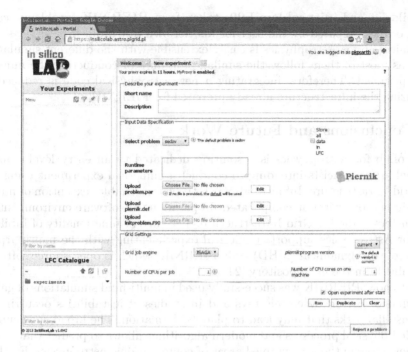

Fig. 4. An empty card of a new experiment

1. **piernik.def** – configuring the list of physical modules selected at the compilation phase,
2. **initproblem.F90** – containing FORTRAN 2003 module to construct the initial condition,
3. **problem.par** – containing numerical runtime parameters, organized in FORTRAN namelists.

The simulation starts after the **Run** command. A current state of the job can be followed in the **'Job execution status'** field. When the job is finished, the results are accessible in the **'Download job files'** field. With default settings, only the last output file (hdf5 format) is stored along with a series of standard plots (png format), generated by a python script of the **yt** package, displaying the gas density and energy density slices through the computational domain. To collect all the output files, one should select the **Store all data in LFC** option before the job execution. All output files together with plot files become available in LFC catalogue.

The described procedure depicts the beginners mode of utilisation of the code, that offers only three simple example test problems. The full list of predefined test problems is available in PIERNIK 'problems' directory available for download from the repository (see [24]). Selection of **USER** in the **Select problem** list opens the possibility to upload a set of problem files (**problem.par,**

piernik.def and **initproblem.F90**) taken from **PIERNIK** 'problems' catalogue, or files prepared by the user for his/her own test problem.

InSilicoLab for Astrophysics is easily extensible with the different simulation
codes as most of them follow the similar procedure of conducting the numerical experiment. Therefore, integrating a new astrophysical code is reduced to
reutilizing the infrastructure already prepared for PIERNIK.

4   Conclusions and Future Work

InSilicoLab for Astrophysics is a solution dedicated to an entry level computational astrophysicists intending to conduct a numerical experiment using the
PL-Grid Infrastructure. InSilicoLab for Astrophysics enables execution of numerical simulations without complicated preparations of software environment on
the clusters of the PL-Grid Infrastructure. The current functionality of InSilico-
Lab for Astrophysics supports numerical experimenting with the multipurpose
magnetohydrodynamical (MHD) code PIERNIK, which is open-source software
accessible from the git repository [24].

Up to now, PIERNIK was successfully used in multi-fluid simulations of galactic dynamos driven by cosmic rays and in studies of instabilities occurring in
circumstellar disks that may lead to planets' formation. The broad spectrum of
included physical processes and modern algorithms allows to predict that it will
gain new users in the yet untamed areas of computational astrophysics. Furthermore, PIERNIK was chosen as a model astrophysical code for integration with
the Polish Grid Infrastructure as a web-based service that will allow to easily
run simulations across all major Polish HPC centers. We believe that the new solution will help computational astrophysicists community to take full advantage
of the PL-Grid Infrastructure.

PIERNIK code grows in parallel with research activities of its developers. The
further development plan is to incorporate new algorithms and functionalities to
transform PIERNIK into a fully universal tool designated for leading-edge research in computational astrophysics. New modules and functionalities planned
for integration into the main branch of the code include: the N-body module
based on particle-mesh (PM) simulation technique, a set of Riemann solvers for
MHD equations, cooling and heating module and – in further plans – also radia-
tive transport module. All these functionalities are oriented towards applications
in collaborative research projects addressing current challenges in the fields of
planet formation, star formation and galaxy evolution.

The integration of PIERNIK into InSilicoLab is a prototype solution for integrating other open-source astrophysical simulation codes. Another astrophysical
simulation code GADGET-2 [26], utilising the Smoothed Particle Hydrodynamics (SPH) simulation technique is being integrated into the InSilicoLab framework.
SPH technique is based on Lagrangian formulation of hydrodynamics, while grid
codes, such as PIERNIK, rely on the Eulerian formulation. Both PIERNIK and
GADGET-2, available through InSilicoLab for Astrophysics framework, will form
together a powerful astrophysical simulation toolbox useful for research experiments as well as for elementary training in the field of computational astrophysics.

References

1. Barnacka, A., Bogacz, L., Gochna, M., Janiak, M., Komin, N., Lamanna, G., Moderski, R., Siudek, M.: PL-Grid e-Infrastructure for the Cherenkov Telescope Array Observatory. In: Bubak, M., Szepieniec, T., Wiatr, K. (eds.) PL-Grid 2011. LNCS, vol. 7136, pp. 301–313. Springer, Heidelberg (2012)
2. Blum, J., Wurm, G.: The Growth Mechanisms of Macroscopic Bodies in Protoplanetary Disks. Annual Review of Astron. and Astrophys. 46, 21–56 (2008)
3. Dullemond, C.P., Dominik, C.: Dust coagulation in protoplanetary disks: A rapid depletion of small grains. Astron. Astrophys. 434, 971–986 (2005)
4. Hanasz, M., Kowalik, K., Wóltański, D., Pawłaszek, R.: The PIERNIK MHD code – a multi-fluid, non-ideal extension of the relaxing-TVD scheme (I). In: Goździewski, K., Niedzielski, A., Schneider, J. (eds.) EAS Publications Series, vol. 42, pp. 275–280 (2010)
5. Hanasz, M., Kowalik, K., Wóltański, D., Pawłaszek, R.: PIERNIK MHD code – a multi-fluid, non-ideal extension of the relaxing-TVD scheme (III). In: de Avillez, M.A. (ed.) EAS Publications Series, vol. 56, pp. 363–366 (2012)
6. Hanasz, M., Kowalik, K., Wóltański, D., Pawłaszek, R.: PIERNIK MHD code – a multi-fluid, non-ideal extension of the relaxing-TVD scheme (IV). In: de Avillez, M.A. (ed.) EAS Publications Series, vol. 56, pp. 367–370 (2012)
7. Hanasz, M., Kowalik, K., Wóltański, D., Pawłaszek, R., Kornet, K.: The PIERNIK MHD code – a multi-fluid, non-ideal extension of the relaxing-TVD scheme (II). In: Goździewski, K., Niedzielski, A., Schneider, J. (eds.) EAS Publications Series, vol. 42, pp. 281–285 (2010)
8. Hanasz, M., Lesch, H.: Incorporation of cosmic ray transport into the ZEUS MHD code. Application for studies of Parker instability in the ISM. Astron. Astrophys. 412, 331–339 (2003)
9. Hanasz, M., Lesch, H., Naab, T., Gawryszczak, A., Kowalik, K., Wóltański, D.: Cosmic Rays Can Drive Strong Outflows from Gas-rich High-redshift Disk Galaxies. ApJL 777, L38 (2013)
10. Hanasz, M., Wóltański, D., Kowalik, K.: Global Galactic Dynamo Driven by Cosmic Rays and Exploding Magnetized Stars. ApJL 706, L155–L159 (2009)
11. Hanasz, M., Wóltanski, D., Kowalik, K., Kotarba, H.: Cosmic-ray driven dynamo in galaxies. In: Bonanno, A., de Gouveia Dal Pino, E., Kosovichev, A.G. (eds.) IAU Symposium, vol. 274, pp. 355–360 (2011)
12. HDF Group: What is hdf5?, http://www.hdfgroup.org/HDF5/whatishdf5.html
13. Huang, J., Greengard, L.: A fast direct solver for elliptic partial differential equations on adaptively refined meshes. SIAM Journal on Scientific Computing 21(4), 1551–1566 (1999), http://epubs.siam.org/doi/abs/10.1137/S1064827598346235
14. InSilicoLab Team, ACK CYFRONET AGH: InSilicoLab (2013), http://insilicolab.cyfronet.pl
15. Jacquet, E., Balbus, S., Latter, H.: On linear dust-gas streaming instabilities in protoplanetary discs. MNRAS 415, 3591–3598 (2011)
16. James, R.A.: The Solution of Poisson's Equation for Isolated Source Distributions. Journal of Computational Physics 25, 71 (1977)
17. Jin, S., Xin, Z.: The relaxation schemes for systems of conservation laws in arbitrary space dimension. Comm. Pure Appl. Math. 48, 235–276 (1995)
18. Johansen, A., Oishi, J.S., Mac Low, M.M., Klahr, H., Henning, T., Youdin, A.: Rapid planetesimal formation in turbulent circumstellar disks. Nature 448, 1022–1025 (2007)

19. Kocot, J., Szepieniec, T., Harężlak, D., Noga, K., Sterzel, M.: InSilicoLab – Managing Complexity of Chemistry Computations. In: Bubak, M., Szepieniec, T., Wiatr, K. (eds.) PL-Grid 2011. LNCS, vol. 7136, pp. 265–275. Springer, Heidelberg (2012)

20. Kowalik, K., Hanasz, M., Wóltański, D., Gawryszczak, A.: Streaming instability in the quasi-global protoplanetary discs. MNRAS 434, 1460–1468 (2013)

21. Masset, F.: FARGO: A fast eulerian transport algorithm for differentially rotating disks. Astron. Astrophys. Suppl. Ser. 141, 165–173 (2000)

22. Mignone, A., Bodo, G., Massaglia, S., Matsakos, T., Tesileanu, O., Zanni, C., Ferrari, A.: PLUTO: A Numerical Code for Computational Astrophysics. ApJS 170, 228–242 (2007)

23. Pen, U.L., Arras, P., Wong, S.: A Free, Fast, Simple, and Efficient Total Variation Diminishing Magnetohydrodynamic Code. ApJS 149, 447–455 (2003)

24. Piernik Developement Team: Piernik mhd code (2013), https://github.com/piernik-dev

25. The PL-Grid Infrastructure Users' Manual: Astrofizyka: InSilicoLab for Astrophysics, https://docs.cyfronet.pl/display/PLGDoc/Astrofizyka (in Polish)

26. Springel, V.: The cosmological simulation code GADGET-2. MNRAS 364, 1105–1134 (2005)

27. Team, J.D.: Jenkins (2011), http://jenkins-ci.org/content/about-jenkins-ci

28. Trac, H., Pen, U.L.: A Primer on Eulerian Computational Fluid Dynamics for Astrophysics. PASP 115, 303–321 (2003)

29. Turk, M.J., Smith, B.D., Oishi, J.S., Skory, S., Skillman, S.W., Abel, T., Norman, M.L.: yt: A Multi-code Analysis Toolkit for Astrophysical Simulation Data. ApJS 192, 9 (2011)

30. Weidenschilling, S.J.: Aerodynamics of solid bodies in the solar nebula. MNRAS 180, 57–70 (1977)

31. Wetzstein, M., Nelson, A.F., Naab, T., Burkert, A.: Vine – A Numerical Code for Simulating Astrophysical Systems Using Particles. I. Description of the Physics and the Numerical Methods. ApJS 184, 298–325 (2009)

32. Wóltański, D., Hanasz, M., Kowalik, K.: Cosmic Ray Driven Dynamo in Spiral Galaxies. MNRAS (2014) (in prep.)

33. Youdin, A.N., Goodman, J.: Streaming Instabilities in Protoplanetary Disks. ApJ 620, 459–469 (2005)

34. yt Developement Team: Grid data form (2011), https://bitbucket.org/yt_analysis/grid_data_format

Services for Astronomical Data Management and Sharing

Tomasz Kundera[1], Greg Stachowski[2], Arkadiusz Wierzbowski[3],
Jerzy Borkowski[4], and Paweł Ciecieląg[5]

[1] Astronomical Observatory of the Jagiellonian University,
ul. Orla 171, 30-244 Kraków, Poland
[2] Mt. Suhora Astronomical Observatory, Pedagogical University of Cracow,
ul. Podchorążych 2, 30-084 Kraków, Poland
[3] Networks and Servers Section of the Jagiellonian University,
ul. Reymonta 4, 30-059 Kraków, Poland
[4] Nicolaus Copernicus Astronomical Center,
ul. Rabiańska 8, 87-100 Toruń, Poland
[5] Nicolaus Copernicus Astronomical Center,
ul. Bartycka 18, 00-716 Warszawa, Poland

Abstract. As part of the AstroGrid-PL project, we have implemented a large scale data management system for the Polish astronomical community within the framework of the PLGrid Plus project, with built-in metadata services, replication and distributed storage based on the well-established iRODS middleware. In parallel, we have implemented the Polish Virtual Observatory, which provides access, search, retrieval and *in situ* processing for this data using the protocols and standards established by the International Virtual Observatory Alliance (IVOA). These standards are already in use at astronomical facilities across the globe, and implementing them within the framework of AstroGrid-PL and the PLGrid Plus project enables us not only to provide advanced data retrieval services to our users, but also to leverage a large body of existing astronomical data analysis software and give our users access to external data resources provided on the same principles.

Keywords: astronomy, data storage, data management, Grid, virtual observatory, data archives.

1 Introduction

1.1 Data-Centric Astronomy

In recent years, astronomy has entered the era of 'big data', with current optical observing programmes regularly producing tens of gigabytes of data per night per instrument, and planned optical survey programmes such as the Large Synoptic Survey Telescope (LSST) projected to generate tens of terabytes per night [1]. Indeed, existing radio astronomy projects using large numbers of antennas in phased arrays, such as Low Frequency Array for Radio Astronomy (LOFAR),

M. Bubak et al. (Eds.): PLGrid Plus, LNCS 8500, pp. 305–316, 2014.

are already generating these kinds of data volumes on a regular basis [2]. This flood of data requires new approaches to data storage and processing. It is no longer possible for users to store and process all of the data they may wish to use locally and neither it is possible to use simple remote storage and transfer the files as required for local processing, even with gigabit-class networks.

Instead, intelligent centralised large-scale data stores have to be provided, with efficient indexing and metadata tagging and search services, which enable the user to extract and transfer only that subsection of the data, which they actually need. Furthermore, powerful processing facilities need to be co-located with the data so that as much initial processing as possible can be performed without the need to transfer the data across the bottleneck of the Internet. These types of services can only be provided efficiently within the framework of a large infrastructure project, such as PL-Grid.

1.2   Astronomical Archives

Within astronomy, there is increasing pressure for storage and processing of archival data, both from modern electronic instruments and from ongoing digitization of analogue sources such as photographic plates. The transient and unpredictable nature of astronomical observations makes this archival data extremely valuable, as there is frequently a need to go back and re-analyse previous observations in light of new discoveries or with newly-developed methods, unavailable when the data was originally collected. The only reasonable way to deal with such a large and growing body of data is by application of grid computing techniques, large databases, intelligent agents and efficient use of metadata tagging and search methods.

1.3   Astronomical Data Standards

File Formats. Standardised file formats for digital data have been established for some time, with the Flexible Image Transport System (FITS) file format, being dominant for image, spectroscopy and – to some extent – tabular data for several decades. A standard library for reading and writing FITS files called CFITSIO [3] exists, available directly for the C and Fortran languages and through hooks in other languages such as Python. However, not only has the FITS standard evolved to some extent over the years; indeed, individual groups and institutions often implement their own variants of the file format, which are not always entirely compatible with the standard CFITSIO library, particularly as regards keyword names and data formats. This presents a particular difficulty with archival data, which may nominally be in the FITS format, but which may require additional pre-processing before it can be shared.

Other data formats, which may need to be dealt with, include proprietary binary or text data files specific to particular instruments.

Virtual Observatory. Over the last decade, the Virtual Observatory concept has emerged as the primary means of data sharing and access within the international astronomical community. Rather than being a single piece of software or library, the Virtual Observatory (VObs) is essentially a set of specifications and standards for protocols, queries, metadata, etc. for data interchange within astronomy, including many field-specific details (such as standard vocabularies or mechanisms for specifying bandpasses for observations). While some reference implementations exist, the idea is to provide a common framework underneath, in which a variety of pre-existing databases and systems can coexist and communicate transparently with each other and with data processing and visualisation software (both "professional" such as NOAO IRAF [4] and "Amateur/educational" such as the Microsoft World Wide Telescope). Collectively, services presenting these common interfaces are known as virtual observatories, and have been implemented on a national level by a number of countries. The International Virtual Observatory Alliance (IVOA) coordinates the development of the standard protocols and specifications.

The VObs brings with it additional file formats (or, more accurately, data structures), which should be accounted for. These include VOtable, which is rapidly becoming the standard interchange format for tabular data.

2 Requirements for Data Services for Polish Astronomy

The Polish astronomical community has historically been comparatively slow to develop data management and data sharing policies and services on an institutional and national level. Data has long been managed and shared on an *ad-hoc* basis through personal collaborations and within small groups, hampered by the wide variety of utilized software and storage systems. National-level software and computing support projects for astronomy along the lines of UK StarLink or the software projects of the National Optical Astronomy Observatory (NOAO) or National Radio Astronomy Observatory (NRAO) did not exist prior to the AstroGrid-PL project described in this book.

In recent years, it has become increasingly apparent to the Polish astronomical community that the trend towards increasingly large data sets (both observational and simulated) and towards large collaborations involving many groups, both national and international, makes this *ad hoc* system unsustainable.

Furthermore, it has become clear that there are large archives of data (both digital and analog), which exist at various institutes and which are in danger of being irretrievably lost (for example photographic plates, floppy disks, old magnetic tapes, optical disks of various types, etc.) Conversion, replication and management of these archives is a particularly pernicious problem for smaller astronomy departments, which lack sufficient hardware and human resources to prepare and publish their archival data.

Therefore, one of the primary goals of the AstroGrid-PL project has been to design, implement and deploy data management services to the community, capable of handling large and small data sets, old (archival) and new data, which will be usable across all of the astronomical institutes in Poland. These data management services must, by design, enable data storage, tagging, search, retrieval, and replication in a manner, which is sufficiently transparent (and efficient) to be easily accepted by the community at all levels, and which can be easily integrated into existing workflows.

In addition, data management services have to be integrated with those developed by other astronomical communities across the globe to allow full bilateral participation in international collaborations. This requires adherence to existing standards and protocols such as those prepared by the IVOA. A side benefit of this policy is the ability to use existing software, reducing development time.

Legacy archives are being handled through a process of digitization of analog data such as photographic plates (as described in a later section) and conversion of digital data stored on obsolete media and/or in obsolete file formats to modern form and storage within the AstroGrid-PL/PL-Grid Infrastructure data management system.

These data services require sufficient disk space, database services (for tagging and indexing), replication/archival mechanisms and access controls. The only feasible way to implement these is within the structure and services of the PLGrid Plus project.

Data storage requirements are difficult to determine accurately because of the aforementioned wide variety of storage media used and their distribution across many *ad-hoc* personal and institutional archives. However, user surveys carried out within the Polish astronomical community at the beginning of the project suggest a present requirement on the order of 100TB for existing data. This requirement is expected to grow rapidly as new large-scale surveys come online in the near future.

Solutions to these requirements have been designed and implemented within the PLGrid Plus project by the AstroGrid-PL project. They are described below.

3   Implementing Astronomical Data Services within the PLGrid Plus Project

We have implemented astronomical data services ("Astro-data") within the AstroGrid-PL/PL-Grid Infrastructure by deploying a data management system (iRODS – see next section), which can be used directly by the users for their own storage needs, but which also provides transparent data replication, distributed storage, indexing and metadata. This has enabled us to build a Virtual Obervatory interface on top of this service, facilitating data queries, retrieval and sharing. Creating a Polish Virtual Observatory allows all of the existing knowledge of the VObs community to be leveraged, both on the national and international levels.

The Polish Virtual Observatory provides:

– local access to data held within institutes through IVOA protocols, necessary for use by local research groups and for preliminary analysis prior to wider sharing (e.g. astrometry of scanned archival photographic plates),

- the ability to work with large (both in terms of number and size) data sets through the use of efficient queries and initial calculations performed at the data storage location prior to any transfer,
- indexing, metadata and search facilities,
- uniform access to archival and new data,
- a consistent interface to varied data types (images, spectra, tables),
- access to existing data collections without the need to transfer them by means of data registry, indexing and standard access protocols (VObs data conversion software can "mine" an existing archive and generate a description and query interface),
- access controls including embargo times,
- access for remote/international collaborators.

The overall structure of the Astro-data service is shown in Fig. 1, while Fig. 2 shows the data path for larger institutes – by definition those, which have local data archives and sufficient resources to present them for sharing without necessarily having to transfer them to an external storage facility. Small institutes are expected to make their data available by transferring it to the centralised storage of the PL-Grid Infrastructure (labelled "KDM" in the figure).

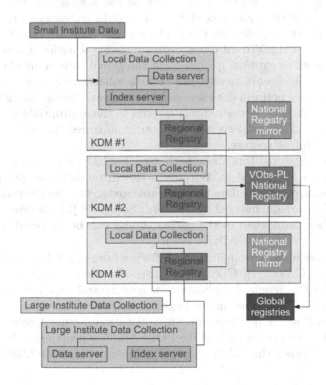

Fig. 1. Overall structure of Astro-data (all Local Data Centers have the same internal architecture)

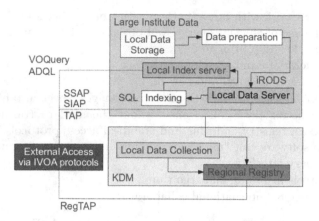

Fig. 2. Data path within large institutes. SSAP, SIAP, and TAP are data access protocols defined by IVOA. RegTAP is a registry access protocol. The indexing service is powered by an SQL server.

As can be seen in the figures, the data collections exist in two parts: a data server, which stores the files themselves, and an indexing server, which supports rapid searching for data and metadata. These data collections are indexed in regional data registries (following the IVOA registry standard [5]), which in turn are registered with the Virtual Observatory registry, a national registry, which is the one exposed to external queries from the global astronomical community. Note that the registries are merely lists of data collections and access protocols, and do not actually perform data searches themselves, thus avoiding a potential bottleneck. The data registries redirect queries to the appropriate index servers. Note that all registries and servers are, of course, mirrored through the resources of the PL-Grid Infrastructure.

Within the large institute data path (see Fig. 2) local storage is used to prepare the data for upload to Astro-data (for example initial pre-processing, adding metadata, etc.). The data is then transfered to the Data Server (using the iRODS middleware) and indexed by the Index Server (SQL). As described above, the data is then catalogued in the registries and can be accessed by standard IVOA protocols (VOQuery, ADQL, etc.).

These services have been built using software from other VObs projects (Astrogrid UK [6], GAVO [7], CDS [8]) on top of a data management backend, which provides the required replication, access control and metadata tagging subsystems. This is described in the next section.

Although still under development, these data management solutions are already being used by groups such as the POLFAR [9] consortium, which manages collaboration between the Polish scientific community and the LOFAR project.

3.1 Data Management Systems

Efficient management of large volumes of data requires a scalable, redundant data management system, which can provide metadata, indexing, search and replication services alongside basic storage space.

While a number of such systems exist, usually implemented as a middleware layer between the user applications and backend filesystem and relational databases, the leading open-source implementation is probably iRODS (integrated rule-oriented data system [10]), derived from the older Storage Resource Broker (SRB) system. It is currently being developed by the Renaissance Computing Institute (RENCI) [11] – the consortium of academic institutions – and the DICE [12] research group, and is used across a large number of large-scale scientific data management projects.

iRODS uses storage provided by an underlying filesystem combined with a PostgreSQL database to manage data files and metadata. The underlying storage can also include slower storage media such as optical disks or magnetic tapes in jukebox-type systems, as well as remote storage, all transparent to the user. iRODS has a well-developed system of rules and policies, which can be adapted for local needs. These provide powerful tools for searching and manipulating the data stored within iRODS. Side projects provide tools such as Java and web-browser based file management tools, which make it easier for users to take advantage of iRODS storage.

Due to its well-developed nature and widespread use, we have selected iRODS as the underlying middleware of the AstroGrid-PL data management system. Initial deployment involved iRODS servers located at five institutions: Jagiellonian University Astronomical Observatory in Kraków, Pedagogical University Department of Astronomy in Kraków, Nicolaus Copernicus Astronomical Center (NCAC) in Warszawa, NCAC in Toruń, and Academic Computer Center Cyfronet AGH in Kraków, all federated into a common system. In addition, development work has been performed in cooperation with PSNC (Poznan Supercomputing and Networking Center) to improve the quality of the iDrop Java-based client software [13]. This data management system is the basis of the Astro-data service and underlies a number of other AstroGrid-PL services, including the Virtual Observatory.

3.2 Architecture and Layers

The architecture of the Astro-data service is based largely around existing and established software, libraries, protocols and toolkits used for data management services and in virtual observatories elsewhere (e.g. GAVO, CDS, Astrogrid UK, etc.). There is, however, no standard overall architecture for these types of systems, with every one having been implemented separately and customised to the needs and capabilities of the local institutions. AstroGrid-PL has gone further than most in terms of integrating both data management and virtual observatory into one system, and providing multiple data access paths to users.

This is a result of the very heterogeneous nature of the Polish astronomical community, much more so than in (for example) the USA or UK where integration and collaboration projects have been ongoing for several decades. Thus users of AstroGrid-PL largely expect to be able to "do things their own way", perhaps more so than elsewhere.

The software layers making up the Astro-data services are shown in Fig. 3.

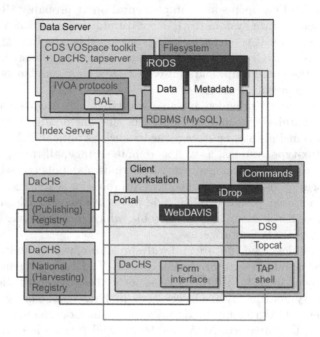

Fig. 3. Software layers for client, server and external services within Astro-data. The data server uses iRODS on top of the filesystem to manage data and metadata. The index server provides indexing via an SQL RDBMS. Data can be accessed directly (iRODS) or indirectly (IVOA protocols provided by VObs middleware). The client has various options for accessing the data, from talking directly to iRODS, through the AstroGrid-PL portal, or via VObs-enabled software such as DS9. Finally, external servers based on the DaCHS middleware provide integrated data registry services. More details is provided in the text.

The data server stores the data and associated metadata on the UNIX filesystem, managed by the iRODS middleware. The index server indexes the data and metadata according to various suitable keys (such as coordinates, object classification, times, etc.), stores the results in a relational database (RDBMS, MySQL in the figure, but PostgreSQL or any other suitable system can be used), which allows rapid SQL queries and searches without the need to search the raw data files themselves.

The client workstation has a wide range of options for accessing the data. Firstly, the data can be reached directly through the iRODS middleware, using either command-line clients (iCommands) reminiscent of the usual UNIX filesystem commands, the Java-based iDrop graphical client (see Fig. 4), which may be installed as a standalone program or as a Java applet on the AstroGrid-PL portal, or finally through the same portal, but using a graphical interface based on the WebDAVIS toolkit [15], without the need for Java.

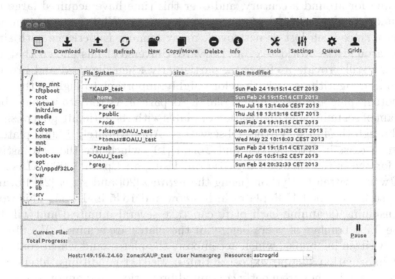

Fig. 4. iDrop Java client for iRODS

Secondly, the data can be reached indirectly through IVOA protocols and the VObs Data Access Layer (DAL). These services are provided on the server-side by a variety of VObs middleware such as the CDS VOSpace toolkit, GAVO DaCHS [14], and tapserver. On the client side they are accessed by Virtual Observatory-enabled applications such as DS9 [16] or Topcat [17], via a form interface on the AstroGrid-PL portal, implemented using the DaCHS middleware, or via a shell, which provides a command-line interface to VObs tabular data (the TAP shell). All of these can also communicate with the data registries, which we have built using the DaCHS toolkit, and which provide a uniform interface for finding data services across the global Virtual Observatory.

The distributed nature of the architecture (multiple data servers, separate index servers with offline indexing, for handling search queries, and separate registry servers to aggregate lists of data sources) combined with the inherent load-balancing/high-availability provided by basing the system on the underlying PL-Grid Infrastructure, provide assurance that the design can withstand heavy load. Furthermore, a general principle is that data servers are co-located in the PL-Grid supercomputing centers alongside computation nodes, so that large data sets do not need to be transferred for processing (only the results are sent to the user).

3.3   Digitization of Analog Archives

Prior to the widespread use of digital camera systems from about the 1990s onward, imaging of astronomical objects and recording of spectra was performed using photographic plates and film. The major astronomical observatories in Poland (at Kraków, Poznań, Toruń, Warszawa and Wrocław) have now been functioning for around a century, and over this time have acquired large numbers (hundreds of thousands) of photographic images. While some percentage of these have since been lost or destroyed, many remain. Experience with similar archives around the world (e.g. at Harvard University) has shown that these plates may still provide useful data, particularly when digitised and processed with modern algorithms. It is therefore highly important to digitise the remaining photographic archives within Poland. As part of Astro-data we have begun a program of scanning and digitisation of plates with the ultimate goal of sharing these through the Polish Virtual Observatory. Approximately 14,000 plates are believed to exist in Kraków [18] and Toruń [19], which are the two institutes chosen for the initial phase of digitization. Using an Epson 10000 XL scanner and software written in Python (using the *astropy* [20] and *scipy* [21] libraries), we have so far scanned 1545 plates in Kraków and 1645 in Toruń. This work is time-consuming (scanning each plate can take several minutes) and will likely continue for a number of years before all the plates are scanned. We also scan the handwritten log books, which accompany the plates, and which contain important information such as exposure times, weather conditions, filters and so on. Unfortunately, they frequently contain abbreviations and annotations, which make transcription difficult. Transcribing this information into the form of standardised digital metadata, which can be attached to the digitised images, is therefore another time-consuming task, which will likely continue into the foreseeable future.

Scanned and metadata-tagged images then undergo initial processing using the *astrometry.net* software [22] to establish astrometry, plate coordinates and object lists, which allows the images to be integrated into the digital archives and used simultaneously with modern data. Fig. 5 shows an image of one of these photographic plates (a wide field image of the Andromeda Galaxy taken in Kraków in the 1970s) after digitisation and tagging with coordinates. The scanned plate has been read by the Aladin applet (a VObs tool created by CDS [23]) and overlaid with a coordinate grid and the location of several exoplanet systems, which have been discovered in this field in recent years (significantly post-dating the photographic plate). Subsequently, photometry of the scanned plate images is carried out using *sextractor* [24]. Finally, additional corrections for precession, background and local instrumental details are performed using in-house software and scripts (mostly using Python and the *astropy* and *numpy* [25] libraries). Both *astrometry.net* and *sextractor* are software packages, which are currently standard in the field for these types of tasks, and are used in similar software pipelines elsewhere, for example in the Digital Sky Century at Harvard (DASCH) project [26].

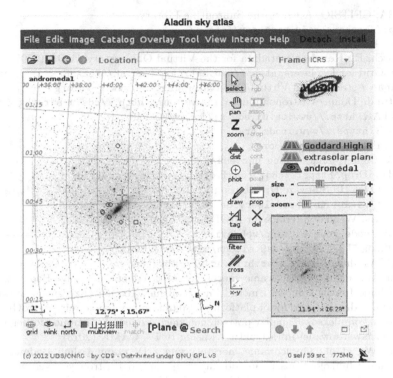

Fig. 5. Digitised photographic plate read into Aladin and overlaid with a coordinate grid and catalog data for exoplanets

4   Conclusions

As part of the AstroGrid-PL project to build a domain-specific grid to support the Polish astronomical community within the framework of the PL-Grid Infrastructure, we have designed and implemented services to provide data management, distributed storage, and data sharing (called "Astro-data"). We have also set up the Polish Virtual Observatory to allow access to the data using standard protocols used by astronomical software and other data providers. Finally, we have begun a program of digitizing the large photographic plate archives existing in Polish observatories. These services will provide a framework for improved national and international collaboration for the Polish astronomical community for the foreseeable future.

References

1. Becla, J., et al.: Organizing the LSST Database for Real-Time Astronomical Processing. In: SPIE, vol. 6270, p. 24 (2004)
2. Holties, H., Renting, A., Grange, Y.: The LOFAR long-term archive: e-infrastructure on petabyte scale. In: SPIE, vol. 8451, p. 17 (2012)

3. NASA: CFITSIO: A FITS File Subroutine Library,
   http://heasarc.gsfc.nasa.gov/fitsio/
4. IRAF Image Reduction and Analysis Facility, http://iraf.noao.edu/
5. Hanisch, R.: Resource Metadata for the Virtual Observatory. IVOA (2007)
6. AstroGrid for Deployers, http://www.astrogrid.ac.uk/RELEASE/
7. German Astrophycical Virtual Observatory, http://www.g-vo.org/
8. Centre de Données astronomiques de Strasbourg, http://cds.u-strasbg.fr/
9. POLFAR, http://www.oa.uj.edu.pl/lofar/POLFAR.pdf
10. iRODS, https://www.irods.org
11. renci, http://www.renci.org/
12. DICE Center, http://dice.unc.edu/
13. iRODS iDrop, https://code.renci.org/gf/project/irodsidrop/
14. GAVO DaCHS Software Distribution,
    http://vo.ari.uni-heidelberg.de/soft/dachs
15. webdavis: Webdav interface for iRODS and SRB,
    http://code.google.com/p/webdavis/
16. SAOImage DS9, http://ds9.si.edu/site/Home.html
17. TOPCAT, http://www.star.bris.ac.uk/~mbt/topcat/
18. Pych, W., et al.: Opracowanie merytoryczne z III etapu Usługi Badawczej pt.
    "Zbadanie funkcjonalności i metod integracji narzędzi astrofizycznych w ramach
    usługi dziedzinowej, gridowej platformy wsparcia pracy naukowej – AstroGrid-PL,
    na bazie kompleksowej analizy potrzeb polskiego środowiska astronomicznego w za-
    kresie zaawansowanej infrastruktury i usług ICT". CAMK (2013)
19. Pych, W., et al.: Opracowanie merytoryczne z IV etapu Usługi Badawczej pt.
    "Zbadanie funkcjonalności i metod integracji narzędzi astrofizycznych w ramach
    usługi dziedzinowej, gridowej platformy wsparcia pracy naukowej – AstroGrid-PL,
    na bazie kompleksowej analizy potrzeb polskiego środowiska astronomicznego w za-
    kresie zaawansowanej infrastruktury i usług ICT". CAMK (2014)
20. Greenfield, P., et al.: Astropy: Community Python Software for Astronomy. In:
    AAS Meeting 223, vol. 255.24 (2014)
21. SciPy.org, http://www.scipy.org/
22. Lang, D., et al.: Astrometry.net: Blind Astrometric Calibration of Arbitrary As-
    tronomical Images. AJ 139, 1782 (2010)
23. Boch, T., et al.: Aladin: An Open Source All-Sky Browser. ASPC 442, 683 (2011)
24. Bertin, E., and Arnouts, S.: SExtractor: Source Extractor. ASCL 1010.064 (2010)
25. NumPy, http://www.numpy.org/
26. Laycock, S., et al.: Digital Access to a Sky Century at Harvard: Initial Photometry
    and Astrometry. AJ 140, 1062 (2010)

A Modern Tool for Modelling and Optimisation of Production in Underground Coal Mine

Edyta Brzychczy

AGH University of Science and Technology,
al. Mickiewicza 30, 30-059 Kraków, Poland

Abstract. A new calculation tool allowing the user to model and optimise production in underground coal mines is presented in the paper. Hard coal plays an essential role in the world economics. Its consumption in 2011 increased faster than for any other energy produced from raw materials (excluding renewable sources). Achieving the planned output levels depends, first of all, on results acquired in the mining design process. It is now possible to support this design process with modern tools, which can significantly increase future mine efficiency as well as the quality of the raw material extracted. The calculation service for optimisation of the production in underground coal mines (OPTiCoalMine) is one of such tools.

Keywords: coal mining, production, optimisation, calculation service.

1 Introduction

Energy produced from coal is one of the primary factors pushing the today's global economy. The global energy needs and consumption are currently increasing more rapidly than at any time in the past. The world's primary energy consumption in the years 1965 to 2011 in Mtoe are presented in Fig. 1.

Coal, along with lignite, covers more than 30% of all primary energy demand, and produces 42% of global electricity [47]. In 2011, its consumption increased faster than any other energy source excluding renewable sources.

According to forecasts, primary global energy consumption will increase to 16,631 Mtoe in 2030 (more than twice the number from 1990). Similarly, the consumption of coal will increase. By 2030, it should amount to more than 4,608 Mtoe, which is equivalent to more than 6 billion tonnes of coal [45].

Coal mining is conducted on all continents in nearly 70 countries around the world. Global production of coal reached 6,637 million tonnes in 2011, and this figure was over 420 million tonnes higher than in the previous year [47].

The main purpose of any coal mine is the extraction of coal in accordance to the approved production plan and the ultimate economic benefits arising from this. Achieving the planned level of production in a mine depends mainly on the results of the design and execution of mining operations at individual mines.

In a hard coal mine, the mining operations design process can be divided into the following stages:

M. Bubak et al. (Eds.): PLGrid Plus, LNCS 8500, pp. 317–334, 2014.

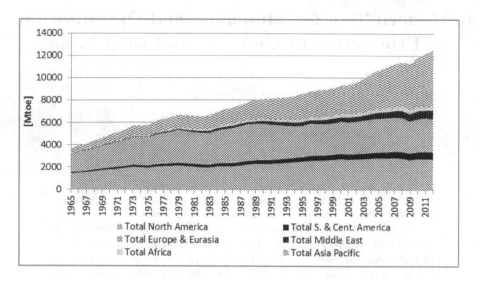

Fig. 1. World's consumption of primary energy in years 1965-2011 (source of data: [46])

1. Design problem formulation.
2. Knowledge gathering.
3. Searching for problem solution.
4. Optimisation.
5. Solution implementation.

A general mining operations design process scheme is presented in Fig. 2.

The design challenge demonstrated here is associated with the following structural components of a mine:

– areas where mining operations will be executed (excavations),
– equipment and organisational elements, which should be provided (technical structure),
– duration of mining operations.

Knowledge gathering related to the design problem (excavation parameters, available equipment, time dependencies between planned excavations) are necessary in the modelling stage of the design process.

This stage consists of the following activities:

– constructing the mining operations model with use of network techniques,
– generating design solutions based on the developed model.

The next step in the design process is the optimisation stage, in which an evaluation of design solutions is carried out, and the best of them selected according to the assumed criteria.

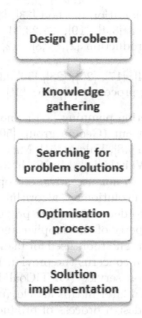

Fig. 2. Mining operations design process scheme

The aim of the solution (variant of mining operations) is distribution of mining operations in the time, which is giving the optimal value for the formulated objective function.

Therefore, the following optimisation problem is formulated:
"Which equipment should be used to conduct mining operations under conditions of designed excavations in a coal mine (or group of mines) and what should be the advance of operations according to the adopted objective function?"

The expected result of searching is a solution, expressed in the form of a matrix (R), where:

- columns represent equipment to be used in the designed excavations,
- rows represent designed excavations,
- the value at the intersection of a column and a row represents the estimated value of the mining operations advance with the allocated equipment.

The chosen solution can be implemented through the mining schedule and realisation of mining operations in the mine.

Results from the design process depend on design methods, which include design procedures and optimisation methods as well as computational methods. A quite detailed review of mine planning methods is presented in [30], [40], however, many of these have been developed for open pits use only.

In the field of the underground mining, methods – which have been developed – are related to the following issues:

- selection of mining or exploitation method [33], [44],
- mine size, model and layout [3,4], [19], [22,23,24], [43],
- optimisation of mining production [2], [7,8], [12], [18], [20], [25], [29], [31], [34,35], [37], [41,42],
- allocation models [11], [14], [17], [26], [28], [36], [39],
- uncertainty of the mining processes [6], [15], [21], [38].

The software used for production planning [27] is mostly designed for map creation, visualisation of deposit cut (Geovia group [50]: Surpac, GEMS, Minex, RockWorks [55], MicroStation [48], Vulcan [51], Micromine [52]) and production scheduling (MineSched [50], Whittle [50], MineSight 3D [54], Minemax [53], CAE Mining [49]). Such programs do not use advanced optimisation methods (such as the Monte Carlo method, evolutionary algorithms or simulated annealing). In some cases, it is difficult to determine their properties due to the fact that detailed algorithms are a property of the supplier and cannot be disclosed [30].

Among the existing methods and tools used for planning of the mining production there is no solution, which concerns the previously formulated optimisation problem. Thus, the calculation service (OPTiCoalMine) has been developed. This service, which is described later in this article, further extends the range of tools available for use in the design process of production in underground hard coal mines.

2   Underground Mining Process of Coal Production

The underground method is based on preparing underground excavations, mining raw material there and transporting it to the surface. The production costs of this method are much higher than with the open pit method. The underground method is currently applied in coal mines giving approx. 60% of the current world production.

Underground mining involves the following steps: providing vertical access to the deposit, providing horizontal access to the deposit, cutting the deposit and its exploitation. Access to the deposit, in practice, is usually achieved through the shifts (vertical) and roadways on mining levels (horizontal). The next step is to divide the deposit into smaller parts (exploitation areas, panels).

There are two main exploitation systems currently used in the underground mining:

- the room-and-pillar system,
- the longwall system.

In the room-and-pillar system the coal deposit is mined by making chambers and leaving pillars of coal at appropriate distances to support the overlying rocks. These pillars can be mined at later, e.g., during liquidation of the mining level or the whole mine. This method is continuously replaced by the longwall system.

The longwall system allows more efficient use of the seam resources by selecting the maximum volume of coal from the longwall panel using longwall shearers. A scheme of longwall excavation is shown in Fig. 3.

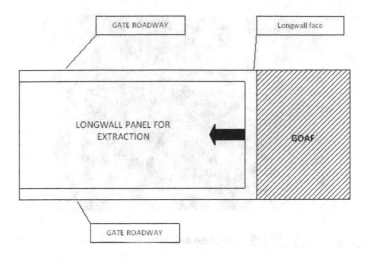

Fig. 3. Longwall excavation scheme

Longwall excavation is characterized by the following parameters:

- longwall length, which corresponds to the length of the longwall face,
- length of the longwall panel, which corresponds to the length of the gate roadways,
- longwall height, which corresponds to horizontal dimension between ceiling and floor of the longwall face.

The basic technical indicator of mining operations in a longwall face is the advance of the longwall face, which corresponds to the number of meters in a unit of time (m/day, m/month) cut along the longwall face.

The advance of the longwall face depends on the dimensions of the excavation and the equipment used. The basic equipment used in a longwall face includes: longwall shearer, chain conveyor and mechanised support. They form a longwall set, which is shown in Fig. 4.

In case of a low height longwall, in place of the shearer, a coal plough is used, which is designed for thin deposits exploitation. The main difference between the plough's and the shearer's construction is the lack of rotating cutting head.

The longwall system uses two main methods of liquidation of the space left after the longwall face passage:

- collapse of roof rocks,
- dry or hydraulic backfilling.

In Poland, the basic method of coal exploitation is the longwall system (used in nearly 99% cases), mainly liquidated using the collapse of roof rocks method.

Fig. 4. Longwall set (source: [56])

3   Input Data to Modelling Process of Mining Production

Modelling the mining process depends on the adopted exploitation system. The main assumptions for any model using the longwall system are presented in this paper.

Gross output of the longwall [Mg/d] could be calculated according to the following formula:

$$W_d = h \cdot ls \cdot \gamma \cdot pos\,, \tag{1}$$

where:

h – the height of the longwall [m],
ls – the length of the longwall [m],
γ – the volume weight of coal [Mg/m^3],
pos – the advance of the longwall face [m/d].

Net output of the longwall [Mg/d] could be calculated according to the following formula:

$$W_{dn} = W_d \cdot ws\,, \tag{2}$$

where:

ws – the coefficient of the exploitation and mineral processing losses.

The advance of the excavation depends on geological and mining conditions and on the mining machinery (mainly longwall shearer).

The advance of the longwall face could be calculated as [5]:

$$pos = p \cdot i\,, \tag{3}$$

where:

p – the effective step of the longwall shearer [m],
i – the number of working cycles of the longwall shearer [1/d].

In case of the mining process modelling, the variability of the longwall advance should be taken into account. For example, by determining the range of variation (from − to) or assuming the distribution function of a random variable with specified parameters. Normal distribution or others can be used sufficiently describing historical data obtained about the longwall advance of similar excavation performed in the past. The variability of the longwall advance is linked to the conditions of uncertainty and risk arising primarily from the risks characterizing the excavation and the actual situation (not known in 100% before the start of works) at the place of operation.

An important element in the mining process model is the arrangement of longwalls. The longwalls carried out in the mine are also related to certain time dependencies. They may arise from the use of the same equipment in subsequent excavations or from territorial affiliation of individual longwall panels (exploitation area). It is, therefore, important to determine the dates for the planned longwalls or to indicate the start of the operation arbitrarily.

Frequently, the start of operations in the first longwalls of each exploitation area is strictly defined, due to the need to maintain continuity of production at the mine, while other longwalls run later in sequence. In case of prospective exploitation areas, these dates are not specified and the modelling process might take place in terms of smaller constraints, which will positively influence the process of finding the best solution. The dates can be determined within the optimisation algorithm calculation stage

When using the same equipment in subsequent longwalls, the next longwall has to wait for the end of operation in preceding excavation.

Hence, the need arises to identify time dependencies between the longwalls. This identification could be done by indication and definition of the so-called production lines, within which suitable mining operations (reinforcement works, exploitation works, liquidation works) are designed.

The production of a multi-plant mining enterprise is a derivative of the operation carried out in each coal mine. In this case, production lines must also be defined, and then, their membership in a particular mine must be indicated.

4   Optimisation Criterion for Mining Production Planning

The most commonly used optimisation criteria in designing of mine elements and the mining process are economic, expressed mostly in form of unit costs or other indicators expressed in monetary units (i.e., NPV).

It should be emphasized that the development of economic values is a derivative of the intensity of mining operations in mining enterprise (involving the costs of resource consumption) giving the product, which is a source of revenue.

The main source of production for a mine are exploitation works carried out in the longwalls, hence, further considerations will apply to this type of work.

The following optimisation criterion was formulated:

$$W = \sqrt{\sum_{i=1}^{lo} (WSR_i - WPLAN_i)^2} \rightarrow \min, \qquad (4)$$

where:

WSR_i – the average value of the net output in a mine (or group of mines) in i-th month [Mg/month].

$WPLAN_i$ – the planned volume of the net output in i-th month [Mg/month].

The proposed criterion allows for the best solution to be found in the conduct of mining operations that will ensure the achievement of the production plan of the mine or mining enterprise. This criterion can be used by those responsible for the execution of the production plan and the persons responsible for the implementation of long-term contracts for supply of coal, whose failure may have certain financial implications to the economic entity (including penalties).

After determining a set of solutions (variants), the most appropriate should be chosen using a selected technique (or techniques) of optimisation. The developed criterion allows to select an optimal configuration of longwalls and equipment that will ensure the planned production is achieved (with some possible deviation).

In a multi-plant mining enterprise, the planned number of longwalls and the capabilities to equip them lead to a large number of variants (even up to tens of millions). Hence, to find a solution, the usage of an evolutionary algorithm presented in [5] is proposed. The algorithm that has been developed, is based on evolutionary programming with elite selection. The main settings of the optimisation algorithm include:

- size of the basic population,
- size of the parental population,
- size of the elite,
- the number of the algorithm iterations (generations).

The stop condition for the algorithm is the lack of significant improvements in the best individual for a predetermined number of iterations.

5 OPTiCoalMine Calculation Service

The current version of the service (Java application [32]) is implemented in the GridSpace2 Virtual Laboratory [10], [16] and shared on the server in ACC Cyfronet AGH.

The GridSpace2 environment, developed in scope of the Polish National Grid Initiative (PL-Grid), is a comprehensive platform, which supports all phases of developing and sharing computational science experiments. GridSpace2 enables a scientist to take advantage of large-scale distributed computing and storage [9].

The main element of the GridSpace2 structure is the Experiment Workbench. The Workbench provides developers with their own research space on a dedicated server (Experiment Host), where experiments can be executed in context of an individual user account. On this server, input files can be stored along with computational results. If necessary, the Experiment Host can delegate the execution of computations to an underlying HPC resource using mechanism such as PBS queues [9].

The access to the calculation service (OPTiCoalMine) is provided by a web platform based on novel mechanism for publishing experiment results, called Collage View (see Fig. 5).

Fig. 5. Calculation service OPTiCoalMine – Collage View implementation

The experiment consists of the following assets:

- input assets,
- code snippets,
- output assets.

The input file (.xml type) consists of the following sections (see Fig. 6):

- "sciany", where parameters of the longwalls are given,
- "ciagi", where production lines are defined and time dependencies are given,
- "zestawy", where longwall sets are given,
- "mws", where possible arrangement of equipment to the planned longwalls is defined (probability of allocation),

- "mps" and "mos" where the parameters of the distribution function of the longwall advance (in each longwall with a defined longwall set) are given (normal distribution of the longwall advance was assumed, therefore, in the "mps" section, the average values of distribution and, in "mos" section, the standard deviations of distribution are introduced).

```
<?xml version="1.0"?>
- <kopalnia>
    + <sciany>
    + <ciagi>
    + <zestawy>
    + <mws>
    + <mps>
    + <mos>
  </kopalnia>
```

Fig. 6. Structure of an .xml file with input data

The input file and the executable application (the JAR file) are stored in a local directory of the service user group (group plgggigi). A code snippet runs the application in the Java virtual machine. The execution of the computations is delegated to **zeus.cyfronet.pl** using the PBS queues mechanism by running an interpreter named "Bash 3.2 via PBS Interactive". After completion of the calculations, the output file (in the .xml format) is generated.

The main elements of the output assets are the output file (see Fig. 7) and the chart (see Fig. 8).

```
<?xml version="1.0" encoding="UTF-8" standalone="true"?>
- <worksPlans>
    - <plan index="1">
        + <productionSeriesList>
          <startTime>2012-01-01</startTime>
          <monthlyOutput>1479977,1039340,947784,938728,1179121,
        </plan>
  </worksPlans>
```

Fig. 7. File structure with experiment results

The output file consists of the following sections:

- the plan index,
- list of the production lines with equipment assigned to the longwalls and the average values of the longwalls' advance [m/d] – calculated on the basis of the performed simulations,
- the date of the beginning of the analysed period (the default analysed period is 24 months),
- the estimated net output in analysed period in the coal mine (or group of mines) [Mg/month].

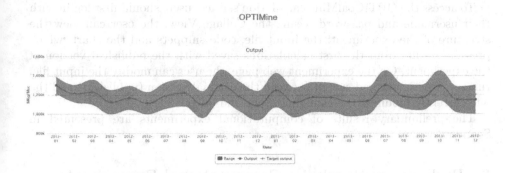

Fig. 8. Output chart for the chosen solution

A chart (based on the output file) is generated with use of the Highcharts library and a prepared application (so-called opener) installed on the machine `gs2.plgrid.pl`. The opener can also be started from the GridSpace2 Workbench during the experiment preparation. It can open files with an "om.xml" extension.

The current scheme of the interaction between the OPTiCoalMine service and GridSpace2 laboratory is presented in Fig. 9.

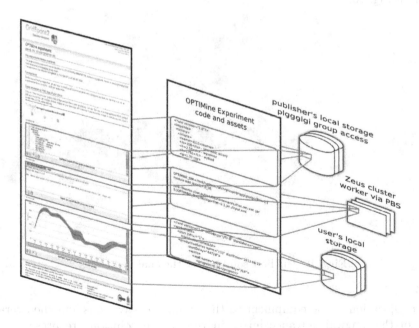

Fig. 9. OPTiCoalMine Service interaction with GridSpace2

To access the OPTiCoalMine calculation service, users should first log in with their username and password. Using the Collage View, the user can view the structure of the experiment: the input file, code snippets and the chart, which presents results from the first calculations saved with the published version of the experiment. On the experiment web page, the user can modify the input file, run the experiment and switch between the original version (published) and the one currently modified (by changing input and output files).

The preliminary results of computational experiments are presented in Section 6.

6   Preliminary Results of Computational Experiments

For the purpose of the service testing, sample data sets (cases), which differ in the degree of complexity of the formulated optimisation problem, have been prepared.

One of the cases concerned a group of four mines, in which 48 excavations were planned in 14 production lines. The possible equipment allocation for the planned excavations is shown in Table 1.

As a result of the calculations, the best solution was found. For this solution, the volume of production in the analysed period with a possible deviation is shown in Fig. 10.

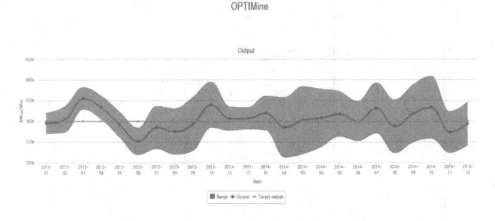

Fig. 10. The best solution for the analysed case

The allocation of the equipment to the planned excavations and the average value of the longwall advance [m/d] in the chosen solution are presented in Table 2.

The prepared data sets and the results obtained drew the author attention to the need for further improvements in the calculation algorithm. Especially, in terms of introducing the possibility of determining the dates of operation start in

Table 1. Possible equipment allocation for the planned excavations

Excavation/longwall set	Z1	Z2	Z3	Z4	Z5	Z6	Z7	Z8	Z9	Z10	Z11	Z12	Z13	Z14	Z15
101	0,2	0,2	0,2	0,2	0,2										
102		0,4	0,4	0,2											
103		0,4							0,6						
104							0,7								0,3
105		0,5					0,5								
106	0,1	0,1	0,1	0,1			0,1	0,1	0,1	0,1	0,1			0,1	
107						0,8							0,2		
108											0,2	0,2	0,4	0,2	
109								0,4					0,6		
201							0,7				0,3				
202				0,7			0,3								
203		0,5					0,5								
204	0,5				0,4	0,1									
205	0,1				0,1		0,3		0,1		0,2				0,2
206			0,2		0,2								0,6		
207		0,3					0,3				0,2			0,2	
208				0,7										0,3	
209						0,7								0,3	
301		0,5					0,5								
302	0,1	0,1	0,1	0,1			0,1	0,1	0,1	0,1	0,1			0,1	
303							0,8						0,2		
304											0,2	0,2	0,4	0,2	
305													0,4		0,6
306			0,3		0,5		0,1						0,1		
307						0,8							0,2		
308											0,2	0,2	0,4	0,2	
309													0,4		0,6
310				0,4				0,5			0,1				
311			0,2		0,2						0,6				
312						1									
313						0,4					0,2			0,4	
314						0,7									0,3
315		0,5					0,5								
401	0,1	0,1	0,1	0,1			0,1	0,1	0,1	0,1	0,1			0,1	
402											0,8		0,2		
403											0,2	0,2	0,4	0,2	
404									0,4						0,6
405											1				
406			0,2		0,2						0,6				
407		0,3					0,3				0,2	0,2			
408				0,7										0,3	
409							0,7								0,3
410		0,5					0,5								
411	0,1	0,1	0,1	0,1			0,1	0,1	0,1	0,1	0,1			0,1	
412					1										
413							0,7				0,3				
414					0,5						0,2	0,3			
415			0,2					0,2			0,2			0,4	

Table 2. Equipment allocation for the planned excavations in the best solution

Exc.	Longwall set	Longwall advance [m/d]	Exc.	Longwall set	Longwall advance [m/d]	Exc.	Longwall set	Longwall advance [m/d]	Exc.	Longwall set	Longwall advance [m/d]
101	Z3	8,96	204	Z1	2,94	307	Z13	3,31	404	Z9	3,64
102	Z4	7,15	205	Z1	6,41	308	Z13	5,54	405	Z12	4,93
103	Z10	4,37	206	Z3	3,29	309	Z12	5,91	406	Z12	3,46
104	Z15	2,6	207	Z14	3,99	310	Z4	4,32	407	Z12	4,88
105	Z7	3,19	208	Z14	6,58	311	Z12	4,75	408	Z4	4,89
106	Z4	4,87	209	Z14	5,97	312	Z6	3,32	409	Z15	4,15
107	Z6	3,09	301	Z2	6,66	313	Z6	4,19	410	Z2	4,76
108	Z13	4,52	302	Z11	6,45	314	Z15	2,77	411	Z8	3,92
109	Z9	8,47	303	Z13	3,38	315	Z6	3,28	412	Z5	3,85
201	Z11	5,41	304	Z13	4,98	401	Z11	4,58	413	Z11	5,23
202	Z8	5,49	305	Z13	7,42	402	Z11	2,43	414	Z11	2,91
203	Z8	7	306	Z7	8,36	403	Z11	3,86	415	Z9	5,41

the production lines, to avoid simultaneous execution of the reinforcement and liquidation works in several production lines, which results in reduced production volume.

7   Conclusions

The main purpose of the presented calculation service, OPTiCoalMine, is to support the process of modelling and optimisation of production in a coal mine (or group of mines) where underground mining method with longwall system is used. The calculation service could be used for evaluation of design solutions (including the uncertainty aspect of the mining process) in terms of:

- proposals of deposit cut,
- determining the order of the production lines,
- equipment selection for the planned excavations.

The OPTiCoalMine calculation service and its implementation on the Grid-Space2 platform within the PLGrid Plus project, allow access to advanced models and numerical simulations for scientists and researchers associated with planning of mining production.

In earlier research on the formulated optimisation problem, an application written in C# was used, which was run on a PC and the available servers. The experiments conducted were very time-consuming, depending on settings of the evolutionary algorithm parameters, and, in some cases, they exceeded the available computing power – which led to the experiments proving unsuccessful.

It should be emphasized, that the tools available within the PLGrid Plus project (calculation services, GridSpace2) and shared computing resources (much needed for complex research problems) allow researchers (distributed in different scientific centers) to model real, complex processes.

The OPTiCoalMine calculation service will be available to scientists after completion of the implementation procedure. Further works on the calculation service development will be aimed at extending the available working scenarios and at visualization of the results of the experiments.

Acknowledgements. The author would like to thank Mr. Bartosz Wilk and the GridSpace2 team for help in preparing the description and drawings related to the implementation of the OPTiCoalMine service on the GridSpace2 platform, and Mr. Tomasz Pędziwiatr for the programmatic implementation of the OPTiCoalMine service idea.

References

1. Abdel Sabour, S.A.: Mine size optimization using marginal analysis. Resources Policy 28, 145–151 (2002)
2. Barbaro, R., Ramani, R.: Generalized multiperiod MIP model for production scheduling and processing facilities selection and location. Mining Engineering 38(2), 107–114 (1986)
3. Brazil, M., Lee, D.H., Van Leuven, M., Rubinstein, J.H., Thomas, D.A., Wormald, N.C.: Optimising declines in underground mines. Mining Technology: IMM Trans. Sect. A 112(3), A164–A170 (2003)
4. Brazil, M., Thomas, D.A.: Network optimization for the design of underground mines. Networks 49(1), 40–50 (2007)
5. Edyta, B.: A New Solution Supporting the Designing Process of Mining Operations in Underground Coal Mines. In: Drebenstedt, C., Singhal, R. (eds.) Mine Planning and Equipment Selection, pp. 53–63. Springer, Heidelberg (2014)
6. Brzychczy, E.: The planning optimization system for underground hard coal mines. Archives of Mining Sciences 56(2), 161–178 (2011)
7. Carlyle, W.M., Eaves, B.C.: Underground planning at Stillwater Mining Company. Interfaces 31(4), 50–60 (2001)
8. Chanda, E.K.C.: An application of integer programming and simulation to production planning for a stratiform ore body. Mining Sci. Tech. 11(2), 165–172 (1990)
9. Ciepiela, E., Nowakowski, P., Kocot, J., Harężlak, D., Gubała, T., Meizner, J., Kasztelnik, M., Bartyński, T., Malawski, M., Bubak, M.: Managing Entire Lifecycles of e-Science Applications in the GridSpace2 Virtual Laboratory – From Motivation through Idea to Operable Web-Accessible Environment Built on Top of PL-Grid e-Infrastructure. In: Bubak, M., Szepieniec, T., Wiatr, K. (eds.) PL-Grid 2011. LNCS, vol. 7136, pp. 228–239. Springer, Heidelberg (2012)
10. Ciepiela, E., Zaraska, L., Sulka, G.D.: GridSpace2 Virtual Laboratory Case Study: Implementation of Algorithms for Quantitative Analysis of Grain Morphology in Self-assembled Hexagonal Lattices According to the Hillebrand Method. In: Bubak, M., Szepieniec, T., Wiatr, K. (eds.) PL-Grid 2011. LNCS, vol. 7136, pp. 240–251. Springer, Heidelberg (2012)
11. Dornetto, L.D.: An adaptive control scheme – expert system – that optimizes the operation of a proposed underground coal mining system with applications to shortwall, longwall and room pillar mining systems. In: Proc. IEEE Internat. Conf. Systems Man, Cybernetics, pp. 209–214. International Academic Publishers, Pergamon Press, Beijing (1988)

12. Epstein, R., Gaete, S., Caro, F., Weintraub, A., Santibanez, P., Catalan, J.: Optimizing long term planning for underground copper mines. In: Proc. Copper 2003-Cobre 2003, 5th Internat. Conf., Santiago, Chile, vol. I, pp. 265–279. CIM and the Chilean Institute of Mining (2003)
13. Fava, L., Millar, D., Maybee, B.: Scenario evaluation through mine schedule optimisation. In: Kuyvenhoven, R., Rubio, E., Smith, M. (eds.) Proceedings of the 2nd International Seminar on Mine Planning, Gecamin, Santiago, Chile, pp. 1–10 (2011)
14. Gamache, M., Grimard, R., Cohen, P.: A shortest-path algorithm for solving the fleet management problem in underground mines. Eur. J. Oper. Res. 166(2), 497–506 (2005)
15. Grieco, N., Dimitrakopoulos, R.: Managing grade risk in stope design optimization: Probabilistic mathematical programming model and application in sublevel stoping. Mining Techology: IMM Trans. Sect. A 116(2), 49–57 (2007)
16. Harężlak, D., Kasztelnik, M., Ciepiela, E., Bubak, M.: Scripting Language Extensions Offered by the GridSpace Experiment Platform. In: Bubak, M., Szepieniec, T., Wiatr, K. (eds.) PL-Grid 2011. LNCS, vol. 7136, pp. 217–227. Springer, Heidelberg (2012)
17. Huang, Y., Kumar, U.: Optimizing the number of load-hauldump machines in a Swedish mine by using queuing theory – A case study. Internat. J. Surface Mining Reclamation Environ. 8(4), 171–174 (1994)
18. Jawed, M.: Optimal production planning in underground coal mines through goal programming: A case study from an Indian mine. In: Elbrond, J., Tang, X. (eds.) Proc. 24th Internat. Appl. Comput. Oper. Res. Mineral Indust (APCOM) Sympos., pp. 44–50. CIM, Montréal (1993)
19. Kumral, M.: Optimal location of a mine facility by genetic algorithms. Mining Technology: IMM Trans. Sect. A 113(2), 83–88 (2004)
20. Kumral, M.: Reliability-based optimisation of a mine production system using genetic algorithms. J. Loss Prevention Process Indust. 18(3), 186–189 (2005)
21. Lemelin, B., Abdel Sabour, S.A., Poulin, R.: An integrated evaluation system for mine planning under uncertainty. In: Magri, E. (ed.) Proc. 33rd Internat. Appl. Comput. Oper. Res. Mineral Indust (APCOM) Sympos., Santiago, pp. 262–269 (2007)
22. Li, Z., Topuz, E.: Optimizing design capacity and field dimensions of under-ground coal mines. In: Proc. 20th Internat. Appl. Comp. Math. Mineral Indust (APCOM) Sympos. Mining, vol. I, pp. 115–122. SAIMM, Johannesburg (1987)
23. Lizotte, Y., Elbrond, J.: Optimal layout of underground mining levels. CIM Bulletin 78(873), 41–48 (1985)
24. Magda, R., Franik, T.: Planning and design of rational parameters of longwall panels in underground hard coal mines. Mineral Resources Management 24(4), 107–117 (2008)
25. Magda, R.: Mathematical model for estimating the economic effectiveness of production process in coal panels and an example of its practical application. Internat. J. Prod. Econom. 34(1), 47–55 (1994)
26. McNearny, R., Nie, Z.: Simulation of a conveyor belt network at an under-ground coal mine. Mineral Resources Engineering 9(3), 343–355 (2000)
27. Miladinovic, M., Cebasek, V., Gojkovic, N.: Computer programs for design and modelling in mining. Underground Mining Engineering 19, 109–124 (2011)

28. Mutagwaba, W., Hudson, J.: Use of object-oriented simulation model to assess operating and equipment options for underground mine transport system. Mining Technology: IMM Trans. Sect. A 102, 89–94 (1993)
29. Newman, A., Kuchta, M.: Using aggregation to optimize long-term production planning at an underground mine. Eur. J. Oper. Res. 176(2), 1205–1218 (2007)
30. Newman, A., Rubio, E., Caro, R., Weintarub, A., Eurek, K.: A review of operations research in mine planning. Interfaces 40(3), 222–245 (2010)
31. Pendharkar, P.C., Rodger, J.A.: Nonlinear programming and genetic search application for production scheduling in coal mines. Ann. Oper. Res. 95(1-4), 251–267 (2000)
32. Pędziwiatr, T.: OPTiCoalMine calculation service: Source code. ACC Cyfronet AGH, Kraków (2014)
33. Qinglin, C., Stillborg, B., Li, C.: Optimization of underground mining methods using grey theory and neural networks. In: Hennies, W., Ayres da Silva, L., Chaves, A. (eds.) 5th Internat. Sympos. Mine Planning Equipment Selection MPES, pp. 393–398, Sao Paulo (1996)
34. Rahal, D., Smith, M., Van Hout, G., Von Johannides, A.: The use of mixed integer linear programming for long-term scheduling in block caving mines. In: Camisani-Calzolari, F. (ed.) Proc 31st Internat. Appl. Comput. Oper. Res. Mineral Indust (APCOM) Sympos., pp. 123–131. SAIMM, Cape Town (2003)
35. Sarin, S.C., West-Hansen, J.: The long-term mine production scheduling problem. IIE Trans. 37(2), 109–121 (2005)
36. Simsir, F., Ozfirat, M.K.: Determination of the most effective longwall equipment combination in longwall top coal caving (LTCC) method by simulation modeling. Internat. J. Rock Mech. Mining Sci. 45(6), 1015–1023 (2008)
37. Smith, M., Sheppard, I., Karunatillake, G.: Using MIP for strategic life-of-mine planning of the lead/zinc stream at Mount Isa Mines. In: Camisani-Calzolari, F. (ed.) Proc. 31st Internat. Appl. Comput. Oper. Res. Mineral Indust (APCOM) Sympos., pp. 465–474. SAIMM, Cape Town (2003)
38. Snopkowski, R.: Longwall output plan considered in probability aspect. Arch. Min. Sci. 47(3), 413–420 (2002)
39. Topuz, E., Breeds, C., Karmis, M., Haycocks, C.: Comparison of two under-ground haulage systems. In: Proc. 17th Internat. Appl. Comput. Oper. Res. Mineral Indust (APCOM) Sympos., pp. 614–619. SME, Littleton (1982)
40. Topuz, E., Duan, C.: A survey of operations research applications in the mining industry. CIM Bulletin 82(925), 48–50 (1989)
41. Trout, L.: Underground mine production scheduling using mixed integer programming. In: Proc. 25th Internat. Appl. Comput. Oper. Res. Mineral Indust. (APCOM) Sympos., pp. 395–400. AusIMM (1995)
42. Winkler, B.: System for quality oriented mine production planning with MOLP. In: Proc. 27th Internat. Appl. Comput. Oper. Res. Mineral Indust (APCOM) Sympos., pp. 53–59. Royal School of Mines, London (1998)
43. Yun, Q., Liu, J., Chen, Y., Huang, G.: Optimization of planning and design in underground mines. In: Proc. 22nd Internat. Appl. Comput. Oper. Res. Mineral Indust (APCOM) Sympos., Berlin, pp. 255–260 (1990)
44. Zhang, H., Zhao, G.: CMEOC – An expert system in the coal mining industry. Expert Systems with Applications 16(1), 73–77 (1999)
45. British Petroleum: BP Energy Outlook 2030 (2013)
46. British Petroleum: Statistical Review of World Energy 2013 (2013)

47. World Coal Association: Coal Facts 2012 (2013)
48. Bentley Systems Inc., http://www.bentley.com
49. CAE Datamine International Ltd., http://www.cae.com
50. Dassault Systémes GEOVIA Ltd., http://www.gemcomsoftware.com
51. Maptec Pty Ltd., http://www.maptek.com
52. Micromine, http://www.micromine.com
53. Minemax, http://www.minemax.com
54. Mintec Inc., http://www.minesight.com
55. RockWare Inc., http://www.rockware.com
56. Teberia Magazine, http://www.teberia.pl

Automatic Monitoring as a Tool for Collection of Information on Fitophenological Cycle

Przemysław Mager[1], Małgorzata Kępińska-Kasprzak[1], Norbert Meyer[2],
Szymon Mueller[2], Dominik Stokłosa[2], Wanda Wójtowicz[3],
and Joanna Jaskulska[3]

[1] Institute of Meteorology and Water Management –
National Research Institute, ul. Dąbrowskiego 174/176, 60-594 Poznań, Poland
{przemyslaw.mager,malgorzata.kepinska-kasprzak}@imgw.pl
[2] Poznan Supercomputing and Networking Center,
ul. Noskowskiego 10, 61-704 Poznań, Poland
{meyer,szymon.mueller,d.stoklosa}@man.poznan.pl
[3] Adam Mickiewicz University Botanical Garden in Poznań,
ul. Dąbrowskiego 165, 60-594 Poznań, Poland
{w.wojtow,indexsem}@amu.edu.pl

Abstract. Study of cyclical biological phenomena influenced by the environment, weather and climate conditions is called phenology. Source of scientific phenological data comes from continuous observations. Performing observations by scientists is often unfeasible due to time and physical constraints. Automated Monitoring project aims at providing users with remote access to elements installed in the observation site: weather monitoring sensors and camera mounted on a turn-plate. User portal allows phenology scientists to choose monitored scenes, schedule repeatable data collection tasks and providing useful description of observed plants and current phenology phase. Other portal components allow to view charts as well as to export weather data and collected phenology photos.

Keywords: environmental education, phenology, remote instrumentation, virtual laboratory, automatic monitoring, remote camera.

1 Introduction

Phenology is an interdisciplinary study of dynamic seasonal life processes of organisms, which are mainly driven by changes of weather and climate conditions [14]. It comprises two research fields: plant phenology, i.e., fitophenology and animal phenology, i.e., zoophenology. Phenological research, as one of the tools for identification of cyclical changes in the environment, is not only of interest to life sciences specialists, but it also provides practical benefits. Phenological research records dynamics of changes occurring in plant and animal worlds, allows to study relationships between living organisms and their habitat, contributes essential information on the diversity of geographic environments and

M. Bubak et al. (Eds.): PLGrid Plus, LNCS 8500, pp. 335–350, 2014.

is useful for determination of site index (SI) of tree stands in forestry, while, in agriculture, it allows to determine and to predict the time of successive life cycle events of crops and to forecast harvesting dates, etc. The results of phenological observations play an important role in climate change investigation, since, which is worth emphasizing, plants exhibit complex response to weather conditions and climate change, i.e., rather than triggered by a single element, e.g. temperature, plants' reaction is set off by all components of climate as a system.

A fundamental part of fitophenology is field research of particular plant species, which, in further process, can be used to determine phenological dynamics of larger plant communities, i.e., populations and biocoenosis [14]. The knowledge of the start dates of successive phenological stages is the basis for determination of dates of phenological seasons. Already in 1895, Egon Ihne, a German naturalist from the Darmstadt University, proposed to distinguish seven seasons (pre-spring, early spring, spring, early summer, summer, early autumn, autumn) in Central Europe. The "measurement instruments", which allowed to separate these seasons, were living organisms (plants and animals). The basic principles of this division, which underwent several modifications over the years, are still applied in the present-day.

In Poland, the idea to distinguish phenological seasons found its support- ers as early as in the 1920s. In 1922, Szafer, a distinguished botanist, pub- lished "Phenological seasons in Poland" in the Polish Naturalist Journal [34]. After the World War II, Polish botanists commenced research initially based on Lastowski [24,25] for the needs of agriculture. The research included recording clearly distinguished phases, i.e., periodical recurrence of annual phenomena of plants life cycle such as opening of leaf buds, flowering, foliation, ripening and falling of fruit and seed, leaf coloration and falling. In the years that followed, the selection of reference species for phenological observations was successively modified and augmented by natural plant stands [21] hence giving the research a more universal scope [10], [26]. For example, Adam Mickiewicz University Botan- ical Garden in Poznań (Poland) conducted a 50-year long research [11]. In the 1940s, the Institute of Meteorology and Water Management created a relatively dense network of over 600 phenological observatories. Their observations were recorded, studied and published in "Phenological Annual Review" up to 1960. In later years, the network was systematically reduced and in 1992, the observations were suspended.

As phenological observations require long-term study of the same reference objects in possibly unchanging environmental conditions, it is increasingly more difficult to conduct them according to the guidelines developed several decades ago. However, naturalists and climatologist still highly value phenology as an important field of knowledge [32]. Indications of "sensitive measurement plant instruments" used to describe plant development within a timeline of phenolo- gical seasons are valuable for inferring the trends and consequences of changes of climate conditions. In a short or long perspective, this knowledge will al- low to forecast trends of transformations in both agriculture and natural plant communities.

Simultaneous analysis of climate factors and plant development provides better understanding of directional climate changes and their impact on plants. For this reason, in the recent years, a growing interest in phenology has been observed, also due to the recognition by the Intergovernmental Panel on Climate Change (IPCC), as one of the most responsive traits to climate change in nature [6]. Recently, there have been many works of authors who studied responses of plants to the continuing increasing trend of air temperature [1], [5], [20], [23], [32,33].

Given the knowledge, practical values and importance of phenological observations, and considering the insufficient number of such observations, a project has been initiated within PLGrid Plus, whose aim is to provide an automatic monitoring system for fitophenological observations. Equipment required by the system has been installed in the observation site in the Wielkopolska National Park and IT system has been created, allowing for remote communication and interaction with observation instruments (a camera, a turn-plate and a weather station). Scientific users are able to schedule cyclic executions of data gathering (weather parameters, photographs) by using a provided user portal customized for phenology observations. All the gathered data can be further accessed by the registered PL-Grid Infrastructure users ranging from biology and phenology scientists, teachers, students to homegrown enthusiasts.

2   State of the Art

The history of phenological observation began decades, and in some regions even hundreds years ago. One of the largest European sources concerning the phenological observation is Plant Phenological Online Database (PPODB). It contains over 16 million observations conducted in years 1880-2009 at over 8000 stations in Central Europe, located mostly in Germany. The majority of PPODB material originates from the Deutsche Wetterdienst resources [8]. The creation of this type of database requires most importantly precise daily field observations carried out according to a standardized protocol by properly trained observers. However, this type of observation is relatively labor intensive and costly. Another disadvantage of this system is also its tendency to discontinuity [19].

The solution that quite successfully removes these inconveniences is the possibility to use satellite products to assess plant status. Presently, the development of satellite-based methods allows to achieve reasonably high resolution images for large areas and at a relatively low cost. Satellite remote sensing provides spatially extensive information, from which signals of green-up and senescence can be extracted, for example. However, satellite images require validation based on the surface measurements and the correlation between these two types of data is very often low. Another weakness of satellite data is also a periodical lack of data, for example, due to clouds. A considerable limitation in satellite product use in phenology is the impossibility to gather information on particular individual plants.

In the recent years, an attempt to find indirect solutions has resulted in the increasingly popular "near-surface" remote sensing, which offers a range of applications in phenological observations. Digital cameras can provide very high spatial and temporal resolutions. Depending on the installation site (towers, platforms, tripods, etc.), they enable the observation of entire plant communities as well as selected parts of plants. One of the earliest observations of phenological phases using this system was implemented in agriculture. The observations performed using digital cameras allow to receive and collect low-cost images, which can be analysed on an ongoing basis or stored for a later use. Recently, also due to the reasonable pricing of photographic equipment, phenological observations using photography are becoming increasingly common. Most of the projects using digital cameras for phenological observations consist of three basic phases: 1) taking pictures at specified frequency (hourly, daily, etc.) and resolution (field, canopy or its part), 2) transferring images to database, 3) analysis of images (type of analysis depends on particulars and aims of a given project).

System of repeat photography can deliver stream of information on emergence of successive phenophases as noted by [6], among others. Repeat photography combined with meteorological observations carried out at the site of phenological photographing provides an opportunity to acquire in-depth knowledge and to understand the intricate relationships between natural conditions and phenological phenomena. An additional advantage of this method is the fact that the observation results include numerical data, which can be further processed mathematically (for example red-green-blue (RGB) color channel information can be separately extracted from digital images as digital numbers). The authors of one of the projects conducted observations using digital camera in Tuscon (USA). The images were then used, e.g., to calculate the "greenness" index as the sum of the differences between the blue and red bands from the green band. It was pointed out that capturing phenologic events and changes by repeat photography offers great opportunities for engaging and educating scientists as well as the general public.

Similar conclusions were reached by Ahrends et al. [2] who identified leaf emergence based on red, green and blue color analysis from the images of mixed beech forest, taken by digital camera located on a flux tower at Lägeren (Switzerland). They concluded that digital cameras could provide spatially representative and objective information with the required temporal resolution for phenological studies.

Gu et al. [13] used data from the analysis of digital images as the input data for the development of model of total VFC (Vegetation fractional coverage) for subtropical forest in Nanjing (China). Bater et al. [3] used ground-based cameras to monitor vegetation in western Alberta (Canada) to demonstrate that specific understorey and overstorey species can be targeted for phenological monitoring in a forested environment, using RGB-based vegetation indices. Sonnentag et al. [31] studied changes of forest canopy using red-green-blue color channel information. The cameras installed in Harvard Forest allowed to collect data for calculation of two indices: excess green (ExG) and green chromatic coordinate (gcc). The results showed that the choice of camera or file format is of minor importance to the quality of the obtained data. Both indicators showed relatively high degree of accordance, especially at identifying end of senescence, however gcc index gave slightly better results.

Zhao et al. [36] introduced, beside greenness index derived from digital cameras, also redness index, which, according to them, was more accurate when estimating leaf senescence while greenness index was superior for estimating leaf development events. However, the authors pointed out that further study was required for the application of this index for a longer period of time and a larger number of species.

Digital cameras are also used for broader analyses. One of the examples includes the installation of standard commercial webcam on the existing flux tower in Bartlett Experimental Forest (USA) by Richardson and Jenkins [30]. The instrument registered the state of canopy each day in order to determine relationships between the canopy structure and the seasonal dynamics of CO2. The authors analysed the changes of relative brightness of the green channel (green %) against the changes in the fraction of incident photosynthetically active radiation that is absorbed by the canopy (fAPAR), a broadband normalized difference vegetation index (NDVI), and the light-saturated rate of canopy photosynthesis (Amax), inferred from eddy flux measurements. In 2009, Richardson and his team [29] published the results of their further investigation based on red, green and blue channels connecting them with the seasonal patterns of gross primary productivity inferred from eddy covariance measurements of surface-atmosphere CO2 exchange.

An example of the use of automated phenological observation for the needs of agriculture was given by Yu et al. [35]. The authors note that there is only a handful of works aimed at the observation of different growth stages of field crops using digital cameras. Yu and his team carried out observation of crop on two different experimental fields in Shandong Province (China) using digital cameras for automated detection of two critical growth stages of maize – emergence and three-leaf stage. The results of the applied analysis method were compared to the observations conducted by a human observer during the same time period. Dates of appearance of specified growth stages determined by automated observation were similar to those indicated by the human observer. The authors proposed that automated methods could successfully fulfill the tasks of phenological observations for the needs of agriculture and farmers.

Ide and Oguma [17] presented results of the analysis of RGB channels used not only for determination of vegetation index (green ratio), but also for detection of snow-cover areas in Japanese Alps. In their earlier work [16], the authors demonstrated the results of analyses of daily images taken by digital cameras installed in national parks in Japan during 8-year long observation period. The calculated vegetation green excess index showed not only phenological patterns of each vegetation type in each year, but also enabled to identify physiological damage caused by typhoons.

A slightly different approach was presented by Graham et al. [12] who used a mobile camera system for calculating leaf area during leaf flush of Rhododendron occidentale in the understory along a 30 m transect. According to Graham and his team, the images from a single viewpoint could not provide complete information in case of a dynamic increase of leaf area. The authors noted that the utility of mobility of sensors had been newly recognized by ecologists and had been included in the designs of new classes of environmental observatories.

Bradley et al. [4] stated that there are many examples of working online cameras, which produce good quality images, but there are no image archives or support for their detailed analysis. In their paper, the authors presented a web site, which provided an application for the archiving and analysis of images from weather cameras. Meteorological stations, presented by the authors, were located in the region of Santa Barbara (California) and were equipped in instruments measuring air temperature and humidity, rainfall, wind speed and direction, solar radiation and leaf wetness. Additionally, such a weather station was also equipped in CC640 digital camera for use in harsh environments (operating temperature is from -40°C to +70°C). The authors emphasize that dynamic web site is an effective and useful tool for both scientific and educational purposes.

Automated phenological observations were also carried out within the IN-CREASE project (An Integrated Network of Climate Research Activities on Shrubland Ecosystems) realized within the FP7 [19] in 2009-2013. One of the project tasks was to design and to start the operation of Automated Phenological Observation System (APOS) using standard, commercially available cameras connected to an automated robotic system. The system was tested in several locations, e.g. in Porto Conte region (Italy) dominated by Mediterranean scrubland species and herbaceous plants.

The above literature review indicates that automated observation fulfills all requirements of phenological observations and while being less time-consuming and costly, it provides the necessary information on, for example, emergence of successive phenological phases. An additional advantage of this method is the possibility to store the images for future reference in archives, thus providing opportunity to carry out analyses with the accuracy to answer other questions in years to come.

An automated phenology observation project requires multidisciplinary knowledge. Physical components of the project (a camera, a turn-plate, microcontrollers) need to be assembled and modified for phenology use case, which requires expertise in engineering and electronics. Implementation of a complex system, which will allow accessing the instruments remotely and storing the data generated by them, as well as that of a portal providing users with control over remote components and tools for accessing phenology data, is a task for IT specialists. The functionality of the proposed solutions must be verified by scientists actively involved in phenology observations.

Remote instrumentation and Internet of Things (IoT) are emerging technologies in the past years as signaled in [9]. Nowadays, sensors are everywhere around us: from home appliances, TVs, cars to sensors integrated in smartphones (sounds, video/photo cameras, temperature, acceleration). Attempts to provide remote control for specialized scientific equipment and even their integration with storage and computational services of e-Infrastructure have been made, as described by Davoli et al. [7]. Data gathered by e.g. floats and gliders were used to monitor and to model chemical and physical aspects of Mediterranean sea.

One of the challenges is to establish universal access to sensors and to store data generated by them, regardless of their type. Various attempts are being made to provide standardization in IoT and instrumentation fields. One of the most widely used is Open Geospatial Consortium's Sensor Web Enablement [28] (OGC SWE). The entire framework consists of standards, which enable developers to make all types of sensors, transducers and sensor data repositories discoverable, accessible and useable via the Web. Among the components interesting from Automatic Monitoring project's point of view, there are: SensorML, which allows describing sensors in a unified way and Observations & Measurements (O&M), which allows for describing the capabilities and nature of gathered data.

To provide interactions with sensors and collected data, SWE exposes two web interfaces. The first one is a Sensor Observation Service (SOS), and is used for querying the sensor metadata and representations of observed features. It also defines means to register new sensors and to remove existing ones. Furthermore, SOS standard is used to insert and query sensor observations. The second interface, a Sensor Planning Service (SPS), allows for querying about the capabilities of a sensor and how to task the sensor. Moreover, it allows interaction with the sensors: submitting sensor tasks, query about task status, update and cancel tasks. Implementation of the task execution is up to developers, and can range from a simple measurement reading to executing a set of operations with specific configuration parameters.

3   Description of Automatic Monitoring Platform

Plants, compared with animals, are more affected by habitat and weather conditions, therefore they are most commonly chosen for phenology observations. Until now, observations were done in-situ by qualified scientists who describe vegetative and reproductive phases of monitored species. The nature of this kind of approach is more local and requires systematic measurements done by human. Our motivation for the Automatic Monitoring project was to provide scientists with a set of tools and equipment allowing not only to schedule remote, automatic observation tasks, but also provide a platform where all the data can be gathered and accessed by all interested users. Our first task was to choose a location surrounded by various species of plants, relevant from the phenological point of view, and installation of the physical equipment. In a next step a portal has been built, allowing remote control over equipment and providing storage and access capabilities to the users. Detailed solutions are described below.

3.1 Location of Phenological Observation

The site of phenological observations has been located in the central part of the Wielkopolska National Park, 20 km to the south-west from Poznan, a city located on the Warta River in the central west of Poland. The choice of this particular site was determined by the necessity to provide appropriate measures for the protection and operation of the installed equipment (see Fig. 1) as well as the possibility to carry out phenological observations. The location of the observation site is at the edge of a sparsely populated plain area bordering with an agricultural field. The plants selected for the observation grow on a typical soil in the region. The observation location features typical hydrographic conditions for the area. The location of the observed plants is not secluded or shaded, which is an important factor for the maintenance of appropriate conditions for phenological monitoring.

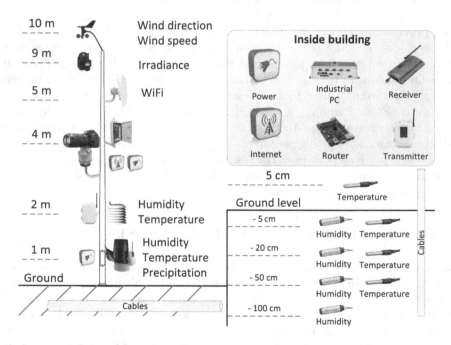

Fig. 1. Installation diagram – represents all components installed at the observation site and monitored parameters

The observed plants grow in a direct vicinity of the observation site. The selected plants are: horse-chestnut (Aesculus hippocastanum), black locust (Robinia pseudoacacia), small-leaved lime (Tilia cordata), dog rose (Rosa canina), European larch (Larix decidua), common lilac (Syringa vulgaris) and a field of crops.

In Poland, modern fitophenological observations are conducted according to the detailed methodology developed by Szennikow and modified by Łukasiewicz [27]. Based on this methodology, the project involves observation of the following plant development stages: beginning of leaf bud opening, beginning of leaf blade emergence, emergence of the first flower or inflorescence buds, emergence of the first flowers, flowering, termination of flowering, beginning of fruit and seed development, beginning of fruit (seed) ripening, termination of fruit (seed) ripening, beginning of fruit (seed) release, termination of fruit (seed) release, the beginning and termination of leaf-fall.

The dynamics of phenological changes in a given area is affected by the total conditions of the environment in the region, however, the most changeable factor is the pattern of weather conditions in a year. For this reason, the analysis and interpretation of the results of fitophenological observation need to include the results of meteorological observations.

3.2 Station Equipment

While considering the equipment of the station, the idea was to select such a set of sensors that would, within the available means, register all those weather elements that affect plant development, i.e., solar radiation, temperature, humidity and rainfall. Therefore, an automatic weather station DAVIS VANTAGE PRO2 has been selected and installed on the site. The station measures the following meteorological elements: barometric pressure (1 m above the ground level), wind speed and wind direction (10 m), solar radiation (9 m), rainfall (1 m), air temperature and relative humidity (1 and 2 m), soil temperature (at depths 5, 20, 50 cm) and soil moisture (5, 20, 50 and 100 cm). In a distance of 80 m from the station, an additional site of precipitation measurements has been installed, i.e., Hellmann rain gauge. At this site, snow cover is also measured during winter.

The analysis of weather conditions of plant growth will also use evapotranspiration values calculated by the meteorological station. Evaporation values are calculated using the Penman-Monteith formula as implemented by California Irrigation Management Information System. Daily precipitation totals (P) and evapotranspiration totals (E) are then used to determine climatic water balance (CWB = P-E).

The species selected for the observation are distributed around the installation site, in various distances. This feature required to use a high quality DSLR camera set on a pan/tilt mount, equipped with telephoto lens, which allows adjusting the zoom and focus settings remotely. A decision has been made to use Nikon D5100 body with Nikkor AF-S 70-300 mm f/4.5-5.6G IF-ED VR lens inside a custom made case (see Fig. 2). To provide zoom and manual focus functionality, a servo mechanism has been added and customized. The contents of the case also include condition sensors (temperature, humidity, dew point), heater as well as controllers and AC. Everything is mounted on a GL-402 pan/tilt turn-plate and, along with weather station components, attached to a 10 m pole.

Fig. 2. Contents of a camera casing: digital camera, servo mechanisms, heater, controller and power cords. Everything is enclosed in weather resistant case.

3.3   Architecture of IT Services and End-User Interfaces

Communication on site is feasible thanks to WiFi coverage. Weather station components connect directly to the network while camera and turn-plate are connected to control computer with internet access. Interaction with components is provided through REST Web Services deployed on a control computer, accessible only from within a secure VPN network. The services are consumed in the next layer of the project architecture – a standardized access to instruments, sensors and observations provided by Open Geospatial Consortium's Sensor Web Enablement. Sensor Planning Service implementation allows describing possible interactions with sensors, scheduling task execution, submitting and modifying tasks as well as checking task status. Data collection tasks (weather parameters or taking photo by a camera) automatically utilize Sensor Observation Service components of access layer, which allows storing and retrieving observation data from the underlying database. For the phenology use case, a special extension of the SOS service has been created, integrating an external data repository with SOS observation data. A special model describing the scene, species, phenology phase and status of photos has also been provided.

Users are not exposed to the access layer directly. A special Liferay [22] portal has been created, extended with phenology-specific portlets, which hides the complexity and OGC communication specific language by providing a graphical user interface with all functionalities. The first group of portlets, operable only by administrators, serve configuration options for the installation (service addresses, settings, etc.). The next group consists of automatic phenology observation settings. Authorized users are able to connect remotely to the

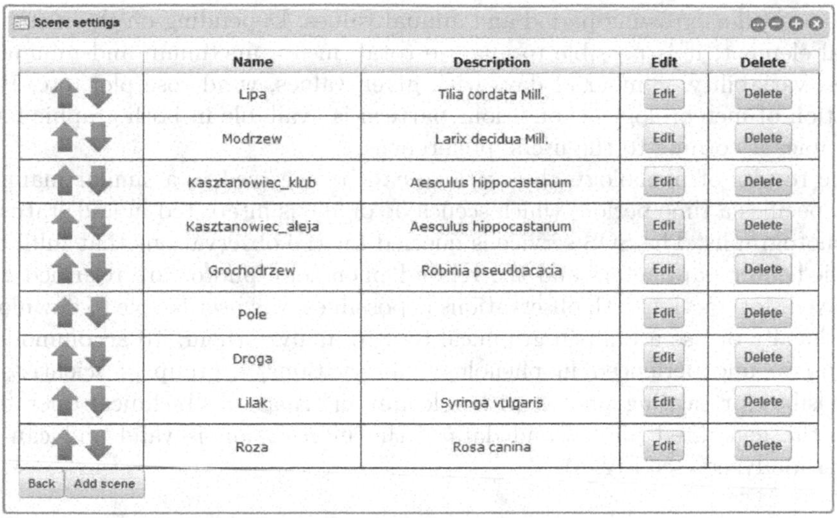

Fig. 3. Scene settings portlet – it allows scientists to manage the existing scenes and add new ones

infrastructure on-site and operate the camera (move to a specified position, move by steps in a selected direction, change the zoom and focus settings) to choose the parameters of the scene. To start periodic observations, the user needs to choose the execution time, specific order and configuration of each scene (see Fig. 3) as well as the period between reading the values from a weather station.

The execution of instrument tasks is handled by the Workflow Manager. At the execution time specified by the user the manager creates an SPS task for a specific instrument (a camera in case of phenology photos or a weather station in case of meteorological readings) with parameters set by the user (e.g. camera position, zoom and focus settings). The task is then submitted to SPS. This service is responsible for the scheduling and running of tasks and makes sure that only one task can be executed by the sensor at any given time. The execution is realised by the sensor-specific implementation.

All the data generated by automatic processes can be displayed using end-user portlets. Weather conditions are displayed in a chart form, representing a chosen characteristic (air temperature, air humidity, wind speed and direction, etc.) in a specified time range. The diagram is displayed using the Highcharts JS library [15] and allows for interaction – zoom in/out, displaying point values in a tooltip on the value line, dynamic changing of the displayed characteristics. The retrieved data can be further exported to a spreadsheet format and easily used in scientific articles and reports.

The measured values of meteorological elements are recorded in the database. Users of the project web site can both follow weather conditions through direct measurements and perform their own calculations of characteristics of interest. This is possible due to the module calculating daily, decadal, monthly, seasonal values as well as growing period and annual values. Depending on the meteorological element, it is possible to analyze total, mean, maximum and minimum values, variability, number of days with given values, wind rose plot, etc. Presentation of meteorological conditions pattern is available in both graphic form and tables according to the users' preferences.

The results of phenology observations can be accessed in a similar manner. User specifies a time period, which scenes he or she is interested in and status of the photographs. The SOS service is queried for the observations that fulfil the specified filter parameters and the related phenology photos are returned and displayed. Interaction with observations is possible – the user is able to download them locally or use a built-in graphical tool to analyze them. To accommodate new users, unexperienced in phenology observations, a group of scientists is responsible for tagging photos with relevant information. Technical operators check the generated photos and data if the information is valid and can be further analyzed (see Fig. 4).

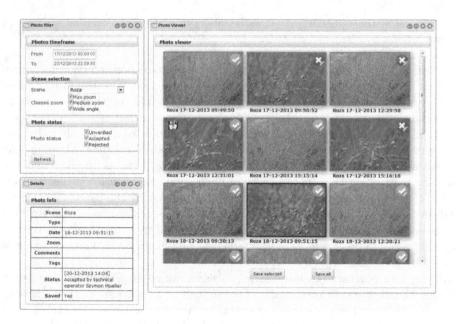

Fig. 4. Technical operator view – it displays all phenology photos fulfilling criteria and allows operators to accept or reject photos

They are also responsible for monitoring if the scenes for periodic observation need to be adjusted (changing zoom/focus setting, changing execution times during short days in winter, etc.), and if the generated photos are in-focus and the observed species are clearly visible. The next step for all validated photos is to receive a scientific description. Phenology operators are responsible for the identification of phenological phase of the observed species. Any additional comments can also be added, informing of peculiar occurrences on the photograph (e.g. anomalies, start of plant disease).

4   Results of Phenology Observations

Within the project, the monitoring system of fitophenological changes in the ecosystem (a camera mounted on a turn-plate and an automated weather station), data storage and data processing center allowing for remote access and ability to change parameters of devices located at the observation site has been activated. A portal, open for public access, has been created, allowing users to take advantage of data (photographs of phenological objects and weather conditions) and the possibility to carry out an analysis of the collected research material.

The activation of instruments (weather station since May 2013 and camera since October 2013) has also started the storage of photographs and values of measured meteorological parameters. The first period has been used for testing purposes, thus a lot of data has been collected. Currently, the installation is working on a daily, production basis and cycle. The number of the total data collected from the beginning of the observation is presented in Table 1.

Table 1. Total amount of data gathered in year 2013

Month	Meteorology reading	Phenology photos
May	32107	N/A
June	110263	N/A
July	121770	N/A
August	118552	N/A
September	121229	N/A
October	154544	4087
November	124597	2701
December	120039	1451
Total	**903101**	**8239**

The observation repository and the tools enabling the analysis of its contents create possibilities to conduct research projects by a wide spectrum of specialists, particularly phenologists, biologists, agrometeorologists or foresters. The scientific program is also carried out by the project authors who provide portal users with instant access to the results. The scientific program is conducted in three time horizons. The information concerning the dates of appearance and duration of successive phenophases of the observed objects are uploaded on an ongoing basis. The analyses of weather patterns, including both the growing seasons and winter rest period, are made accessible. On an ongoing basis, the impact of extreme weather conditions on the status and development of plants is monitored. Over a 1-2 year period since the activation of the weather station, a preliminary characteristic of topoclimatic conditions at the observation site will be developed through the comparison of meteorological data with the long term meteorological time series from the closest, representative for the analyzed region weather station. In a long time perspective, after a few years of observation, research of relationships between weather conditions and the appearance dates and duration of phenophases of the observed objects will be examined.

5   Conclusion and Future Work

The project involving the development of a system comprising IT services and infrastructure enabling fitophenological monitoring is one of the first endeavors of this type attempted in Poland. The Automatic Monitoring platform also presented unique requirements for the PLGrid Plus project, extending its IT infrastructure with physical sensors and instruments. Long-term phenological observation generates a large quantity of data, which is stored in the PL-Grid Infrastructure resources. Automatic Monitoring is also integrated into PL-Grid portal: users are able to apply for access and log in using their PL-Grid OpenID credentials. Deployment of the pilot installation in the Wielkopolski National Park provided invaluable experience in solving a number of technical problems as well as creating the procedures in the activation of observations systems of similar type in the future. It will allow for extending the current platform by a reference observation site, which would allow to observe the same species in two different environments, comparing the influence of local conditions on fitophenological lifecycle.

While using the system and conducting scientific research, the project authors collect information concerning the system functionality and the scope of available information. The daily routine of both technical and phenological operators consists of monitoring and tagging observations with a current phenological stage of the species. The Automatic Monitoring application is available to PL-Grid Infrastructure users who can use this basic information and meteorological data as an entry point for further scientific work. This data attracts the attention not only of scientific researchers, but also of practitioners, especially in the fields of agriculture and forestry. The project has also an educational value – it is the basis for an e-learning system supporting the environmental education in schools at all levels and the development of amateurs interested in life sciences.

Additionally, the data and observations as well as proposals submitted by users, scientists, practitioners and teachers are and will be used for further improvement of the research platform. The project authors are also working on popularization of the platform among the potential users.

References

1. Ahas, R., Aasa, A.: The effects of climate change on the phenology of selected Estonian plant, bird and fish populations. International Journal of Biometeorology 51, 17–26 (2006)

2. Ahrends, H.E., Brügger, R., Stöckli, R., Schenk, J., Michna, P., Jeanneret, F., Wanner, H., Eugster, W.: Quantitative phenological observations of a mixed beech forest in northern Switzerland with digital photography. Journal of Geophysical Research 113, G04004 (2008)
3. Bater, C.W., Coops, N.C., Wulder, M.A., Hilker, T., Nielsen, S.E., McDermid, G., Stenhouse, G.B.: Using digital time-lapse cameras to monitor species-specific understorey and overstorey phenology in support of wildlife habitat assessment. Environmental Monitoring and Assessment 180, 1–13 (2011)
4. Bradley, E., Roberts, D., Still, C.: Design of an image analysis web site for phenological and meteorological monitoring. Environmental Modelling & Software 25, 107–116 (2010)
5. Chmielewski, F.M., Müller, A., Bruns, E.: Climate changes and trends in phenology of fruit trees and field crops in Germany, 1961-2000. Agricultural and Forest Meteorology 121, 69–78 (2004)
6. Crimmins, M.A., Crimmins, T.M.: Monitoring Plant Phenology Using Digital Repeat Photography. Environmental Management 41, 949–958 (2008)
7. Davoli, F., Meyer, N., Pugliese, R., Zappatore, S. (eds.): Remote Instrumentation Services on the e-Infrastructure. Springer, Heidelberg (2011)
8. Dierenbach, J., Badeck, F.W., Schaber, J.: The plant phenological online database (PPODB): an online database for long-term phenological data. International Journal of Biometeorology 57, 805–812 (2013)
9. EPoSS: European Technology Platform on Smart Systems Integration, joint EU-EPoSS workshop, Brussels, BE (2013), http://www.smart-systems-integration.org/public/internet-of-things
10. Górska, M.: Przebieg fenologicznych pór roku w Poznańskim Ogrodzie Botanicznym w latach 1958–1967 (Patterns of phenological seasons in Adam Mickiewicz University Botanical Garden in Poznań). Wiadomości Botaniczne 13(3), 215–221 (1969) (in Polish)
11. Górska-Zajączkowska, M., Wójtowicz, W.: Odzwierciedlenie zmian klimatycznych w przebiegu fenologicznych pór roku w Poznaniu w latach 1958–2009 (Effects of climate changes on phenological seasons in Poznań in 1958-2009). Annales Universitatis Mariae Curie-Skłodowska Lublin, Vol. LXVI, 1 Sectio B 2011, pp. 103–114 (2011)
12. Graham, E.A., Yuen, E.M., Robertson, G.F., Kaiser, W.J., Hamilton, M.P., Rundel, P.W.: Budburst and leaf area expansion measured with a novel mobile camera system and simple color thresholding. Environmental and Experimental Botany 65, 238–244 (2009)
13. Gu, Z.J., Zeng, Z.Y., Shi, X.Z., Li, L., Weindorf, D.C., Zha, Y., Yu, D.S., Liu, Y.M.: A model for estimating total forest coverage with ground-based digital photography. Pedosphere 20(3), 318–325 (2010)
14. Harmata, W.: Fenologia ogólna (General phenology). Uniwersytet Jagielloński, Skrypty Uczelniane nr 729, 1–61 (1995) (in Polish)
15. Highcharts (2013), http://www.highcharts.com/
16. Ide, R., Oguma, H.: Use of digital cameras for phenological observations. Ecological Informatics 5, 339–347 (2010)
17. Ide, R., Oguma, H.: A cost-effective monitoring method using digital time-lapse cameras for detecting temporal and spatial variations of snowmelt and vegetation phenology in alpine ecosystems. Ecological Informatics 16, 25–34 (2013)
18. Ihne, E.: Über phänologishe Jareszeiten. Naturwissenschaftliche Wochenschrift. Bd. X. no. 4 (1895) (in German)

19. INCREASE, APOS technique documentation (2013),
    http://www.increase-infrastructure.eu/
20. Karlsen, S.R., Solheim, I., Beck, P.S.A., Hogda, K.A., Wielgolaski, F.E., Tom-
    mervik, H.: Variability of the start of the growing season in Fennoscandia, 1982–
    2002. International Journal of Biometeorology 51, 513–524 (2007)
21. Krotowska, T.: Pory roku w życiu roślin: obserwacje fenologiczne w zespołach
    roślinnych (Seasons in plant life cycle: phenological observations of plant communi-
    ties). PWN, Seria: Wydawnictwa Popularnonaukowe – PTPN. Nauki Biologiczne,
    no. 1, p. 69 (1958)
22. Liferay portal (2013), http://www.liferay.com
23. Linderholm, H.W., Walther, A.: Twentieth-century trends in the thermal growing
    season in the Greater Baltic Area. Climatic Change 87, 405–419 (2008)
24. Łastowski, W.: Masowe obserwacje fenologiczne, ich zadania i wykonywanie (Mass
    phenological observations, their purpose and procedure). Rocznik Nauk Rol-
    niczych 51, 379–395 (1948) (in Polish)
25. Ł.: astowski, W.: Podział roku na fenologiczne sezony (Year division into phenolo-
    gical seasons). PTPN 1(4), Poznań (1951) (in Polish)
26. Łukasiewicz, A.: Uwagi o gatunkach wskaźnikowych dla wyznaczania fenologicz-
    nych pór roku (Reference species for phenological season determination). Wiad.
    Bot. 2(11), 129–135 (1967) (in Polish)
27. Łukasiewicz, A.: Potrzeba ujednolicenia metodyki fenologicznej w Polskich Ogro-
    dach Botanicznych i Arboretach. Wiad. Bot. 28(2), 153–158 (1984)
28. Open Geospatial Consortium Sensor Web Enablement (2013),
    http://www.opengeospatial.org/domain/swe
29. Richardson, A.D., Braswellm, B.H., Hollingerm, D.Y., Jenkinsm, J.P., Ollinger,
    S.V.: Near-surface remote sensing of spatial and temporal variation in canopy phe-
    nology. Ecological Applications 19(6), 1417–1428 (2009)
30. Richardson, A.D., Jenkins, J.P.: Use of digital webcam images to track spring
    green-up in a deciduous broadleaf forest. Oecologia 152, 323–334 (2007)
31. Sonnentag, O., Hufkens, K., Teshera-Sterne, C., Young, A.M., Friedl, M., Braswell,
    B.H., Milliman, T., O'Keefe, J., Richardson, A.D.: Digital repeat photography
    for phenological research in forest ecosystems. Agricultural and Forest Meteorol-
    ogy 152, 159–177 (2012)
32. Sparks, T.H., Górska-Zajączkowska, M., Wójtowicz, W., Tryjanowski, P.: Pheno-
    logical changes and reduced seasonal synchrony in western Poland. International
    Journal of Biometeorology 55, 447–453 (2011)
33. Sparks, T.H., Mizera, T., Wójtowicz, W., Tryjanowski, P.: Synchrony in the pheno-
    logy of a culturally iconic spring flower. International Journal of Biometeorology 56,
    407–409 (2012)
34. Szafer, W.: O fenologicznych porach roku w Polsce (Phenological seasons in
    Poland). Kosmos 47(1-3), Kraków (1992) (in Polish)
35. Yu, Z., Cao, Z., Wu, X., Bai, X., Qin, Y., Zhuo, W., Xiao, Y., Zhang, X., Xue,
    H.: Automatic image-based detection technology for two critical growth stages of
    maize: Emergence and three-leaf stage. Agricultural and Forest Meteorology 174-
    175, 65–84 (2013)
36. Zhao, J., Zhang, Y., Tan, Z., Song, Q., Liang, N., Yu, L., Zhao, J.: Using digital
    cameras for comparative phenological monitoring in an evergreen broad-leaved
    forest and a seasonal rain forest. Ecological Informatics 10, 65–72 (2012)

Preliminary Data Classification in COMPASS Experiment Using HEP-Grid Tools

Anna Padée

Interdisciplinary Centre for Mathematical and Computational Modelling ICM,
Warszawa, Poland

Abstract. Preliminary classification of Monte Carlo data in the high
energy physics experiments can significantly reduce the computational
cost needed for simulation and reconstruction. The commonly used method of rectangular cuts has a limited efficiency in many cases. In this
work, an attempt has been made to address the problem by using the
multilayer perceptron neural network. In order to speed up the tests and
further processing of the data, the network has been developed in a parallel environment using Proof on Demand on the grid resources. The
results show that the usage of a neural network can significantly improve
the efficiency of the classification.

Keywords: neural networks, artificial intelligence, high energy physics,
grid computing.

1 Introduction

1.1 Goals of the Experiment

The COMPASS experiment, commissioned in 2001 at the SPS at CERN, was
designed to investigate hadron structure and spectroscopy. COMPASS was originally planned as two separate experiments (HMC and CHEOPS), therefore it
consists of two independent parts. One of them, utilizing a high-intensity polarized muon beam, is focused on how the proton spin is carried by its constituents.
The other one is based on various nuclear targets and hadron beams – this
setup is aimed to study exotic baryons, such as pentaquarks. The classification
problem presented in this paper is based on the data from the muon beam run,
therefore only that part of the experiment is described in detail here. Deep inelastic scattering (DIS) experiments have contributed to better understanding
of particle physics ever since the discovery of the inner structure of nucleon. The
COMPASS experiment uses lepton-nucleon scattering to determine the contribution of nucleon constituents to its overall spin. It is known that nucleon spin
is composed of helicity contributions from quarks ($\Delta\Sigma = \sum \Delta q + \Delta\bar{q}$), gluons
(ΔG) and orbital angular momentum of quarks (L_q) and gluons (L_g). All these
contributions sum up to the overall nucleon spin which equals $\frac{1}{2}$ [1]

$$S_n = \frac{1}{2} = \frac{1}{2}\Delta\Sigma + \Delta G + L_q + L_g. \tag{1}$$

M. Bubak et al. (Eds.): PLGrid Plus, LNCS 8500, pp. 351–363, 2014.

Meanwhile, other experiments have established the contribution from the quarks ($\Delta\Sigma$) to be 20-30%, which is well below theoretical predictions. In order to further investigate this issue, named the "Spin Crisis of the nucleon", it is needed to measure the gluon spin and the orbital angular momentum of the partons. In the COMPASS experiment, a process called Photon Gluon Fusion (PGF) is used for direct measurement of gluon helicity. In the PGF process, the high energy muon from the beam interacts, by the virtual photon, with a quark (or an antiquark) from the pair created from the gluon. The struck quark is removed from the initial nucleon by creation of another quark-antiquark pair (to retain color singlet state), so a meson is created as an output particle. The problem with PGF events is that they occur rarely, among other background processes. The most common is the leading order DIS ($\gamma q \to q$) and another is QCD-Compton process ($\gamma q \to qg$). In these processes, the muon from the beam interacts with one of the quarks of the nucleon, and not one of the gluons. Another such process are so-called resolved photon events, in which the hadronic contents of the photon react with a parton of the nucleon. These resolved photon events, however, can be easily screened by selecting only the events with high photon virtuality ($Q^2 > 1\ GeV^2$).

Two methods are used to extract PGF events from the data. The first one, called open-charm method, is based on the selection of events where the fusion process was mediated by a charm quark. The $c\bar{c}$ quark pair hadronises into mesons and baryons, usually resulting in the production of D_0 meson. The decay of the D_0 meson into pion and kaon allows the selection of these events experimentally. The main advantage of open-charm production is the fact that because the intrinsic charm content in the target nucleon is virtually nonexistent, such events are the certain result of the PGF process and the method is relatively free of background. However, because of the high mass of the c quark, these events are extremely rare. Another method is selecting PGF events comprising the production of light quark pairs. In this case, due to the light quark content in the nucleon, the contributions from other processes cannot be neglected and they have to be taken into account during Monte Carlo simulations. This approach is called high-p_t hadron pairs method, because only the events with two outgoing hadrons are considered, and also there are constrains on the transverse momentum of these hadrons. The requirement of high transverse momentum of outgoing hadrons allows to filter much of the LO-DIS events. The classification problem presented in this paper is based only on the high-p_t events data [2,3].

1.2   The Experiment Setup

The COMPASS experiment uses the beam from the SPS accelerator to create a secondary beam. The SPS proton beam hits the beryllium production target, creating pions and kaons that further decay into muons and neutrinos. The parity violation decay of hadrons produces polarized muons. Through a series of bending magnets, muons of 160GeV momentum are selected and guided to COMPASS experimental hall. This procedure provides 80% (with relative error 5%) polarized beam with momentum spread of 160 GeV±5% and intensity of $2 * 10^8 \mu^+/spill$. Because of that high momentum spread, the exact momentum of incoming particles is measured by the detectors of the beam momentum station (BMS). The target consists of three cylinders (two 30 cm long and one 60 cm long), 4 cm in diameter, made of ^{6}LiD and separated by 5 cm gaps. The two shorter cylinders are polarised in the same direction and the longest one in the middle has reverse polarisation. To achieve the state called "frozen spin", in which the polarisation decay is very slow, the target is cooled to a very low temperature of 50 mK and kept in a homogenous magnetic field of 2.5 T. To detect the outgoing particles, a two stage spectrometer has been set up. The whole COMPASS spectrometer is about $4x5$ m^2 in size and 50 m long. Each part consists of a spectrometer magnet, tracking detectors and particle identification detectors. The first part, directly after the target, covers a range of ±180 rad, so it is referred to as the Large Angle Spectrometer (LAS). Further away, after the stronger SM2 magnet, there is a small angle spectrometer (SAS), which covers the inner 30 mrad angle. In both parts of the spectrometer there are different types of detectors:

Tracking Detectors:

- *Scintillating Fibre Detectors (SciFi)*. They have the best time resolution (400 ps), however, their active area is very small (5×5 or 12×12 cm^2). They can also handle high intensity of the beam, therefore they are used for tracking of particles very close to the beam axis. These detectors are also used for so called Beam Telescope (BT) to measure kinematic parameters of scattered and unscattered muons from the beam.
- *Silicon Strip Detectors*. Due to their small active area and good performance in high intensity of the beam, they are used in the same areas as SciFi detectors.
- *Micromesh Gaseous Structure Detectors (Micromegas) and Gas Electron Multiplier (GEM)*. Gas detectors that use high voltage to provide amplification of the number of ionized particle in the gas. Micromega detectors can measure particles up to 40 cm from the beam axis, and with cutting off the high voltage in the central part of the detector, they can handle the high intensity of the beam. Therefore, they are used for tracking the particles between the target and the first magnet. GEM detectors are used for tracking in all segments of the spectrometer.
- *Multi-Wire Proportional Chamber (MWPC)*. A layer of wires, approximately 1 m long, is used to gather charge from ionized gas. The resolution of these detectors is 500 μm, but they have large active surface, therefore they are used to track particles scattered at bigger angles.
- *Drift Chambers*. Multi-wire gas detectors measuring time of flight of the ionised gas to the electrodes, which results in a better resolution than MWPCs. In the COMPASS experiment, drift chambers have approximate dimensions of 140x120 cm and their spatial resolution is around 180 μm.
- *Straw Tube Chambers*. Multi-wire gas detectors, in which each wire is enclosed in Kapton-aluminum tube, which works also as the cathode of the detector. In COMPASS, there are two sizes of the straw tubes, 6 mm in the

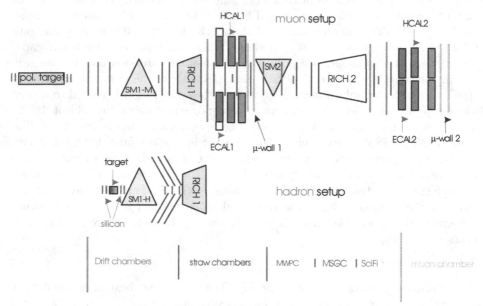

Fig. 1. The COMPASS spectrometer [4]

area closer to the beam axis and 9 mm in the outer regions. Straw chamber planes in COMPASS measure about 3x3 m and have spatial resolution about 220 μm.

Particle identification:

- *The RICH Detector.* To identify the particles passing through the spectrometer, besides the reconstructed tracks, additional parameters are needed. The momentum of a particle can be determined from its track in the magnetic field of the bending magnets. However, to distinguish between different types of particles, either their velocity or energy is needed. The RICH (Ring Imaging Cherenkov) employs Cherenkov effect in a pressurized cavity surrounded by multiple photon detectors to measure particles' velocity.
- *Muon detection.* The part of the spectrometer designed for muon detection consists of detectors placed behind so-called muon filters. These filters are basically blocks of iron or concrete that absorb incoming hadrons, so only muons reach the detectors behind them. The detectors (Iarocci tubes and aluminum drift tubes) have relatively low spatial resolution, but they can determine whether a muon has passed or not.
- *Calorimetry.* There are two types of calorimeters in the COMPASS spectrometer. Hadronic calorimeters are used for discrimination between hadrons and muons. They are also used to trigger events if hadrons are detected in the final state. Electromagnetic calorimeters are used to detect electrons and photons.

The spectrometer has also a trigger system, which performs preliminary selection of the events. Within 500 ns it decides whether a potentially interesting event has occurred and then triggers the readout from the detectors. The purpose of this system is to store only the valuable events candidates on the tapes and reduce the data flow so that Data Acquisition System can handle it [5].

Even with the readout of events selected by the trigger only, with the trigger rate of 5-10 kHz and event size of approximately 40 kByte, the data collected by the experiment add up to 300 TByte per year[1]. The data is then processed, first online and later offline. The online part has to be done in real time. First, the readouts from all detectors are combined into one event. The events in this stage go through preliminary filtering, monitoring and are copied to the tapes for long-term storage.

1.3   Data Analysis

Events in the form described in the previous section are called "raw data". They contain digitized signals from the detectors and calibration information. Further processing of these events, due to the complexity of the process, is done offline. In the COMPASS experiment, offline processing is performed by the package named CORAL (COmpass Reconstruction and anALysis). The first stage of the reconstruction of each event is called decoding. It converts raw signals from the detectors to the information about activated channels in the detectors. The next step is called clustering, at which the channels activated by the same particle are grouped together. The resulting information contains the positions where tracks of the particles cross the detector planes. These positions are called hits. The next stage is called segment reconstruction, because it tries to find straight segments of the tracks by grouping hits coming from different detectors in the same section. The segments from different sections are then extrapolated to the areas, in which there are no detectors (e.g. in the magnet section) and linked together. This process is called bridging. After that, the software tries to calculate the charge and the momentum of the particles (by measuring the curvature of the track in the magnetic field). The last stage of the reconstruction is grouping the tracks belonging to one event and calculating the coordinates of the primary interaction vertex by extrapolating them into the target area.

The reconstruction process, due to its complexity, is controlled by many parameters. These include geometrical and time tolerances, number of planes required to accept the track segments, etc. In order to calibrate all these parameters, a detailed simulation of all the physical processes in the detector is needed. The simulation uses Monte Carlo method and it is done in two steps:

- event generation,
- tracking of the particles through the detector.

---

[1] The data taking time is limited, due to the non-continuous muon beam and also the fact that data is not produced on every day of the year. Therefore, the final amount taken per year is lower than $5kHz * 40kB * 60s * 60 * 24 * 356$.

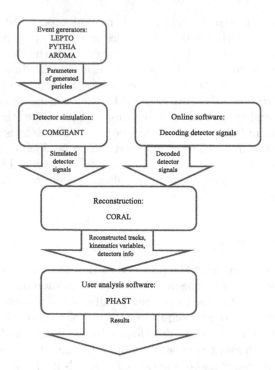

Fig. 2. Data flow in COMPASS experimental and Monte Carlo events

The first step simulates an interaction of a muon from the beam with a nucleon from either of the parts of the target. It is done in several stages, each of them controlled by a separate program. LEPTO is responsible for the scattering of the muon, AROMA for the creation of heavy quarks in photon-gluon fusion and POLDIS for the effect of the spin asymmetries. This is supplemented by the background simulation done by PYTHIA. The result of the whole event generation process is the list of the particles created in the event, together with their kinematic parameters.

This list is passed to the second step of the simulation, in which the particles are tracked through the detector. This step is performed by the COMGEANT program, which is built on the basis of the popular GEANT 3 simulation package. For this step, the detector is described by detailed material and field maps. The secondary particles that appear as products of the simulated reactions are added to the event and simulated as well. As a result of this recursive procedure, a data file is created, similar to the real data coming from the detectors, but supplemented with the reference parameters of the simulated particles. This data is called Monte Carlo (MC) data. Having the original information about the particles, it is possible to compare it with the reconstructed data and check the efficiency and accuracy of the reconstruction. This is done automatically by CORAL when working on MC data.

However, the reconstruction process, even though the algorithm itself is simple, encounters a number of difficulties. The main problem is the high noise level during data acquisition. The reconstruction algorithm in each detector has to check each hit several times, even though vast majority of hits come from the background radiation or particles created by interactions in the material of the spectrometer itself. Another problem is the limited detectors efficiency, when high-energy particles coming from the PGF process might not be detected at all. Limited time resolution of the detectors creates so called pile-ups, where particles coming from the two separate events are detected in the same time frame. Because of the limited space resolution of the detectors, the reconstruction algorithm repeats the procedure several times, increasing the spatial tolerance with each step. Even if the event can be reconstructed successfully, it often cannot be used in the analysis, because some essential particles cannot be identified. In such cases, the computing time devoted to the simulation and reconstruction of the event is wasted. Therefore, pre-selection of the events to eliminate unreconstructable events before the simulation stage, would greatly reduce the need for computational resources.

2   Description of the Problem's Solution

2.1   Neural Networks Approach

Artificial neural networks are one of the modern methods of multivariate analysis, used especially in classification and parametrization problems [6]. Their design is inspired by biological nervous systems, particularly by the structure of the brain. The neural networks approach has many advantages. Firstly, neural networks are capable of adaptive learning, which enables them to solve problems where instructions needed to create a conventional program are not known a priori. Neural networks extract essential characteristic of the data from the training examples given to the network. Secondly, neural networks enable the processing of different input vectors in parallel, which allows for good performance in parallel environment, such as computing grid. It also allows the application to run normally even if it fails on one particular piece of data. Finally, multi-layer neural networks are capable of modeling non-linear, complex functions in problems where linear approximation fails. The most simple neural network example, called perceptron, consists of only one neuron and divides the space of input variables with one $n - 1$ dimensional hyperplane. The perceptron has $n + 1$ inputs (where n is the number of input variables) and each input has a weight w_i associated with it. The extra input (x_0) is always set to 1 and is called bias or threshold. For each input vector, the products of input variables and their corresponding weights are summed up and the neuron activation function determines the output value

$$y_k(\mathbf{x}) = \varphi(\sum w_{ki}x_i + w_{k0}).\tag{2}$$

The activation function $\varphi(a)$ in the McCulloch-Pitts perceptron model was originally a binary step function, however, presently differentiable, asymptotic

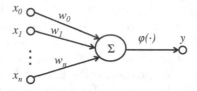

Fig. 3. Single neuron model

functions, such as the sigmoid function, are often used. An example of such function is

$$\varphi(a) = \tanh a = \frac{1 - e^{-\beta a}}{1 + e^{-\beta a}}. \tag{3}$$

The weights w_i are in the beginning set up with random values. Then, in the process of training of the network, for each input vector the output value is computed. The calculated output values are then subtracted from the desired output value for that vector (in signal-background separation problems usually 1 for the signal and 0 for the background) to determine the error value. The error is then used to modify the weights:

$$w_i(k + 1) = w_i(k) + \alpha \varphi'(a(k)) x_i(k)(t(k) - y(k)), \tag{4}$$

where $\alpha \in (0, 1)$ is the learning rate parameter.

Of course, the applications of perceptron are very limited, because it divides the variable space with just one $n - 1$ dimensional hyperplane and most problems cannot be solved that way. However, by creating a layer of d neurons, the variable space can be divided into $2d$ linearly independent sections. The performance of such 2-layered network is limited to convex regions, however, by adding another layer of neurons, a neural network with 3 layers is capable of approximating regions of any shape, with precision limited only by the number of neurons in hidden layers. Such networks called multilayer perceptron (MLP) are commonly used in classification tasks and that type of network is also used in this analysis. The layers of multilayer network are sets of parallel neurons. The neurons are connected in such a way that the output vector of each layer is the input of the next layer, with no feedback loops. The weight modification algorithm for multilayer network in the training phase is called the error back-propagation algorithm, because after computing the error value for each training vector, starting from the output layer, the error is propagated backwards through the network. The weight modification algorithm for input i of neuron n in layer l is:

$$w_{n,i}^{(l)}(k + 1) = w_{n,i}^{(l)}(k) + \alpha x_i(k) \delta_n^{(l)}(k), \tag{5}$$

where $\delta_n^{(l)}$ is the error value for the output of the neuron n:

$$\delta_n^{(l)}(k) = \begin{cases} t_n(k) - y_n(k) & \text{for output layer} \\ \varphi'(a_n(k)) \sum_{m=1}^{N_{l+1}} \delta_m^{(l+1)}(k) w_{mn}^{(l+1)}(k) & \text{for hidden layers.} \end{cases} \qquad (6)$$

The weights can be updated either after each training vector or the weight corrections can be summed up for all vectors (without updating after each one), and the weights are updated once with cumulative Δw. The training of the network requires a large set of sample vectors, with a desired output value for each vector. This set is divided into two parts: the training set and the testing set. The training set is used to train the network, while the testing set is used to monitor the training process.

2.2 Kinematic Variables

In this classification task, a large amount of training data has been obtained from the Monte Carlo simulation in the form of training vectors consisting of 20 kinematic variables for one event and the information whether the event had been successfully reconstructed or not.

Table 1. Kinematic variables used as neural network inputs

vX, vY, vZ	position of the primary vertex
x_{Bj}	fraction of the nucleon momentum carried by the struck quark
Q^2	momentum transferred from the lepton to the nucleon
kY	fraction of the lepton momentum carried by the virtual photon
mP, mPx, mPy	momentum of the scattered muon
bP	initial momentum of the muon
hPt0, hPt1	transverse momentum of the two fastest hadrons
hP0, hP1	momentum of the hadrons
hQ0, hQ1	charges of the hadrons
$h\theta$	scattering angles of the hadrons, measured from the beam axis
$h\varphi$	scattering angles of the hadrons, measured in the plane perpendicular to the beam axis

2.3 ROOT and TMVA

The neural network was implemented using the TMVA toolkit, which is a part of ROOT framework [7]. TMVA provides C++/ROOT classes for several methods of multivariate analysis, but it also provides tools for pre-processing the data, evaluation of the algorithms and support of ROOT tree files [8]. As part of the ROOT framework, TMVA can be run in the PoD (Proof on Demand) parallel environment [9].

3   Results

Each of the input variables has been normalised to distribution in <-1,1>. After testing various network architectures, a network with 10 neurons in the first layer and 5 neurons in the second layer provided the best performance. The best $S/\sqrt{S+B}$ ratio was 25.37 with the cut at network output of 0.32.

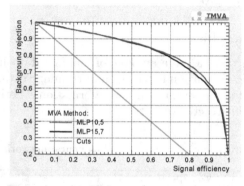

Fig. 4. Signal efficiency vs background rejection for 20 input variables case

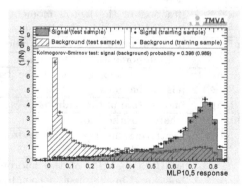

Fig. 5. Output distribution of the network for training and testing samples for 20 input variables case

However, by examining the correlations between the input variables and the network response, it turned out that some variables had little influence on the network's performance.

Table 2. Ranking of the variables after training and testing the network

Rank	Variable	Importance
1	hPt1	33.27
2	hPt0	32.66
3	hTheta1	12.31
4	kQ2	11.37
5	hP0	9.442
6	hP1	9.199
7	hTheta0	7.803
8	kXbj	7.745
9	kY	$617.3 * 10^{-3}$
10	vZ	$193.8 * 10^{-3}$
11	bP	$33.66 * 10^{-3}$
12	vX	$24.75 * 10^{-3}$
13	hQ1	$23.41 * 10^{-3}$
14	hQ0	$20.75 * 10^{-3}$
15	mP	$8.903 * 10^{-3}$
16	mPx	$3.697 * 10^{-3}$
17	mPy	$1.131 * 10^{-3}$
18	hPhi0	$126.4 * 10^{-6}$
19	hPhi1	$66.11 * 10^{-6}$
20	vY	$3.156 * 10^{-6}$

Some variables have been therefore removed from further analysis:

- vX and vY: Because the target is symmetrical with respect to the beam axis, the exact point of the interaction in the given cross-section of the target does not influence the result.
- mP: It has 99% anti-correlation with kY, therefore only one of these variables is needed.
- bP: The beam momentum itself does not determine the fraction of the momentum transferred by the virtual photon, therefore it is not relevant.
- hQ: The charges of the hadrons (that have only discrete values: -1 or 1) do not influence the probability of detection or the reconstruction process.
- $h\varphi$, mPx, mPy: The spectrometer is virtually symmetrical with respect to the beam axis, therefore the scattering angles $h\varphi$ as well as the components x and y of mP do not influence the result.

After reducing the number of the input variables by ten, the best performance has been achieved for a network with 8 neurons in the first layer and 4 neurons in the second layer.

The best $S/\sqrt{S+B}$ ratio of 25.68 has been achieved for cut of the output signal at 0.29.

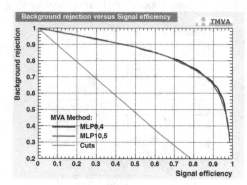

Fig. 6. Signal efficiency vs background rejection for the networks with reduced number of input variables

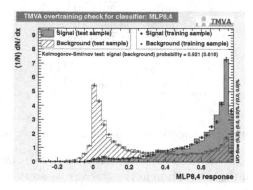

Fig. 7. Output distribution of the network for training and testing samples with reduced number of input variables

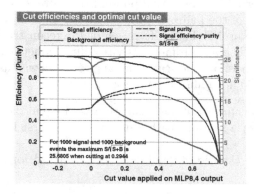

Fig. 8. Cuts efficiency for the network with reduced number of input variables

4   Conclusions and Future Work

The achieved efficiency of the method, shown in Fig. 6, proves that the neural network approach can be very useful for the preliminary classification of the Monte Carlo data. Even though the method requires some manual work in picking the network input variables, as well as the network architecture, the results can be much better than the simple kinematic cuts method, which has been commonly used for this task so far. Although the processing of a single vector is computationally inexpensive, the amount of the input data makes the parallelization of the task very useful. Usage of the ROOT framework in the parallel environment of HEP-oriented services developed in PLGrid Plus makes the processing much faster [10]. It also helps considerably during the design phase, because many different architectures of the network can be tested at the same time. Despite the good overall efficiency of the proposed method, there is a room for improvement in changing the network training algorithm. The method used in the presented experiments was the simple gradient descent, which in many cases can be outperformed by more sophisticated methods such as Levenberg-Marquadt procedure or evolutionary algorithms. Some more effort can also be put in the selection and further decorrelation of the input variables, although the preliminary tests with the PCA method were rather discouraging.

References

1. van der Steenhoven, G.: Polarized structure functions. In: Proc. Baryons 2002, Newport News, USA (2002)
2. Hedicke, S.: Determination of the gluon polarisation in the nucleon using hadron pairs with high transverse momentum at COMPASS. Albert-Ludwigs-Universität Freiburg (2005)
3. Klimaszewski, K.: Determination of gluon polarisation in the nucleon from events with high-pT hadron pairs in COMPASS experiment. Soltan Institute for Nuclear Studies, Warsaw (2010)
4. COMPASS site, http://wwwcompass.cern.ch/compass/
5. Abbon, P., Albrecht, E., Alexakhin, V.Y., et al.: The COMPASS Experiment at CERN. CERN-PH-EP/2007-001 (2007)
6. Bishop, C.M.: Neural Networks for Pattern Recognition. Clarendon Press, Oxford (1995)
7. TMVA Toolkit, http://tmva.sourceforge.net/
8. The ROOT System Home Page, http://root.cern.ch
9. Malzacher, P., Manafov, A.: PROOF on Demand. In: CHEP 2009 (2010)
10. Binczewski, A., et al.: Polish Contribution to the Worldwide LHC Computing. In: Bubak, M., Szepieniec, T., Wiatr, K. (eds.) PL-Grid 2011. LNCS, vol. 7136, pp. 285–300. Springer, Heidelberg (2012)
11. Brona, G.: Hadron production and polarisation of gluons in the nucleon in the $\mu-$ N interactions in the COMPASS experiment at CERN (2007)

Application of Sensitivity Analysis to Grid-Based Procedure Dedicated to Creation of SSRVE

Łukasz Rauch, Danuta Szeliga, Daniel Bachniak,
Krzysztof Bzowski, and Maciej Pietrzyk

AGH University of Science and Technology,
al. Mickiewicza 30, 30-059 Kraków, Poland
{lukasz.rauch,danuta.szeliga,daniel.bachniak,kbzowski,
maciej.pietrzyk}@agh.edu.pl

Abstract. The methods of sensitivity analysis allow to reduce computational cost of multi-iterative optimization procedures by finding the most influential parameters of the particular model. The article presents details of implementation of the numerical library, which is dedicated to sensitivity analysis and can be used by middleware in e-infrastructures. Then, the application of implemented methods to parallel and distributed models is presented on the example of Statistically Similar Representative Volume Element (SSRVE) in the field of metal forming. The influence of parameters, used in the SSRVE methodology, on accuracy of obtained results and performance of calculations is analyzed. The results of sensitivity analysis are presented in the article as well.

Keywords: HPC computing, sensitivity analysis, SSRVE.

1 Introduction

The most of numerical models applied in simulations of real phenomena, e.g. economical processes, biological species habits or material behavior under loading conditions, are used in computational costly optimization procedures. Such procedures have multiple objectives. In the case of metallurgical aspects, they are performed to design production processes and cycles. Growing complexity of models used in these simulations is usually related to a large number of input parameters, which not necessarily influence the results in the same way. Reduction of computational complexity can be obtained by fixing constant values of less important parameters in a set of optimization variables. This approach reduces not only computational cost, but also increases the reliability of applied optimization method by decrease of input space dimensionality. Such aim can be obtained by application of sensitivity analysis (SA) methods, allowing to list input parameters of the model in descending order by their influence on model output. Nevertheless, SA still requires multiple performance of investigated models with different input parameters, which have to be determined according

M. Bubak et al. (Eds.): PLGrid Plus, LNCS 8500, pp. 364–377, 2014.
© Springer International Publishing Switzerland 2014

to selected SA method. However, capabilities of currently available middleware are not sufficient to achieve this aim, due to the complexity of rules allowing determination of proper set of input parameters. Therefore, the main objective of this work is to design and implement the numerical library containing SA procedures. The functionality of the library allows to generate a set of input parameters for different SA methods, which can be passed further to middleware dedicated to submit and monitor numerical models in a grid infrastructure. The Scalarm platform [1] is an example of such middleware, which is used as the development platform for this purpose.

The proposed SA numerical library will be applied to SSRVE analysis to determine the influence of SSRVE procedure parameters on its computational performance and the accuracy of rheological model estimation. From the sensitivity analysis point of view, the SSRVE is treated as a model. Input of this model is composed of three parameters, i.e., number of inclusions in SSRVE, degree of interpolation polynomial function and number of Non-uniform Relational B-Splines (NURBS) control points. Output of the model is represented by two coefficients, i.e., number of SSRVE procedure iterations, which influences computing time, and Mean Square Error of equivalent stress estimation showing accuracy of the model.

The article contains five sections. The second section describes sensitivity analysis methods, their advantages and disadvantages as well as their requirements and functional assumptions. Afterwards, the implementation details of the SA numerical library are presented. The fourth section contains information about SSRVE idea and realization of this procedure as a grid service. Then, the results of the analysis performed by application of Morris Design approach and Sobol's method to SSRVE, are presented. The article ends with conclusions and the description of further work.

2   Sensitivity Analysis

Sensitivity Analysis (SA) is the field of knowledge investigating the model behavior for various input data and model parameters [2]. It determines how the variations of input data and parameters are distributed on the variations of model outputs and influence them. In this article, global sensitivity methods were applied, which calculate one (global) value expressing the sensitivity of a parameter for the whole parameter domain; these methods are derived from statistics and the probability theory. Global SA requires a definition of the following terms:

- expression, which characterizes the measure of model output/outputs (it should be a scalar value),
- definition of the variation interval for each input parameter,
- selection of the points in the parameters domain (a design of experiment techniques is applied),
- sensitivity measure – the sensitivities are estimated based on the model outputs measure variations, caused by changes in the model parameters.

Two algorithms were selected in the work: Morris Design, which is a screening method, and Sobol's algorithm based on analysis of variance.

2.1   An Algorithm Based on the Morris Design

The term "screening design" characterizes the method of the input parameters domain processing. The methods of this group calculate the parameter sensitivities as the global indices and they search systematically the whole parameters domain, thus, they are called screening methods. The main idea of these algorithms is to investigate the model parameters, which have the biggest influence on variability of the model output, and to keep computational costs as low as possible. The methods deal with the question, which model parameters are really important. The assumption of not high calculation costs makes these procedures estimate the importance of the input parameters qualitatively, not quantitatively, i.e., they state that one parameter is more important than another one. The One-At-a-Time (OAT) approach, originally developed by Morris [3], was selected. This technique investigates the impact of the variation of each parameter in turn. The OAT design is called a global sensitivity analysis, because the algorithm explores the entire space, over which the parameters vary. In the algorithm, the term of "parameter main effect" is introduced and it is determined by computing a number of local measures at different points in the input space and next estimated by mean value and standard deviation. The key definitions and steps of Morris design are presented below.

Assumptions and Definitions. Let $\mathbf{X}$ be a n-dimensional vector of model parameters x_i. The primary assumption of the algorithm is that all x_i components are defined on [0,1] interval. In most practical problems, x_i components are of various physical units and the parameters have to be rescaled to the mentioned range. Linear or logarithmic transformation can be applied. The conversion is necessary to compare the results obtained for various parameters. It is feasible only if estimated elementary effects are expressed with the same units for all parameters.

Let the components x_i, $i=1,..,$n, accept k values in the set $\{0, 1/(k-1), 2/(k-1), ..., 1\}$. Then, the parameters domain $\Omega \subseteq \mathbb{R}$ forms an n-dimensional k-level grid. The elementary effect x_i of the ith parameter at a given point $\mathbf{x}$ calculated for y model output is defined as:

$$\xi_i(\mathbf{x}) := \frac{\widetilde{y}(x_1, ..., x_{i-1}, x_i + \widetilde{\Delta}_i, X_{i+1}, ..., x_n) - \widetilde{y}(\mathbf{x})}{\Delta} , \tag{1}$$

where $\mathbf{x}$ is any value in the Ω domain such that the perturbed point $\mathbf{x}+\Delta$ is also in Ω, $\widetilde{\Delta}_i = \Delta(x_{i,s} - x_{i,e})$ and $x_{i,s}, x_{i,e}$ are start and end points of parameter x_i variation interval, respectively, Δ depends on k and describes the side length of the grid element. A finite distribution F_i for each parameter x_i is obtained by sampling $\mathbf{x}$ in Ω. The number of elements of F_i is equal to $(k-1)k^{n-1}$.

Distribution F_i of elementary effects is described by mean μ and standard deviation σ. A mean characterizes the sensitivity of the model output with respect to i^{th} parameter. A high mean indicates that the parameter is important and it substantially influences the output. A high standard deviation implies that the parameter interacts with other parameters or its effect to the model is nonlinear.

The naive algorithm calculates in sequence r values from distribution F_i of each parameter x_i and in summary there are $2rn$ solver runs to determine elementary effects. Another, more effective procedure with the orientation matrix $\mathbf{B}^*$ introduced to the algorithm was proposed by Morris [3]. The rows of the matrix $\mathbf{B}^*$ represent input vectors $\mathbf{x}$ and n corresponding model runs providing n elementary effects ξ_i, one for each parameter x_i, are computed for them. Thus, the dimension of the matrix $\mathbf{B}^*$ is $(n+1) \times n$. The orientation matrix $\mathbf{B}^*$ is randomly and independently selected r times. As a result, $r(n+1)$ model outputs are obtained, forming an rn-elements set of F_i distribution for elementary effects ξ_i.

The mean of elementary effects will be incorrect (underestimated) for the effects obtained simultaneously with positive and negative signs, therefore, instead of the elementary effect defined as 1, the absolute value of ξ_i is taken:

$$\xi_i(\mathbf{x}) := \left| \frac{\tilde{y}(x_1, ..., x_{i-1}, x_i + \widetilde{\Delta}_i, X_{i+1}, ..., x_n) - \tilde{y}(\mathbf{x})}{\Delta} \right| . \tag{2}$$

The results of the sensitivity of the model output with respect to the input model parameters expressed as the estimated mean of elementary effects are dependent on Δ value, which is selected arbitrarily. This dependence rises with the nonlinearity of the model and the sensitivity calculations may be not reliable. Thus, the calculations with the Morris design algorithm are performed for various Δ and next the results are compared. The comparison is feasible for normalized quantities:

$$\tilde{\mu}_i = \frac{\mu_i}{||\boldsymbol{\mu}||} \tilde{\sigma}_i = \frac{\sigma_i}{||\boldsymbol{\sigma}||} , \tag{3}$$

where $\boldsymbol{\mu} = (\mu_1, ..., \mu_n), \boldsymbol{\sigma} = (\sigma_1, ..., \sigma_n)$ are vectors of means and standard deviations calculated for all the input parameters $x_i, i = 1, ..., n$. If means and standard deviations computed for various Δ are close to each other, the sensitivities are properly estimated. If not, the value of Δ should be narrowed down and the procedure is repeated. Another solution is to define Δ for each input parameter separately, keeping in mind that the whole interval for each parameter should be screened (the value of r should be carefully examined).

2.2 Sobol's Method

Sobol in [4] developed the method of the global SA based on the variance analysis and the Monte Carlo algorithm. Let us assume that the domain of the input model parameters $x_i, i = 1, ..., n$, is defined as an n-dimensional cube Ω:

$$\Omega = \{\mathbf{x} : 0 \leq x_i \leq 1 \quad \forall_i = 1, ..., n\} . \tag{4}$$

Let the function $y = y(x)$ represents a model. Sobol defined the decomposition of $y(x)$ as the sum of the increasing dimensionality addends:

$$y(x_1, ..., x_n) = y_0 + \sum_{i=1}^{n} y_i(x_i) + \sum_{1 \leq i < j \leq n} y_{ij}(x_i, x_j) + ... + y_{1,2,...,n}(x_1, ..., x_n) \ . \ (5)$$

The decomposition (5) is held if y_0 is constant and the integrals of every addend over its own variables is zero:

$$\int_0^1 y_{i_1,...,i_s}(x_{i_1}, ..., x_{i_s}) dx_{i_k} = 0 \quad \forall k : 1 \leq k \leq s \ . \tag{6}$$

From (5) and (6) it is concluded that all the addends in (5) are orthogonal:

$$\int_0^1 y_{i_1,...,i_s}(x_{i_1}, ..., x_{i_s}) y_{j_1,...,j_k}(x_{j_1}, ..., x_{j_k}) dx = 0 \quad \forall (i_1, ..., i_s) \neq (j_1, ..., j_k)$$
$$\tag{7}$$

and

$$y_0 = \int_\Omega y(\mathbf{x}) dx \ . \tag{8}$$

Sobol in [5] proved that the decomposition (5) is unique and all the decomposition addends can be evaluated as multidimensional integrals:

$$y_i(x_i) = -y_0 + \int_0^1 ... \int_0^1 y(\mathbf{x}) dx_{\sim i}$$
$$\tag{9}$$
$$y_{ij}(x_i, x_j) = -y_0 - y_i(x_i) - y_j(x_j) + \int_0^1 ... \int_0^1 y(\mathbf{x}) dx_{\sim(ij)} \ ,$$

where $dx_{\sim i}$ and $dx_{\sim(ij)}$ denote integration over all the variables except x_i and x_i, x_j, respectively. Following that, the total variance Var is of the form:

$$Var = \int_\Omega y^2(\mathbf{x}) dx - y_0^2 \tag{10}$$

and partial variances are estimated based on the terms in equation (5):

$$Var_{i_1...i_s} = \int_0^1 ... \int_0^1 y_{i_1...i_s}^2(x_{i_1}...x_{i_s}) dx_{i_1}...x_{i_s} \ , \tag{11}$$

where $1 \leq i_1 < ... < i_s \leq n, s = 1, ..., n$. Squared and integrated over Ω equation (5) gives:

$$Var = \sum_{i=1}^{n} Var_i + \sum_{1 \leq i < j \leq n} Var_{ij} + ... + Var_{1,2,...,n} \ . \tag{12}$$

Thus, the sensitivity measures $S_{i_1...i_s}$ are defined by:

$$S_{i_1...i_s} = \frac{Var_{i_1...i_s}}{Var} \ . \tag{13}$$

S_i is called the first order sensitivity index for the parameter x_i and it measures the main effect of x_i on the model output. $S_{ij}, i \neq j$, is the second order sensitivity index and it measures the interacted effect of the two parameters x_i and x_j on the model output. The higher order sensitivity indices can be defined in the same way.

The multidimensional integration in calculations of variances (11) and (12) is performed with the Monte Carlo method, hence the efficiency of Sobol's algorithm depends mostly of efficiency of the Monte Carlo procedure.

3   SA Numerical Library

The proposed library has two fundamental functionalities:

- it prepares the input data for grid-based applications by sampling the space of application parameters,
- it calculates input-output dependencies on the basis of data received from a grid-based application.

The interface between the library and the grid side is covered by Scalarm platform used to submit and monitor distributed computational tasks. The sequence diagram of the solution is presented in Fig. 1.

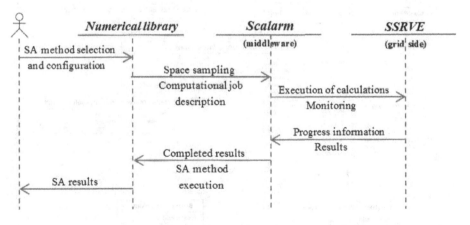

Fig. 1. Sequence diagram of numerical library and dependent software

The methods mentioned in the previous section were implemented as a part of the SA numerical library. The library is composed of:

- core classes – elements responsible for the main functionality of particular methods,
- supporting classes – elements allowing flexible management of SA methods and offering functionality of randomization, file management or statistical calculations.

The core part of the library is divided into classes dedicated to configuration, sampling, statistical investigation of model output and sensitivity analysis. The library is flexible and open for newly developed SA methods included by inheritance of the base classes. Moreover, the presented solution contains communication interfaces, which facilitate usage of the core functionality by external computer applications like grid middleware used for authorization, job scheduling and monitoring. Data generated by the SA library is submitted as input to a grid-based SSRVE service, and the functionality of this MPI-based application allows to calculate SSRVEs for different parameters. The results are returned to the specific SA method, executed by the library. The main class diagram is presented in Fig. 2. The classes cover the functionality described in the following paragraphs of this section.

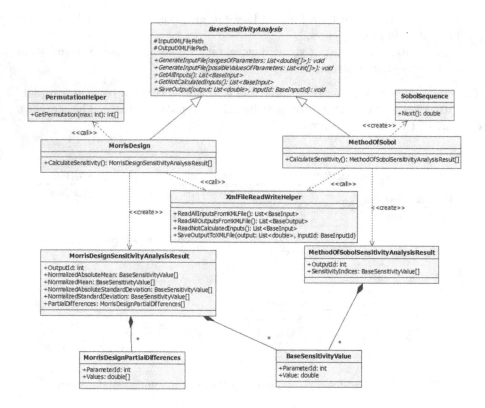

Fig. 2. Class diagram of the SA library

Sampling of the Parameters Space. Implemented methods of sensitivity analysis require to make multi-iterative calculations of the model for different inputs. The results of the calculations are used to investigate influence of inputs on the model outputs. All methods require a specific input data set, therefore the library is equipped with algorithms to generate input records and to save this set to a file afterwards. The simplest way is to use main classes for Morris Design or Sobol's method, which are presented in Fig. 2. To create objects of mentioned classes, paths of input and output files have to be set. Values of input model parameters are specified by ranges of parameters or by the set of acceptable values for each parameter.

Input/Output Management. Generated and saved input sets are read from a file of XML format by using the *GetAllInputs* method. Each of inputs has a unique identifier and values of parameters set as a vector, parsed to an object by *MorrisDesignInput* or *MethodOfSobolInput*. The methods return a list of objects. The format of XML input files is similar for both methods, therefore, one procedure dedicated to read inputs was implemented. The similar procedures were defined for saving inputs to files. The basic methods for reading and writing data are located in the static helper class called *XmlFileReadWriteHelper*.

Model Execution. The subsequent step is execution of model calculations for all inputs generated by the library. The *SaveOutput* function was implemented for Morris Design and Sobol's method to save results of the model to a file of XML format. The function saves data to a file specified as the second argument of the main classes of the sensitivity analysis library. The model has MPI-based implementation, which allows to execute calculations on many computing nodes in a grid environment. Data management methods are thread safe, preventing from many operations on files in the same time by different threads.

Calculations Management and Collection of Results. The calculations can be stopped after execution of the model covering only a part of inputs. Afterwards, it can be resumed at any time. The restart of calculations requires to deliver the files containing inputs and outputs saved before stopping. The library provides *GetNotCalculatedInputs* method to check the input parameters, which were not used in the calculations. The method analyzes two files delivered to resume calculations. Their structures are presented in Fig. 3 (a – input set, b – output set). The approach allows to properly react in the case of unexpected failures of a computer system, while the results are stored immediately after each execution of the model.

Sensitivity Analysis Performance. When all the results are gathered, the sensitivity analysis is started. The *GetNotCalculatedInputs* method is run first to check whether all necessary data was obtained. Afterwards, the *Calculate-Sensitivity* method, provided by the main classes of the library, is executed. The Morris Design method delivers many useful results, from which the most important is contained in *MorrisDesignNormalizedAbsoluteMean* objects. The number of the objects is equal to a number of output variables of the model. Morris Design also delivers model information (see Fig. 4) crucial for detailed

```xml
<?xml version="1.0" encoding="UTF-8"?>
- <Data DataType="Moriss Design Inputs File">
  - <SettingsOfAnalysis>
      <ParametersVectorCount>3</ParametersVectorCount>
    + <ValuesOfParameters>
      <SamplesCount>10</SamplesCount>
    </SettingsOfAnalysis>
  - <Inputs>
    - <Input Id="sampleId=0; inputId=0">
        <Value Id="0">4</Value>
        <Value Id="1">13</Value>
        <Value Id="2">3</Value>
      </Input>
    - <Input Id="sampleId=0; inputId=1">
        <Value Id="0">4</Value>
        <Value Id="1">10</Value>
        <Value Id="2">3</Value>
      </Input>
```

a) input set

```xml
<?xml version="1.0" encoding="UTF-8"?>
- <Data DataType="Moriss Design Outputs File">
  - <Outputs>
    - <Output Id="sampleId=0; inputId=0">
        <Value Id="0">290</Value>
      </Output>
    - <Output Id="sampleId=0; inputId=1">
        <Value Id="0">221</Value>
      </Output>
    - <Output Id="sampleId=0; inputId=2">
        <Value Id="0">141</Value>
      </Output>
    - <Output Id="sampleId=0; inputId=3">
        <Value Id="0">151</Value>
      </Output>
    - <Output Id="sampleId=1; inputId=0">
        <Value Id="0">265</Value>
      </Output>
```

b) output set

Fig. 3. A part of data files for Morris Design

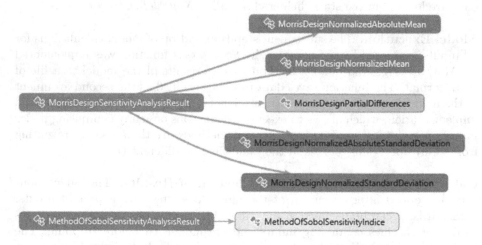

Fig. 4. Information delivered as the results of the library for Morris Design and Sobol's method

interpretation of the results. The Sobol's algorithm provides information about impact of input parameters on the model output. All obtained results are stored in a file of text format to facilitate visualization of the data with charts by using external software.

4   SSRVE Methodology

The SSRVE grid-based computational service is treated as the model for sensitivity analysis calculations in this work. The section describes the main idea of SSRVE and the optimization procedure dedicated to SSRVE creation in detail.

4.1   The Idea of SSRVE

In the micro-macro modelling approach, an RVE representing the underlying micro-structure is attached at each Gauss point of the macroscopic solution. The constitutive law describing material behavior in the macro scale is obtained by averaging the first Piola-Kirchoff stresses with respect to the RVE. The theoretical basis of the micro-macro modelling is well described in the scientific literature, see e.g. [6]. Considering micro-heterogeneous materials, the continuum mechanical properties at the macro scale are characterized by the morphology and by the properties of the particular constituents in the micro scale. In the present work, the DP microstructures composed of soft ferrite (70-80%) and hard martensite (20-30%) are considered. In the analysis, we concentrate on the measures characterizing the hard martensite islands only. The material models of the individual constituents are assumed to be known. The description of the microstructure is based on statistical considerations [7].

A usual RVE is determined by the smallest possible sub domain, which is still able to represent the macroscopic behavior of the material. Although these RVEs are the smallest as possible by the definition, they can be too complex for the efficient calculations. Therefore, the construction of statistically similar RVEs, characterized by a lower complexity than the smallest possible substructure, was proposed in [6]. The basic idea is to replace an RVE with an arbitrary complex inclusion morphology by a periodic one composed of optimal unit cells, see Fig. 5. This idea is applied in the present work to the analysis of the DP steel microstructures.

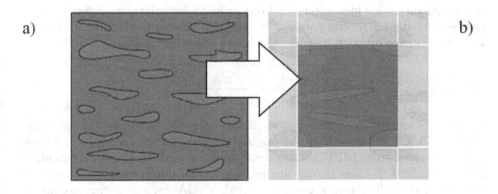

a)   b)

Fig. 5. Schematic illustration of the basic concept of the SSRVE [8]: a) RVE, b) periodically arranged SSRVE

4.2   The Procedure of SSRVE Generation

The scheme of the procedure dedicated to the SSRVE creation is presented in Fig. 6. It starts with analysis of original micrographs [9] to obtain binary images with separated martensitic inclusions. In case of 2D procedure, the shape

coefficients of inclusions in original images are estimated. In case of 3D procedure, the reconstruction of three dimensional microstructure on the basis of 2D
images has to be performed [10]. Then, the shape coefficients of 3D inclusions
are estimated. Additionally, statistical coefficients and rheological coefficients
are calculated to obtain the full set of reference coefficients used further in an
optimization procedure.

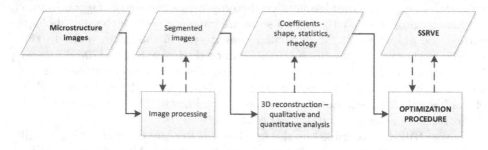

Fig. 6. Procedure of SSRVE generation

The optimization procedure is based on the approach proposed in [6]. Originally, a method for the construction of simple periodic structures for the special
case of randomly distributed circular inclusions with constant equal diameters
was proposed by Povirk [11]. The positions of circular inclusions of a given
diameter were found by minimizing the objective function, defined as a square
root error between spectral density of the periodic RVE and non-periodic real
microstructure. This idea inspired Schroeder [6] to formulate the objective function accounting for several parameters, which characterize the microstructure.
In this work, the function was adapted in the following form:

$$\Phi = \sqrt{\sum_{i=1}^{n} \left[w_i \left(\frac{\varsigma_i - \varsigma_{iSSRVE}}{\varsigma_i} \right)^2 \right]}, \tag{14}$$

where: w_i – weights, n – number of coefficients, a sum of all $w_i = 1$, $\varsigma_i - i^{th}$ reference coefficient obtained from the original microstructure, $\varsigma_{iSSRVE} - i^{th}$ coefficient obtained from SSRVE. The calculations are performed with assumption
that inside SSRVE there is only one inclusion. The implementation of the optimization procedure uses a genetic algorithm (GA), where a chromosome is
composed of m elements representing coordinates of control points determining
the SSRVE shape. These points are connected with spline functions forming the
smooth shape of the SSRVE inclusion. Calculation of the objective function is
performed iteratively for each proposition of the new SSRVE shape.

5   Results

Two experiments of sensitivity analysis were performed, i.e., by using Morris
Design and Sobol's method. The influence of three input parameters on output

was analyzed. The number of inclusions per cell, the degree of NURBS basic functions and number of control points were selected for that purpose. The output parameters of the model were represented by the number of iterations and mean square error between reference equivalent tensile stress and SSRVE equivalent tensile stress. The reference stress value was calculated from the rule of mixture for the original microstructure, while equivalent tensile stress for SSRVE was calculated from results of virtual uniaxial compression, tensile and shear deformation tests. The selected output parameters reflect the quantitative and qualitative character of the model, respectively.

The results obtained for Morris Design are presented in Fig. 7a and Fig. 7b. The former figure presents standard deviation of both output parameters for all the input coefficients. The latter plot shows sensitivity index calculated for the same configurations.

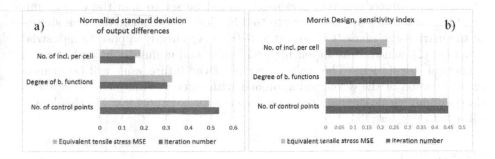

Fig. 7. Results of sensitivity analysis by using Morris Design: a) normalized standard deviation, b) sensitivity index

The second experiment was performed with the Sobol's method. The obtained results are presented in Fig. 8. They are characterized by the similar trend as in the case of Morris Design, however, the final values of sensitivity index are slightly different.

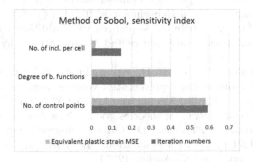

Fig. 8. Results of sensitivity analysis by using Sobol's method

6   Conclusions and Future Work

The paper presents the application of sensitivity analysis methods to support the procedure of SSRVE generation. The SA numerical library, containing two different methods, was designed and implemented for this purpose. As a model for sensitivity analysis, the grid-based optimization procedure for construction of SSRVE was used. The analysis was performed to determine the influence of three input model parameters on qualitative and quantitative model output. The results obtained for Morris Design and Sobol's method proved that the highest influence on both output parameters is provided by the number of control points used to describe shapes of inclusions. This parameter is also very unstable, what is shown by the highest value of standard deviations of outputs. On the other hand the lowest influence on the qualitative and quantitative SSRVE results has the number of inclusions. Therefore, to increase computational performance of the whole procedure, this parameter should be set to 1 in the case of microstructures, which are not characterized by clearly visible two different shapes of the martensitic phase. Calculated SSRVEs were already applied in industrial practice [12], which proved their high reliability and usefulness in sophisticated numerical calculations. The main objective of the future work will be focused on integration of the developed approach with software solutions dedicated to design of multiscale simulations on modern e-infrastructures, e.g. Multiscale Application Designer [13].

References

1. Król, D., Wrzeszcz, M., Kryza, B., Dutka, Ł., Kitowski, J.: Scalarm: massively self-scalable platform for data farming. In: Bubak, M., Turała, M., Wiatr, K. (eds.) CGW 2012 Proceedings, pp. 53–54. ACK Cyfronet AGH, Kraków (2012)
2. Saltelli, A., Ratto, M., Andres, T., Campolongo, F., Cariboni, J., Gatelli, D., Saisana, M., Tarantola, S.: Global Sensitivity Analysis. The Primer. John Wiley & Sons Ltd. (2008)
3. Morris, M.D.: Factorial sampling plans for preliminary computational experiments. Technometrics 33, 161–174 (1991)
4. Sobol, I.M.: Sensitivity analysis for non-linear mathematical models. Mathematical Modelling and Computational Experiment 1, 407–414 (1993)
5. Sobol, I.M.: Uniformly distributed sequences with additional uniformity properties. USSR Computational Mathematics and Mathematical Physics 16(5), 236–242 (1976)
6. Schroeder, J., Balzani, D., Brands, D.: Approximation of random microstructures by periodic statistically similar representative volume elements based on lineal-path functions. Archives of Applied Mechanics 81, 975–997 (2011)
7. Beran, M.: Statistical continuum theories. Wiley, New York (1968)
8. Brands, D., Schroder, J., Balzani, D.: On the incorporation of microstructural information in dual phase steel simulations. In: Hirt, G., Tekkaya, A.E. (eds.) Proc. 10th ICTP, pp. 823–826. Aachen (2011)
9. Rauch, L., Madej, L.: Application of the automatic image processing in modeling of the deformation mechanisms based on the digital representation of microstructure. International Journal for Multiscale Computational Engineering 8, 343–356 (2010)

10. Rauch, L., Bachniak, D., Bzowski, K., Pietrzyk, M.: Reconstruction of 3D microstructures of one phase materials. Rudy i Metale Nieżelazne 58, 789–794 (2013)
11. Povirk, G.L.: Incorporation of microstructural information into models of two-phase materials. Acta Metallurgica 43, 3199–3206 (1995)
12. Ambrozinski, M., Bzowski, K., Rauch, L., Pietrzyk, M.: Application of statistically similar representative volume element in numerical simulations of crash box stamping. Archives of Civil and Mechanical Engineering 12, 126–132 (2012)
13. Rycerz, K., Bubak, M., Ciepiela, E., Harężlak, D.: Gubała, T., Meizner, J., Pawlik, M.: Composing, Execution and Sharing of Multiscale Applications. Submitted to Future Generation Computer Systems, after 1st review (2013)

Optimization of Profile Extrusion Processes Using the Finite Element Method and Distributed Computing

Andrzej Milenin and Piotr Kustra

AGH University of Science and Technology,
al. Mickiewicza 30, 30-059 Kraków, Poland
milenin@agh.edu.pl

Abstract. This paper is dedicated to the development of a FEM model of the extrusion process of tubes and profiles made from Mg alloys. Mg alloys are characterized by low technological plasticity during extrusion. The model is designed to optimize the parameters of extrusion tubes on mandrel and profiles using the ductility of alloy as an objective function and the maximum value of temperature in the deformation zone as a limitation condition. Optimization of extrusion parameters requires a large number of FEM simulations that is why the solution based on distributed computing capabilities was used. The developed software generates a vector of simulation variants and runs them on a computer cluster in parallel mode in the PL-Grid Infrastructure. In this work, an example of optimization process and a procedure for obtaining the needed materials data for simulation using the case of Mg alloy were shown.

Keywords: extrusion, optimization, FEM, distributed computing.

1 Introduction

As shown in the papers [1,2,3], the metallurgical community has a high demand for modeling and optimization of extrusion profiles problems. This resulted in the widespread use of FEM in the development of numerical tools for the extrusion and also causes the evolution of appropriate numerical techniques [4,5,6].

Extrusion processes of tubes and profiles from low plastic materials (for example biocompatible magnesium alloys) have their peculiarities. In addition to the well-known optimization criteria, based on the geometric dimensions of the profile, limitations must be fulfilled, related to the limited technological ductility of alloys. The addition of such restrictions is possible after development and implementation of appropriate material models to FEM code [7,8].

Because the extrusion is a process of deep plastic deformation, the related numerical calculations are time consuming. Optimization of extrusion processes requires the run several instances of codes with different initial conditions. Therefore, it seems sensible to launch another instance of the program on separate

M. Bubak et al. (Eds.): PLGrid Plus, LNCS 8500, pp. 378–390, 2014.

processors in parallel mode. This solution is possible using the PL-Grid Infrastructure.

The aim of this work is to develop and verify a parallel FEM code for the modeling and optimization of extrusion of magnesium tubes and profiles.

2   State of the Art

One of FEM-based software for the simulation and optimization of extrusion profiles is Extrusion3d [9,10], which was developed in cooperation with the company Quantor [11,12] and was a commercial prototype of the Qform-Extrusion [12]. The sequential version of the program has been developed [9], [11]. That computer program was used for the optimization of extrusion profiles of aluminum alloys [11], [13,14,15]. In this software, a user has to prepare simulation data, analyze the results and also has to decide what would be the next step of the optimization. Another modern FEM software (FEM Qform-Extrusion, Forge3, Deform) designed for modeling the extrusion processes is working analogously. Specific features of FEM tasks related to the modeling of extrusion profiles in comparison with most of the three-dimensional modeling tasks for forming processes are:

- high number of degrees of freedom of the task (because the high gradients of strain rate require the use of a dense FEM mesh),
- high sensitivity of the solutions to the quality and density of the FE mesh and also to the geometric dimensions of the matrix.

These factors caused that the optimization based on sequential calculations is significantly limited by the computing power. On the other hand, the optimization process in this case involves a large amount of conventional simulations independent of each other (for example, a simulation of the extrusion process at different positions of channel on the die). This opens a wide range of possibilities for the use of parallel and distributed computation to perform the optimization of the extrusion process (for example "inverse" analysis). Using supercomputers network (the PL-Grid Infrastructure) and the parallel run of the multiple task simulation, optimization results can be obtained over one simulation. Unfortunately, performing the calculations using the resources of PL-Grid requires a significant modification of the sequential FEM code [9,10,11].

3   Description of the Solution

3.1   Formulation of the Boundary Value Problem and the Finite Element Implementation

The solution of the boundary problem of extrusion tubes and profiles involves a mechanical model, which is based on the theories of the plastic flow and heat transfer problem. We will present the basic mathematical formulation of the thermo-mechanical solver. The basic differential equation contains the following equations:

equilibrium equations:

$$\sigma_{ij,i} = 0, \tag{1}$$

compatibility condition:

$$\xi = \frac{1}{2}(v_{i,j} + v_{j,i}), \tag{2}$$

constitutive equations:

$$\sigma'_{ij} = \frac{2\bar{\sigma}}{3\bar{\xi}}\xi_{ij}, \tag{3}$$

incompressibility equation:

$$v_{ij} = 0, \tag{4}$$

energy balance equation:

$$k(t_{,i})_{,i} + \beta\bar{\sigma}\bar{\xi} = 0, \tag{5}$$

yield stress model:

$$\bar{\sigma} = \bar{\sigma}(\bar{\varepsilon}, \bar{\xi}, t), \tag{6}$$

where: σ_{ij} – stress tensor, ξ_{ij} – strain rate tensor, v_i – components of flow vector, σ'_{ij} – deviator of stress tensor, $\bar{\sigma}, \bar{\varepsilon}, \bar{\xi}$ – effective stress, effective strain and effective strain rate, t – temperature, β – heat generation ratio that is commonly accepted within the limits, $\beta = 0.9$ - 0.95 (0.9 value was used [16]) k – thermal conductivity.

Yield stress model is a function of strain, strain intensity and temperature. The model that is used for numerical calculation is presented in Section 4. Equations (1) – (4) are converted using the principle of virtual work and techniques for the nonlinear FEM algebraic equation. They contain the flow velocities and average tension as unknown parameters. To solve the system of equations, the frontal method and iterative calculations of the distribution of parameters is used. The algorithm used to solve the system of nonlinear equations is presented in detail in the work [17].

The finite element, which is used in the extrusion code, is shown in Fig. 1. For the interpolation of the metal flow rate and temperature, a 15-node element was used, while the interpolation of mean stress was done using a 6-node linear element. This interpolation results in the stability of the solution [18]. In the existing FEM programs [12], [14] for the modeling of hot extrusion process, solutions of thermal and mechanical boundary problems usually are obtained on different FEM grids, which was caused by different areas of grid density. For example, there may be deformation zones of high temperature gradients, requiring to thicken FEM mesh to solve the heat transfer problem (T-grid), while not requiring a dens fine mesh for mechanical solution (M-grid). A reverse situation is also possible. This approach allows for minimizing the simulation time of thermo-mechanical problem. Therefore, in this code two different grids T and M are used. They exchange data during calculations. In sequential programs, mechanical and thermal parts are solved one after another (on a single processor) and the exchange of data takes place immediately after the end of each solution.

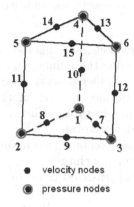

●   velocity nodes

◉   pressure nodes

Fig. 1. Prismatic finite element with 15(6) nodes

A modification of the program code for parallel mode was done by a distribution of the thermal and mechanical problems on two different processors. So in the parallel mode, the heat transfer problem and mechanical problem are solved on separate processors and the exchange of data between T and M grids is possible after completion of both tasks. That is why the parallel solutions of thermal and mechanical part significantly (almost twice as much) accelerate the solution of a single thermo-mechanical task.

The optimization process in the developed service is based on the parallel execution of the generated task variants vector obtained by the factorial experiment algorithm. In this case, also a modification of the program code was carried out being aimed at parallel execution of program variants (the number of variants is dependent of the size of task variants vector). In the optimization mode the user must select the parameters of the extrusion, which will be changed during the process, and set the range and the number of intervals of each parameter change. Examples of the parameters are: extrusion velocity, billet temperature, die temperature, pre chamber temperature, etc. and the geometric parameters of the matrix. In the latter case, the user must prepare several variants of the geometry of the matrix channel in form of files in a special format that is compatible with the format of the graphic files in Qform [12]. Because the FEM mesh generation for each variant of the calculation is performed in parallel mode, the interference of the user with this process is impossible.

3.2   Automatic Generation of FE Mesh for Variants of the Optimization Process

The developed code for generating the volume FEM mesh is based on the idea of extracting a 2d mesh to obtain the appropriate dimensions in 3d space. This approach requires the development of an automatic and effective program for 2d mesh generation for complex cross-sections. To solve this problem, the following algorithm was used:

1. The contours of the die channels, pre chamber and container geometry are analyzed in order to determine the points, which separate them into closed areas to generate the 2d grid independently (see Fig. 2a).
2. 2d mesh generation is performed in each of the closed area as shown in (see Fig. 2b). Grids are built in subdomains in such a way that they have common nodes at the border of areas.
3. 2d grids obtained in step 2 are combined to obtain a 2d mesh for the container sections, extruded profiles or pre chamber.
4. 2d mesh quality analysis is performed based on the following criteria:

$$k_{2d} = max(\frac{L_{max}}{L_{min}}),$$ (7)

where: L_{max} and L_{min} are maximum and minimum side length of the finite element. Parameter k_{2d} is calculated for each element of FEM grid.

5. If the value k_{2d} is above the limit (empirical data indicates a value of 20), the grid is generated again by modification of contours and by setting more nodes in order to obtain a more uniform grid. As the 2d mesh generator, the program from the sequential version of Extrusion3d is used [11], [13,14].
6. 2d grids are "extruded" to the appropriate dimensions in 3d for different variants of extrusion (see Fig. 2c). If needed, grids are modified to obtain roundings, fillets or to change surface of matrix.

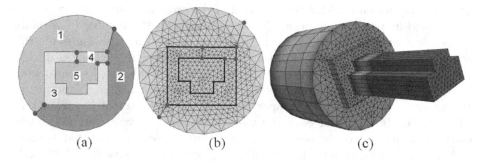

(a)   (b)   (c)

Fig. 2. Diagram of FE mesh generation for the matrix with prechamber: (a) the results of the algorithm search of the geometry split at the closed domains, (b) the result of 2d mesh generation for the domains, (c) generated 3d mesh

The separate categories of matrices are those, which are used for extrusion tubes and profiles on mandrel. Such a process needs more contours to characterize the geometry of the process.

For each variant of simulation two different grids are generated – for mechanical solution (M) and thermal (T) problem. For a sequential program, the exchange of data between grids takes place after completion of a single task. Once a solution of the boundary problem for current temperature distribution (on M-grid) is obtained, the following data: velocity, strain rate tensor and stress tensor are transferred to T-grid, where the heat transfer problem is solved. Because solving the stationary thermal problem with convection is difficult, T-grid is more dens than M-grid. The procedure described above is working differently in parallel mode. The data exchange between T and M grids is done at the end of each task (T and M tasks are solved in the same time – parallel mode).

The algorithm used for automatic control of mesh quality was tested with an example of profiles of complex shape. Fig. 3 shows the optimization process of the position of a profile channel at the mirror of die (a real profile to the window system) [15].

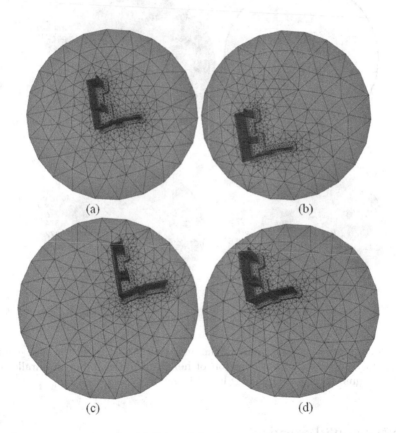

Fig. 3. Automatic generation of FEM grid during optimizing in parallel mode. Different positions of profile channel on die (a) – (d)

3.3   Test Simulations

Test simulations are performed to determine the influence of geometric parameters on the non-isothermal flow of material. As an example of optimization
height of pre chamber for profile made from AD31 alloy was analyzed (see Fig. 4).
Three variants of pre chamber height are considered – 5, 10 and 15 mm. The
simulation results (see Fig. 4b–d) allow to conclude that the smallest bend of
profile after extrusion is obtained at a height of 10 mm (see Fig. 4c).

The data presented in Fig. 4 also shows that the change in the geometry of
the pre chamber has influence on the temperature in the process. The reason is
the change of material flow velocity, which results in a different distribution of
generation of the heat deformation.

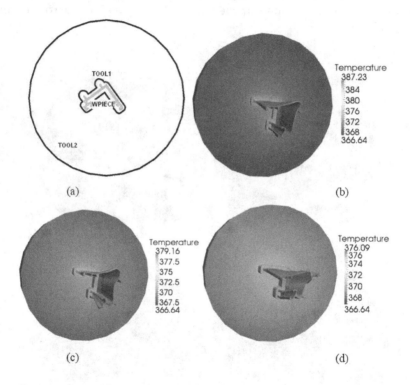

Fig. 4. Cross section of the matrix channel (WPIECE) and the pre chamber
(TOOL1): (a) the results of optimization of height of pre chamber in parallel mode
for (b) h = 5 mm, (c) h = 10 mm, (d) h = 15 mm

4   Extrusion3d Service

The Extrusion3d service has been developed within the PLGrid Plus project.
This service consists of a computational engine, which was written in Fortran
language and a preprocessor, which was developed using Excel software and

VBA (Visual Basic for Applications) language. The service has been installed in the PL-Grid Infrastructure.

The user generates batch files with geometry and boundary conditions using Excel preprocessor. This task is performed on the user's computer. To submit a calculation task, QCG-Icon (QosCosGrid-Icon) is used [19]. Based on the boundary conditions file and the file(s) (dependent on simulation type) with geometry, a vector of extrusion tasks is generated. Then, each task is run on a separate processor in the PL-Grid Infrastructure. Such a solution caused that the optimization time is comparable with the time needed to perform one numerical simulation of the extrusion process. The results of numerical calculations are returned to the user's computer as a *vtk* format file(s). The results can be read using ParaView software, which is an open source code and allows for visualization and analysis of simulation results [20].

5   Methods of Obtaining Material Models

The flow stress model for MgCa08 magnesium alloy is introduced using Hansel-Spittel equation:

$$\sigma_s = Aexp(-m_1t)\bar{\varepsilon}^{m_2}\bar{\xi}^{m_3}exp(\frac{m_4}{\bar{\varepsilon}})(1+\bar{\varepsilon})^{m_5t}exp(m_7\bar{\varepsilon})\bar{\xi}^{m_8t}t^{m_9}. \tag{8}$$

The proposed ductility model states that only a limited amount of strain, called critical deformation, can be introduced to the material without damaging it. The fracture is not observed as long as the effective strain is smaller than the critical deformation:

$$\Psi = \frac{\bar{\varepsilon}}{\varepsilon_p(k_\sigma, t, \bar{\xi})} < 1, \tag{9}$$

where: Ψ – ductility function, ε_p – critical deformation function.

Critical deformation was proposed [21] as a function of stress triaxiality $k_\sigma = \sigma_0/\sigma_s$, temperature t and effective strain rate $\bar{\xi}$:

$$\varepsilon_p(k_\sigma, t, \bar{\xi}) = d_1exp(-d_2k_\sigma)exp(d_3t)\xi^{\bar{d}_4}, \tag{10}$$

where: d_1 - d_2 – empirical coefficients.

It was assumed that two conditions must be satisfied to avoid material damage during processing. The maximum value of ductility function (9) is less than one and the maximum calculated temperature is less than the incipient melting temperature of MgCa08 alloy, which is 516°C.

5.1   Flow Stress Model

The compression tests results were used to identify parameters of the flow stress model. The Hooke-Jeeves algorithm was used to minimize the objective function, defined as the root mean square error between the load curves obtained from experiment and predicted by FEM simulation [7], [21]. Friction factor in the simulation was equal to 0.1. The coefficients of the equation (8), determined using the optimization method, are as follows: A=405.85; m_1=-0.00826428; m_2=-0.0281807; m_3=0.020492; m_4=-0.0114059; m_5=0.00521939; m_7=-0.69316; m_8=0.0001636; m_9=0.192958.

5.2   Ductility Model

The generalized reduced gradient algorithm for nonlinear problems implemented in MS Excel Solver was used to determine the empirical coefficients of the critical deformation function. According to equation (9), the ductility function in a fracture initiation zone should be equal to or greater than one to correctly predict the material damage. Therefore, the objective function was defined using the following equation:

$$\Theta = \frac{1}{n} \sum_{i=1}^{n} (1 - \Psi_i)^2 \,, \tag{11}$$

where: – Ψ_i value of ductility function in fracture initiation zone obtained from FEM simulation, n – number of measurements.

The empirical coefficients of equation (10) are as follows: d_1=0.04611; d_2=0.4759; d_3=0.01265; d_4=-0.07009. The total percentage error between real and calculated values was 7.8%.

Fig. 5 shows the comparison between the results obtained from FEM simulation and tensile test carried out at 300°C with tool velocity 1 mm/s. The model predicted that the ductility function value is greater than one when the total tool displacement reached 22 mm (see Fig. 5a). During the experimental testing, the sample fractured at displacement 22.5 mm (see Fig. 5b).

5.3   Results of Optimization of Extrusion Process of MgCa08 Tube

Based on the developed code, an optimization of the extrusion process of tubes made from MgCa08 alloy was done. The experimental part was made in IMN in Skawina, Poland. The extruded tube had a diameter of 5 mm (internal diameter 4 mm). The size of rod was 20 mm and the extrusion velocity was 1 mm/s.

The reason for optimizing the thermal conditions in extrusion process is formation of defects (cracks) in the final tube (see Fig. 6). Therefore, the optimization of billet temperature was performed. Some example results obtained for the billet temperature of 400°C, 300°C and 200°C are shown in Fig. 7,8,9.

The simulation results for the billet temperature 400°C allow to conclude that the ductility function reaches a value less than one (see Fig. 7). It is worth noting of the nonlinear dependence of the temperature of tube after extrusion of the billet temperature. By lowering the billet temperature, heat generation is increasing and a more intense temperature rising can be observed. Based on the accepted variant of the extrusion process, tubes without defects were obtained. An example of the obtained tubes is shown in Fig. 10.

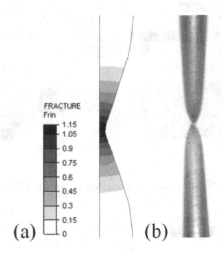

(a)   (b)

Fig. 5. Tensile test at 300°C with tool velocity equal to 1 mm/s: (a) ductility function; (b) fractured specimen

Fig. 6. An example of the formation of defects during the extrusion of the tube

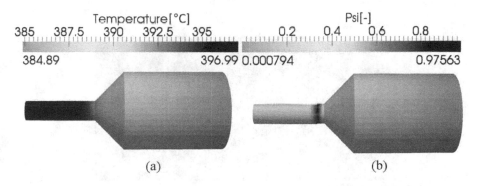

(a)   (b)

Fig. 7. The temperature distribution (a) and ductility function distribution (b) for the billet temperature of 400°C (Option 1)

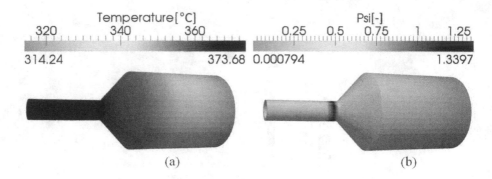

(a)   (b)

Fig. 8. The temperature distribution (a) distribution of ductility function (b) for the billet temperature of 300°C (Option 2)

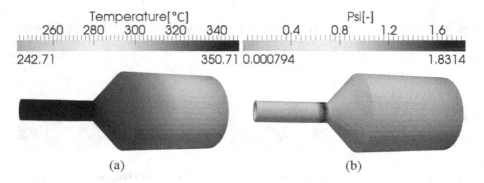

(a)   (b)

Fig. 9. The temperature distribution (a) distribution of ductility function (b) for the billet temperature of 200°C (Option 3)

Fig. 10. Tube made from MgCa08 alloy obtained experimentally in the extrusion process for the conditions corresponding to numerical calculations (Option 1)

6   Conclusions and Future Work

6.1   Conclusions

1. The proposed concept of optimization of the extrusion process of Mg alloys is based on solving in parallel mode the simulations task generated in the space factor. This allowed to solve the optimization task over one simulation.
2. The verification of the program was made on the basis of the experimental extrusion process of biocompatible tubes made of MgCa08 alloy.
3. The developed program is available in the PL-Grid Infrastructure as the Grid-Extrusion service.

6.2   Future Work

The authors plan to extend the service to other deformation processes of magnesium alloys, e.g., the drawing process of thin magnesium wires with a low diameter ca. 0.1mm.

References

1. Machado, P.: Extrusion Die Design. In: Proceedings of Fifth International Extrusion Technology Seminar, Chicago, USA, vol. 1, pp. 385–389 (1992)
2. Kiuchi, M., Yanagimoto, J., Mendoza, V.: Three-dimensional FE simulation and extrusion die design. Journal of The Japan Society For Technology of Plasticity 39, 27–32 (1998)
3. Herberg, J., Gundeso, K., Skauvic, I.: Application of numerical simulation in design of extrusion dies. In: 6 Int. Aluminium Extrusion Technology Seminar, pp. 275–281 (1996)
4. Chenot, J.L., Bay, F.: An overview of numerical modeling techniques. Journal of Materials Processing Technology 80-81, 8–15 (1998)
5. Chenot, J.L.: Resent contributions to the finite element modelling of metal forming processes. Journal of Materials Processing Technology 34, 9–18 (1992)
6. Rens, B.J.E., Brekelmans, W.A.M., Baaijens, F.P.T.: A semi-structured mech generator applied to extrusion. In: Proc. of the 7 Int. Conf. on Numerical Methods in Industrial Forming Processes, Enschede, Netherlands, pp. 621–626 (1998)
7. Milenin, A., Gzyl, M., Rec, T., Płonka, B.: Computer aided design of wires extrusion from biocompatible Mg-Ca magnesium alloy. Archives of Metallurgy and Materials 59(2), 561–566 (2014)
8. Milenin, A., Kustra, P.: Numerical and experimental analysis of wire drawing for hardly deformable biocompatible magnesium alloys. Archives of Metallurgy and Materials 58, 55–62 (2013)
9. Milenin, A.: Mathematical modeling of operations of correcting the dies for section extruding. Metallurgicheskaya i Gornorudnaya Promyshlennost 1-2, 64–66 (2000)
10. Milenin, A., Berski, S., Banaszek, G., Dyja, H.: Theoretical analysis and optimisation of parameters in extrusion process of explosive cladded bimetallic rods. Journal of Materials Processing Technology SPEC. ISS 157-158, 208–212 (2004)

11. Lishnij, A.I., Biba, N.V., Milenin, A.: Two levels approach to the problem of extrusion optimization. Simulation of Materials Processing Theory, Methods and Applications. In: Proceedings of the 7 Int. Conf. on Numerical Methods in Industrial Forming Processes, pp. 627–631 (1998)

12. Biba, N., Stebunov, S., Lishny, A., Vlasov, A.: New approach to 3D finite-element simulation of material flow and its application to bulk metal forming. In: Proceedings of the 7th International Conference on Technology of Plasticity, pp. 829–834 (2002)

13. Milenin, A.: Modelowanie numeryczne procesów wyciskania profili z zastosowaniem gęstości dyslokacji jako zmiennej wewnętrznej w modelu reologicznym materialu. Informatyka w Technologii Materiałów 1(2), 26–33 (2002) (in Polish)

14. Milenin, A., Biba, N., Stebunow, S.: Modelowania procesów wyciskania cienkościennych kształtów z wykorzystaniem teorii dyslokacji do opisania właściwości reologicznych stopow aluminium. In: Proceedings of the 9th Conference "Informatyka w Technologii Metali", pp. 217–224 (2002) (in Polish)

15. Milenin, A., Golovko, A.N., Mamuzic, I.: The application of three-dimensional computer simulation when developing dies for extrusion of aluminium shapes. Metallurgija 41(1), 53–55 (2002)

16. Bell, J.F.: The Experimental Foundations of Solid Mechanics. In: Encyclopedia of Physics, Mechanics of Solids VIa/1, Berlin (1973)

17. Kopernik, M., Milenin, A.: Two-scale finite element model of multilayer blood chamber of POLVAD_EXT. Archives of Civil and Mechanical Engineering 12(2), 178–185 (2012)

18. Zienkiewicz, O.C., Taylor, R.L.: The Finite Element Method. The Fluid Mechanics, vol. 3. Butterworth, Oxford (2000)

19. QCG-Icon, http://www.qoscosgrid.org/trac/qcg-icon

20. ParaView, http://www.paraview.org/

21. Milenin, A., Kustra, P.: Optimization of extrusion and wire drawing of magnesium alloys using the finite element method and distributed computing. In: Proc. Int. Conf. InterWire, Atlanta, USA. Wire Association International (2013)

Adaptive Finite Element Modelling of Welding Processes

Krzysztof Banaś, Kazimierz Chłoń, Paweł Cybułka,
Kazimierz Michalik, Przemysław Płaszewski, and Aleksander Siwek

AGH University of Science and Technology,
al. Mickiewicza 30, 30-059 Kraków, Poland
kbanas@agh.edu.pl

Abstract. We describe the ModFEM_met service within the PL-Grid Infrastructure, designed to model welding processes using adaptive finite element method (FEM). The code aims at utilizing modern computing environments to produce high quality results for large scale problems. It exploits different forms of parallelism to improve the performance of simulations. The program uses a three-dimensional model of laser welding for materials with different chemical compositions.

Keywords: finite element method, adaptivity, parallel computations, laser welding, weld pool.

1 Introduction

The ModFEM_met service within the PL-Grid Infrastructure described below belongs to the family of parallel adaptive finite element codes, used for simulations in various domains of science and engineering. The main efforts related to the development of the service are twofold: first, the service tries to incorporate advanced numerical models related to its domain of application, second, it is designed to be easily adapted to new computer architectures and to exploit the related opportunities for high performance execution.

The subject of high performance parallel finite element simulations has always been an active area of research. We mention here the investigations of two kinds. First, there is a problem of code design that combines advanced numerical methods with the ease of maintenance, modification and extension. Recent, interesting developments in that field include, among others, the FENICS project, the Dune framework and the Deal.II library.

The FENICS project [15] emphasizes component architecture with the common goal of enabling an automated solution of differential equations. The proposed components provide scientific computing tools for working with computational meshes, finite element variational formulations of ordinary and partial differential equations as well as numerical linear algebra. The FENICS project takes advantage of many available HPC libraries, like MPI, PETSC, Trilinos, uBlas, UMFPACK, ParMetis, and others. In the Dune framework [6] the leading

M. Bubak et al. (Eds.): PLGrid Plus, LNCS 8500, pp. 391–406, 2014.

design principle was one-to-one correspondence between the mathematical objects within grid-based discretization schemes for stationary and non-stationary partial differential equations and C++ interface classes. The goal has been accomplished thanks to advanced C++ programming techniques and the reported experiments demonstrated both the efficiency of the created code and its applicability to a very large class of problems. A similar approach to avoiding computational overhead, while still taking advantage of OO-programming, is presented in the Deal.II library [5]. The design of the library tries to achieve a proper separation of FEM concepts such as meshes, finite element spaces and degrees of freedom, as well as the possibility to arbitrarily combine finite element spaces, numerical quadratures, and mapping information.

The second important field of research is the use of modern computer architectures for simulation software. Within this field main efforts are concerned with providing the optimal implementations for computational kernels – the key components from the point of view of the performance of codes. Traditionally, such investigations include the problem of proper mapping of numerical linear algebra routines to computer architectures [17], [28]. Also, the implementation of algorithms typical for finite elements, such as procedures for element matrix creation and assembly have been investigated for different architectures [8,9]. Recently, the issue of heterogeneous computing, with the use of accelerators, has gained importance, both for linear algebra (see e.g. [27]), as well as for finite element computing in general [11], [22].

2   Finite Element Modelling of Welding Processes

The process of joining materials by laser welding has been used in industry for many years. The development of this joining method depends on the increasing knowledge of the physical phenomena that occur during welding. Mathematical models of welding try to describe these processes and to predict the structure of the weld. Numerical simulations based on mathematical models give insight into the details of welding processes impossible to obtain by experimental methods [23], [25]. The accuracy of numerical models depends on the involved physical and chemical phenomena specific to the welding process, assumed boundary conditions, energy source characteristics and material models.

The ModFEM_met service was created to simulate formation of a weld pool during the laser beam welding. Moving laser beam illuminates the surface of welded materials (see Fig. 1) that are locally melted into a weld pool. The pool, after cooling for some time, when the laser beam moves further, forms a solid weld. The phenomena inside the weld pool can be described using many mathematical descriptions. In the model selected for the ModFEM_met service, the following assumptions have been made [26]:

- flow in the weld pool is laminar and incompressible
- weld pool surface is flat
- thermophysical properties of the materials used in the model are piecewise linear or constant

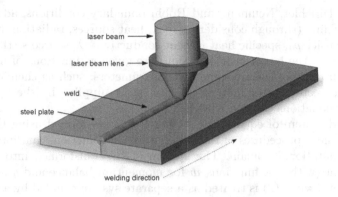

Fig. 1. A schematic illustration of the modelled welding process

– such physical phenomena are taken into account as: Marangoni effect [12], mushy zone formation [24], buoyancy force (the last using the Boussinesq approximation)
– different forms of power density distribution of the laser beam (such as single-mode TEM_{00} or multi-mode TEM_{01}, TEM_{10}, TEM_{11}) can be assumed according to the classification proposed in [13].

The mathematical model used by the ModFEM_met service consists of unsteady Fourier and Navier-Stokes equations, approximated by the adaptive finite element method. The system of Navier-Stokes equations for the unknown fluid velocities $u(x,t)$ and pressures $p(x,t)$ has the form:

$$\rho_0 \left(\frac{\partial u}{\partial t} + (u \cdot \nabla)u - \nu \nabla^2 u \right) + \nabla p + Ku = f \quad \text{in } \Omega \tag{1}$$

$$\nabla \cdot u = 0 \quad \text{in } \Omega$$

with boundary conditions:

$$u = \hat{u}_0 \quad \text{on } \Gamma_D$$

$$(\nu \nabla u)n - pn = g \quad \text{on } \Gamma_N.$$

In Equation (1) ν denotes kinematic viscosity of fluid, K is related to momentum changes in the mushy zone, f is a source term that includes gravity forces and forces resulting from Boussinesq approximation. The vector fields $\hat{u}_0$ and g are given on disjoint parts of the computational domain Ω, Γ_D for velocities and Γ_N for pressures, respectively. As a separate type of boundary condition, a free surface is specified, with several complex phenomena, such as surface tension and Marangoni effects, taken into account.

Heat conduction equation for the unknown temperature field $T(x,t)$ has the form:

$$\rho_0 c \left(\frac{\partial T}{\partial t} + u \cdot \nabla T \right) - \nabla \cdot (\lambda \nabla T) = s \quad \text{in } \Omega \tag{2}$$

with classical Dirichlet, Neumann and Robin boundary conditions, adapted to the case of welding (through considering, e.g., heat sources, radiation, etc). Parameters of density ρ_0, specific heat c, heat conductivity λ, source s (that takes into account, e.g., the latent heat of fusion) are given as functions of materials and temperature (and possibly some other parameters, such as chemical composition). The vector of conductive velocity, $\boldsymbol{u}$, is supplied by the system of Navier-Stokes equations coupled with (2).

The coupled system of equations (1) and (2) is transformed using the standard finite element procedures of multiplying by test functions and integrating over the computational domain. The system (1) is transformed into a single weak statement (with test functions $\boldsymbol{w}$ for momentum balance and q for divergence condition), while (2) is treated as a separate system coupled by a solution procedure that provides the field $\boldsymbol{u}$ to (2) and the field T to (1).

For both systems, the same triangulation of the domain Ω into elements Ω_e is introduced, and the same approximation based on linear shape functions assumed. For the Navier-Stokes equations, the spaces V_u^h and V_p^h of continuous piecewise linear polynomials satisfying Dirichlet boundary conditions for velocities and pressure, together with the corresponding function spaces V_w^h and V_q^h with zero values on respective parts of the boundary are defined. Similar spaces are defined for the heat equation.

Both systems (1) and (2) in a standard Galerkin form are unstable, so both are stabilized using the SUPG method [10]. Using the index notation and the summation convention for repeated indices, together with ",$_i$" denoting space differentiation with respect to i-th space coordinate, the final weak formulation for the system of the Navier-Stokes equations is given as:

Find approximate functions $u_i^h \in V_u^h$ and $p^h \in V_p^h$ such that the following statement:

$$\rho_0 \int_\Omega \frac{\partial u_j^h}{\partial t} w_j^h d\Omega + \int_\Omega \left\{ \rho_0 u_{j,k}^h u_k^h w_j^h + \rho_0 \nu u_{j,k}^h w_{j,k}^h - p^h w_{j,j}^h + K u_j^h w_j^h \right\} d\Omega$$

$$+ \int_\Omega u_{j,j}^h q^h d\Omega + \sum_e \int_{\Omega_e} \left\{ R_j(\boldsymbol{u}^h, p^h) \tau_{jk} R_k(\boldsymbol{w}^h, q^h) + u_{j,k}^h \delta w_{j,k}^h \right\} d\Omega \quad (3)$$

$$= \int_\Omega f_j w_j d\Omega - \int_{\Gamma_N} g_j w_j d\Gamma$$

holds for every function $w_i^h \in V_w^h$ and $q^h \in V_q^h$.

Above, $R_j(\boldsymbol{u}^h, p^h)$ and $R_k(\boldsymbol{w}^h, q^h)$ denote the residuals of Navier-Stokes equations computed for respective arguments, while τ_{jk} and δ are coefficients of the SUPG stabilization [10].

In a similar fashion, the statement for the heat equation is obtained, with the same stabilization and its own specific boundary terms.

The resulting weak statements are non-linear and time dependent. The standard α-method of time integration is used for both of them and the procedure of simple (Picard's) iterations is used for solving the system of non-linear equations [16].

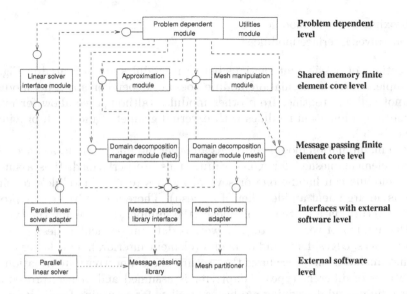

Fig. 2. Structure of FEM applications created by the ModFEM framework

3   ModFEM Framework for Parallel Adaptive Finite Element Simulations

ModFEM (from Modular Finite Element Method) is a framework for creating applications that perform adaptive finite element approximations of various problems in science and engineering. Its design principles have been described in several papers [1,2], [18], [19] and are briefly summarized below.

The main assumption of ModFEM is that every code created within the framework is composed of several modules of different types. The structure of such a code is shown in Fig. 2, with rectangular boxes representing an instance of a module of particular type. For each module type, a specifically designed, narrow but extensive interface is defined, and interactions between modules are limited to procedure calls exclusively. As an obvious consequence of such a design, the modules of the same kind are fully interchangeable, which makes it possible to create many applications with different combinations of modules' instances. From the technical point of view, the idea behind the design is that each module operates on its own, possibly large, data structure that is fully independent of the data structures of other modules.

3.1   Finite Element Core Modules

The modules forming an application are grouped into several levels. The most fundamental modules constitute a finite element core level. There are three such modules:

– mesh manipulation module

- approximation field module
- linear solver interface module.

The directions of possible interactions between modules are indicated in Fig. 2. For example, a mesh manipulation module does not depend on any other module, it does not call any routines from other modules (although we allow for interfacing mesh manipulation modules with external geometry and mesh providing components [3]).

A mesh manipulation module provides all other modules with data concerning the finite element meshes, for which simulations are performed. It is assumed that the module can handle one or several meshes (each of module's routines accepts as an argument an identifier of a mesh). There are interfaces for procedures that return data on the whole mesh (the number of elements, the type of mesh, the number of vertices, etc.), as well as data on particular mesh entities, such as vertices, edges, faces and elements (element interiors). This latter group of routines includes the procedures that return the connectivity information for mesh entities of different types. Adaptivity is assumed and, hence, procedures exist for refining and de-refining meshes, as well as for returning family information for mesh entities (assuming that from the division of one father mesh entity there emerge several child entities).

An approximation module performs operations related to the degrees of freedom associated with mesh entities (higher order approximations are allowed and degrees of freedom can be associated with mesh entities of any kind). Different approximation modules are usually related to different approximation spaces (the sets of shape functions and degrees of freedom), with the ModFEM interface allowing for such techniques as hp-adaptivity and discontinuous Galerkin methods. Approximation module routines use extensively mesh manipulation procedures, and, due to this strong dependence, there are usually specific instances of approximation modules for particular types of meshes (although there may be several different approximation modules properly interacting with a single mesh manipulation module). The main role of an approximation module in the finite element solution process is to perform numerical integration of terms in a finite element weak formulation, an essential ingredient of the creation of the finite element system of linear equations. There exist also important procedures for projecting the values of degrees of freedom between mesh entities of different types and generations.

The main purpose of linear solver interface routines is to provide solvers with properly structured element matrices and vectors, from which the global system matrix and the global right hand side vector are created. Moreover, the interface module often has to interact with solvers during the linear system solution process (these interactions depend on the type of the solver, e.g., for frontal solvers, local matrices are supplied during the solution procedure, while for iterative solvers with geometric multigrid preconditioning, additional restriction and prolongation operators are provided by the FEM part of the code). To keep the design of ModFEM codes clean and limit the number of modules' interactions, a linear solver interface module does not call the mesh manipulation and approximation procedures. All the necessary data for solvers are provided by problem dependent routines, being often only wrappers for particular mesh manipulation and approximation routines.

3.2   Problem Dependent Modules

The procedures from within the modules forming the finite element core level are used by problem dependent modules to form the whole finite element specific part of simulation applications. The procedures from within the problem dependent modules control and manage the processes of:

- reading input files and writing output files
- time integration and solution of nonlinear equations (if they are required in simulations)
- creation and solution of systems of linear equations
- mesh adaptations.

Apart from steering and control procedures, each problem dependent module contains procedures used for creating local element matrices and vectors, according to the particular weak formulation associated with the module. This design allows to use the problem dependent modules related to different problems to create a simulation code for coupled problems. What is necessary, is to create a so called "super-module", with steering and control procedures, but without procedures related to the weak formulation. The weak formulation related part of the application is composed of the proper weak formulation routines from coupled sub-problems using additional procedures that perform suitable coupling.

A super-module must provide all the control and steering procedures for its sub-problems, taking into account such implementation details as whether the sub-problems use the same mesh or different meshes, whether they are approximated using the same spaces or different ones, what are the strategies for time integration and solution of nonlinear equations (if they are required), what adaptation strategy should be employed for the coupled problems.

Some control and management procedures at this level of the code may be used for different problems without modifications. Several such procedures are gathered in the special utilities module, the same for all problems, and – due to this – differentiated from the problem dependent module, visible in Fig. 2. The procedures from within the utilities module may be used for:

- initialization of meshes and approximation fields
- exporting output data in different formats (e.g. for graphics)
- performing mesh adaptations according to one of common strategies (like, e.g., equidistribution of errors)
- estimation of a posteriori global and local errors by derivative recovery (Zienkiewicz-Zhu method).

3.3 External Software Level

There is only one external module required to complete a basic version of each application – a solver of linear equations. The FEM part of ModFEM codes is designed to work with sequential and parallel solvers, within shared and distributed memory environments. Both direct (e.g. multi-frontal) and iterative (e.g. Krylov space with different preconditioning) solvers are supported. The codes can interact with multigrid solvers and preconditioners by providing prolongation and restriction operators for particular finite element meshes and approximation spaces used in simulations.

3.4 Parallel Execution

ModFEM codes can run on different types of parallel computers and are designed to efficiently exploit the opportunities for high performance execution offered by the hardware. It is assumed that all finite element core modules utilize shared memory multithreading at proper places (e.g. loops over mesh entities). OpenMP is considered as the standard programming environment, but different modules employ multithreading independently (hence, they can use other parallelization models, like OpenACC or Pthreads).

At the same level, but with more effort, low level programming techniques to access massively multicore accelerators are employed. For architectures like GPUs or Xeon Phi coprocessors, OpenCL and CUDA programming models are used for the main computational task of finite element codes, i.e., global linear system creation (assuming that system solution is performed by external software) [4], [14].

Special care is taken to allow for flexible adaptation of finite element core modules to execution on machines with distributed memory. The standard modules are required only to provide several additional procedures used in distributed memory environment. Main tasks are performed by special modules, designed to support the selected standard parallelization strategy – the domain decomposition approach.

There are two types of domain decomposition modules (see Fig. 2), one for mesh modules and the second one for approximation modules. These domain decomposition modules can be described as suitable overlays that adapt different core modules to the execution in distributed memory environments. A domain decomposition module for meshes provides global (inter-subdomain) identifiers for mesh entities, controls mesh partition and repartition, performs the exchange of mesh entities between sub-domains for load balancing, provides parallel solvers with necessary data on the mesh entities belonging to neighbouring subdomains. A domain decomposition module for fields provides global identifiers to degrees of freedom, allows for the exchange of degrees of freedom between subdomains and performs simple operations on global vectors of degrees of freedom, such as norm or scalar product. As indicated in Fig. 2, the module for fields can use the information provided by the module for meshes, i.e., it can base its global identifiers for degrees of freedom on global identifiers for mesh entities.

Domain decomposition modules may use external software for particular tasks, such as mesh partition and repartition. The message passing calls in ModFEM are abstracted to special message passing library interface. Different implementations of interface procedures can therefore exist, including different variations of MPI implementations (blocking or non-blocking, buffered, synchronous, etc.). Thanks to this, the separation of concerns between the algorithmic and computational sides of the distributed memory version of the code is achieved.

ModFEM codes can utilize special adapters for parallel, distributed memory solvers of linear equations, to interact according to the model defined by the ModFEM interfaces. The interfaces, for example, specify the way for performing some global operations (ranging from simple vector product and norm to restriction and prolongation for the whole mesh in geometric multigrid), as well as the exchange of degrees of freedom associated with ghost mesh entities for subdomains.

The two modes of parallelization, for the shared memory and distributed memory environments, are designed as orthogonal concepts. Shared memory parallelism is implemented for core modules. In principle, each module can use an independent parallelization model. There are, however, special mechanisms (in form of special procedures in the utilities module) that allow for sharing a common platform for parallelization within several modules. This way, several versions or extensions of core modules for different parallel architectures can be implemented and employed, once again using a mechanism of compile time selection, typical for ModFEM.

All these variations of core modules can be used without changes in shared memory and distributed memory environments. Each variant of core modules must conform to the specification that allows for domain decomposition overlays to interact with the modules. In such a way, a particular application created within the ModFEM framework can be flexibly adapted to different computer architectures and parallel programming environments. In particular, such combinations as OpenMP/OpenCL/MPI or OpenMP/CUDA/MPI are possible for heterogeneous clusters with accelerators in form of graphics processors or Xeon Phi coprocessors.

4   ModFEM_met Service within the PLGrid Plus Project

The structure of the ModFEM computational framework described in the previous section, allows for the use of ModFEM ready-made modules for the Mod-FEM_met service. Due to the nature of the welding process, some of the modules have been partially modified or extended for the deployment in the service. The functionality of the modified modules has not been changed and the modules can still be used in other services. The ModFEM_met service uses the following modules provided by the ModFEM computational framework:

- the part of the stabilized Streamline Upwind Petrov-Galerkin (SUPG) problem dependent module supplying a weak formulation for the approximation of incompressible fluid flows

- the part of the convection-diffusion problem dependent module supplying a weak formulation for the approximation of the temperature field
- a super-module coupling the above two modules to model the welding processes
- a hybrid mesh management module for meshes composed of tetrahedral and prismatic elements
- an iterative solver module for linear equations implementing the GMRES (Generalized Minimal Residuals) method with different forms of preconditioning
- an interface module for the external direct solver PARDISO and the solver itself.

For the purpose of deploying the service in the PL-Grid Infrastructure, a special procedure for running the code using the QosCosGrid middleware for job management [7] has been created. The procedure allows for preparing input data files, sending them to computational infrastructure, running the service and transferring the results back to the user.

The files required for the execution of the code include:

- a single file with a scenario of the service usage
- two files with control data, one for each subproblem – incompressible fluid flow and thermal convection-diffusion
- a file with mesh data (the same mesh is used for all approximation fields)
- a file with material data, again, only one file with the characteristics of the media necessary for approximating all the fields
- two files describing the boundary conditions to be imposed on the boundary of computational domain, a separate file for incompressible fluid flow and thermal convection-diffusion
- solver configuration files (one or several, depending on how many parameter sets are specified in problem control files).

When the service starts, the super module reads the data from input files and initializes proper data structures. The basic data structures used by the ModFEM_met service include:

- physico-chemical data structure for the materials used in the model – part of the properties are stored as constant; other, temperature dependent data, are linearly approximated in the successive temperature ranges
- mesh data structure – depending on the shape of the model, the calculations can be performed on prismatic, tetrahedral or hybrid meshes
- data structure for velocity, pressure and temperature approximation fields.

After initializing the data structures, the ModFEM_met super module proceeds to integration in time, performing the following actions at each time step:

- Courant-Friedrichs-Lewy (CFL) condition is tested and the length of time step possibly modified; thanks to the use of implicit methods for time integration, the length of time step can be set to be a multiple of the length determined by the CFL condition

- time dependent boundary conditions are updated
- iterative GMRES solver module or external direct solver PARDISO is called
- mesh adaptation and de-adaptation conditions are tested; when the conditions are fulfilled, division or merging of mesh elements are performed
- condition of recording the results in an internal ModFEM format or VTK format is checked and suitable data are written to output files when required.

At each time step, the most time consuming part of the calculations is the solution of two systems of linear equations – one for each subproblem (due to the use of adaptive meshes, implicit time integration methods are used to allow for larger time steps). In the case of using the direct solver, only shared memory computations can be performed. For distributed memory environments the service is equipped with the GMRES iterative solver that can operate in both sequential and parallel modes.

The effectiveness of the iterative solver is largely determined by the preconditioner employed, the method of improving condition number for the matrix of the system of equations. Block Jacobi (additive Schwarz) preconditioner is used globally and block Gauss-Seidel (multiplicative Schwarz) preconditioner is applied locally for each MPI process/subdomain. Several variants of block-GS preconditioning with different algorithms for block construction are available in ModFEM_met [20,21]. Parallel execution of the solver is accomplished by only several small changes in the sequential code. In each GMRES iteration the solver delegates to the FEM part of the code three operations whose implementation vary depending on the operating mode. The problem module, which has the knowledge of the operating mode – sequential or parallel – is responsible for providing appropriate implementation. These operations are:

- exchange of the updated values of the current residual, after preconditioned residual calculations in each GMRES iteration
- calculations of vector scalar products and norms, for global vectors of unknowns that correspond to the whole computational domain.

When the calculations are completed, the user has a range of files with results:

- text files with data for successive steps of calculations (data read from configuration files, mesh information data, solution error values for Navier-Stokes and heat module for each iteration, mesh adaptation data) – in the case of distributed memory calculations each node can produce its own file
- field dump files in ModFEM or VTK format.

The files are transferred back to the user and can be further post-processed or visualised, using the modules provided by the ModFEM framework or some external programs (e.g. ParaView visualisation software).

5   ModFEM_met Service – A Case Study

To show the capabilities of the code, we present a case study of welding of two plates made of steel (HS625). For applying a heat source, the model proposed

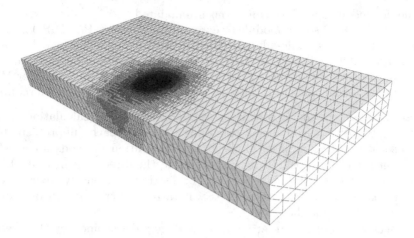

Fig. 3. The adapted mesh at time t=0.06s for the example case of two plates welding

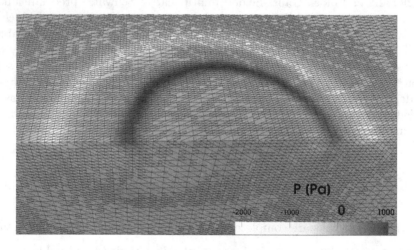

Fig. 4. The pressure field on the cross-section of the mesh from Fig. 3 in the neighbourhood of the welding pool

in [13] was used with the laser mode of Gaussian intensity profile TEM_{00}. The same adaptive mesh is used for the approximation of all fields: temperature, pressure and velocity. Computations are performed for several thousands of variable length time steps, with adaptations of the mesh after each ten steps. Fig. 3 shows the mesh obtained at time instant t=0.06s. The next two figures present the pressure field (see Fig. 4) and the velocity field (see Fig. 5) on the cross section of the mesh from Fig. 3, in the neighbourhood of the welding pool.

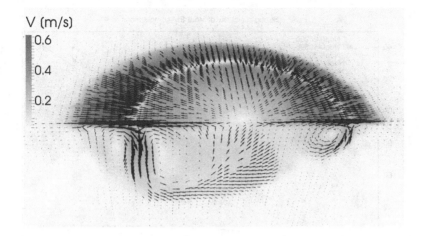

Fig. 5. The velocity field on the cross-section of the mesh from Fig. 3 in the neighbourhood of the welding pool

6   Scalability Study

We present a strong scalability study to show the performance of the Mod-FEM_met code in cluster environments. For the purpose of the study, we solve a sequence of test problems using a growing number of processors. Test problems consist in performing the creation of a system of linear equations and several (10) iterations of the GMRES solvers. By doing this, we consider only computational performance of the code, neglecting the problem of numerical performance (i.e., solver convergence) that may depend on the physical problem solved.

We use the meshes with the growing number of nodes (proportional to the number of unknowns in the solved linear systems) from 20,000 up to 1,280,000. We use the number of MPI processes from 1 (the code employed was the parallel code) to 128 (32 cluster nodes, 4 processes per node). Fig. 6 presents the speed-up obtained for test cases. The code presents a typical behaviour. For small problems, the communication cost early starts to dominate the solution time and the speed-up curve becomes flat. For large problems, we obtain speed-ups close to the perfect one. In fact, for large problems and small numbers of processors we get super-linear speed-up. This can be associated with the performance of sparse matrix-vector product, the essential ingredient of the solver from the performance point of view. For large problems, there is little spatial locality when accessing the main memory and the local performance is relatively low. With the number of processes growing, the problem size per process decreases, the locality of references in sparse matrix-vector product increases and the performance of the solver grows. For large problems and large numbers of processes, the local performance becomes constant, the communication time is outweighed by the computation time and we obtain the speed-up curves parallel to the perfect speed-up line.

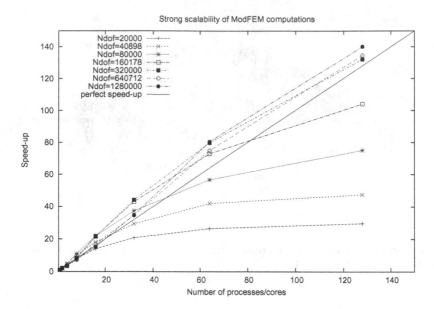

Fig. 6. The speed-up of the ModFEM_met solver for several different meshes (strong scaling)

7 Conclusions

The purpose of the ModFEM_met service is to help students, engineers and scientists to simulate and design welding processes. The model currently employed by the service should be understood as the first step towards accurate simulations of these complex phenomena. Further steps should take into account the modelling of electromagnetic field, moving free surface and several additional processes such as turbulence and multi-scale interactions, not yet accounted for in our models. New numerical techniques, e.g. discontinuous approximations, variational turbulence models, moving mesh formulations, provide opportunities for improvement of modelling capabilities and are also planned for future extensions of the framework. Last but not least, another direction of development will be aimed at increasing the computational capabilities of the code, by utilizing the progress in hardware and programming models. Not yet included into the ModFEM_met service are the ModFEM extensions allowing for the use of accelerators, such as GPUs or Xeon Phi coprocessors. The list of modifications is not closed, different programming models and hardware solutions are considered for the future, in order to adapt to the quickly changing landscape of contemporary computer architectures.

References

1. Banaś, K.: A modular design for parallel adaptive finite element computational kernels. In: Bubak, M., van Albada, G.D., Sloot, P.M.A., Dongarra, J. (eds.) ICCS 2004, Part II. LNCS, vol. 3037, pp. 155–162. Springer, Heidelberg (2004)
2. Banaś, K.: On a modular architecture for finite element systems. I. Sequential codes. Computing and Visualization in Science 8, 35–47 (2005)
3. Banaś, K., Michalik, K.: Design and development of an adaptive mesh manipulation module for detailed FEM simulation of flows. In: Sloot, P.M.A., van Albada, G.D., Dongarra, J. (eds.) Proceedings of the International Conference on Computational Science, ICCS 2010, University of Amsterdam, The Netherlands, May 31-June 2. Procedia Computer Science, vol. 1, pp. 2043–2051. Elsevier (2010)
4. Banaś, K., Płaszewski, P., Macioł, P.: Numerical integration on {GPUs} for higher order finite elements. Computers and Mathematics with Applications 67(6), 1319–1344 (2014)
5. Bangerth, W., Hartmann, R., Kanschat, G.: Deal.II – A general-purpose object-oriented finite element library. ACM Transactions on Mathematical Software 33(4), 24 (2007)
6. Bastian, P., Blatt, M., Dedner, A., Engwer, C., Klofkorn, R., Kornhuber, R., Ohlberger, M., Sander, O.: A generic grid interface for parallel and adaptive scientific computing. Part II: implementation and tests in DUNE. Computing 82(2), 121–138 (2008)
7. Bosak, B., Komasa, J., Kopta, P., Kurowski, K., Mamoński, M., Piontek, T.: New Capabilities in QosCosGrid Middleware for Advanced Job Management, Advance Reservation and Co-allocation of Computing Resources – Quantum Chemistry Application Use Case. In: Bubak, M., Szepieniec, T., Wiatr, K. (eds.) PL-Grid 2011. LNCS, vol. 7136, pp. 40–55. Springer, Heidelberg (2012), http://dl.acm.org/citation.cfm?id=2184180.2184184
8. Cecka, C., Lew, A.J., Darve, E.: Assembly of finite element methods on graphics processors. International Journal for Numerical Methods in Engineering 85(5), 640–669 (2011), http://dx.doi.org/10.1002/nme.2989
9. Dziekonski, A., Sypek, P., Lamecki, A., Mrozowski, M.: Generation of large finite-element matrices on multiple graphics processors. International Journal for Numerical Methods in Engineering 94(2), 204–220 (2013), http://dx.doi.org/10.1002/nme.4452
10. Franca, L., Frey, S.: Stabilized finite element methods ii: The incompressible Navier-Stokes equations. Computer Methods in Applied Mechanics and Engineering 99, 209–233 (1992)
11. Georgescu, S., Chow, P., Okuda, H.: GPU acceleration for FEM-based structural analysis. Archives of Computational Methods in Engineering 20(2), 111–121 (2013)
12. Ha, E., Kim, W.: A study of low-power density laser welding process with evolution of free surface. International Journal of Heat and Fluid Flow 26, 613–621 (2005)
13. Han, L., Liou, F.W.: Numerical investigation of the influence of laser beam mode on melt pool. International Journal of Heat and Mass Transfer 47, 4385–4402 (2004)
14. Krużel, F., Banaś, K.: Vectorized OpenCL implementation of numerical integration for higher order finite elements. Computers and Mathematics with Applications 66(10), 2030–2044 (2013)
15. Logg, A., Mardal, K.A., Wells, G.N., et al.: Automated Solution of Differential Equations by the Finite Element Method. Springer (2012)

16. Löhner, R.: Applied Computational Fluid Dynamics Techniques: An Introduction Based on Finite Element Methods. Wiley (2008)
17. Marker, B., Poulson, J., Batory, D., van de Geijn, R.: Designing linear algebra algorithms by transformation: Mechanizing the expert developer. In: Daydé, M., Marques, O., Nakajima, K. (eds.) VECPAR. LNCS, vol. 7851, pp. 362–378. Springer, Heidelberg (2013)
18. Michalik, K., Banaś, K., Płaszewski, P., Cybułka, P.: ModFEM – a computational framework for parallel adaptive finite element simulations. Computer Methods in Materials Science 13(1), 3–8 (2013)
19. Michalik, K., Banaś, K., Płaszewski, P., Cybułka, P.: Modular FEM framework ModFEM for generic scientific parallel simulations. Computer Science 14(3) (2013), https://journals.agh.edu.pl/csci/article/view/262
20. Płaszewski, P., Paszyński, M., Banaś, K.: Architecture of iterative solvers for hp-adaptive finite element codes. Accepted for publication in Computer Assisted Methods in Engineering and Science 20(1), 43–54 (2013)
21. Płaszewski, P., Banaś, K.: Performance analysis of iterative solvers of linear equations for hp-adaptive finite element method. In: Alexandrov, V.N., Lees, M., Krzhizhanovskaya, V.V., Dongarra, J., Sloot, P.M.A. (eds.) Proceedings of the International Conference on Computational Science, ICCS 2013, Barcelona, Spain, June 5-7. Procedia Computer Science, vol. 18, pp. 1584–1593. Elsevier (2013)
22. Reguly, I., Giles, M.: Finite element algorithms and data structures on graphical processing units. International Journal of Parallel Programming, 1–37 (2013), http://dx.doi.org/10.1007/s10766-013-0301-6
23. Rońda, J., Siwek, A.: Modelling of laser welding process in the phase of keyhole formation. Archives of Civil and Mechanical Engineering 3, 739–752 (2011)
24. Roy, G., Elmer, J., DebRoy, T.: Mathematical modeling of heat transfer, fluid flow, and solidification during linear welding with a pulsed laser beam. Journal of Applied Physics 100 (2006)
25. Siwek, A.: Model of surface tension in the keyhole formation area during laser welding. Computer Methods in Material Science 13(1), 166–172 (2013)
26. Siwek, A., Banaś, K., Rońda, J., Chłoń, K., Cybułka, P., Michalik, K., Płaszewski, P.: Modelowanie procesu spawania z wykorzystaniem programu adaptacyjnej metody elementów skończonych ModFEM. Hutnik 80(4), 248–253 (2013) (in Polish)
27. Tomov, S., Dongarra, J., Baboulin, M.: Towards dense linear algebra for hybrid GPU accelerated manycore systems. Parallel Computing 36(5-6), 232–240 (2010)
28. Williams, S., Oliker, L., Vuduc, R., Shalf, J., Yelick, K., Demmel, J.: Optimization of sparse matrix-vector multiplication on emerging multicore platforms. Parallel Comput. 35(3), 178–194 (2009)

Numerical Simulation of the Continuous Casting of Steel on a Grid Platform

Lechosław Trębacz, Katarzyna Miłkowska-Piszczek,
Krzysztof Konopka, and Jan Falkus

AGH University of Science and Technology,
al. Mickiewicza 30, 30-059 Kraków, Poland
{trebacz,kamilko,kkonopka,jfalkus}@agh.edu.pl

Abstract. The process of continuous casting of steel is a modern and
the most effective method of obtaining steel cast strands due to its standardization, automation and production process continuity, which brings
about high quality and very high yield. The presented paper shows the
Procast service, a distributed solver that is explicitly designed for the
simulation of the continuous casting of steel on a grid platform. This
service calculates temperature and solid fraction distributions for the selected machine geometry and user-specified material data and boundary
conditions. This article presents a continuous casting simulation for the
S235 steel cast with an industrial continuous casting machine. In addition, the speed-up and efficiency of calculations for various numbers
of calculation nodes and sizes of finite element mesh is presented. We
characterize some commercial programs for parallel computing of the
continuous casting model as well.

Keywords: continuous casting of steel, Grid, speed-up, FEM, ProCAST.

1 Introduction

Computing grid is a distributed system that supports a virtual research environment across different institutions [1]. Grid computing is an emergent field in
computer science that focuses, in part, on the aggregation of geographically distributed and federated computational resources [2]. These resource aggregations
can be harnessed by grid applications to solve problems in science and engineering, which require considerable computing power. Solving such challenging
problems, and subsequently, obtaining new scientific results, is an integral part
of the grid computing vision.

In recent years, the possibilities surrounding numerical modelling of metallurgical processes have been very important for creating new technologies, along
with modifying those already existing. Modelling of the continuous process of
steel casting (CCS) is generally acknowledged in literature as this subject has
been addressed by many authors [3,4]. In the continuous casting process, molten
metal is poured from the ladle into the tundish and then through a submerged
entry nozzle into a mould cavity. The mould is water-cooled so that enough

M. Bubak et al. (Eds.): PLGrid Plus, LNCS 8500, pp. 407–418, 2014.
© Springer International Publishing Switzerland 2014

heat is extracted to solidify a shell of sufficient thickness. The shell is withdrawn from the bottom of the mould at a casting speed that matches the inflow of metal so that the process ideally operates at a steady state. Below the mould, water is sprayed to further extract heat from the strand surface, and the strand eventually becomes fully solid when it reaches the metallurgical length.

Continuous casting of steel is a prevailing and progressive casting method that is applied in the steel industry. It is amongst new and continually developing casting processes, their purpose being to improve the steel cast strand quality. Due to the global scale of steel production, any studies that can improve the effectiveness of the casting process are vital from the business point of view.

The presented paper shows the Procast Service, a distributed and complete satisfiability solver that is explicitly designed for simulating continuous casting of steel. The purpose of this paper is to show the use of the developed service for temperature field and the solid fraction calculation for selected CC machine. An additional aim of this paper is to determine the speed-up and efficiency of this service for various numbers of processors.

2   State of the Art

The method of continuous casting of steel – due to its ability to maximize the utilization of the equipment capacity, along with the possibility of mechanization, automation and computer control of the process – has become the fundamental and prevailing method for obtaining steel semi-products. In order to obtain the correct course of the continuous casting process, steel with a specific chemical composition and an adequate temperature should be supplied to the continuous casting machine [4], [6,7]. The formulation of a numerical model of the continuous casting process requires knowledge of a number of process parameters, i.e., the casting speed, the amount of heat taken away in individual cooling zones, the technical parameters of the continuous casting machine. In addition, it is necessary to be aware of the material-related parameters for the selected steel grade [8]. The key material-related parameters are: specific heat, heat of solidification, thermal conductivity, density, and liquidus and solidus temperatures [9].

At present, the numerical modelling also includes the prediction of cast strand defects such as cracks, porosity or element segregation.

Nowadays, the advanced computer programs are used for the numerical modelling of the continuous casting of steel. The commercially available computer applications for the modelling of crystallization processes are mostly based on the Finite Element Method [5]. There are a few systems on the market for modelling the continuous casting of steel:

- ProCAST (ESI) for Windows and Linux OS [10],
- THERCAST (Transvalor) for Windows and Linux OS [11,12],
- FLOW-3D Cast (Flow Science Inc.) for Windows OS [13],
- CC Master (Expresslab) [14].

Only the first two packages enable calculations to be performed on a number of processors/machines.

THERCAST of Transvalor is software for three-dimensional modelling of ingot casting and continuous casting of steel and other metals, using the finite element method. It contains a database of thermal and mechanical parameters, and therefore it is a comprehensive solution that does not require any external sources of thermo-mechanical data. This package models the process of heat transfer through metal in contact with ladles, nozzles, tundishes, rolls, sprays and by air, with great accuracy. The software also enables metal bulging between rollers and hot tearing effects to be modelled. These capabilities enable the package to optimize the continuous casting process by selecting the proper casting speed and the strand cooling conditions. This software is supported on x86 and x86-64 platforms (Intel or AMD) from a simple workstation up to an HPC cluster. The Windows operating system, as well as Red Hat Enterprise Linux (RHEL) and SUSE Linux Enterprise Server (SLES), are fully supported.

ProCAST provides a complete program solution enabling the progress of the whole casting process to be traced, including the mould filling, solidification, forming of the microstructure, and simulating the thermo-mechanical properties [15]. The ProCAST software enables the distribution of temperature, pressure and speed vectors to be modelled along the whole strand length, along with the strand metallurgical length (the length of the liquid core), and the shell thickness to be modelled both for the straight and curved geometry of the continuous casting machine. Furthermore, the influence of the casting speed and the submerged entry nozzle design on the temperature distribution, in addition to the vector speed field distribution, may be analysed. This software may also use methods utilizing simultaneously the Euler's and Lagrange's approaches (MiLE) [16]. The purpose of such a solution is simultaneous modelling of a number of other effects, for example the thermal shrinkage, the shrinkage related to a phase transition, the distribution of stresses in the strand in the zone under the mould, or the formation of a gap between the mould and the strand. The ProCAST software operates in both Windows and Linux systems.

Due to the ability to run the solver on the PL-Grid environment and configuration options, the ProCAST software was selected for the further development of the service. The result of the simulation of CCS (by ProCAST software) is the distribution of temperature and pressure. In addition, the result of modelling is a liquid core length and thickness of the shell in the mould.

3   Procast Service

The calculation solver included in the ProCAST package has been used in the implemented service. The ProCAST software allows the user to conduct calculations with the use of a DMP and combined SMP/DMP architecture. The user may also use the solver on a platform with an SMP architecture – the calculations will be performed by a few processes running in parallel. The communication is performed with the MPI protocol that is supplied together with the package. In order to perform calculations on N-processors, the finite element mesh is divided into N parts. The division of the geometry is executed directly

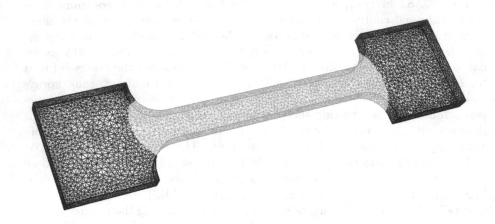

Fig. 1. Partitioning of FE mesh into three parts

by the solver, and one of the criteria taken into account is the minimization of the number of elements shared by individual parts. This approach enables to minimize the demand for communication between the individual solver processes. Fig. 1 shows an example of FE mesh partitioning.

The Procast service in the grid environment uses only the numerical solver of the ProCAST software. The preprocessor that was used for the creation of the continuous casting process model has been implemented by the Authors of the service. However, for the visualisation of the simulation results, the Paraview open-source tool has been used, for which the input data was generated by the solver, and is based on a script prepared by the Authors of the Procast service.

In order to allow the users to use the ProCAST software in the grid environment, a tool for preparing the continuous casting process model had to be introduced. Using the geometric model (created in SolidWorks) and CompuTherm LLC thermodynamic databases, a preliminary model of continuous casting process was created, including initial conditions, boundary and material properties. The initial and boundary conditions have been calculated on the basis of industrial data coming from two CC machines, which are presented in Table 1. In the preprocessor of the Procast service, the user can select the continuous casting machine geometry and the steel grade cast, or independently, determine the material-related parameters in the function of the temperature of the material cast:

– conductivity, density, specific heat, solid fraction, viscosity as a function of temperature,
– latent heat, liquidus and solidus temperature as a value.

Additionally, the user may set the following boundary conditions:

– heat transfer coefficients between steel and water in the secondary cooling zone,

Table 1. Geometric parameters of CC machines

Parameter	First machine	Second machine
Strand dimensions	220 x 1100 mm	160 x 160 mm
Mould height	900 mm	900 mm
Mould wall thickness	40 mm	14 mm
Machine/strand arc radius	10500 mm	10000 mm
Number of spray zones within the secondary cooling zone	7	4

– heat transfer coefficients between steel and mould in the primary cooling zone,
– external heat transfer coefficients of mould,

and initial conditions:

– temperature of steel,
– temperature of mould,
– casting speed.

In addition, the number of iterations should be specified, after which the steady state will be achieved in the simulation and the calculations will be terminated.

The preprocessor module has been implemented with the GridSpace2 platform, which is available in the PL-Grid Infrastructure. GridSpace2 is a virtual laboratory framework, enabling researchers to conduct virtual experiments on Grid-based resources. GridSpace2 facilitates the exploratory development of experiments by means of scripts, which can be expressed in a number of popular languages, including *bash*, Ruby, Python and Perl [17,18,19]. The preprocessor module of the service enabling the continuous casting model to be prepared from the Internet browser level was completed with this platform. Fig. 2 presents examples of HTML sites, which allow the user to enter the input data to the continuous steel casting process modelling.

The part of the Procast service concerning the input data entry has been implemented in the Ruby language. Based on the data entered by the user, which has been described above, the subsequent preprocessor script implemented in the Perl language prepares the input files for the ProCast calculation solver, which is then called by the final component of the preprocessor written as a *bash* script. Launching the ProCast solver and interaction with the PL-Grid Infrastructure is based on Portable Batch System (PBS). PBS provides a functionality of job scheduling and control. A dedicated algorithm (wrapper) was implemented by the authors of the ProCAST service to provide appropriate communication between the user interface (written in Ruby language) and the PBS on PL-Grid. The wrapper accepts several parameters (e.g. mytasks, submit, status) and returns data provided by the PBS. The data provided by PBS are filtered in order to remove headers, etc. The wrapper also provides a functionality of reporting current progress of selected calculation – the current step and the walltime used

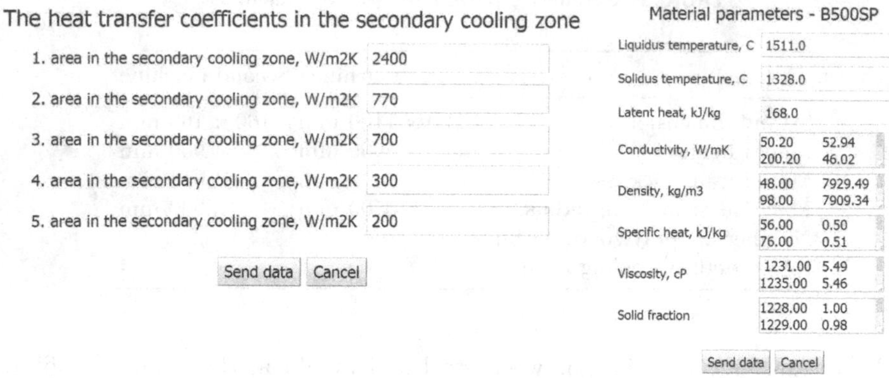

The heat transfer coefficients in the secondary cooling zone

1. area in the secondary cooling zone, W/m2K   2400

2. area in the secondary cooling zone, W/m2K   770

3. area in the secondary cooling zone, W/m2K   700

4. area in the secondary cooling zone, W/m2K   300

5. area in the secondary cooling zone, W/m2K   200

Send data   Cancel

Material parameters - B500SP

Liquidus temperature, C	1511.0	
Solidus temperature, C	1328.0	
Latent heat, kJ/kg	168.0	
Conductivity, W/mK	50.20	52.94
	200.20	46.02
Density, kg/m3	48.00	7929.49
	98.00	7909.34
Specific heat, kJ/kg	56.00	0.50
	76.00	0.51
Viscosity, cP	1231.00	5.49
	1235.00	5.46
Solid fraction	1228.00	1.00
	1229.00	0.98

Send data   Cancel

Fig. 2. Examples of HTML sites of the Procast service

by each of solver's processes. These two parameters are obtained from output files generated by the ProCAST solver. The wrapper is implemented in *bash* language and is executed on behalf of the user of the service. After the completion of calculations, the ProCast solver executes the script developed by the Authors, which saves the calculation results to a file. The results can be read by the Paraview software, which is an open-source, multi-platform data analysis and visualization application [20].

Fig. 3 presents a sequence flow chart that shows individual preprocessing stages, calculation start-up, and creating the simulation results. In conclusion, preprocessor and postprocessor scripts were implemented by the Authors, while the solver calculation stays part of the ProCast software.

4   Results

The Procast service allows the calculation of parameters such as temperature and solid fraction distribution of a strand. This data can be used to calculate the metallurgical length and thickness of the shell. The above parameters are important technological parameters in the continuous casting of steel.

For the following conditions, the temperature and solid fraction distributions have been calculated across the whole volume of the solidifying continuously cast strand, and these distributions are presented in Figs. 4-6. Table 2 shows the values of the heat transfer coefficient in a mould.

In the secondary cooling zone, different values of the heat transfer coefficient for each cooling area had been set up, according to Table 3.

Another set of boundary conditions was assumed:

− geometric parameters – first CC machine (see Table 1),
− material – steel grade S235 (chemical composition in Table 4),
− casting speed – 1m/min,
− inlet temperature – 1550°C.

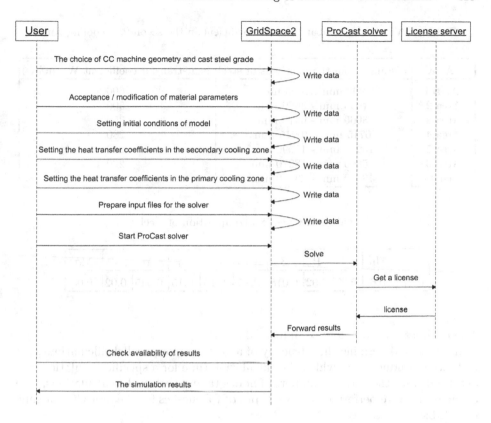

Fig. 3. The Procast service sequence flow chart

Table 2. Values of the heat transfer coefficient in a mould

Temperature, °C	Heat transfer coefficient, W/(m²K)
860	856
870	891
880	926
890	960
900	994
910	1027
920	1600
1600	1600

The numerical calculations were verified based on the analysis of:

— the thickness of the shell leaving the mould equal to 2.51 cm,
— the metallurgical length equal to 17 m.

Table 3. Values of the heat transfer coefficient in the secondary cooling zone

Area	distance from the meniscus of steel	heat transfer coefficient W/(m²K)
Area 1	900 mm - 1095 mm	600
Area 2	1095 mm - 3060 mm	500
Area 3	3060 mm - 6715 mm	350
Area 4	6715 mm - 10915 mm	280
Area 5	10915 mm - 15090 mm	250
Area 6	15090 mm - 18270 mm	220
Air cooling	18270 mm - 23300 mm	86

Table 4. Chemical composition of steel

C	Mn	Si	P	S	Cr	Ni	Cu	Al	V	Mo
0.07	0.6	0.03	0.02	0.018	0.15	0.15	0.15	0.045	0.02	0.05

These values are very close to industrial data.

In order to determine the efficiency of algorithms for parallel calculations, the tests were conducted, in which the calculation time for a specific simulation was determined for the various numbers of nodes taking part in the calculations. The calculations were performed for two types of FE meshes for the first CC machine (see Table 1):

— a big mesh with 930,000 tetrahedral elements,
— a small mesh with 273,000 tetrahedral elements.

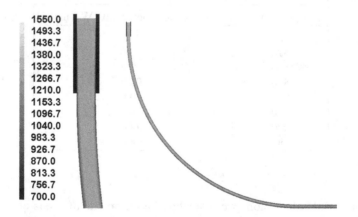

Fig. 4. Visualisation of the cast strand temperature distribution

Fig. 5. Visualisation of the solid fraction distribution

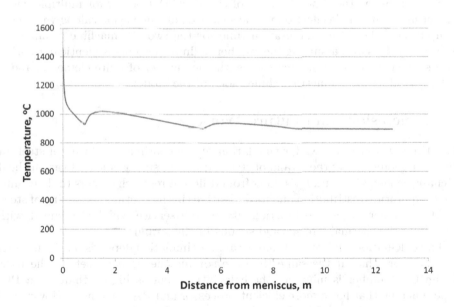

Fig. 6. The temperature distribution on the strand's surface

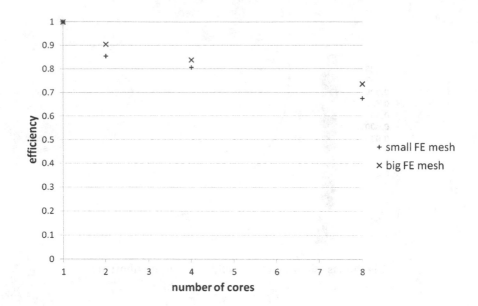

Fig. 7. Efficiency of the Procast service

Fig. 7 presents the time efficiency of the ProCAST solver for multiple cores. FE mesh size has little effect on the acceleration of calculations along with more computing nodes. The computation time for the two CC machine geometry is practically the same, assuming the number of finite elements is identical. In other words, the calculation time increases with the number of finite elements, and is independent of the geometrical dimensions of the model.

5   Conclusions and Future Work

The Procast service allows for simulation of the continuous casting of steel for different geometries of the strand of steels, different steel grade and various heat exchange coefficients. It allows users from different research centers to determine the temperature distribution and its derivatives in the continuous casting of steel.

At a further stage, the functionality of the service will be extended with modelling the thermal stresses and strains in the strand.

The calculation time of continuous casting simulation depends on the number of processors that at the same time are solving the problem set by the user. When this number is minimal, the calculation time is higher than for a PC-type machine that has a more efficient processor and RAM memory. However, if more processors are used in the grid environment for calculating the continuous casting process simulation, the time needed for these calculations is reduced, and in this configuration the grid environment – despite the additional time overheads needed to exchange information due to the division of the finite element mesh – proves more effective than a sequential environment.

Based on the results concerning the effectiveness, one can conclude that the ProCAST software, in particular its solver, has low communication and synchronization overhead as its efficiency for 8 calculation nodes falls down to about 70%. This efficiency is further increased when more finite elements are involved in the process model. Nevertheless, the use of the grid environment enables to obtain the results faster than in the case of sequential calculations.

The main advantage of the presented service and running it in the PL-Grid environment is enabling a broad community of scientists – dealing with the continuous casting issues – to conduct simulations of this process with the software dedicated to the continuous casting process.

This service is restricted by the number of available licences for a calculation solver, which in turn limits the number of nodes that can be used for such calculations. The second disadvantage of the presented solution is the constraint of the preprocessor module, which enables the continuous steel casting process conditions to be modified only for the machine geometry that was previously implemented in the service. In order to expand the service capabilities by a new geometry, a continuous caster geometrical model should be prepared and a finite element mesh should be applied to this model.

References

1. Schwiegelshohn, U., Badia, R., Bubak, M., Danelutto, M., Dustdar, S., Gagliardi, F., Geiger, A., Hluchy, L., Kranzlmueller, D., Laure, E., Priol, T., Reinefeld, A., Resh, M., Reuter, A., Rienhoff, O., Rueter, T., Sloot, P., Talia, D., Ullmann, K., Yahyapour, R., Voigt, G.: Perspectives on grid computing. Future Generation Computer Systems 26, 1104–1115 (2010)
2. Berman, F., Fox, G., Hey, T.: The grid: past, present, future. In: Berman, F., Fox, G.C., Hey, A.J.G. (eds.) Grid Computing: Making the Global Infrastructure a Reality. Wiley Series in Communications, Networking and Distributed Systems, pp. 9–50. Wiley, Chichester (2003)
3. Rywotycki, M., Miłkowska-Piszczek, K., Trębacz, L.: Identification of the boundary conditions in the continuous casting of steel. Archives of Metallurgy and Materials 57, 385–393 (2012)
4. Falkus, J., Buczek, A., Burbelko, A., Drozdz, P., Dziarmagowski, M., Karbowniczek, M., Kargul, T., Milkowska-Piszczek, K., Rywotycki, M., Solek, K., Slezak, W., Telejko, T., Trebacz, L., Wielgosz, E.: Modelowanie procesu ciaglego odlewania stali: monografia. Wydawnictwo Naukowe Instytutu Technologii Eksploatacji – Państwowy Instytut Badawczy, Radom (2012) (in Polish)
5. Zienkiewicz, O.C., Taylor, R.L., Zhu, J.Z.: The Finite Element Method: Its Basis and Fundamentals, 6th edn. Butterworth-Heinemann, Oxford (2005)
6. Milkowska-Piszczek, K.: Development and application the numerical model of the CCS process to determine technological parameters of casting for steel S235. PhD Thesis. AGH University of Science and Technology, Krakow (2013) (in Polish)
7. Schwerdtfeger, K.: The Making, Shaping and Treating of Steel. Casting Volume, 11th edn. The AISE Steel Foundation (2013)
8. Falkus, J., Milkowska-Piszczek, K., Rywotycki, M.: The influence of the selected parameters of the mathematical model of steel continuous casting on the distribution of the solidifying strand temperature. Journal of Achievements in Materials and Manufacturing Engineering 55, 668–672 (2012)

9. Milkowska-Piszczek, K., Korolczuk-Hejnak, M.: An analysis of the influence of viscosity on the numerical simulation of temperature distribution, as demonstrated by the CC. Archives of Metallurgy and Materials 58, 1267–1274 (2013)
10. Procast software, https://www.esi-group.com/software-services
11. THERCAST software, http://www.transvalor.com/
12. Vollrath, K.: Casting simulation using numerical processing becomes more important in steel mills. Stahl und Eisen 133, 45–53 (2013)
13. Liu, X.J., Bhavnani, S.H., Overfelt, R.A.: Simulation of EPS foam decomposition in the lost foam casting process. J. Mater. Process. Technol. 182, 333–342 (2007)
14. CC Master, http://www.expresslab.co.kr/home/products/?view=CC-Master
15. Procast software – user manual
16. Solek, K., Trebacz, L.: Thermo-mechanical model of steel continuous casting process 57, 355–361 (2012)
17. GridSpace2 Virtual Laboratory, https://gs2.plgrid.pl/
18. Jadczyk, T., Malawski, M., Bubak, M., Roterman, I.: Examining Protein Folding Process Simulation and Searching for Common Structure Motifs in a Protein Family as Experiments in the GridSpace2 Virtual Laboratory. In: Bubak, M., Szepieniec, T., Wiatr, K. (eds.) PL-Grid 2011. LNCS, vol. 7136, pp. 252–264. Springer, Heidelberg (2012)
19. Ciepiela, E., Zaraska, L., Sulka, G.D.: GridSpace2 Virtual Laboratory Case Study: Implementation of Algorithms for Quantitative Analysis of Grain Morphology in Self-assembled Hexagonal Lattices According to the Hillebrand Method. In: Bubak, M., Szepieniec, T., Wiatr, K. (eds.) PL-Grid 2011. LNCS, vol. 7136, pp. 240–251. Springer, Heidelberg (2012)
20. Paraview software, http://www.paraview.org/

Experimental and Numerical Database of EU Research Projects Investigating Shock Wave-Boundary Layer Interaction in Transonic/Supersonic Flows

Piotr Doerffer and Oskar Szulc

Institute of Fluid-Flow Machinery, ul. Fiszera 14, 80-231 Gdańsk, Poland
{piotr.doerffer,oskar.szulc}@imp.gda.pl

Abstract. One of the achievements of the PLGrid Plus project is the development of a new web service called "Projects' Database" (pol. *Baza Danych Projektowych "BDP"*) located at https://bdp.plgrid.pl within the PL-Grid Infrastructure. The service is designed as a unique medium for sharing the experimental and numerical results obtained during European research projects related to shock wave-boundary layer interaction and its control in transonic/supersonic flows. User access to valuable data is granted and managed through PL-Grid mechanisms and Open ID authorization allowing for an extensive validation of new physical models, advanced numerical methods and Computational Fluid Dynamics (CFD) codes applied to shock wave-boundary layer interaction phenomenon.

Keywords: database, transonic and supersonic flow, shock wave-boundary layer interaction.

1 Introduction

The shock wave-boundary layer interaction (SWBLI) phenomenon inherent in high-speed transonic/supersonic conditions is commonly encountered in various aeronautical applications, both in external and internal aerodynamics, leading to the boundary layer separation, which downgrades the efficiency of the aircraft or propulsion system, or even causes structural damage. A development of new flow control strategies would limit the physical risks for the aircraft, therefore a physical mechanism of the interaction of the shock wave with the boundary layer developing at the surface/wall is of a major concern in terms of the aerodynamic performance and is still under extensive research in Europe.

The Projects' Database (pol. *Baza Danych Projektowych "BDP"*) – the web service located at https://bdp.plgrid.pl within the PL-Grid Infrastructure and developed during the PLGrid Plus project – delivers a unique opportunity for researchers dealing with SWBLI to access necessary experimental and numerical data for validation of physical models, numerical methods and CFD codes introducing not only academic value, but also strong research quality. Due to

M. Bubak et al. (Eds.): PLGrid Plus, LNCS 8500, pp. 419–428, 2014.

a limited public availability of the data, access to BDP is restricted and granted only through a secure mechanism of the PL-Grid platform. The contents shared by BDP is a result of the coordination of European research projects and delivers a raw and first-hand set of complete experimental and CFD data focused on investigation of steady/unsteady SWBLI and its control (SWBLIC).

2   State of the Art

The shock wave generated by flow of air past the aircraft wing/profile, in the inlet of a jet-engine or in a supersonic nozzle (all important basic flow cases governed by normal and oblique shocks) has been investigated extensively within European projects in the past. Just to mention a few: Efficient Turbulence Models for Aeronautics (ETMA, 1992–1995) [1], Drag Reduction by Passive Shock Control (Euroshock, 1993–1995) [2], Drag Reduction by Shock and Boundary Layer Control (Euroshock II, 1996–1999) [3] and Unsteady Viscous Flow in the Context of Fluid-Structure Interaction (UNSI, 1998–2000) [4]. None of these project's consortia has built an easily accessible and complete database of results. So far, only the recently coordinated by IMP PAN[1] UFAST project (Unsteady Effects of Shock Wave Induced Separation, 2005–2009) [5,6] made an effort to create a database of the experimental data related to all investigated cases/problems. This database supplied with the results of the numerical simulations is currently a main content of the Projects' Database (BDP) and is described in more detail below. The follow-up TFAST project (Transition Location Effect on Shock Wave Boundary Layer Interaction, 2012–2015) [7], also coordinated by IMP PAN, will be added to BDP in the future as well.

3   UFAST Project (Unsteady Effects of Shock Wave Induced Separation, 2005–2009)

3.1   UFAST Project Overview

Aligned with the needs of the aeronautics industry, the general aim of the UFAST project was to foster experimental and theoretical work in the highly non-linear area of unsteady shock wave-boundary layer interaction. Although previous EU projects concentrated on transonic/supersonic flows, they did not examine unsteady shock wave-boundary layer interaction. Important developments in experimental and numerical methods in recent years have now made such research possible.

The main cases of study, shock waves on wings/profiles, nozzle flows and inlet flows, provided a sound basis for open questions posed by the aeronautics industry and can easily be exploited to enable more complex applications to be tackled. In addition to basic flow configurations, control methods (synthetic jets, electro-hydrodynamic actuators, stream-wise vortex generators and transpiration flow) have been investigated for controlling both interaction and inherent

---

[1] Institute of Fluid-Flow Machinery, Poland.

flow unsteadiness. The interaction unsteadiness is initiated and/or generated by SWBLI itself, but it is often destabilized by the outer/downstream flow-field. Therefore, the response of shock wave and separation to periodic excitations was of utmost importance and has been included in the research program.

Before UFAST, not enough had been done to accurately predict and control flows dominated by unsteady shock wave-boundary layer interaction. Even where advanced CFD techniques were applied to predict the flow around full aircraft configurations, they only dealt with the steady flow features and often only extrapolated from incompressible/subsonic domains to transonic/supersonic flow regimes. It is obvious that there was a lack of understanding of the flow-physics involved in unsteady SWBLI phenomena. There was also clearly a need for appropriate modelling and – even more importantly – for a control of the flows in order to limit the physical risks for an aircraft.

There was a pertinent need to improve the predictive capability of CFD methodologies, such as URANS (Unsteady Reynolds Averaged Navier-Stokes), LES (Large-Eddy Simulation), and hybrid RANS-LES approaches. Using RANS, URANS and hybrid RANS-LES methods, UFAST has cast new light on turbulence modelling in unsteady, shock dominated flows. Moreover, LES methods were applied to resolve the large coherent structures that govern SWBLI. This way, UFAST provided the "range of applicability" between RANS, URANS and LES. The UFAST project has delivered a deeper insight into the physics governing the unsteadiness of the shock, the shock/boundary layer interaction, the development of buffeting, together with a study on efficient methods for controlling these phenomena.

One of the main objectives of the UFAST project was to provide a comprehensive experimental Data Bank, documenting both low frequency events and the properties of the large scale coherent structures in the context of SWBLI. It should again be stressed that before the project almost no experimental information had been available, especially in industrially relevant flow cases. Therefore, flows in the important Mach number range going from transonic conditions to Mach number 2.25 were investigated. The measured flow configurations correspond to generic geometries that can be easily exploited in more complex geometries, such as airfoils/wings, nozzles, curved ducts/inlets. This wide shock configuration platform was necessary to identify general interaction unsteady features. And it should be repeated that the realisation of this objective in a short space of time could only be achieved by involving a sufficiently large number of laboratories sharing an enormous amount of crucial experimental work.

3.2   Project Structure

The UFAST project divided its funds and research work into two main areas. The one concerned experiments, which delivered the Data Bank on SWBLI and its control. The other area concerned numerical simulations, including the modelling of SWBLI, using URANS, hybrid RANS-LES and LES methods, and delivered an assessment of their applicability to the problem. To consider the general features of unsteady SWBLI, most of the typical flow configurations with shock waves had to be included in the investigation. Three flow configurations were selected, as shown in Fig. 1. The selection of three configurations implied a high number of flow cases. Three different experiments were designed for each configuration (see Table 1).

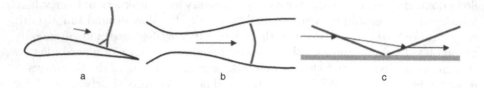

Fig. 1. UFAST configurations of flow with shock waves: a) transonic interaction, b) nozzle flow, c) oblique shock reflection

In order to manage this in a three-year project, a number of experimental facilities were engaged and various theoretical methods, e.g. CFD codes, were used.

Table 1. UFAST experiments

Transonic interaction

bump at the wall (QUB[2])
biconvex airfoil (INCAS[3])
NACA 0012 with aileron (IoA[4])

Nozzle flow

nozzle with a bump, forced shock oscill. (ONERA[5])
nozzle with rectilinear wall, forced shock oscill. (UCAM[6])
nozzle with flat wall, curved duct (IMP PAN)

Oblique shock reflection

$Ma = 1.7$ (TUD[7])
$Ma = 2.0$ (ITAM[8])
$Ma = 2.25$ (IUSTI[9])

---

[2] Queens University of Belfast, United Kingdom.
[3] Romanian Institute for Aeronautics.
[4] Institute of Aviation, Poland.
[5] Office National d'Études et de Recherches Aérospatiales, France.
[6] University of Cambridge, United Kingdom.
[7] Delft University of Technology, The Netherlands.
[8] Russian Academy of Science.
[9] Centre National de la Recherche Scientifique, France.

That was the main reason why as many as 18 partners participated in the realisation of the ambitious goals of the UFAST project. For the present article,
only exemplary experimental and numerical results are presented for a transonic
interaction (buffet) at the biconvex airfoil obtained by INCAS and IMFT[10].

3.3 Transonic Interaction at Biconvex Airfoil

Buffeting is a severe problem in airplane service, which can lead to reduced
comfort, life cycle limitations or even structural fatigue. Therefore, it is very
important during design to predict accurately and control the buffet onset. The
present test case is that of a biconvex symmetric airfoil in a wind tunnel at
buffeting flow conditions. Three partners: EADS[11], IMFT and INCAS have participated in this task. All of them have performed flow simulations while INCAS
was also responsible for the new experiments. Structured and unstructured grids
and codes were used as well as URANS, DES and LES models were applied.

The experiments were performed by INCAS in their 1.2 m × 1.2 m Trisonic
Wind Tunnel at shock induced buffeting conditions. The flow field configuration
was based on a classical biconvex aerofoil (18%) at transonic speeds in the range
of Mach 0.7–0.9. The experiments were designed in order to enable buffeting.
The photograph of the model is given in Fig. 2. The rectangular model having an
800 mm span, a 400 mm chord and a biconvex profile of 18% relative thickness
was attached on its lower side to a rigid 72 mm diameter sting. The sting was
installed in the model support pitch system so that its angle of attack could
be varied during the run. The model was designed to accommodate pressure
scanning devices, Kulite pressure transducers and Synthetic Jet (SJ) actuators.

Fig. 2. Biconvex airfoil model inside the INCAS test section

In order to identify the buffeting on the model, the detailed global schlieren
images were recorded. The schlieren pictures provided qualitative information on

---

[10] Institut de Mécanique des Fluides de Toulouse, France.
[11] European Aeronautic Defence and Space Company, Germany.

the flow field configuration and proper identification of buffeting phenomenon. The buffeting conditions were established for $Ma = 0.76$, $Re = 6.78 \cdot 10^6$ and $1°$ of incidence (see Fig. 3) and this was defined as the reference test case for the biconvex symmetric profile.

A strong shock in the rear part of the profile leads to shock induced boundary layer separation. The increasing boundary layer thickness and separation force the shock to move upstream and it becomes weaker till the separation vanishes and the flow reattaches. Then, the movement starts from the beginning again. As a result, the shock location on the model was varying from 55% to 85% of the chord length on both upper and lower surfaces, alternating in the buffeting phenomena. A series of tests were devoted to measurements of static pressure at transducers placed on the top surface of the model at 40%, 50%, 60%, 70% and 80% of the profile chord at $Ma = 0.76$ in buffeting conditions (see Fig. 4). The frequency of the shock wave oscillation was found to be 78 Hz.

In an attempt to control the SWBLI, a number of 5 Synthetic Jet (SJ) actuators were installed on the biconvex symmetric airfoil at 65% of the chord on the top surface of the model. The model was equipped with piezoelectric SJ actuators having a body diameter of 25 mm, a diaphragm diameter of 20 mm, a 1 mm hole diameter and 1.1 mm hole height. The effects of the flow control by SJ actuators were expected to be seen as alterations in the amplitude and frequency of the unsteady pressure signals recorded by the Kulite transducers. At all runs with $Ma = 0.76$ the Kulite transducers indicated the presence of the buffeting. However, there were changes in the amplitude and frequency of the signals recorded by the Kulite sensors, depending on the excitation of the SJ actuators.

IMFT performed CFD simulations for this test case with the URANS (Spalart-Allmaras) model, and especially devoted a special attention to take into account the exact 3d wind tunnel geometry. The computations have been performed using the NSMB (Navier-Stokes Multi-Block) software [8], which is a structured multi-block code created and upgraded by means of a European consortium since early 90's, including IMFT since 2002. The final 3d geometry taken into account by IMFT was the full wind tunnel with curved nozzle and diffuser. The difference between this computational domain and the real geometry was the absence of the sting for the computation, because this would require a high increase in the number of grid points in respect of the structured grid configuration. The IMFT's grid contained about $5 \cdot 10^6$ nodes and is presented in Fig. 5.

The IMFT results obtained using the URANS/Spalart-Almaras model for $\alpha = 1°$, $Ma = 0.762$, $Re = 6.78 \cdot 10^6$ efficiently capture the buffet phenomenon and compare quite well with the physical experiment in respect of the predominant frequency and of the amplitude of oscillations due to the shock wave motion. It can be seen in example Fig. 6, presenting pressure fluctuations in time at the spanwise station of 150 mm and the chordwise location of $x/c = 0.6$ on the suction side of the airfoil obtained by IMFT (URANS) and by EADS using URANS (SA URANS) and DDES (SA DDES). The calculated buffet frequency of 78 Hz is in good agreement with the experimental data.

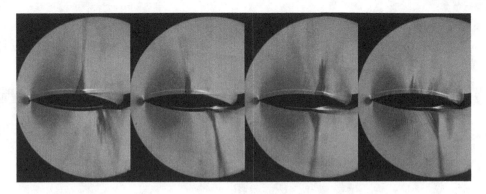

Fig. 3. Schlieren pictures for biconvex airfoil (experiment, $\alpha = 1°$, $Ma = 0.762$, $Re = 6.78 \cdot 10^6$)

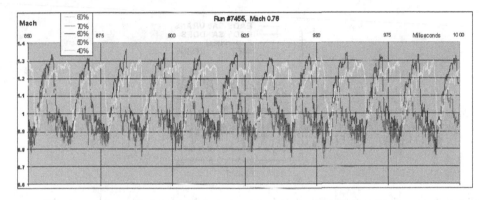

Fig. 4. Instantaneous value of local Mach number at biconvex airfoil (experiment, $\alpha = 1°$, $Ma = 0.762$, $Re = 6.78 \cdot 10^6$)

The results efficiently capture the buffet phenomenon and compare quite well with the physical experiment, not only in respect of the predominant frequency and of the amplitude of oscillations due to the shock motion, but for the mean value and extrema of the shock motion as well presented in Fig. 7 – for the spanwise station of 100 mm located on the suction side of the airfoil.

The BDP database contains a comprehensive set of data files regarding the flow conditions and recorded flow parameters during the experiment, while the CFD results are presented in the form of figures and tables (due to large amount of simulation output data). For the first series of basic tests, the measured parameters for each run are given in ASCII format in files identified by the run number "XXXX" and the extension "TAB", including schlieren visualisation of the flow (see example in Fig. 3). The values represent averages of readings taken for each pitch angle or convenient time intervals. For the tests for profile pressure distributions, the maximum, minimum and mean c_p and p/p_{inf} values at each pressure hole of the respective section are given in the database as TECPLOT

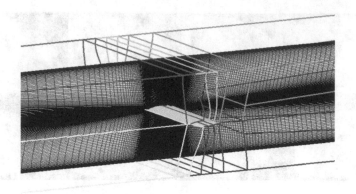

Fig. 5. Computational grid for biconvex airfoil

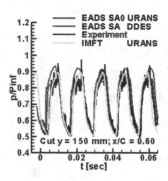

Fig. 6. Comparison between calculated and measured pressure fluctuations at biconvex airfoil ($\alpha = 1°$, $Ma = 0.762$, $Re = 6.78 \cdot 10^6$)

ASCII data files, identified by the run number "XXXX" and suffix "_Cp" or "_ppinf" followed by the extension ".DAT" (see example data plotted in Fig. 7). For the unsteady pressure measurements, the data from the Kulite transducers was reduced to pressure coefficients and "p/p_{inf}" values, and recorded into the ASCII TECPLOT data files "XXXX_Cp_time.dat" and "XXXX_ppinf_time.dat" (see example data plotted in Fig. 4 and Fig. 6). The data collected during the SJ flow control experiments are included as ASCII files with the extension ".CSV", which can be opened, used and saved with Microsoft Excel. For each run, there is a "pretare" file (Run number followed by the suffix "_0") containing 8 000 readings of all channels a few seconds before the run, and a "runtime" file (Run number followed by the suffix "_1") containing 32 000 readings of all channels at 32 microseconds intervals. The first row of each CSV file contains the name of the parameter in the respective column.

A more complete set of the experimental data obtained for the transonic interaction and its control at the biconvex airfoil has been published in the UFAST Data Bank [5] and Springer book [6], with raw data files included in

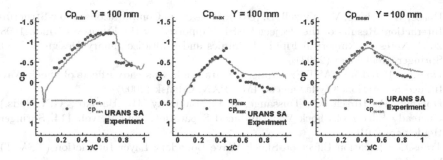

Fig. 7. Comparison between calculated and measured pressure coefficient distributions at biconvex airfoil ($\alpha = 1°$, $Ma = 0.762$, $Re = 6.78 \cdot 10^6$)

the Projects' Database (BDP) of the PLGrid Plus project. The extended results of the numerical simulations of IMFT, supplemented by two additional sets of data from INCAS and EADS are included in the BDP as well. Apart from the biconvex airfoil test case, two other configurations of transonic interaction with flow control present at the wall mounted bump and on the NACA 0012 airfoil equipped with aileron were investigated during the UFAST project and are fully represented in [5,6] and in the Projects' Database (BDP).

4   Conclusions

Thanks to the PLGrid Plus project and the PL-Grid Infrastructure, an extensive database of results of the European research projects related to SWBLI and SWBLIC has been developed and is shared among PL-Grid users (scientists) dealing with shock wave dominated flows. The included, complete results of the UFAST project currently build a basis of a new service, awaiting for future research projects (e. g. TFAST) to join the platform. The presented experimental and numerical exemplary data obtained within the UFAST project for the buffet phenomenon at the biconvex airfoil constitute only a fraction of the full material, available in the Projects' Database (BDP), concerning SWBLI and its control.

References

1. Dervieux, A., Braza, M., Dussauge, J.-P. (eds.): Computation and Comparison of Efficient Turbulence Models for Aeronautics – European Research Project ETMA. NNFM, vol. 65. Vieweg, Braunschweig (1998)
2. Stanewsky, E., Délery, J., Fulker, J., Geißler, W. (eds.): EUROSHOCK – Drag Reduction by Passive Shock Control; Results of the Project EUROSHOCK, AER2-CT92-0049 Supported by the European Union, 1993–1995. NNFM, vol. 56. Vieweg, Braunschweig (1997)
3. Stanewsky, E., Délery, J., Fulker, J., Matteis, P. (eds.): Drag Reduction by Shock and Boundary Layer Control; Results of the Project EUROSHOCK II Supported by the European Union 1996–1999. NNFM, vol. 80. Springer, Heidelberg (2002)

4. Haase, W., Selmin, V., Winzell, B. (eds.): Progress in Computational Flow-Structure Interaction; Results of the Project UNSI, Supported by the European Union 1998-2000. Notes on Numerical Fluid Mechanics and Multidisciplinary Design, vol. 81. Springer, Heidelberg (2003)
5. Doerffer, P. (ed.): UFAST Experiments Data Bank; Unsteady Effects of Shock Wave Indued Separation. Wydawnictwo IMP PAN, Gdańsk (2009)
6. Doerffer, P., Hirsch, C., Dussauge, J.-P., Babinsky, H., Barakos, G.N. (eds.): Unsteady Effects of Shock Wave Induced Separation. NNFM, vol. 114. Springer, Heidelberg (2010)
7. Transition Location Effect on Shock Wave Boundary Layer Interaction (TFAST), http://tfast.eu
8. Vos, J., Chaput, E., Arlinger, B., Rizzi, A., Corjon, A.: Recent advances in aerodynamics inside the NSMB (Navier-Stokes Multi-Block) consortium. AIAA Paper, 1998–0802 (1998)

Aerodynamic and Aero-acoustic Analysis of Helicopter Rotor Blades in Hover

Piotr Doerffer, Oskar Szulc,
Fernando Tejero Embuena, and Javier Martinez Suarez

Institute of Fluid-Flow Machinery, ul. Fiszera 14, 80-231 Gdańsk, Poland
{piotr.doerffer,oskar.szulc,fernando.tejero,javier.martinez}@imp.gda.pl

Abstract. One of the achievements of the PLGrid Plus project is development of new services and tools designed for numerical prediction of aerodynamic performance and aero-acoustic signature of helicopter rotor blades. A novel approach is based on the integration and automation of all stages of a numerical simulation (pre-processing, processing and post-processing) within a single tool available in the HPC environment of the PL-Grid Infrastructure. A well-established set of professional commercial software packages (developed by Numeca Int. and Tecplot Inc.), combined with knowledge and experience, ensure high quality of the overall service. Two initial "demonstrators" are designed to deliver aerodynamic performance (Aero-H) and aero-acoustic data (Aku-H) for the High-Speed Impulsive (HSI) noise generated by the two-bladed model of a helicopter rotor in high-speed, transonic hover conditions. An Euler or RANS structured approach to numerical simulation of the flow past a hovering rotor poses many challenges for Computational Fluid Dynamics (CFD). Still, the predictions of Aero-H and Aku-H correspond well with the experimental databases of Caradonna-Tung and Purcell.

Keywords: shockwave, helicopter rotor, transonic hover, high-speed impulsive noise.

1 Introduction

The article presents details of the implementation and application of a new set of tools named Aero-H and Aku-H (based on the commercial software packages) designed for integration of all stages of a numerical simulation of flow and acoustic near-field generated by hovering helicopter blades within the HPC environment of the PL-Grid Infrastructure. The accurate Aero-H prediction of the aerodynamic performance of the rotor (flow-field) is a key element for the Aku-H solution of the generated High-Speed Impulsive (HSI) noise (acoustic pressure), hence both tools are interlinked.

Two new and unique numerical tools: Aero-H and Aku-H developed in the PLGrid Plus project and designed for integrating and automating all stages of the numerical simulation of a hovering helicopter rotor aerodynamics and aero-acoustics using commercial CFD software and PL-Grid supercomputers introduce not only academic value, but also strong engineering and research quality.

M. Bubak et al. (Eds.): PLGrid Plus, LNCS 8500, pp. 429–444, 2014.

2   State of the Art

It is known that the RANS (Reynolds-Averaged Navier-Stokes) numerical simulation of flow past a helicopter rotor in lifting hover poses many difficulties.
A rotating blade induces high down-wash of air below the rotor, while the spiral
tip vortex and trailing edge vortex sheets interact with the preceding blades. As a
result, both the local flow in the vicinity of the blades and the far wake of the rotor have to be resolved by CFD. Additionally, a normal shock wave, terminating
a local supersonic area near the blade tip, not only limits aerodynamic performance, but also becomes a significant source of HSI noise. A combination of a
helicopter rotor flow-field with the presence of a shock wave and boundary layer
separation leads to large numerical models (in terms of memory consumption)
and long parallel computing times even when using the most efficient supercomputers of the PL-Grid Consortium. A literature survey of the RANS results
obtained for a transonic lifting hover (tip Mach number of 0.88 and collective
of 8°) of the Caradonna and Tung (1981) [1] model helicopter rotor reveals significant scatter according to experimental data [2,3,4,5,6]. However, the Aero-H
prediction of this transonic flow-field is acceptable as one of the best RANS
solutions that can be found in the literature thus far.

The shock wave induced HSI noise phenomenon is very often studied experimentally in "non-lifting" hover conditions (zero collective). When the acoustic
signal is measured in the rotor plane, it is independent of the blade loading [7].
However, during operation, a low collective angle (e.g. 1.5°) is set for the rotor
blades in order to avoid room recirculation and to redirect the rotor wake outside of the test stand. The "low-lifting" conditions provoke generation of regular
tip vortices and weak rotor wake degrading the performance of the numerical
scheme leading to even longer computing times. The shock wave induced HSI
noise may be directly resolved in the near-field of the rotor by using the Euler (inviscid) method. Acoustic pressure impulses are less dissipated and tend
to be detectable over longer distances in the flow-field compared to RANS solutions. Unfortunately, the Euler method has a slight negative impact on the
aerodynamic performance of the rotor – negligible from the point of view of the
HSI noise study. A literature survey of the Euler results obtained for HSI noise
emitted by the tip of the blade of the Purcell (1988) [8] model helicopter rotor
(tip Mach number of 0.9) reveals good agreement with experimental data at the
location of $r/R = 1.11$ [9,10,11]. The Aku-H prediction of this phenomenon is
satisfactory and gives confidence for future applications.

The Caradonna-Tung experimental database, which was used for verification
of the Aero-H flow prediction in hover conditions, is extensively utilized within
the helicopter community in process of the validation of CFD codes applied
to rotorcraft problems. The blade shape of the model rotor is based on the
NACA0012 cross-section – the most comprehensively tested aerodynamic profile
in the history of aviation. On the other hand, the experimental data published
by Purcell, which was used for verification of the Aku-H predictions, is equally
popular among scientists developing and validating CFD codes focused on the
simulation of the HSI noise emitted by the helicopter rotor in high-speed hover.

It is worth mentioning that the model rotor (based again on the NACA0012 profile) is a 1/7th scale main rotor of the U. S. Army UH-1H version of the Bell UH-1 Iroquois (Huey) – one of the most popular helicopters ever produced. Two separate test cases of Caradonna-Tung and Purcell are used for validation of the Aero-H and Aku-H numerical result, since the combined measurements of the aerodynamic performance (thrust, blade pressure distributions and tip vortex trajectories) and the HSI noise (acoustic pressure) in high-speed hover are not freely available. Moreover, cross-validation of the Aero-H and Aku-H simulation results (based on Fine/Turbo package from Numeca Int.) against CFD results obtained using the academic general purpose SPARC code [12] from the University of Karlsruhe and the aviation oriented FLOWer solver [13] from DLR is presented.

3   Aero-H and Aku-H Numerical Tools for Simulating Helicopter Rotors in Hover

3.1   What Are Aero-H and Aku-H?

The Aero-H and Aku-H tools consist of a set of Linux shell and python scripts designed to control commercial CFD software in order to semi-automatically complete a numerical simulation of a flow and acoustic field generated by a helicopter rotor in hover. These demonstrators are not conceived as separate applications, but constitute supplements of the Fine/Turbo package from Numeca Int. (pre-processing and flow solution) and Tecplot 360 software from Tecplot Inc. (post-processing). Currently, direct functionality of Aero-H and Aku-H is limited to the helicopter rotors having two untwisted and untapered blades with the NACA0012 cross-section. This type of rotor was extensively tested by Caradonna-Tung [1], Purcell [8] and Caradonna-Laub-Tung [14] in hover and forward flight conditions. Other rotors may be implemented with variable effort from the user depending on the actual shape of the blade (e.g. rotor of the Bell AH-1G Huey Cobra helicopter [15]). Still, some flexibility is explicitly hardcoded allowing for manipulation of the dimensions of the rotor and computational domain, grid size, operating conditions, numerical and physical modeling. Additionally, all features of Aero-H and Aku-H implemented in the scripts and macros are available as plain text, allowing for even more accurate adaptation to user needs.

A simulation process by Aero-H or Aku-H is initiated by building of a numerical model of the geometry of the rotor, creation of a computational domain limited by a set of boundary conditions and generation of a grid. This preprocessing phase is based on a set of parameterised python scripts developed exclusively for IGG (Interactive Grid Generator) from the Fine/Turbo package. Depending on the user-supplied rotor operating conditions, a new project is set up for the flow solver and the test case is sent to PL-Grid supercomputers for efficient parallel execution. This processing phase is controlled by another set of parameterised python scripts developed exclusively for Euranus flow solver from

Fine/Turbo package. Finally, the post-processing of the output data obtained for the aerodynamic performance and acoustic prediction of the HSI noise for a hovering helicopter rotor is based on a set of macros developed exclusively for Tecplot 360 visualisation software.

One of the main advantages of the Aero-H and Aku-H tools is the possibility to accelerate a numerical simulation process by automating pre-processing, solution and post-processing phases, thus minimizing the necessary user effort. The usage of Aero-H and Aku-H instead of the manual (interactive) preparation of the numerical model, solution on a desktop computer and local post-processing of the results ensures significant speed-up. A single run is reduced from 6 weeks to approximately 1 week of pure calculation using an HPC cluster with very limited user effort (see Tab. 1). Taking into account that complete prediction of the aerodynamic performance and HSI noise signature of the rotor in hover requires more than one simulation, the expected savings are even more significant.

Table 1. Approximate runtime of Aero-H and Aku-H vs. interactive work

	interactive run[1] by user	automated run[2] by Aero-H and Aku-H
pre-processing	3 weeks	5 minutes
parallel solution	2 weeks	1 week
post-processing	1 week	1 minute

The pre-processing and solution functionality of the Aero-H and Aku-H services are analogous. The preparation of the rotor geometry and computational domain, setting of boundary conditions, grid generation and project setup for the flow solver are based on a similar engine and are described together. Only the final stage of the post-processing of the simulation data is unique and differs between Aero-H and Aku-H.

3.2 Experimental Set-Ups

The validation of Aero-H is performed against the experimental data obtained by F. X. Caradonna and C. Tung in 1981 [1]. The model rotor consists of 2 rectangular, untwisted and untapered NACA0012 rigid blades mounted on a tall column containing a drive shaft located in a large chamber with special ducting designed to eliminate room recirculation (see Fig. 1). The aspect ratio of the rotor $AR = 6$, the chord length of the blade $c = 0.1905$ m and the diameter $2R = 2.286$ m. A large set of test conditions has been applied with tip Mach number Ma_T ranging from 0.23 to 0.89 and the collective pitch θ ranging from $0°$ to $12°$ at atmospheric conditions. The pressure distributions were measured

---

[1] Using a modern desktop computer equipped with a single 4-core processor.
[2] Using one node of the PL-Grid supercomputer equipped with two 6-core processors.

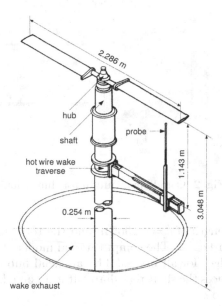

Fig. 1. Experimental set-up of the Caradonna-Tung two-bladed model rotor [1]

at 5 cross-sections of the blade and the tip vortex trajectory was extracted using a hot-wire technique. For a detailed validation a transonic test-case was chosen with the experimental tip Mach number equal to $Ma_T = 0.877$, the tip Reynolds number of $Re_T = 3.931 \cdot 10^6$, the rotation speed of 2500 RPM and the collective pitch of $\theta = 8°$.

The validation of Aku-H is performed against the experimental data obtained by T. Purcell in 1988 [8]. The 1/7th scale model of the UH-1H helicopter main rotor consists of 2 rectangular, untwisted NACA0012 blades. The aspect ratio of the rotor $AR = 13.71$, the chord length of the blade $c = 0.0762$ m and the radius $R = 1.045$ m. A large set of test conditions has been applied with tip Mach number Ma_T ranging from 0.85 to 0.95 and a low collective pitch θ at atmospheric conditions. The acoustic pressure was measured at 4 radial locations off the tip of the blade ($r/R = 1.11, 1.78, 2.18$ and 3.09) at the rotor plane. For a detailed validation a transonic, delocalized test-case was chosen with the experimental tip Mach number equal to $Ma_T = 0.9$, the tip Reynolds number of $Re_T = 1.7 \cdot 10^6$ and the collective pitch of $\theta = 1.5°$.

3.3   Geometrical Model of a Helicopter Rotor in Hover

The currently available geometrical model of the rotor implemented in Aero-H and Aku-H using IGG (Interactive Grid Generator) scripts consists of 2 rectangular, untwisted and untapered NACA0012 rigid blades (see Fig. 2). As an example, the modeled geometry of the Caradonna-Tung rotor is presented having a radius $R = 6 \cdot c$, a chord length $c = 1$ and a collective $\theta = 8°$. The original,

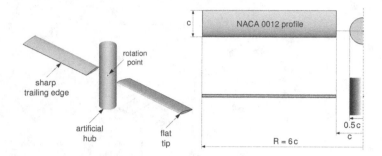

Fig. 2. Caradonna-Tung rotor dimensions

experimental chord length of $c = 0.1905$ m and the rotor radius of $R = 1.143$ m
are re-scaled to a chord $c = 1$. The computational model utilizes flat tip surfaces
and sharp trailing edges for all blades. The artificial hub cylindrical surface of
a radius of $0.5 \cdot c$ replaces the shaft real shape. It is assumed that the inner radius
of the rotor is equal to c.

The flexibility of the scripting approach allows for direct modification of the
rotor radius R (or aspect ratio), blade chord length c and collective angle θ.
The inner rotor radius and the artificial hub dimensions may be modified as
well. This kind of approach may be used to generate the geometry of a popular
class of rotors based on the NACA0012 profile. Setting a certain value of the
aspect ratio provides the Caradonna-Tung [1] rotor ($AR = 6$), the Caradonna-
Laub-Tung [14] rotor ($AR = 7$) and finally the UH-1H model rotor of Purcell [8]
($AR = 13.71$). Additionally, by linearly twisting the blade (from the root to the
tip by -10 degrees) the main rotor of the AH-1G [15] helicopter ($AR = 9.8$)
may be modeled.

3.4 Computational Domain and Boundary Conditions

A computational domain implemented in Aero-H and Aku-H using IGG scripts
consists of a half-cylinder enclosing a single blade of the 2-bladed rotor (see Fig. 3).
The flow field of the hovering rotor is quasi steady with respect to the blade and
periodic in nature – only one blade needs to be accounted for, decreasing time requirements for the simulation. The location of the outer surface, being a parameter
of the scripts, is based on the choice of the radius of the rotor, thus adapting itself
automatically. As an example, the computational domain designed for a numerical simulation of the Caradonna-Tung hovering rotor is presented. The distance
between the rotor plane and the location of the outer surfaces is fixed to $3 \cdot R$.

For small computational domains, Froude-type [16] boundary conditions are
usually applied away from the rotor. In Aero-H and Aku-H a different approach
is implemented. The computational domain is surrounded by the boundary conditions of 4 types: viscous and inviscid walls, rotational periodicity and pressure inlet/outlet. The surface of the blade is modeled using a non-slip adiabatic

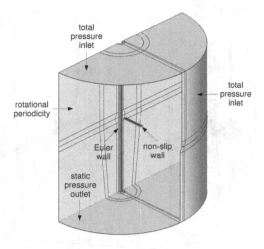

Fig. 3. Caradonna-Tung rotor computational domain and boundary conditions

wall condition. Due to natural periodicity of the flow, a rotational periodicity boundary condition is applied. To save computational resources, a surface of the artificial hub is modeled as an inviscid wall. The outer surface is approximated by a pressure inlet/outlet boundary condition. It is based on the assumption of a constant inlet/outlet total/static pressure and temperature far from the blades. Pressure inlet/outlet boundary conditions allow for an induced flow through the outer boundaries being a part of the solution with intensity dependent on the flow-field generated by the rotating blades.

3.5   Grid Topology

The computational domain of the hovering rotor setup by Aero-H and Aku-H (again using IGG parameterised scripts) is divided into 80 structured blocks with a C-topology in streamwise and H-topology in normal and spanwise directions (see Fig. 4). The C-H-H topology proves able to capture the rotor wake system with sufficient accuracy. A computational body-fitted structured grid is generated automatically with grid clustering enforced at the locations of the boundary layer development, along the path of the tip and root vortices and the exhaust wake of the rotor (see Fig. 5). As an example, the computational grid generated for the Caradonna-Tung rotor is presented. It consists of 5.7 million of volumes per blade. The distance of the first grid point away from a solid wall is constant and set to be below $y^+ = 3$ for a turbulent RANS simulation.

There are many features of the numerical grid that may be explicitly modified by the user, for example the type of the mesh in terms of the physical modeling (Euler vs RANS), the number of cells in each direction, cell size distribution along block edges, y^+ of the first layer of cells above the non-slip walls, etc. The same grid, having a sufficiently high boundary layer resolution for a RANS simulation,

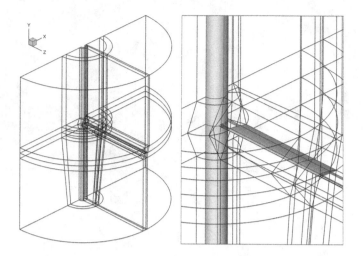

Fig. 4. Caradonna-Tung rotor multi-block grid topology

is generated for the Aero-H aerodynamic predictions as for the inviscid Euler solutions implemented in Aku-H. Hence, results obtained from both tools are complementary and may be directly confronted without any need for a mesh difference study.

3.6   Aerodynamic and Aero-acoustic Solutions

The Aero-H or Aku-H test case is created and set up based on the outcome of the previous preprocessing stages (geometry modeling and grid generation) for a cell-centered, block-structured, parallel CFD code Euranus developed as a part of the Fine/Turbo package from Numeca International. The code solves numerically the Euler or the compressible, mass-weighted, Reynolds-Averaged Navier-Stokes (RANS) equations closed by a one-equation, low-Reynolds number turbulence model of Spalart-Allmaras. The algorithm incorporates a semi-discrete approach, utilizing a finite volume method for the spatial discretisation (central scheme, 2nd order of accuracy) and the steady-state multistage Runge-Kutta type integration in time. In order to increase the convergence rate, the local time stepping, the implicit residual averaging and the full multigrid techniques are included in the explicit approach. The only difference in physical modeling between Aero-H and Aku-H is the choice of equations describing the fluid motion. The aerodynamic predictions of Aero-H are based on the RANS equations (including turbulence modeling), while the acoustic pressure simulations of Aku-H are obtained using the Euler equations (inviscid). All other physical parameters are kept as similar as possible.

The rotor modeled by Aero-H and Aku-H is placed in a quiescent environment described by the atmospheric pressure and temperature (p_{atm} and T_{atm}). When the blades start to rotate with a positive collective pitch θ, a non-zero velocity is

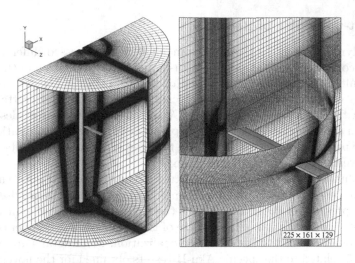

Fig. 5. Caradonna-Tung rotor C-H-H grid

induced at the boundaries. At locations where air is entering the computational domain (inlet) the atmospheric conditions p_{atm} and T_{atm} become stagnation parameters. At the outlet (below the rotor) where the air is exiting the computational domain the static pressure is equal to the atmospheric pressure p_{atm}. The example flow conditions set for the Caradonna-Tung hovering rotor simulation are presented in Tab. 2. The difference between the experimental and the actual value of the atmospheric pressure p_{atm} set for the computation is related to the scaling of the geometry of the rotor to assure a chord length equal to 1.

Table 2. Flow conditions for the Caradonna-Tung rotor simulation

	experiment	Aero-H
tip Mach number Ma_T	0.877	0.877
tip Reynolds number Re_T	$3.93 \cdot 10^6$	$3.93 \cdot 10^6$
atmospheric pressure p_{atm}	103 027 Pa	19 627 Pa
atmospheric temperature T_{atm}	289.75 K	289.75 K

By properly adjusting the atmospheric conditions (p_{atm} and T_{atm}) and rotation speed (RPM) the tip Reynolds and Mach numbers may be controlled explicitly by the user. The collective angle has already been built into the rotor geometry. A basic computation steering is based on the control of the convergence criteria of reaching the steady-state (number of iterations and order of magnitude reduction of the density residual), the full multigrid parameters and the CFL number of the scheme. A fully prepared Aero-H or Aku-H test-case is submitted to a queuing system of the PL-Grid supercomputer for a parallel solution. After approximately one week of a simulation the output data files are written for automatic post-processing of results.

3.7   Post-processing of Results

The aerodynamic (flow-field) Aero-H output is post-processed differently from the aero-acoustic (acoustic pressure) Aku-H data. The evaluation of the aerodynamic results of the simulation is based on the total thrust C_T and torque C_Q coefficients of the rotor, pressure coefficient c_P distribution at certain cross-sections of the blade, spanwise loading C_L of the blade, tip vortex descent and contraction rates supplemented by the tip vortices and wake visualisation. More details are presented in Section 4 related to the specific Aero-H results obtained for the hovering rotor of Caradonna-Tung.

The evaluation of the aero-acoustic Aku-H results of the HSI noise simulation is based on the extraction of the quasi time-dependent pressure impulse, generated by the presence of the shock wave at the tip of the blade and emitted in the rotor plane. A visualization of the surface of the relative Mach number equal to 1 allows for detection of transonic flow delocalization. More details are presented in Section 5 related to the specific Aku-H results obtained for the hovering rotor of Purcell.

4   Aero-H Results of a Numerical Simulation of Flow past the Caradonna-Tung (1981) Model Helicopter Rotor in Hover

4.1   SPARC and FLOWer Flow Solvers

The multi-code cross-validation of Aero-H (Fine/Turbo, Numeca Int.) is based on a comparison with the numerical results obtained using two additional flow solvers: Structured Parallel Research Code SPARC from the University of Karlsruhe (Germany), maintained by F. Magagnato [12] and FLOWer solver from DLR (Germany) developed during the MEGAFLOW project [13].

The SPARC setup incorporates identical rotor and artificial hub geometry, computational domain, grid topology and boundary conditions [17]. The simulation is based on the RANS equations, Spalart-Allmaras turbulence model and a central numerical scheme of a 2nd order accuracy in space as well. The presented material is a direct extension of the 1st order accurate numerical results published in [18,19,20]. A slightly better resolved shock wave is the effect of local grid refinement of 2 blocks located at the suction side of the tip (enclosing the transonic flow and shock wave – boundary layer interaction) increasing the number of cells from 5.7 to 7.0 million. SPARC adopts a time-accurate, implicit dual-time-stepping scheme of a 2nd order accuracy, which has no noticeable effect (when limited to small time-steps) on the results compared to a steady solution implemented in Aero-H.

The FLOWer setup is based on the chimera overlapping grids technique incorporating identical rotor geometry, but without the artificial hub surfaces [21].

Inclusion of a slightly larger computational domain, a chimera grid topology with a total of 112 blocks (for 2 blades) and the Froude-type far-field boundary conditions resulted in an increase of the number of cells to 12.7 million. As in Aero-H and SPARC, the simulation is based on the RANS equations, Spalart-Allmaras turbulence model and a central numerical scheme of a 2nd order accuracy in space.

4.2   Aerodynamic Wake and Tip Vortex Trajectory

A fully turbulent, steady numerical simulation of the flow-field of the Caradonna-Tung rotor in high-speed hover requires approximately 250 000 iterations on the finest grid to reach a steady state (Aero-H). One of the most important aspects of this simulation is to properly capture the rotor wake including the path and strength of the tip vortices shed from the blade tip. It is worth noticing that when using Aero-H the wake of the rotor is not externally set, but is part of the global solution. The surface of a constant vorticity reveals the tip vortices that follow a helical path by slowly contracting and descending in close proximity of the blades (see Fig. 6). A strong induced velocity field associated with the tip vortex significantly alters the effective angle of attack seen by the rotor blades. This interference directly affects the rotor performance.

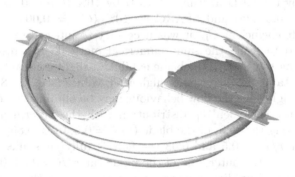

Fig. 6. Aerodynamic wake

The RANS method is known to be very dissipative, causing vorticity to be quickly diffused. Approximately 450° of a tip vortex age is resolved in the current simulation, which is sufficient to capture the interaction of the shed vortex with the following blade at 180°. Below 180° the tip vortex descent and contraction rates (based on the location of the vorticity maximum) are accurately predicted by Aero-H, SPARC and FLOWer (see Fig. 7).

After 180° the FLOWer solution deviates slightly compared to the Aero-H and SPARC solutions and the measured tip vortex trajectory, possibly due to insufficient background chimera component grid refinement.

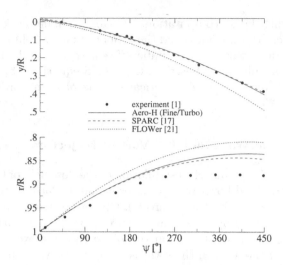

Fig. 7. Tip vortex descent and contraction

4.3 Blade Loading

The experimental value of the thrust coefficient $C_T = 0.00473$ of the rotor is overpredicted by the CFD utilizing: Aero-H by 16% ($C_T = 0.00548$), FLOWer by 14% ($C_T = 0.00538$) and SPARC by 10% ($C_T = 0.00521$). To compare the sectional lift coefficient C_L, it was necessary to integrate the experimental and numerical data using the same numerical method. The resulting loading distribution along the span of the blade exhibits a slight constant shift from the experimental data in the direction of higher C_L values (see Fig. 8).

A detailed insight into the flow behaviour may be obtained by comparing the predicted pressure coefficient c_P distribution with the experimental data at 5 cross-sections along the span of the blade ($r/R = 0.5, 0.68, 0.80, 0.89$ and 0.96) (see Fig. 9). At $r/R = 0.5$ and 0.68 the flow is fully subsonic, while a shock system builds up at the outer 20% of the blade (at $r/R = 0.80, 0.89$ and 0.96). The shock location is predicted correctly in accordance with the measurements for all transonic radial locations and for all numerical flow solvers. Only a slight downstream shift of the shock wave is observed in the Aero-H and FLOWer results compared to the SPARC solution and the experimental data. These barely visible deviations between different flow solutions and the test data integrated over the whole surface of the blade cause significant differences in the total thrust of the rotor and the spanwise loading distribution presented in Fig. 8. It is worth to emphasize that the rotor wake (vertical inflow) affects mainly the inner part of the blade radius, where only small velocities are induced by the rotation. At the outer part of the blade the rotational velocity dominates.

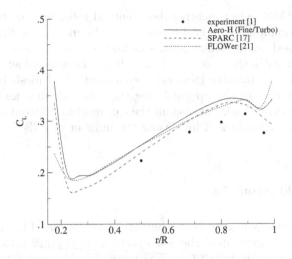

Fig. 8. Blade sectional lift coefficient

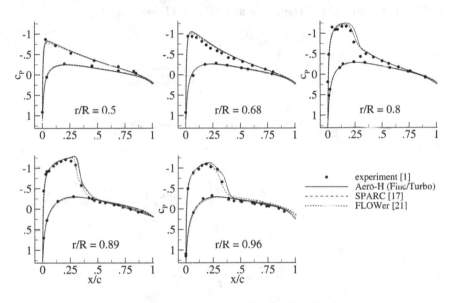

Fig. 9. Blade pressure coefficient distributions

5   Aku-H Results of a Numerical Simulation of High-Speed Impulsive (HSI) Noise of the Purcell (1988) UH-1H Model Helicopter Rotor in Hover

5.1   SPARC Flow Solver

Multi-code cross-validation of Aku-H (Fine/Turbo, Numeca Int.) is based on a comparison with the numerical results obtained using the academic flow solver

SPARC. The SPARC setup incorporates identical rotor and artificial hub geometry, computational domain, grid topology and boundary conditions [17]. The simulation is based on the Euler equations and a central numerical scheme of a 2nd order accuracy in space as well. A slightly better resolved acoustic pressure peak is an effect of a massive local grid refinement of all mesh blocks located not only at both sides of the tip (enclosing the transonic flow and shock wave-boundary layer interaction), but also off the tip, reaching the outer boundary of the computational domain and increasing the number of cells from 5.7 to 18.2 million.

5.2 Near-Field Acoustics

The main functionality of Aku-H is a numerical prediction of the acoustic pressure impulse caused by a tip of the helicopter blade rotating with a sufficiently high tip Mach number to initiate the HSI noise. For $Ma_T = 0.9$ the Purcell experimental data is well reproduced by the numerical simulations of Aku-H and SPARC in the near-field of the blade at $r/R = 1.11$ (see Fig. 10).

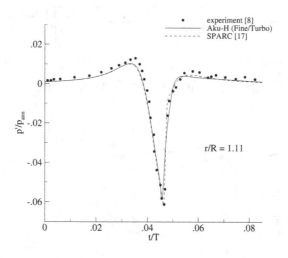

Fig. 10. Acoustic pressure at $r/R = 1.11$ at the rotor plane

For this delocalized case, a very intensive HSI phenomenon generates an acoustic pressure peak of approximately 6 kPa appearing two times per rotor revolution (with the blade passing frequency BPF). The recorded overall sound pressure level (OASPL) of 149.3 dB is underpredicted by numerics using: SPARC by 0.9 dB (148.4 dB) and Aku-H by 1.2 dB (148.1 dB). The slightly better SPARC solution results from extensive grid refinement.

5.3 Sonic Cylinder

Delocalization of the shock wave may be readily detected by visualizing the iso-surface of a relative Mach number. When the local, supersonic pocket generated above the tip of the rotating blade is connected with an imaginary surface of $Ma = 1$ (in a relative frame of reference), the HSI noise becomes extremely loud, annoying and easily detectable over long distances dominating all other sources of noise associated with a flying helicopter. The flow over the tip of the Purcell rotor operating with a tip Mach number of $Ma_T = 0.9$ is delocalized, i.e., the local supersonic area (1) is connected with the sonic cylinder (2) and the shock wave extends off the tip of the blade (see Fig. 11).

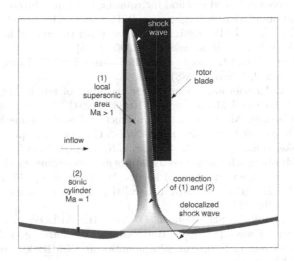

Fig. 11. Shock wave delocalization

6   Conclusions

The Aero-H and Aku-H tools proved capable of capturing the aerodynamics and aero-acoustics of two-bladed model rotors under high-speed transonic hover conditions. Comparison of simulation results with experimental data is accep-table, hence the described methodology and tools might be used with confi-dence in future numerical studies of helicopter rotor blades. The main objective of this article, i.e., validation of Aero-H and Aku-H results against the avail-able experimental data using the PL-Grid Infrastructure, has been successfully accomplished.

References

1. Caradonna, F.X., Tung, C.: Experimental and analytical studies of a model heli-copter rotor in hover. NASA Technical Memorandum, 81232 (1981)

2. Kang, H.J., Kwon, O.J.: Unstructured mesh Navier-Stokes calculations of the flow field of a helicopter rotor in hover. J. of the American Helicopter Society 47(2), 90–99 (2002)
3. Sun, H., Lee, S.: Response surface approach to aerodynamic optimization design of helicopter rotor blade. J. Numer. Meth. Engng. 64, 125–142 (2005)
4. Song, W.P., Han, Z.H., Qiao, Z.D.: Computational aeroacoustic prediction of transonic rotor noise based on Reynolds-Averaged Navier-Stokes flow simulation. In: 25th Congress of the International Council of the Aeronautical Sciences, Paper ICAS 2006-2.10.3, Hamburg (2006)
5. Xu, J.H., Song, W.P., Xie, F.T.: Application of high-resolution scheme in rotor flow simulation. In: 27th Congress of the International Council of the Aeronautical Sciences, Paper ICAS 2010-2.1.3, Nice (2010)
6. Sheng, C.: A preconditioned method for rotating flows at arbitrary Mach number. Modelling and Simulation in Engineering 2011, Article ID 537464 (2011)
7. Schmitz, F.H., Yu, Y.H.: Helicopter impulsive noise: theoretical and experimental status. NASA Technical Memorandum, 84390 (1983)
8. Purcell, T.W.: CFD and transonic helicopter sound. In: 14th European Rotorcraft Forum, Paper No. 2, Milano (1988)
9. Baeder, J.D.: Euler solutions to nonlinear acoustics of non-lifting hovering rotor blades. NASA Technical Memorandum, 103837 (1991)
10. Strawn, R., Garceau, M., Biswas, R.: Unstructured adaptive mesh computations of rotorcraft high-speed impulsive noise. NASA Contractor Report, 195090 (1993)
11. Usta, E., Wake, B.E., Egolf, T.A., Sankar, L.N.: Application of a symmetric total variation diminishing scheme to aerodynamics and aeroacoustics of rotors. In: 57th American Helicopter Society Annual Forum, Washington, pp. 1712–1722 (2001)
12. Magagnato, F.: KAPPA – Karlsruhe parallel program for aerodynamics. TASK Quarterly 2(2), 215–270 (1998)
13. Rossow, C.-C., Kroll, N., Schwamborn, D.: The MEGAFLOW project – numerical flow simulation for aircraft. In: Di Bucchianico, A., Mattheij, R.M.M., Peletier, M.A. (eds.) Progress in Industrial Mathematics at ECMI 2004, vol. 8, pp. 3–33. Springer, Heidelberg (2006)
14. Caradonna, F.X., Laub, G.H., Tung, C.: An experimental investigation of the parallel blade-vortex interaction. NASA Technical Memorandum, 86005 (1984)
15. Cross, J.L., Watts, M.E.: Tip aerodynamics and acoustics test. NASA Reference Publication, 1179 (1988)
16. Srinivasan, G.R.: A free-wake Euler and Navier-Stokes CFD method and its application to helicopter rotors including dynamic stall. JAI Associates, Technical Report, 93-01 (1993)
17. Szulc, O.: Passive control of shock wave – boundary layer interaction. Ph.D. thesis, Institute of Fluid-Flow Machinery, Poland (2014)
18. Doerffer, P., Szulc, O.: Numerical simulation of model helicopter rotor in hover. TASK Quarterly 12(3-4), 227–236 (2008)
19. Doerffer, P., Szulc, O.: Passive control of shock wave applied to helicopter rotor high-speed impulsive noise reduction. TASK Quarterly 14(3), 297–305 (2010)
20. Doerffer, P., Szulc, O.: Application of the passive control of shock wave to the reduction of high-speed impulsive noise. J. of Engineering Systems Modelling and Simulation 3(1-2), 64–73 (2011)
21. Doerffer, P., Tejero Embuena, F., Szulc, O.: Numerical simulation of model helicopter rotor in hover using chimera overlapping grids technique. Report No. 29/2014, Institute of Fluid-Flow Machinery, Poland (2014)

Parallelization of the Monte Carlo Static Recrystallization Model

Łukasz Madej and Mateusz Sitko

AGH University of Science and Technology,
al. Mickiewicza 30, 30-059 Kraków, Poland
{lmadej,msitko}@agh.edu.pl

Abstract. Implementation of parallel version of the Monte Carlo (MC) static recrystallization algorithm for application in the PL-Grid Infrastructure is presented in this work. General assumptions of the algorithm are described first. This is followed by presentation of modifications that were introduced and are required for the parallel execution. Monte Carlo space division schemes between subsequent computing nodes are particularly addressed. Implementation details are also presented. Finally, influence of size and geometry of the MC space on calculations efficiency is discussed.

Keywords: Monte Carlo, static recrystallization, parallelization.

1 Introduction

Metallic polycrystalline materials are commonly used in many practical engineering applications, because of their variety and possibility to obtain final products characterized by required behavior under processing and exploitation conditions. In this case, the microstructure of investigated material plays crucial role in controlling its final mechanical properties. Controlling of the microstructure evolution during processing conditions is possible mainly due to phase transformation and recrystallization processes. The latter phenomena are temperature activated that leads to restoration of the deformed microstructure, reduction of the effect of strain hardening and allows to obtain desirable grain size. Unfortunately, finding the correlation between recrystallization parameters and the material properties is not an easy task. It can be done mainly by means of the experimental investigation, but it is rather expensive and time consuming procedure. The solution is to support costly experimental investigation by a series of numerical simulations. The increasing computing power of computers and the economic aspects make the simulation a powerful investigation tool, which recently is often used in the steel industry. The simulation of the recrystallization (e.g. static recrystallization SRX) can be performed with various numerical approaches based on the conventional continuum as well as discrete models. The most popular discrete models used for SRX modelling are cellular automata (CA) and Monte Carlo techniques, described in detail in [1]. Unfortunately, the drawback of these approaches is excessive computing time, especially

M. Bubak et al. (Eds.): PLGrid Plus, LNCS 8500, pp. 445–458, 2014.

in 3D space. That is why, this paper is focused on the possibility of parallelization of the Monte Carlo static recrystallization algorithm, to take advantages of
the PL-Grid Infrastructure and make computing time acceptable from industrial
point of view.

2   Description of the MC Static Recrystallization Algorithm

The model for SRX operates in the specific domain called MC space that includes
geometry of the microstructure as well as properties of the analyzed material.
Explicit combination of these two elements is called the digital material representation (DMR) [2,3]. The MC is a general name for a group of algorithms
based on a completely random sampling of a solution space for an application
in mathematical and physical simulations. The algorithm is composed of several
major steps (for details please refer to [4]):

 - Preparation of input data that describe an initial state of the material in the
   form of two or three-dimensional matrix of cells. A random state Q_i – that
   belongs to $\Omega = \{Q_0, \ldots, Q_{n-1}\}$ – is assigned to each cell in the investigated
   space.
 - Random sampling of the entire space is performed in order to calculate the
   energy change of the subsequent cells. Sampling can be performed according
   to the Metropolis algorithm until all cells are analyzed.
 - Random change in the cells state from the n available states is another step
   of the algorithm. After the change of the state, the energy of the system is
   again calculated.
 - Calculation of the probability of the change in the cell state is performed. If
   the calculated difference of energy takes a negative value, a new value of the
   cell state is accepted, otherwise the state is accepted with a probability p.

These principles were adapted within the research to requirements of static recrystallization. Implemented algorithm of the SRX is presented in Fig. 1.

As seen in Fig. 1, the first stage in the static recrystallization model is a nucleation process. As reported in the literature [5], there is no single model that
can describe this phenomenon. This is due to the fact that nucleation is very
complex and it is hard to measure and investigate it experimentally. As a result,
several nucleation models are widely used. In order to give a deeper insight into
this process, four nucleation models have been implemented within the present
work. Generally, nucleation can be described by two approaches. The first is
a function of the nucleation time and the second takes into account the nucleation sites:

 - site saturated nucleation – the N_{ss} number of nuclei is introduced at the
   beginning of the simulation,
 - constant rate nucleation – the constant number of nuclei (N_{const}) is introduced in the same time intervals,

– continuous ascending nucleation – the ascending number of nuclei is introduced in the same time intervals until the number of N_{max} nuclei is reached:

$$N = sMCS,\qquad(1)$$

where: s – scaling factor, MCS – the actual number of Monte Carlo step.

– continuous descending nucleation – the descending number of nuclei is introduced in the same time intervals:

$$N = N_{init} - sMCS,\qquad(2)$$

where: N_{init} – the initial number of the nuclei.
In the case of site dependent algorithm two options are possible:

– homogeneous nucleation – nuclei are located in the random lattice sites,
– heterogeneous nucleation – nuclei are placed in the sites with the highest amount of stored energy.

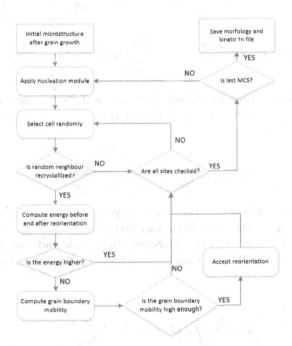

Fig. 1. The Monte Carlo static recrystallization algorithm schema

The second stage of static recrystallization is the grain growth phenomenon. The nuclei grow into the deformed matrix. The energy stored in the material due to deformation is the main driving force of that process. Implemented MC model is based on the arbitrary units of the energy as similar approaches that are reported in the literature [7,8,9,10]. The simulation procedure follows presented above several subsequent steps. At the beginning, the particular lattice site is selected randomly. Once the lattice site is selected, it cannot be selected again in the same simulation Monte Carlo step (MCS). This modification of the classical MC approach is implemented to reduce computing time. Then, the energy for that lattice site is computed using the formula:

$$E_i^{preSRX} = -J \sum_{j=1}^{Z} (\delta_{S_i S_j} - 1) + H_i , \tag{3}$$

where: J – grain boundary energy, Z – the number of neighbours, $\delta_{S_i S_j}$ – Kronecker delta, H_i – value of the energy stored in the lattice site. Selected lattice site is then set to the temporary state Q_i. It is reoriented to the crystallographic orientation chosen randomly from within its recrystallized neighbors orientations and its state is marked as recrystallized. Then, the energy is computed once again:

$$E_i^{postSRX} = -J \sum_{j=1}^{Z} (\delta_{S_i S_j} - 1) . \tag{4}$$

The H_i is omitted, because the energy is released due to the recrystallization process. The change in the energy is computed as:

$$\triangle E_i = E_i^{postSRX} - E_i^{preSRX} . \tag{5}$$

New crystallographic orientation and recrystallized state are accepted with some probability when the condition is satisfied. The probability is determined by the equation, which correlates the misorientation angle and the grain boundary mobility. It can be found in [8] that there is the dependency between them:

$$M(\theta) = M_m \left[1 - exp\left(-B \frac{\theta}{\theta_m} \right)^n \right] , \tag{6}$$

where: M_m – high angle grain boundary mobility (the value of 1 is assumed [7,8]), B, n – equation parameters (the values of 1 and 3 are assumed respectively [5,6]), θ – misorientation angle between two lattice sites, θ_m – misorientation angle of a high angle grain boundary (the value of 15° is assumed [6]).

The values generated by equation (6) are within the $[0; 1]$ range for the assumed values of parameters. Then, the random value is generated from within the same range and compared with the value from equation (6). If generated value is lower than the value from the equation, then the recrystallized state and the new site orientation are accepted. The whole procedure is repeated until all of the lattice sites are recrystallized. Examples of application of the described algorithm to SRX simulations are presented in the next section.

3   Results of the MC SRX Model

The first step in creation of the required DMR is to obtain an appropriate morphology and size of the investigated grains. In that stage, also the Monte Carlo grain growth algorithm is used to meet that requirement. All simulations were performed in the two-dimensional (300×300 sites) and three-dimensional ($100 \times 100 \times 100$ sites) MC spaces. Initial microstructure morphology is presented in Fig. 2.

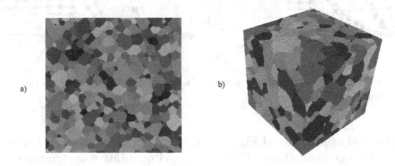

Fig. 2. Initial microstructure morphology generated by the Monte Carlo grain growth algorithm

In the Monte Carlo static recrystallization simulations, the parameter, which has a crucial influence on the recrystallization kinetics, is H/J ratio (where H is the energy stored in the lattice site and J is the grain boundary energy). That ratio is used to describe the deformation and the annealing temperature. Higher values indicate higher level of deformation and higher annealing temperature. For the first simulation the following values were assumed: $H/J = 3.5$ for the 2D model and $H/J = 10$ for the 3D model. The nucleation was homogeneous with the energy distributed uniformly in the lattice and the grain boundary mobility was independent from the misorientation angle. Remaining parameters, which were used in the simulation, are presented in Table 1.

The recrystallization kinetics (MC model) and Avrami's exponent plots (conventional JMAK model) are presented for the 2D and 3D simulations in Fig. 3a and Fig. 3b, respectively. Corresponding results of obtained microstructure morphologies are presented in Fig. 4–7.

Table 1. The parameters of the nucleation in 2D and 3D models

The nucleation type:	The parameters values:		
site saturated nucleation	$N_{ss}= 200$		
constant rate nucleation	interval: 10 MCS	$s = 1$	$N_{const}= 10$
continuous ascending nucleation			$N_{max}=100$
continuous descending nucleation			$N_{init}=100$

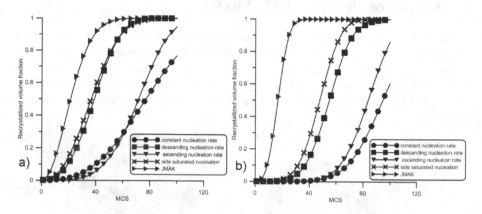

Fig. 3. The static recrystallization kinetics in: a) the 2D model, b) the 3D model; homogeneously stored energy

As presented in Fig. 3a and Fig. 3b, the recrystallization kinetics curves have characteristic sigmoidal shape. There is a good qualitative agreement between the JMAK and MC models. However, some distortions are also observed. On the other hand, there are inhomogeneities in the real deformed materials [11] and they have a big influence on the recrystallization kinetics. This is due to the fact that the MC method has probabilistic character.

Another approach to modeling SRX with the MC method can take into account heterogeneous distribution of the stored energy and influence of the misorientation angle on grain boundary mobility (for details see [1]). As seen, developed model can provide wide range of results that are of interest when designing real manufacturing operation in industrial condition. However, as mentioned, the limiting factor of wider application of the model is excessive computing time. Thus, authors proposed the use of modern computer infrastructure developed within the PL-Grid project to speed up calculations. The process of parallelization of the SRX model, to meets PL-Grid requirements, is presented next.

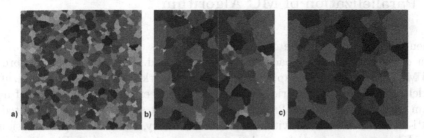

Fig. 4. Microstructure morphology after SRX with side saturated nucleation rate, after: a) 30MCS, b) 60MCS, c) 90MCS

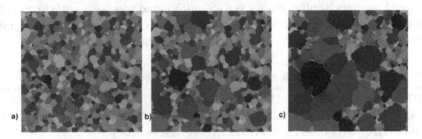

Fig. 5. Microstructure morphology after SRX with constant nucleation rate, after: a) 30MCS, b) 60MCS, c) 90MCS

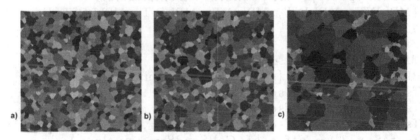

Fig. 6. Microstructure morphology after SRX with continuous ascending nucleation rate, after: a) 30MCS, b) 60MCS, c) 90MCS

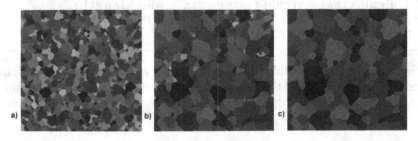

Fig. 7. Microstructure morphology after SRX with continuous descending nucleation rate, after: a) 30MCS, b) 60MCS, c) 90MCS

4   Parallelization of MC Algorithm

When parallelization of the MC SRX algorithm is discussed, a problem of efficient division of the MC space has to be addressed. The master-slave approach and MPI standards are adapted in the present work. Adapting recrystallization model to parallel use on grid platform required certain modifications of algorithm described in Section 2. Due to the fact that simulations are executed on multi-node infrastructure with distributed-memory, the first step is division of the MC space into equal layers between computing nodes (see Fig. 8). In this case, each computing node receives the same size of the MC space for further processing. After that, the new *MPIdatatype* is created (see Listing 1.1) and additional memory (buffer send – *cellsSendSrx* and receive – *cellsReceiveSrx* arrays), that stores information about sent and received node boundary information, is allocated.

Listing 1.1. MPI data type creation

```
MPI_Datatype mpi_cell_srx_type;
const int CellSrxElementsNumber = 6;
const int nitemsSrx=CellSrxElementsNumber;
int blocklengthsSrx[CellSrxElementsNumber]
= {1,1,1,1,1,1};
MPI_Datatype typesSrx[CellSrxElementsNumber]
= {MPI_INT, MPI_INT, MPI_INT, MPI_INT, MPI_DOUBLE,
MPI_DOUBLE};

//MPI_Datatype mpi_cell_srx_type;
MPI_Aint offsetsSrx[CellSrxElementsNumber];
offsetsSrx[0] = offsetof(CellSendSrx, id);
offsetsSrx[1] = offsetof(CellSendSrx, orientation);
offsetsSrx[2] = offsetof(CellSendSrx, recrystallized);
offsetsSrx[3] = offsetof(CellSendSrx, nucleon);
offsetsSrx[4] = offsetof(CellSendSrx, storedEnergy);
offsetsSrx[5] = offsetof(CellSendSrx, rxFraction);
MPI_Type_create_struct(nitemsSrx, blocklengthsSrx,
offsetsSrx, typesSrx, &mpi_cell_srx_type);
MPI_Type_commit(&mpi_cell_srx_type);
```

Crucial element in the modified version of the algorithm is introducing changes to the nucleation models. At the beginning of simulation, initial nucleation parameter s is modified according to (7):

$$s = s/n \qquad (7)$$

where n – number of nodes.

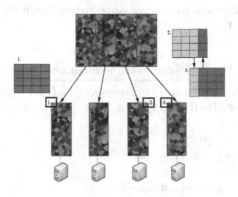

Fig. 8. MPI space division concept

Then, at the beginning of each MCS, nuclei number for particular node is recalculated from modified nucleation formulas (1) and (2):

$$N_n = \lfloor sMCS \rfloor + counter \tag{8}$$

$$N_n = N_{init} - \lfloor sMcs \rfloor + counter, \tag{9}$$

where *counter* in formulas (8) and (9) is calculated by (10):

$$\begin{cases} counter = 1 & if \ \lfloor N * 100 \rfloor \%100 \geq random\,integer\%100 \\ counter = 0 & if \ \lfloor N * 100 \rfloor \%100 < random\,integer\%100. \end{cases} \tag{10}$$

In subsequent MC steps, arrays that store boundary information for each node are updated and sent to the neighboring nodes (see Listing 1.2).

Listing 1.2. Non-blocking information updated and sent to neighboring nodes

```
void MPIElements :: BoundarySendSrx (
CellSendSrx ** cellsSendSrx , int boundarySize ){
int leftSend ;
if ( mpi_node_num==0)
leftSend = mpi_num_of_nodes -1;
else
leftSend = mpi_node_num -1;

MPI_Isend ( cellsSendSrx [0] , boundarySize , mpi_cell_srx_type ,
leftSend , tag2 , MPI_COMM_WORLD,
&mpi_send_boundary_request [0]);
MPI_Isend ( cellsSendSrx [1] , boundarySize , mpi_cell_srx_type ,
( mpi_node_num+1)%mpi_num_of_nodes , tag1 , MPI_COMM_WORLD,
&mpi_send_boundary_request [1]);
}
```

Then, each of nodes awaits to receive appropriate feedback from neighbouring nodes (see Listing 1.3).

Listing 1.3. Blocking information received from neighboring nodes

```
void  MPIElements :: BoundaryReceiveSrx (
CellSendSrx** cellsReceiveSrx , int  boundarySize){
int  leftReceive ;
if ( mpi_node_num==0)
leftReceive  =  mpi_num_of_nodes −1;
else
leftReceive  =  mpi_node_num −1;

MPI_Recv( cellsReceiveSrx [1] ,  boundarySize ,
mpi_cell_srx_type , ( mpi_node_num+1)%mpi_num_of_nodes , tag2 ,
MPI_COMM_WORLD, &mpi_status_boundary [1]);
MPI_Recv( cellsReceiveSrx [0] ,  boundarySize ,
mpi_cell_srx_type ,  leftReceive  , tag1 ,
MPI_COMM_WORLD, &mpi_status_boundary [0]);
}
```

When all nodes got the boundary information (blocking received), the particular MC step is finished, the MC space is updated and the algorithm goes to the next MCS. Illustration of the message passing algorithm used in the present work is presented in Fig. 8. The modified MC static recrystallization algorithm is shown in Fig 9.

Moreover, within a single computing node, simulation can be executed on multiple treads, using the OpenMP technology. The approach with different MC space division schemes was implemented and presented in earlier authors' work [12].

As mentioned, the developed algorithm is designed to work at the PL-Grid platform in a user friendly manner. To use the provided functionality of the developed SRX model, several steps are required:

- Generation of the input file → dedicated application.
- Transferring of the input file to the server → QCG-Icon.
- Calculation of the SRX on the Zeus supercomputer.
- Automatic download of the obtained result to a user computer → QCG-Icon.
- Visualization of obtained results (microstructure morphology, kinetics and energy distribution) → dedicated application.

The flow chart of this procedure is schematically presented in Fig. 10.

As seen, modified SRX model is compatible with the PL-Grid Infrastructure and can provide results in significantly lower time that makes it interesting for practical applications even in industrial conditions. Detailed discussion of obtained reduction in computing time is presented next.

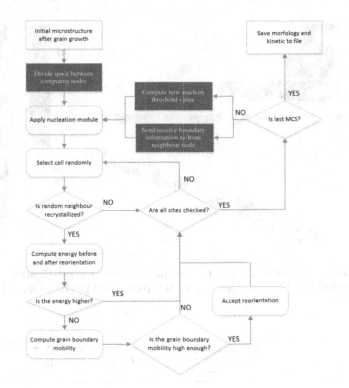

Fig. 9. The Parallel Monte Carlo static recrystallization algorithm schema

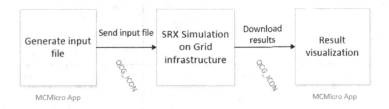

Fig. 10. Flow chart of the SRX model execution at the PL-Grid Infrastructure

4.1 Results

To evaluate efficiency of parallelization, different MC space sizes (9 and 20 million cells) and geometries (3000×3000, 9000×1000, 1000×9000 and 20000×1000, 1000×20000, 2000×100×100) were considered during static recrystallization modeling (see Fig. 12). Influence of queuing time was omitted in order not to disrupt final results. During simulation, constant nucleation rate (N_{const}= 100) and Moore neighborhood were used.

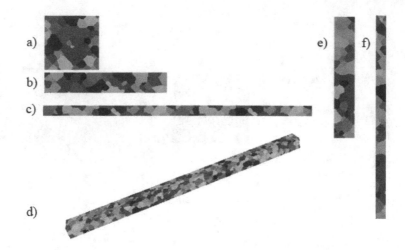

Fig. 11. Initial geometries used to compare static recrystallization execution times: a) 3000x3000, b) 9000x1000, c) 20000x1000, d) 2000x100x100, e)1000x9000, f) 1000x20000

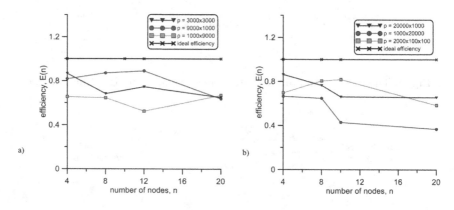

Fig. 12. Efficiency for different space size: a) 9m., b) 20m. MC cells space

Computations with different numbers of nodes were performed to evaluate possible decrease in computing time. Obtained results in the form of efficiency as a function of number of nodes are shown in Fig. 12.

As presented in Fig. 12, with increasing number of nodes, efficiency of calculations decreases, because the application needs to send more data packages and spends less time on the pure calculations. Moreover, the best efficiency is observed in spaces with dimension $x > y$ and $x > z$.

5   Conclusions and Future Work

Based on the presented investigation, it can be concluded that:

- Various types of nucleation model provide a possibility to replicate different material behavior under thermo-mechanical processing conditions.
- Parallelization of the code based on MPI and OpenMP standards provides significant decrease in computing time.
- When the number of computing nodes increases, the computing time decreases to some extent. This is associated with the efficiency of the calculations, and strictly depends on the number of nodes and the geometry of space. Computing time reduction for more than 10–12 nodes is insignificant. Such behavior is not beneficial from the practical point of view. However, running several different calculations at the same time for various processsing conditions may be a solution to this issue.
- With increasing number of nodes the efficiency decreases. This is related to the increasing number of messages passing between nodes.
- The applied client-server architecture easily allows to prepare the input files and starts simulation in the grid environment.

References

1. Sieradzki, L., Madej, L.: A perceptive comparison of the cellular automata and Monte Carlo techniques in application to static recrystallization modeling in polycrystalline materials. Computational Material Science 67, 156–173 (2013)
2. Madej, Ł., Rauch, Ł., Perzyński, K., Cybułka, P.: Digital Material Representation as an efficient tool for strain inhomogeneities analysis at the micro scale level. Archives of Civil and Mechanical Engineering 11, 661–679 (2011)
3. Szyndler, J., Madej, L.: Effect of number of grains and boundary conditions on digital material representation deformation under plain strain. Archives of Civil and Mechanical Engineering (2013), http://dx.doi.org/10.1016/j.acme.2013.09.001
4. Kalos, M.H., Whitlock, P.A.: Monte Carlo Methods. Wiley-VCH (2008)
5. Humphreys, M.J., Hatherly, M.: Recrystallization and related annealing phenomena, 2nd edn. Elsevier, Oxford (2004)
6. Doherty, R.D., Hughes, D.A., Humphreys, F.J., Jonas, J.J., Juul Jensen, D., Kassner, M.E., King, W.E., McNelley, T.R., McQueen, H.J., Rollett, A.D.: Current issues in recrystallization: a review. Materials Science and Engineering 238, 219–274 (1997)
7. Chun, Y.B., Siemiatin, S.L., Hwang, S.K.: Monte Carlo modeling of microstructure evolution during the static recrystallization of cold-rolled, commercial-purity titanium. Scripta Materialia 54, 3673–3689 (2006)
8. Ivasishin, O.M., Shevchenko, S.V., Vasiliev, N.L., Semiatin, S.L.: A 3-D Monte Carlo (Potts) model for recrystallization and grain growth in polycrystalline materials. Materials Science and Engineering A 422, 216–232 (2006)

9. Rollett, A.D., Manohar, P.: The Monte Carlo method. In: Raabe, D., Roters, F., Chen, L.-Q. (eds.) Continuum Scales Simulation of Engineering Materials, pp. 76–113. Wiley-VCH (2004)
10. Walasek, T.A.: Experimental verification of Monte Carlo recrystallization model. Journal of Material Processing Technology 157- 158, 262–267 (2004)
11. Goetz, R.L., Seetharaman, V.: Static recrystallization kinetics with homogeneous and heterogeneous nucleation using a cellular automata model. Metallurgical and Materials Transactions A 29A, 1998–2307 (1997)
12. Sitko, M., Dybich, D., Szyndler, J., Madej, Ł.: Parallelization of the Monte Carlo grain growth algorithm. Materials Science & Technology 2013, 1657–1667 (2013)

Convergence of Explicitly Correlated
Gaussian Wave Functions

Piotr Kopta[1], Tomasz Piontek[1], Krzysztof Kurowski[1],
Mariusz Puchalski[2], and Jacek Komasa[2]

[1] Poznan Supercomputing and Networking Center,
ul. Noskowskiego 10, 61-704 Poznań, Poland
[2] Adam Mickiewicz University, Faculty of Chemistry,
ul. Umultowska 89b, 61-614 Poznań, Poland
{pkopta,piontek,krzysztof.kurowski,mpuchals,komasa}@man.poznan.pl

Abstract. Results of high precision quantum-chemical calculations on
selected diatomic molecular systems are reported. The wave function is
expanded in the basis of exponentially correlated Gaussian functions. For
each of the systems the Schrödinger equation is solved variationally with
several lengths of this expansion, which enables the energy convergence
to be studied as well as an extrapolation to infinite basis set size and
an error estimation to be performed. The algorithms applied to evaluate
matrix elements and the matrix diagonalization are analyzed for their
scalability, and their strong and weak points are revealed.

Keywords: quantum mechanics, explicitly correlated wave functions,
energy convergence, general symmetric eigenvalue problem, inverse iteration method, scalability.

1 Introduction

In the last half of the 20th century, quantum chemistry became a widespread tool
for experimental chemists. Its role has been appreciated by awarding J. Pople
"for his development of computational methods in quantum chemistry" and
W. Kohn "for his development of the density-functional theory" with the Nobel
Prize in 1998. Last year, three other quantum and computational chemists have
been distinguished with the Prize "for the development of multiscale models
for complex chemical systems". The software created on the basis of the Prize
winners' ideas enabled modelling of huge biomolecular systems. Another, complementary trend in theoretical methods focuses on high accuracy description
of small diatomic molecules. Such an approach to the interaction between particles often involves a theory more fundamental than quantum chemistry – the
quantum electrodynamics (QED). The high precision theory enables studying
tiny effects resulting, e.g., from coupling between the movement of electrons and
the nuclei, from relativistic behaviour of electrons, or even from interactions of
the particles with the vacuum. Apart from testing the fundamental theory, such
accurate calculations supply data for molecular spectroscopy – a very demanding experimental discipline, which has recently made an enormous progress in

M. Bubak et al. (Eds.): PLGrid Plus, LNCS 8500, pp. 459–474, 2014.

increasing the accuracy of acquired information. The theoretical data is used to interpret and complement the measurements [1,2]. Quantum-mechanical calculations, when sufficiently accurate, enable determination of fundamental physical constants and many vital parameters of nuclei, atoms, and molecules. Moreover, the knowledge of accurate interaction between atoms can be translated onto the properties of bulk matter or even utilized to calibrate the measuring devices [3]. Quite recently, the results of high accuracy calculations on H_2 were employed to study so-called 'fifth-force', a new hypothetical weak interaction between elementary particles [4].

An essential question, which accompanies high accuracy quantum-chemical calculations, is: How to determine the accuracy? A prompt answer, which comes to mind, is: By comparison with an experiment. Unfortunately, this seemingly obvious answer solves the problem only occasionally. It is not so rare, when the experiment is less accurate than the theory. Quite often too, one deals with quantities unavailable from a measurement. In such cases, some kind of internal means of the accuracy assessment is needed. In many theoretical models it is possible to formulate the problem in such a way that the target quantity converges regularly to the exact value with a parameter of the model. The extrapolation allows reaching beyond what is directly calculable and, additionally, an estimation of the error.

In this contribution, we present the results of our study on the energy convergence in selected diatomic molecules built of 2-6 electrons. In several cases, the results presented here are the most accurate ones available to date. Apart from the quantum-chemical observables, we also discuss some numerical issues related to these particular calculations.

2   Quantum-mechanical Model and Formulation of the Convergence Problem

In quantum mechanics, the system under investigation is described by its wave function, Ψ, which is a solution to the Schrödinger equation $H\Psi = E\Psi$. The Hamiltonian H represents an energy as a physical property of the system and E is its numerical value. In our study, we use the so-called clamped nuclei Hamiltonian

$$H = -\frac{1}{2}\sum_{i=1}^{n}\nabla_i^2 + V\,,\tag{1}$$

which describes the kinetic energy of n electrons and the Coulomb interaction V between all the particles comprising the molecule: resting nuclei and moving electrons. Since, in general, exact solutions to the Schrödinger equation are unknown, one has to rely on some approximate methods of solving the equation. The approximate wave function is commonly assumed as a linear combination of some known basis functions

$$\Psi = \sum_{k=1}^{K} c_k\,\phi_k\,.\tag{2}$$

As the basis functions ϕ_k we employ multielectron, exponentially correlated Gaussian (ECG) functions [5]

$$\phi_k = \exp\left[-(\boldsymbol{r} - \boldsymbol{s}_k)\mathbf{A}_k(\boldsymbol{r} - \boldsymbol{s}_k)\right] . \qquad (3)$$

They have proven in many studies their applicability in high accuracy calculations [6,7] and form a basis set of choice for the few-electron systems considered here. The size of the expansion, K, plays an important role in our study of convergence. We expect that with growing K the approximate solutions (E_K, Ψ_K) to the Schrödinger equation become more and more accurate. This intuitive expectation is confirmed by a mathematically strict theorem called the variational principle [8]. This principle is also employed to determine optimal values of the linear parameters c_k of Eq. (2) and the non-linear parameters collected in the matrices $\mathbf{A}_k$ and vectors $\boldsymbol{s}_k$ of Eq. (3). Details of the optimization algorithm can be found in [9].

Although we have the guarantee that the energy error $\Delta E_K = E_K - E_\infty$ tends to zero with increasing K, the real issue is how fast this convergence is. From the experience gained over the years [10] it is known that the energy error converges with the size of the ECG basis according to the inverse power law

$$\Delta E_K = A K^{-B} . \qquad (4)$$

The purpose of our work was to verify this convergence pattern and subsequently to employ it to estimate: firstly, the energy E_∞ in the limit of the infinite basis set size; and secondly, the threshold K_0 of the basis set size, above which the convergence pattern ceases to obey the power law of Eq. (4), which indicates, in turn, that the optimization of the variational parameters defining the basis becomes ineffective. Achieving this goal required a very time consuming optimization of the energy with respect to the variational parameters c, $\mathbf{A}_k$, and $\boldsymbol{s}_k$ of the wave function and was possible owing to the access to PL-Grid resources and services.

The basis set size and the number of electrons of the molecule determine the computational complexity of the optimization. The complexity of a matrix element evaluation increases exponentially with the number of electrons, while the basis set size determines the size of the matrix. The matrix diagonalization is the main part of the optimization process. Thus, the optimization scalability is limited by the characteristics of the two aforementioned steps. Since the matrix elements are independent of each other, they can be computed in parallel, with almost linear scalability. On the other hand, the matrix-vector multiplication along with solving the triangular system of equations – the main parts of the diagonalization algorithm, do not scale very well. The lack of an alternative diagonalization algorithm is the 'bottleneck' of the entire optimization scalability.

3 Extrapolation Procedure and Results

The computations were performed for several diatomic molecules of growing size. The smallest, two-electron systems, for which very accurate solutions are already known [11,12], were used as benchmarks to validate our extrapolation procedure. Then, the procedure was applied to larger, three-, four- and six-electron systems. The energy was evaluated starting with a small basis set, which was being successively doubled reaching the largest size, for which the calculations were still feasible in reasonable time.

For a particular molecule, members of the energy series E_K differ very little from each other. Extrapolation from such a set of very similar data would be contaminated with a relatively large error. To avoid this, we converted the raw energies E_K (expressed in units of hartree, E_h) to a new series ε_K with the meaningful digits exposed – first the energies were shifted by η to the vicinity of the scale origin, then were scaled by a factor γ according to the following formula

$$\varepsilon_K = \gamma (E_K + \eta). \tag{5}$$

The results of such a series of calculations were then fitted to a linearized form of Eq. (4) obtained by taking the logarithm of both sides

$$\ln(\varepsilon_K - \varepsilon_\infty) = -B \ln K + \ln A. \tag{6}$$

The unknown parameter ε_∞ was adjusted to maximize the squared correlation factor r^2 and finally converted back to E_∞ using Eq. (5).

While increasing the expansion length K, we noticed that at a certain size the fit distinctly deteriorated, which indicated that the threshold value K_0, defined in previous section, has been exceeded. Such values were rejected from the fit and the procedure was finished.

In the following subsections, we shall present some results obtained for six distinct diatomic molecules. The first two systems (H_2, HeH^+) will be treated as a testing ground for the extrapolation procedure described above. For these systems there is extremely accurate data available in literature, which was obtained with the wave functions dedicated to two-electron diatomic molecules only. The ECG functions employed in our study are not limited with respect to the number of electrons or nuclei. Therefore, they could have been applied to larger diatomic systems built of three (He_2^+), four (He_2, LiH), or six (CH^+) electrons. Atomic units are used in referring to the length (bohr) and energy (hartree, E_h).

3.1 H_2

Hydrogen molecule is the simplest neutral molecule. It is built of only two electrons and for its relative simplicity is very often used to test new computational methods. Not long ago Pachucki developed a new method of treating two-center two-electron integrals over exponential functions [13,14]. This new methodology allowed him to push the accuracy of molecular energy calculations to an unprecedented level of 16 significant digits [11]. The calculations based on the ECG functions [15] cannot compete with these results. Nevertheless, energy accurate to a fraction of nanohartree (nE_h) has been obtained (see E_∞ in Table 1). Such an accuracy is often more than sufficient to most needs. The extrapolation was performed from just four energies with an absolute error given in the last column of Table 1. The quality of the fit is measured by the squared correlation factor $r^2 = 0.9953$ and can be assessed visually from Fig. 1.

Table 1. Convergence of the energy E_K of H_2 at $R = 1.4$ bohr. The conversion formula (5) reads $\varepsilon_K = -10^9(E_K + 1.17447571)$.

K	ε_K	$\ln K$	$\ln \Delta \varepsilon_K$	$\Delta E_K / nE_h$
75	-1200.944	4.32	7.09	1205.16
150	-73.483	5.01	4.35	77.70
300	2.797	5.70	0.34	1.42
600	4.146	6.40	-2.88	0.07

Regression parameters:
$$r^2 = 0.9953$$
$$\ln A = 28.5$$
$$B = 4.9$$

Extrapolated energy:
$$E_\infty = -1.174\,475\,714\,2(4)\ E_h$$

Reference energy from [11]:
$$E_{\text{ref}} = -1.174\,475\,714\,220\,443\,4(5)\ E_h$$

3.2 HeH$^+$

The hydrohelium is a heteronuclear molecular cation, which is isoelectronic with H_2 and the calculations for both molecules seem to be analogous. However, there are also some differences, which are significant from the computational point of view. The concentration of the electronic charge distribution close to helium nucleus and the lack of inversion symmetry in HeH$^+$ make the wave function Ψ more complicated than in the case of H_2. As a consequence, longer expansions (2) have to be used in order to preserve accuracy similar to that obtained for H_2. The large permanent dipole moment of this cation enables acquisition of highly accurate spectra, which stimulates interest in high accuracy theoretical studies [16].

As in previous subsection, we refer to the benchmark results published by Pachucki [12] who used exponential functions and obtained the energy with 12 exact digits. The parameters of our extrapolation procedure are collected in Table 2 and shown graphically in Fig. 1. As we can see from this Table, our extrapolated energy recovers 8 figures of the exact value.

We have shown that for both two-electron systems the energy series obey the inverse power law of Eq. (4), which opens up the possibility of reasonable extrapolation using the procedure described in the previous section. In the following subsections we shall supply the results of such an extrapolation for larger systems, for which no reference calculations of a significantly better quality exist.

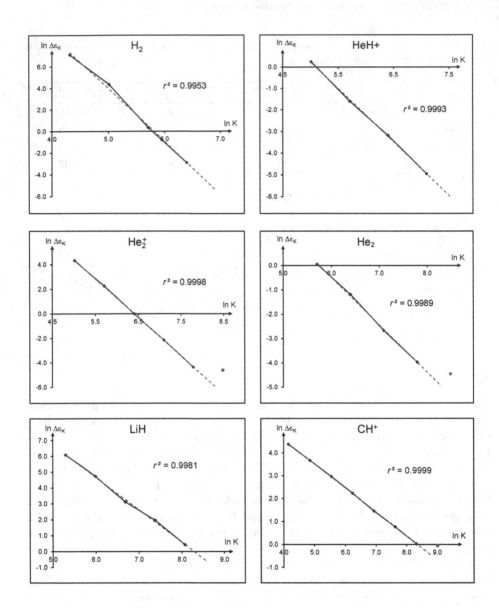

Fig. 1. Graphical representation of the linear regression for all six molecular systems (at their equilibrium internuclear distance) described in this section. r^2 is the squared correlation factor. Please, refer to text for description of the axes. The dot (if present) separated from the regression line locates the entries rejected from the fit.

Table 2. Convergence of the energy E_K of HeH$^+$ at $R = 1.46$ bohr. The conversion formula (5) reads $\varepsilon_K = -10^6(E_K + 2.978705)$.

K	ε_K	$\ln K$	$\ln \Delta\varepsilon_K$	$\Delta E_K/\text{mE}_\text{h}$
150	0.28097	5.01	0.24	1.32
300	1.35367	5.70	−1.59	0.25
600	1.51566	6.40	−3.19	0.08
1200	1.54993	7.09	−4.95	0.05

Regression parameters:
$$r^2 = 0.9993$$
$$\ln A = 12.6$$
$$B = 2.5$$

Extrapolated energy:
$$E_\infty = -2.978\,706\,56(7)$$

Reference energy from [12]:
$$E_\text{ref} = -2.978\,706\,600\,341(1)$$

3.3 He$_2^+$

The helium dimer cation, according to the standard Big Bang model, is one of the first molecules formed in the Universe. Astronomical observations though are hindered by a low abundance of He$_2^+$ in space. Therefore, a theoretically predicted spectrum of high quality would be of great value for astronomers. The first step towards obtaining such a spectrum is a high precision interaction energy curve with well-established error bars. Among the most accurate calculations reported to date there are those by Cencek and Rychlewski [17] and by Tung et al. [18]. As can be inferred from Table 3, in comparison with their results, the extrapolated energy is an order of magnitude more accurate.

Our energy obtained from the largest 4800-term expansion was excluded from the fit as it was illustrated by a red dot in Fig. 1. Adding this value to the fitted series lowered significantly the quality of the regression. This is an indication of deviation from the inverse power low. Of course, such energy E_{4800} is still a valuable one as the most accurate variational estimation of the energy to date. From this observation we can locate the threshold K_0 in the range (2400,4800).

3.4 He$_2$

Despite having only four electrons, helium dimer, for its unusually small binding energy and extremely large spatial extent, is one of the most interesting and difficult to accurately model molecules. To be more specific, common equilibrium distance in a diatomic molecule is less than 3 bohrs whereas in He$_2$ it amounts to 5.6 bohr; the average internuclear distance is as large as 89 bohrs and the nuclear wave function has significant values as far as 2000 bohrs from the middle of the molecule. Moreover, the binding energy of the only bound state of He$_2$ is 10^4 times smaller than the interaction well depth, which means that the rovibrational level is located just below the dissociation threshold. This short characteristics

Table 3. Convergence of the energy E_K of He_2^+ at $R = 2.042$ bohr. The conversion formula (5) reads $\varepsilon_K = -10^3(E_K + 4.994)$.

K	ε_K	$\ln K$	$\ln \Delta\varepsilon_K$	$\Delta E_K/mE_h$
150	568.038	5.01	4.33	76.020
300	634.359	5.70	2.27	9.699
600	643.050	6.40	0.01	1.008
1200	643.942	7.09	−2.15	0.116
2400	644.045	7.78	−4.34	0.013
4800	644.048	8.48	−4.61	0.010

Regression parameters:
$$r^2 = 0.9998$$
$$\ln A = 20.1$$
$$B = 3.1$$
Extrapolated energy:
$$E_\infty = -4.994\,644\,06(5)$$
References:
Cencek and Rychlewski [17] $E_\infty = -4.994\,644\,2(2)$

shows how sensitive the molecular parameters are to the quality of the wave function. Therefore, this system is very demanding from the point of view of the accuracy of the quantum-mechanical calculations.

To date, the most accurate prediction of the energy has been published by Cencek and Szalewicz [15] using ECG wave functions. The comparison of the extrapolation method used by Cencek and Szalewicz (see Table 4) with the method investigated here shows that their computations are an order of magnitude more accurate. In this case we have also rejected the E_{4800} contribution from the fitting procedure as shown in Fig. 1 and the estimation of K_0 threshold is the same as in the case of He_2^+.

3.5 LiH

Lithium hydride is the smallest heteronuclear neutral diatomic molecule. It is willingly studied both theoretically and experimentally. One of the reasons for the wide spread interest in LiH is a discovery of the role it plays in astrochemistry of the recombination era and in the formation of the first cosmological objects [19]. There exists rich spectroscopic data, see e.g. [20] and [21], concerning the most abundant isotopomers of LiH.

The most accurate previous calculations on the energy of LiH at the equilibrium distance come from Cencek and Rychlewski [17] and from Tung et al. [22], but only the first reference contains an extrapolated value together with the error estimation. When compared, our extrapolated value seems to be one order of magnitude more accurate than that of Ref. [17] (see Table 5). The quality of our fit can be assessed visually in Fig. 1. The energy E_{3200} obtained from our largest expansion fits well to our regression model and was not excluded, hence we can conclude that the threshold $K_0 > 3200$.

Table 4. Convergence of the energy E_K of He_2 at $R = 5.6$ bohr. The conversion formula (5) reads $\varepsilon_K = -10^7(E_K + 5.807483)$.

K	ε_K	$\ln K$	$\ln \Delta\varepsilon_K$	$\Delta E_K/mE_h$
300	4.861	5.70	0.05	1.052
600	5.608	6.40	−1.19	0.305
1200	5.844	7.09	−2.67	0.069
2400	5.894	7.78	−3.97	0.019
4800	5.901	8.48	−4.46	0.012

Regression parameters:
$$r^2 = 0.9989$$
$$\ln A = 11.2$$
$$B = 2.0$$

Extrapolated energy:
$$E_\infty = -5.807\,483\,591(7)$$

References:
Cencek and Szalewicz [15] $E_\infty = -5.807\,483\,590\,9(6)$

Table 5. Convergence of the energy E_K of LiH at $R = 3.015$ bohr. The conversion formula (5) reads $\varepsilon_K = -10^3(E_K + 8.070)$.

K	ε_K	$\ln K$	$\ln \Delta\varepsilon_K$	$\Delta E_K/mE_h$
200	109.719	5.30	6.09	439.411
400	435.878	5.99	4.73	113.252
800	526.652	6.68	3.11	22.478
1600	542.016	7.38	1.96	7.114
3200	547.600	8.07	0.43	1.530

Regression parameters:
$$r^2 = 0.9981$$
$$\ln A = 16.8$$
$$B = 2.0$$

Extrapolated energy:
$$E_\infty = -8.070\,549\,1(2)$$

References:
Cencek and Rychlewski [17] $E_\infty = -8.070\,553(5)$

3.6   CH$^+$

The methylidyne cation was discovered in 1937 by Dunham who recorded an electronic spectrum of the interstellar space. Only recently, after intensive laboratory studies on its infrared spectrum, CH$^+$ fundamental rotational line has been detected by *Herschel* Space Observatory. To date, the presence of methylidyne cation has also been confirmed in the Large Magellanic Clouds and in many other interstellar and cometary species. According to modern astrochemistry, CH$^+$ plays a central role in the formation of hydrocarbons in the interstellar medium. Intensive studies on this cation are propelled by a significant disagreement between the theoretically predicted and observed rate of association in

Table 6. Convergence of the energy E_K of CH^+ at $R = 2.1$ bohr. The conversion formula (5) reads $\varepsilon_K = -10^3(E_K + 38.0)$.

K	ε_K	$\ln K$	$\ln \Delta\varepsilon_K$	$\Delta E_K/mE_h$
64	8.34	4.16	4.38	79.660
128	48.68	4.85	3.67	39.320
256	68.66	5.55	2.96	19.344
512	78.72	6.24	2.23	9.281
1024	83.71	6.93	1.46	4.294
2048	85.85	7.62	0.77	2.149
4096	86.98	8.32	0.02	1.025
8192	87.05	9.01	−0.05	0.950

Regression parameters:
$$r^2 = 0.9999$$
$$\ln A = 8.8$$
$$B = 1.0$$

Extrapolated energy:
$$E_\infty = -38.088\,00(2)$$

formation of CH^+. Unexpectedly large abundance of this cation observed in the interstellar medium is another puzzle, which remains to be explained.

CH^+ is the smallest "organic" molecular system, which can be currently studied using accurate, explicitly correlated quantum chemical methods. We present here the first approach to a high precision (of a fraction of millihartre) study of this 6-electron system. For this reason, we have no reference data of comparable accuracy and the estimation given in Table 6 is the most accurate available. The energy from the largest basis set ($K = 8192$) was rejected from the fit yielding $4096 < K_0 < 8192$ and the remaining 7 entries fits perfectly ($r^2 = 0.9999$) to the linearized inverse power model of Eq. (6).

4   Numerical Aspects of the Computations

Each energy value used in this work was a result of time consuming calculations, in which the variational parameters c_k, $A_{k,ij}$ and $s_{k,i}$, defining the wave function Ψ (see Eq. (2) and (3)), were optimized to variationally minimize the energy. The optimization was performed under control of the Powell's conjugate direction algorithm [23]. The computationally most time consuming case we encountered here, was the optimization of the energy of CH^+ with 8192-term expansion (see ε_{8192} in Table 6). This task required the energy to be evaluated about 20 million times. From the numerical point of view, a single energy evaluation, the so-called energy shot, comprises two distinct phases: 1) the evaluation of matrix elements – a scalar process, which due to the mutual independence of particular matrix elements, ideally undergoes parallelization; and 2) the diagonalization, or more strictly speaking, solution of a general symmetric eigenvalue problem, using the inverse iteration method – a linear algebra task built of several distinct steps discussed below in detail. The computations were performed in the PL-Grid Infrastructure with a support from QCG services newly developed for the quantum chemistry and molecular physics domain grid. These services significantly simplified job submission and flow control. In particular, the QCG-Monitoring service enabled tracing the task progress in real time. In this section we shall present our experience, strong and weak sides of our algorithm, and efficiency tests on available platforms.

With this kind of time consuming calculations every source of improvement translates immediately to a significant lowering of the computational costs. One of the most crucial savings was obtained by implementing an updating of the diagonalization. If the wave function is optimized term by term, then only one row and column of the 8192×8192 matrices vary in the course of the optimization. As a consequence, the whole matrices have to be evaluated just once at the beginning and in the following steps the selected row and column are updated. The same concerns the diagonalization phase as the updating scales as K^2 in contrast to K^3 for full diagonalization.

4.1 Evaluation of Matrix Elements

We consider two symmetric matrices, $\mathbb{S}$ and $\mathbb{H}$, whose elements are defined by integrals over the ECG basis functions of Eq. (3)

$$\mathbb{S}_{ij} = \int \phi_i \phi_j \, d\boldsymbol{r} \,, \tag{7}$$

$$\mathbb{H}_{ij} = \int \phi_i H \phi_j \, d\boldsymbol{r} \,. \tag{8}$$

For the case introduced above, a single computation of $8192(8192+1) \approx 67 \cdot 10^6$ integrals is needed at the very beginning of the optimization, then, at each energy shot, $2 \cdot 8192$ integrals is evaluated. Approximately 200 shots are required to optimize a single basis function out of total 8192. Such a cycle over all the basis function was repeated several tens of times. In summary, the overall optimization procedure required ca. 10^{12} evaluations of the integrals $\mathbb{S}_{ij}$ and $\mathbb{H}_{ij}$. As mentioned above, this time consuming task can be very efficiently performed in parallel and, indeed, we observed nearly linear scalability.

In Table 7 we present an efficiency for a thousand of pairs of the matrix elements measured for several hardware platforms. The efficiency is defined as a ratio of the evaluation time using all available cores to a single core divided by the number of cores. The higher the 'Efficiency' is, the better is the scalability offered by the platform. Another parameter characterising the core usage in these platforms is the 'Efficiency per core' expressed in core-hours. This parameter says how many hours are needed to evaluate the number of matrix elements (full symmetric matrices $\mathbb{S}$ and $\mathbb{H}$ in this case) with a given number of cores and the smaller is its value the more efficient a single core is.

4.2 Diagonalization

The second phase of the energy evaluation is a typical linear algebra problem. The Schrödinger equation (1) written in the matrix notation has a form of well-

Table 7. Efficiency of evaluation of 6-electron molecular integrals on selected platforms

	AMD	AMD	Intel	Intel
CPU type	Opteron 2435	Opteron 6272	Xeon L5640	Xeon E5-2670
Clock speed	2600 MHz	2100 MHz	2260 MHz	2600 MHz
Last level cache	6 MB	16 MB	12 MB	20 MB
No. of CPUs	2	4	2	2
No. of cores	2 x 6	4 x 16	2 x 6	2 x 8
Memory	16 GB	512 GB	16 GB	128 GB
Efficiency	0.97	0.78	0.86	0.92
Efficiency per core (in core-hour)	55	89	53	34

known general symmetric eigenvalue problem

$$\mathbb{H}\mathbf{c} = E\,\mathbb{S}\,\mathbf{c}\,, \tag{9}$$

which can be solved using one of the standard procedures available, e.g. in LA-PACK library. In order to make use of the updating mentioned above, we have selected the inverse iteration algorithm [24] to solve Eq. (9). It relies on iterative searching of the vector $\mathbf{c}$ according to the following scheme:

$$(\mathbb{H} - E_0\,\mathbb{S})\,\mathbf{c}_{k+1} = \mathbb{S}\,\mathbf{c}_k\,. \tag{10}$$

The iterative process converges quickly (in 3-5 iterations) provided that reasonable starting values of E_0 and $\mathbf{c}_0$ are supplied. The left hand side matrix $\mathbb{H} - E_0\,\mathbb{S}$ remains constant during the iteration – it is Cholesky decomposed

$$\mathbb{H} - E_0\,\mathbb{S} = \mathbb{L}\,\mathbb{L}^T \tag{11}$$

at the beginning of the process and the triangular factor $\mathbb{L}$ is further employed in solving successively two sets of linear equations

$$\mathbb{L}\,\mathbf{y} = \mathbb{S}\,\mathbf{c}_k\,, \tag{12}$$

$$\mathbb{L}^T\,\mathbf{c}_{k+1} = \mathbf{y}\,. \tag{13}$$

The whole inverse algorithm iterations are realized by three most time-consuming base operations: the Cholesky decomposition, symmetric matrix-vector multiplication (symv) and triangular system solution (trsv). The former one features $O(K^3)$ compute complexity, where the other two – $O(K^2)$. Due to the applied algorithmic optimizations, the number of $O(K^3)$ Cholesky decomposition calls was reduced to only one for about 60-400 inverse iteration method requests (energy shots). In summary, the number of the most time-consuming operations can be estimated as follows: Cholesky decomposition – one for 60-400 energy shots (i.e., for a single basis function optimization); symmetric matrix-vector multiplication – twice per energy shot; triangular system solution – three times per energy shot.

The computing complexity of all the other operations is linear. Due to the iterative property of the algorithm, the only possible way of parallelization of the inverse iteration method is parallelization of particular steps of the algorithm. To reach this goal and to achieve an optimal efficiency, we employed parallel implementations of linear algebra BLAS and LAPACK libraries.

Cholesky Decomposition. To perform this algorithm, we used the dpotrf function from LAPACK library. We assumed the amount $K^3/3$ for the number of floating point operations (FLOPS) for Cholesky decomposition algorithm. As it operates only on half of the matrix, its space complexity is $[K(K+1)]/2$ words.

Table 8. Estimated number of floating point operations (FLOPS) and memory space complexity of basic procedures comprising the inverse iteration method algorithm

Procedure	FLOPS	Memory	FLOPS / words
dpotrf	171 GFlops	256 MB	5461
backsub	64 MFlops	256 MB	2
dsymv	64 MFlops	256 MB	2
dtrsv	64 MFlops	256 MB	2

Cholesky Decomposition Update. This algorithm is employed in order to update the previously calculated matrix decomposition at the point when one row and one column of a source matrix change. It is performed with the use of three operations: vector updates, triangular systems solutions and scalar product of two vectors. For this reason, as the number of operations (FLOPS), $K^2 + 4K$ value was assumed. We assume that the space complexity equals to $[K(K+1)]/2 + 2K$.

Multiplying Matrices by Vectors. In order to perform this algorithm, the dsymv subroutine from BLAS library was employed. We assumed the amount of $K(K+1)$ for the number of operations for the multiplying triangular matrix algorithm. This method operates on half of the matrix and two vectors, hence we assume that space complexity equals to $[K(K+1)]/2 + 2K$.

Triangular Systems Solutions. To perform this algorithm we employed the dtrsv routine from BLAS library. We assumed the amount K^2 for the number of operations for backward substitution triangular systems solution algorithm. We assume that space complexity equals to $[K(K+1)]/2 + 2K$.

Analysis. Cholesky decomposition algorithm exhibits a good scalability, reaching on one node (2 x CPU) acceleration from x8 (for 2 x 6 cores L5640, 2435) to x13 (2 x 8 cores E5). Only on machines with AMD 6272 processors its scalability breaks after 16 threads, which may be caused by a specific construction of AMD Bulldozer processors, in which two physical cores share one FPU unit.

Unfortunately, the two other algorithms, i.e., the back substitution (triangular system) and multiplication of a symmetric matrix by a vector do not scale well. In some cases, optimal efficiency is achieved for two threads. Both the aforementioned algorithms can be characterized by a low FLOPS/words ratio (see Table 8), which in connection with relatively small matrices result in a poor scalability. It is worth noticing that the platforms based on Intel processors achieve much better scalability.

When comparing the efficiency of BLAS library implementations, it is worth noticing that for multiplication of a symmetric matrix by a vector the efficiency is higher for OpenBLAS library than that for MKL. It has to be borne in mind that the tested OpenBLAS library employed a multithreading standard – pthreads and not OpenMP, which may be beneficial in the cases of applications frequently employing the synchronizing operations.

Scalability of the Inverse Iteration Method. Assuming that for optimization of a single basis function one hundred of executions of the inverse iteration algorithm are required, we can estimate the number of runs of the basic subroutines as follows:

$$C + 5(2S + 2T) + 99(T + 3(2S + 2T)) = C + 703T + 604S, \qquad (14)$$

where C stands for a number Cholesky decomposition executions, S – for symmetric matrix-vector multiplications, and T – triangular system solutions. Filling the variables in the above equation with the best results obtained for all of the algorithms, a share of particular algorithms in the total time of optimizing the basis function may be assessed: Cholesky – 6%, trsv – 71%, and symv – 22%. We can conclude that the most computationally complex and time-consuming algorithm is responsible for only 6% of computing time, therefore if its runtime could be cut by half, it will result in a 3% reduction of computing time. The most influential factor on the optimization time is the number of **backsub** and **symv** executions. Due to their very limited scalability, they are the bottleneck of the whole optimization process. Without improvements in their time execution, the current implementation of inverse iteration method cannot be further accelerated.

Constraints of the Algorithm. The biggest constraint of scalability of the diagonalization algorithm run on state-of-the-art processors is in the algorithm optimization. Owing to the reduction in the amount of runs of the most time-consuming algorithm, that is Cholesky decomposition $(O(K^3))$ and replacing it by less computationally complex algorithms $(O(K^2))$, the complexity of the whole process was reduced to such an extent that the characteristics of the whole algorithm became more "memory bound". In order to achieve the maximal efficiency, processors require at least 5 operations per byte (Intel Xeon E5), which in the case of computations on double precision numbers gives 40 operations per word. The most time-consuming operations of our inverse iteration method, are characterized by value 2 (about 20 times less), making them highly memory bandwidth dependent. An increase in the diagonalization algorithm scalability may be achieved only by employing the computing architectures with a significantly bigger memory bandwidth, such as GPU or Intel Xeon Phi.

Acknowledgments. This research was supported by NCN grant No. 2011/01/B /ST4/00733 as well as by a computing grant from Poznan Supercomputing and Networking Center and by the PL-Grid Infrastructure.

References

1. Komasa, J., Piszczatowski, K., Lach, G., Przybytek, M., Jeziorski, B., Pachucki, K.: Quantum Electrodynamics Effects in Rovibrational Spectra of Molecular Hydrogen. J. Chem. Theory Comput. 7, 3105–3115 (2011)
2. Kassi, S., Campargue, A., Pachucki, K., Komasa, J.: The absorption spectrum of D_2: Ultrasensitive cavity ring down spectroscopy of the (2-0) band near 1.7 μm and accurate ab initio line list up to 24 000 cm^{-1}. J. Chem. Phys. 136, 184309 (2012)
3. Cencek, W., Przybytek, M., Komasa, J., Mehl, J.B., Jeziorski, B., Szalewicz, K.: Effects of adiabatic, relativistic, and quantum electrodynamics interactions on the pair potential and thermophysical properties of helium. J. Chem. Phys. 136, 224303 (2012)
4. Salumbides, E.J., Koelemeij, J.C.J., Komasa, J., Pachucki, K., Eikema, K.S.E., Ubachs, W.: Bounds on fifth forces from precision measurements on molecules. Phys. Rev. D 87, 112008 (2013)
5. Singer, K.: The Use of Gaussian (Exponential Quadratic) Wave Functions in Molecular Problems. I. General Formulae for the Evaluation of Integrals. Proc. R. Soc. London, Ser. A 258, 412 (1960)
6. Rychlewski, J., Komasa, J., Rychlewski, J. (eds.): Explicitly Correlated Wave Functions in Chemistry and Physics. Kluwer Academic Publisher, Dordrecht (2003)
7. Mitroy, J., Bubin, S., Horiuchi, W., Suzuki, Y., Adamowicz, L., Cencek, W., Szalewicz, K., Komasa, J., Blume, D., Varga, K.: Theory and application of explicitly correlated Gaussians. Rev. Mod. Phys. 85, 693–749 (2013)
8. Epstein, S.T.: The Variation Method in Quantum Chemistry. Academic Press, New York (1974)
9. Kopta, P., Kulczewski, M., Kurowski, K., Piontek, T., Gepner, P., Puchalski, M., Komasa, J.: Parallel application benchmarks and performance evaluation of the Intel Xeon 7500 family processors. Procedia Computer Science 4, 372–381 (2011)
10. Cencek, W., Komasa, J., Rychlewski, J.: Benchmark calculations for two-electron systems using explicitly correlated Gaussian functions. Chem. Phys. Lett. 246, 417–420 (1995)
11. Pachucki, K.: Born-Oppenheimer potential for H_2. Phys. Rev. A 82, 032509 (2010)
12. Pachucki, K.: Born-Oppenheimer potential for HeH$^+$. Phys. Rev. A 85, 042511 (2012)

13. Pachucki, K.: Two-center two-electron integrals with exponential functions. Phys. Rev. A 80, 032520 (2009)
14. Pachucki, K.: Correlated exponential functions in high-precision calculations for diatomic molecules. Phys. Rev. A 86, 052514 (2012)
15. Cencek, W., Szalewicz, K.: Ultra-high accuracy calculations for hydrogen molecule and helium dimer. J. Quantum Chem. 108, 2191 (2008)
16. Pachucki, K., Komasa, J.: Rovibrational levels of helium hydride ion. J. Chem. Phys. 137, 204314 (2012)
17. Cencek, W., Rychlewski, J.: Benchmark calculations for He_2^+ and LiH molecules using explicitly correlated Gaussian functions. Chem. Phys. Lett. 320, 549–552 (2000)
18. Tung, W.-C., Pavanello, M., Adamowicz, L.: Very accurate potential energy curve of the He_2^+ ion. J. Chem. Phys. 136, 104309 (2012)
19. Lepp, S., Stancil, P.C., Dalgarno, A.: Atomic and molecular processes in the early Universe. J. Phys. B: At. Mol. Opt. Phys. 35, R57–R80 (2002)
20. Stwalley, W.C., Zemke, W.T.: Spectroscopy and Structure of the Lithium Hydride Diatomic Molecules and Ions. J. Phys. Chem. Ref. Data 22, 87 (1993)
21. Coxon, J.A., Dickinson, C.S.: Application of direct potential fitting to line position data for the $X^1\Sigma^+$ and $A^1\Sigma^+$ states of LiH. J. Chem. Phys. 121, 9378 (2004)
22. Tung, W.-C., Pavanello, M., Adamowicz, L.: Very accurate potential energy curve of the LiH molecule. J. Chem. Phys. 134, 064117 (2011)
23. Powell, M.J.D.: An efficient method for finding the minimum of a function of several variables without calculating derivatives. Comput. J. 7, 155 (1964)
24. Kiełbasiński, A., Schwetlick, H.: Numeryczna algebra liniowa. Wprowadzenie do obliczeń zautomatyzowanych. Wydawnictwa Naukowo-Techniczne, Warszawa (1992) (in Polish)

Analysing a Power Generation Sector Using the MILP Approach

Jacek Kamiński[1], Przemysław Kaszyński[1], and Tomasz Mirowski[2]

[1] Mineral and Energy Economy Research Institute of the Polish Academy of Sciences, ul. Wybickiego 7, 31-261 Kraków, Poland
kaminski@meeri.pl

[2] AGH University of Science and Technology, The Faculty of Energy and Fuels, al. Mickiewicza 30, 30-059 Kraków, Poland

Abstract. The paper presents a computable model of the Polish power generation sector implemented as a Mixed Integer Linear Programming problem. As the optimisation process of power generation systems needs substantial computing resources and normally both specialised knowledge on modelling and expensive modelling systems are required, we decided to make the tool available to the scientific community via the PL-Grid Infrastructure. Consequently, users are allowed to transfer their tasks to computing clusters, hence all of the key numerical calculations are done on the computing clusters of ACC Cyfronet AGH. For interfacing with users we selected the QosCosGrid middleware, which is an efficient programming and execution tool. We present exemplary results based on designed scenario simulations carried out using the developed tool. Some potential improvements, such as transposition to a non-linear model, are also proposed for the future.

Keywords: power generation, computable model, GAMS, MILP, mathematical programming.

1 Introduction

The power sector continues to be considered a key sector in contemporary society owing to the fact that electricity is now treated as a public good without which it would be difficult to imagine a developed economy functioning. It is obvious that development of the power sector (the energy sector, if taken in a broader context) is directly related to the economic development of any country. Due to its features, the power sector needs long-term planning, yet such analyses are often complex to carry out since the numbers of elements in the power system and relations between them are both enormous.

One of the options considered when demand for electricity is under discussion is the contribution of renewables to the fuel mix for power generation. Regardless of the pros and cons of the deployment of renewable energy sources, one of the consequences that comes from the use of renewables is a general difficulty in managing and operating a power system, a difficulty which results from the intermittent production of power by renewable technologies. Due to the impact of

M. Bubak et al. (Eds.): PLGrid Plus, LNCS 8500, pp. 475–488, 2014.
© Springer International Publishing Switzerland 2014

weather conditions, power generation facilities need to be more elastic to be able to respond to rapid changes in availability of wind or sunlight. Thus, simulations are needed that allow one to tackle such issues in order to foresee whether the stability of the power system is ensured or needs improvement. Such issues are of key importance when we consider the prospects for the long-run development of the power sector. Consequently, appropriate tools are required to simulate the functioning of the power system with sufficiently high resolution. Normally the testing of long term models is based on the input of representative loads. However, when variable weather conditions are considered, it is absolutely necessary to get down to an hourly resolution. This directly leads to computational problems, since the number of variables and interlinked constraints soars when the number of time slices grows.

Another important issue that very often needs to be analysed, and where application of computable models is highly recommended, is the impact of the deployment of new power generation units from the perspective of the whole power generation system. Usually it is not known in advance what would be the consequence of the development of a new gas-fired or coal-fired unit. Also the impact on the costs of electricity generation or emission levels expressed in quantitative terms, which are of utmost importance to scientists who deal with energy and the environment nowadays, is very complex to estimate. Ultimately, it is not known whether a unit being deployed would be competitive when compared with the existing units. In this case simulations carried out using the computable models are to be highly recommended in order to analyse the consequences of the introduction of new units into the system.

On the other hand, when there are power generation units that need to be decommissioned, analyses of the impact of such activities on the ability of the power generation system to meet the demand for power are required. Also, the economic and environmental consequences of such decommissioning need to be assessed in advance, so that one is able to point out in advance potential problems with the adequacy of power generation. Moreover, as virtually all companies consume electricity for their own economic activities (and the energy-intensive sectors in particular are very exposed to price risk), the prices of electricity are also of significant importance. And since they are very often based on costs, analyses of the costs of power generation under certain scenario assumptions are highly appreciated.

If we look at the power sector from another perspective, it has to be emphasized that it is responsible for a substantial quantity of emissions. Therefore, considerations and discussions about power generation-related emissions of SO_2, NO_x, PM, and CO_2 are also of particular interest to the scientific community. The application of a computable model gives the scientific community a huge opportunity to test the outcomes of certain environmental policies prior to their implementation. Thus, it can be quantitatively estimated in advance what would be the effects of: (i) changes to the price of a CO_2 emission permit, (ii) a reduction in emissions factors or (iii) obligatory phase-out of certain technologies (or particular units) on the basis of their emissions levels, both at national level and at company level.

The aforementioned problems faced by researchers that investigate the development of the power generation sector require appropriate methods and tools, in particular when numerical results rather than general replies and discussions are required. One of the so far identified key obstacles to using such tools was the fact that the process of development of a computable model is usually a time-consuming and complex task that is almost never undertaken by non-modellers. Taking into account the circumstances outlined, no model has yet been made available to the scientific community that would enable non-modellers to carry out scenario analyses of the Polish power generation sector. The main scientific objective of this paper is to present the key assumptions and the framework of such a tool, together with characteristic results and possible applications. As regards the methods, we applied the Mixed Integer Linear Programming (MILP) approach, which will be discussed later on.

The remainder of this article is structured as follows. In Section 2 the most important relevant work is presented and briefly discussed. Section 3 describes the solution that was applied in order to develop a computable model of the Polish power generation sector with hourly resolution and in addition the method adopted for making this service available to final users (the scientific community) is discussed. Section 4 presents some typical results of scenario-based analyses. Finally, Section 5 concludes the findings and sets out the scope of further research.

2   State of the Art

There have been several examples of the implementation of the MILP approach cited in the literature, as described hereinafter. However, to the best of our knowledge none have addressed this issue for a power generation sector like the Polish one (there are also other approaches such as the agent-based approach, presented by Kaleta et al. – please see [7] as an example).

In 2000, Arroyo and Conejo proposed using the MILP approach for solving a problem of the optimal bidding strategy for a thermal unit on the spot market [4]. They also reported that the MILP approach can be useful for modelling the unit commitment problem, in particular in representing the specific constraints such as start-up costs, ramp rate limitations or available spinning reserve. Such a research was conducted by Gollmer et al. [5], who formulated a simplified model of the power generation unit commitment problem.

Carrion and Arroyo [2] used the MILP approach for the formulation of the unit commitment problem. Their approach was quite innovative as the number of binary variables and constraints was decreased and thus both time and computable problems were reduced. In addition, through the MILP approach, time-dependent variables such as start-up costs, ramping rates (up and down) or minimum on and off times were more accurately implemented. The authors also tested their algorithm on a realistic case study, which consisted of one hundred thermal units. The quality of the results obtained was evaluated through a comparison with other widely used approaches and the Carrion and Arroyo algorithm proved to produce better optimal solutions in a much shorter time. To a certain extent, the above mentioned formulation of the problem was developed by Frangioni et al. [3].

A new MILP approach for solving the unit commitment problem was proposed by Viana and Pedroso [6]. They presented a quadratic formulation of the problem and also a MILP algorithm based on a piecewise linear approximation of the fuel cost function. The calculation of the optimal solution is an iterative process where the precision of the result increases with each step. This new approach was tested on several benchmark examples, giving an optimal solution in a short time.

The MILP approach can be applied to large-scale unit commitment problems considered from the perspective of the whole power system (like in previous examples). At the same time, it can be used for a self-scheduling problem of a single power unit or power plant. Such an approach was presented by Martens et al. [1], who built a MILP model of an ultra-supercritical coal plant with post combustion carbon capture. Likewise, in this formulation of the model the focus was put on the different power modes of the plant, namely normal work, start-up, off-state and stand-by. In addition, the carbon capture part of the power plant can be turned off or on, depending on external conditions such as a low CO_2 price on the market, peak electricity demand, etc.

The self-scheduling problem of the gas-fired power plant under various price scenarios was the subject of research conducted by Jiri Šumbera [10]. The MILP was used and several approaches to formulation of constraints were presented. The technical characteristics of the power plant, including the minimum up and down times, ramp rates or start-up costs (from hot, warm and cold start) were described in detail.

A comprehensive source of knowledge on the power generation and electricity industry modelling, including the application of the MILP approach, was provided by Christoph Weber in a book on decision support tools in power industry [11].

Although the above mentioned publications do not fully cover the issue of MILP approach in solving unit commitment or self-scheduling problems, they can serve as a useful basis to develop a model of the Polish power generation sector. This sector consists of over 100 power generation units, which are different in terms of age, technology, used fuel, emission factors, related costs, etc. In the sections that follow, we present the application of the MILP modelling approach to the development of a model tailored to the conditions of the Polish power sector.

3   Description of the Solution

In the current organisation of the power sector, electricity generation activity is carried out by the power generation sector. Conventional power plants and Combined Heat and Power (CHP) plants generate power using their own units which are characterised by several technical, economic and environment-related parameters. Moreover, there are intermittent (renewable) technologies whose generation levels are complex to predict, and which may change significantly over time. Therefore, in order to allow one to analyse the operation of power generation sectors with a higher deployment of renewables, it is necessary to select an appropriate approach. In practice, the only method that allows one to carry out quantitative analyses of the power generation sector from the perspective of the whole system is *modelling*.

As regards the objectives of the model, we assumed that the model to be developed will allow the running of scenario-based analyses of the power generation sector with hourly resolution taking into account the most important technical, economic and environmental constraints. The literature review, together with the authors' own experience, resulted in the selection of the Mixed-Integer Linear Programming (MILP) approach as the one that is the best possible option to solve the problem of power sector operation when hourly resolution is required. This is due to the fact that power generation units are either set On-Line (which is logical 1) or Off-Line (which is logical 0). This means that binary variables are required to be introduced into the model and the MILP approach allows to define these. As regards the objective function, in our model we defined it as the minimisation of the total variable costs of power generation over the period analysed, which is a typical approach when addressing short-term problems of the power generation system. It is assumed that the MILP approach allows to adequately represent the power generation sector for the planned application of the model. Since the domestic power sector relies heavily on hard and brown coals (approx. 90% of power generation), technologies based on these fuels have to be introduced with especial care taking into consideration several technical, economic and environmental aspects of power production, such as coal prices, ramp rates, emissions, etc. Moreover, since biomass co-combustion plays a special role as a contributor to the fuel-mix, it needs to be explicitly considered in the model.

In order to fulfill the objectives, it was necessary to develop a model that would enable users to differentiate the following technical, economic and related to environment parameters (data) of the power generation sector: installed capacity, net efficiency, PM emissions factor, SO_2 emissions factor, NO_x emissions factor, CO_2 emissions factor, biomass co-combustion factor, availability factor, own power consumption factor, technical minimum, ramp up rate, ramp down rate, minimal up time, minimal down time, start-up cost, operational and maintenance costs, and capacity factor. These parameters are set individually for each particular power generation unit or for aggregates of similar units. Moreover, the following parameters are also defined by users: hourly demand for power, hourly availability factors for wind- and solar-based power generation technologies, monthly fuel prices (separately for hard coal, brown coal, natural gas, oil and nuclear fuel), emission charges or emission permit prices and transmission power losses. The concept of the model assumed setting the following variable blocks (optimised in the model solution): (i) Power Generation (unit- and hour-dependent), (ii) On-Line (unit- and hour-dependent), (iii) Off-Line (unit- and hour-dependent), and (iv) Total Cost. Furthermore, the following equation blocks were introduced into the model:

- Demand for Power (hour-dependent);
- Capacity Constraint Max (unit- and hour-dependent);
- Capacity Constraint Min (unit- and hour-dependent);
- Ramping Up Constraint (unit- and hour-dependent);
- Ramping Down Constraint (unit- and hour-dependent);
- On1, (unit- and hour-dependent);
- On2 (unit- and hour-dependent);
- On3 (unit- and hour-dependent);
- Off1 (unit- and hour-dependent);
- Off2 (unit- and hour-dependent);
- Off3 (unit- and hour-dependent);
- Minimal Up Time Constraint (unit- and hour-dependent);
- Minimal Down Time Constraint (unit- and hour-dependent);
- Capacity Factor Constraint (power plant-dependent);
- Generation Cost Function – the objective function.

Based on the defined sets, parameters, variables and equation naming systems, equations and inequalities were worked out, which constitute the formal mathematical representation of the system (as the complete set of mathematical formulae for the model is rather extensive, we decided not to include it in this paper). Then, the mathematical model is implemented in the General Algebraic Modeling System (GAMS). A numerical solution is reached by applying the CPLEX solver, one of the most efficient solvers used for Linear Programming, and Mixed Integer Linear Programming models. The tests performed when developing the model together with the sensitivity analyses proved that the model correctly responds to the changes enforced at the level of parameters (assumptions). This confirmed the robustness of the model developed.

It was intended to design a system of interfacing with the user that is as user-friendly as possible. To do this, we decided that the input data file (the file that users fill in with their scenario assumptions – parameters) must be in a well-known format, namely xlsx. We provide the user with a default scenario that includes data that represent the Polish power generation system as of 2011. The user is enabled to make changes to these parameters, thus defining their own scenarios. As regards the results file (the output of the model – model solution), it is also generated and saved as an xlsx file. This simplifies the process of using and analysing the results of model runs.

As far as the process of sending tasks to the computing grid is concerned, we selected the QosCosGrid middleware, which is an efficient programming and execution tool allowing the user to run large scale parallel simulations [8,9]. Therefore, a desktop application called QCG-Icon with a graphical user interface was involved to carry out the computing tasks. The work scheme is depicted in Fig. 1. First, the default InputData file is downloaded and saved in a local hard disk drive. Then, depending on the scenario designed, users are allowed to change the default settings of the scenario with their data series. Once done, users submit the task to the grid computing clusters and are waiting for the results file to be sent back to their local hard disk drives via the QCG-Icon application. The QCG-Icon application allows the following parameters to be set: task name, target cluster, wall time, queue type, memory limit and type of solving method (sequential or parallel). When all is set up, the task can be submitted. Firstly, the task goes to the Portable Batch System (PBS), which is a task queuing system. When the computing resources are released, the task is performed and afterwards, the calculation process results are sent back to users via the used middleware.

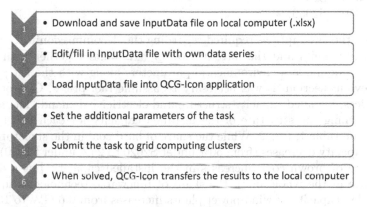

Fig. 1. Scenario for using the MILP model of the Polish power generation sector, available to the scientific community via grid computing

4   Results

The model allows the user to obtain numerical solutions under assumed scenarios, hence it allows to analyse and discuss the outcomes of any configuration of the Polish power generation sector. The results that are available for consideration are listed below:

- power generation production by individual units assumed to be operating in the power generation sector, separately for each hour in the period considered (at an aggregated level for CHPs),
- hourly power generation fuel-mixes,
- the state of each individual unit (1: On-Line, 0: Off-Line),
- hourly SO_2, NO_x, PM, and CO_2 emissions, by each individual power generation unit,
- total SO_2, NO_x, PM, and CO_2 emissions in the period considered,
- costs of generating the electricity (hourly, average of the period considered, total).

In this section we show some examples of the results of the model's functioning under four different scenarios. These scenarios were developed to investigate how the power generation system in Poland will function in the future. Particular attention was paid to exploring the influence of changing the Polish fuel mix, and more specifically – to the decreasing of the share of coal and replacing it by renewable sources. To a certain extent, the scenarios described herein, being based on the assumptions adopted in the national energy and environmental policies, predict power generation system configurations in particular years, namely:

− year 2020 – S2020;
− year 2030 – S2030;
− year 2040 – S2040;
− year 2050 – S2050.

Apart from the assumptions required regarding the decommissioning of the currently existing units and the introduction of new units together with all the technical, economic and environmental parameters along with the list provided in the previous section, it was necessary to assume fuel prices, CO_2 emissions permit prices, installed capacity structure and electricity demand. The assumptions concerning the structure of the installed capacity for each fuel type are illustrated in Table 1, Fig. 2. While the share of hard coal in the structure of the installed capacity decreases (from 50% under S2020 to 25% under S2050) as well as the share of brown coal (increases in the installed capacity, but a decrease of the share in the whole mix), the share of renewable technologies increases. The installed capacity of wind power plants increases from 6.6 GW to 15.4 GW whereas for solar power plants it grows from 0.003 GW to 9.6 GW.

Table 1. Installed capacity by primary fuel type in different scenarios, GW

	S2020	S2030	S2040	S2050
	$[GW]$			
Hard Coal	21.1	20.7	17.0	15.6
Brown Coal	7.4	7.4	11.6	9.6
Heavy Oil	0.5	0.5	0.5	0.5
Biomass	1.6	1.9	1.8	1.8
Biogas	0.4	0.6	0.6	0.7
Natural Gas	2.1	2.0	2.2	6.5
Wind	6.6	12.0	13.3	15.4
Hydro	2.4	2.4	2.5	2.6
PV	0.003	0.003	2.0	9.6
Total	42.1	47.6	51.5	62.2

Also the electricity demand, fuel prices and CO_2 emission allowance prices were different in each scenario. Apart from natural gas (for which a decline in price was assumed) there are slight changes between scenarios in the prices of the most important fuels. The increasing demand for electricity was another

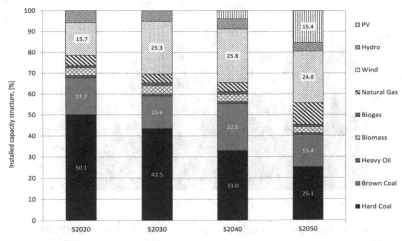

Fig. 2. Fuel-mix of installed capacity under different scenarios, %

assumption and this changed from a level of 164 TWh in S2020 to 227 TWh in 2050 (Table 2).

Table 2. CO_2 emissions allowance price and annual electricity demand under different scenarios

	Unit	S2020	S2030	S2040	S2050
CO_2 allowance price	PLN/tCO_2	62	70	78	87
Electricity demand	TWh	164	185	210	227

The aggregated hourly power generation fuel-mixes of each scenario (in relation to the same week) are illustrated in Figs. 3-6. Analysis of these results for the whole period indicates that even during the high hourly volatility of power produced in wind power plants, it is preferable to use the more flexible, hard and brown coal-fired generating units. Pumped storage and gas-fired plants are only used in periods of peak demand. This is particularly visible in S2040 and S2050, in which the share of coal-fired power plants in power generation structure is reduced. Changing the power generation fuel mix of the energy system (understood as a change in the installed capacities of power plants based on different fuels) directly affects the costs of power generation. The modelling results show that the average weekly variable costs of electricity in the scenarios analysed are decreasing due to the drastic increase in the share of wind and solar technologies in the energy mix. While in scenarios S2020 and S2030 this cost equals 174.0 and 171.1 PLN/MWh, respectively, in scenarios S2040 and S2050 it is only 156.3 and 161.7 PLN/MWh (see Fig. 7). The situation illustrated in S2050 is particularly interesting as despite the share of wind and solar technologies being larger, the average weekly variable costs of electricity generation are higher than in S2040. Even though in some hours (when favourable weather conditions occur)

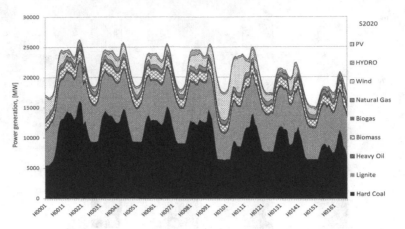

Fig. 3. Aggregated hourly power generation fuel-mix in S2020

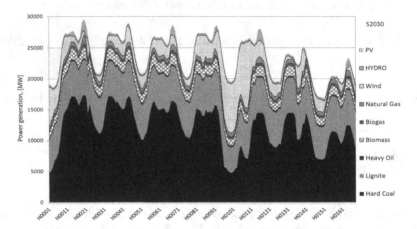

Fig. 4. Aggregated hourly power generation fuel-mix in S2030

the variable costs of electricity generation are decreasing to negligible values, they significantly increase during windless periods and nights. This is due to the necessity to start up more expensive gas-fired power units, which secure the generating work of the renewable technologies.

To describe more precisely what happens in particular hours of the power generation system under different generation capacity mixes, two very different scenarios (S2020 and S2050) were analysed for an hour with low power demand (H0100, Table 3) and for one of the peak hours with high demand (H0066, Table 4). Parameters such as average utilization rate, power generation and average technical availability factor (AF) were included into the analysis. In S2020, for low power demand, the model chose an optimal mix using all the units. In S2050, with a high share of wind and solar power and favourable wind conditions (AF equals 0.66), wind energy generation was high enough (10 132 MW) to allow the model to exclude all the units based on brown coal.

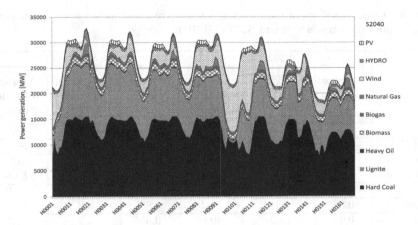

Fig. 5. Aggregated hourly power generation fuel-mix in S2040

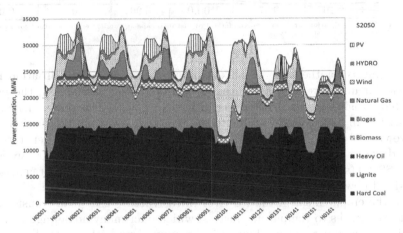

Fig. 6. Aggregated hourly power generation fuel-mix in S2050

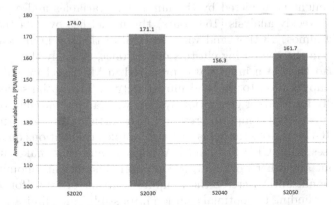

Fig. 7. Average week variable cost of electricity production in the scenarios analysed

Table 3. Detailed analysis of the power generation fuel mix in one hour of low power demand under scenarios S2020 and S2050 (H0100)

	S2020			S2050		
	Average technical AF	Generation in hour H0100	Average utilisation rate[†]	Average technical AF	Generation in hour H0100	Average utilisation rate[†]
	-	MW	%	-	MW	%
Hard Coal	0.84	6420	67.2	0.87	11136	81.7
Brown Coal	0.82	4380	73.4	0.84	0	0.0
Heavy Oil	0.83	285	70.1	0.8	3 222	54.5
Biomass	0.84	807	76.3	0.83	815	51.9
Biogas	0.83	184	74.4	0.83	321	57.1
Natural Gas	0.94	669	49.8	0.95	32	22.5
Wind	0.66	4345	100.0	0.66	10132	100.0
Hydro	0.84	313	41.4	0.86	289	55.2
PV	0.10	0.37	100.0	0.00	0	0.0

[†] e.g for wind 100% utilisation rate means maximum use of installed capacity under certain weather conditions (it is NOT 100% of installed capacity)

The analysis for the hour of peak demand shows that the utilisation rates of particular units are high and, even despite low wind availability, the power generated satisfies power demand, as proved in S2020. The power demand is also satisfied in S2050, however, due to the relatively low wind production, hard and brown coal energy units work intensively and additional power generation in gas-fired power plants is high. The average generation costs in S2050 are lower than in S2020 (see Fig. 7), but still higher than in S2040, where power generation in gas-fired power plants was less intense.

With the employment of the PL-Grid Infrastructure users can transfer their optimisation tasks to computing clusters, which offer many advantages, such as the ability to conduct advanced numerical computation without purchasing specialised software or very efficient (hence usually expensive) computers. The size of the model might be depicted by the number of variables and equations. In our case, for a weekly analysis (168 hours) the model has over 34 thousand of equations and almost 13 thousand variables. All of the key numerical calculations are done in the computing clusters of Cyfronet, the only thing users need to do is to load their own input data (prepared in MS Excel format) through a middleware application to the grid infrastructure. The optimisation process itself, especially for a power generation system with a large number of working hours, needs substantial computing resources, in particular in the form of internal memory (RAM). Furthermore, launching complex calculations on a personal computer causes a full CPU load and RAM usage, and thus makes it impossible to carry out any other work on this computer. Insufficient amount of RAM memory can significantly increase the computation time or even (for large scale problems) make finding the optimal solution impossible. Such limitations do not occur when the PL-Grid Infrastructure is used.

Table 4. Detailed analysis of the power generation fuel mix in one hour of peak power demand under scenarios S2020 and S2050 (H0066)

	S2020			S2050		
	Average technical AF	Generation in hour H0066	Average utilisation rate[†]	Average technical AF	Generation in hour H0066	Average utilisation rate[†]
	-	MW	%	-	MW	%
Hard Coal	0.84	13030	92.3	0.88	14418	93.7
Brown Coal	0.82	6642	100.0	0.85	7399	100.0
Heavy Oil	0.83	285	70.1	0.83	222	54.5
Biomass	0.84	807	76.3	0.83	815	51.9
Biogas	0.83	267	87.2	0.83	562	100.0
Natural Gas	0.94	669	49.8	0.95	2304	30.2
Wind	0.16	1103	100.0	0.16	2572	100.0
Hydro	0.84	313	41.4	0.87	690	80.8
PV	0.10	0	100.0	0.12	1148	100.0

[†] e.g for wind 100% utilisation rate means maximum use of installed capacity under certain weather conditions (it is NOT 100% of installed capacity)

5   Conclusions and Future Work

Development of the MILP approach-based model of the power generation sector allows one to analyse the functioning of the domestic power generation sector represented at a disaggregated level (each unit as an individual item reflected in the model) with hourly resolution. There are several technical, economic and environmental constraints reflected in the model and the model mimics the real Polish power generation sector in a way that enables the scientific community (in particular non-modellers) to run and analyse scenarios of power generation system development. One of the biggest advantages of using this service is the fact that users do not need to know how to develop computable models or how to use complicated tools. They simply design a scenario, then on this basis they fill in input datasets with the required figures in a well-known xlsx file and after submitting a task to the grid space they receive results in an xlsx file. The results are ready for comparisons, analyses, or interpretations. Another advantage is that users do not have to purchase expensive licenses for modelling systems and/or solvers as model computation and solution is carried out in the grid space. Summarizing, the service and the model itself are recommended for quantitative analyses of user-defined scenarios of power generation systems, and to the best of our knowledge this is the first tool of that type made available to the scientific community via grid computing systems.

As is usual in such cases, there are certain technical particularities that could be considered for introduction to the current version of the model, yet it may lead to further complicating of the process of numerical solution and therefore a significant increase to the computation time. One of them that could be identified at this stage is differentiation into cold-, warm-, and hot-startup. Also when dealing with very large MILP tasks, tasks for periods exceeding half a year, namely 4380 hours, could be tackled. However, this is not a key problem at this stage, as the whole year could be split and run in two half-year sessions. Another challenging issue that needs further study is the potential transformation to a Mixed Integer Non-Linear Programming model, which would be worth considering in the future, as the relationship between load and the efficiency of power generation is nonlinear and linear approximations are usually applied due to the problems that occur in obtaining numerical solutions to the model.

References

1. Martens, P., Delarue, E., D'haeseleer, W.: A Mixed Integer Linear Programming Model for a Pulverized Coal Plant With Post-Combustion Carbon Capture. IEEE Transactions on Power Systems 27(2), 741–751 (2012)
2. Carrion, M., Arroyo, J.M.: A computationally efficient mixed-integer linear formulation for the thermal unit commitment problem. IEEE Transactions on Power Systems 21(3), 1371–1378 (2006)
3. Frangioni, A., Gentile, C., Lacalandra, F.: Tighter approximated MILP formulations for unit commitment problems. IEEE Transactions on Power Systems 24(1), 105–113 (2009)
4. Arroyo, J.M., Conejo, A.J.: Optimal response of a thermal unit to an electricity spot market. IEEE Transactions on Power Systems 15(3), 1098–1104 (2000)
5. Gollmer, R., Nowak, M.P., Römisch, W., Schultz, R.: Unit commitment in power generation – a basic model and some extensions. Annals of Operations Research 96, 167–189 (2000)
6. Viana, A., Pedroso, J.P.: A new MILP-based approach for unit commitment in power production planning. International Journal of Electrical Power & Energy Systems 44, 997–1005 (2013)
7. Kaleta, M., Pałka, P., Toczyłowski, E., Traczyk, T.: Electronic trading on electricity markets within a multi-agent framework. In: Nguyen, N.T., Kowalczyk, R., Chen, S.-M. (eds.) ICCCI 2009. LNCS, vol. 5796, pp. 788–799. Springer, Heidelberg (2009)
8. Bosak, B., Komasa, J., Kopta, P., Kurowski, K., Mamoński, M., Piontek, T.: New Capabilities in QosCosGrid Middleware for Advanced Job Management, Advance Reservation and Co-allocation of Computing Resources – Quantum Chemistry Application Use Case. In: Bubak, M., Szepieniec, T., Wiatr, K. (eds.) PL-Grid 2011. LNCS, vol. 7136, pp. 40–55. Springer, Heidelberg (2012)
9. Radecki, M., Szymocha, T., Harężlak, D., Pawlik, M., Andrzejewski, J., Ziajka, W., Szelc, M.: Integrating Various Grid Middleware Components and User Services into a Single Platform. In: Bubak, M., Szepieniec, T., Wiatr, K. (eds.) PL-Grid 2011. LNCS, vol. 7136, pp. 15–26. Springer, Heidelberg (2012)
10. Šumbera, J.: Modelling generator constraints for the self-scheduling problem (2012), http://energyexemplar.com/wp-content/uploads/publications/Modelling-generator-constraints-for-the-self-scheduling-problem.pdf
11. Weber, C.: Uncertainty in the Electric Power Industry: Methods and Models for Decision Support. International Series in Operations Research & Management Science, vol. 77. Springer (2005)

Modelling the Long-Term Development of an Energy System with the Use of a Technology Explicit Partial Equilibrium Model

Artur Wyrwa[1,2], Marcin Pluta[1,2],
Szymon Skoneczny[2], and Tomasz Mirowski[1,2]

[1] AGH University of Science and Technology,
al. Mickiewicza 30, 30-059 Kraków, Poland
{awyrwa,mpluta,mirowski}@agh.edu.pl
[2] AGH University of Science and Technology, ACC Cyfronet AGH,
ul. Nawojki 11, 30-950 Kraków, Poland
skoneczny@gmail.com

Abstract. The paper presents the results of a study on the modelling of the development of the power system in Poland in the long-term time horizon. Four scenarios were considered, differentiated according to four parameters, notably price evolution of CO_2 emission allowances, targets for renewable energy technologies, limits on new nuclear capacity additions and availability of carbon capture and storage technology. The analysis was conducted with the πESA service developed within the Energy Sector domain grid within the PLGrid Plus project. The main analytical tool used was the TIMES energy model generator. The results of the analysis show that the Polish power sector is very vulnerable to the EU climate policy. The changes in the fuel and technology structure, total CO_2 emissions and the electricity generation costs for each scenario were presented.

Keywords: energy system, energy mix, modelling, bottom-up approach.

1 Introduction

In recent years, the development of energy systems has been receiving considerable and increasing attention by scientists and policy makers. Often, there is a lack of a general consensus on what would be the best mix of fuels and energy generation technologies in the coming decades. This ongoing debate should be supported by analytical tools, which are able to thoroughly analyse the multidimensional problems related to energy systems. An analytical tool, called Platform for an Integrated Energy System Analysis (πESA), developed within the Energy Sector domain grid [1], is dedicated to the modelling of mid-term development of the energy system. It provides quantitative results in the 4E dimensions (Energy, Engineering, Environment, Economy) that can be used to support the decision making process.

M. Bubak et al. (Eds.): PLGrid Plus, LNCS 8500, pp. 489–503, 2014.

The main element of πESA in the area of energy system evolution is TIMES, an economic model generator for local, national or multi-regional energy systems. It provides a technology-rich basis for estimating energy dynamics over a long-term, multi-period time horizon [2]. In this paper, we demonstrate the capabilities of πESA for optimizing the energy mix of the power sector in Poland for different scenarios in the time perspective up to 2050.

2   Related Work

The issue of the modelling of the development of energy systems has been present in multi-disciplinary research since the first energy crisis in the early 1970's. Many countries and international organizations have taken part in the construction of tools for forecasting and optimization of energy systems development.

A variety of models have been developed, ranging from simple simulation models for individual sectors by country-level, regional and global models. These include, i.a., the bottom-up dynamic Linear Programming energy models, e.g. MARKAL [3], Mixed Integer Programming models such as MESSAGE [4] and Non-linear Programing models like e.g. PRIMES [5]. Depending on the inclusion of market mechanisms they can be further split into Partial-Equilibrium, e.g. POLES [6], TIMES [7] or Computable General Equilibrium models, which construct the behaviour of economic agents based on the micro-economic principle, such as GEM-E3 [8]. These models were often used to estimate the impacts of different policies related to the development of renewables, energy efficiency and climate change mitigation [9–12].

In Poland, research on the mid- and long-term development of the energy system was the subject of the [13], in which the MESSAGE model was used to analyse the investments plans for coal fired power plants. Preliminary study on the long-term development of the power system in Poland was the subject of [14]. In [15] the MARKAL model was used to analyse the mechanisms to promote renewable energy sources and high-efficiency cogeneration. The role of hard coal and brown coal in the power sector in the time perspective up to 2050 was the subject of the study done with the use of the TIMES-PL model in [16]. It should be emphasized that in Poland there is still a lack of comprehensive energy tool, which could be easily accessible for conducting the integrated energy system analysis.

3   Description of the Solution

3.1 πESA Service in the PL-Grid Infrastructure

πESA can be used to solve problems related to the optimization of the fuel and technological structures of energy systems twofold:

- for users experienced in the energy system modelling, who use TIMES with the VEDA data handling system [17], it offers solving the VEDA-generated models in the Zeus cluster of the PL-Grid Infrastructure [18],

- for users unexperienced in VEDA it offers an in-built model of the Reference Energy System (RES), which can be used to analyse the impacts of changes to the different techno-economic parameters of fuels and energy technologies, political and environmental constraints, etc.

Both user groups operate πESA through a web interface created by the use of Java Server Pages and Ajax technology.

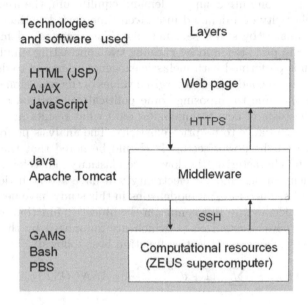

Fig. 1. Schema of πESA implementation in the PL-Grid Infrastructure

The created application has three tiers. The presentation tier is a web page (see Fig. 1). Using this web page, the user is able to send the files of a model to the Zeus cluster or change the data of an existing model. For the purpose of changing the data of an existing model, the user makes use of HTML forms. Each page has its own description in English. Connection between web page and middleware is secure. The second tier (middleware) prepares HTML forms for the user, and processes the data obtained from them. The changes made by the user through the web page are translated into a TIMES language code. The third tier, i.e. the computational resources one, is used for running the simulations. Every job is started using Portable Batch System (PBS), a queuing system running on the PL-Grid servers.

3.2   General Methodology

Research on the perspectives for the development of energy systems requires to use appropriate tools. The complexity and extent of the problems make mathematical models the only tools capable to adequately address them. TIMES, which is the main element of πESA, is a bottom-up, technology-explicit energy system model generator, which assumes competitive markets for all commodities. TIMES optimizes system performance across the entire modelling horizon with the complete knowledge of the present and future market parameters, i.e., with a perfect foresight. Producers are represented by energy technologies while consumers by demand (or energy end-use devices, etc.). TIMES allows self-adjustment of demand in reaction to the changes in price of a given energy service. In order to compute a supply-demand equilibrium, the user has to specify the price elasticity of a demand in a given time period (in fact the demand curve is approximated by staircase functions). The change in demand in reaction to a change in price is found by running two contrasting simulations. First preliminary run is performed with inelastic exogenous demand to determine the reference price. In a second run the marginal values of the provision of the energy service change (e.g. due to imposing some political constraints, a different assumption on the costs of new technologies, etc.) what results in adjustment of the demand in accordance to its price elasticity. The analysis performed in this study is focused on the power sector. It should be noted that the demand for electricity can be characterized by low price elasticity. Therefore, inclusion of the price elasticity of demand for electricity will have a very little, if any, impact on the results. Therefore, all model runs in this study have been performed with an inelastic demand. In this condition the objective function represents the total discounted power system costs, which are minimized by the model. The mathematical formula of the objective function is as follows:

$$NPV = \sum_{y \in years} (1+d)^{REFYR-y} \cdot ANNCOST\,(y)\,, \tag{1}$$

where:

NPV – the net present value of the total system cost,
$ANNCOST\,(y)$ – total annual cost in year y,
d – discount rate,
$REFYR$ – the reference year for discounting,
$years$ – the set of years for which there are costs.

The total annual cost includes:

$$ANNCOST\,(y) = INVCOST\,(y) + FIXCOST\,(y)$$
$$+ VARCOST\,(y) + DECOM\,(y)\,, \tag{2}$$

where:

INVCOST – investment costs including the capital costs incurred
during construction,
FIXCOST – fixed costs (independent of the production rate, e.g.
administration),
VARCOST – variable costs (dependent on the production, e.g. fuel costs),
DECOM   – decommissioning costs.

Investment costs incurred in the year y are transformed into streams of annual payments with the use of the Capital Recovery Factor. When the technical lives of the investments exceed the modelling time horizon, the unused portion of their lifetime (the sum of streams of annual payments after the end of the modelling) forms the salvage value, which is deducted from the total cost. This is particularly important in the case of investment decisions at the end of the modelling horizon that would otherwise be heavily distorted. The model takes into account also the time of construction and capital costs incurred during the construction.

The main equations of the model include: an efficiency relationship for power plants, commodity balances (energy, pollutants), capacity-activity constraints (e.g. available capacity limits in certain time periods), peaking capacity constraints (guaranteeing reserve capacity at peak load). There are also scenario specific constraints such as the emission reduction targets, required quota for renewables, etc. The main decision variables include: activity variables (e.g. production of electricity and heat in given technologies), energy flows, investments in the new capacities. Detailed descriptions of equations, variables and model parameters that describe the processes can be found in [2], [19].

All the energy technologies in the model are characterized by a number of technical and economic parameters, which are presented in more detail in Section 4.2. It should be noted that the results of TIMES, which include emissions of SO_2, NO_x and PMs, are further processed with the πESA environmental impacts assessment module [20].

3.3 Description of the Reference Energy System

In this study the model of the national energy system, which has been developed at AGH-UST, was used. The structure of the model that represents the subsystem of centralized power and heat generation is presented in Fig. 2.

This subsystem covers all the existing power plants (PP) with the net electric capacity equal to 23.5 GW in 2011. These are mainly hard and brown coal fired units. In some of them coal was co-fired with biomass. Investments in new units in Pątnów 2, Łagisza and Bełchatów 2 have been taken into account. Each power plant is represented in the model separately. Also, each gas fired combined heat and power plant is represented individually. All other existing CHPs were aggregated into four main types according to the fuel used (hard coal, natural gas, biomass or biogas) and the type of installed turbine (condensing or back pressure). Their total installed net electric capacity in 2011 exceeded 7 GW.

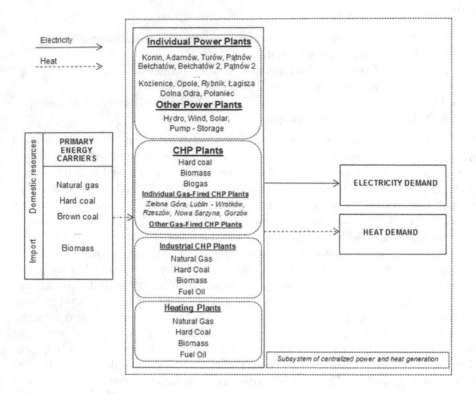

Fig. 2. Structure of the model representing the subsystem of centralized power and heat generation

The model includes existing renewable energy technologies such as photovoltaic cells, wind turbines and hydro plants.

The total power of these technologies in the base year was about 4 GWe. New energy technologies are also available, which are discussed in more detail in Section 4.2.

4   Simulation Settings

πESA service for advanced users (see Section 3.1) was used to model the development of the energy system in Poland. The qualitative and quantitative input data were generated with the use of VEDA 4.3.45. TIMES V334 was used to generate the LP mathematical model in GAMS 23.9. Finally, CPLEX solver, set up for parallel computing on 12 threads using the barrier algorithm, was used to solve the model on the Zeus cluster.

The modelling horizon in this study covered the period from 2011 to 2050. The temporal resolution covering five-year periods was used, and the results were given for the central, so called *modelling year*. The selected base year for calibration was 2011. Each modelling year was split into 224 time slices in order to improve the temporal characteristics of demand and supply sides (in the latter case this is particularly related to the increasing share of intermittent renewable technologies) [21]. For instance, a time slice named W_MON_01 covered the total demand for electricity in all Mondays of the year y during winter in the time period: 00:00-03:00.

The variability of electricity generation in wind turbines and solar photovoltaic in each time slice was taken into account. Electricity generation in wind turbines was based on the meteorological data for 2008 provided by the European Centre for Medium-range Weather Forecasting [22] for the location in West Pomeranian Voivodeship (16.0° E and 54.1° N). Electricity generation in PV was calculated for the same location based on the data provided by Photovoltaic Geographical Information System [23]. The reserve capacity was set to 25% of the peak demand. A rate of 8% is used for discounting.

4.1   Scenario Definition

This study considered four energy scenarios: REF, NUC, NO-CCS and RES, which were differentiated according to four parameters, notably the evolution pathway of prices of EU CO_2 Emission Allowances (EUAs), targets for renewable energy technologies, limits on new nuclear capacity additions, and the availability of carbon capture and storage technology (CCS). The first two parameters, which could have the reference or high value, are discussed in more detail in the next paragraph. In the case of nuclear capacity extension, a constraint was applied in all of the scenarios but NUC that 1.5 GW of net electric capacity can be built every five years starting from 2025 to 2035. In NUC scenario, nuclear capacity could be added till the end of the modelling time horizon. In NO-CCS scenario, it was assumed that CCS technology will not be available commercially in the period under consideration, whereas in other scenarios it could be applied starting from 2030. The summary of parameter settings is presented in Table 1.

Table 1. Summary of the scenarios settings

Scenario	EUAs price	RES target	NUC limit	CCS
REF	REF	REF	YES	YES
NUC	HIGH	REF	NO	YES
NO-CCS	HIGH	REF	YES	NO
RES	HIGH	HIGH	YES	YES

4.2   Assumptions

The key assumptions of this study concern the potential of domestic fuel supply, fuel prices, technology data (specific investments and efficiencies), electricity and heat demand, mandatory RES quotas in the electricity mix and prices of CO_2 allowances.

Potential of the Domestic Fuel Supply. The present analysis assumes that the supply of domestic steam coal will be reduced from around 64 Mt in 2011 to approximately 44 Mt in 2050. The supply of domestic brown coal will decrease from 63 Mt in 2011 to 50 in 2050. The values presented in Table 2 are based on [16] and assume a production growth stemming from the exploitation of new levels of opened mines and the opening of new coal mines. The potential of renewable energy sources is adopted based on the document [24] prepared at the request of the Polish Ministry of Economy. There is no constraint on import of natural gas and crude oil. Due to large uncertainties related to the potential of shale gas in Poland, and to the costs of its extraction, the current analysis does not include the possibility of using this fuel in the modelling period considered.

Table 2. Potentials of hard coal and brown coal

Fuel/year	2015	2020	2025	2030	2035	2040	2045	2050
Hard coal [Mt]	73	74	79	73	70	65	48	44
Hard coal [PJ]†	1679	1702	1817	1679	1610	1495	1104	1012
Brown coal [Mt]	62	66	79	83	86	62	52	50
Brown coal[PJ]†	527	561	671.5	705.5	731	527	442	425

†Conversion assuming the LHV of: 23 and 8.5 GJ/t for hard and brown coal, respectively.

Fuel Prices. The price of crude oil, natural gas, hard coal and uranium is based on the study published in [16]. The price of uranium includes the cost of enrichment and the cost of storage of the spent fuel. The price of brown coal is differentiated between the existing and new coal mines and equals to 65% and 85% of the hard coal price, respectively. The price of biomass and biogas is based on [25].

Table 3. Forecast of fuel prices expressed in terms of energy content [€' 11/GJ]

Fuel/year	2011	2015	2020	2025	2030	2035	2040	2045	2050
Oil crude	13.48	14.83	16.07	17.00	17.67	18.16	18.98	19.63	20.78
Natural gas	7.26	8.47	9.15	9.76	10.14	10.36	10.87	11.63	12.39
Hard coal	3.55	3.16	3.30	3.43	3.52	3.59	3.39	3.39	3.49
Brown coal – existing	2.30	2.05	2.15	2.23	2.29	2.33	2.20	2.20	2.27
Brown coal – new	3.01	2.69	2.81	2.91	2.99	3.05	2.88	2.88	2.97
Uranium	0.47	0.47	0.47	0.49	0.51	0.52	0.54	0.60	0.73
Biomass	6.75	6.55	6.07	6.19	6.07	6.17	6.29	6.38	6.51
Biogas	10.44	10.44	10.44	10.44	10.44	10.44	10.44	10.44	10.44

† Exchange rate: 1.3920 USD'2011/1EUR'2011.
Exchange NBP rate: 4.1198 PLN'2011/1EUR'2011.

Technology Data. Technical and economic parameters for energy technologies are among the most important factors determining the structure of generating capacity and electricity production. The main parameters used in this

Table 4. Technical and economic parameters of new thermal power plants

Fuel/Technology	Electric capacity[†]	Investment costs	Fixed O&M	Variable O&M	Electric efficiency 2010/30/50	Lifetime	CO$_2$ emission factor[††]
	MW	$\frac{\text{kEUR}}{\text{MW}_{net}}$	$\frac{\text{kEUR}}{\text{MW}_{net}}$	$\frac{\text{kEUR}}{\text{MWh}_{net}}$	%	years	kg/GJ
HC/PC	800	1432	29	2	45/46.5/47	40	94.19
HC/PC+CCS	800	2437	50	8	n.a./36.5/38	40	11.30
HC/IGCC	600	1942	51	3	44/51/52	40	94.19
HC/IGCC+CCS	600	3000	71	8	n.a./43/45	40	11.30
BC/PC	800	1723	33	2	44/45/46.6	40	109.08
BC/PC+CCS	800	2961	56	9	33/36	40	13.09
BC/IGCC	600	1942	51	3	43/49/51	40	109.08
BC/IGCC+CCS	600	3068	71	9	n.a./41/44	40	13.09
NG/GT	150	388	15	1	38/39.5/40.5	25	55.82
NG/CCGT	450	728	19	1	60/62/62	25	55.82
NG CCTG+CCS	450	1536	39	6	n.a./53/54	25	6.70
NUC/PWR	1500	4491	76	2	36/37/37	50	-
Wind onshore	2	1456	39	-	-	25	-
Wind offshore	3	3277	78	-	-	25	-
PV (Open space)	0.5	1796	32	-	-	25	-
Biomass/CHP	20-50	2354	51	4	30/80	25	0.00
Biogas/CHP	2-5	1966	30	2	38/85	25	0.00

[†] Approximate installed electric power.
[††] The CO$_2$ emission factors depend on the calorific value of the fuel and are based on the data available on http://www.kobize.pl/. Only direct emissions are included.

study – based on [16] and [26] – include: unit investment costs, operation and maintenance costs (fixed & variable), efficiency and the economic lifetime of a technology, and are represented in Table 4.

Electricity Demand. In order to determine the future electricity demand, a method proposed in [29] was used. This method assumed convergence of the electricity intensity of the Polish economy (i.e. a ratio of the total final electricity consumption to Gross Domestic Product, which was equal to 0.08 kWh/PLN in 2011) to the level determined by the least energy-intensive Western economies, according to the following formula:

$$E_{t+1} = \alpha E_t + (1 - \alpha)\bar{E}, \tag{3}$$

where:

E_t – electricity intensity of the economy in year t,
$\bar{E}$ – target electricity intensity assumed to be equal to two fifths of the value in 2011,
α – correction coefficient equal to 0.965.

Such an evolution pathway will enable Poland to reach the present electricity intensity of United Kingdom in 2050. Next, the final electricity demand was estimated based on the equation:

$$D_t = GDP_t \cdot E_t, \tag{4}$$

where:

D_t – final electricity demand in year t,
GDP_t – GDP in year t (long-term forecast of the Polish Ministry of Finance, May 2013).

The final electricity demand in 2050 increases by approximately 50% compared to 2011, reaching the level of ca. 181 TWh, as presented in Table 5.

Table 5. Final electricity demand [TWh]

Item	2011	2015	2020	2025	2030	2035	2040	2045	2050
Final electricity demand	121.9	129.4	139.4	151.9	161.0	163.7	169.0	175.1	181.1
Conversion sector	11.5	10.2	10.6	11.1	11.7	9.1	9.6	10.2	10.9
Line losses	12.1	12.4	12.9	13.2	13.0	12.6	12.0	11.4	11.2

The annual demand for electricity in each modelling year was distributed into time slices based on the historical data provided by the transmission system operator – PSE (http://www.pse-operator.pl).

Mandatory Quotas of Electricity Produced from Renewable Energy Sources. The targets for RES in the period 2015-2050 were expressed as the share of the electricity generated from renewable sources in the total final electricity consumption. Until 2020 these targets were in line with the National Renewable Energy Action Plan, which has been drawn up to meet a commitment of Directive 2009/28/EC. After 2020, two pathways for RES development were assumed, i.e. REF and HIGH with the final RES target for 2050, equal to 35% and 50%, respectively as presented in Table 6.

Table 6. Required share of electricity generated from renewable energy sources in final electricity consumption [%]

RES Pathway	2015	2020	2025	2030	2035	2040	2045	2050
REF	15%	23%	25%	27%	29%	31%	33%	35%
HIGH	15%	23%	25%	30%	35%	40%	45%	50%

Prices of CO$_2$ Allowances. The prices of CO$_2$ emission allowances under the European ETS are one of the parameters, which have a significant impact on the shape of the future fuel mix. The subject of the forecasting of the future EAUs prices has been the center of many studies, whose summary can be found in, e.g., [16]. Two pathways for the evolution of EUAs prices were assumed in this study. The first one, REF, corresponds to the pathway presented in [29]. The second one, HIGH, refers to the Current Policy Initiatives scenario presented in [30]. These forecasts are presented in Table 7.

Table 7. Forecast of CO$_2$ emission allowances under the EU ETS [€' 11/t$_{CO2}$]

Scenario	2015	2020	2025	2030	2035	2040	2045	2050
REF	10.0	15.0	15.0	17.0	18.0	18.9	19.9	21.1
HIGH	10.0	15.0	23.1	32.0	40.1	49.0	50.0	51.0

5   Results

With the decommission of the existing capacities and growth of energy demand, new electric capacities are needed. Fig. 3 presents new capacity additions for different scenarios.

In all the scenarios but NO-CCS there are investments in new coal power plants. In NO-CCS, high prices of EUAs and lack of CCS make natural gas to substitute coal in base-load power plants. Renewable energy technologies, mainly wind and in the later period also solar, have a significant share in new capacity additions. In the scenarios assuming high EUAs prices there are investments in new nuclear units, particularly in NUC, in which the total capacity installed over the entire period equals to 6 GW.

Hard and brown coal is most widely used for electricity generation in the REF scenario, providing ca. 134 TWh of electricity in 2050 (see Fig. 4). In this scenario, low EUAs prices do not provide incentive for installation of CCS. On the contrary, in NUC and RES new coal based units are being equipped with CCS. In NO-CCS coal based generation is gradually substituted for natural gas, which in 2050 has the highest share in the total electricity generation, i.e., 76 TWh. The high share of RES in new capacity additions does not translate directly to the level of electricity generation. The main reason is the low capacity factor of RES-based technologies in the Polish geographical conditions. The total amount of electricity generated from renewables in 2050 exceeds 63 TWh in all the scenarios, as required by the imposed RES constraint.

The emission of CO$_2$ is dropping in the period from 2011 to 2050 for all the scenarios (see Fig. 5). This decrease follows a similar reduction pathway for RES and NUC, reaching ca. 74%. The REF, which relies strongly on coal, has the highest CO$_2$ emissions of 135 Tg in 2050. The CO$_2$ emissions for NO-CCS are in between. It should be noted, however, that the emissions of other pollutants, i.e. SO$_2$, NO$_x$ and PMs, are the lowest in NO-CCS, as presented in [20].

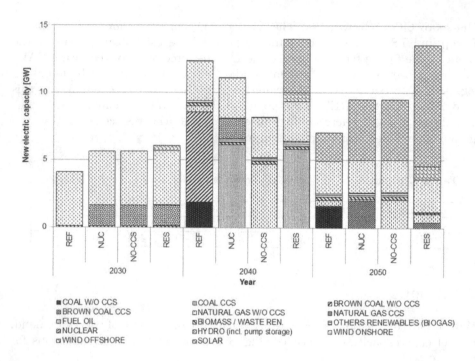

Fig. 3. New net electric capacity additions (GW) split into technologies and fuels

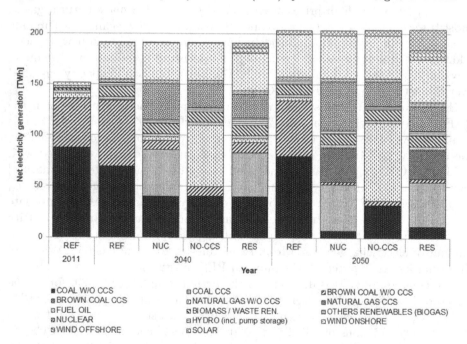

Fig. 4. Net electricity generation [TWh] split into technologies and fuels

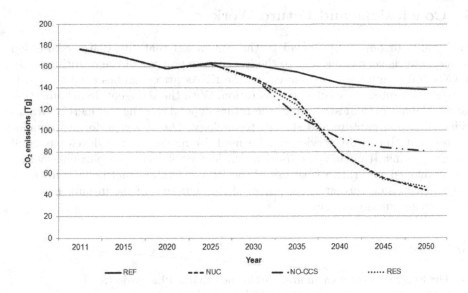

Fig. 5. CO_2 emissions by scenario in [Tg CO_2]

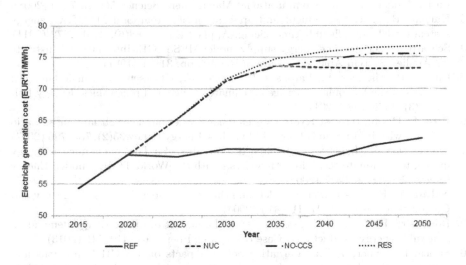

Fig. 6. Total electricity generation cost (including power plants and CHPs) in [EUR/MWh]

Finally, as presented in Fig. 6, the lowest electricity generation costs are in the REF scenario. One should bear in mind, however, that this scenario assumes low prices of EUAs. For other three scenarios with high EAUs prices the electricity generation costs were the lowest ones in NUC, followed by NO-CCS and RES.

6 Conclusions and Future Work

The results of our analysis lead to the conclusion that the Polish coal-based power sector is very vulnerable to the EU climate policy and the resulting prices of CO_2 emission allowances. Increasing the EUAs prices implies a shift towards a less carbon intensive electricity generation. With the stringent decarbonisation target, the use of domestic coal in the future depends on the commercial availability of carbon capture and storage technology. The study performed demonstrates that the πESA service can be used for modelling the development of energy systems. It enables the users to efficiently solve the complex energy models developed in TIMES with use of the PL-Grid Infrastructure. Future work will be focused on further development of the structure of the in-built model of the reference energy system.

References

1. The Energy Sector domain grid within the PLGrid Plus project, http://www.plgrid.pl/en/projects/plus/science_domains
2. Loulou, R., Labriet, M.: ETSAP-TIAM: The TIMES integrated assessment model Part I: Model structure. Computational Management Science 5(1-2), 7–40 (2008)
3. Kannan, R.: The development and application of a temporal MARKAL energy system model using flexible time slicing. Applied Energy 88(6), 2261–2272 (2011)
4. Schrattenholzer, L.: The energy supply model MESSAGE. International Institute for Applied System Analysis, Research Report, pp. 31–81 (1981)
5. Capros, P., Mantzos, L., Parousos, L., Tasios, N., Klaassen, G., van Ierland, T.: Analysis of the EU policy package on climate change and renewables. Energy Policy 39(3), 1476–1485 (2011)
6. Russ, P., Criqui, P.: Post-Kyoto CO_2 emission reduction: The soft landing scenario analysed with POLES and other world models. Energy Policy 35(2), 786–796 (2007)
7. Vaillancourt, K., Labriet, M., Loulou, R., Waaub, J.-P.: The role of nuclear energy in long-term climate scenarios: An analysis with the World-TIMES model. Energy Policy 36(7), 2296–2307 (2008)
8. Nakata, T.: Energy-economic models and the environment. Progress in Energy and Combustion Science 30(4), 417–475 (2004)
9. Rosenberg, E., Lind, A., Espegren, K.A.: The impact of future energy demand on renewable energy production – Case of Norway. Energy 61, 419–431 (2013)
10. Sarica, K., Tyner, W.E.: Alternative policy impacts on US GHG emissions and energy security: A hybrid modeling approach. Energy Economics 40, 40–50 (2013)
11. Labriet, M., Kanudia, A., Loulou, R.: Climate mitigation under an uncertain technology future: A TIAM-World analysis. Energy Economics 34(suppl. 3), S366–S377 (2012)
12. Blesl, M., Kober, T., Bruchof, D., Kuder, R.: Effects of climate and energy policy related measures and targets on the future structure of the European energy system in 2020 and beyond. Energy Policy 38(10), 6278–6292 (2010)
13. Radovic, U., Skwierz, S., Tatarewicz, I.: Application of the MESSAGE Model in Long-Term Generation Capacity Scenarios in Poland. In: Problems of Energy Resources in Domestic Economy, pp. 91–101. The Mineral and Energy Economy Research Institute of the Polish Academy of Sciences, Zakopane (2012)

14. Pluta, M., Wyrwa, A., Mirowski, T., Zyśk, J.: Results of preliminary studies on the long-term development of the power system in Poland. Polityka Energetyczna 15(4), 85–96 (2012)
15. Jaskolski, M.: Application of MARKAL model to optimisation of electricity generation structure in Poland in the long-term time horizon. Acta Energetica 3(13), 4–13 (2012)
16. Gawlik, L., Grudziński, Z., Kamiński, J., Kaszyński, P., Kryzia, D., Lorenz, U., Mirowski, T., Mokrzycki, E., Olkuski, T., Ozga-Blaschke, U., Pluta, M., Sikora, A., Stala-Szlugaj, K., Suwała, W., Szurlej, A., Wyrwa, A., Zyśk, J., Gawlik, L. (eds.): Coal for the Polish power sector in the time perspective up to 2050 – scenario analysis, vol. I. Wydawnictwo Instytutu Gospodarki Surowcami Mineralnymi i Energią PAN, Katowice (2013)
17. Gargiulo, M.: Getting started with TIMES-VEDA. ETSAP, International Energy Agency, pp. 1–145 (2009)
18. Kitowski, J., Turała, M., Wiatr, K., Dutka, Ł.: PL-Grid: Foundations and Perspectives of National Computing Infrastructure. In: Bubak, M., Szepieniec, T., Wiatr, K. (eds.) PL-Grid 2011. LNCS, vol. 7136, pp. 1–14. Springer, Heidelberg (2012)
19. Loulou, R.: ETSAP-TIAM: The TIMES integrated assessment model. Part II: Mathematical formulation. Computational Management Science 5(1-2), 41–66 (2008)
20. Wyrwa, A., Zyśk, J., Mirowski, T.: Assessment of Environmental Impacts of Energy Scenarios Using the πESA platform. In: Bubak, M., Kitowski, J., Wiatr, K. (eds.) PLGrid Plus. LNCS, vol. 8500, pp. 504–517. Springer, Heidelberg (2014)
21. Kannan, R., Turton, H.: A Long-Term Electricity Dispatch Model with the TIMES Framework. Environmental Modeling and Assessment 18(3), 325–343 (2013)
22. ECMWF. Provides medium-range weather forecast support to European meteorological organizations, http://www.ecmwf.int
23. JRC. Photovoltaic Geographical Information System (2013)
24. Andrzejewska, M., Grabias, M., Kassenberg, A., Kubski, P., Kupczyk, A., Michałowska, K., Mroszkiewicz, T., Oniszk-Popławska, A., Ruciński, D., Więcka, A., Włodarski, M., Wójcik, B., Wiśniewski, G. (eds.): Possibility of use of renewable energy sources in Poland until 2020, pp. 1–57. EC BREC IEO, Warszawa (2007)
25. Ciżkowicz, P., Gabryś, A., Baj, K., Bawół, M.: The impact of wind energy on economic growth in Poland. In: Ernst & Young (2012)
26. Andreas, S., Friedrich, K., Jan, M., Roman, M., von Christian, H.: Current and Prospective Costs of Electricity Generation until 2050. German Institute for Economic Research, DIW Berlin (2013)
27. Suwała, W.: Modeling of fuel and energy systems, vol. I. Wydawnictwo Instytutu Gospodarki Surowcami Mineralnymi i Energią PAN, Katowice (2011)
28. IEA, Energy Technology Perspectives, Scenarios & Strategies to 2050 (2010), http://www.worldenergyoutlook.org/
29. DAS, Optimimal Polish energy mix by 2060. Strategic Analysis Department, Polish Prime Minister's Office (2013)
30. European Commission: Energy Roadmap 2050. SEC(2011) 1565/2, http://eur-lex.europa.eu/legal-content/EN/TXT/?uri=CELEX:52011DC0885

Assessment of Environmental Impacts of Energy Scenarios Using the πESA Platform

Artur Wyrwa[1,2], Janusz Zyśk[1,2], and Tomasz Mirowski[1,2]

[1] AGH University of Science and Technology,
al. Mickiewicza 30, 30-059 Kraków, Poland
{awyrwa,jazysk,mirowski}@agh.edu.pl
[2] AGH University of Science and Technology, ACC Cyfronet AGH,
ul. Nawojki 11, 30-950 Kraków, Poland

Abstract. The πESA service developed within the Energy Sector domain grid of the PLGrid Plus project with its main element – a full air quality modelling system Polyphemus – was used to analyse changes in ambient concentration and deposition of pollutants for four energy scenarios. The simulations of atmospheric transport of pollutants were run for a domain centered around Poland with a horizontal resolution of 0.25°. Changes in annual concentrations and depositions of SO_2, NO_x, PMs for different years as well as energy scenarios were presented. The scenarios were compared as regards to the total deposition of sulphur in the modelling domain. A grid cell, in which the highest hourly concentration of a given pollutant occurred during a year, could be identified. The results show that due to the improvement of emission controls in large combustion plants, which is required to fulfill future EU regulations, they will have much lower negative impact on the environment. The study has shown that establishing a hard link between Polyphemus and TIMES energy model makes it possible to take into account environmental dimension in decisions making for energy policy.

Keywords: energy system, environmental impact, modelling, air quality.

1 Introduction

The energy demand is growing worldwide and in the absence of new policies it will double by 2050 [1]. The current pattern of exploitation of energy resources places considerable pressure on the environment. Emissions released from fuel consumption have a negative impact on air quality and lead to significant damage to the environment, health and materials [2]. These negative impacts are to a large extent the result of human activity and, thus, can be subject to change. The problem is multidisciplinary and complex. Therefore, the decision makers need scientific support in the preparation of energy development strategies, which also take into account the environmental aspects. Responding to those needs, an analytical tool – the so called Platform for an Integrated Energy System Analysis (πESA) has been developed within the Energy Sector domain grid [3]. Its

M. Bubak et al. (Eds.): PLGrid Plus, LNCS 8500, pp. 504–517, 2014.

concept is based on the Driver-Pressure-State-Impact-Response (DPSIR) framework. Based on the chain of causality, πESA links human-caused drivers (use of primary energy sources) to pressures on the environment (emissions), changes of environmental states (air quality) and eventually responses to correct the situation (constraints imposed on energy scenarios). πESA is performing real time computations of atmospheric dispersion of air pollutants with the use of the full air quality modeling system Polyphemus. Employing the Zeus cluster of the PL-Grid Infrastructure [4] makes it possible to have almost instant results on changes of environmental states related to ambient concentration and deposition of pollutants for each energy scenario elaborated by the user.

2   Related Work

πESA belongs to the category of integrated assessment modelling tools. Integrated assessment models have been developed to support energy and environment policy development [5]. They are able to assess the environmental impacts of energy (and resulting emission) scenarios. They have been used at the global [6], regional [7], national [8] and local level [9]. They can work either in a simulation, e.g. EcoSense [10], or optimization mode [11].

The atmospheric dispersion of air pollutants within integrated assessment models is commonly performed with the use of emission transfer matrices (ETM) that represent source-receptor relationships. ETMs are derived from hundreds of runs of the full atmospheric dispersion models with systematically changed emissions of the individual sources around a reference level.

Dispersion models are typically based on one or two frameworks: (i) Eulerian, e.g. EMEP [12], DEHM [13], CMAQ [14], Lotos-Euros [15] or (ii) Lagrangian, e.g. HYSPLIT [16]. In the Eulerian approach, the frame of reference is fixed to the Earth whereas in the Lagrangian approach, the frame of reference is moving with the air parcel. Additionally, models based on the Gaussian equitation are widely used for near-field calculations [17]. At present, many air quality modelling systems often combine both type of models. Near source emission dispersion is tackled with the Gaussian plum or puff models and, subsequently, in larger distances from the source, the Eulerian type models are used [18].

Works on modelling of air pollution have been widely undertaken in Poland. The results can be found e.g. in [19,20,21]. Several research groups have been involved in integrated assessment modelling (http://www.niam.scarp.se/). The Warsaw University of Technology developed a single-pollutant regional model ROSE [22]. The integrated assessment model focused on environmental impact of emissions from power sector was developed by [23]. Recently, a study was conducted by [24] on adverse health effects caused by fine particulate matter air pollution. However, there is lack of an integrated assessment framework consisting of an energy-economic and full dispersion models coupled with a hard-link, which could be easily accessible for conducting assessment of environmental impacts of the exploitation of energy resources for different energy scenarios for Poland.

3   Description of the Problem Solution

3.1   Environmental Impacts Assessment in πESA

The assessment of environmental impacts of energy scenarios in relation to the changes in ambient concentrations and deposition of pollutants in πESA is conducted with the use of the full air quality modelling system Polyphemus. A hard-link has been created between Polyphemus and the TIMES energy model. TIMES is a technology-rich, bottom-up model generator used for constrained optimization of the development of energy systems over mid- to long-term time horizons. It served as a tool for preparation of the energy emission scenarios. More information on TIMES can be found in [25]. The Polyphemus software was installed as a module on the Zeus cluster. Bash scripts were prepared, which automate intermediate tasks performed in computations. The data flow and computational steps are presented in Fig. 1.

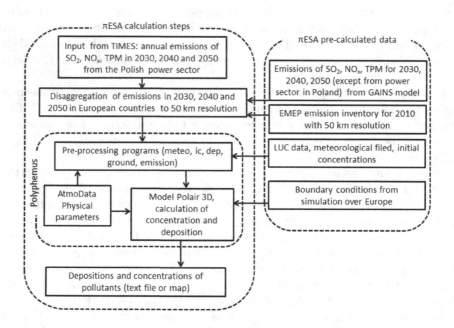

Fig. 1. Data flow and computational steps of πESA for the assessment of impacts of energy scenarios on air quality

3.2   General Methodology

Polyphemus is a complex modelling system for air quality [26]. Its main element is an Eulerian chemistry-transport-model: Polair3D, used for both gaseous and aerosol species. Polair3D tracks multiphase chemistry: (i) gas, (ii) water and (iii) aerosols. The gas-phase chemical scheme is RACM and aerosol chemistry is treated differently depending on the cloud liquid water content [27].

Inside clouds, aqueous-phase chemical reactions are modelled using the Variable Size-Resolution Model (VSRM) [28]. Otherwise, a size-resolved aerosol model (SIREAM) treats the effects of condensation/evaporation (including the inorganic aerosol thermodynamics, ISORROPIA), coagulation and nucleation upon the particle size distribution [29]. Polyphemus is also composed of a library of physical parameterizations called AtmoData and a set of programs using AtmoData designed to generate data required by Polair3D, e.g. deposition velocities, vertical diffusion coefficients, emissions, etc. [30,31]. Polair3D is a numerical solver for the chemistry transport equation 1:

$$\frac{\partial c_i}{\partial t} = -\underbrace{\operatorname{div}(Vc_i)}_{\text{advection}} + \underbrace{\operatorname{div}\left(\rho K \nabla \frac{c_i}{\rho}\right)}_{\text{diffusion}} + \underbrace{\aleph_i(c)}_{\text{chemistry}} + S_i - L_i. \tag{1}$$

The concentration of the $i-$th species is c_i. The transport driven by wind V is the advection term. The diffusion term $\operatorname{div}\left(\rho K \nabla \frac{c_i}{\rho}\right)$ essentially accounts for turbulent mixing in the vertical. Chemical production and losses of the $i-$th species are introduced with $\aleph_i(c)$. Additional sources (Si, emissions) and losses (Li, wet and dry deposition) are included.

The operational evaluation of Polyphemus results for runs performed over Poland showed that the correlation coefficients between simulated and observed data from EMEP and AirBase are 47% for NO_2, 46% for SO_2, 30% for PM_{10} [20]. These results are in agreement with the results of the operational evaluation for 9 years air quality simulation conducted over Europe with the use of Polyphemus, presented in [32] (only in the case of PM_{10} the correlation is significantly lower). The modelling results for the Kraków area showed a slight overestimation in the case of SO_2 (26.7 $\mu g/m^3$ simulated against 24.7 $\mu g/m^3$ in the measurements) and NO_2 (37.8 $\mu g/m^3$ simulated against 34.3 $\mu g/m^3$ in the measurements). By contrast, results were much underestimated for PM_{10} (33.6 $\mu g/m^3$ simulated against 74.3 $\mu g/m^3$ in the measurements), what can be explained by significant uncertainty regarding PMs emissions from fuel combustion for heating in the domestic sector.

4   Simulation Settings

4.1   Domain of Simulation

The simulations were run for a domain centered around Poland on a grid consisting of 61 x 41 cells starting from 12.175° E longitude and 46.7750° N latitude with a horizontal resolution of 0.25°. Five vertical layers were used with the following limits [in meters above the surface]: 0; 50; 600; 1200; 2000; 3000.

4.2   Input Data

Land Use Coverage. For the disaggregation of emissions and the calculation of the dry deposition velocities, the data on land use coverage [33], which includes 24 categories of LUC provided by [34], was used.

Meteorological Data. In all simulations, the meteorological data for the year 2008 of the European Centre for Medium-range Weather Forecasting [35] was used. The ECMWF data is provided with a resolution of 0.25° on 54 vertical hybrid levels every 3 hours. The parameters for vertical diffusion were taken from [36] and [37].

Initial Condition. The results for the year 2000 of the global model MOZART were used as the initial concentrations [38].

Boundary Condition. A nesting approach was used to generate the boundary conditions. A mother domain consisted of 40 x 25 cells starting from 5.0° W longitude and 38.0° N latitude with a horizontal resolution of 1.0°. As the boundary conditions in these simulations, results for 2000 of the global model MOZART [38] for gaseous species and for 2001 of GOCART for aerosol species [39] were used. Other input data was generated in the same way as for the simulation over Poland. The simulations ran utilizing emission for 2010, 2030, 2040 and 2050 from the study of [40]. The results of simulations were stored every 3 hours.

Dry Deposition Velocity. Dry deposition velocity was generated with a time step of 3 hours based on models and parameters of [41] for gases and [42] for aerosols. It was calculated in each cell for each LU category with separate resistance components. Subsequently, the final dry deposition velocity was calculated taking into account the share of different LU categories in a given cell.

Natural Emission. The emission of terpenes and isoprenes are estimated based on the parameters provided by [43]. The emission of the sea salt was generated based on [44].

Anthropogenic Emission Data. As the main goal of this study was to analyse the impacts of energy scenarios, emissions from the Polish power sector played the central role. Four energy-emissions scenarios elaborated with the use of the πESA energy module were considered: REF, NUC, NO-CCS and RES [25]. The analysis of scenarios in terms of their impact on the concentration and deposition of pollutants was conducted for the energy mix in 2030, 2040 and 2050. It was assumed that all energy technologies will fulfill emission limit values specified in Part II of Annex V of the IED Directive [45]. In order to convert the IED emission limits value expressed as a mass of pollutant per unit volume of exhaust gas $[mg/m^3]$ for the mass of pollutant per unit of chemical energy of consumed fuel $[kg/GJ]$, conversion coefficients presented in [46] were used. As the IED emission limits value depends on the magnitude of the thermal input of combustion plants, a breakdown of the total nominal thermal input into the size categories presented in Table 1 was used.

The obtained total national emissions of SO_2, NO_x and PM_{TSP} for different energy scenarios are presented in Fig. 2–4.

Table 1. Assignment of plants into thermal input classes [%]

Type of plant	Thermal input [MW]		
	50 − 100	100 − 300	> 300
Power plant	0%	14%	86%
CHP	13%	39%	48%
Heating plant	63%	36%	2%

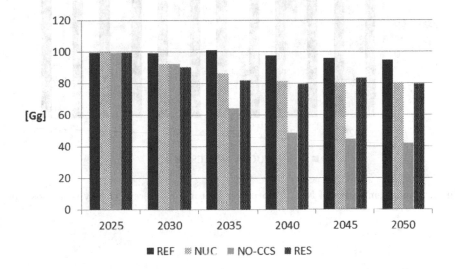

Fig. 2. Annual emissions of SO_2 from power sector for different energy scenarios [Gg]

Subsequently, the annual emissions from the power sector were spatially disaggregated into the Polyphemus grid with the assumption that 62.7% and 37.3% of them were released in vertical layers with the height 50–600 and 600–1200 meters, respectively. Emissions from other sectors in Poland that are not represented in πESA, and for other countries belonging to the model domain, were taken from the Baseline Scenario presented in [40]. The gridding process was, at first, based on the EMEP (Co-operative Programme for Monitoring and Evaluation of the Long-range Transmission of Air Pollutants in Europe, http://www.emep.int) emission inventory. The EMEP dataset includes anthropogenic emissions for countries in Europe with a spatial resolution of 50 km split into the SNAP (Standardized Nomenclature for Air Pollutants) categories. Similar allocation of national emissions into the gridded emissions was assumed to one existing in 2010. In the second step, the emissions from the 50 km x 50 km grid were further disaggregated into the Polyphemus modelling grid with the use of land use coverage data. As the EMEP temporal resolution is 1 year, the temporal distribution into months, days of the week and hours of the day was done based on the sector emission profiles presented in [47].

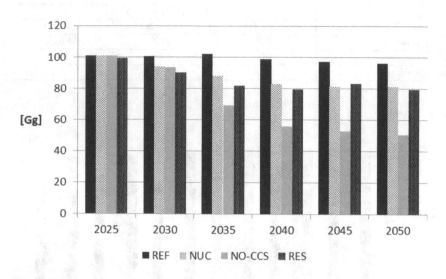

Fig. 3. Annual emissions of NO_x from power sector for different energy scenarios [Gg]

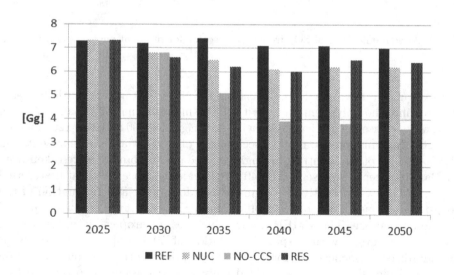

Fig. 4. Annual emissions of PM_{TSP} from power sector for different energy scenarios [Gg]

5   Results

Results of πESA include i.a. information on changes in annual concentrations and depositions of SO_2, NO_x, PMs for different years as well as energy scenarios. Fig. 5 illustrates the absolute SO_2 concentration in 2040 for the REF scenario and the difference between REF and NO-CCS. The latter, as presented in Fig. 2, was the scenario with lowest emissions. Similar results are presented for NO_x in Fig. 6.

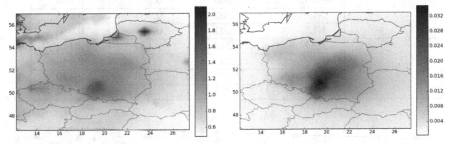

Fig. 5. Average annual concentration of SO_2 at ground level in 2040 (left) for REF and the difference between REF and NO-CCS (right) $[\mu g/m^3]$

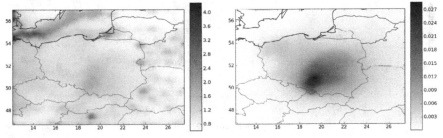

Fig. 6. Average annual concentration of NO_x at ground level in 2040 (left) for REF and the difference between REF and NO-CCS (right) $[\mu g/m^3]$

The comparison of mean concentration of pollutants over Poland at ground level for different energy scenarios is presented in Table 2.

The model results for SO_2 and NO_x show that halving the Polish power sector emissions in 2040 (please compare results for REF and NO-CCS scenarios) provides only a few percent change in their ambient ground-level concentrations. One should bear in mind, however, that the overall emissions of SO_2 and NO_x assumed for 2040 from other sectors amounted to ca. 240 and ca. 170 kt, respectively. The scenarios were compared as regards to the total deposition of sulphur in the modelling domain (see Fig. 7). The scenario with the lowest sulphur deposition in years after 2030 is: NO-CCS followed by RES, NUC and REF. It could be seen that emissions from the Polish power for all the scenarios considered in this study have only marginal impact on the value of the total S deposition.

Table 2. Annual mean concentration of pollutants over Poland at ground level $[\mu g/m^3]$

Pollutant	Scenario	2030	2040	2050
SO$_2$	REF	1.156	1.083	1.071
	NUC	1.137	1.079	1.068
	NO-CCS	1.138	1.070	1.057
	RES	1.137	1.078	1.067
NO$_2$	REF	1.204	0.980	0.982
	NUC	1.202	0.996	0.980
	NO-CCS	1.202	0.991	0.974
	RES	1.201	0.996	0.980
PM$_{2.5}$	REF	2.233	2.134	2.145
	NUC	2.222	2.132	2.146
	NO-CCS	2.222	2.128	2.139
	RES	2.221	2.132	2.144

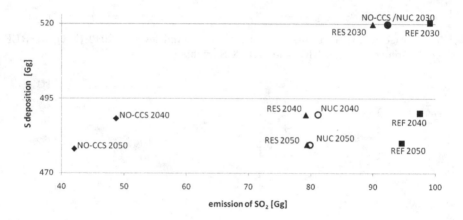

Fig. 7. Emissions of SO$_2$ from the Polish power sector and total annual sulphur deposition in the modelling domain [Gg]

For instance, a comparison of the REF and NO-CCS scenarios for 2050 shows a 55% difference in SO$_2$ emissions from the power sector but only 0.4% change in total S deposition. One should bear in mind that the total deposition is reported for the entire modelling domain and accounts for emissions from other sectors and countries.

Finally, πESA makes it possible to identify the grid cell, in which the highest concentration of a given pollutant occurs. This could be particularly useful to identify the areas where people exposure to air pollution is the highest. For illustration, Fig. 8 presents the difference in hourly concentration of SO$_2$ in 2040, between REF and NO-CCS as well as between REF and RES scenarios.

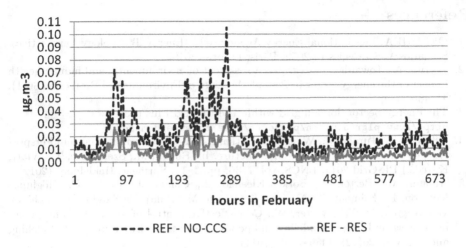

Fig. 8. Difference in hourly concentration of SO_2 at ground level in February 2040 between scenarios for a grid-cell with highest concentration $[\mu g/m^3]$

6   Conclusions and Future Work

πESA can be used to compare changes in pollutants concentrations and depositions resulting from different energy scenarios. In this way, their environmental dimension can be taken into account in decision making for energy policy. The results show that due to the improvement of emission controls in large combustion plants, which is required to meet future EU regulations, they will have a much lower negative impact on the environment. The study demonstrates that the πESA service can be applied for modelling the atmospheric dispersion of air pollutants for the energy scenarios elaborated by the users. Future work will be focused on integration of health impacts of people's exposure to fine particulate matter ($PM_{2.5}$) and calculation of exceedance of critical loads for acidification by deposition of nitrogen and sulphur compounds. The present version of πESA uses a relatively coarse resolution for air quality modelling. This was a compromise between the accuracy of results and computation time, bearing in mind that also other πESA functionalities related to the energy system modelling are included in simulation runs. To improve the representativeness of air quality results, particularly for urban areas, increments in urban background air concentration due to local emission sources need to be taken into account. This can be done, e.g., by increasing the spatial resolution of Polyphemus and its input data or by applying a generalized methodology that describes these increments, which has been elaborated within the City-Delta project [48]. It is also planned to use temporal emission profiles provided by a coupled TIMES-PL energy model as they are scenario-specific. Temporal emission profiles used at present were developed based on the historical activity data. In the future, when more energy will be generated from intermittent RES technologies (e.g. wind and solar) the emission profiles will change as the activity of thermal units will be affected.

References

1. OECD/IEA, International Energy Agency (ed.): Energy Technology Perspectives, Scenarios & Strategies to 2050. Paris, France (2010)
2. Wyrwa, A.: Towards an integrated assessment of environmental and human health impact of the energy sector in Poland. Archives of Environmental Protection 36(1), 41–48 (2010)
3. The Energy Sector domain grid within the PLGrid Plus project, http://www.plgrid.pl/en/projects/plus/science_domains
4. Kitowski, J., Turała, M., Wiatr, K., Dutka, Ł.: PL-Grid: Foundations and Perspectives of National Computing Infrastructure. In: Bubak, M., Szepieniec, T., Wiatr, K. (eds.) PL-Grid 2011. LNCS, vol. 7136, pp. 1–14. Springer, Heidelberg (2012)
5. Amann, M., Bertok, I., Borken-Kleefeld, J., Cofala, J., Heyes, C., Höglund-Isaksson, L., Klimont, Z., Nguyen, B., Posch, M., Rafaj, P., Sandler, R., Schöpp, W., Wagner, F., Winiwarter, W.: Cost-effective control of air quality and greenhouse gases in Europe: Modeling and policy applications. Environmental Modelling and Software 26(12), 1489–1501 (2011)
6. Blaschke, T., Mittlböck, M., Biberacher, M., Gadocher, S., Vockner, B., Hochwimmer, B., Lang, S.: The GEOSS – ENERGEO portal: towards an interactive platform to calculate, forcast and monitor the environmental impact of energy carriers. Integration of Environmental Information in Europe. Shaker Verlag (2010)
7. Syri, S., Amann, M., Capros, P., Mantzos, L., Cofala, J., Klimont, Z.: Low-CO_2 energy pathways and regional air pollution in Europe. Energy Policy 29(11), 871–884 (2001)
8. Oxley, T., Dore, A.J., ApSimon, H., Hall, J., Kryza, M.: Modelling future impacts of air pollution using the multi-scale UK Integrated Assessment Model (UKIAM). Environment International 61, 17–35 (2013)
9. Liu, F., Klimont, Z., Zhang, Q., Cofala, J., Zhao, L., Huo, H., Nguyen, B., Schöpp, W., Sander, R., Zheng, B., Hong, C., He, K., Amann, M., Heyes, C.: Integrating mitigation of air pollutants and greenhouse gases in Chinese cities: Development of GAINS-City model for Beijing. Journal of Cleaner Production 58, 25–33 (2013)
10. Czarnowska, L., Frangopoulos, C.A.: Dispersion of pollutants, environmental externalities due to a pulverized coal power plant and their effect on the cost of electricity. Energy 41(1), 212–219 (2012)
11. Schöpp, W., Amann, M., Cofala, J., Heyes, C., Klimont, Z.: Integrated assessment of European air pollution emission control strategies. Environmental Modelling & Software 14(1), 1–9 (1998)
12. Simpson, D., Benedictow, A., Berge, H., Bergström, R., Emberson, L.D., Fagerli, H., Flechard, C.R., Hayman, G.D., Gauss, M., Jonson, J.E., Jenkin, M.E., Nyúri, A., Richter, C., Semeena, V.S., Tsyro, S., Tuovinen, J.P., Valdebenito, A., Wind, P.: The EMEP MSC-W chemical transport model; Technical description. Atmospheric Chemistry and Physics 12(16), 7825–7865 (2012)
13. Brandt, J., Silver, J.D., Frohn, L.M., Geels, C., Gross, A., Hansen, A.B., Hansen, K.M., Hedegaard, B., Skjøth, A., Villadsen, H., Zare, A., Christensen, J.H.: An integrated model study for Europe and North America using the Danish Eulerian Hemispheric Model with focus on intercontinental transport of air pollution. Atmospheric Environment 53, 156–176 (2012)
14. Appel, K.W., Chemel, C., Roselle, S.J., Francis, X.V., Hu, R.-M., Sokhi, R.S., Rao, S.T., Galmarini, S.: Examination of the Community Multiscale Air Quality (CMAQ) model performance over the North American and European domains. Atmospheric Environment 53, 142–155 (2012)

15. de Ruiter de Wildt, M., Eskes, H., Manders, A., Sauter, F., Schaap, M., Swart, D., Velthoven, P.: Six-day PM_{10} air quality forecasts for the Netherlands with the chemistry transport model Lotos-Euros. Atmospheric Environment 45, 5586–5594 (2011)

16. Draxler, R.R., Rolph, G.D.: HYSPLIT (HYbrid Single-Particle Lagrangian Integrated Trajectory) Model access via NOAA ARL READY (2014), http://ready.arl.noaa.gov/HYSPLIT.php

17. Mehdizadeh, F., Rifai, H.S.: Modeling point source plumes at high altitudes using a modified Gaussian model. Atmospheric Environment 34, 821–831 (2004)

18. Korsakissok, I., Mallet, V.: Development and application of a reactive plume-in-grid model: evaluation over Greater Paris. Atmos. Chem. Phys. 2010b, 8917–8931 (2010)

19. Cieślińska, J., Łobocki, L.: Comparison of the Polish regulatory dispersion model with AERMOD. International Journal of Environment and Pollution 40(1-3), 62–69 (2010)

20. Wyrwa, A., Zyśk, J., Stężały, A., Śliż, B., Pluta, M., Buriak, J., Jestin, L.: Towards an Integrated Assessment of Environmental and Health Impact of Energy Sector in Poland. In Environmental Informatics and Systems Research. Shaker Verlag, Warsaw (2007)

21. Kryza, M., Dore, A.J., Błaś, M., Sobik, M.: Modelling deposition and air concentration of reduced nitrogen in Poland and sensitivity to variability in annual meteorology. Journal of Environmental Management 92(4), 1225–1236 (2011)

22. Juda-Rezler, K.: Risk assessment of airborne sulphur species in Poland. Air Pollution Modeling and Its Application: International Technical Meeting on Air Pollution Modeling and Its Application 16, 23 (2003)

23. Wyrwa, A.: Integrated Impact Assessment of Emissions from the Polish Energy Sector for Determination of the Optimal Mix of Energy Generation and Pollution Control Technologies. In: Faculty of Energy and Fuels. AGH University of Science and Technology, Kraków (2009)

24. Tainio, M., Juda-Rezler, K., Reizer, M., Warchałowski, A., Trapp, W., Skotak, K.: Future climate and adverse health effects caused by fine particulate matter air pollution: Case study for Poland. Regional Environmental Change 13(3), 705–715 (2013)

25. Wyrwa, A., Pluta, M., Skoneczny, S., Mirowski, T.: Modelling the Long-term Development of an Energy System with the Use of a Technology Explicit Partial Equilibrium Model. In: Bubak, M., Kitowski, J., Wiatr, K. (eds.) PLGrid Plus. LNCS, vol. 8500, pp. 489–503. Springer, Heidelberg (2014)

26. CEREA. Polyphemus Air Quality Modeling System (2011), http://cerea.enpc.fr/polyphemus/introduction.html

27. Stockwell, W.R., Middleton, P., Chang, J.S., Tang, X.: The second generation regional acid deposition model chemical mechanism for regional air quality modelling. J. Geophys. Res. 95, 16343–16367 (1990)

28. Fahey, K.M., Pandis, S.N.: Optimizing model performance: variable size resolution in cloud chemistry modeling. Atmospheric Environment 35(26), 4471–4478 (2001)

29. Debry, E., Fahey, K., Sartelet, K., Sportisse, B., Tombette, M.: Technical Note: A new Size Resolved Aerosol Model (SIREAM). Atmos. Chem. Phys. 37, 950–966 (2007)

30. Mallet, V., Sportisse, B.: 3-D chemistry-transport model Polair: numerical issues, validation and automatic-differentiation strategy. Atmospheric Chemistry and Physics Discussions 4, 1371–1392 (2004)
31. Mallet, V., Quello, D., Sportisse, B., Ahmed de Biasi, M., Debry, E., Korsakissok, I., Wu, L., Roustan, Y., Sartelet, K., Tombette, M., Foudhil, H.: Technical Note: The air quality modeling system Polyphemus. Atmos. Chem. Phys. 7(20), 5479–5487 (2007)
32. Lecœur, E., Seigneur, C.: Dynamic evaluation of a multi-year model simulation of particulate matter concentrations over Europe. Atmospheric Chemistry and Physics 13, 4319–4337 (2013)
33. GLCC/USGS. Global Land Cover Characteristics (2008), http://edc2.usgs.gov/glcc/glcc.php
34. USGS. U.S Geological Survey (2011), http://www.usgs.gov/
35. ECMWF. Provides medium-range weather forecast support to European meteorological organizations, http://www.ecmwf.int
36. Louis, J.F.: A parametric model of vertical eddy fluxes in the atmosphere. Bound Layer Meteor. 17, 187–202 (1979)
37. Troen, I.B., Mahrt, L.: A simple model of the atmospheric boundary layer; sensitivity to surface evaporation. Boundary-Layer Meteorology 37, 129–148 (1986)
38. Horowitz, L.W., Walters, S., Mauzerall, D.L., Emmons, L.K., Rasch, P.J., Granier, C., Tie, X., Lamarque, J.-F., Schultz, M.G., Tyndall, G.S., Orlando, J.J., Brasseur, G.P.: A global simulation of tropospheric ozone and related tracers: description and evaluation of MOZART version II. Journal of Geophysical Research: Atmospheres 108(D24), 4784 (2003)
39. Chin, M., Rood, R.B., Lin, S.-J., Muller, J.-F., Thompson, A.M.: Atmospheric sulfur cycle simulated in the global model GOCART: Model description and global properties. Journal of Geophysical Research: Atmospheres 105(D20), 24671–24687 (2000)
40. Rafaj, P., Cofala, J., Kuenen, J., Wyrwa, A., Zyśk, J.: Benefits of European Climate Policies for Mercury Air Pollution. Atmosphere 5(1), 45–59 (2014)
41. Zhang, L., Brook, J.R., Vet, R.: A revised parameterization for gaseous dry deposition in air-quality models. Atmos. Chem. Phys. 3, 2067–2082 (2003)
42. Zhang, L., Gong, S., Padro, J., Berrie, L.: A size-segregated particle dry deposition scheme for an atmospheric aerosol module. Atmospheric Environment 35, 549–560 (2001)
43. Simpson, D., Winiwarter, W., Borjesson, G., Cinderby, S., Ferreiro, A., Guenther, A., Hewitt, C.N., Janson, R., Khalil, M.A.K., Owen, S., Pierce, T.E., Puxbaum, H., Shearer, M., Skiba, U., Steinbrecher, R., Tarrason, L., Oquist, M.G.: Inventorying emissions from nature in Europe. J. Geophys. Res. 104, 8113–8152 (1999)
44. Monahan, E.C., Spiel, D.E., Davidson, K.L.: A Model of Marine Aerosol Generation Via Whitecaps and Wave Disruption. Oceanographic Sciences Library 2, 167–174 (1986)
45. EU, The European Parliament and of the Council of the European Union (ed.): Directive 2010/75/EU of the European Parliament and of the Council of 24 November 2010 on industrial emissions (integrated pollution prevention and control). Official Journal of the European Union, p. 103 (2010)

46. Gawlik, L., Grudziński, Z., Kamiński, J., Kaszyński, P., Kryzia, D., Lorenz, U., Mirowski, T., Mokrzycki, E., Olkuski, T., Ozga-Blaschke, U., Pluta, M., Sikora, A., Stala-Szlugaj, K., Suwała, W., Szurlej, A., Wyrwa, A., Zyśk, J., Gawlik, L. (eds.): Coal for the Polish power sector in the time perspective up to 2050 – scenario analysis, vol. I. Wydawnictwo Instytutu Gospodarki Surowcami Mineralnymi i Energią PAN, 299, Katowice (2013)

47. Friedrich, R., Reis, S.: Emissions of Air Pollutants – Measurements, Calculation, Uncertainties – Results from the EUROTRAC-2 Subproject GENEMIS. Springer (2004)

48. Thunis, P., Rouil, L., Cuvelier, C., Stern, R., Kerschbaumer, A., Bessagnet, B., Schaap, M., Builtjes, P., Tarrason, L., Douros, J., Moussiopoulos, N., Pirovano, G., Bedogni, M.: Analysis of model responses to emission-reduction scenarios within the city delta project. Atmospheric Environment 41(1), 208–220 (2007)

Author Index

Subject Index